A reader on Islam

A Reader on Islam

A Reader on Islam

Edited by
Arthur Jeffery

AYER COMPANY, PUBLISHERS, INC.
SALEM, NEW HAMPSHIRE 03079

Reprint Edition, 1987
AYER Company, Publishers, Inc.
382 Main Street
Salem, New Hampshire 03079

Editorial Supervision: Steve Bedney

Reprint Edition 1980 by Books for Libraries, a Division of
Arno Press Inc.

Reprinted from a copy in the University of Illinois Library
ISLAM
ISBN for complete set: 8369-9259-8
See last pages of this volume for titles.
Manufactured in the United States of America

Library of Congress Cataloging in Publication Data

Jeffery, Arthur, ed.
A reader on Islam.

(Islam)
Reprint of the ed. published by Mouton, 's-Gravenhage, which was issued as ser. A 2 of Publications in Near and Middle East studies, Columbia University.
Bibliography: p.
1. Islamic literature. 2. Islam. I. Title.
II. Series: Islam (New York) III. Series: Columbia University. Publications in Near and Middle East Studies ; ser. A, 2.
BP20.J4 1980 297 79-52557
ISBN 0-8369-9264-4

A READER ON ISLAM

PUBLICATIONS IN NEAR AND MIDDLE EAST STUDIES

COLUMBIA UNIVERSITY

Editorial Board

Chairman

Tibor Halasi-Kun

Members

Jacob C. Hurewitz
Ishtiaq H. Qureshi
Charles P. Issawi
Joseph Schacht
Aert H. Kuipers
Schuyler C. Wallace
Ehsan Yar-Shater

Series A

II

This series, published under the auspices of the Department of Near and Middle East Languages and of the Near and Middle East Institute of Columbia University, consists of monographs, readers and other studies designed to promote systematic research on the Near and Middle East and to further public understanding of the problems of the area. The opinions expressed are those of the individual authors and do not necessarily reflect those of the Department or the Institute.

A READER ON ISLAM

PASSAGES FROM
STANDARD ARABIC WRITINGS
ILLUSTRATIVE OF THE
BELIEFS AND PRACTICES OF MUSLIMS

Edited by

ARTHUR JEFFERY †

MOUTON & CO · 1962 · 'S-GRAVENHAGE

PRINTED IN THE NETHERLANDS

CONTENTS

INTRODUCTION

Islam is the religion which has developed from a movement of reform started in seventh century Arabia by the preaching of Muḥammad, a townsman of Mecca who died at Madīna in 632 A. D. ten years after his "Flight" (Hijra) to that city from Mecca, an event from which the Muhammadan world still dates its era. Muḥammad himself referred to the religion which he was preaching as Islam, i.e. "submission", and one who accepted the teaching, submitting himself to Allah, was a Muslim, i.e. "one who submits". In his later years, after he had broken with the Jews and Christians of his environment, he claimed that the religion he was preaching was a restoration of the original religion of Abraham, so that he refers to various Biblical characters as Muslims, i.e. those who had submitted themselves to Allah. Everyone who accepted the new teaching became thereby a "believer" *(mu'min)* and each of the Caliphs who succeeded Muḥammad as head of the Muslim community bore the title Amīr al-Mu'minīn, i.e. "Prince of the believers". One who did not accept the teaching was an unbeliever *(kāfir)*.

The first four Caliphs, viz. Abū Bakr, 'Umar, 'Uthmān and 'Alī, were elected and ruled from Madīna. During the Caliphate of 'Alī there was a split in the community resulting in the formation of the two great groups, the Shī'a, the smaller group of legitimists who held that the headship in Islam should remain always in the Prophet's own family, and the larger group of the Sunnis, who follow the Prophet's rule of life *(sunna)*, but do not accept the claim of his family to authority among them. As a result we have the Umayyad Dynasty ruling from 661–750 from Damascus, followed by the 'Abbāsid Dynasty ruling from Baghdad from 750–1258, after which effective power passed into the hands of the Turks, who held it till the Caliphate was abolished by them in 1924.

Muḥammad's own religious pronouncements, his "revelations", were collected after his death into the Qur'ān, but this was soon supplemented by a vast body of Tradition *(ḥadīth)*, which professed to set forth his *sunna*, or way of life, as the pattern to be followed by the community. With the inevitable changes brought about by the natural development of the Muslim community this again had to be supplemented, this time by what was called *ijmāʿ*, or the consensus of the community, and *qiyās* (analogy), which covered anything that could be deduced logically from the other three. These provide the four sources *(uṣūl* = bases, roots) for the whole structure of Islamic theology and jurisprudence, the various schools and sects differing for the most part only in the different ways in which they have developed the material from these sources.

Students of Comparative Religion frequently complain that Islam has much less of interest to offer them than the other great religions of the Ancient and the Oriental worlds. The chief ground of the complaint is that they find Muḥammad showing no special profundity of thought and no great spiritual insight, dealing for the most part in a rather hackneyed way with religious matters that are dealt with far more adequately in earlier religions, and very often giving only a jejune recapitulation of Jewish or Christian teaching, while Islam as it developed in later days generally represents religion at a pretty low level. Only in the writings of the Ṣūfīs do they find anything that really challenges their interest, and then find that the Ṣūfīs are looked at askance by orthodox Islam.

It must be admitted that for the most part those plumbings of the depths of religious experience and those soaring attempts at the heights which so fascinate the student in some of the other religions we study are conspicuous by their absence in Islam. Yet Islam is today the living faith of some two hundred and eighty million believers in our modern world, and is, as it always has been, remarkable for the firmness of its hold over its followers. A religious system which satisfies the needs of so many millions, and which is a missionary religion still gaining adherents by conversion from other groups, cannot but make its claim on our attention. Perhaps the basis of our judgment on it has been wrong. Perhaps we ought to have been seeking to understand how it functions in its own societies, and judging it on the ground of how it serves the practical needs of people in terms of their particular environment. Islam has always claimed to be a practical religion teaching a practical way of life.

It is with this in mind that the present Reader has been compiled. All the material in it save the notes and explanatory rubrics has been written by Muslims, and all the translation has done is attempt to make what they say intelligible to the English-speaking student. The selections begin with the Qurʾān, which is the Scripture of Islam, pass on to the Traditions, which give what the early generations of believers reported as the sayings and doings of their Prophet, and which they set forth in explanation of his teaching, and then take up some more systematic statements of what the beliefs and practices of Islam are. This is followed by selections from various types of religious writings which illustrate the practical and devotional life of Islam.

One pitfall in the compilation of such a Reader as this is that the selections represent only what a non-Muslim thinks are passages representative of the religion of Islam. An attempt to avoid this has been made by having a Muslim select the actual passages to be used. An outline was constructed to indicate what the Reader was meant to cover and then a practising Muslim was asked to select what passages from the Qur'ān, what material from the Traditions, what popular catechism, etc., etc., he would think best illustrated what his religion meant to him. Thus the skeleton framework is that of the Editor, but the flesh to clothe the skeleton was chosen by someone from within the Islamic tradition. Some of the passages chosen were rather surprising, but they have been followed with two exceptions. From the "Stories of the Prophets" the one chosen was the story of Dhū'l-Qarnain, i.e. Alexander the Great, whose story is interesting enough in itself, but would have meant little to those who will use this Reader, so in place of it has been taken the story of Jesus from the same collection. The second is the case of a *fatwā* where the one chosen involved so highly technical a matter of Islamic Law that it seemed wiser to substitute a *fatwā* by the famous divine al-Ghazzālī which would be more meaningful to a non-Muslim reader. The Editor also took the liberty of suggesting one or two short Qur'ānic passages and one or two prayers in common use which had not been originally chosen but which it seemed wise to include.

In every case the passage chosen has been translated completely, with no omissions save on odd occasions where the text got into technicalities which would be meaningless to a non-Muslim. Such places are distinctly marked. There are at times rather tedious repetitions, at times a certain crudity and uncouthness, and often enough the texts deal with very earthy matters which most of us would never dream of regarding as coming under the head of religion. Yet these are the things a Muslim reads in these texts and to omit them from the translation would mean that to that extent we are deforming the picture of Islam as a Muslim meets it in the literature.

There will always, of course, be objections from one quarter or another to any selection of passages that could be made, and there will likewise always be objections to the way in which a translator has rendered such and such phrases. It can only be said that an attempt has been made to see that the passages selected cover the main areas of Muslim religious life and to give them as literally as possible in English. Footnotes have been reduced to the minimum and the rubrics to the various sections made as concise as possible. Explanatory additions by the translator have been put in round brackets (), and words not in the original but assumed by it, and necessary to the sense in English, have been put in square brackets [ ]. Where Arabic technical terms are important they have been included in brackets. All Qur'ānic references are to the standard Egyptian edition of 1344 A. H. (= 1925 A. D.), but Flügel's verse numbering, which is followed in almost all European works, is also given where it differs from that of the 1344 text; thus VII, 31/29 means Sūra VII verse 31 in the Egyptian edition but verse 29 in Flügel.

The translations presented in this Reader have all been made directly from the Arabic texts, and have been checked for accuracy with the assistance of Dr. Butrus 'Abd al-Malik of the School of Oriental Studies of the American University at Cairo, to whose conscientious care all users of the Reader are under obligation.

ARTHUR JEFFERY †

A few weeks before his untimely death on August 2, 1959, Professor Arthur Jeffery handed over the manuscript of his *A Reader on Islam* to be printed in this series, with the intention of making slight alterations at the proof stage. With the concurrence of Mrs. Jeffery, the Editorial Board decided to have the manuscript printed as it stood, making only such small technical corrections as they felt sure the author would have approved. Several members of the Editorial Board were assisted in reading the proofs by Professor S. A. Bonebakker.

JOSEPH SCHACHT

CHRONOLOGICAL TABLE

c. 570	Birth of Muḥammad.
622	The "Flight" to Madīna. 622 A.D. = 1. A.H.
624	Battle of Badr.
625	Battle of Uḥud.
628	Destruction of Jewish settlements at Khaibar.
630	Battle of Ḥunain.
632	Death of the Prophet Muḥammad.
632–634	Caliphate of Abū Bakr aṣ-Ṣiddīq.
633	Death of Fāṭima, wife of ʿAlī and daughter of the Prophet.
634–644	Caliphate of ʿUmar b. al-Khaṭṭāb.
639	Muslim conquest of Egypt under ʿAmr b. al-ʿĀṣ.
644–656	Caliphate of ʿUthmān b. ʿAffān.
c. 653	Official recension of the Qur'ān issued by ʿUthmān.
656–661	Caliphate of ʿAlī b. Abī Ṭālib.
661–750	Umayyad Dynasty ruling from Damascus.
677	Death of Abū Huraira, the source of many Traditions.
678	Death of ʿĀ'isha, the Prophet's favourite wife.
680	The massacre at Kerbela. Death of al-Ḥusain b.ʿAlī.
728	Death of the theologian al-Ḥasanal-Baṣrī.
746	Death of Jahm b. Ṣafwān, the her etic.
748	Death of Wāṣil b.ʿAṭā', the early rationalist Muʿtazilite.
750–1258	ʿAbbāsid Dynasty ruling from Baghdad.
756–1037	Umayyad Dynasty in Spain.
767	Death of Abū Ḥanīfa, founder of the Ḥanīfite rite.
775–785	Caliphate of al-Mahdī. Persecution of heretics.
785	Building of the great Mosque at Cordova.
786–809	Caliphate of Hārūn ar-Rashīd.
795	Death of Mālik b.Anas, founder of the Mālikite rite.
813–833	Caliphate of al-Ma'mūn. Controversies with the Muʿtazilites.
820	Death of ash-Shāfiʿī, founder of the Shāfiʿite rite.
834	Death of Ibn Hishām, author of the Biography of Muḥammad.

836	Founding of the city of Sāmarrā.
845	Ibn Sa'd wrote his *Ṭabaqāt*.
855	Death of Aḥmad b. Ḥanbal, founder of the Ḥanbalite rite.
c. 858	Death of al-Azraqī, historian of the city of Mecca.
861	Death of the Caliph al-Mutawakkil, with whom orthodoxy triumphed.
870	Death of al-Bukhārī, compiler of the *Ṣaḥīḥ*.
871	Death of the Ṣūfī Master, Yaḥyā b. Mu'ādh ar-Rāzī.
874	Death of the Ṣūfī Bayāzīd al-Bisṭāmī.
875	Death of Muslim, the Traditionist.
878	The twelfth Shī'ite Imām goes into occultation.
886	Death of Ibn Māja, compiler of the *Sunan*.
888	Death of Abū Dāwūd the Traditionist.
890	Appearance of the Qarmaṭians in 'Irāq.
892	Death of at-Tirmidhī, compiler of the *Jāmi'*.
909–1171	Fāṭimid Dynasty in North Africa.
915	Death of al-Jubbā'ī the heretic. Death of an-Nasā'ī the Traditionist.
923	Death of aṭ-Ṭabarī the historian, and of the philosopher ar-Rāzī (Rhazes).
929	Death of the astronomer al-Battānī.
930	The Qarmaṭians conquer Mecca.
935	Death of Abū'l-Ḥasan al-Ash'arī, the theologian.
942	Death of aṭ-Ṭaḥāwī, the theologian.
944	Death of Abū Manṣūr al-Māturīdī, the theologian.
949	Death of Abū Ja'far an-Naḥḥās.
951	Death of the philosopher al-Fārābī.
969	Fāṭimid conquest of Egypt.
983	Death of Naṣr b. Muḥammad as-Samarqandī.
987	Death of al-Malaṭī.
991	Death of Ibn Bābawaih, the Shī'ite theologian.
996–1021	Al-Ḥākim, the mad Caliph, rules in Egypt.
998–1030	Rule of Maḥmūd of Ghazna.
1013	Death of the theologian al-Bāqillānī.
1020	Death of Firdawsī, author of the *Shāh-nāmeh*.
1035	Birth of ath-Tha'labī, author of the *Qiṣaṣ al-Anbiyā'*.
1037–1610	Rule of petty Moorish dynasties in Spain.
1037	Death of Ibn Sīnā (Avicenna), and of 'Abd al-Qāhir al-Baghdādī.
1039	Death of the hagiographer Abū Nu'aim of Iṣfahān.

1048	Death of al-Bīrūnī.
1055	Tughril Beg the Seljuq takes over rule in Baghdad.
c. 1060	Al-Kisā'ī, author of the *Qiṣaṣ al-Anbiyā'*.
1074	Death of al-Qushairī the hagiographer.
1085	Death of the theologian al-Juwainī, Imām al-Ḥaramain.
1099	Capture of Jerusalem by the Crusaders.
1111	Death of the theologian al-Ghazzālī.
1122	Death of al-Farrā' al-Baghawī.
1138	Death of the philosopher Ibn Bājja (Avempace).
1142	Death of Najm ad-Dīn 'Umar an-Nasafī.
1193	Death of Saladin.
1198	Death of the philosopher Ibn Rushd (Averroes).
1209	Death of Fakhr ad-Dīn ar-Rāzī.
1229	Death of the geographer Yāqūt al-Ḥamawī.
1234	Death of Ibn al-Athīr the historian.
1240	Death of the Ṣūfī Muḥyī ad-Dīn b. al-'Arabī.
1254–1517	Mameluke rule in Egypt.
1258	Hūlāgū the Mongol takes Baghdad.
1273	Death of the grammarian Ibn Mālik, and of the Ṣūfī Jalāl ad-Dīn ar-Rūmī.
1274	Death of Nāṣir ad-Dīn aṭ-Ṭūsī.
1277	Death of an-Nawawī the traditionist.
1295	Death of al-Būṣīrī, author of the poem in honour of Muḥammad.
1316	Death of al-Baiḍāwī, the Commentator on the Qur'ān.
1326	Death of Taqī ad-Dīn Ibn Taimiyya.
1336	Compilation of the *Mishkāt al-Maṣābīḥ*.
c. 1350	Death of al-Qummī an-Naisābūrī.
1356	Death of the Muslim traveller Ibn Batūṭa.
1370	Death of Tāj ad-Dīn as-Subkī, Qāḍī of Damascus.
1390	Death of Sa'd ad-Dīn at-Taftāzānī.
1406	Death of the historian Ibn Khaldūn.
1422	Death of Sulaimān Chelebī, author of the eulogy on the Prophet.
1429	Death of Muḥammad al-Jazarī.
1453	Fall of Constantinople to the Turks.
1470	Death of Ibn Makhlūf, the writer on practical theology.
1490	Death of as-Sanūsī, author of the Credal statement.
1492	Fall of Granada, and end of Moorish domination in Spain.
1505	Death of the polygraph Jalāl ad-Dīn as-Suyūṭī.

1517	Selīm I conquers Egypt for the Turks.
1565	Death of ash-Shaʿrānī, the theologian.
1573	Death of the theologian Muḥammad b. Pīr ʿAlī al-Birkawī.
1574	Death of the historian ad-Diyārbekrī.

QUR'ĀN

INTRODUCTION

The Qur'ān is the sacred Scripture of the religion of Islam, and as such is the subject of the same reverential treatment and devout study as the Bible is among Jews and Christians, and other Scriptures among the followers of religions which have such sacred writings. It is referred to as the "Glorious Qur'ān", the "Noble Qur'ān", the "Illustrious Qur'ān", but never the "Holy Qur'ān" save by modern Indian Muslims who in that are imitating the Christian use of "Holy Bible". Until recent days the memorizing of the Qur'ān was the first stage in formal education among Muslim peoples, and it is still considered highly meritorious to learn it by heart. It is in Arabic, and contains the material promulgated by the Prophet Muḥammad during the years of his active ministry among his people. A great many of the personages mentioned in its pages, and much of its religious teaching, will be familiar to readers of the Bible. This is because Muḥammad's conception of his mission was that he was called to bring to his people the Arabs, who had had no prophet, the substance of the Scriptural religion of the "People of the Book", i.e. the Jews and Christians, who were commonly to be met with in Arabia in his day. He died before he had his Book ready, so that the Qur'ān which we have is what was gathered together of his pronouncements after his death and issued in a standard form by the third Caliph 'Uthmān (644–656).

The Muslim theory of Scripture is that the Qur'ān is uncreate. As the eternal Word of God it was pre-existent. Long before the creation of the world it was written on the Preserved Tablet in heavenly places, whence the archangel Gabriel, who is the Angel of Revelation, revealed such portions of its message as were needful to each prophet in the long succession of inspired prophets who were chosen to reveal the will of Allah to mankind. When Muḥammad, the final prophet, the seal of the prophets, came, Gabriel revealed to him piecemeal over some twenty odd years the final form of this material from the Tablet, and, since this was to be the last Scripture given to mankind, Gabriel collated it carefully with him. As it was revealed Muḥammad had amanuenses write it all down. It was this collated, collected, carefully arranged body of material which the Caliph 'Uthmān published in his official recension of the text, and which has been transmitted unchanged to the present day.

Critical scholarship knows that many other collections of the Prophet's "revelations" were in circulation in the early days after the Prophet's death, and that what the Caliph 'Uthmān did was to canonize a collection made at Madina, after which he took measures to see to the destruction of all other collections, about which only fragmentary evidence has survived to us. What 'Uthmān canonized was a bare skeleton consonantal text, with no points to distinguish similar consonants, as is now the custom, and with no vowel signs. The possibilities of interpreting this consonantal text in various ways were of course great, but gradually certain famous Schools of interpretation arose, whose tradition as to the pointing and vowelling of the text came to be the authoritative systems. Seven such systems were ultimately canonized as orthodox systems, so that to recite the Qur'ān according to any one of these seven is allowable. Only two, however, survive in the lithographed and printed texts of the Qur'ān available to us today. The Madinan system of Warsh still has some following in North Africa, but the Kūfan system of Ḥafṣ has come to be the *textus receptus* in the world of Islam, and is the system to be found in practically all the Qur'āns in circulation at the present time.

If the Qur'ān is uncreate its words are necessarily all words of Allah. The Prophet was only the mouthpiece, so that it is Allah who is speaking in the Qur'ān from beginning to end. From this it follows that Arabic is the sacred language, so that the Qur'ān is the ultimate authority for matters of Arabic grammar and rhetoric. This is the reason for Muslim insistence that Scripture be recited only in Arabic, and that translations should be accompanied by the Arabic text, which alone has authority. Its literary style is a rhymed prose. It is not poetry, for it follows no metre, but it is rhythmical, rhymed prose, such as was used by the pre-Islamic soothsayers for their utterances, and which was apparently regarded as the appropriate literary form for religious pronouncements.

The word *Qur'ān* is used in the book itself to mean a passage of revelation. It is a borrowed word in Arabic, coming from the Syriac *qeryānā* "Scripture Lesson". Muḥammad uses the words *Qur'ān* and *Sūra* in this sense of "a passage of revelation", but as the book was assembled and published after his death, the word *Qur'ān* was used as a name for the whole collection, and *Sūra* for each of the one hundred and fourteen sections into which it was divided. The arrangement of these Sūras as we have it is the work of 'Uthmān's collectors, who seem to have arranged their material roughly on the principle of longest first shortest last. It is obvious even to the casual reader that the present order of the material is not chronological. In 1860 Theodor Nöldeke, completing earlier work by Gustav Weil, worked out a set of criteria whereby we can distinguish material belonging to four periods of the Prophet's activity:

I. EARLY MECCAN – the poetical rhapsodies of his earliest preaching.

II. MIDDLE MECCAN – the material of his preaching as he was formulating his religion and dealing with his opponents.

III. LATE MECCAN – the somewhat prosaic material from the period when he was busy building his community.

IV. MADINAN – the decidedly prosaic material from the period when he was head of a community at Madina and legislating for the life of a community.

Rodwell's translation of the Qur'ān in *Everyman's Library* arranges the Sūras chronologically according to the criteria of Nöldeke. Most Sūras, however, are composite, containing material from different periods, so that Richard Bell in his translation (2 vols. Edinburgh, 1937–39) has used printing devices to show how this material may be separated out in accordance with the results of critical analysis.

To Muslims the Qur'ān is primarily a book of devotion, in the reading of which they are as little conscious of critical problems as are readers of the Pentateuch. To them each Sūra is a whole, whose message is to be understood as a whole. In the following selections, therefore, we have neglected critical analysis, but as chronological order is important to show the development of the religion at the Prophet's hands, we have translated passages which may give some idea of the kind of material belonging to each of the aforementioned stages.

SELECTIONS FROM EARLY MECCAN SŪRAS

SŪRA XCIII

(To give some idea of how the rhymed, rhythmic prose sounds in the original Arabic we have given here this Sūra in a translation which appeared in the *Edinburgh Review* for July, 1866, in which an attempt has been made to imitate it in English).

I swear by the splendour of the light,
And by the silence of the night,
That the Lord shall never forsake thee,
Nor in His hatred take thee;
Truly for thee shall be winning
Better than all beginning.
Soon shall the Lord console thee, grief no longer control thee,
And fear no longer cajole thee.
Thou wert an orphan boy, yet the Lord found room for thy head,
When thy feet went astray, were they not to the right path led?
Did He not find thee poor, yet riches around thee spread?
Then on the orphan boy, let thy proud foot never tread,
And never turn away the beggar who asks for bread,
But of thy Lord's bounty ever let praise be sung and said.

SŪRA I[1]

SŪRAT AL-FĀTIḤA: THE OPENER

1. In the Name of Allah, the Merciful, the Compassionate.
2/1. Praise be to Allah, Lord of Mankind,
3/2. The Merciful, the Compassionate,
4/3. Master of the Day of Judgment.
5/4. Thee do we worship, and to Thee do we turn for help.

[1] This Sūra is really a prayer composed in Early Meccan style of phrases reminiscent of material used elsewhere in the Qur'ān, and placed at the head of the collection as a little Preface, whence its name—the Opener.

6/5. Guide us [in] the straight path,
7/6. The path of those to whom Thou hast been gracious,
7. Not [that] of those with whom Thou art angered, nor of those who go astray.

XC

SŪRAT AL-BALAD: THE LAND

In the Name of Allah, the Merciful, the Compassionate

1. I swear not [1] by this land,
2. And thou art a free inhabitant in this land,
3. Nor by a parent and what he has begotten.
4. We, indeed, have created man in trouble.
5. Does he think that no one will ever have power over him?
6. He says: "I have squandered enormous wealth."
7. Does he think that no one saw him?
8. Did We not give him his two eyes,
9. And a tongue, and two lips?
10. And give him guidance to the two highways? [2]
11. But he has made no attempt at the steep.
12. And what will teach thee what the steep is?
13. [It is] the setting free of someone in bondage,
14. Or feeding someone in a day of famine,
15. An orphan who is near of kin,
16. Or some unfortunate person in destitution.
17. Then to be, besides, one of those who believe, and who counsel one another to endure patiently, and counsel one another to compassionateness.
18. These are the Companions of the Right Hand.
19. But those who disbelieve in Our signs, they are the Companions of the Left Hand,
20. Upon whom [will come] a fire that is closed in.

[1] Some take this particle not as negative but as asseverative: "I swear, indeed, by this land."

[2] *najd* means an elevated road; *'aqaba* in the next line means a steep mountain path, and here we have one statement of the Qur'ānic version of the Two Paths, the easy path and the difficult path of duty and endeavour.

XCII

SŪRAT AL-LAIL: THE NIGHT

In the Name of Allah, the Merciful, the Compassionate

1. By the night when it spreads its veil,
2. By the day when it brightly shines,
3. By Him who created the male and the female,
4. Your course,[1] indeed, is diverse.
5. So as for him who gives [in alms] and acts piously
6. And puts his trust in that which is best,
7. His [path] to ease We shall facilitate.
8. But as for him who is niggardly, yet boasts in [his] riches,
9. And treats the best as a lie,
10. We shall facilitate his [path] to lack of ease,
11. And not a whit will his wealth profit him when he falls.
12. It is Ours [to give] guidance,
13. For to Us, indeed, belong both the Last and the First.
14. So I give you warning of a Fire that blazes,
15. None will be roasted thereat save the one, most wretched,
16. Who has counted [the message] false and has turned away.
17. But the one who is truly pious will avoid it,
18. He who gives his wealth [in charity] to purify himself,
19. And is under obligation to no one for a favour that is to be recompensed,
20. Desiring only the face of his Lord, the Most High,
21. So anon he will assuredly be well-pleased.

XCVI

SŪRAT AL-'ALAQ: THE BLOOD-CLOTS

In the Name of Allah, the Merciful, the Compassionate

1. Recite! in the name of thy Lord, Who has created,
2. Created man from blood-clots.[2]

[1] *sa'y* is lit. "running", but is used for a man's life endeavour, and so means his life "course". What follows is another version of the Two Paths.

[2] *'alaqa* is said to mean a minute nodule of clotted blood. The word is used in other passages which deal with the process of human reproduction (e.g. XXII, 5; XXIII, 14;

3. Recite! seeing that thy Lord is the most generous,
4. Who has taught by the Pen,
5. Taught man what he did not know.[1]
6. Nay! indeed, man assuredly acts insolently,
7. Because he considers himself self-sufficient.
8. Verily, to thy Lord is the return.
9. Hast thou considered [O Muḥammad], him who hinders
10. A servant when he is saying prayers?
11. Hast thou considered if he is in the way of guidance,
12. Or of commanding piety?
13. Hast thou considered if he counted [the message] false and turned away?
14. Did he not know that Allah sees?
15. Nay, indeed! if he desist not We shall drag [him] by the forelock,
16. A lying, sinful forelock.
17. So let him summon his party,
18. We shall summon the Zabāniyya.[2]
19. Nay, indeed! obey him not, but do obeisance [to Allah], and draw near.

LXXIV

SŪRAT AL-MUDDATHTHIR: THE ENWRAPPED

In the Name of Allah, the Merciful, the Compassionate

1. O thou who enwrappest thyself in a mantle,
2. Arise! Warn!
3. And thy Lord, magnify [Him].[3]
4. And thy garments, purify [them].
5. And the wrath, flee from it.
6. And do not do favours in order to seek increase,
7. But for thy Lord wait patiently.

XL, 67/69; LXXV, 38), and seems intended to represent the earliest stage of the formation of the embryo in the womb.

[1] Some think that this refers to the art of writing. Others, with more likelihood, take it to mean that through the pen He was able to teach men by Scripture revelation many things that otherwise they would never have known.

[2] The Zabāniyya are said to be the assistants of Mālik, the Grand Chamberlain of Hell.

[3] *kabbir* lit. "make great", which later came to mean "repeat the words *Allahu akbar*" (Allah is very great), whence the term *takbīr* which we shall meet again.

8. So when there shall come a trump on the Trumpet,
9. That then will be a difficult day,
10. For the unbelievers it will be far from easy.
11. Leave Me alone with him whom I have created,
12. Since I have appointed for him extensive wealth,
13. And sons as witnesses,
14. And I have smoothed out everything for him smoothly.—
15. Then is he covetous that I do more.
16. Nay, indeed! he at Our signs was obstinate.
17. But I shall overtake him with something grievously difficult.
18. He, indeed, thought and pondered.
19. Death to him! how he pondered.
20. Then, death to him! how he pondered.
21. Then he looked;
22. Then he frowned and looked crossly;
23. Then he turned back and showed his pride,
24. And said: "This is naught but magic being employed:
25. This is naught but human speech."
26. I shall roast him at Saqar.[1]
27. And what will teach thee what Saqar is?
28. It lets nothing remain, and desists not,
29. Scorching the skins.[2]
30. Over it are nineteen.[3]
31. We have not set as masters of the Fire any save angels, nor have We
fixed their number save as a testing for those who disbelieve, that
those who have been given the Book may be certain, and that those
who believe may increase in belief, (32) that those who have been
given the Book and the believers may not be in doubt, (33) and that
those in whose hearts is disease, and the unbelievers, may say: "What
does Allah mean by such a similitude as this?" (34) Thus does
Allah lead astray whom He will, and guide whom He will. Yet no
one knows the hosts of thy Lord save Him Himself, so this is naught
but a reminder to humans.[4]

[1] This is said to be a name of Hell or of a part thereof. The word itself is from the verb meaning "to scorch".

[2] There is a play on words here for the word *bashar* "epidermis" is the same word as was used for "a human" in v. 25.

[3] These are said to be the Zabāniyya, mentioned in XCVI, 18, and who are the special assistants of Mālik in the infernal regions.

[4] Though the original passages of this Sūra are early Meccan this is a later gloss of the Madinan period intended to explain the mysterious nineteen.

32/35. Nay, indeed! by the moon,
33/36. By the night when it retreats,
34/37. By the morning when it shines bright,
35/38. It is one of the great things,
36/39. A warning to humans,
37/40. To whosoever of you wishes to push forward or to lag behind.
38/41. Every soul for what it has gained is a pledge,
39/41. Except the Companions of the Right Hand.
40/42. In gardens they will be asking one another
41/42. About the sinners. [They will ask them]:
42/43. "What led you into Saqar?"
43/44. They will say: "We were not of those who prayed,
44/45. Nor were we feeding the unfortunate,
45/46. But we were engaging [in disputes] with those who so engaged,
46/47. We were treating as false the Day of Judgment,
47/48. Until the certainty came upon us."
48/49. So the intercession of those who intercede will not benefit them.
49/50. Now what is the matter with them that they are turning from the reminder,
50/51. As though they were startled asses
51/51. Who flee from a lion?
52. Yet every man among them desires that he be given scrolls unfolded.
53. Nay, indeed! but they do not fear the hereafter.
54. Nay, indeed! it is a reminder,
55. And he who wills will remember it,
56. But they will not remember save should Allah so will. He is worthy of your piety, and He is worthy to forgive.

LXXXVI

SŪRAT AṬ-ṬĀRIQ: THE SHINING STAR

In the Name of Allah, the Merciful, the Compassionate

1. By the heaven, and by the Ṭāriq.
2. And what will teach thee what the Ṭāriq is?
3. [It is] the shining star.[1]

[1] Some think that the reference is to the morning or to the evening star, but others think it means a shooting star or a meteor. The word we have translated "shining" might also have been translated "burning", and another possible meaning from the same root is "piercing".

4. Assuredly each soul has over it a guardian.
5. Let man then look at that from which he was created.
6. He was created from water [1] that pours forth,
7. Which comes from between the loins and the ribs.
8. He, (i.e. Allah) is quite capable of bringing him back
9. On the Day when the secrets will be tried,
10. And he will have no strength and no helper.
11. By the heaven which has [its] return,
12. And by the earth which has [its] splitting,[2]
13. It is, indeed, a saying, a statement,
14. It is no piece of frivolity.
15. It is they who are devising a stratagem,
16. And I, [Allah], shall also devise a stratagem.
17. So do thou show forbearance to the unbelievers; grant them a little respite.

LXXX

SŪRAT 'ABAS: HE FROWNED

In the Name of Allah, the Merciful, the Compassionate

1. He frowned and turned his back,
2. Because the blind man had come to him.
3. And what will teach thee? Maybe he will purify himself,
4. Or be reminded, so that the reminding will profit him.
5. As for him who is rich,
6. Why, to him thou didst give much attention,
7. And what dost thou care that he does not purify himself?
8. But as for him who comes to thee in earnest search,
9. While he is in fear [for his soul]
10. Of him thou art neglectful.
11. Nay, indeed! it is a reminder,
12. So whoever wills remembers it.
13. [It is] in honoured scrolls *(ṣuḥuf)*,
14. Exalted, purified,
15. [Written] by the hands of scribes,

[1] *mā'* is the word for "water", but it is often used for "semen", though some lexicographers think that that meaning is derived from its use in this passage.

[2] The "return" of v. 11 is said to refer to the annual recurrence of the celestial phenomena, and the "splitting" here to the annual return of the vegetation, shooting up through the soil.

16/15. Honoured, pious.
17/16. Death to man! How ungrateful he is!
18/17. From what thing did He create him?
19/18. From a drop of semen (19) He created him, and gave him his allotment.
20. Then the way He made easy;
21. Then He caused him to die and buried him;
22. Then, when He wills, He will raise him up.
23. Nay, indeed! not yet has he fulfilled what He commanded him.
24. So let man have a look at his food.
25. We it was who poured out the water copiously,
26. Then We split the ground in cracks.
27. So that therein We caused grain to grow up,
28. Also grapes and nutritious plants,
29. And olives and palms,
30. And orchards thick with trees,
31. And fruits and herbage,
32. A provision for you and for your flocks.
33. So when the crack [of doom] arrives,
34. A Day when a man will flee from his brother,
35. And his mother and his father,
36. And his wife and his sons,
37. Every man of them on that Day will have a concern to occupy him.
38. [Some] Faces on that Day will be radiant,
39. Laughing, joyous.
40. And [there will be] faces on that Day with dust upon them;
41. Black dust will cover them.
42. These are the unbelievers, the wicked.

LXXXI

SŪRAT AT-TAKWĪR: THE REMOVAL

In the Name of Allah, the Merciful, the Compassionate

1. When the sun has been removed,
2. And the stars have fallen down,
3. When the mountains have been moved away,
4. And the she-camels in their tenth month have been abandoned,[1]

[1] The tenth month of their pregnancy is when they particularly need attention.

5. And when the wild beasts have been gathered together,
6. And when the seas have been set boiling,
7. And when the souls have been paired again [with their bodies].[1]
8. And then the female infant who was buried alive has been asked
9. For what sin she was put to death.[2]
10. And when the scrolls have been opened out,[3]
11. When the heaven has been stripped away,[4]
12. And al-Jaḥīm [5] has been set blazing,
13. And the garden [of Paradise] has been brought near,
14. [Each] soul will know what it has got ready.
15. So I swear not [6] by the planets
16. Which swiftly move and conceal themselves,
17. By the night when it draws on,
18. By the morn when it comes in.
19. It, indeed, is the speech of a noble messenger,[7]
20. One possessed of power, established beside the Lord of the Throne,
21. Obeyed there, faithful.
22. And your companion (i.e. Muḥammad) is not jinn-possessed,
23. For, indeed, he saw him (i.e. Gabriel) on the clear horizon.
24. Nor was he niggardly concerning the unseen.
25. It is not the speech of a stoned satan.
26. So where are ye going?
27. It is naught but a reminder to mankind,
28. To such among you as are willing to go straight,
29. But ye will not [so] will, save if Allah, Lord of mankind, wills.

LXXXIV

SŪRAT AL-INSHIQĀQ: THE RENDING

In the Name of Allah, the Merciful, the Compassionate

1. When the heaven has been rent,

[1] At the resurrection soul and body are to be joined together again that man may face the Judgment as once more a whole man.

[2] This is said to refer to a pre-Islamic Arab custom of exposing female infants.

[3] Apparently this means the records of men's deeds. See Dan. VII, 10; Rev. XX, 11–15.

[4] On the Day the lower heaven will be rolled up like a scroll. See Isa. XXXIV, 4; Rev. VI, 14.

[5] *jaḥīm* is one of the names of Hell, or of a section thereof.

[6] Again this particle may be asseverative not negative.

[7] This and the following verses are generally thought to refer to Gabriel.

2. And has given ear to its Lord and become worthy.
3. And when the earth has been stretched out, flat,
4. And has cast forth what was in it and become empty,
5. And has given ear to its Lord and become worthy.
6. [Then] O man, thou [wilt be] toiling painfully unto thy Lord, for thou art going to meet Him.
7. Then as for him who is given his [record] book in his right hand,
8. He will be reckoned with by an easy reckoning,
9. And he will turn back happily to his kindred.
10. But as for him who is given his [record] book behind his back,
11. He will invoke destruction,
12. But will roast in Saʿīr (i.e. Hell).
13. He, indeed, had been happy amongst his kindred,[1]
14. He, indeed, thought that he would never be brought back [to a reckoning].
15. Aye! but his Lord was watching him.
16. So I swear not by the twilight glow,
17. Nor by the night and what it gathers,
18. Nor by the moon when it is full,
19. Assuredly ye shall ride on stage after stage.
20. So what is the matter with them that they do not believe?
21. And when the lesson (Qur'ān) is recited to them they do not do obeisance?
22. Nay, those who have disbelieved count the message false.
23. Allah, however, knows well what they have in mind,
24. So give thou to them good tidings of a painful punishment
25. [Which awaits all] save those who have believed, and worked righteous works. For them is a reward that will not be cut off.

LXXXV

SŪRAT AL-BURŪJ: THE TOWERS

In the Name of Allah, the Merciful, the Compassionate

1. By the heaven furnished with towers,[2]
2. By the promised Day,

[1] Verses 13, 14, 15 seem to be a Madinan addition inserted into this Sūra.
[2] *burūj* is the plu. of *burj* which is an Arabic adaptation of the Greek πύργος (Lat. *burgus*), a tower on a city wall. It was used in astronomy in connection with the Zodiac, and is said in this Sūra to mean "constellations",

3. By a witness and that which is witnessed,
4. Death take the Masters of the Trench,[1]
5. Of the fire fed with fuel.
6. Lo! they were sitting around it,
7. And they were witnesses to what they were doing to the believers.
8. They were wreaking vengeance on them for no other reason than that they believed in Allah, the Sublime, the Praiseworthy,
9. To Whom belongs the kingdom of the heavens and the earth. But Allah is a witness of everything.
10. Verily, those who vexed the believing men and the believing women, and then did not repent, for them is the punishment of Gehenna, for them is the punishment of the burning.
11. But those who have believed and worked works of righteousness, for them are the gardens beneath which rivers flow. That is the great success.
12. Verily thy Lord's assault is terrible.
13. He it is Who originates and restores.
14. And He is the Forgiving, the Loving One,
15. Lord of the Throne, the Glorious One,
16. He Who accomplishes that which He intends.
17. Has there come to thee, [O Muḥammad], the story of the hosts
18. Of Pharaoh, and of [those of] Thamūd?
19. Nay, but those who disbelieve are at [their perverse way of] counting false.
20. But Allah from behind them is encompassing [them].
21. Nay, but it is a glorious lesson (Qur'ān),
22. [Inscribed] on a preserved tablet.

LXXVII

SŪRAT AL-MURSALĀT: THOSE WHO ARE SENT

In the Name of Allah, the Merciful, the Compassionate

1. By those[2] sent forth one after the other,
2. By those that blow in violent gusts,

[1] This and the following verses seem to refer to the famous persecution of the Christians of Najrān in South Arabia in the year 524.

[2] The "those" in verses 1–5 are all grammatically feminine and are generally taken to refer to various classes of angelic beings. Others say they are winds.

3. By those that scatter scatterings,
4. By those that divide up into parts,
5. By those that cast down reminders,
6. [Whether it be] as excuse or as warning,
7. Verily, that which ye are promised is about to happen.
8. So when the stars are blotted out,
9. And when the sky is rent asunder,
10. When the mountains are crumbled,
11. And when the Messengers have a time set;
12. For what day is [all this] being arranged?
13. For the day of Severance.
14. And what will teach thee what the day of Severance is?
15. Woe on that Day to those who count [the message] false! [1]
16. Did We not destroy those of former times?
17. Then We shall cause those of later times to follow them,
18. For thus do We deal with sinners.
19. Woe on that Day to those who count it false!
20. Did We not create you from contemptible water
21. Which We placed in a repository secure
22. Until a known measure [of time]?
23. We determined it, and what excellent determiners are We!
24. Woe on that Day to those who count it false!
25. Did We not appoint the earth as a gathering-place,
26. For the living, and for the dead?
27. And We placed upon it firmly fixed mountains, rising lofty, and gave you water sweet to drink.
28. Woe on that Day to those who count it false!
29. Off with you to that which ye were counting false!
30. Off with you to a three-branched shadow,
31. Which gives no shade and protects not against the flame,
32. Which casts out sparks, [in size] like castles.
33. [A shadow which is] as though it were tawny camels.
34. Woe on that Day to those who count it false!
35. This is the Day on which they will not speak,
36. Nor will permission be given them to make excuses.
37. Woe on that Day to those who count it false!
38. This is the Day of Severance. We have gathered you along with those of former times.

[1] Lit. "giving it the lie".

39. So if you have any stratagem, then try your stratagem on Me.
40. Woe on that Day to those who count it false!
41. Verily, the pious will be amid shades and fountains,
42. And fruits of whatever [kinds] they may desire.
43. [We shall say]: "Eat and drink with full enjoyment [as a reward] for what ye have been doing.
44. Thus it is that We recompense those who do good."
45. Woe on that Day to those who count it false!
46. Eat and take your enjoyment for a little. Ye, indeed, are sinners.
47. Woe on that Day to those who count it false!
48. For when it is said to them: "Bow down!", they do not bow down.
49. Woe on that Day to those who count it false!
50. For in what discourse after this will they believe?

LXXXIX

SŪRAT AL-FAJR: THE DAWN

In the Name of Allah, the Merciful, the Compassionate

1. By the dawn
2/1. And ten nights.
3/2. By the double and the single.
4/3. By the night when it runs its course.
5/4. Is there in that an oath for a man of intelligence?
6/5. Hast thou not seen, [O Muḥammad], how thy Lord dealt with ʿĀd
7/6. At Iram, adorned with pillars,
8/7. The like of which has not been created in the land?
9/8. And with Thamūd, who hewed out the rocks in the valley [for dwellings],
10/9. And with Pharaoh, Lord of the stakes?
11/10. Who [all of them] acted presumptuously in the land,
12/11. And increased corruption therein,
13/12. So thy Lord poured out upon them the scourge of chastisement.
14/13. Verily, thy Lord is assuredly lying in a place of snare.
15/14. But as for man, whenever his Lord tries him, then honours him and is graciously bountiful to him, he says: (15) "My Lord has honoured me."
16. But whenever He tries him and sets a measure to His provision for him, (17) he says: "My lord has humiliated me."

17/18. Nay, indeed! but ye do not honour the orphan,
18/19. And do not urge one another to feed the unfortunate,
19/20. But ye do devour heritages greedily,
20/21. And ye love wealth with an ardent affection.
21/22. Nay, indeed! When the earth is pounded [to dust], pounding, pounding,
22/23. And thy Lord comes along, and the angels, rank by rank,
23/24. And Gehenna on that Day is brought in; Man, on that Day, would fain be reminded, but whence shall the reminder come to him?
24/25. He will say: "O would that I had sent ahead [provision] for my life."
25. But on that Day no one will chastise with His chastisement,
26. And no one will bind with His binding.
27. [Then will it be said]: "O tranquil soul,
28. Return to thy Lord, approving and approved;
29. And enter among My servants,
30. And enter My garden" (i.e. Paradise).

LXXV

SŪRAT AL-QIYĀMA: THE RESURRECTION

In the Name of Allah, the Merciful, the Compassionate

1. I swear not [1] by the Day of Resurrection,
2. Nor do I swear by the self-accusing soul.
3. Does man think that We shall never reassemble his bones?
4. Aye! We are quite well able to rearrange even his fingers.
5. But man desires to deny what is ahead of him.
6. He asks: "When is the Day of Resurrection?"
7. So when the sight is dazzled,
8. And the moon is darkened [in eclipse],
9. And the sun and moon are brought together,
10. On that Day man will say: "Where is a place to which to flee?"
11. Nay, indeed! there is no refuge.
12. With thy Lord on that Day is the resting-place.

[1] Some take the particle here as asseverative, not negative, i.e. "I swear, indeed, by the Day".

13. On that Day man will have announced to him what he has sent forward and what he has held back.
14. Nay, but man will be a clear demonstration against himself,
15. Even though he put forward his excuses.[1]
16. Move not thy tongue [therein, O Muḥammad, to hasten with it,
17. The assembling of it and reciting it is Our affair,
18. So when We recite it do thou follow its recitation.
19. Then it is Our affair to make it clear.[2]
20. Nay, indeed! but ye love this transitory [world],
21. And neglect the hereafter.
22. On that Day [some] faces will be beaming,
23. Looking towards their Lord.
24. But [other] faces on that Day will be dismal,
25. So you would think they are being subjected to nose-slitting.
26. Nay, indeed, when it (i.e. the departing soul) reaches the collar-bones,
27. And there is a cry: "Who can give a charm?"
28. And he thinks that it is the parting,
29. For leg is entwined with leg,
30. On that Day the driving-on will be to thy Lord.
31. So he did not consider it true, and he did not say prayers,
32. But counted it as false, and turned away.
33. Then he went to his folk, walking haughtily.
34. Near to thee, ever nearer [is the Hour].
35. Then nearer to thee, still nearer.
36. Does man think that he will be left forsaken?
37. Was he not a drop of semen emitted?
38. Then he was a blood-clot. So did He create and fashion,
39. And make of him the two sexes, the male and the female.
40. Is that One not powerful enough to bring to life the dead?

[1] Verses 13–15 are apparently a much later addition to an early passage.

[2] These verses 16–19 are quite disconnected from the rest of the material in this Sūra, and, though they may be from an early period, are apparently a scrap of extraneous material from the Prophet which has come to be inserted here.

SELECTIONS FROM MIDDLE MECCAN SŪRAS

XXXVII

SŪRAT AṢ-ṢĀFFĀT: THOSE WHO SET IN ARRAY

In the name of Allah, the Merciful, the Compassionate

1. By those who set the ranks in array,[1]
2. By those who scare away by a cry,
3. By those who recite a warning,
4. Verily your God is One,
5. Lord of the heavens and of the earth and of what is between them, and Lord of the rising-places [of the sun].
6. Truly We have adorned the lower heaven with an adornment of stars,
7. And [We have set] a guard against every rebellious satan.
8. They (i.e. the Satans) do not listen in at the Highest Council, but are pelted away from every side.
9. Banished [are they], and for them is a continuing punishment.
10. [They learn naught] save such an one as may snatch a chance phrase, but there follows him a gleaming flame.[2]
11. So question thou them.[3] Are they a stronger creation, or those whom We have created? Indeed, We have created them (i.e. humans) of sticky clay.
12. Nay, but thou art amazed [at Allah's signs] while they make mock,
13. And when they are reminded they do not pay heed.
14. And when they see a sign they set to making mock [of it].
15. And they say: "This is naught but manifest sorcery.

[1] Verses 1–3 are thought to refer to angelic groups, those who arrange the ranks of angels for their celestial duties (or dress the ranks of men for Judgment); those who chide the Jinn who try to listen in on the heavenly councils (or chide men for their evil ways); and those who recite warnings from the heavenly Book.

[2] This refers to the shooting stars which are thought to be cast at the satans who seek to listen in at what goes on in the heavenly Council.

[3] The "them" the Prophet is bidden question would seem to be the unbelieving Meccans.

16. Is it that when we have died and have become dust and bones we are to be raised up?
17. And also our sires, those of former times?"
18. Say: "Yes! and ye will be abashed."
19. For it is only a single blast, and behold! they are looking [about them].
20. And they will say: "O woe to us! This is the Day of Judgment."
21. This is the Day of Severance which ye were counting false.
22. Gather together those who have done wrong, and their consorts, and what they used to worship
23. In place of Allah, and guide them to the path to al-Jaḥīm.[1]
24. And make them stand, for they are to be questioned, [by one who will ask]:
25. "How is it that ye do not help one another?"[2]
26. Nay, but they are today seeking [their own] safety.
27. They will approach one another making inquiry.
28. They (i.e. men) will say: "Verily ye used to come to us from the right hand."[3]
29. They (i.e. the false gods) will say: "Nay, but ye were not believers.
30/29. We had no authority over you. Nay, it was ye who were a people given to transgression.
31/30. So the sentence of our Lord has come true upon us; we, indeed, are tasting [it].
32/31. We made you err [because] we were ourselves erring."
33/32. So they, on that Day, are sharing in the punishment.
34/33. Thus do We deal with sinners.
35/34. They, when it was said to them: "There is no deity but Allah", were haughty,
36/35. And were saying: "Shall we abandon our gods for a crazy poet?"
37/36. Nay, but he came with the truth and confirmed the envoys.[4]
38/37. It is ye who will be tasting the painful punishment,
39/38. Nor will ye be receiving recompense save for the works ye have been doing:

[1] One of the names of Hell, or of a part thereof. The word means "fiercely burning". See p. 28.

[2] From here to v. 39/38 it is a question of men and the false gods they used to worship (v. 22), but who on the Day prove their worthlessness.

[3] The right hand was the side of good omen.

[4] *al-mursalūn*, "those who have been sent", i.e. the envoys, the messengers from Allah to mankind. The meaning is that the Meccans retorted to Muḥammad's preaching that he was a "crazy poet", jinn-possessed *(majnūn)*, as the poets and soothsayers were, but the reply to them is that since the message of his preaching confirms the things about which the former Prophets preached he must be in the prophetic succession.

40/39. Save Allah's servants the single-hearted,
41/40. Those have a well-known provision,
42/41. Fruits [to eat] while they are being honoured
43/42. In gardens of delight,
44/43. Upon couches, facing one another.
45/44. Borne around among them is a cup [filled] from a spring,
46/45. White, a pleasure to those who drink,
47/46. In which is no headache, nor from it will they be intoxicated.
48/47. And beside them are wide-eyed damsels, restrained of glance,
49/47. As though they were sheltered eggs.
50/48. So they will approach one another, making enquiry.
51/49. One of them will say: "I, indeed, had a close friend,
52/50. [Who used] to say: 'Are you of those who consider it true?
53/51. Is it that when we have died and become dust and bones we are going to be judged?'"
54/52. He will say: "Are ye able to look down?"
55/53. So he will look down and see him (i.e. his doubting friend) in the midst of al-Jaḥīm.
56/54. He will say [to him]: "By Allah, you came near to causing me to perish also.
57/55. Had it not been for the favour of my Lord, I too should have been among those brought [to torment]!"
58/56. "Is it then that we do not die
59/57. Save our first death, and are we not to be punished?
60/58. Truly this is the great success;
61/59. For the like of this, then, let the workers work."
62/60. Is that a better repast, or the tree of Zaqqūm?
63/61. Verily, we have appointed [this tree] as a trial [1] for the wrong-doers.
64/62. It is a tree which emerges from the bottom of al-Jaḥīm,
65/63. Its fruit [2] is as though it were satans' heads.
66/64. Indeed they will be eating it and from it filling their bellies,
67/65. Then they shall have on top of it a drink of scalding water.
68/66. Then, indeed, the place to which they will return will be al-Jaḥīm.
69/67. Truly they found their fathers erring,
70/68. Yet they in their footsteps are hastening along.

[1] *fitna* a "trial", a "testing". (See p. 90). This tree of the infernal regions is mentioned again in XLIV, 43 ff; LVI, 51 ff.

[2] *ṭal'* is literally the spathe of the palm tree, but here it must mean the fruit of the tree Zaqqūm.

71/69. Indeed, before them most of those of former times had erred,
72/70. Even though We had sent among them warners.
73/71. So see what the latter end was of those who were warned,
74/72. Save Allah's servants, the single-hearted.
75/73. Verily, Noah had called upon Us, and right good were those who responded.
76/74. We delivered him and his household out of the great distress,
77/75. And We appointed his offspring to be the survivors.
78/76. And We left for him with those of later times [the saying]:
79/77. "Peace be upon Noah in the worlds."
80/78. Thus, indeed, do We reward those who do well.
81/79. Truly, He was among Our servants, the believers.
82/80. Then We drowned the others.
83/81. Verily, of his (i.e. Noah's) party was Abraham,
84/82. When he came to his Lord with a sound heart. (Cf. Sūra XXVI, 89).
85/83. When he said to his father and to his people: "What is this ye are worshipping?
86/84. Is it some false devising ye prefer as gods instead of Allah?
87/85. What is your thought then of the Lord of mankind?"
88/86. Then he gave a look at the stars
89/87. And said: "I am sick."
90/88. So they turned from him, departing.
91/89. He went in alone to their gods, and said: "Do ye not eat?
92/90. What is the matter with you that ye do not speak [in reply to me]?"
93/91. Alone [among them he began] striking them with [his] right hand.
94/92. Then [the people] came towards him, moving hastily.
95/93. He said: "Is it that ye worship that which ye carve,
96/94. Although Allah created both you and what ye make?"
97/95. They said: "Build for him a pyre and cast him into the blaze."[1]
98/96. They wished [to find] some stratagem against him, but We made them the inferior ones.
99/97. And he said: "I, indeed, am going to my Lord. He will guide me.
100/98. O my Lord, give me one of the righteous [as a son]."
101/99. So We gave him the good tidings of a meek-tempered youth.
102/101.[2] Then when he (i.e. the son) had reached the age of working with him, (101) he said: "O my son, I see in a dream that I am to sacrifice thee. So look! what is it that thou dost see?" (102)

[1] The word used here for "blaze" is *jaḥīm*, the same word used above several times for the blazing fires of Hell. Doubtless the choice of word was intentional. See pp. 28, 36.
[2] Verses 102/100–113 seem to be a Madinan addition to this Meccan Sūra.

He said: "O my father, perform what thou art bidden. Thou wilt find me, if Allah wills, one of those who patiently endure."

103. So when the two had thus resigned themselves, and he had laid him face downwards,
104. We called to him: "O Abraham!
105. Thou hast treated the vision as worthy of trust. Thus do We recompense those who do well.
106. This, indeed, was the clear testing."
107. So We redeemed him (i.e. the son) by an excellent sacrifice,
108. And We left for him (i.e. the father) with those of later times [the saying]:
109. "Peace be upon Abraham."
110. Thus, indeed, do We reward those who do good.
111. Truly, he was among Our servants, the believers.
112. And We gave him the good news of Isaac, a Prophet, one of the righteous.
113. And We bestowed Our blessing upon him and upon Isaac. Of the offspring of these two some were well-doers and some were doers of manifest wrong to themselves.
114. We also showed favours to Moses and Aaron,
115. And delivered them both, along with their people, out of the great distress.
116. And We aided them, so that it was they who were the conquerors.
117. And We gave to both of them the Book that makes clear,
118. And guided them both to the straight path,
119. And We left for them both with those of later times [the saying]:
120. "Peace be upon Moses and Aaron."
121. Thus do We reward those who do well.
122. Truly, both of them were among Our servants, the believers.
123. Verily Elias was one of the envoys,
124. When he said to his people: "Will ye not be pious?
125. Do ye call upon Baʿal and leave the Best One of those who create,
126. Allah, your Lord, and the Lord of your fathers, those of former times?"
127. But they counted him false, so it is they who will be brought in [to judgment],
128. Save Allah's servants, the single-hearted.
129. And We left for him with those of later times [the saying]:
130. "Peace be upon Elias."
131. Thus do We reward those who do well.

132. Truly, he was among Our servants, the believers.
133. And, verily, Lot was one of the envoys,
134. When We rescued him and his household, all of them
135. Save an old woman among those who hung behind.
136. Then We destroyed the others.
137. Ye, indeed, pass by them as ye go in the morning,[1]
138. And by night. Will ye not then understand?
139. And, verily, Jonah was one of the envoys,
140. When he fled to the laden ship.
141. So he took part in the casting of lots but he was one of those condemned,
142. And so the fish [2] swallowed him, and he was blameworthy.
143. And had it not been that he was one of those who glorify [Allah]
144. He would have remained in its belly till the Day when they are raised.
145. But We cast him up on the naked shore, and he was a sick man,
146. But We caused to grow over him a plant of the gourd species,
147. And We sent him to a hundred thousand, or maybe more.
148. Then they believed, so We gave them enjoyment [of life] for a while.

149. So do thou consult them.[3] Is it that thy Lord has daughters and they sons?
150. Or did We create the angels females while they were watching?
151. Is it not a fact that it is out of their own false devising [4] that they say:
152. "Allah has begotten?" They, indeed, are speaking lies.
153. Did He give preference to daughters over sons?
154. What is the matter with you? How are ye judging?
155. Will ye not be reminded?
156. Or do ye have some clear authority?
157. Bring out your Book if ye are speaking the truth.
158. Moreover they have made kinship between Him and the jinn, though the jinn know already that they are to be brought [to judgment].
159. Glory be to Allah! [He is far removed] from what they describe,

[1] The caravan route to the north passed by ruins which, it is suggested here, were the ruins of the settlement to which Lot was sent as a messenger.
[2] *ḥūt*, which is the word for Pisces in the Zodiac.
[3] Verses 149 ff. are a separate piece of revelation material, perhaps earlier in date than what precedes. It is the Meccans Muḥammad is bidden consult, for their notion that the angels are daughters of Allah is referred to elsewhere in the Qur'ān. See XLIII, 16/15–19/18.
[4] This is the same word *ifk* as is used in verse 86/84.

160. Save Allah's servants, the single-hearted.
161. Ye, indeed, and what ye worship [1]
162. Will not tempt [any to rebellion] against Him,
163. Save such a person as is [destined] to roast in al-Jaḥīm.
164. There is not one of us [angels] but has an appointed place.
165. We are those who arrange the ranks in order,
166. We are those who give glory [to Allah]."
167. And though they (i.e. the unbelievers) were saying:
168. "Had we had with us a reminder from those of former times
169. We should have been Allah's servants, the single-hearted."
170. Yet they have disbelieved in it;[2] but anon they will know.
171. Our word came of old to Our servants the envoys.
172. They are the ones who should have been aided.
173. And, indeed, it is Our armies that are the conquerors.
174. So turn thou from them for a while, [O Muḥammad,]
175. And observe them. Anon it is they who will observe.
176. Is it that they would hasten on Our punishment?
177. When it descends at their courts an evil morning will it be for those who were warned.
178. Now turn thou from them for a while,
179. And observe. Anon it is they who will observe.
180. Glory be to thy Lord, Lord of the greatness. [He is far removed] from what they describe.
181. Peace be upon the envoys.
182. And praise be to Allah, Lord of mankind.

LXXI[3]

SŪRAT NŪḤ: THE SŪRA OF NOAH

In the name of Allah, the Merciful, the Compassionate

1. We, indeed, sent Noah to his people, [saying]: "Warn thy people before a painful punishment come upon them."
2. He said: "O my people, I am to you a plain warner.
3. Worship Allah and act piously towards Him, and obey me,
4. [Then] He will forgive you your sins and defer you till a fixed time.

[1] Verses 161–166 are spoken to men by the angels.
[2] I.e. in Muḥammad's message that is being preached to them.
[3] This is a Meccan Sūra worked over later at Madina. See Bell, *Qur'ān,* p. 607.

Truly, Allah's time, when it comes, is not to be deferred, did ye only know."

5. He said: "O my Lord, I have summoned my people night and day,

6/5. But my summoning has only increased them in [their eagerness to be] fleeing.

7/6. Indeed, whenever I summon them that Thou mayest forgive them, they put their fingers in their ears, and wrap their garments around them, and they persist [in their evil ways] and act disdainfully.

8/7. Then I, indeed, summoned them plainly,

9/8. Then I addressed them in public, and secretly I addressed them in private,

10/9. And I said: 'Ask pardon of your Lord, for He has become forgiving.

11/10. He will send down the skies upon you in copious rain,

12/11. And will expand you in wealth and children, and will appoint for you gardens, and appoint for you streams.

13/12. What is the matter with you that ye put no hope in Allah's benevolence?

14/13. Seeing that it was He who created you stage by stage.

15/14. Have ye not seen how Allah created the seven heavens one above the other?

16/15. And in them set the moon as a light, and set the sun as a lamp?

17/16. Also Allah made you spring plant-like out of the earth,

18/17. Then He will make you return into it, and will bring you out again.

19/18. Also Allah has set the earth for you like a carpet spread,

20/19. That thereon ye may walk in open paths.'"

21/20. Said Noah: "O my Lord, they have disobeyed me, and have followed one whose wealth and children have increased him only in loss,

22/21. And they have worked out a mighty stratagem,

23/22. And say: 'Leave not your deities. Leave not Wadd, nor Suwāʿ
(23) nor Yaghūth and Yaʿūq and Nasr.'[1]

24. And they have, indeed, led many astray, though they increase the wrong-doers in naught but error."

25. Because of their sins they were drowned, and were made to enter
a fire, (26) for they did not find for themselves any helpers apart from Allah.

[1] These are supposed to be the names of deities worshipped by the pagans in Noah's day. Three of the names, viz. Wadd, Yaghūth and Nasr, have been found in South Arabian inscriptions.

26/27. Said Noah: "O my Lord, leave not on the earth any house of the unbelievers,
27/28. For shouldst Thou leave them they will lead Thy servants astray, and beget only wicked unbelievers.
28/29. O my Lord, forgive me, and my parents, and every believer who enters my house, and the male and female believers, but increase not the wrong-doers save in destruction."

XLIV

SŪRAT AD-DUKHĀN: THE SMOKE

In the Name of Allah, the Merciful, the Compassionate

1. Ḥā' Mīm.[1]
2/1. By the Book which makes clear,
3/2. Lo! We have sent it down during a blessed night. Lo! We were warning.
4/3. Therein each wise affair is disposed of.
5/4. An affair from with Us. Lo! We have been sending [envoys]
6/5. As a mercy from thy Lord. He, verily, is the One who hears, the One who knows;
7/6. Lord of the heavens and of the earth and of whatever is between them, if ye are convinced.
8/7. There is no deity save Him. He brings to life, and He puts to death. [He is] your Lord, and the Lord of your fathers of former times.
9/8. Nay, they in doubt are but playing,
10/9. So just wait for the Day when the heavens will bring along a palpable smoke
11/10. Which will cover the people. [They then will cry]: "This is the painful punishment.
12/11. O our Lord, lift from us the punishment: we, indeed, are believers."
13/12. How comes it that they had the reminder, when there came to them a clear-speaking messenger,

[1] Mysterious letters such as these stand at the beginning of some twenty-nine Sūras. What they mean is still quite uncertain. A discussion of some of the theories may be found in the *Moslem World*, vol. XIV (1924), pp. 247–260.

14/13. But then they turned their backs on him and said: "One who has been taught; one jinn-possessed." [1]
15/14. We, now, are lifting the punishment a little; ye are doing it again.[2]
16/15. The day [is coming when] We shall make the great assault. Then, truly, We shall be taking vengeance.
17/16. Now assuredly, before their time, We made trial of Pharaoh's people, and there came to them a noble messenger.[3]
18/17. [Saying]: "Deliver to me Allah's servants. I am, indeed, to you a faithful messenger,
19/18. And exalt not yourselves against Allah. Behold I come to you with clear authority.
20/19. And I have taken refuge with my Lord and your Lord against your stoning me.
21/20. So if you do not believe me, then separate yourselves from me."
22/21. Then he called upon his Lord: "Verily these are a sinful people."
23/22. [The Lord answered]: "Set out by night with My servants. Ye will assuredly be followed;
24/23. And leave the sea cleft open. They, indeed, are an army that will be drowned."
25/24. How many gardens and springs they left!
26/25. And plantations and noble station!
27/26. And a pleasant life in which they were enjoying themselves!
28/27. Thus it was, but We gave them as inheritance to another people.
29/28. The skies did not weep over them, nor did the earth, nor were they given respite.
30/29. But We certainly rescued the Children of Israel from humiliating punishment,
31/30. From Pharaoh. He, indeed, was a haughty fellow, one of the extravagant.
32/31. And we certainly chose them, knowingly, above the worlds,[4]
33/32. And gave them such signs [5] as had in them a clear testing.
34/33. Yet these [unbelievers] are saying:
35/34. "There is naught but our first death. We shall not be raised.

[1] The messenger here is Muḥammad, and the charge against his contemporaries is that they declared he was taught by others all that he was preaching, and that he was jinn-possessed *(majnūn)* like the soothsayers and poets.

[2] I.e. Were We to lift the punishment ye would but fall back into your old ways.

[3] The messenger here is Moses.

[4] I.e. above all mankind.

[5] *āyāt*, a word often used for "miracles".

36/35. Produce our sires if ye are those who speak the truth."
37/36. Are they better, or the people of Tubbaʿ?[1] (37) And those before their time whom We destroyed? Verily they were sinners.
38. We have not created the heavens and the earth and what is between them in sport.
39. We created them only in truth, but most of them do not know.
40. Verily the Day of Distinction is a rendezvous for them all,
41. A Day when a patron will be of no avail for a client at all, nor will they be helped,
42. Save those on whom Allah has mercy. He, indeed, is the Mighty One, the Compassionate.
43. Verily, the tree of Zaqqūm[2]
44. [Shall be] the food of the sinful.
45. It will boil in [their] bellies like *muhl*,[3]
46. Like the boiling of hot water.
47. "Seize him[4] and cast him into the midst of al-Jaḥīm.
48. Then pour out on the top of his head some of the punishment of the hot water."
49. "Taste! Verily, thou art the mighty, the noble![5]
50. This is that about which ye were doubting."
51. But the pious [will be] in a secure position,
52. Among gardens and springs,
53. Clothed in *sundus* and *istabraq*,[6] facing one another.
54. Thus shall it be! And We shall mate them with *ḥūr ʿīn*.[7]
55. Therein, in security, they will call for every kind of fruit.
56. They shall not taste of death therein, except the first death, for He has preserved them from the punishment of al-Jaḥīm.
57. [That is] a gracious bounty from thy Lord. That is the great felicity.
58. We have but made it (i.e. the Qur'ān) easy for thy tongue that perhaps they may be reminded,
59. So wait thou. They indeed are waiting.

[1] *tubbaʿ* is the title of the ancient rulers of the South Arabian kingdoms.
[2] See n. 2 p. 37.
[3] This word occurs again in XVIII, 29/28 and LXX, 8. Some say it means molten metal, but others take it to mean the dregs of oil.
[4] This may be the command of Mālik to his attendants in charge of Hell, or it may be Allah's command to the Angels of Chastisement.
[5] Verses 49 and 50 are the words of the infernal angels addressing the Damned, and in mockery using for them titles appropriate only to Allah.
[6] Iranian words suggesting richly brocaded garments.
[7] These are the Ḥūrīs, the fair-skinned, dark-eyed maidens of Paradise.

L

SŪRAT QĀF[1]

In the name of Allah, the Merciful, the Compassionate

1. Qāf. By the glorious Qur'ān.
2. Nay, but they marvel that there has come to them a warner from among themselves. So the unbelievers say: "This is a strange thing.
3. Is it that when we have died and become dust [we shall be raised]? That is a far off return."
4. Now We know what the earth consumes from them, and with Us is a Book that preserves [a record of them].
5. Nay, but they counted the truth false when it came to them, and they are in a perplexed affair.
6. Have they never looked at the sky above them, how We have built it and adorned it, and [how that] there are no rents in it?
7. And the earth which We have spread out and cast mountains upon it, and caused to grow up in it every beautiful species of plant,
8. As a demonstration and a reminder to every servant who will turn in penitence.
9. And We have sent down from heaven blessed water, and thereby caused gardens to spring up and the grain of harvest,
10. And tall palm trees with compact spathes,
11. As a provision for [Our] servants, and thereby We brought life to a dead country. Thus shall be the resurrection.[2]
12. Before their times the people of Noah counted [the message] false, and the Companions of ar-Rass,[3] and Thamūd,
13. And 'Ād and Pharaoh, and the brethren of Lot,

14/13. And the Companions of al-Aika, and the people of Tubba'. All counted the messenger false, and [on them] My promise came true.

[1] Qāf is the 21st letter of the Arabic alphabet. Some regard it here as a reference to the mythical mountains of Qāf which surround the circumambient ocean and in which the Jinn have their habitations.

[2] Lit. "the coming forth", i.e. the coming forth of the bodies from their graves on the Day, which will be like vegetation shooting up from dead land.

[3] These folk of ar-Rass are mentioned again along with 'Ād and Thamūd in XXV, 38/40 as among those ancient peoples of Arabia to each of whom a messenger had been sent, but who rejected their messenger and so perished. The Companions of al-Aika in verse 14/13 are the people of Midian, since we learn from XXVI, 176, 177 that Shu'aib was the name of their messenger, and Shu'aib was the messenger to Midian. For the Tubba' in the same verse see the note on XLIV, 37/36, (p. 45, n. 1).

15/14. Were We wearied by the first creation? Nay, but they are in doubt about a new creation.
16/15. We indeed created man, and We know what his soul whispers within him, and We are closer to him than his neck vein.[1]
17/16. When the two who are to meet sitting meet on the right hand and on the left,[2]
18/17. He does not utter a word but beside him is a ready watcher.
19/18. The stupor of death in truth will come. That is what thou hast been shunning.
20/19. And there will be a blast on the Trump. That is the threatened Day.
21/20. And every soul will come, accompanied by a driver and a witness.[3]
22/21. [They will say]: "Verily thou wast in heedlessness about this, but we have lifted from thee thy covering, so sharp will be thy sight today."
23/22. And his *qarīn*[4] will say: "This is what I have ready."
24/23. [Allah will say to the driver and the witness]: "Cast into Gehenna, O ye two, every obstinate unbeliever,
25/24. Hinderer of the good, hostile, doubter,
26/25. Who set up another deity along with Allah. So cast him into the fierce punishment."
27/26. His *qarīn* will say: "O our Lord, I did not make him transgress, but he was himself far astray in error."
28/27. He (i.e. Allah) will say: "Do not wrangle in My presence, for I had sent beforehand to you the menace."
29/28. What has once been said does not change with Me, nor am I one who would do wrong to [My] servants.
30/29. On a Day when We say to Gehenna: "Art thou filled up?", and it will say: "Are there some more?"
31/30. And the Garden shall be brought along for the pious, not far off,
32/31. [And Allah will say]: "This is what ye were promised; [it is] for every contrite one who keeps [Allah's law],

[1] This is thought to mean the jugular vein.
[2] The reference seems to be to the Recording Angels who daily record man's good and evil. Their names Raqīb and 'Atīd are derived from the words "watcher" and "ready" in the next verse. See pp. 426–427.
[3] This is said to refer to two angels who accompany each soul to judgment, the one driving him along, and the other witnessing to his deeds.
[4] A *qarīn* is a mate or a companion of equal age. Here it refers to the satan who will be chained to every unbeliever on the Day (see Sūra XLIII, 36/35), though others say it refers to the Recording Angel.

33/32. Who feared the Merciful One in the unseen, and came with a penitent heart.
34/33. Enter it in peace." That is the Day of Eternity.
35/34. In it they shall have what they will, and with Us there is more [in reserve].
36/35. How many a generation have We destroyed before their time, people who were mightier than they are, but they went searching in the land, [saying]: "Is there some sheltering place?"
37/36. Verily in that there is a reminder for whosoever has a heart, or gives ear while he is a witness.
38/37. We, indeed, created the heavens and the earth and what is between them in six days, yet We were not touched by weariness.
39/38. So do thou, [O Muḥammad], bear patiently what they are saying, and give glory with praise to thy Lord before the rising of the sun and before the setting,
40/39. And during the night glorify Him, and at the end of the prostration;
41/40. And be listening for the Day when the Herald will proclaim from a nearby place,
42/41. The Day when they will hear the Shout in truth. That will be the day of coming forth [from the graves].
43/42. We indeed bring to life and put to death, and to Us is the arrival,
44/43. On a Day when the earth will be split over them suddenly. That is an assembling. To Us it is easy.
45/44. We well know what they are saying; but thou art not a tyrant over them, (45) so remind by the Qur'ān whosoever fears My threat.

SELECTIONS FROM LATE MECCAN SŪRAS

XXXVI

SŪRAT YĀ' SĪN

In the name of Allah, the Merciful, the Compassionate

1. Yā' Sīn.[1]
2/1. By the wise lesson (Qur'ān),
3/2. Thou, [O, Muḥammad], art indeed one of the envoys,
4/3. Upon a straight path,
5/4. [Bringing] a revelation of the Sublime, the Compassionate,
6/5. That thou mayest warn a people whose fathers were not warned, so they were heedless.
7/6. Verily the sentence has come true on most of them, so they will not believe.
8/7. We, indeed, have set shackles on their necks, which reach to the chins, so that they perforce hold up [their heads].
9/8. And We have set a rampart before them and a rampart behind them, and We have covered them over so that they do not see.
10/9. Thus it is alike to them whether thou warn them or warn them not, they will not believe.
11/10. Only such as follow the reminder wilt thou warn, such as fear the Merciful in the unseen; so to such give good tidings of forgiveness and of a generous reward.
12/11. It is We who bring to life the dead, and write down what they have sent ahead and the traces they have left behind. Everything have We reckoned up in a Codex *(Imām)*[2] that makes clear.
13/12. Set forth for them, [O Muḥammad], a parable. The people of a certain town[3] [were there] when the envoys came to it,

[1] These are the 28th and the 12th letters of the Arabic alphabet, and provide the name for the Sūra. This is the Sūra commonly recited at funerals and at the visitation of tombs.

[2] This is doubtless the Record Book which is to be opened at Judgment. See p. 426.

[3] The town is said to be Antioch, and the Commentaries tell of two disciples of Jesus being sent to preach to that city, and then joined by a third.

14/13. When We sent to them two, but they counted them both false, so We strengthened [the mission] by a third. Then they (i.e. the messengers) said: "We are indeed [Allah's] envoys to you."
15/14. They (i.e. the people) said: "Ye are naught but humans like ourselves; and the Merciful has not sent down a thing. It is only that ye are lying."
16/15. [The messengers] said: "Our Lord knows that we are indeed [His] envoys to you,
17/16. But we have no obligation beyond the clear proclamation [of the message]."
18/17. [The people] said: "We augur [1] ill of you. If ye do not desist we shall most assuredly stone you, and assuredly there will touch you from us a painful punishment."
19/18. [The messengers] said: "Your ill augury is with yourselves. Since ye have been warned [will ye still be unbelieving?]. Nay, but ye are prodigal people."
20/19. Then there came from the farthest end of the city a man running.[2] Said he: "O my people, follow ye the envoys,
21/20. Follow those who do not ask of you any wage, and who are rightly guided.
22/21. Why should I not worship Him who created me?; It is to Him ye are to be brought back.
23/22. Am I to take [other] gods instead of Him? Should the Merciful wish to harm me their intercession would not avail me a thing, nor would they deliver me.
24/23. I should indeed then be in manifest error.
25/24. Lo! I have believed in your Lord,[3] so hearken ye to me."
26/25. It was said [to him]: "Enter the Garden." Said he: "Would that my people could know
27/26. How my Lord has forgiven me [my sins] and made me one of the honoured ones."
28/27. Now We did not send down upon his people after him any army from the skies, nor have We been sending such down,
29/28. There was naught but a single shout, and lo! They were extinct.

[1] The verb used here suggests taking auguries from birds.

[2] Tradition names him Ḥabīb the Carpenter. Verse 26/25 suggests that he was martyred, and in later times his tomb at Antioch became a place of visitation.

[3] In this verse he turns from his people and is addressing the envoys. The assumption is that the people of Antioch were polytheists, but the envoys preached of the One God, and when Ḥabīb believed, and was martyred for his belief, he was taken to Paradise.

30/29. O what sorrow for humans![1] There comes not to them any messenger but they are making mock of him.
31/30. Have they not seen how many generations before them We have destroyed? (31) They, indeed, will not return to them.
32. Yet assuredly all will be brought together before Us.
33. Moreover the dead earth is a sign to them. We gave it life and brought forth from it grain, so that of it they eat.
34. And We set therein gardens of date-palms and grape-vines, and therein caused springs to gush forth,
35. That they might eat of its fruits and of that for which their hands have laboured. Will they not then be thankful?
36. Glory be to Him who created all the pairs from which the earth has its productivity, and [is the Creator] of themselves, and of things they know not.[2]
37. The night also is a sign for them. We strip from it the day, and behold! they are in darkness.
38. Also the sun which runs to a place of rest it has. That is the decreeing of the Sublime, the Knowing One.
39. And for the moon We have decreed stations, so that it comes back like an ancient bent palm-branch.
40. It behooves not the sun to overtake the moon, nor the night to outstrip the day, but, each in an orbit, they swim along.
41. And a sign for them [is the fact] that We carried their progenitors[3] in the fully-laden ark.
42. And We have created for them the like whereon they embark;
43. And if We will We drown them, so no cry for help [will avail] them, nor will they be rescued,
44. Unless as an act of mercy from Us, and an enjoyment for a while.
45. Yet, when it is said to them: "Fear ye what is before you and what is behind you, maybe ye will obtain mercy", [they pay no heed].
46. Not a sign of the signs of their Lord comes to them but they turn away from it.
47. And when it is said to them: "Give a contribution out of that with which Allah has provided you", those who disbelieve say to those

[1] Lit. "servants", but it means humans who are all servants of Allah.
[2] The meaning is that there are male and female elements in nature, among mankind, and also in other areas of which man is ignorant, but in each area the "pairs" are the cause of new life.
[3] *dhurriyya* normally means "progeny", but here seems to refer to their progenitors who were in the ark with Noah.

who believe; "Shall we feed one whom Allah could feed if He so willed? Ye are only in clear error."

48. And they are saying: "When will this threat [come to pass]?, if ye are those who speak the truth."
49. What do they expect save a single shout? It will seize them while they are still disputing.
50. So they will be able to make no testamentary deposition, nor will they return to their families.
51. But there will be a blast on the Trump, and lo! from the sepulchres to their Lord will they be speeding.
52. They will say: "Ah! alas for us! Who has raised us from our place of rest? This is what the Merciful promised, and the envoys spoke the truth."
53. There was naught but a single blast, and behold! all of them are brought into Our presence.
54. Today no soul will be wronged in anything, and ye will not be recompensed save for what ye have been doing.
55. Verily, the inmates of the Garden today are joyously busy,
56. They and their spouses are in shade, reclining on couches.
57. They have therein fruit, and they have whatsoever they call for.
58. "Peace!" a word [of greeting] from a compassionate Lord.
59. But [to the others He will say]: "Separate yourselves out, today, O ye sinners."
60. Did I not make a covenant with you, O ye sons of Adam, that ye should not serve Satan—he, indeed, is a manifest enemy to you—
61. And [did I not say]: "Worship ye Me. This is a straight path?"
62. But now, indeed, he has led astray a great host of you. Did ye then have no sense?
63. This is Gehenna with which ye were threatened.
64. Roast in it today because of the way ye were disbelieving.
65. Today We shall set a seal upon their mouths, and their hands will speak to Us, and their feet will bear witness to what they have been acquiring.
66. And did We please We should put out their eyes, so that they would be trying to get ahead on the path, but how would they see?
67. And did We please We should metamorphose them where they stand, so that they would not be able to move on or to go back.
68. And no matter to whom We give long life, him shall We reverse in nature. Is it that they do not have intelligence?
69. We have not taught him (i.e. Muḥammad) poetry, nor would that

beseem him. It is naught but a reminder and a lesson (Qur'ān) that makes clear,

70. That he may warn whosoever is alive, and that the sentence against the unbelievers may be justified.
71. Do they not see that We have created cattle for them out of what Our hands have made, so that they may have dominion over them?
72. And We have made them subject to them, so that from them they may have their riding beasts, and from them they may eat,
73. And have of them advantages and beverages. Will they not be thankful?
74. Yet they have taken for themselves deities apart from Allah, that mayhap they may be aided by them.
75. They are not able to aid them, though they are for them a host that will be brought forward.
76. So do not let their speech grieve thee. We know, indeed, what they keep secret and what they reveal.
77. Does not man see that We have created him from a drop? Yet, behold, he is a manifest disputer,
78. And has set forth for Us a parable, and forgotten his creation, saying: "Who will bring the bones to life when they are decayed?"
79. Say: "He will bring them to life Who produced them the first time, since He knows about every created thing."
80. He who gave you fire from the green tree, so that, behold, ye kindle flame from it,
81. Is not He Who created the heavens and the earth powerful enough to create their like? Yea, indeed, He is the Creator, the Knower.
82. His only command when He wishes anything is to say to it: "Be!", and it is.
83. So glory be to Him in Whose hand is the dominion over everything, seeing that to Him ye will be brought back.

XII

SŪRAT YŪSUF: SŪRA OF JOSEPH[1]

In the name of Allah, the Merciful, the Compassionate

1. Alif. Lām. Rā'. These are the signs of the Book that makes clear.

[1] This is the only Sūra of the Qur'ān of any length which deals with the same subject from beginning to end. It was well known that though Meccan it was retouched during the Madinan period.

2. We have sent it down an Arabic lesson (Qur'ān). Maybe ye will understand.
3. We are relating to thee, [O Muḥammad], one of the best of stories in revealing to thee this lesson (Qur'ān), though before it thou wert one of the heedless.
4. When Joseph said to his father: "O my father, I, indeed, have seen eleven stars and the sun and the moon. I saw them doing obeisance to me."
5. Said he: "O my son, relate not thy vision to thy brethren, lest they plot against thee a stratagem. Verily, Satan is a manifest enemy to man.
6. Thus is thy Lord choosing thee, and He will teach thee the interpretation of hard sayings, and will perfect His favour upon thee, and upon the House of Jacob, as He perfected it earlier on thy two forefathers, Abraham and Isaac. Verily thy Lord is knowing, wise."
7. Now indeed in Joseph and his brethren were signs for those who question.
8. When they said: "Joseph and his brother are dearer to our father than we are, though we are a band. Verily our father is in manifest error.
9. Kill ye Joseph, or drive him out of the country, then the face of your father will be free for you, and ye may be thereafter honest people."
10. A speaker from among them said: "Kill ye not Joseph, but cast him into the bottom of a cistern.[1] One of the passing caravans will pick him up if ye do that."
11. They said: "O our father, what is the matter with Thee? Thou dost not trust us with Joseph, although we are his sincere advisers.
12. Send him with us tomorrow. He will enjoy himself and play, and we shall be watching over him."
13. Said he: "It assuredly grieves me that ye should go off with him, and I fear that the wolf may eat him while ye are careless of him."
14. They said: "Should the wolf eat him while we are a band [of men], in that case we should indeed be the losers."
15. So when they went off with him, and agreed together to put him in the bottom of the cistern, then We spoke by revelation to him, [saying]: "Thou wilt most assuredly inform them of this matter of theirs [at a time] when they are not aware."
16. Then in the evening they came to their father weeping.

[1] A *jubb* is a large catchment cistern for water such as are to be found along the caravan trails.

17. They said: "O our father, we went off to race one another and we left Joseph with our baggage, but the wolf ate him. Yet thou wouldst not be believing us, even were we telling the truth."
18. And they brought lying blood upon his shirt. He (i.e. their father) said: "Nay, indeed! your souls have enticed you into an affair; but patience is a seemly thing, and Allah is the One to be asked for help against what ye tell."
19. Now a caravan came along, and they sent ahead their water-drawer, who let down his water-bucket. Said he: "O best of news! here is a youth", and they concealed him as a piece of merchandise; but Allah was well aware of what they were doing.
20. So they sold him for a trifling price, some dirhams counted out, for they were but rough appraisers with regard to him.
21. The Egyptian who bought him said to his wife: "Lodge him honourably, for it may be that he will be useful to us, or we may take him as a son." Thus did We make a place for Joseph in the land, and that was so that We might teach him the interpretation of hard sayings. Allah has the mastery over His affair, though the most part of the people do not know.
22. Now when he reached his mature strength We gave him wisdom and knowledge. Thus do We reward those who do well.
23. But she in whose house he was lusted for his person. She locked her doors and said: "Come along!" Said he: "Allah forbid! Truly, my Lord has lodged me in excellent fashion. Moreover, wrong-doers will not prosper."
24. But she wanted him, and he had wanted her, had it not been that he saw a demonstration of his Lord.[1] It was thus in order that We might turn from him evil and turpitude. He, indeed, was one of Our single-hearted servants.
25. The two of them raced for the door, and she tore his shirt from behind. At the door they met her husband. Said she: "What is the recompense for one who has desired evil of thy household, unless it be that he be put in prison, or [suffer] a painful punishment?"
26. [Joseph] said: "She lusted for my person." A witness[2] from her household bore witness, [saying]: "If his shirt has been torn in front then she has told the truth and he is among the liars,

[1] The Commentaries tell how he saw an apparition of his old father. This is an element in the Jewish legendary accounts of Joseph in Egypt.

[2] This, we are told, was a babe that was lying there in its cradle, and this is one of the four cases where infants in the cradle have spoken. See p. 623.

27. But if his shirt has been torn from behind then she is lying and he is of those who tell the truth."
28. So when he saw that his shirt had been torn from behind, he said: "This, indeed, is of your female scheming. Verily, the scheming of you women is great.
29. O Joseph, shun this; and do thou [O woman] ask pardon for thy sin, for thou hast, indeed, been among those who commit faults."
30. Women in the city said: "The Prince's wife lusts after her servant's person. He has made her sick with love. In our opinion she is in manifest error."
31. Now when she heard of their plotting, she sent them [a message] and prepared for them a banquet. [When they came] she gave to each one of them a knife. Then she said: "Come forth to them, [O Joseph]." When they saw him they were amazed at him, and cut their hands. They said: "Allah forbid! This is no man. This is naught but a noble angel."
32. She said: "This is the one with regard to whom ye were blaming me. I, indeed, did lust for his person, but he abstained. Yet if he does not do what I bid him he will most assuredly be imprisoned, and be one of the paltry ones."
33. He said: "O my Lord, to me the prison is preferable to that to which they are inviting me. Yet if Thou dost not avert from me their scheming I shall act the youth with them, and shall be one of the ignorant."
34. So his Lord answered him, and averted from him their scheming. He, indeed, is the Hearer, the Knower.
35. Then it seemed good to them, after they had seen the signs, to imprison him for a while.
36. Now there entered the prison with him two youths. Said one of them: "As for me, I see myself pressing out wine." Said the other: "As for me, I see myself carrying on my head bread of which the birds are eating. Tell us its interpretation. We, indeed, consider thee one of those who do good."
37. Said he: "No food with which ye are provided will come to you ere I have told you its interpretation before it comes to you. That is part of what my Lord has taught me. I, indeed, have forsaken the religion of a people who do not believe in Allah and are disbelieving in the Hereafter,
38. And I have followed the religion of my fathers Abraham and Isaac and Jacob. It was not for us to associate anything with Allah. That

is Allah's bounty to us and to the people, but the most part of the people do not render thanks.

39. O my two prison companions, are various Lords better, or Allah the One, the allovercoming?
40. What ye worship apart from Him are naught but names which ye and your fathers have named. Allah has sent down no authority for them. Wisdom is with Allah alone. He has given command that ye worship none but Himself. That is the right religion, but the most part of the people do not know.
41. O my two prison companions; as for one of you, he will pour out wine for his lord; as for the other, he will be crucified and birds will eat from his head. Decreed is the matter about which ye made enquiry."
42. Then he said to the one of them he thought was going to escape: "Mention me before thy lord." But Satan made him forget to mention him to his lord,[1] so he continued in prison for some years.
43. Said the king: "I see [in my vision] seven fat cows which seven lean ones devour, and seven green ears of grain and others dried up. O courtiers, instruct me with regard to my vision, if ye are such as can expound visions."
44. They said: "Confusions of dreams! We are not such as know about the interpretation of dreams."
45. Said the one who had escaped, remembering after a time: "I will get you information as to its interpretation, so send me!"
46. [Going to the prison he said]: "O Joseph, O thou trusty one, instruct us about seven fat cows which seven lean ones devour, and seven green ears of grain and others dried up. Perchance I may return to the people, that maybe they will know."
47. Said he: "Seven years will ye sow according to custom, but what ye harvest, leave in its ear, save a little from which ye may eat.
48. Then there will come after that seven hard [years] which will devour what ye have laid up for them, save a little of what ye preserve in store.
49. Then, after that, there will come a year in which the people will have abundant rain, and in which they will express the juice of grapes."

[1] The reference of the pronoun is ambiguous in the original. Some translate it: So Satan caused him (i.e. Joseph) to forget the remembrance of his Lord (i.e. Allah), so he remained in prison some years longer for the sin of putting his trust in man instead of in Allah. The original story, however, had it that the released servant forgot to mention Joseph to Pharaoh till the incident of the dream reminded him of the dream-interpreter he had known in prison.

50. Said the king: "Bring him to me." But when the messenger came to him, he said: "Return to thy lord, and ask him what was the matter with the women who cut their hands. My lord, indeed, knows about their scheming."
51. He (i.e. the king) said: "What is this affair of yours when ye lusted after Joseph's person?" They answered: "Allah forbid! We know no evil against him." The wife of the prince said: "Now has the truth come to light. It was I who lusted after his person, and he, indeed, is one of those who speak the truth."
52. "That," [said Joseph], "is that he may know that I did not betray him in his absence, and that Allah guideth not the plotting of those who are betrayers.
53. Yet I do not declare myself innocent. Verily, the soul has a natural inclination towards evil, save in so far as my Lord shows mercy. Truly, my Lord is forgiving, compassionate."
54. Said the king: "Bring him to me! I appropriate him for myself." So when he spoke with him, he said: "Behold, thou art today before us, [in a position] established, secure."
55. He said: "Appoint me over the store-houses of the land. I, indeed, am a knowing keeper."
56. Thus did We make a place for Joseph in the land, that he might settle down therein wheresoever he might desire. We make Our mercy alight on whom We will, and We allow not the reward of those who do good to be lost.
57. Nevertheless, the reward of the Hereafter is better for those who believe and have been pious.
58. Now [when the days of famine arrived] Joseph's brethren came and entered to him, and he recognized them but they were ignorant of who he was.
59. When he supplied them with their [needed] supplies, he said: "Bring me a brother of yours from your father. Do ye not see that I give full measure, and that I am the best of hosts?
60. But if ye do not bring him to me there will be no measure for you with me, nor will ye draw near me."
61. They said: "We shall beseech his father for him. We are those who will do it."
62. He said to his servants: "Put their merchandise [back] in their packs. Maybe they will recognize it when they get back to their families, and maybe they will return."
63. Now when they returned to their father, they said: "O our father,

measure is refused us, but send our brother along with us and we shall get measure, and we shall be sure guardians of him."

64. Said he: "Shall I entrust you with him save as I entrusted you formerly with his brother? But Allah is the best guardian, and He is the most merciful of those who shew mercy."
65. Then when they opened up their belongings they found that their merchandise had been returned to them. They said: "O our father, what [more could] we desire? This merchandise of ours has been returned to us, so we can supply our families, and preserve our brother, and get an extra camel-load of measure. That will be an easy measure."
66. Said he: "Never will I send him with you until ye give me an assurance from Allah that ye will bring him back to me, unless ye are prevented." Then when they had given him their assurance, he said: "Allah is trustee over what ye say."
67. He said: "O my sons, enter not in by a single gate, but enter by different gates. Yet I avail you naught against Allah. The judgment is with Allah alone. On Him have I set my trust, and on Him let those who trust set their trust."
68. So when they entered according as their father had bidden them, it availed them naught against Allah, though it satisfied a need in Jacob's soul, and he was a possessor of knowledge because of what We had taught him, but most of the people do not know.
69. When they entered to Joseph he took his brother to be with him, saying: "I, truly, am thy brother, so do not be distressed at what they have been doing."
70. Then when he prepared for them what they wanted prepared, he put the [king's] drinking-cup in his brother's saddle-bag. Then a herald made cry: "O Caravan! ye are surely thieves."
71. Said they, as they approached them: "What do ye find missing?"
72. They said: "We miss the king's goblet. To him who brings it [will be given] a camel's load, and I am surety for that."
73. They said: "By Allah, ye well know that we did not come to do evil in the land, and we are no thieves."
74. They said: "And what will the recompense for it be if ye are lying?"
75. They answered: "Let the recompense for it be that he in whose saddle-bag it is found be himself the recompense for it. Thus would we recompense wrong-doers."
76. He made a beginning with their packs before [coming to] his brother's pack. Then he drew it forth from his brother's pack. Thus did We

work a scheme for Joseph. Because of the king's religion he could not have taken his brother, had not Allah so willed. We raise the ranks of whom We will, and above every possessor of knowledge there is One who knows.

77. They said: "If he has stolen, nevertheless a brother of his stole before", but Joseph kept it secret to himself and did not let it appear to them. He said: "Ye are in an evil spot, and Allah knows best about what ye tell."

78. They said: "O Prince, he has a father, a very old man, so take one of us in his stead. We, indeed, see that thou art one of those who do good."

79. Said he: "Allah forbid that we should take anyone save him with whom we found our property, for otherwise we should be oppressors."

80. So when they despaired of him they drew aside to take counsel in private. Said the eldest of them: "Know ye not that your father has taken an assurance against you from Allah, and how previously ye acted iniquitously with regard to Joseph? I shall never leave the land till my father gives me permission, or till Allah gives judgment for me, for He is the best of those who give judgment.

81. Go back to your father, and say: 'O our father, thy son hath stolen, and we testify only to that which we know, nor could we have guarded against the unseen.

82. So question the town in which we were, and the caravan in which we have come, for we, indeed, are those who speak the truth.'"

83. [This they did, but their father] said: "Nay! but your souls have framed up a matter for you. Patient endurance, however, is a beautiful thing. Maybe Allah will bring them all to me together. He it is who is the Knowing, the Wise."

84. Then he turned from them and said: "O what grief is mine for Joseph." And his eyes went white from sorrow, and he was inwardly grieving.

85. They said: "By Allah, thou wilt keep on making mention of Joseph till thou art become decrepit, or art become one of those about to perish."

86. Said he: "I take my complaint of my sorrow and my grief to Allah alone, but I know from Allah what ye know not.

87. O my sons, go and seek for news of Joseph and his brother, and despair not of Allah's mercy. None, indeed, despair of Allah's mercy save the unbelieving people."

88. Then when they came into him (i.e. to Joseph) they said: "O Prince,

distress has touched us and our households, and we have brought naught but scanty merchandise, but give us full measure, bestowing it as charity upon us, for Allah, indeed, recompenses those who give in charity."

89. He said: "Know ye what ye did to Joseph and his brother when ye were ignorant [of what ye were doing]!"

90. They said: "Art thou, can it be that thou art Joseph?" Said he: "I am Joseph, and this is my brother. Allah has been gracious to us. The fact is, if one shows piety and patiently endures, Allah lets not the reward of those who do good perish."

91. They said: "By Allah, Allah has, indeed, given thee the preference over us, and we have been those who were committing faults."

92. Said he: "Let there be no blame upon you this day. Allah will forgive you, for He is the most merciful of those who show mercy.

93. Go ye with this shirt of mine and cast it on my father's face, [and] he will see again. And bring to me your households, all of them."

94. When the caravan set out [from Egypt] their father said: "I should declare that I perceive the smell of Joseph, were it not that ye would think me doting."

95. They said: "By Allah, there thou art at thine ancient error."

96. But when the bearer of good tidings came he cast it on his face, so he saw again.
(97) Said he: "Did I not say to you: 'I know from Allah what ye know not?'"

97/98. They said: "O our father, ask pardon for us for our sins. We have been those who were committing faults."

98/99. Said he: "Anon I shall ask pardon for you from my Lord. He it is who is the Forgiving, the Merciful."

99/100. When they entered to Joseph he took his two parents to be with him, and he said [to the others]: "Enter ye Egypt in safety, if Allah wills."

100/101. Then he brought his two parents up to the throne. They [all] fell down before him doing obeisance. He said: "O my father, this is the interpretation of my dream heretofore. My Lord has made it [come] true. He has treated me well indeed, since He brought me out of prison, and has brought you from the desert, after Satan had stirred up strife between me and my brothers. My Lord, indeed, is kindly disposed in what He wills. He it is who is the Knowing, the Wise.

101/102. O my Lord, Thou hast given me dominion and taught me the interpretation of hard sayings. O Creator of the heavens and the earth, Thou art my guardian in this world and the next. Cause me to die as one who submits, and join me with the Just."

102/103. This is one of the announcements of the unseen. We reveal it to thee [O Muḥammad], for thou wast not with them when they agreed on their matter and were scheming.

103. But the most part of the people, even though thou art urgent, are not believers.

104. Yet thou askest no reward for it. It is naught but a reminder to the worlds.

105. How many a sign in the heavens and the earth they pass by, yet they are turning away from them.

106. Most of them believe not in Allah without associating [others with Him].

107. Are they then secure from there coming upon them a calamity of Allah's punishment, or from the Hour coming on them suddenly, when they are not aware?

108. Say—: "This is my way. I summon to Allah by way of clear proof, I and whosoever follows me. So glory be to Allah, I am not one of the associators."

109. We have not sent before thee any save men of the townspeople to whom We gave revelation. Have they not travelled in the land and seen what the final issue was for those who preceded them? The abode of the hereafter is better, indeed, for those who show piety. Will ye then not understand?

110. Until when the messengers were in despair and thought they were being counted false, Our help came to them. Thus we rescue whomsoever We will, and Our violence is not to be turned back from the sinful people.

111. Now, indeed, there has been in their story a lesson for such as are possessed of insight. It was not a tale newly invented, but a confirmation of that which is there present, and an explanation of everything, a guidance and a mercy to a people who believe.

SELECTIONS FROM MADINAN SŪRAS[1]

XXIII

SŪRAT AL-MU'MINŪN: THE BELIEVERS

1. The believers have indeed prospered.
2. [They are] those who in their prayer are humble,
3. And those who turn away from loose talk,
4. And those who are active at giving Zakāt (i.e. the legal alms),
5. And those who keep guard over their genitals
6. Save with their wives or what their right hands possess,[2] for [with them] they are not under blame.
7. But he who lets his desires go beyond that, such are the transgressors.
8. And those who give attention to their pledges and their covenants,
9. And those who are watchful about their prayers.
10. These are the ones who will be inheritors,
11. Who will inherit Paradise,[3] in which they will live for ever.

CIII

SŪRAT AL-'AṢR: THE AFTERNOON[4]

In the Name of Allah, the Merciful, the Compassionate

1. By the afternoon,
2. Verily man is in loss,
3. Save those who have believed and worked righteous works, and have enjoined on one another truth, and enjoined on one another patient endurance.

[1] Since these are in general long Sūras it has not been possible to give more than selections from them.

[2] I.e. slave-girls.

[3] *firdaus*, which may mean Paradise as such, though some take it to mean a special section of Paradise. See p. 241.

[4] A Meccan fragment to which verse 3 was added during the Madinan period.

CIV

SŪRAT AL-HUMAZA:[1] THE BACKBITER

In the Name of Allah, the Merciful, the Compassionate

1. Woe to every backbiter, maligner,
2. Who gathers wealth and hoards it up.
3. He thinks that his wealth has made him immortal.
4. Nay, indeed! but he will assuredly be flung into al-Ḥuṭama.[2]
5. And what will teach thee what al-Ḥuṭama is?
6. [It is] Allah's kindled fire.
7. Which mounts up over the hearts.
8. Verily it [shall be] a vault over them
9. In outstretched columns [of flame].

XXII

SŪRAT AL-ḤAJJ: THE PILGRIMAGE

The closing verses

77/76. O ye who believe, bow down and do obeisance and worship your Lord, and do good, maybe ye will prosper.

78/77. And strive in [the way of] Allah with such striving as He is worthy of. He has chosen you, and has not laid on you in religion any narrowness, [only] the religion[3] of your father Abraham. He has named you Muslims (78) both aforetime and in this, that the Apostle might be a witness against you, and that ye might be witnesses against the people. So observe the prayer, and give the legal alms *(zakāt)*, and take tight hold on Allah. He is your patron, so what a patron [you have], and what a helper.

CXII

SŪRAT AL-IKHLĀṢ:[4] SINCERE [WORSHIP]

In the name of Allah, the Merciful, the Compassionate

1. Say: The fact is Allah is One,

[1] Some authorities consider this as an Early Meccan Sūra.
[2] One of the names of Hell, or of a portion thereof.
[3] *milla*, a religious party, sect. Bell translates it "creed".
[4] This is the Sūra most commonly recited as part of the daily prayer services. Many authorities consider it an early Meccan passage.

2. Allah is the Eternal.[1]
3. He did not beget and He was not begotten,
4. And no one has ever been his peer.[2]

XLIX

SŪRAT AL-ḤUJURĀT: THE APARTMENTS

In the name of Allah, the Merciful, the Compassionate

1. O ye who believe! be not froward before Allah and His Apostle, but fear Allah. Verily Allah is One who hears and knows.
2. O ye who believe! raise not your voices above the voice of the Prophet, and do not shout in speaking to him as ye shout to one another, lest your works come to naught, while ye are unaware.
3. Verily those who lower their voices when with the Apostle of Allah, they are those whose hearts Allah has tested for piety. They have forgiveness and a mighty reward.
4. Verily those who call out to thee [O Muḥammad] from behind the apartments,[3] most of them [are people who] do not understand.
5. Had they had patience till thou shouldst come out to them it would have been better for them, but Allah is forgiving, merciful.
6. O ye who believe! if there come to you some reprobate with a report, then make [the matter] clear, lest by ignorance ye harm folk, and have to repent for what ye have done.
7. And know that among you is Allah's Apostle. Were he to obey you in many an affair ye would be in distress, but Allah has made the faith dear to you, and made it appear beautiful in your hearts, whereas He has made unbelief and reprobate conduct and disobedience hateful to you. These are they who are rightly guided.

[1] *aṣ-ṣamad.* The translation is merely a guess. The word occurs only here and its meaning is quite uncertain.

[2] This seems to be a conscious rejection of the Christian teaching that Jesus was the Son of God and was on an equality with the Father. If so, the first verse may be intended to reject the doctrine of the Trinity.

[3] The apartments are those of the Prophet's various wives. These verses are said to refer to some rude Beduin who came to the Prophet and disrespectfully called to him while he was engaged in the apartment of one of his wives.

8. A bounty from Allah, and a favour. And Allah is knowing, wise.
9. Now if two parties of the believers fight one another, make ye peace between them, and if one of the two acts wrongfully against the other, fight ye that one that acts wrongfully till it comes back to Allah's command. Then if it returns make ye peace between them with justice, and be impartial. Verily Allah loves those who act impartially.
10. Believers are indeed brethren, so make peace between your brethren, and fear Allah; maybe ye will have mercy shown you.
11. O ye who believe! let not one [group of] people make mock of [another group of] people who perhaps are better than themselves, nor women [make mock of other] women who perhaps are better than themselves. And do not speak ill of one another nor use disparaging nicknames. Bad is a name for reprobate conduct after [profession of] faith, and such as do not repent, they it is who are the wrong-doers.
12. O ye who believe! avoid frequent suspicion, for sometimes suspicions are sin, and do not pry, nor traduce one another behind your backs. Would anyone of you like to eat the flesh of his dead brother? Nay, ye would loathe it. So fear Allah, for Allah is One who relents, is compassionate.
13. O ye people! We created you from a male and a female, and made you races and tribes that ye might know one another. Verily the noblest of you in Allah's sight is the most pious of you. Verily Allah is knowing, well-informed.
14. The Beduin say: "We believe." Say: "Ye believe not. Say rather: 'We have submitted', for not yet has the faith entered your hearts. But if ye obey Allah and His Apostle He will not have you lose aught of your works. Allah, indeed, is forgiving, compassionate."
15. The [true] believers are those who believe in Allah and His Apostle, then have no more doubts, who strive with their property and their persons in the way of Allah. Those it is who speak the truth.
16. Say: "Will ye teach Allah about your religion, when Allah knows whatever is in the heavens and what is in the earth, seeing that Allah knows everything?"
17. They would do thee a favour by becoming Muslims. Say: "Do me no favour by your becoming Muslims. It is Allah who does you a favour by having guided you to the faith, if ye are those who speak the truth."
18. Verily Allah knows the hidden things of the heavens and the earth, and Allah knows what ye are doing.

II

SŪRAT AL-BAQARA: THE COW

In the name of Allah, the Merciful, the Compassionate

1. Alif, Lām, Mīm.
2/1. That is the Book. There is no doubt about it. [It is] a guidance to those who shew piety.
3/2. Who believe in the unseen, and observe prayer, and give generously [in charity] of that with which We have provided them,
4/3. And who believe in what has been sent down to thee [O Muḥammad], and in what was sent down before thee, and concerning the Hereafter have sure conviction.
5/4. Such have guidance from their Lord, and those are they who prosper.

135/129. They say: "Be Jews or Christians [and] ye will be [rightly] guided". Say: "Nay, but the religion [1] of Abraham, a Ḥanīf,[2] and he was not one of the polytheists."
136/130. Say ye: "We believe in Allah and in what has been sent down to us, and what was sent down to Abraham, and to Ishmael and Isaac and Jacob and the Patriarchs, and in what was given to Moses and Jesus, and in what was given to the prophets from their Lord. We make no distinction between any of them, and to Him we submit ourselves."[3]
137/131. So, if they believe in the like of what ye believe, then they are indeed guided, and if they turn away it is only they who are in schism. Allah will be thy sufficiency against them. He is the One who hears, the One who knows.
138/132. Allah's *ṣibgha*,[4] and who has a better *ṣibgha* than Allah? Him are we worshipping.
139/133. Say: "Will ye dispute with us about Allah, when He is both our Lord and your Lord? We have our works, and ye have your works, and we devote ourselves single-heartedly to Him.

[1] *milla.* See n. 3 p. 64.
[2] A word of Syriac origin often used in the Qur'ān of Abraham, and apparently meant to suggest that he was a strict monotheist.
[3] *muslimūn* "those who submit themselves" is the plu. of *muslim*, so when thus understood the last clause could be translated "to Him we are Muslims."
[4] The verb means to dye a cloth a deep colour, so this noun seems to mean that true religion steeps a man, as it were, in Allah, as a cloth in a dye-vat, so that he is dyed with Allah's dye.

140/134. Or do ye say: 'Verily Abraham, and Ishmael, and Isaac, and Jacob, and the Patriarchs were Jews or Christians'. Say: 'Are ye the more learned or Allah?' Who is a greater wrong-doer than he who conceals a testimony he has from Allah? Allah is not neglectful of what ye are doing.

141/135. That is a community which has passed away. It has what it earned, and ye will have what ye have earned, and ye will not be questioned about what they were doing."

142/136. The foolish among the people will say: "What has turned them from the *qibla* they were wont to make use of?"[1] Say: "To Allah belong both East and West. He guides whom He wills to a straight path."

143/137. Thus have We made you (i.e. the Muslims) an intermediate community, that ye may be witnesses against the people, and that the Apostle may be a witness against you. (138) We appointed the *qibla* ye used to make use of only that We might know who would follow the Apostle from him who would turn on his heel. If it be a great matter it is not so to those whom Allah has guided. Allah was not One to let your faith come to naught. With the people Allah is indeed gentle, compassionate.

144/139. We, indeed, see thee turning thy face towards the skies, so We shall assuredly make thee, [O Muḥammad], turn around to a *qibla* that will please thee. Turn, therefore, thy face towards the sacred shrine,[2] and wherever ye [Muslims] may be, turn your faces towards it. Verily those to whom the Book has been given know that it is the truth from their Lord, and Allah is not heedless of what they are doing.

145/140. Even shouldst thou bring to those to whom the Book has been given every sign they would not follow thy *qibla*. Thou art not now a follower of their *qibla*, even as some of them are not followers of the *qibla* of others, and shouldst thou follow their desires, after the knowledge that has come to thee, thou wouldst in that case be among the wrong-doers.

[1] This and the following verses refer to the change in the *qibla* or direction to which the worshipper turns in prayer, a change which took place in the second year of the Hijra. Before that Muḥammad had been accustomed to have his followers face towards Jerusalem in their daily prayer services, but after his breach with the Jews he had them turn to face the shrine in his own city Mecca, which is still the *qibla* to which all Muslims turn during their prayers.

[2] *masjid* means a place where *sujūd*, or prostration in worship, is practised, and is the word from which our word "mosque" is derived. Here it means the ancient shrine at Mecca, which was apparently a very ancient centre of worship.

146/141. Those to whom We have given the Book recognize it as they recognize their own sons, yet a party among them conceals the truth, and they know [that they are doing so].

147/142. The truth is from thy Lord, so on no account be thou among those who doubt.

148/143. To each [has been given] a direction to which he turns [in prayer], so strive for pre-eminence in the good things. Wheresoever ye may be, Allah will bring you together. Allah, indeed, is powerful over everything.

149/144. So from wherever thou hast gone forth, turn thy face to the sacred shrine; for it, indeed, is the truth from thy Lord, and Allah is not heedless of what ye are doing.

150/145. So from wherever thou hast gone forth turn thy face towards the sacred shrine, and wheresoever ye [Muslims] may be, turn your faces towards it, that the people may have no argument against you, save those among them who do wrong. Do not fear them, fear Me, and [do this] that I may perfect My favour upon you, and maybe ye will be guided.

151/146. Accordingly We have sent among you an Apostle from among yourselves to recite to you Our signs, and purify you, and teach you the Book and the Wisdom, and teach you what ye did not know.

152/147. So remember Me, I will remember you, and give thanks to Me, and be not ungrateful to Me.

159/154. Verily, those who conceal the evidential signs and the guidance that We have sent down, after We have made it clear to the people in the Book, they are the ones Allah will curse, and those who curse will also curse them,

160/155. Save those who repent and reform and make [this] clear, for they are those towards whom I shall relent, for I am He who relents, the Compassionate.

161/156. They, indeed, who disbelieve and die as infidels, they are those on whom is the curse of Allah, of the angels, and of the people altogether,

162/157. Under which they will be for ever, their punishment never lightened for them, and having no expectancy [of deliverance].

163/158. Your God is One God, there is no deity save Him, the Merciful, the Compassionate.

164/159. Assuredly in the creation of the heavens and the earth, in the alternation of night and day, in the ships that run in the sea with what may be useful to people, in the rain that Allah sends down from the sky, whereby He quickens the earth after its deadness and spreads abroad in it every [kind of] animal, in the changing about of the winds, and in the clouds set to serve between sky and earth, [in all of these] are signs for a people who have intelligence.

165/160. Yet among the people are some who in place of Allah take substitutes which they love as one loves Allah. Nevertheless those who believe have an even stronger love for Allah. Could those who do wrong but see [that Day] when they will see the punishment, [see] that the power is wholly with Allah, and that Allah is severe in punishment!

166/161. [It will be a Day] when those who have been followed [1] will declare themselves innocent of those who have followed, and they will see the punishment, while [all] means [of relief] are cut off from them.

167/162. And those who have followed will say: "Could we but have another chance we would keep ourselves free from them, as they declare themselves free from us." In this way doth Allah show them their works. For them are [in store] sighings, but they will not get out from the Fire.

168/163. O ye people! eat of what is lawful and good in the earth, but do not follow in the footsteps of Satan, for he is a manifest enemy to you.

169/164. He enjoins on you only evil and wickedness, and that ye say about Allah what ye do not know.

170/165. When it is said to them: "Follow what Allah has sent down", they say: "Nay, but we shall follow what we found our fathers at." What! even though their fathers understood naught and had no guidance?

171/166. The similitude of those who disbelieve is that of one who addresses a creature which hears nothing but a summons and a call. Deaf, dumb, blind are they, so they do not understand.

172/167. O ye who believe! eat of the good things which We have given you as provision, and be thankful to Allah, if ye really worship Him.

173/168. He has made forbidden to you only that which is dead,[2] and

[1] Some say that this refers to the false gods, the "substitutes" *(andād)* of the previous verse, but others claim that it refers to the leaders of religious sects.

[2] Anything that is found already dead and has not been properly killed for food according to the ritual prescriptions.

blood, swine's flesh, and that which has been offered to any other than Allah;[1] though should anyone be compelled, not lusting for it nor wilfully [transgressing], then there is no guilt on him [if he eat of such food], for Allah, indeed, is forgiving, compassionate.

174/169. Verily those who conceal what Allah has sent down of the Book, and thereby purchase a little gain, such take naught but fire as food into their bellies. Then on the Resurrection Day Allah will not speak to them, and will not clear them, but for them will be a painful punishment.

175/170. Those are the ones who purchase error at the expense of guidance, and punishment at the expense of forgiveness. How patiently enduring will they be at the Fire!

176/171. That is because Allah sent down the Book with the truth, so those who differ among themselves about the Book are indeed far gone in schism.

255/256.[2] Allah, there is no deity save Him, the Living, the Self-subsistent, slumber takes Him not nor sleep. His is whatever is in the heavens and whatever is on earth. Who is it that will intercede with Him save by His leave? He knows what is before them and what is behind them, whereas they comprehend naught of His knowledge save what He wills. Wide stretches His Throne over the heavens and the earth, yet to guard them both wearies Him not, for He is the High, the Mighty.

282.[3] O ye who believe! when ye contract a debt [payable] at a fixed term, write it down. Let a scribe write it down fairly between you, and let no scribe refuse to write, as Allah has taught him. Let him do the writing and let the one who owes the debt dictate, and let him fear

[1] When a beast is slaughtered ritually the name of Allah is pronounced over it. The verb for this ritual invocation is *hallala*, a word familiar to us from the cognate Hebrew *Hallelujah*. Apparently the ancient Arabs pronounced the names of other deities in this ritual invocation, so the prohibition here is against using as food the flesh of animals slaughtered in the name of any other than Allah.

[2] This is the Throne Verse *(āyat al-kursī)* which is commonly memorized by young children all over the Muslim world.

[3] These are the last verses of Sūra II, which are mentioned in many traditions as verses of special excellence and virtue.

Allah, His Lord, and not diminish aught thereof. Should he who owes the debt be feeble in mind or body, or be unable himself to dictate, then let his guardian dictate with fairness, and call to witness two witnesses from among your men, or if there be not two men [available] then a man and two women from among those looking on whom ye think suitable, that if one of them should err the other may remind her. Let not the witnesses refuse when they are called upon. Disdain not to put it in writing, whether it be little or much, with its [agreed upon] term. That is more equitable for you with Allah, more accurate for the witnessing, and more likely to save you from doubts [about it]. [This is the proper procedure] unless it be [a matter of] present merchandise which you are circulating among yourselves. In that case it is no fault on your part if ye do not write it down, but [be sure to] have witnesses when ye are buying and selling with each other. Let not either scribe or witness do any injury [to the parties involved], for if ye do, that is a crime on your part. Show ye piety towards Allah and Allah will instruct you, for Allah knows about everything.

283. Should ye be on a journey and find no scribe, then [let there be] a pledge taken; but should any one of you trust another, let him who is trusted pay back what has been entrusted to him, and let him fear Allah, his Lord. Do not conceal the evidence. Whosoever conceals it, his heart is guilty, and Allah knows what ye are doing.

284. Allah's is whatever is in the heavens and whatever is in the earth. Whether ye disclose what is in your souls or conceal it, Allah will reckon with you for it. He forgives whom He will, and He punishes whom He will, and Allah is powerful over everything.

285. The Apostle believes in what has been sent down to him from his Lord, as do the believers. Each believes in Allah, and in His angels, and His Books, and His messengers. We make no distinction between one [and another] among His messengers. And they say: "We hear and obey. [Grant us] Thy forgiveness, O our Lord, for to Thee is the return."

286. Allah does not impose upon a soul more than it is capable [of bearing]. To its credit is what it has earned and against it is what it has stored up. O our Lord, do not take us to task if we should forget or make a mistake. O our Lord, do not burden us with what is beyond our capacity, but pardon us, and forgive us, and have mercy upon us. Thou art our patron, so assist us against the unbelieving people.

IV

SŪRAT AN-NISĀ': THE WOMEN

105/106. We have, indeed, sent down to thee, [O Muḥammad], the Book with the truth, that thou mayest judge between the people according to what Allah has shown thee, so be not an advocate for treacherous men,

106/106. But seek Allah's forgiveness, [for] Allah, indeed, is forgiving, compassionate.

107. And stand not up on behalf of those who are traitors to themselves. Allah, indeed, loves not one who is a traitor, a guilty person.

108. They may conceal themselves from the people, but they do not conceal themselves from Allah, for He is with them when they spend the night at speech that is not seemly, and Allah comprehends what they are doing.

109. There ye are! Ye have stood up for these in this worldly life, but who is going to stand up for them against Allah on Resurrection Day? or who then will be an advocate for them?

110. Whosoever does evil, or wrongs himself, then asks Allah's forgiveness, will find Allah forgiving, compassionate,

111. But whoso makes a guilty gain, gains it only to his own hurt, for Allah is knowing, wise.

112. Whoso makes a sinful or a guilty gain, then casts it on an innocent person, has indeed laid on himself calumny and manifest guilt.

113. Had it not been for Allah's bounty and mercy to thee, [O Muḥammad], a party of them would have succeeded in leading thee astray, but they lead astray none but themselves, and they will not harm thee in any way. Allah has sent down to thee the Book and the Wisdom, and has taught thee what thou knewest not, so Allah's bounty to thee has been great.

114. In much of their secret talk there is no good, save [in the case of] him who enjoins the giving of charitable alms or [the doing] of that which is approved, or making peace among the people. To the one who does that, out of a desire to be well-pleasing to Allah, We shall anon give a great reward.

115. But whosoever severs himself from the Apostle after the guidance has been made clear to him, and follows some path other than that of the believers, We shall turn Our back to him just as he has turned his back [to Us], and We shall roast him in Gehenna, and how evil a place to arrive at [that will be].

116. Allah assuredly will not forgive any associating [of others] with Him, but He will forgive anything short of that to whomsoever He will. He who associates [any other] with Allah has indeed gone far into error.
117. What they invoke in place of Him are but females. What they invoke is naught but a rebellious satan.[1]
118. Allah cursed him (i.e. Satan), so he said: "I shall assuredly take of Thy servants a prescribed portion.
119/118. I shall lead them astray; I shall move them with desire; I shall command them and they will cut the camels' ears; I shall command them and they will alter Allah's creation."[2] He who takes Satan as a patron *(walī)* instead of Allah has indeed suffered a manifest loss.
120/119. [Satan] gives them promises and he moves them with desire, but what Satan promises them is naught but delusion.
121/120. These have Gehenna as their abode, from which they will find no escape.
122/121. But those who believe and work the works of righteousness We shall cause to enter into gardens beneath which rivers flow, therein to abide for ever. Allah's promise is sure, for who is more truthful than Allah in what He says?
123/122. It is not according to your wishes, nor the wishes of the People of the Book. Whosoever does evil will be recompensed therefor, and will find for himself no patron *(walī)* and no helper apart from Allah.
124/123. And whosoever does works of righteousness, whether he be male or female, provided he is a believer, such shall enter the Garden and will not be wronged [so much as] the skin of a date-stone.
125/124. Who is better in the matter of religion than he who submits his face to Allah, and is a doer of good, and follows the religion *(milla)* of Abraham as a Ḥanīf,[3] for Allah took Abraham as a friend.
126/125. To Allah belongs what is in the heavens and what is in the earth, and Allah encompasses all things.

[1] The reference in this verse is to the objects of worship among the pagan Arabs, probably to the chief deities of the Meccan shrine, one of which was a male, named Hubal, and three were females, named Allāt, Manāt and al-'Uzzā.

[2] The reference is to a pagan Arab custom of making small mutilations on the bodies of animals or humans for supposedly religious reasons. The common custom of circumcision could also, of course, be considered such a mutilation of Allah's creation.

[3] For *milla* and *ḥanīf* see notes on pp. 64 and 67.

127/126. They will ask thee for a decision in regard to women. Say: "Allah gives you a decision in regard to them. What now is recited to you in the Book concerning female orphans to whom ye do not give what is prescribed for them but whom ye desire to marry, and regarding the weak among the children, and that ye should establish justice for the orphans? Whatever good ye do Allah knows about it.

128/127. Should a woman fear ill-treatment from her husband or aversion, then it is no crime for the pair of them to make a mutual agreement. A mutual agreement is a good thing, for souls are prone to avarice. If ye do well and act piously then Allah is well aware of what ye do.

129/128. Ye will never be able to deal evenly among the women even though ye are eager [to do so], but do not incline entirely [to one] so that ye leave another like one forsaken, and if ye make a mutual agreement then act piously, for Allah is forgiving, compassionate.

130/129. And if the two separate, Allah will enrich both out of His abundance, for Allah is wide-reaching, wise.

TRADITION

INTRODUCTION

Next in importance to the Qur'ān as a source for Muslim belief and practice comes the Corpus of Tradition. The Qur'ān, which to the Muslim is the word of Allah, gives him a primary rule of life, but there are many matters where guidance for practical living is necessary but about which the Qur'ān says nothing. In such cases the obvious thing was to follow custom *(sunna)*. There was ancient custom which could be a guide in many matters, but in matters peculiar to the new religion there was the custom of the earliest believers, who had been in contact with the Prophet and who presumably would act in matters of religion according to the custom of the Prophet and the earliest Muslim community. Very soon traditions began to circulate giving formal statement of what the *sunna* of the earliest Muslims on a variety of matters was, and such traditions formed, unconsciously perhaps at first, a supplement to the Qur'ān as a rule of life. In this earliest stage the traditions which gave the *sunna* of the Prophet were no more important, perhaps not even so important, as those which gave the *sunna* of the earliest believers. Ere long, however, attention came to be concentrated on the Prophet, as his manner of life became in their eyes the ideal Muslim life to be imitated by his followers. Very soon after the Prophet died there began to circulate stories of his wonderful sayings and doings. Then as new converts and younger members of the community, who had not known Muḥammad in the flesh, began to turn to the Companions and those who had been nearest to him, to tell them about the Prophet, not only would tales about him increase, but as they passed from mouth to mouth would be subject to standardization and selection, till presently there was in existence a more or less well-known body of traditions about the sayings and doings of the Prophet which represented the Word of the Prophet as supplement to the Word of Allah.

This body of traditions circulated orally for some time, as is indicated by the word *ḥadīth*, commonly used for tradition, which originally meant "some thing new", and was a normal word for "conversation", i.e. the telling of something new. The demand for such traditions naturally created a supply which put into circulation a vast number of spurious traditions. Moreover, once it was recognized that tradition was coming to have a place of authority as a supplement to the Qur'ān, every group, every party, every movement developing with the community supplied itself with a selection of traditions which would give Prophetic authority for its particular point of view. Ere long the situation was such that we find the great collector Sa'īd al-Qaṭṭān sadly remarking: "In nothing will you find pious men greater liars than in *ḥadīth*." It was thus inevitable that sooner or later an attempt would have to be made to form some sort of authoritative collection of such traditions as could be reasonably considered genuine, and which were of a nature to give guidance to the community in matters where no sufficient rule of life could be found in the Qur'ān. In this way the *sunna* of the Prophet came to take its place beside the Qur'ān as normative for Muslim teaching and practice.

The earliest formal collections of traditions were generally in the form known as *Musnad.* In these each *ḥadīth*, or statement which gave the saying or described the action of the Prophet, was preceded by an *isnād*, or chain of transmitters taking it back to the Companion or intimate of the Prophet who had himself heard the statement or witnessed the event given in the *matn*, or text of the *ḥadīth*, as authority for the *sunna* of the Prophet. These were then listed under the name of the final link in the *isnād.* A more practical arrangement, however, was by subject-matter, and as at an early period the working jurists needed collections of traditions which they might use in rendering decisions on practical cases, there grew up the practice of arranging collections under the rubrics suggested by the needs of the jurists —marriage, inheritance, debts, cult practice, etc.

There was never any formal canonization in Islam of a Corpus of Tradition, comparable to 'Uthmān's canonization of the Madinan text of the Qur'ān, but gradually six collections, made in the latter part of the third Islamic century, succeeded in gaining such general approval that later generations tacitly accepted them as the six canonical collections. They are the *Ṣaḥīḥ* of al-Bukhārī (d. 256 A.H. = 870 A.D.), the *Ṣaḥīḥ* of Muslim (d. 261 A.H. = 875 A.D.), the *Sunan* of Ibn Māja (d. 273 A.H. = 887 A.D.), the *Sunan* of Abū Dāwūd (d. 275 A.H. = 888 A.D.), the *Jāmi'* of at-Tirmidhī (d. 279 A.H. = 892 A.D.), and the *Sunan* of an-Nasā'ī (d. 303 A.H. = 915 A.D.).

In making their collections these Traditionists obviously used a critical technique of selection to decide what they would include and what they would reject. Bukhārī, for example, is said to have examined some six hundred thousand traditions of which he accepted only 7,397. Their purpose was to assemble a body of traditions which would serve as a rule of life for practising Muslims, so their primary interest was in selecting such traditions as gave clear guidance concerning what Muslim belief and practice should be, what things were permissible and approved, and what were not permissible and disapproved. In the second place the presence of so much spurious material in circulation made them anxious to set up tests of authenticity which would exclude unauthentic material. Unfortunately they picked on the *isnād* as the testing point and worked out an elaborate system for testing the trustworthiness of these "chains", and of the individuals who formed the links therein, so that an *isnād* could be labelled "excellent", "good", "fair", "weak", etc., and the tradition itself rated accordingly. To a Muslim, therefore, the *isnād* is quite as important an element in a *ḥadīth* as the *matn* itself.

In the following pages selections are presented both from the canonical collections, from the later compendiums based on these, and from the much richer uncanonical collections which, since they were not concerned with the rubrics of jurisprudence, were freer to include a great deal of *ḥadīth* material which did not interest the canonical collectors, but which is of the first importance as illustration of religious thought and life in Islam.

SELECTED TRADITIONS FROM AL-BUKHĀRĪ'S *AL-JĀMI' AṢ-ṢAḤĪḤ*[1]

Said the Apostle of Allah—upon whom be Allah's blessing and peace—: "The [true] Muslim is he from whose tongue and whose hand [other] Muslims are safe, and the [true] Muhājir is he who has fled from those things Allah has forbidden."[2]

Islam is built upon five things: on testifying that there is no deity save Allah and that Muḥammad is his Apostle, on performing prayer, on paying the legal alms *(zakāt)*, on the pilgrimage [to Mecca], and on the fast of Ramaḍān.

The Apostle of Allah—upon whom be Allah's blessing and peace— was asked which [good] work was the most excellent, and he answered: "Belief in Allah and in His Apostle." He was asked: "And then which?" He replied: "Jihād in the way of Allah."[3] He was again asked: "And then what?" and he replied: "An acceptable pilgrimage."[4]

No one ever bears witness that there is no deity save Allah and that Muḥammad is the Apostle of Allah, [testifying to it] sincerely from his heart, but Allah will preserve[5] him from Hell-fire.

There is no Muslim who plants a tree or cultivates a plot from which birds or man or domestic beasts [may gather food to] eat, but has therein an act of charitable alms [recorded to his merit].

If a man seizes the property of others with intent to restore it, Allah

[1] From the text in V. Rosen's *Chrestomathia Arabica* (St. Petersburg, 1875), Vol. I, pp. 1–6. In this text the *isnāds* have for the most part been omitted. — Abū 'Abdallah Muḥammad b. Ismā'īl al-Bukhārī, 194–256 A. H. = 810–870 A.D., a savant of Iranian origin, is by far the most famous of all the collectors of Islamic Tradition. He wandered far in making his collection and out of the 600,000 he gathered, he accepted 7,397 into his *Ṣaḥīḥ*, an edition of which by Krehl and Junyboll was published in four volumes at Leiden, 1862–1908.

[2] A *muhājir* was one who had emigrated from his home in Mecca to join Muḥammad and the young Muslim community in Madina, so the Tradition is playing on the meaning of the verb *hajara* "to flee", just as in the first clause it played on the verb forms *aslama* "to become a Muslim" and *salima* "to be safe".

[3] *jihād* is the technical term for going out on Holy War.

[4] Literally "an approved pilgrimage", i.e. one which has fulfilled all the proper requirements, and so is acceptable to Allah.

[5] Lit. "make him something forbidden to Hell-fire".

will settle with him, but if he seizes it with intent to waste it Allah will make waste of him.

If a slave serves honestly his [earthly] master and worships earnestly his [heavenly] Lord, he will have a double recompense.

He who shows concern for the widows and the unfortunate [ranks as high] as one who goes on Jihād in the way of Allah, or one who fasts by day and who rises at night [for prayer].

A [true] believer views his sins as though he were sitting beneath a mountain which he fears may fall on him, but an evil-doer views his sins as a fly that moves across his nose.

In this world be as a stranger, or as one who is just passing along the road.

In two things an old man's heart never ceases to be that of a youth, in love of this world and in hoping long.

Were a man to possess two valleys full of gold he would be wanting a third, for nothing will ever really fill man's belly but the dust.

To look at a woman is forbidden, even if it is a look without desire, so how much the more is touching her.

Said he—upon whom be Allah's blessing and peace—: "Avoid seven pernicious things." [His Companions] said: "And what are they, O Apostle of Allah?" He answered: "Associating anything with Allah, sorcery, depriving anyone of life where Allah has forbidden that save for just cause, taking usury, devouring the property of orphans, turning the back on the day of battle, and slandering chaste believing women even though they may be acting carelessly."

No one who enters Paradise will ever want to return to this world, even could he possess the earth and all that is on it, save the martyrs who desire to return to this world and be killed ten times so great is the regard in which they find themselves held.

To be stationed on the frontier for one day during Holy War is better than [to possess] this world and all that is on it. A place in Paradise the size of one of your whip-lashes is better than this world and all that is on it. A night or a day that a man spends on Holy War is better than this world and all that is on it.

The similitude of a stingy man and a generous giver of alms is that of two men wearing cloaks of mail in which the hand-pieces are fastened to the collar-piece. Whenever the generous giver starts to give an alms it stretches for him so that it is as though it were not, but when the stingy man starts to give an alms every link clings to the one next it so contracting that his hands are kept tight by his collar-bone and however much he strives it will not stretch.

It is right to "hearken and obey"[1] so long as one is not bidden disobey [Allah], but should the command be to disobedience let there be no "hearken and obey".

Travelling is part of one's punishment, for one is deprived of one's sleeping, one's eating, one's drinking thereby, so whenever any one of you has finished what he had to do let him hurry home.

Allah desires to meet those who desire to meet with Him, but is disinclined to meet those who are disinclined to meet with Him.

The man who has the lightest punishment on the Day will be the one who has live coals placed under the soles of his feet [so hot that] his brains will boil from the heat thereof.

If a man sees something in [the conduct of] his ruler which he dislikes let him put up with it patiently, for there is no one who separates himself even a span from the community and dies [in that separation], but dies a pagan [2] death.

When Friday comes angels take their seat over every mosque gate and write down in order those who come in, but when the prayer-leader sits they fold their sheets and come to hearken to the words.

Said the Prophet—upon whom be Allah's blessing and peace—: "I had a look into Paradise and I saw that the poor made up most of its inhabitants, and I had a look into Hell and saw that most of its inhabitants were women."

When [the month of] Ramaḍān begins the gates of heaven are set open, the gates of Hell are locked shut, and the satans are chained.

Treat women-folk kindly for woman was created of a rib. The crookedest part of a rib is its upper part. If you go to straighten it out you will break it, and if you leave it alone it will continue crooked. So treat women in kindly fashion.

Whosoever testifies that there is no deity save Allah, that Muḥammad is His servant and His Apostle, that Jesus is His servant and His Apostle and His word which He cast to Mary and a Spirit from Him,[3] that Paradise is a reality and Hell-fire a reality, him will Allah bring into Paradise in accordance with his works.

Only two men are really to be envied, namely, a man to whom Allah has given Scripture and who sits up at nights with it, and a man to whom

[1] The reference is to the common response "to hear is to obey" which is the polite response to make when one is bidden do something or other.

[2] Literally "the death of the Jāhiliyya", this being the name used for the pagan pre-Islamic period of Arab history.

[3] This statement about Jesus is reproducing Sūra IV, 171/169.

Allah has given wealth which he distributes in charitable alms day and night.

Said the Apostle of Allah—upon whom be Allah's blessing and peace—: "O band of youths, let him among you who is able to make a home get married, and let him who is not able betake himself to fasting for he will find in that a quencher [of his passions]."

The worst of foods is that of a feast to which the rich have been invited and the poor overlooked, yet anyone who overlooks an invitation is in rebellion against Allah and His Apostle.

Said the Apostle of Allah—upon whom be Allah's blessing and peace—: "Do not wear silks and satins, and do not drink from gold and silver vessels nor eat from dishes made thereof, for these things are theirs in this world but ours in the world to come."

Said the Apostle of Allah—upon whom be Allah's blessing and peace—: "Gabriel said to me: 'Whosoever of your community dies without ever having associated any other with Allah will enter Paradise' (or perhaps he said: 'will not enter Hell-fire'). Someone said: 'Even if he is an adulterer or a thief?' He replied: 'Even if.'"

The similitude of a good companion and a bad one is [that of] a man who carries musk and one who blows a blacksmith's bellows, for one who is carrying musk may give you a share, or you may purchase some of it, or in any case enjoy the delightful smell, but one who blows the blacksmith's bellows will either set your clothes on fire or accost you with an evil smell.

Said the Prophet—upon whom be Allah's blessing and peace—: "The first group to enter Paradise will have faces like the moon on the night of its fullness, will neither spit nor blow their noses nor defecate therein, their utensils there will be of gold, their combs of gold and silver, their censers of aloes wood, their sweat will be musk, and each of them will have two spouses so beautiful that the marrow of their leg-bones will be visible through the flesh. There will be no differences or disputings among them for they will all be of one heart, glorifying Allah morning and evening."

'Ā'isha said: "I was stuffing a pillow for the Prophet—upon whom be Allah's blessing and peace—on which were images like those on a saddle-cushion, when he came and stood in the doorway. His countenance started to alter, so I said: 'What is it, O Apostle of Allah?' He said: 'What are you doing with this pillow?' 'It is a pillow', I answered, 'that I have made for you on which you may recline.' Said he: 'Do you not know that angels will not enter a house in which there is a picture? On the Day makers of [such] pictures will be punished, for [Allah] will say to them: 'Give life to that which you have created.'"

Among the signs of the coming of the Hour are these: ignorance will be apparent and learning inconspicuous, fornication will be rampant and the drinking of wine, men will be few but women many so that fifty women will have but one husband between them.

Said the Prophet—upon whom be Allah's blessing and peace—:"He who drinks wine in this world and repents not of it will be forbidden it in the world to come."

There is no misfortune befalls a Muslim but Allah will atone for some sin of his thereby, even if it be only [so small a misfortune as] his being pricked by a thorn.

Said the Prophet—upon whom be Allah's blessing and peace—:"Visions are from Allah but dreams are from Satan, so if any one of you sees anything disagreeable [during sleep] let him spit three times when he wakens up and take refuge [with Allah] from its evil, and then it will do him no harm."

Said the Apostle of Allah—upon whom be Allah's blessing and peace—: "Among the greatest of mortal sins is that a man curse his parents." They said: "O Apostle of Allah, how could a man curse his parents?" He replied: "The man who reviles another man's parents is reviling his own father and mother."

Abū'l-Yamān related to us [saying]: Shuʿaib informed us on the authority of az-Zuhrī, [who said]: Abū Salama b. ʿAbd ar-Raḥmān related to us that Abū Huraira—with whom may Allah be pleased—said: The Apostle of Allah—on whom be Allah's blessing and peace—once kissed al-Ḥasan the son of ʿAlī while al-Aqraʿ b. Ḥābis of Tamīm was sitting there. Al-Aqraʿ said: "I have ten sons but never have I kissed any one of them." The Apostle of Allah—upon whom be Allah's blessing and peace—looked at him, and then said: "He who does not show tenderness will not have tenderness shown him."

Said the Prophet—upon whom be Allah's blessing and peace—: "Whoever casts himself down from a mountain so as to kill himself will be in Hell continually casting himself down thus for ever and ever. Whoever sips poison so as to kill himself will in Hell have poison in his hand which he will go on sipping there for ever and ever. Whoever kills himself with a knife will in Hell have a knife in his hand which he will go on continually plunging into his bowels for ever and ever."

Said he—upon whom be Allah's blessing and peace—:"Let none of you wish for death because of any hardship that has befallen him. If he needs must say something, let him say: 'Allahumma! let me live so long as life is best for me, and let me pass away when passing away is the best thing for me.'"

Said the Prophet—upon whom be Allah's blessing and peace—:"Allah made mercy in a hundred parts. Ninety-nine of these parts He kept with Himself and one single part He sent down on earth. It is by reason of this one part that creatures show mercy to one another, so that a mare carefully lifts her hoof fearing lest with it she harm her foal."

Said the Apostle of Allah—on whom be Allah's blessing and peace—: "Let him who believes in Allah and the Last Day refrain from doing harm to his neighbour. Let him who believes in Allah and the Last Day see to it that he properly honours his guest. Let him who believes in Allah and the Last Day either speak what is good or hold his tongue."

Said the Prophet—upon whom be Allah's blessing and peace—:"No one will ever experience the sweetness of faith till he loves a man solely for the sake of Allah, till he feels that he would rather be cast into Hell-fire than return to unbelief once Allah has delivered him from it, till Allah and His Apostle are dearer to him than anything besides."

Muḥammad b. Muqātil Abū'l-Ḥasan has related to me [saying]: ʿAbdallah informed us on the authority of Ḥumaid b. ʿAbd ar-Raḥmān, on the authority of Abū Huraira—with whom may Allah be pleased—that a man came to the Apostle of Allah—upon whom be Allah's blessing and peace—saying: "O Apostle of Allah, there is no hope for me."[1] He replied: "Too bad for you." Said [the man]: "I had intercourse with my wife during Ramaḍān." [The Prophet] answered: "Then set free a slave." Said he: "I have none." [The Prophet] answered: "Then fast for two months on end." Said he: "But I could not." [The Prophet] answered: "Then feed sixty poor people." Said he: "I have not the wherewithall." Just then there was brought to [the Prophet] a basket of dates, so he said to the man: "Take this and distribute it as charitable alms [in expiation for your sin]." Said he: "O Apostle of Allah, [am I to distribute it] to other than my own family? when by Him in whose hand is my soul there is no one between the gateposts of the city more needy than I am." Thereat the Prophet laughed till his canine teeth showed, and he said: "Go along and take it."

ʿUmar b. Ḥafṣ has related to me [saying]: My father related to us [saying]: al-Aʿmash related to us [saying]: Ibrāhīm at-Taimī related to me

[1] Literally "I have perished," i.e. I have committed a sin for which I am doomed to destruction. The Tradition given here illustrates the principle of expiation for sins committed wittingly. See pp. 102–103 for this same Tradition.

on the authority of al-Ḥārith b. Suwaid, who said: ʿAbdallah said that the Prophet—upon whom be Allah's blessing and peace—said: "To which of you is the wealth of his heir preferable to his own wealth?" They answered: "O Apostle of Allah, there is no one but finds his own wealth more precious." He replied: "Yet one's wealth is what one sends on ahead, and the heir's wealth is what one leaves behind."

Al-Ḥumaidī has related to us [saying]: Sufyān related to us [saying]: ʿAbdallah b. Abī Bakr b. ʿAmr b. Ḥazm has related to us that he heard Anas b. Mālik say: Said the Apostle of Allah—upon whom be Allah's blessing and peace—: "Three follow the corpse. Two return but one remains with him. His family and his wealth and his deeds follow him. His family and his wealth return but his deeds go on with him."

THE SECTION ON FASTING, FROM THE *ṢAḤĪḤ* OF AL-BUKHĀRĪ[1]

1. *On the necessity of the Fast of Ramaḍān, and on the verse (II, 183/179): "O ye who have believed, fasting is prescribed for you, just as it was prescribed for those who were before you. Maybe ye will show piety."*

Qutaiba related to us, saying: Ismāʿīl b. Jaʿfar related to us from[2] Abū Suhail, from his father, from Ṭalḥa b. ʿUbaidallah, that a nomad Arab came to the Apostle of Allah—on whom be Allah's blessing and peace—with dishevelled head, saying: "O Apostle of Allah, inform me of what Allah has laid on me as incumbent duty in the matter of saying prayers." He answered: "The five prayer-services, unless you would voluntarily add thereto." Then [the Arab] said: "O Apostle of Allah, inform me of what Allah has laid on me as incumbent duty in the matter of fasting." He answered: "The month of Ramaḍān, unless you would voluntarily add thereto." Said [the Arab]: "Inform me of what Allah has laid on me as incumbent duty in that matter of alms." So the Apostle of Allah informed him of the legal prescriptions of Islam [with regard thereto]. Said he: "By Him who has honoured you with the truth, I will not voluntarily add aught, but neither will I come short of what Allah has prescribed as incumbent duties for me." Then the Apostle of Allah—upon whom be Allah's blessing and peace—said: "He will be one of the fortunate ones, if he means that." Or [according to another version, he said]: "He will be brought into Paradise, if he means that."

Musaddad related to us, saying: Ismāʿīl related to us from Ayyūb, from Nāfiʿ, from Ibn ʿUmar, who said: "The Prophet—upon whom be Allah's blessing and peace—fasted ʿĀshūrā'[3] and bade it be kept as a fast, but when Ramaḍān was made an incumbent duty [on the Muslims] it was abandoned. ʿAbdallah used not to fast therein save when it happened to coincide with his [voluntary] fasts.

[1] In the Krehl–Junyboll edition. Vol. I. pp. 472–498.

[2] The particle *ʿan* used in these *isnāds* really means "on the authority of", but as the transmission of the Tradition was "from" one authority to another, we translate it throughout by "from" for brevity's sake.

[3] A fast said to have been observed by the Jews and some of the Arabs in the pre-Islamic days as commemoration of their deliverance from their enemies. See. pp. 122–3.

Qutaiba b. Sa'īd said: al-Laith has related to us from Yazīd b. Abī Ḥabīb, that 'Irāk b. Mālik related to him that 'Urwa informed him from 'Ā'isha [1] that the Quraish [2] used to fast the Day of 'Āshūrā' in the pre-Islamic days, and then the Apostle of Allah—upon whom be Allah's blessing and peace—bade it be kept as a fast, [which it was] till Ramaḍān was made an incumbent duty. Said the Apostle of Allah—upon whom be Allah's blessing and peace—: "If anyone so wishes, let him still keep it as a fast, but if anyone so wishes, let him eat thereon."

2. *On the Merits of the Fast*

'Abdallah b. Maslama related to us from Mālik, from Abū'z-Zinād, from al-A'raj, from Abū Huraira, that the Apostle of Allah—upon whom be Allah's blessing and peace—said: "Fasting is a protective covering [from the fires of Hell], so let there be no unseemly speech, no foolish acting [during it]. If a man is attacked or vilified [during it], let him say twice: 'I am fasting;' for by Him in Whose hand is my soul, the odour from the mouth of him who fasts is sweeter to Allah than the perfume of musk. [Allah says to Himself]: 'He is giving up his food and his drink and his body lusts for My sake when he is fasting unto Me, so I shall reward him, and for each good deed [that he does] grant him the merit of ten.'"

3. *On Fasting as an Expiation*

'Alī b. 'Abdallah related to us, saying: Sufyān related to us, saying: several have related to us from Abū Wā'il, from Ḥudhaifa, who said: 'Umar once asked: "Who is there who has memorized a Tradition from the Prophet—upon whom be Allah's blessing and peace—about discord?" Ḥudhaifa answered: "I heard him say that discord arises for a man from [three sources, from] his family, from his property, and from his neighbour, but prayer, fasting and gifts of charity may be its expiation." Said ['Umar]: "I am not asking about this [general matter of discord arising among men], but about that [which will come at the Last Days] billowing like the billows of the sea." "Facing that", said [Ḥudhaifa], "there is a gate shut." "Will it be opened", asked ['Umar], "or broken down?" "It will be broken down", answered [Ḥudhaifa]. "Then", said he, "it is not likely to be shut again until the Day of Resurrection." We said to

[1] The Prophet's youngest wife who is quoted as the source for a vast number of Traditions.
[2] The ruling Arab tribe in Mecca in the days of the Prophet.

Masrūq: "Ask him if 'Umar knew who the 'Gate' would be?"[1] So he asked him, and he answered: "Yes, [he knew that] just as he knew that night is before morning."

4. *On how ar-Rayyān is for those who fast*

Khālid b. Makhlad related to us, saying: Sulaimān b. Bilāl related to us, saying: Abū Ḥāzim related to us from Sahl, from the Prophet—upon whom be Allah's blessing and peace—who said: "In Paradise there is a gate named *ar-Rayyān* through which, on the Day of Resurrection, those who fast will enter, and through which none but they will enter. The call will come: 'Where are the Fasters?', and they will rise. None other than they will enter by it, for when they have entered it will be locked, so that no one else can enter by it."

Ma'n related to us, saying: Mālik related to me from Ibn Shihāb, from Ḥumaid b. 'Abd ar-Raḥmān, from Abū Huraira, that the Apostle of Allah—upon whom be Allah's blessing and peace—said: "Whoever has expended a pair [of anything] in the way of Allah will hear a call from the gates of Paradise, 'O Servant of Allah, this is good.' Whosoever has been constant at prayer will be summoned from the Prayer Gate, and whosoever has been diligent in Holy War will be summoned from the Jihād Gate. Whosoever has been diligent in fasting will be summoned from the Gate *ar-Rayyān,* and whosoever has been diligent in charity will be summoned from the Charity Gate." Said Abū Bakr: "I give for you my father and my mother, O Apostle of Allah. There is nothing against anyone who may be summoned from any of these gates, but could anyone be summoned from all the gates?" "Surely", said he, "and I hope that you will be one of them."

5. *On whether one should say Ramaḍān or Month of Ramaḍān; and on those who say that either is allowable. The Prophet—upon whom be Allah's blessing and peace—said: "He who fasts during Ramaḍān", and "Do not outrun Ramaḍān."*

Qutaiba has related to us, saying: Ismā'īl b. Ja'far has related to us from Abū Suhail, from his father, from Abū Huraira, that the Apostle of

[1] The technical word in this Tradition is *fitna,* (see, p. 37) "dissension," "discord," and in Muslim accounts of the events of the Last Days preceding the great Day of Judgment, there are innumerable stories about the dissensions which will arise among the people. The "gate" *(bāb)* is the individual who will usher in any particular dissension.

Allah—upon whom be Allah's blessing and peace—said: "When Ramaḍān has come the gates of Paradise are opened." Also Yaḥyā b. Bukair related to me, saying: al-Laith related to us from 'Uqail, from Ibn Shihāb [who said], Ibn Abī Anas, the client of the Tamīmites, related to me that his father related to him that he had heard Abū Huraira say: The Apostle of Allah—upon whom be Allah's blessing and peace—said: "When Ramaḍān has commenced the gates of heaven are opened, and the gates of Hell are shut, and the Satans are chained."

Yaḥyā b. Bukair related to us, saying: al-Laith related to us from 'Uqail, from Ibn Shihāb, who said: Sālim b. 'Abdallah b. 'Umar informed me that Ibn 'Umar said: I heard the Apostle of Allah—upon whom be Allah's blessing and peace—say: "When you have seen it (i.e. the new moon of the month Ramaḍān) then fast, and when you have seen it, (i.e. the new moon of the month Shawwāl) then break the fast; and if it is cloudy compute the time." Another narrator from al-Laith [has him say]: "'Uqail and Yūnus related to me from Ibn Shihāb: 'At the new moon of Ramaḍān....'"

6. *On him who fasts during Ramaḍān in faith, in hope of recompense, and with [sincere] intention. 'Ā'isha—with whom may Allah be pleased—[quoted] from the Prophet—upon whom be Allah's blessing and peace—[the saying]: "Men will be raised [on the Last Day] in accordance with their intentions."*

Muslim b. Ibrāhīm related to us, saying: Hishām related to us, saying: Yaḥyā related to us from Abū Salama, from Abū Huraira, from the Prophet—upon whom be Allah's blessing and peace— who said: "Whosoever rises up [for vigil and prayers] during the night of al-Qadr,[1] with faith, and in hope of recompense, will have all his previous sins forgiven him, and whosoever fasts during Ramaḍān with faith, in hope of recompense, and with [sincere] intention, will have all that is past forgiven him."

7. *On how the Prophet—upon whom be Allah's blessing and peace— was never more generous than he was during Ramaḍān*

Mūsā b. Ismā'īl related to me, saying: Ibrāhīm b. Sa'd related to us,

[1] The "Night of Power", or "Night of Decree", which falls towards the end of the month of Ramaḍān. It is mentioned in the Qur'ān in Sūra XCVII, and is popularly believed to be the night on which the fates for the coming year are fixed.

saying: Ibn Shihāb informed us from ʿUbaidallah b. ʿAbdallah b. ʿUtba that Ibn ʿAbbās said: "The Prophet—upon whom be Allah's blessing and peace—was the most generous of men with his goods, but he was never more generous than during Ramaḍān, when Gabriel would meet with him. Gabriel was wont to meet with him each night during Ramaḍān until [the month] was ended, and [at these meetings] the Prophet would collate with him the Qur'ān. So at these times when Gabriel met with him he would be more generous than the rain-bringing wind."

8. *On him who does not give up saying false words and doing false deeds during Ramaḍān*

Ādam b. Abī Iyās related to us, saying: Ibn Abī Dhi'b related to us, saying: Saʿīd al-Maqburī related to us from his father, from Abū Huraira, who said: Said the Prophet—upon whom be Allah's blessing and peace—:"If one does not give up saying false words and doing false deeds in Ramaḍān, his giving up eating and drinking means nothing to Allah."

9. *On whether, if one is reviled, he should say: "I am fasting"*

Ibrāhīm b. Mūsā related to us, saying: Hishām b. Yūsuf informed us from Ibn Juraij, who said: ʿĀṭā' informed me from Abū Ṣāliḥ az-Zayyāt, that he heard Abū Huraira say: The Apostle of Allah—upon whom be Allah's blessing and peace—said: "Allah, mighty and majestic is He, has said: 'Every deed of a child of Adam is his [and will be recorded and rewarded in due measure] save fasting, which is Mine, and which I will reward [in My own measure].' Fasting is a protective covering, so when the day comes for anyone of you to fast, let there be no unseemly speech, no clamouring. If anyone reviles such an one, or attacks him, let him say: 'I am fasting.' By Him in whose hand is my soul, the odour from the mouth of him who fasts is sweeter to Allah than the perfume of musk. He who fasts has two occasions of rejoicing. He will have joy when he breaks his fast, and when he meets his Lord he will have joy because of his fasting."

10. *On Fasting [as a help] for one who fears [the temptations of one who remains] celibate*

ʿUbdān related to us from Abū Ḥamza, from al-Aʿmash, from Ibrāhīm, from ʿAlqama, [who said]: While I was walking with ʿAbdallah he said: "I was once with the Prophet—upon whom be Allah's blessing and peace—when he said: 'Let him who is able to marry take a wife, for it is the best way of averting lascivious glances and of providing chaste enjoyment, but let him who is not able [to marry] fast, for it will be a remover [of unseemly passions] for him.'"

11. *On the saying of the Prophet—upon whom be Allah's blessing and peace—: "When ye see the new moon, fast, and when ye see it, break your fast." Ṣila quoted from ʿAmmār: "Whosoever fasts on a doubtful day is disobeying Abū'l-Qāsim,[1]—upon whom be Allah's blessing and peace*

ʿAbdallah b. Maslama related to us from Mālik, from Nāfiʿ, from ʿAbdallah b. ʿUmar, that the Apostle of Allah—upon whom be Allah's blessing and peace—mentioned Ramaḍān, and said: "Do not fast until ye see the new moon, and do not break the fast until ye see it, and if it is cloudy make a computation for it."

ʿAbdallah b. Maslama related to us, saying: Mālik related to us from ʿAbdallah b. Dīnār, from ʿAbdallah b. ʿUmar, that the Apostle of Allah—upon whom be Allah's blessing and peace—said: "The month is twenty-nine nights, so do not fast till ye see it (i.e. the new moon), and if it is cloudy then compute the number to thirty."

Abū'l-Walīd related to us, saying: Shuʿba related to us from Jabala b. Suḥaim, who said: I heard Ibn ʿUmar say that the Prophet—upon whom be Allah's blessing and peace—said: "The month is so-and-so", and he tucked in [his] thumb the third time.

Ādam related to us, saying: Shuʿba related to us, saying: Muḥammad b. Ziyād related to us, saying: I heard Abū Huraira say that the Prophet—upon whom be Allah's blessing and peace—said:—or may be he said: Abū'l-Qāsim, upon whom be, etc. said:—"Fast when it (i.e. the moon) becomes seeable, and break your fast when it becomes seeable, and if it is cloudy then complete the number of Shaʿbān,[2] [viz.] thirty."

Abū ʿĀṣim related to us from Ibn Juraij, from Yaḥyā b. ʿAbdallah b. Ṣaifī, from ʿIkrima b. ʿAbd ar-Raḥmān from Umm Salama, that the Prophet—upon whom be Allah's blessing and peace—took an oath to abstain from his women for a month. When twenty-nine days had elapsed he came in the morning—or may be it was in the evening—[to ʿĀ'isha].

[1] Abū'l-Qāsim means "Father of Qāsim", and Muḥammad was familiarly so called because Qāsim was the name of his first-born son.

[2] Shaʿbān is the month which precedes the fasting month of Ramaḍān.

Someone objected, "But you swore that you would not enter for a month", and he replied: "A month is of twenty-nine days."

'Abd al-'Azīz b. 'Abdallah related to us, saying: Sulaimān b. Bilāl related to us from Ḥumaid, from Anas, who said: "The Apostle of Allah—upon whom be Allah's blessing and peace—took an oath to abstain from his women. As his foot was injured he stayed in an upper chamber for twenty-nine nights. Then he came down, but they said: 'O Apostle of Allah, you took an oath for a month', whereat he said: 'The month is twenty-nine [days].'"

12. *On how the two months of festival may not be curtailed*

Musaddad has related to us, saying: Mu'tamir related to us, saying: I heard Isḥāq b. Suwaid [quoting] from 'Abd ar-Raḥmān b. Abī Bakra, from his father, from the Prophet—upon whom be Allah's blessing and peace—[or according to another *isnād*], Musaddad related to me, saying: Mu'tamir related to us from Khālid al-Ḥadhdhā', who said: 'Abd ar-Raḥmān b. Abī Bakra related to me from his father, from the Prophet—upon whom be Allah's blessing and peace—who said: "There are two months which may not be curtailed, the two months of festival, Ramaḍān and Dhū'l-Ḥijja."[1] Said Abū 'Abdallah: "Isḥāq said: 'Twenty-nine complete days.' Aḥmed b. Jundub said: 'If Ramaḍān is curtailed, complete Dhū'l-Ḥijja, and if Dhū'l-Ḥijja is curtailed, complete Ramaḍān.' Abū'l-Ḥasan said: 'Isḥāq b. Rāhuwaih used to say, Let neither be curtailed in [their] meritoriousness, whether it is twenty-nine or thirty [days].'"

13. *On the saying of the Prophet—upon whom be Allah's blessing and peace—:"We do not write and we do not calculate"*

Ādam related to us, saying: Shu'ba related to us, saying: Al-Aswad b. Qais said: Sa'īd b. 'Amr related to us that he heard Ibn 'Umar [relate] from the Prophet—upon whom be Allah's blessing and peace—how he said: "We are an unlettered community, we neither write nor calculate, the month is thus and thus." He meant that one time it has twenty-nine [days] and another thirty.

[1] Ramaḍān, the month of fasting, is the ninth month in the Islamic calendar, and Dhū'l-Ḥijja is the twelfth month, the month during which takes place the annual pilgrimage to Mecca. See p. 489.

14. *That Ramaḍān ought not to be preceded by a day or two days of fasting*

Muslim b. Ibrāhīm related to us, saying: Hishām related to us from Yaḥyā b. Abī Kathīr, from Abū Salama, from Abū Huraira, from the Prophet—upon whom be Allah's blessing and peace—how he said: "Let not any one of you bring in a day or two of fasting ahead of Ramaḍān, unless it be a man who has been wont to fast [voluntarily] on that day. Such a man may fast on it."

15. *On the verse (II, 187/183): "Going into your wives on the night of the fast is lawful for you. They are a clothing for you and you are a clothing for them. Allah knows that ye have been defrauding yourselves, so He has relented toward you and has pardoned you. So now lie with them, and seek what Allah has prescribed for you."*

'Ubaidallah b. Mūsā related to us from Isrā'īl, from Abū Isḥāq, from al-Barā' who said: "It was the custom of the Companions of Muḥammad—upon whom be Allah's blessing and peace—that when one was fasting, as the time for breaking the fast drew near he would sleep before breaking the fast, so he would not eat [that] night or day till evening came. Now Qais b. Ṣirma al-Anṣārī was fasting, and when the time for breaking the fast drew near he came to his wife, saying to her: 'Have you some food?' 'No', said she, 'but I shall go and seek some for you.' Now he had been working that day so his eyes got the better of him. Presently his wife came back to him, and when she saw him she said: 'What a disappointment for you.' When the day was but half over he fainted, and when that fact was brought to the attention of the Prophet—upon whom be Allah's blessings and peace—this verse (II, 187/183) was revealed: 'Going into your wives on the night of the fast is lawful for you.' At this they rejoiced greatly, and then was revealed [the rest of the verse] 'so eat and drink till at the dawning a white thread is distinguishable by you from a black thread.'"

16. *On the verse (II, 187/183): "Eat and drink till at the dawning a white thread is distinguishable by you from a black thread. Then fulfil the fast till night." It was in regard to this that [we had the Tradition of] al-Barā' from the Prophet*

Ḥajjāj b. Minhāl related to us, saying: Hushaim related to us, saying: Ḥuṣain b. 'Abd ar-Raḥmān informed us from ash-Sha'bī, from 'Adī b.

Ḥātim, who said: "When the verse (II, 187/183), 'until a white thread is distinguishable by you from a black thread' was revealed, I made off to get a black cord and a white cord, which I placed under my pillow. Then during the night I began to look at them, and they were not distinguishable to me. In the morning, therefore, I went to the Apostle of Allah and mentioned that to him. He said: 'That is but the blackness of night and the whiteness of day.'"

Sa'īd b. Abī Maryam related to us saying: Ibn Abī Ḥāzim related to us from his father, from Sahl b. Sa'd, [or according to another *isnād* it is] Sa'īd b. Abī Maryam related to me, saying: Abū Ghassān b. Muḥammad b. Muṭarrif related to us, saying: Abū Ḥāzim related to me from Sahl b. Sa'd, who said: "When [the verse] was revealed: 'Eat and drink till a white thread is distinguishable by you from a black thread', the words 'at the dawning' were not revealed, so there were some men who, when they wished to keep the fast, would bind on their two feet a white thread and a black thread, and would continue to eat as long as they could distinguish them. So Allah afterwards revealed [the words] 'at the dawning' that they might know that it meant only night and day."

17. *On the saying of the Prophet—upon whom be Allah's blessing and peace—: "Let not Bilāl's call to prayer* [1] *prevent you from having your daybreak meal"*

'Ubaid b. Ismā'īl related to me from Abū Usāma, from 'Ubaidallah, from Nāfi', from Ibn 'Umar and al-Qāsim b. Muḥammad, from 'Ā'isha—with whom may Allah be pleased—that Bilāl used to give the call to prayer while it was still night, so the Apostle of Allah—upon whom be Allah's blessing and peace—said: "Eat and drink till Ibn Umm Maktūm gives the call to prayer, for he does not give the call till dawn has broken." Al-Qāsim said: "Between the two calls to prayer there was naught but the time for the one to mount up [to the place from which the call was made] and the other to descend."

18. *On hastening the delayed daybreak meal*

Muḥammad b. 'Ubaidallah related to us, saying: 'Abd al-'Azīz b. Abī Ḥāzim related to us from his father, from Sahl b. Sa'd, who said: "I was

[1] The call to prayers precedes each of the five canonical prayer services each day. The Abyssinian Bilāl was the muezzin appointed to call the prayer times at the mosque built for the Prophet after his emigration to Madīna.

taking my daybreak meal in [the midst of] my family, and then had to make haste to be present at the prostration [in prayer] with the Apostle of Allah—upon whom be Allah's blessing and peace."

19. *On how much time should elapse between the daybreak meal and the dawn prayer service*

Muslim b. Ibrāhīm related to us, saying: Hishām related to us from Qatāda, from Anas, from Zaid b. Thābit, who said: "We took our daybreak meal with the Apostle of Allah—upon whom be Allah's blessing and peace. Then he rose for the prayer service. I said: 'How long a time was there between the call to prayer and the daybreak meal?' He replied: 'As much as [would be necessary to recite] fifty verses.'"

20. *That the blessing attached to the daybreak meal is not a necessary one, for the Prophet—upon whom be Allah's blessing and peace—and his Companions, kept uninterrupted [fast for more than one day] and there is no mention of the daybreak meal [in connection therewith]*

Mūsā b. Ismā'īl related to us, saying: Juwairiya related to us from Nāfi', from 'Abdallah, that the Prophet—upon whom be Allah's blessing and peace—kept uninterrupted [fast for more than one day], and the people kept it uninterruptedly, but it was distressing to them so he forbade them. They said: "But you keep uninterrupted fast." He answered: "I am not quite in your position. I am continually fed and watered" (i.e. supernaturally).[1]

Ādam b. Abī Iyās related to us, saying: Shu'ba related to us, saying: 'Abd al-'Azīz b. Suhaib related to us, saying: I heard Anas b. Mālik say: The Prophet—upon whom be Allah's blessing and peace—said: "Take the daybreak meal, for in the daybreak meal there is blessing."

21. *On when one purposes to keep fast on a [particular] day*

Umm ad-Dardā' said that [her husband] Abū'd-Dardā' used to say: "Do you have any food?", and if we said "No," he would say: "Well I shall be a faster today." This was so, and Abū Ṭalḥa, Abū Huraira, Ibn 'Abbās and Ḥudhaifa imitated him in this.

Abū 'Āṣim related to us from Yazīd b. Abī 'Ubaid, from Salama b. al-

[1] See pp. 111 and 112.

Akwaʿ, that the Prophet—upon whom be Allah's blessing and peace—sent a man to announce among the people on the Day of ʿĀshūrā':[1] "Whoever has eaten let him complete [the day as a non-fast day], or let him fast, but whoever has not eaten let him not eat."

22. *On the faster who awakes in the morning in a state of sexual pollution*

ʿAbdallah b. Maslama related to us from Mālik, from Sumayy, a client of Abū Bakr b. ʿAbd ar-Raḥmān b. al-Ḥārith b. Hishām b. al-Mughīra, that he heard Abū Bakr b. ʿAbd ar-Raḥmān say: "I was with my father when we entered to ʿĀ'isha and Umm Salama", [or as another *isnād* has it], Abū'l-Yamān related to us, saying: Shuʿaib informed us from az-Zuhrī, who said: Abū Bakr b. ʿAbd ar-Raḥmān b. al-Ḥārith b. Hishām informed me that his father ʿAbd ar-Raḥmān informed Marwān that ʿĀ'isha and Umm Salama had both informed him, that the Apostle of Allah—upon whom be Allah's blessing and peace—would be overtaken by the dawn while he was still in a state of pollution from [sex contact with] his wives, but he would bathe and then fast. Marwān said to ʿAbd ar-Raḥmān b. al-Ḥārith: "I swear by Allah you shall surely [go and] disturb Abū Huraira by that [information]." Marwān was at that time [Governor] over Madīna. Said Abū Bakr: "ʿAbd ar-Raḥmān, however, disliked [the idea of doing] that, so it was decided among us that we would foregather at Dhū'l-Ḥulaifa, where Abū Huraira had some land. Then ʿAbd ar-Raḥmān said to Abū Huraira: 'I am about to mention to you a matter that I should never have mentioned to you had not Marwān sworn that I should.' Then he mentioned what ʿĀ'isha and Umm Salama had said. Said [Abū Huraira]: 'That is so. Al-Faḍl b. ʿAbbās related [it] to me, and no one would know better than him.'" Said Ḥammām and Ibn ʿAbdallah b. ʿUmar [quoting] from Abū Huraira: "The Prophet—upon whom be Allah's blessing and peace—used to order [in such a case that] the fast be broken", but the first [version] has the better *isnād*.

23. *On the [restrictions of] sex relations for one who is fasting. ʿĀ'isha said: "It is her vulva which is forbidden to him"*

Sulaimān b. Ḥarb related to us from Shuʿba, from al-Ḥakam, from Ibrā-

[1] For 'Ashūrā' see pp. 122–123.

hīm, from al-Aswad, from ʿĀ'isha, who said: "The Prophet—upon whom be Allah's blessing and peace— used to kiss and handle [his wives] while he was fasting, but he had more control over his *irb* than any of you." [As to this word *irb*], Ibn ʿAbbās said that [the derivative from it] *ma'ārib* means "need", and Ṭāwūs used to use the phrase "one who possesses no *irba*" for a defective who has no need of women. Jābir b. Zaid said: "If one looks [at a woman] and has an emission let him go on with his fast."

24. *On the [legitimacy of] kissing for one who is fasting*

Muḥammad b. al-Muthannā related to us, saying: Yaḥyā related to us from Hishām, who said: My father informed me from ʿĀ'isha—with whom may Allah be pleased—from the Prophet—upon whom be Allah's blessing and peace—[or by another *isnād*], ʿAbdallah b. Maslama related to us from Mālik, from Hishām, from his father, from ʿĀ'isha—with whom may Allah be pleased—who said: "There were times when the Apostle of Allah—upon whom be Allah's blessing and peace—would kiss certain of his wives while he was fasting." Then she laughed.

Musaddad related to us, saying: Yaḥyā related to us from Hishām b. Abī ʿAbdallah, who said: Yaḥyā b. Abī Kathīr related to us from Abū Salama, from Zainab daughter of Umm Salama, from her mother,[1] who said: "While I was with the Prophet—upon whom be Allah's blessing and peace—in bed, my menses started, so I slipped out and put on my menstrual clothes. He asked: 'What is the matter with you? has your period come on?' 'Yes', I replied, and I entered the bed with him again." Now she and the Apostle of Allah—upon whom be Allah's blessing and peace—used both to bathe at the same [water] vessel, and he used to kiss her when he was fasting.

25. *On the bathing of one who is fasting*

Ibn ʿUmar soiled his garment with urine but put it on him while he was fasting. Ash-Shaʿbī entered the [public] baths while he was fasting. Ibn ʿAbbās said: "There is no harm in tasting [what is in] the cooking pot [while fasting] or [any other] thing." Al-Ḥasan said: "There is no harm in the faster gargling or cooling himself off" (i.e. provided he does not drink the water). Ibn Masʿūd said: "When the day comes around for any one of

[1] Her mother was one of the Prophet's wives.

you to fast he may, as he rises in the morning, use oil and comb." Anas said: "I had a copper wash-basin in which I used to plunge even while I was fasting, and Ibn 'Umar used to brush his teeth at the beginning and at the end of the day [while he was fasting]." Ibn Sīrīn said: "There is no harm in the use of the tooth-brush if it is fresh." The objection was raised: "But it has taste", and [he replied]: "and so does the water have taste when you gargle with it, [yet that is not considered to be breaking the fast]. Anas, al-Ḥasan and Ibrāhīm also saw no harm in the faster making use of koḥl [for the eyes]

Aḥmad b. Ṣāliḥ related to us, saying: Ibn Wahb related to us, saying: Yūnus related to us, from Ibn Shihāb, from 'Urwa and Abū Bakr, who said: 'Ā'isha—with whom may Allah be pleased—said: "The dawn used to overtake the Prophet in Ramaḍān when he was polluted—and not from an [erotic] dream—but he would bathe and [then commence the] fast."

Ismā'īl related to us, saying: Mālik related to me from Sumayy, a client of Abū Bakr b. 'Abd ar-Raḥmān b. al-Ḥārith b. Hishām b. al-Mughīra, that he heard Abū Bakr b. 'Abd ar-Raḥmān say: "I was with my father and went along with him till we entered to 'Ā'isha—with whom may Allah be pleased—who said: 'I bear witness of the Apostle of Allah—upon whom be Allah's blessing and peace—that he used to wake up in the morning polluted [by sperm] from intercourse, not from dreaming, and then he would fast [that day].'" Then we entered to Umm Salama, who said the same thing.

26. *On the faster who eats and drinks from forgetfulness*

'Aṭā' said: "If one snuffs up water and some of it enters the throat so that one is not able to reject it, no harm is done [thereby to one's fast]." Also al-Ḥasan said: "If a fly should get into one's throat, that is nothing", and al-Ḥasan and Mujāhid both said: "If one should have sex intercourse forgetfully, that is nothing"

'Abdān related to us [saying], Yazīd b. Zurai' informed us, saying: Hishām related to us, saying: Ibn Sīrīn related to us from Abū Huraira, from the Prophet—upon whom be blessing and peace—that he said: "If anyone forgets and eats or drinks, let him complete his fast, for it was Allah who caused him thus to eat or drink."

27. *On the fresh and the dry tooth-brush for him who is fasting*

It is reported from ʿĀmir b. Rabīʿa, who said: "I have seen the Prophet—upon whom be Allah's blessing and peace—using the tooth-brush while he was fasting more times than I can reckon or count." ʿĀʾisha said, quoting the Prophet—upon whom be Allah's blessing and peace—: "The tooth-brush is a purifier for the mouth and a thing well-pleasing to the Lord." ʿAṭāʾ and Qatāda said: "One may swallow one's saliva [without thereby breaking one's fast]." Abū Huraira said, quoting the Prophet—upon whom be Allah's blessing and peace—: "Were it not that I might be causing distress to my community I should bid them use the tooth-brush at every ablution." The like of this Tradition is transmitted from Jābir and Zaid b. Khālid from the Prophet—upon whom be Allah's blessing and peace—who [in this matter] did not particularize the one fasting from anyone else

ʿAbdān related to us, saying: ʿAbdallah informed us, saying: Maʿmar informed us, saying: az-Zuhrī related to us from ʿAṭāʾ b. Yazīd, from Ḥumrān, who said: "I saw ʿUthmān (i.e. the third Caliph) performing ablutions. He poured [the water out] over his hands three times. Then he gargled and snuffed up [the water]. Then he washed his face three times. Then he washed his right arm up to the elbow three times. Then he washed his left arm up to the elbow three times. Then he rubbed his head [with his moist hands]. Then he washed his right foot three times. Then he washed his left foot three times. Then he said: 'I have seen the Apostle of Allah—upon whom be Allah's blessing and peace—performing ablution just like this ablution of mine, after which he (i.e. the Prophet) said: 'Whosoever performs [his] ablutions as I have done here, and prays a two-bow prayer, not allowing anything to distract him during them, will have all his past sins forgiven him.'"

28. *On the statement of the Prophet—upon whom be Allah's blessing and peace—: "When anyone performs ablutions let him snuff up the water into his nostrils", where he makes no distinction between one who is fasting and any other*

Al-Ḥasan said: "There is no harm in a faster making use of medicinal snuff so long as it does not reach the throat. Also he may make use of *koḥl*." ʿAṭāʾ said: "He who gargles and then ejects the water that is in his mouth does not damage [his fasting] even if he should swallow his saliva or what [water] may remain in his mouth. He who chews chewing-resin, if he swallows the resin-impregnated saliva [is in a different case], I do not say that he has broken his fast, but he is doing something that is forbidden."

29. *[On what would happen] should one have sexual intercourse during [the fasting hours of] Ramaḍān*

It is recounted on the authority of Abū Huraira, who traced it back [to the Prophet]: "Whosoever breaks the fast for a single day during Ramaḍān, without due cause or on account of illness, would not redeem it were he to fast for the rest of time." Ibn Mas'ūd held this [point of view], but Sa'īd b. al-Musayyab, ash-Sha'bī, Ibn Jubair, Ibrāhīm, Qatāda, and Ḥammād taught that he might make up for it by [fasting for] another day in place of it

'Abdallah b. Munīr related to me that he heard Yazīd b. Hārūn say: Yaḥyā, i.e. Ibn Sa'īd, related to us that 'Abd ar-Raḥmān b. al-Qāsim informed him, from 'Abbād b. 'Abdallah b. az-Zubair, who informed him that he heard 'Ā'isha say: "A man came to the Prophet—upon whom be Allah's blessing and peace—and said: 'I am going to be burned [in Hell].' Said [the Prophet]: 'What is the matter with you?' Said he: 'I had to do with my wife during [the fasting hours of] Ramaḍān.' The Prophet—upon whom be Allah's blessing and peace—brought out a palm-leaf date basket, of the kind called *'araq*, and asked: 'Where is the fellow who is going to be burned?' 'It is I', said he. [The Prophet] said: 'Give these in alms [as a redemption for your fault].'"

30. *On how if one has had sexual intercourse during [the fasting hours of] Ramaḍān, and has nothing to give in alms, one should make an expiatory fast*

Abū'l-Yamān related to us, saying: Shu'aib informed us from az-Zuhrī, saying: Ḥumaid b. 'Abd ar-Raḥmān informed me that Abū Huraira said: "While we were sitting with the Prophet—upon whom be Allah's blessing and peace—there came to him a man who said: 'O Apostle of Allah, I am lost.' Said [the Prophet]: 'What is the matter with you?' He answered: 'I came at my wife while I was fasting.' Said the Apostle of Allah—upon whom be Allah's blessing and peace—'Could you find a slave you might set free?' 'No', said he. 'Well, could you fast for two months in succession [as an expiatory fast]?' 'No', said he. 'Well, could you find the wherewithall to feed sixty unfortunates?' 'No', said he. The Prophet—upon whom be Allah's blessing and peace—paused, and while we were at that point there was brought to the Prophet—upon whom be Allah's blessing and peace—an *'araq* in which were dates. An *'araq* is a palm-leaf date basket. He said: 'Where is the one who asked the question?' 'It is I', said [the man]. So [the Prophet] said: 'Take this and give it as alms.' Said the man: '[Am I to give it as alms] to someone poorer than myself, O Apostle of Allah? By Allah, between its two stony fields—he meant the two Ḥarras of Madina—there is no family poorer than my family.' Thereat the Prophet—upon whom be Allah's blessing and peace—laughed till his back teeth shewed, then he said: 'Feed it to your family.'"

31. *On whether one who has had sexual intercourse during [the fasting hours of] Ramaḍān may use his expiatory gift to feed his own family if they are in need*

'Uthmān b. Abī Shaiba related to us, saying: Jarīr related to us from Manṣūr, from az-Zuhrī, from Ḥumaid b. 'Abd ar-Raḥmān, from Abū Huraira: A man came to the Prophet—upon whom be Allah's blessing and peace—saying: "[I] the least [of men] came at my wife during [the fasting hours of] Ramaḍān." Said [the Prophet]: "Could you find a slave to set free?" "No", said he. "Well, would you be able to fast for two consecutive months?" "No", said he. "Well, could you find [the wherewithall] to feed sixty unfortunates?" "No", said he. Just then there was brought to the Prophet—upon whom be Allah's blessing and peace—an *'araq* in which were dates, i.e. a leaf basket [of dates]. So [the Prophet] said: "Feed this [to someone as an expiation] for yourself." Said he: "To someone more needy than ourselves? Why there is not between [Madina's] two stony fields a family more needy than ourselves." [The Prophet] answered: "Then feed it to your family."

32. *On blood-letting and vomiting in the case of one fasting*

Yaḥyā b. Ṣāliḥ said to me: Mu'āwiya b. Sallām related to us, saying: Yaḥyā b. Abī Kathīr related to us from 'Umar b. al-Ḥakam b. Thawbān [who said]: I heard Abū Huraira say: "If one vomits that does not break the fast, for that is only causing something to come out not making something enter." It is reported from Abū Huraira that [he said] that it does break the fast, but the former is the more reliable [version]. Ibn 'Abbās and 'Ikrima also said that the fast is broken by what goes in not by what comes out. Ibn 'Umar used to be cupped while he was fasting, but then he gave it up and used to have the cupping done at night. So also Abū Mūsā had his cupping done at night, and it is recorded of Saʿd and Zaid b. Arqam and Umm Salama that they had cuppings when they were fasting. Bukair reported that Umm ʿAlqama [said]: "We used to be cupped at ʿĀʾisha's [house] and were not forbidden." Traditions have come down from al-Ḥasan, from more than one source claiming to go back to the Prophet, that he said: "Both he who does the cupping and he who is cupped have broken the fast." ʿAyyāsh said to me: ʿAbd al-Aʿlā related to us, saying: Yūnus related to us from al-Ḥasan the like of what [we have just recorded], and he was asked: "Was that from the Prophet—upon whom be Allah's blessing and peace?"—and he said "Yes", but then added, "Allah knows best."

*

Muʿallā b. Asad related to us, saying: Wuhaib related to us from Ayyūb, from ʿIkrima, from Ibn ʿAbbās, that the Prophet—upon whom be Allah's blessing and peace—used to submit to cupping when he was in the *iḥrām*,[1] and when he was fasting.

Ādam b. Abī Iyās related to us, saying: Shuʿba related to us, saying: I heard Thābit al-Bunānī say: Anas b. Mālik was asked: "Did you folk disapprove of cupping for one who is fasting?" He answered: "No, save in the case of a feeble person." Shabāba added [to the wording of this Tradition]: "Shuʿba related to us that at the time of the Prophet—upon whom be Allah's blessing and peace—[I heard Thabit...]."

33. *On fasting and breaking the fast while on a journey*

ʿAlī b. ʿAbdallah related to us, saying: Sufyān related to us from Abū Isḥāq ash-Shaibānī [who said]: I heard Ibn Abī Aufā say: "We were with the Apostle of Allah—upon whom be Allah's blessing and peace—on a journey, when he said to a man: 'Dismount, and mix me a drink.' [The man] replied: 'O Apostle of Allah, the sun.'[2] But he said: 'Dismount, and mix me a drink.' Again the man said: 'O Apostle of Allah, the sun.' But he said: 'Dismount, and mix me a drink', saying it twice. So the man dismounted and mixed him a drink, which he drank. Then, throwing out his hand in this direction (i.e. to the East), he said: 'When you see the night approaching from this direction, then indeed the faster may break his fast.'"

[1] I.e. while he was in the sacrosanct state of one performing the rites of pilgrimage. The *iḥrām* is the special garb worn by the pilgrims. See p. 497.

[2] Meaning that in his judgment the sun was still far too high for it to be time to break the fast. There is another version of this Tradition on pp. 109, 110.

Jarīr and Abū Bakr b. ʿAyyāsh follow him [in this line of transmission] from ash-Shaibānī, from Ibn Abī Aufā, who said: "I was with the Prophet on a journey, etc."

Musaddad related to us, saying: Yaḥyā b. Hishām related to us, saying: My father related to me from ʿĀʾisha—with whom may Allah be pleased—that Ḥamza b. ʿAmr al-Aslamī said: "O Apostle of Allah, I am continuing the fast", [or according to another line of transmission] ʿAbdallah b. Yūsuf related to us, saying: Mālik informed us from Hishām b. ʿUrwa, from his father, from ʿĀʾisha, the wife of the Prophet—upon whom be Allah's blessing and peace—that Ḥamza b. ʿAmr al-Aslamī said to the Prophet—upon whom be Allah's blessing and peace—: "I am fasting on the journey." He was one who fasted much. [The Prophet] said: "Fast if you wish, or if you wish break the fast."

34. *On [the case] when one has fasted some days of Ramaḍān and then goes on a journey*

ʿAbdallah b. Yūnus related to us, saying: Mālik informed us from Ibn Shihāb, from ʿUbaidallah b. ʿAbdallah b. ʿUtba, from Ibn ʿAbbās, that the Apostle of Allah—upon whom be Allah's blessing and peace— went to Mecca during Ramaḍān and fasted till he reached al-Kadīd, where he broke the fast, so the people also broke it. Said Saʿīd b. ʿAbdallah: "Kadīd is [a place] between ʿUsfān and Qudaid [on the route between Madina and Mecca]."

35. *A section. ʿAbdallah b. Yūsuf related to us, saying: Yaḥyā b. Ḥamza related to me from ʿAbd ar-Raḥmān b. Yazīd b. Jābir, that Ismāʿīl b. ʿUbaidallah related to him from Umm ad-Dardāʾ, from Abūʾd-Dardā, who said: "We went out with the Prophet—upon whom be Allah's blessing and peace—on one of his journeys, on a day so hot that a man would put his hand on his head [to protect it] from the severity of the heat, and there was no one among us fasting save the Prophet—upon whom be Allah's blessing and peace—and Ibn Rawāḥa"*

36. *On the saying of the Prophet—upon whom be Allah's blessing and peace—[addressed] to those who sought shade [for their heads] when the heat was severe: "Fasting while on a journey is no part of piety"*

Ādam related to us, saying: Shuʿba related to us, saying: Muḥammad b. ʿAbd ar-Raḥmān al-Anṣārī related to us, saying: I heard Muḥammad b.

ʿAmr b. al-Ḥasan b. ʿAli [reporting] from Jābir b. ʿAbdallah, who said: "The Apostle of Allah—upon whom be Allah's blessing and peace—was on a journey when he saw a crowd gathered around a man who was shading himself. 'What is this?' he asked. They answered: 'Someone who is fasting', and he said: 'Fasting while on a journey is no part of piety.'"

37. *On how the Companions of the Prophet—upon whom be Allah's blessing and peace—did not upbraid one another whether about fasting or about breaking the fast*

ʿAbdallah b. Maslama related to us from Mālik, from Ḥumaid aṭ-Ṭawīl, from Anas b. Mālik, who said: "We were journeying with the Prophet —upon whom be Allah's blessing and peace—and he who was fasting did not upbraid him who ate, nor did he who ate [upbraid] him who kept fasting."

38. *On him who breaks the fast during a journey so that the people may see it*

Mūsā b. Ismāʿīl related to us, saying: Abū ʿUwāna related to us from Manṣūr, from Mujāhid, from Ṭāwūs, from Ibn ʿAbbās, who said: "The Apostle of Allah—upon whom be Allah's blessing and peace—went from Madina to Mecca, and fasted till he reached ʿUsfān. Then he called for water, which he raised in his two hands so that the people might see it. Then he broke fast till he came to Mecca, though it was in Ramaḍān." Ibn ʿAbbās used to say: "The Apostle of Allah—upon whom be Allah's blessing and peace—fasted and broke the fast [while on a journey], so let whosoever wishes fast and let whosoever wishes break the fast."

39. *[On the verse] "But those who are able [to fast, yet do not] must pay a redemption" (II, 184/180)*

Ibn ʿUmar and Salama b. al-Akwaʿ say that this verse is abrogated by (II, 185/181): "The month of Ramaḍān in which the Qur'ān was sent down... for the way He has guided you, and maybe ye will be thankful." Ibn Numair al-Aʿmash said: He said [to us]: ʿAmr b. Mūsā related to us saying: Ibn Abī Lailā related to us, saying: the Companions of Muḥammad—upon whom be Allah's blessing and peace—have related to us, that [the verse about] Ramaḍān was revealed and was distressing to them, so whosoever was able to feed some unfortunate each day gave up the fasting. That was permitted them, but [presently] it was abrogated by [the verse] (II, 184/180): "... but that you should fast would be better for you." Thus they were bidden fast.

*

'Ayyāsh related to us, saying: 'Abd al-A'lā related to us, saying: 'Ubaidallah related to us from Nāfi', from Ibn 'Umar, that he recited [the words]: "... a redemption [by] feeding an unfortunate" (II, 184/180). Then he said: "That is abrogated."

40. *On when one should discharge the [obligation of a fast of] replacement for [a fast omitted during] Ramaḍān*

Ibn 'Abbās said: "There is no harm in splitting up [the days of a fast of replacement], because Allah has said (II, 184/180): "... then a number of other days." Sa'īd b. al-Musayyab said with regard to the fast of the ten [days of Dhū'l-Ḥijja]: "No [fast] is suitable unless it is a substitute for Ramaḍān." Ibrāhīm said: "If one neglects it until the next Ramaḍān has come, let him fast them both", for he did not consider that the feeding [of poor people would be adequate compensation] for it. It is recorded from Abū Huraira, but with imperfect *isnād*, and from Ibn 'Abbās, that he should feed [poor people]. The words of Allah [in the Qur'ān], however, make no mention of the feeding [of the poor], but say: "... then a number of other days."

*

Aḥmad b. Yūnus related to us, saying: Zuhair related to us, saying: Yaḥyā related to me from Abū Salama, who said: I heard 'Ā'isha—with whom may Allah be pleased—say: "I used to have some fasting from Ramaḍān to make up, but would not be able to discharge [the obligation] till in [the month of] Sha'bān." Yaḥyā said [that the reason why she missed out days of fasting during Ramaḍān was because she was] busied with affairs for the Prophet—upon whom be Allah's blessing and peace—or was with the Prophet—upon whom be Allah's blessing and peace.

41. *On a menstruating woman neglecting fasting and prayer*

Said Abū'z-Zinād: "Customs [recorded as those of the Prophet] and aspects of truth often come into contradiction with reason, but the Muslims have nevertheless no excuse for not following them. Among such is the [regulation] that the menstruating woman makes up for the fast [that she had to miss], but does not make up for [missed] prayers."

Ibn Abī Maryam related to us, saying: Muḥammad b. Ja'far informed us, saying: Zaid informed me from ʿIyāḍ, from Abū Saʿīd, who said: "The Prophet—upon whom be Allah's blessing and peace—said: 'Is it not [a fact that] when she has her menses she does not pray and does not fast? That is a falling short in her religion.'"

42. *On him who dies while still having some fasting to make up.*

Said al-Ḥasan: "If thirty men were to fast one day in his stead, [to make up what he owed], that would be allowable"

Muḥammad b. Khālid related to us, saying: Muḥammad b. Aʿyan related to us, saying: My father related to us from ʿAmr b. al-Ḥārith, from ʿUbaidallah b. Abī Jaʿfar, that Muḥammad b. Jaʿfar related to him, from ʿUrwa, from ʿĀʾisha, that the Apostle of Allah—upon whom be Allah's blessing and peace—said: "If any one should die with days of fasting still to make up, let his *walī* [1] fast in his stead." Ibn Wahb follows him [in this Tradition] from ʿAmr, [but] Yaḥyā b. Ayyūb transmitted it from Ibn Abī Jaʿfar.

Muḥammad b. ʿAbd ar-Raḥīm related to us, saying: Muʿāwiya b. ʿAmr related to us, saying: Zāʾida related to us from al-Aʿmash, from Muslim al-Baṭīn, from Saʿīd b. Jubair, from Ibn ʿAbbās, who said: "A man came to the Prophet—upon whom be Allah's blessing and peace—saying: 'O Apostle of Allah, my mother has died owing a month's fast which she had not made up. Can I redeem it for her?' 'Yes', he replied. 'For a debt owed to Allah has more claim to be redeemed [than any other].'" Said Sulaimān: "Al-Ḥakam and Salama said: 'We were all sitting together there when Muslim related this Tradition', and they both added, 'and we heard Mujāhid recount this from Ibn ʿAbbās.'" It is also recorded from Abū Khālid [that he said]: al-Aʿmash related to us from al-Ḥakam and Muslim al-Baṭīn and Salama b. Kuhail from Saʿīd b. Jubair and ʿAṭāʾ and Mujāhid from Ibn ʿAbbās [that] a woman said to the Prophet —upon whom be Allah's blessing and peace—: "My sister has died...", but Yaḥyā and Abū Muʿāwiya said: al-Aʿmash related to us from Muslim, from Saʿīd, from Ibn ʿAbbās [that] a woman said to the Prophet—upon whom be Allah's blessing and peace—: "My mother has died owing a fast that she had vowed [to perform]." Abū Ḥarīz said: ʿIkrima related to me from Ibn ʿAbbās [that] a woman said to the Prophet—upon whom be Allah's blessing and peace—: "My mother died still owing a fast of fifteen days."

[1] The *walī* here would mean the heir. See p. 206.

43. *On when it is lawful for a faster to break his fast*

Abū Sa'īd al-Khudrī broke his fast when the sun's disk disappeared

Al-Ḥumaidī related to us, saying: Sufyān related to us, saying: Hishām b. 'Urwa related to us, saying: I heard my father say: I heard 'Āṣim b. 'Umar b. al-Khaṭṭāb [relate] from his father, who said: Said the Apostle of Allah—upon whom be Allah's blessing and peace—: "When night approaches from here (i.e. the East), and day departs from here (i.e. the West), and the sun has set, then let the faster break his fast."

Isḥāq b. Shāhīn al-Wāsiṭī related to us, saying: Khālid related to us from ash-Shaibānī, from 'Abdallah b. Abī Awfā, who said: "We were with the Apostle of Allah—upon whom be Allah's blessing and peace—on a journey while he was fasting, and when the sun set he said to one of the people: 'O So-and-So, rise and prepare a drink for us.' Said [the man]: 'O Apostle of Allah, if you will wait till evening.' [The Prophet] repeated: 'Descend and prepare a drink for us.' Again he answered: 'O Apostle of Allah, if you will wait till evening.' Said [the Prophet]: 'Descend and prepare a drink for us.' [The man answered]: 'But you still have daylight.' [However, when the Prophet] reiterated: 'Descend and prepare a drink for us', the man alighted and prepared a drink for them, whereat the Apostle of Allah—upon whom be Allah's blessing and peace—drank. Then he said: 'When you see the night approach from here (i.e. from the East), then let the faster break his fast.'"

44. *On breaking the fast with whatever is easiest, whether with water or something else*

Musaddad related to us, saying: 'Abd al-Wāḥid related to us, saying: ash-Shaibānī Sulaimān related to us, saying: I heard 'Abdallah b. Abī Awfā say: "We were journeying with the Apostle of Allah—upon whom be Allah's blessing and peace—while he was fasting, and when the sun set he said [to one of the men]: 'Descend and prepare a drink for us.' Said [the man]: 'O Apostle of Allah, if you will wait till the evening.' Said [the Prophet]: 'Descend and prepare a drink for us.' [The man] answered: 'O Apostle of Allah, but you still have daylight.' Said he: 'Descend and prepare a drink for us.' So [the man] alighted and prepared a drink. He [the Prophet] said: 'When you see the night approaching from here, then let the faster break his fast', and he motioned with his finger to the East."

45. *On haste to break the fast*

'Abdallah b. Yūsuf related to us, saying: Mālik informed us from Abū Ḥāzim, from Sahl b. Sa'd, that the Apostle of Allah—upon whom be Allah's blessing and peace—said: "Folk will continue in good ways so long as they hasten the breaking of the fast."

Aḥmad b. Yūnus related to us, saying: Abū Bakr related to us from Sulaimān, from Ibn Abī Awfā, who said: "I was with the Prophet—upon whom be Allah's blessing and peace—on a journey, and he fasted till it was evening, when he said to a man: 'Descend and prepare a drink for me.' Said [the man]: 'If you will wait expectantly till it is evening.' But [the Prophet] said: 'Descend and prepare a drink for me. When you see that the night has approached from here, then let the faster break his fast.'"

46. *On [the case] when in Ramaḍān one has broken one's fast and then the sun [re]appears*

'Abdallah b. Abī Shaiba related to me, saying: Abū Usāma related to us from Hishām b. 'Urwa, from Fāṭima, from Asmā' the daughter of Abū Bakr, who said: "In the time of the Apostle of Allah—upon whom be Allah's blessing and peace—we broke our fast on a cloudy day, and then the sun appeared." Someone asked Hishām: "Were they ordered to make it up?", and he said: "There was no escape from making it up." Ma'mar said: "I heard Hishām [say]: 'I do not know if they made it up or not.'"

47. *On children fasting*

'Umar said to a drunken man during Ramaḍān: "Woe to you! why even our children are fasting", and he struck him

Musaddad related to us, saying: Bishr b. al-Mufaḍḍal related to us, saying: Khālid b. Dhakwān related to us from ar-Rubayya' daughter of Mu'awwidh, who said: "The Prophet—upon whom be Allah's blessing and peace—sent on the morning of 'Āshūrā' to the villages of the Anṣār [saying]: 'Let whosoever has eaten this morning continue thus the rest of the day, but let whosoever commenced the morning fasting fast [for the rest of it].'" She said: 'We were fasting [during] it and we made our children fast. We had made for them playthings of *'ihn,* so that when one of them cried for food we would give him one of these, [and thus we kept them quiet] till the time for breaking the fast." *ʿihn* means [dyed] wool.

48. *On Wiṣāl (i.e. combining day and night fasting), and on him who says that there is no night fasting, because of these words of Allah (II, 187/183): "... then fulfil the fast till night", and [because] the Prophet—upon whom be Allah's blessing and peace—as an act of mercy to them (i.e. to the Believers), and for their preservation, prohibited it. Also on that excess which is reproved*

Musaddad related to us, saying: Yaḥyā related to us from Shuʿba, who said: Qatāda related to me from Anas, from the Prophet—upon whom be Allah's blessing and peace—who said: "Do not practise *wiṣāl.*" They said: "But you practise *wiṣāl.*" To which he replied: "But I am not as one of you." He said: "I am given food and drink" (i.e. I am supernaturally supplied), or [according to another *isnād*, he said]: "I pass the night supplied with food and drink."[1]

ʿAbdallah b. Yūsuf related to us, saying: Mālik informed us from Nāfiʿ, from ʿAbdallah b. ʿUmar, who said: "The Apostle of Allah—upon whom be Allah's blessing and peace—forbade *wiṣāl.* They said: 'But you practise *wiṣāl*', and he answered: 'But I am not like you. I am supplied food and drink.'"[1]

ʿAbdallah b. Yūsuf related to us, saying: al-Laith related to us, saying: Ibn al-Hād related to me from ʿAbdallah b. Khabbāb, from Abū Saʿīd, that he heard the Prophet—upon whom be Allah's blessing and peace—say: "Do not practise *wiṣāl*, but if any one among you wants to practise *wiṣāl*, then let him do it till the *saḥar*" (i.e. the meal normally eaten at daybreak). They said: "But you practise [complete] *wiṣāl*, O Apostle of Allah." He replied: "But I am not in your case. I pass the night with a supplier of food who feeds me, and with a supplier of drink who gives me drink."

ʿUthmān b. Abī Shaiba and Muḥammad who is the son of Sallām related to us, saying: ʿAbda informed us from Hishām b. ʿUrwa, from his father, from ʿĀ'isha—with whom may Allah be pleased—who said: "The Apostle of Allah, as an act of mercy to them, forbade *wiṣāl.* They said: 'But you practise *wiṣāl*', and he replied: 'But I am not in your case, for my Lord supplies me with food and drink.'" Said Abū ʿAbdallah: ʿUthmān did not mention [the words] "as an act of mercy to them" [in his account of this Tradition].

[1] See p. 97.

49. *On the exemplary punishment [to be inflicted] on one who excessively practises wiṣāl. Anas related this from the Prophet—upon whom be Allah's blessing and peace*

Abū'l-Yamān related to us, saying: Shu'aib informed us from az-Zuhrī, who said: Abū Salama b. 'Abd ar-Raḥmān informed me that Abū Huraira said: "The Apostle of Allah—upon whom be Allah's blessing and peace—forbade *wiṣāl* in fasting. A man from among the Muslims said to him: 'But you practise *wiṣāl,* O Apostle of Allah', to which [the Prophet] replied: 'But which of you is like me? I pass the night with my Lord supplying me with food and drink.' Since they refused to give up practising *wiṣāl* [the Prophet] did it with them for a day and then [another] day, [and then immediately after that] they saw the new moon (i.e. the sign that the month of fasting was over). Said he: 'Had the [new moon] been delayed [in appearing] I would have made you keep on [at it] as an exemplary punishment for you, as you refused to give it up.'"

Yaḥyā b. Mūsā related to us, saying: 'Abd ar-Razzāq related to us from Ma'mar, from Hammām, that he heard Abū Huraira [quote] from the Prophet—upon whom be Allah's blessing and peace—who said: "Beware of *wiṣāl.*" [This he said] twice, so someone said: "But you practise *wiṣāl*", to which he replied: "But I pass the night with my Lord supplying me food and drink. Take ye, therefore, upon yourselves [only] such labour as ye are capable of [bearing]."

50. *On wiṣāl until the saḥar (i.e. the daybreak meal)*

Ibrāhīm b. Ḥamza related to us, saying: Ibn Abī Ḥamza related to me from Yazīd, from 'Abdallah b. Khabbāb, from Abū Sa'īd al-Khudrī, that he heard the Apostle of Allah—upon whom be Allah's blessing and peace—say: "Do not practise *wiṣāl,* but if anyone wishes to practise *wiṣāl* let him do it [only] till the *saḥar* [meal]." They said: "But you practise *wiṣāl,* O Apostle of Allah", and he answered: "I am not in your case, for I pass the night with a supplier of food who gives me to eat and a supplier of drink who gives me to drink."

51. *On him who puts his brother under oath to break a voluntary fast, and does not consider that there is any obligation to make it up, if this [breaking of the fast] were the more suitable thing for him, (i.e. for the one who was fasting)*

Muḥammad b. Bashshār related to us, saying: Ja'far b. 'Aun related to us, saying: Abū'l-'Umais related to us from 'Aun b. Abī Juḥaifa, from his father, who said: "The Prophet—upon whom be Allah's blessing and peace—had established a brotherhood between Salmān and Abū'd-Dardā'. Now Salmān visited Abū'd-Dardā' and saw [his wife] Umm ad-Dardā' in poor attire, so he said to her: 'What is the matter with you [that you are dressed so poorly]?' She answered: 'Your brother Abū'd-Dardā' has no care for [the things of] this world.' Then Abū'd-Dardā' came in and prepared food for him, saying: 'Eat.' But he said: 'I am fasting.' Abū'd-Dardā' answered: 'Well, I shall not eat till you eat', so he ate. When it was night [and everyone wanted to sleep] Abū'd-Dardā' set about getting up, but [Salmān] said: 'Sleep!' So he slept [for a while] but then started to get up, and [Salmān again] said: 'Sleep!' Then when the night was almost over Salmān said: 'Now get up, and let us say prayers.' Then [after they had said prayers] Salmān said to him: 'You have duties which you owe to your Lord, and which you owe to yourself, but you also have duties which you owe to your family, so give to each what you owe to him.' Then he came to the Prophet—upon whom be Allah's blessing and peace—and recounted this to him. The Prophet—upon whom be Allah's blessing and peace—said: 'Salmān has spoken the truth.'"

52. *On the fast of Sha'bān* [1]

'Abdallah b. Yūsuf related to us, saying: Mālik informed us from Abū'n-Naḍr, from Abū Salama, from 'Ā'isha, who said: "The Apostle of Allah—upon whom be Allah's blessing and peace—used to fast [so long] that we would say he was not going to break the fast, and [on the other hand] he would continue eating [so long] that we would say he was not going to fast, but never have I seen the Prophet—upon whom be Allah's blessing and peace—complete a fast of a whole month save at Ramaḍān, nor have I seen him fast more [days in any other month] than in Sha'bān."

Mu'ādh b. Fuḍāla related to us, saying: Hishām related to us from Yaḥyā, from Abū Salama, that 'Ā'isha related to him, saying: "The Prophet—upon whom be Allah's blessing and peace—used not to fast in any month more than he did in Sha'bān, for he used to fast the whole of Sha'bān, and he used to say: 'Take [upon yourselves] such pious works as ye are able [to bear], for Allah will not grow weary till ye grow weary.' The prayer-service most agreeable to the Prophet—upon whom be Allah's blessing and peace—was one that lasted long, even though it

[1] Sha'bān is the eighth month, during which a certain amount of fasting is considered meritorious. See n. 2 p. 93.

be [one that was] seldom performed. Whenever he said prayers he would lengthen them."

53. *On what is recounted about the Prophet's fasting and breaking fast*

Mūsā b. Ismā'īl related to me, saying: Abū 'Uwāna related to us from Abū Bishr, from Sa'īd b. Jubair, from Ibn 'Abbās, who said: "The Prophet—upon whom be Allah's blessing and peace—never at any time fasted a whole month save Ramaḍān. He would go on fasting till one would say that, by Allah, he was not going to break it, and he would go on eating till one would say, by Allah, that he was not going to fast." 'Abd al-'Azīz b. 'Abdallah related to us, saying: Muḥammad b. Ja'far related to me from Ḥumaid, that he heard Anas say: "The Apostle of Allah—upon whom be Allah's blessing and peace—used to continue eating during a month so long that we would think that he was not going to fast therein, and he would fast so long [during a month] that we would think that he was not going to eat at all during [that month]. Never would you want to see him praying during the night but you would see him praying, or want to see him sleeping but you would see him sleeping." Sulaimān said, quoting Ḥumaid, that he asked Anas about the fasting.

Muḥammad, namely Ibn Sallām, related to me, saying: Abū Khālid al-Aḥmar informed us, saying: Ḥumaid informed us, saying: I asked Anas about the fasting of the Prophet—upon whom be Allah's blessing and peace—and he said: "Never did I want to see him fasting in any month but I saw him, or [want to see him] eating but I saw him; not was there any night [when I wanted to see him] up for prayers but I saw him, or sleeping but I saw him. Never have I touched silk-wool tissue or [pure] silk softer than the hand of the Prophet—upon whom be Allah's blessing and peace—nor have I smelled musk or ambergris sweeter than the [body] scent of the Prophet—upon whom be Allah's blessing and peace."

54. *On a guest's rights in the matter of fasting*

Isḥāq related to us, saying: Hārūn b. Ismā'īl informed us, saying: 'Alī b. al-Mubārak related to us, saying; Yaḥyā related to us, saying: Abū Salama related to me, saying: 'Abdallah b. 'Amr b. al-'Āṣ related to us, saying: "The Apostle of Allah—upon whom be Allah's blessing and peace—entered to me...", then he recounted the Tradition, viz. "Verily you have duties towards your visitors; verily you have duties towards your wife." So I said: "What was David's fast?" and he answered: "Half the time."

55. *The rights of the body in [the matter of] fasting*

Muḥammad b. Muqātil related to us, saying: ʿAbdallah informed us, saying: al-Awzāʿī informed us, saying: Yaḥyā b. Abī Kathīr related to me, saying: Abū Salama b. ʿAbd ar-Raḥmān related to me, saying: ʿAbdallah b. ʿAmr b. al-ʿĀṣ related to me, saying: "The Apostle of Allah —upon whom be Allah's blessing and peace—said to me: 'O ʿAbdallah, am I not informed that you fast by day and stay up at night [for prayer]?' I answered: 'Yea, O Apostle of Allah.' Said he: 'Then do not do it. Fast, then break the fast. Be up [for prayers], then sleep, for you have duties towards your body, towards your eyes, towards your wife, and towards your visitors. It is sufficient for you to fast three days every month. Then you will have for each good work ten like it, and that will be as though you were fasting all the time.' But I was obstinate, so he was obstinate with me. I said: 'O Apostle of Allah, I find [that I have the] strength.' He replied: 'Then fast the fast of Allah's Prophet David, and go not beyond that.' I asked: 'And what was the fast of Allah's Prophet David?' He answered: 'Half the time.' When he became old ʿAbdallah used to say: 'Would that I had accepted the indulgence of the Apostle of Allah—upon whom be Allah's blessing and peace.'"

56. *On continuous fasting*

Abū'l-Yamān related to us, saying: Shuʿaib informed us from az-Zuhrī, who said: Saʿīd b. al-Musayyab and Abū Salama b. ʿAbd ar-Raḥmān informed me that ʿAbdallah b. ʿAmr said: "The Apostle of Allah—upon whom be Allah's blessing and peace—was informed that I used to say: 'By Allah, I will assuredly fast by day and stay up at night [for prayers] as long as I live.' So I said to him: 'By my father and my mother, I did say that.' He said: 'But you are not capable of that, so fast, then break the fast, rise up [for prayers] then sleep. Fast each month three days, for thus each good deed [of yours] will have ten like it [added to your merit], and that will be like fasting continuously.' I replied: 'But I am capable of even better than that.' So he said: 'Then fast for one day and eat for two days.' I replied: 'I am capable of better than that.' So he said: 'Then fast a day and eat a day, for that was the fasting of David, and is the best [kind of] fasting.' I answered: 'But I am capable of better than that', but the Prophet—upon whom be Allah's blessing and peace—answered: 'There is nothing better than that.'"

57. *On the rights of the family in [the matter of] fasting*

Abū Juḥaifa related it from the Prophet—upon whom be Allah's blessing and peace

ʿAmr b. ʿAlī related to us, saying: Abū ʿĀṣim related to us from Ibn Juraij who said, I heard ʿAṭā' [saying] that Abū'l-ʿAbbās the poet informed him that he had heard ʿAbdallah b. ʿAmr [say]: "It reached the Prophet—upon whom be Allah's blessing and peace—that I fasted continuously and spent the night at prayers. Either he sent for me, or I encountered him, and he said: 'Have I not been informed that you fast and do not eat? that you keep saying prayers and do not sleep? Fast, but then break the fast. Get up for prayers, but then sleep. You have a duty towards your eyes, towards yourself, and towards your family.' 'But,' I replied, 'I have the strength for that.' 'Then,' said he, 'fast the fast of David.' 'How [was that],' I asked, and he answered: 'He used to fast one day and eat the next, yet he did not flee when he encountered [the enemy].'[1] I said: 'O Prophet of Allah, who will give me the like of this?'" ʿAṭā' said: "I do not know how there can be talk of perpetual fasting, for the Prophet—upon whom be Allah's blessing and peace—said: 'He does not fast who fasts perpetually,' [a statement which he made] twice."

58. *On fasting one day and eating one day*

Muḥammad b. Bashshār related to us, saying: Ghandar related to us, saying: Shuʿba related to us from Mughira, who said: I heard Mujāhid [relate] from ʿAbdallah b. ʿAmr, from the Prophet—upon whom be Allah's blessing and peace—who said: "Fast for three days out of the month." He (i.e. ʿAbdallah) answered: "I am capable of more than that." [The Prophet] continued [to repeat his statement] till [finally] he said: "Fast for a day, and break fast for a day." He also said (presumably to the same ʿAbdallah): "Make a recitation of the Qur'ān each month." He answered: "But I am capable of more." [The Prophet] continued [to repeat his statement] till [finally] he said: "Well on three [nights each month]."

59. *On the fasting of David—upon whom be peace*

Ādam related to us, saying: Shuʿba related to us, saying: Ḥabīb b. Abī Thābit related to us, saying: I heard Abū'l-ʿAbbās the Meccan, who was a poet, but of whom no one was suspicious in the matter of Traditions

1 The point is that though he fasted every other day that did not sap his strength nor impair his martial valour.

which he related, say: I heard ʿAbdallah b. ʿAmr b. al-ʿĀṣ say: "The Prophet—upon whom be Allah's blessing and peace—said to me: 'You fast perpetually, and stay up at night for prayers.' 'Yes', I answered. Said he: 'If you do that your eye will grow dim and your soul become wearied. He does not fast who fasts perpetually. Fasting for three days [each month] is [the true] perpetual fast.' I answered: 'But I am capable of more than that.' He replied: 'Then fast the fast of David. He used to fast one day and break it the next day, yet he fled not when he encountered [the enemy].'"

Isḥāq b. Shāhīn al-Wāsiṭī related to us, saying: Khālid b. ʿAbdallah related to us from Khālid al-Ḥadhdhā', from Abū Qilāba, who said: Abū'l-Malīḥ related to me, saying: I went in with your father to ʿAbdallah b. ʿAmr, who related to us [the following]: "The Apostle of Allah—upon whom be Allah's blessing and peace—had had my fasting called to his attention, so he came in to me. I placed for him a leather cushion stuffed with palm-fibre, but he sat on the ground so that he had the cushion between me and himself. He asked: 'Are not three days [of fasting] each month sufficient for you?' I replied: 'O Apostle of Allah.' 'Then five', said he. I replied: 'O Apostle of Allah.' 'Then seven', said he. I replied: 'O Apostle of Allah.' 'Then nine', said he. I replied: 'O Apostle of Allah.' 'Then eleven', said he. Finally he said: 'There is no fast higher than the fast of David, namely half the time, for he fasted one day and broke the fast one day.'"

60. *On fasting on the days of white [moonlight, i.e.] the thirteenth, fourteenth and fifteenth*

Abū Maʿmar related to us, saying: ʿAbd al-Wārith related to us, saying: Abū't-Tayyāḥ related to us, saying: Abū ʿUthmān related to me, from Abū Huraira, who said: "My dear friend—upon whom be Allah's blessing and peace—recommended me three things—to fast three days each month, to make the fore-noon prayer service one of two bows, and to perform a *witr* [1] prayer before sleeping."

61. *On one who visits people but does not break the fast while he is with them*

Muḥammad b. al-Muthannā related to us, saying: Khālid, i.e. the son of al-Ḥārith, related to us, saying: Ḥumaid related to us from Anas, who said: "The Prophet—upon whom be Allah's blessing and peace—entered to Umm Sulaim, who brought him dates and butter, but he said: 'Return

[1] A *witr* is a prayer service with an odd number of *rakʿas* (bowings). See p. 464.

the butter to its jar and the dates to their basket for I am fasting.' Then he rose [and went] to a corner of the house where he performed a non-canonical prayer,[1] in which he made supplication for Umm Sulaim and her household. Umm Sulaim said: 'O Apostle of Allah, I have a special [favour to ask].' 'What is it', he asked, and she replied: 'Your servant Anas.'[2] Thereat [said Anas], he left no good thing of this world or the next which he did not implore might be granted to me, [saying]: 'Allahumma, prosper him in wealth and in children, and bless him in them.' So [as a result of his prayer], here I am the wealthiest of the Anṣār, and my daughter Umaima has related to me that at the time of al-Ḥajjāj's coming to Baṣra there were buried [there] one hundred and twenty [children who were the product] of my loins." Ibn Abī Maryam said: Yaḥyā b. Ayyūb related to us, saying: Ḥumaid related to me, saying: I heard Anas quoting from the Prophet [the above Tradition].

62. *On fasting at the end of the month*

Aṣ-Ṣalt b. Muḥammad related to us, saying: Mahdī related to us from Ghailān, [or another *isnād* reads] and Abū'n-Nu'mān related to us, saying: Mahdī b. Maimūn related to us, saying: Ghailān b. Jarīr related to us from Muṭarrif, from 'Imrān b. Ḥuṣain, from the Prophet—upon whom be Allah's blessing and peace—that he asked him, or he asked some man and 'Imrān heard it, saying to him: "O son of So-and-So, did you not fast the last day of this month?" I think the [narrator] said that his meaning was Ramaḍān. "No, O Apostle of Allah", said the man. "Then", said he, "you have broken the fast. Fast two days" (i.e. two extra days to make up for thus breaking it). Aṣ-Ṣalt did not say: "I think he meant Ramaḍān." Saith Abū 'Abdallah (i.e. al-Bukhārī himself): Thābit said, [quoting] from Muṭarrif, from 'Imrān, from the Prophet—upon whom be Allah's blessing and peace—"of the last days of Sha'bān."

63. *On fasting on Friday*

If, on a Friday, one rises in the morning fasting he must break it, i.e. if he was not previously fasting and has no intention of fasting after it

Abū 'Āṣim related to us from Ibn Juraij, from 'Abd al-Ḥamīd b. Jubair b. Shaiba, from Muḥammad b. 'Abbād, who said: "I asked Jābir: 'Did the Prophet—upon whom be Allah's blessing and peace—forbid

[1] There are five canonical prayer services each day, but pious men often add non-canonical prayer services in between the canonical hours. See pp. 463 ff.

[2] Anas was her son.

fasting on Friday?' 'Yes', said he." [Some Traditionists] other than Abū 'Āṣim added [the words]: "That is to say, that he should particularize that day for his fasting."

'Umar b. Ḥafṣ b. Ghiyāth related to us, saying: My father related to us, saying: al-A'mash related to us, saying: Abū Ṣāliḥ related to me from Abū Huraira, who said: I heard the Prophet—upon whom be Allah's blessing and peace—say: "Let no one of you fast on Friday, unless [he fast also] the day before it and the day after it."

Musaddad related to us, saying: Yaḥyā related to us from Shu'ba, [or according to another *isnād*], Muḥammad related to me, saying: Ghandar related to us, saying: Shu'ba related to us from Qatāda, from Abū Ayyūb, from Juwairiya the daughter of al-Ḥārith, that the Prophet—upon whom be Allah's blessing and peace—entered to her one Friday when she was fasting, and said: "Did you fast yesterday?" "No", she answered. "And do you intend to fast tomorow?" "No," she answered. "Then", said he, "break your fast." Ḥammād b. al-Ja'd said that he heard Qatāda say: Abū Ayyūb related to me that Juwairiyya related to him that he commanded her, so she broke her fast.

64. *Are there any particular days [for fasting]?*

Musaddad related to us, saying: Yaḥyā related to us from Sufyān, from Manṣūr, from Ibrāhīm, from 'Alqama, [who said]: "I said to 'Ā'isha: 'Did the Apostle of Allah—upon whom be Allah's blessing and peace—have any particular days [on which he fasted]?' 'No', said she, 'it was a constant practice with him, but which of you is capable of that of which the Apostle of Allah—upon whom be Allah's blessing and peace—was capable?'"

65. *On fasting on the day of 'Arafa* [1]

Musaddad related to us, saying: Yaḥyā related to us from Mālik, who said: Sālim related to me, saying: 'Umair, the client of Umm al-Faḍl, related to me, that Umm al-Faḍl had related to him, [or according to another *isnād*] 'Abdallah b. Yūsuf related to us, saying: Mālik informed us, from Abū'n-Naḍr, the client of 'Umar b. 'Ubaidallah, from 'Umair, the client of 'Abdallah b. 'Abbās, from Umm al-Faḍl the daughter of al-Ḥārith, that some folk were discussing at her place on the day of 'Arafa about the fasting of the Prophet—upon whom be Allah's blessing

[1] This is one of the more solemn days of assembly during the annual pilgrimage to Mecca. See pp. 499–500.

and peace. Some said that he used to fast [on that day], but others said that he did not fast [then]. So she sent him (i.e. the Prophet) a jar of milk, there where he was upright on his camel, and he drank it.

Yaḥyā b. Sulaimān related to us, saying: Ibn Wahb informed me, or it was read to him, saying: ʻAmr informed me from Bukair, from Kuraib, from Maimūna, that the people were in doubt about the Prophet's fasting on the day of ʻArafah, so she sent him a milk jug while he was standing there at the [pilgrim] station, and he drank from it while the people were watching.

66. *On fasting on the day of al-Fiṭr* [1]

ʻAbdallah b. Yūsuf related to us, saying: Mālik informed us from Ibn Shihāb, from Abū ʻUbaid, the client of Ibn Azhar, who said: I attended the feast [of al-Fiṭr] with ʻUmar b. al-Khaṭṭāb (i.e. the second Caliph), who said: "There are two days on which the Apostle of Allah—upon whom be Allah's blessing and peace—forbade fasting, viz. the day of al-Fiṭr when you end your fasting, and the other is the day on which you eat of your sacrificial victims." [2] Saith Abū ʻAbdallah (i.e. al-Bukhārī himself): Said Ibn ʻUyaina: "If one says: 'client of Ibn Azhar', that is correct, and if one says: 'client of ʻAbd ar-Raḥmān b. ʻAuf', that also is correct."

Mūsā b. Ismāʻīl related to us, saying: Wuhaib related to us, saying: ʻAmr b. Yaḥyā related to us from his father, from Abū Saʻīd, who said: "The Apostle of Allah—upon whom be Allah's blessing and peace—forbade fasting on the day of al-Fiṭr and on that of the sacrifice." According to aṣ-Ṣammā' [he also forbade] a man to dress in a single garment, and [forbade] the performance of prayer after the morning and evening prayer services.

67. *On fasting on the day of Sacrifice*

Ibrāhīm b. Mūsā related to us, saying: Hishām informed us from Ibn Juraij, who said, ʻAmr b. Dīnār informed me from ʻAṭā' b. Mīnā', who said: I heard him reporting from Abū Huraira, who said: "Two fasts are forbidden and two kinds of sale. [The fasts are those of] al-Fiṭr and the Sacrifice; [the two kinds of sale are those where the bargain is concluded] by touching [the commodity], and by throwing [a commodity]."

[1] The great feast day which marks the end of the month of fasting.

[2] The Feast of Sacrifice falls on the tenth day of the twelfth month, the day on which the victims are slaughtered during the Pilgrimage ceremonies.

Muḥammad b. al-Muthannā related to us, saying: Muʿādh related to us, saying: Ibn ʿAun informed us from Ziyād b. Jubair, who said: "A fellow came to Ibn ʿUmar, saying: 'A man took a vow that he would fast on a certain day—I think he said Monday—but that fell on a feast day'. Ibn ʿUmar said: 'Allah has commanded that vows be fulfilled, but the Prophet—upon whom be Allah's blessing and peace—forbade fasting on such a day.'"

Ḥajjāj b. Minhāl related to us, saying: Shuʿba related to us, saying: ʿAbd al-Malik b. ʿUmair related to us, saying: I heard Qazʿa say: I heard Abū Saʿīd al-Khudrī, who went on twelve military expeditions with the Prophet—upon whom be Allah's blessing and peace—say: "There are four things which I heard from the Prophet—upon whom be Allah's blessing and peace—which pleased me. He said: 'Let not a woman journey two days without having with her her husband or some male who is legally forbidden to her.[1] Let there be no fast on the two days of al-Fiṭr and the Sacrifice. Let there be no prayer services after morning prayer till the sun is up, nor after evening prayers till it has set. Let no riding beasts be saddled [for going to mosques], save in the case of three mosques, viz. the Masjid al-Ḥarām [at Mecca], the Masjid al-Aqṣā [at Jerusalem], and my mosque here [at Madina]."

68. *On fasting during the days of Tashrīq* [2]

Saith Abū ʿAbdallah (i.e. al-Bukhārī himself): Now Muḥammad b. al-Muthannā said to me: Yaḥyā related to us from Hishām, who said: My father informed me that ʿĀʾisha used to fast during the days at Munā,[3] *and her father* [4] *also used to fast during them*

Muḥammad b. Bashshār related to us, saying: Ghandar related to us, saying: I heard ʿAbdallah b. ʿĪsā b. Abī Lailā [reporting] from az-Zuhrī, from ʿUrwa from ʿĀʾisha, and from Sālim from Ibn ʿUmar, both of whom said: "It was not considered allowable that there should be fasting on the days of Tashrīq save for him who could not procure a victim [to sacrifice]."

[1] I.e. a father, or a brother, or some male within the circle of those whom she may not marry.

[2] The 11th, 12th and 13th days of the twelfth month. They are days on which certain ceremonies are being performed by those on Pilgrimage.

[3] Munā is one of the places at which the pilgrims stop for the performance of certain rites during their Pilgrimage. See pp. 505–508.

[4] I.e. Abū Bakr, the first Caliph.

ʿAbdallah b. Yūsuf related to us, saying: Mālik informed us from Ibn Shihāb, from Sālim b. ʿAbdallah, from Ibn ʿUmar, who said: "He who is enjoying the ʿUmra and then the Ḥajj [1] must fast until the day of ʿArafah. If he could not get a sacrificial victim and did not fast let him fast the days of Munā." From Ibn Shihāb from ʿUrwa, from ʿĀʾisha comes the like [account], and Ibrāhīm b. Saʿd follows it from Ibn Shihāb.

69. *On fasting on the day of ʿĀshūrāʾ*

Abū ʿĀṣim related to us from ʿUmar b. Muḥammad, from Sālim, from his father, who said: The Prophet—upon whom be Allah's blessing and peace—said: "If anyone so wishes, let him fast on the day of ʿĀshūrāʾ."

Abū'l-Yamān related to us, saying: Shuʿaib informed us from az-Zuhrī, who said: ʿUrwa b. az-Zubair informed me that ʿĀʾisha said: "The Apostle of Allah—upon whom be Allah's blessing and peace—used to command that there be fast on the day of ʿĀshūrāʾ, but when Ramaḍān was made an incumbent duty, those who wished to fast [on the day of ʿĀshūrāʾ] continued to do so, but those who wished to eat did so."

ʿAbdallah b. Maslama related to us from Mālik, from Hishām b. ʿUrwa, from his father, that ʿĀʾisha said: "The Quraish used to fast on the day of ʿĀshūrāʾ in pre-Islamic days, and the Apostle of Allah—upon whom be Allah's blessing and peace—used also to fast on it at that time, so that when he went to Madina he kept it as a fast and ordered that there be fasting on it, but when Ramaḍān was made an incumbent duty the day of ʿĀshūrāʾ was abandoned [as a fast day]. Whoever so wished fasted on it, but whoever so wished abandoned it."

ʿAbdallah b. Maslama related to us from Mālik, from Ibn Shihāb, from Ḥumaid b. ʿAbd ar-Raḥmān, that he heard Muʿāwiya b. Abī Sufyān say from the pulpit on the day of ʿĀshūrāʾ, in the year on which he went on pilgrimage: "O people of Madina, where are your theologians? I heard the Apostle of Allah—upon whom be Allah's blessing and peace—say: 'This is the day of ʿĀshūrāʾ. Allah has not prescribed for you fasting thereon, but I am fasting, so if anyone wishes let him fast, and if anyone wishes let him eat.'"

Abū Maʿmar related to us, saying: ʿAbd al-Wārith related to us, saying: Ayyūb related to us, saying: ʿAbdallah b. Saʿīd b. Jubair related to us from his father, from Ibn ʿAbbās, who said: "The Prophet—upon whom be Allah's blessing and peace—came to Madina and saw the Jews

[1] The *ʿumra*, or visitation, is the Lesser Pilgrimage; the *ḥajj* is the Greater Pilgrimage, i.e. the Pilgrimage proper. See p. 496.

fasting on this day of 'Āshūrā', so he asked: 'What is this?' They said: 'This is a holy day. This is the day when God saved the Children of Israel from their enemy, so Moses fasted thereon.' Said he: 'I have more right with Moses than you have'; so he fasted thereon and gave orders [to his community] that it be kept as a fast."

'Alī b. 'Abdallah related to us, saying: Abū Usāma related to us from Abū 'Umais, from Qais b. Muslim, from Ṭāriq b. Shihāb, from Abū Mūsā, who said: "The Jews used to count the day of 'Āshūrā' as a feast day. The Prophet—upon whom be Allah's blessing and peace—said: 'Fast ye on it also.'"

'Ubaidallah b. Mūsā related to us from Ibn 'Uyaina, from 'Ubaidallah b. Abī Yazīd, from Ibn 'Abbās, who said: "I have not seen the Prophet —upon whom be Allah's blessing and peace—select one day of fasting to give it preference over another save [in the case of] this day, the day of 'Āshūrā', and this month", meaning by that Ramaḍān.

Al-Makkī b. Ibrāhīm related to us, saying: Yazīd b. Abī 'Ubaid related to us from Salama b. al-Akwa', who said: "The Prophet—upon whom be Allah's blessing and peace—gave orders to a man of Aslam, [saying]: 'Have this announced among the people: Whosoever has eaten let him fast the rest of the day, and let him who has not eaten fast likewise, for this day is the day of 'Āshūrā'.'" [1]

[1] This was the Jewish fast for the Day of Atonement which Muḥammad had adopted from the Jews on coming to Madina before he appointed the Muslim fast of Ramaḍān. See p. 88 and Wensinck in *Ency. Islam*², I, 705.

FROM THE *SUNAN* OF ABŪ DĀWŪD [1]

SECTION ON CLOTHING [2]

'Amr b. 'Aun has related to us, relating from Ibn al-Mubārak, from al-Jarīrī, from Abū Naḍra, from Abū Sa'īd al-Khudrī, who said that the Apostle of Allah—upon whom be Allah's blessing and peace—was accustomed, when he put on a new garment, to name it by its name, *qamīṣ* (long-shirt) or *'imāma* (turban) [or whatever it might be], and then say: "Allahumma, praise be to Thee. Thou hast clothed me with this, so I ask Thee for the good that there is in it and the good that there is in that for which it was made, and I seek refuge with Thee from the evil there may be in it, and the evil there may be in that for which it was made." Abū Naḍra said that it was the custom when any one of the Companions of the Prophet—upon whom be Allah's blessing and peace—put on a new garment, folk would say: "Thou wilt wear out, but Allah—exalted be He—will remain." Musaddad has related to us, relating from 'Īsā b. Yūnus, from al-Jarīrī, on his line of transmission, much the same Tradition. Muslim has related to us, relating from Muḥammad b. Dīnār, from al-Jarīrī, on his line of transmission, what amounts to the same thing. Saith Abū Dāwūd: 'Abd al-Wahhāb ath-Thaqafī does not mention therein Abū Sa'īd or Ḥammād b. Salama, but reported it from al-Jarīrī, from Abū'l-'Alā', from the Prophet—on whom be Allah's blessing and peace. Nuṣair b. al-Faraj has related to us, relating from 'Abdallah b. Yazīd, relating from Sa'īd, that is, Ibn Abī Ayyūb, from Abū Marḥūm, from Sahl b. Mu'ādh b. Anas, from his father, that the Apostle of Allah

[1] The *Sunan* of Abū Dāwūd is usually classed as the fourth of the six canonical collections of Muslim Tradition. Abū Dāwūd Sulaimān b. al-Ash'ath as-Sijistānī (d. 275 A.H. = 889 A. D.), is said to have collected some five hundred thousand *ḥadīth* of which he selected some four thousand eight hundred for inclusion in his book. His work at first had great popularity, but as it was somewhat limited in the range of subjects it covered, and was not very critical in testing the authenticity of the Traditions, it came to be less highly regarded than the collections of al-Bukhārī and Muslim.

[2] Translated from *Ṣaḥīḥ Sunan al-Muṣṭafā* (Cairo, 1348 A.H.), vol. II, pp. 171–181, which covers about one half of the traditions in this section.

—upon whom be Allah's blessing and peace—said: "Whoever partakes of food and says: 'Praise be to Allah who has given me this food to eat, giving it to me for my sustenance, without any power or might on my part', Allah will pardon him his former and his latter sins. Also whoever puts on a garment and says: 'Praise be to Allah, who has clothed me with this and given it to me as my sustenance, without any might or power on my part', He will pardon him his former and latter sins."

On what is to be said to one who puts on new clothes

Isḥāq b. al-Jarrāḥ al-Udhnī has related to us, relating from Abū'n-Naḍr, relating from Isḥāq b. Sa'īd, from his father, from Umm Khālid, the daughter of Khālid b. Sa'īd b. al-'Āṣ, that some garments were brought [as a gift] to the Apostle of Allah —upon whom be Allah's blessing and peace—among which was a little blackbordered cloak. He said: "Who do you think is the most deserving of this?" The people were silent, so he said: "Bring me Umm Khālid." She was brought and he put it on her, saying: "Wear out and become shabby." This he said twice, and looking at a red and yellow ornament on the cloak he said: "Sanāh! sanāh! O Umm Khālid." Now *sanāh* in the Abyssinian language means "beautiful". [1]

On the qamīṣ (long shirt)

Ibrāhīm b. Mūsā has related to us, relating from al-Faḍl b. Mūsā, from 'Abd al-Mu'min b. Khālid al-Ḥanafī, from 'Abdallah b. Buraida, from Umm Salama, who said that the garment most beloved by the Apostle of Allah—upon whom be Allah's blessing and peace—was the *qamīṣ*. Isḥāq b. Ibrāhīm al-Ḥanẓalī has related to us, relating from Mu'ādh b. Hishām, from his father, from Budail b. Maisara, from Shahr b. Ḥawshab, from Asmā', daughter of Yazīd, who said: "The sleeve of the *qamīṣ* of the Apostle of Allah—upon whom be Allah's blessing and peace—used to tuck in at the wrist."

On the aqbiya (full-sleeved gowns)

Qutaiba b. Sa'īd and Yazīd b. Khālid b. Mawhib al-Ma'nī have related to us that al-Laith related to them, from 'Abdallah b. 'Ubaidallah b. Abī Mulaika, from al-Miswar b. Makhrama, that he said that the Apostle

[1] The reference is doubtless to the Ethiopic word *shanay* (sometimes written *sanay*) which means "beautiful".

of Allah—upon whom be Allah's blessing and peace—distributed some full-sleeved gowns but did not give Makhrama anything. Said Makhrama: "O my son, go to the Apostle of Allah [and enquire about this]." So I went along with him. He said: "Enter and make request of him for me." So I went in and made request for him, and [the Prophet] went out to him wearing one of the full-sleeved gowns, and said: "I have been saving this one for you." Then he inspected it. Ibn Mawhib here reads "Makhrama" (i.e. that it was Makhrama who inspected it). They both agree that he said that Makhrama was well-pleased, but Qutaiba, relating from Ibn Abī Mulaika, does not mention any name [of who it was inspected it]. Muḥammad b. ʿĪsā has related to us, relating from Abū ʿUwāna, and Muḥammad, i.e. Ibn ʿĪsā, has related to us, relating from Sharīk, from ʿUthmān b. Abī Zurʿa, from al-Muhājir ash-Shāmī, from Ibn ʿUmar, who said that in the Tradition from Sharīk, which he took up, it said: "Whosoever clothes himself in startling garments, him will Allah clothe in the like on the Day of Resurrection." To this he added on the authority of Abū ʿUwāna, "then in it he will be burned in the Fire". Musaddad has related to us, relating from Abū ʿUwāna, who said: "There are clothes which abase [a man]." ʿUthmān b. Abī Shaiba has related to us, relating from Abū Naḍr, relating from ʿAbd ar-Raḥmān b. Thābit, relating from Ḥassān b. ʿAṭiyya, from Abū Munib al-Jurashī, from Ibn ʿUmar, who said that the Apostle of Allah—upon whom be Allah's blessing and peace—said: "He who imitates [any group of] people belongs to them."

On woollen and hair clothing

Yazīd b. Khālid b. Yazīd b. ʿAbdallah ar-Ramlī and Ḥusain b. ʿAlī have related to us, saying that Ibn Abī Zā'ida related to them from his father, from Muṣʿab b. Shaiba, from Ṣafiyya the daughter of Shaiba, from ʿĀ'isha—with whom may Allah be pleased—who said: "The Apostle of Allah—upon whom be Allah's blessing and peace—went out [one day] wearing a *mirṭ* (wrapper) of black hair with ornamented border." Ḥusain said: Yaḥyā b. Zakariyā' has related to us, relating from Ibrāhīm b. al-ʿAlā' az-Zubaidī, relating from Ismāʿīl b. ʿAyyāsh, from ʿUqail b. Mudrik, from Luqmān b. ʿĀmir, from ʿUtba b. ʿAbd as-Sulamī, who said: "I begged the Apostle of Allah—upon whom be Allah's blessing and peace—for clothing, and he put on me two [gowns of] coarse flax-cloth, and you, indeed, have seen me as I was clothing my friends." ʿAmr b. ʿAun has related to us, relating from Abū ʿUwāna, from Qatāda, from Abū Burda, who said: My father said to me: "O my son, would that you could have seen us when we were with our Prophet—upon whom be Allah's blessing and peace—for when the rain came on us you would have thought that we smelled like sheep." 'Amr b. 'Aun has related to us, giving report from 'Ammāra b. Zādhān, from Thābit, from Anas b. Mālik, that the king of Dhū Yazan sent as a gift to the Apostle of Allah —upon whom be Allah's blessing and peace—a cloak *(ḥulla)* for which he had paid thirty-three camels, or thirty-three she-camels, and he accepted it. Mūsā b. Ismā'īl has related to us, relating from Ḥammād, from 'Alī b. Zaid, from Isḥāq b. 'Abdallah b. al-Ḥārith, that the Apostle of Allah—upon whom be Allah's blessing and peace—purchased a *ḥulla* for twenty and some young she-camels *(qalūṣ)*, and gave it as a gift to Dhū Yazan. Mūsā b. Ismā'īl has related to us, relating from Ḥammād, and Mūsā has also related to us relating from Sulaimān, that is Ibn al-Mughīra, from Ḥumaid b. Hilāl, from Abū Burda, who said: "I entered to 'Ā'isha—with whom may Allah be pleased—who brought out to us a thick *izār* (waist-wrapper) of the kind made in Yemen, and a garment *(kisā')* of the kind called felt *(mulabbada)*, and she swore by Allah that the Apostle of Allah—upon whom be Allah's blessing and peace—died while wearing these two garments." Ibrāhīm b. Khālid Abū Thawr has related to us, relating from 'Umar b. Yūnus b. al-Qāsim al-Yamāmī, relating from 'Ikrima b. 'Ammār, relating from Abū Zumail, relating from 'Abdallah b. 'Abbās, who said: "When the Ḥarūriyya[1] went out I came to 'Alī—with whom may Allah be pleased—who said: 'Go to these folk.' So I dressed myself in the finest of Yemenite *ḥullas*." Abū Zumail said: "Now Ibn 'Abbās was a handsome, fine looking man." Ibn 'Abbās said: "I came to them, and they said: 'Welcome to you, O Ibn 'Abbās, but what is this *ḥulla*?' I answered: 'Now do not cry shame upon me [for wearing such a garment], for I have seen the Apostle of Allah—upon whom be Allah's blessing and peace—wearing the most beautiful of *ḥullas*.'"

On the use of khazz[2]

'Uthmān b. Muḥammad al-Anmāṭī al-Baṣrī has related to us, relating from 'Abd ar-Raḥmān b. 'Abdallah ar-Rāzī, and Aḥmad b. 'Abd ar-Raḥmān ar-Rāzī has related to us, relating from his father, who was

[1] The Ḥarurīyya are more commonly known as the Khawārij (Kharijites). They were a group who, at the time of the conflict between 'Alī and Mu'āwiya for the Caliphate, deserted the cause of 'Alī because he agreed to submit his case to arbitration rather than settling it by the sword.

[2] *khazz* is a tissue of silk and wool.

informed by Abū ʿAbdallah b. Saʿd, from his father Saʿd, who said: I saw a man at Bukhārā [riding on] a white she-mule having on him a turban of black *khazz*, and who said: "The Apostle of Allah—upon whom be Allah's blessing and peace—placed this on me." These are the very words of ʿUthmān and the report is in his Tradition. ʿAbd al-Wahhāb b. Najda has related to us, relating from Bishr b. Bakr, from ʿAbd ar-Raḥmān b. Yazīd b. Jābir, relating from ʿAṭiyya b. Qais, who said: I heard ʿAbd ar-Raḥmān b. Ghanam al-Ashʿarī say: Abū ʿĀmir or Abū Mālik related to me, and by Allah he lied not to me, that he had heard the Apostle of Allah—upon whom be Allah's blessing and peace—say: "There will assuredly be in my community folk who will consider *khazz* and *ḥarīr* (silk) to be lawful." Then he reported some further words in which he (i.e. the Prophet) said: "and there will be others of them who will be metamorphosed into apes and pigs till the Day of Resurrection."

On clothing of silk (ḥarīr)

ʿAbdallah b. Maslama has related to us from Mālik, from Nāfiʿ, from ʿAbdallah b. ʿUmar, that ʿUmar b. al-Khaṭṭāb saw a striped yellow *ḥulla* for sale at the mosque gate, and he said: "O Apostle of Allah, would that I could buy this and wear it Fridays and for the delegations when they come to you", but the Apostle of Allah—upon whom be Allah's blessing and peace—said: "Only a man who has no share in the future life would wear this." Presently there came [as a gift] to the Apostle of Allah—upon whom be Allah's blessing and peace—some *ḥulla*s of that same kind, so he gave one of them to ʿUmar b. al-Khaṭṭāb. Said ʿUmar: "O Apostle of Allah, you have put this on me, and yet you said about the *ḥulla* of ʿUṭārid what you said." The Apostle of Allah—upon whom be Allah's blessing and peace—answered: "I did not put it on you that you should wear it", so ʿUmar put it on a brother of his at Mecca who was a polytheist. Aḥmad b. Ṣāliḥ has related to us, relating from Ibn Wahb, who reported it from Yūnus and ʿAmr b. al-Ḥārith, from Ibn Shihāb, from Sālim b. ʿAbdallah, from his father, about this story. He said it was a brocaded *ḥulla*, and added that [the Prophet] sent to him a full-sleeved upper gown of silk brocade *(dībāj)*, saying: "You may sell it and thereby satisfy your need." Mūsā b. Ismāʿīl has related to us, relating from Ḥammād, relating from ʿĀṣim al-Aḥwal, from Abū ʿUthmān an-Nahdī, who said: ʿUmar wrote to ʿUtba b. Farqad that the Prophet—upon whom be Allah's blessing and peace—forbade [the use of] silk save what was thus and so, two fingers and three and four.[1] Sulaimān b. Ḥarb has related to us, relating from Shuʿba, from Ibn ʿAun, who said: I heard Abū Ṣāliḥ relate from ʿAlī—with whom may Allah be pleased—who said: "There was sent as a gift to the Apostle of Allah—upon whom be Allah's blessing and peace—a striped yellow *ḥulla*, which he sent to me. I put it on and came to him, but I saw anger in his face, and he said: 'I did not send you that for you to wear it.' Then at his command I cut it up among my women-folk."

On those who disapprove of it

Al-Qaʿnabī has related to us from Mālik, from Nāfiʿ, from Ibrāhīm b. ʿAbdallah b. Ḥunain, from his father, from ʿAlī b. Abī Ṭālib—with whom may Allah be pleased—that the Apostle of Allah—upon whom be Allah's blessing and peace—forbade the wearing of Egyptian cloth, the wearing of anything dyed yellow, the use of gold seal-rings, and the recitation [of the Qur'ān] while in the bowing position.[2] Aḥmad b. Muḥammad, namely al-Marwazī, has related to us, relating from ʿAbd ar-Rāziq, reporting from Maʿmar, from az-Zuhrī, from Ibrāhīm b. ʿAbdallah b. Ḥunain, from his father, from ʿAlī—with whom may Allah be pleased—that the Prophet—upon whom be Allah's blessing and peace—said this with regard to reciting [the Qur'ān] both during the bowing position *(rukūʿ)* and that of prostration *(sujūd)*. Mūsā b. Ismāʿīl has related to us, relating from Ḥammād, relating from Muḥammad b. ʿAmr, from Ibrāhīm b. ʿAbdallah about this, where he added: "But I do not say he forbade you." Mūsā b. Ismāʿīl has related to us, relating from Ḥammād, from ʿAlī b. Zaid, from Anas b. Mālik, that the king of Byzantium sent as a gift to the Prophet—upon whom be Allah's blessing and peace—a *mustaqa* [3] of silk brocade *(sundus)*. He put it on and I can even now see his hands dangling. Then he sent it to Jaʿfar who put it on and came to him, but the Prophet—upon whom be Allah's blessing and peace—said: "I did not give it to you for you to wear it." "Then what shall I do with it?", he asked. [The Prophet] answered: "Send it to your brother the

[1] The meaning apparently is that he allowed a silk border to a garment, as much as two to four fingers' width.

[2] The reference is to the liturgical recitation of passages from the Qur'ān during prayers, the prohibition here being against reciting while in the bowing of the *rukūʿ* or the prostration of the *sujūd*. See pp. 68, 199, 477.

[3] A *mustaqa* is said to be a long-sleeved fur garment. As it is a question here of *sundus*, not of fur, the meaning must be that the garment was in appearance like a *mustaqa*.

Najāshī."[1] Makhlad b. Khālid has related to us, relating from Rauḥ, relating from Sa'īd b. Abī 'Arūba, from Qatāda, from al-Ḥasan, from 'Imrān b. Ḥaṣīn, that the Prophet—upon whom be Allah's blessing and peace—said: "I do not ride on purple, nor do I wear anything dyed yellow, nor put on a *qamīṣ* that is selvaged with silk." Then al-Ḥasan motioned with his head to the collar of his own *qamīṣ* and continued: "And then he said: 'Is not the perfume for men one which has odour but no colour, and the perfume for women one which has colour but no odour?'" Said Sa'īd: "My opinion is that they understood his saying with regard to the perfume for women to apply only to when she was going out, but if she is at home with her husband then let her perfume herself with anything she pleases." Yazīd b. Khālid b. 'Abdallah b. Mawhib al-Hamdānī has related to us, relating from al-Mufaḍḍal, i.e. Ibn Faḍāla, from 'Ayyāsh b. 'Abbās, from Abū'l-Ḥuṣain, i.e. al-Haitham b. Shafī, who said: "I went out with one of my friends named Abū 'Āmir, a man of the Ma'āfir, to pray at Īliyā." Now their *qāṣṣ*[2] was a man of the Azd named Abū Raiḥāna, one of the Companions [of the Prophet]. "My companion reached the mosque before me", continued Abū'l-Ḥuṣain, "And when I came along and sat down beside him he asked me had I heard the stories Abū Raiḥāna was telling. I said that I had not, whereat he said: 'I heard him say that the Apostle of Allah—upon whom be Allah's blessing and peace—forbade ten things: (1) haste; (2) tattooing; (3) plucking out the hair; (4) men sleeping with men without their undergarments on; (5) women sleeping with women without their undergarments on; (6) a man putting silk at the bottom of his garments like the Persians do; (7) or putting silk on his shoulders like the Persians do; (8) plundering; (9) riding on the skins of wild animals; (10) wearing a signet ring, unless he is a man of authority.'" Yaḥyā b. Ḥabīb has related to us, relating from Rauḥ, relating from Hishām, from Muḥammad, from 'Ubaida, from 'Alī—with whom may Allah be pleased—who said that [the Prophet] forbade [the use of] purple coverings. Ḥafṣ b. 'Umar and Muslim b. Ibrāhīm have related to us, saying: Shu'ba related to us from Abū Isḥāq, from Hubaira, from 'Alī—with whom may Allah be pleased—that the Apostle of Allah—upon whom be Allah's blessing and peace—forbade [the use of] gold signet-rings, the wearing of Egyptian cloth, and red coverings. Mūsā b. Ismā'īl has related

[1] *najāshī* is the Arabic word for the Negus of Abyssinia with whom many of the early Muslims had taken refuge when persecuted in Mecca.

[2] A *qāṣṣ* was a professional story-teller, but here apparently it means a narrator of Traditions about the Prophet.

to us, relating from Ibrāhīm, relating from Ibn Sa'd, relating from Ibn Shihāb, from 'Urwa, from 'Ā'isha—with whom may Allah be pleased—that the Apostle of Allah—upon whom be Allah's blessing and peace—said his prayers in a black-bordered cloak with ornamentation, but he looked at its ornamentation and when he had finished he said: "Take this black-bordered cloak of mine [and give it] to Abū Jahm, for it has bothered me in my praying, and bring me one of coarse wool." Saith Abū Dāwūd: "This Abū Jahm was the son of Ḥudhaifa of the Banū 'Adī b. Ka'b."

On Permission to use silk ornament and thread

Musaddad has related to us, relating from 'Īsā b. Yūnus, relating from al-Mughīra b. Ziyād, relating from 'Abdallah Abū 'Umar, the client of Asmā', daughter of Abū Bakr, who said: "I saw Ibn 'Umar in the market-place buy a Syrian garment, in which he noticed a red thread so he returned it. I came to Asmā' and reported that to her, whereat she said [to one of her slaves]: 'O girl, bring me the long-sleeved cloak of the Apostle of Allah—upon whom be Allah's blessing and peace.' So she brought forth a long-sleeved Persian cloak with collar and sleeves and openings hemmed with silk brocade *(dībāj)*." Ibn Nufail has related to us, relating from Zuhair, relating from Khaṣīf, from 'Ikrima, from Ibn 'Abbās, who said that the Apostle of Allah—upon whom be Allah's blessing and peace—forbade only [the use of] a garment made wholly of silk, but saw no harm in [garments with] ornamentation of silk or with a silk warp.

On wearing silk for an excusable reason

An-Nufailī has related to us, relating from 'Īsā, i.e. Ibn Yūnus, from Sa'īd b. Abī 'Arūba, from Qatāda, from Anas, who said: "The Apostle of Allah—upon whom be Allah's blessing and peace—permitted 'Abd ar-Raḥmān b. 'Auf and az-Zubair b. al-'Awwām to use a silk *qamīṣ* on a journey because of an itch from which they both suffered."[1]

On the use of silk by women

Qutaiba b. Sa'īd has related to us, relating from al-Laith, from Yazīd b. Abī Ḥabīb, from Abū Aflaḥ al-Hamdānī, from 'Abdallah b. Zurair,

[1] The skin trouble from which they were suffering would have been aggravated by woollen material touching the skin, which was an excuse for wearing silk.

that he heard ʿAlī b. Abī Ṭālib—with whom may Allah be pleased—say that the Prophet—upon whom be Allah's blessing and peace—took a piece of silk and held it in his right hand, then took a piece of gold and held it in his left hand, and said: "These two things are forbidden to the males of my community." ʿAmr b. ʿUthmān and Kathīr b. ʿUbaid, both of whom were from Ḥimṣ, have related to us, saying: Baqiyya has related to us from az-Zubaidī, from az-Zuhrī, from Anas b. Mālik, that he related how he had seen Umm Kulthūm the daughter of the Apostle of Allah—upon whom be Allah's blessing and peace—wearing a cloak of striped yellow cloth, and he remarked that this striped yellow cloth is figured with silk *(qazz)*. Naṣr b. ʿAlī has related to us, relating from Abū Aḥmad, i.e. az-Zubaidī, relating from Misʿar, from ʿAbd al-Malik b. Maisara, from ʿAmr b. Dīnār, from Jābir, who said: "We used to strip such from the slave-boys *(ghilmān)* [if we saw them wearing it], but would leave it on the slave-girls". Misʿar said: "I asked ʿAmr b. Dīnār about this and he said he did not know it".

On wearing a striped garment (ḥibara)

Hudba b. Khālid al-Azdī has related to us, relating from Hammām, from Qatāda, who said: "We asked Anas what kind of garment the Apostle of Allah—upon whom be Allah's blessing and peace—liked best, or which was the most pleasing to him, and he answered: 'The *ḥibara*.'"

On wearing white

Aḥmad b. Yūnus has related to us, relating from Zuhair, relating from ʿAbdallah b. ʿUthmān b. Khuthaim, from Saʿīd b. Jubair, from Ibn ʿAbbās, who said that the Apostle of Allah—upon whom be Allah's blessing and peace—said: "Wear your white garments for they are the best clothes you have, and shroud your dead in them. Also the best *koḥl* for the eyes is antimony *(ithmid)*, for it clears the vision and makes the lashes grow."

On washing clothes, and on [wearing] shabby garments

An-Nufailī has related to us, relating from Miskīn, from al-Awzāʿī, and ʿUthmān b. Abī Shaiba has related to us, relating from Wakīʾ from al-Awzāʿī likewise, from Ḥassān b. ʿAṭiyya, from Muḥammad b. al-Munkadir, from Jābir b. ʿAbdallah who said: "The Apostle of Allah—upon whom be Allah's blessing and peace—came to us [one day] and saw a man with dishevelled hair, i.e. his hair was disordered, so he said: 'Could not this fellow find something to keep his hair smoothed down?' Also he saw another man who was wearing a dirty garment, and he said: 'Could not this man find water to wash his clothes?' An-Nufailī has related to us, relating from Zuhair, relating from Abū Isḥāq, from Abū'l-Aḥwaṣ, from his father, who said: "I came to the Prophet—upon whom be Allah's blessing and peace—in a poor garment. He said: 'Do you have wealth?' 'Yes,' I replied. 'What kind of wealth?' he asked. 'Allah', I answered, 'has given me camels and small cattle, horses and slaves.' He said: 'Then if Allah has given you wealth, let the evidences of Allah's bounty be seen on you.'"

On that which is dyed

'Abdallah b. Maslama has related to us, relating from 'Abd al-'Azīz, i.e. Ibn Muḥammad, from Zaid, i.e. Ibn al-Aslam, that Ibn 'Umar used to dye his beard with a yellow substance so that all his clothing got covered with yellow. Someone asked him why he dyed it with yellow, and he said: "I saw the Apostle of Allah—upon whom be Allah's blessing and peace—use it as a dye, and there was nothing he liked better, so that he used to dye all his clothes with it, even his turban." [1]

On [the use of] green

Aḥmad b. Yūnus has related to us, relating from 'Ubaidallah, i.e. Ibn Iyād, relating from Iyād, from Abū Rimtha, who said: "I went with my father to the Prophet—upon whom be Allah's blessing and peace—and saw him wearing two green cloaks."

On [the use of] red

Musaddad has related to us, relating from 'Īsā b. Yūnus, relating from Hishām b. al-Ghāz, from 'Amr b. Shu'aib, from his father, from his grandfather, who said: "We came down from a mountain pass with the Apostle of Allah—upon whom be Allah's blessing and peace—when he looked at me and saw that I was wearing a *raiṭa* [2] dyed with yellow. He

[1] The reference to yellow in these Traditions is apparently to the yellow-brown henna colour, which is popularly associated with the Prophet Muḥammad.

[2] A *raiṭa* is a garment made from a single-weave cloth.

said: 'What is this *raiṭa* you have on?' I knew what displeased him, so when I came to my people who were heating an earthen oven of theirs I threw it into it. On the morrow I went to him and he said: 'O 'Abdallah, what have you done with the *raiṭa*?' I informed him, whereat he said: 'Why did you not put it on someone of your family, for there is no harm in women wearing such." 'Amr b. 'Uthmān al-Ḥimṣī has related to us, relating from al-Walīd, who said that Hishām, i.e. Ibn al-Ghāz said: "He [meant] a dyed garment which is neither saturated with dye nor dyed with saffron." Muḥammad b. 'Uthmān ad-Dimashqī has related to us, relating from Ismā'īl b. 'Ayyāsh, from Shuraḥbīl b. Muslim, from Shuf'a, from 'Abdallah b. 'Amr b. al-'Āṣ, who said: "The Apostle of Allah—upon whom be Allah's blessing and peace—saw me wearing a yellow-dyed garment of deep saffron, and he said: 'What is this?' So I went off and burned it. Anon the Prophet—upon whom be Allah's blessing and peace—said: 'What have you done with your garment?' 'I burned it', I answered. 'Why', said he, 'did you not put it on one of your family?' Saith Abū Dāwūd: Thawr has related [this Tradition] from Khālid and has 'dyed a deep saffron', but Tā'ūs says: 'dyed yellow.'" Muḥammad b. Ḥuzāba has related to us, relating from Isḥāq i.e. Ibn Manṣūr, relating from Isrā'īl, from Abū Yaḥyā, from Mujāhid, from 'Abdallah b. 'Amr, who said: "A man passed by the Prophet—upon whom be Allah's blessing and peace—wearing two red garments. He gave a greeting, but the Prophet—upon whom be Allah's blessing and peace—did not return it." Muḥammad b. al-'Alā' has related to us, reporting from Abū Usāma, from al-Walīd, i.e. Ibn Kathīr, from Muḥammad b. 'Amr b. 'Aṭā', from a man of the Banū Ḥāritha, from Rāfi' b. Khudaij, who said: "We went out with the Apostle of Allah—upon whom be Allah's blessing and peace—on a journey, when the Apostle of Allah—upon whom be Allah's blessing and peace—saw on our riding beasts, i.e. on our camels, garments in which were threads of red wool. Said he: 'Do I not see that this red has diverted you?' We rose in such haste at this word of the Apostle of Allah—upon whom be Allah's blessing and peace—that some of our camels shied, but we took the garments and removed them from them." Ibn 'Auf aṭ-Ṭā'ī has related to us, relating from Muḥammad b. Ismā'īl, who said: 'My father (Ismā'īl) related to me; and Ibn 'Auf said he had seen the original of Ismā'īl where he said: Ḍamḍam, i.e. Ibn Zur'a, related to me from Shuraiḥ b. 'Ubaid, from Ḥabīb b. 'Ubaid, from Ḥuraith b. al-Ablaj as Salīḥī, that a woman of the Banū Asad said: "I was one day with Zainab, the wife of the Apostle of Allah—upon whom be Allah's blessing and peace—and we were dyeing clothes belonging to her with a reddish dye. While we were busy at this the Apostle of Allah—upon whom be Allah's blessing and peace—came upon us, but when he saw the red dye he went away. When Zainab saw this she knew that the Apostle of Allah—upon whom be Allah's blessing and peace—was displeased and disapproved of what she was doing, so she took the clothes and washed them and hid everything red. Presently the Apostle of Allah—upon whom be Allah's blessing and peace—returned and looked in, and when he did not see anything [red] he entered."

On the permissibility [of using red]

Ḥafṣ b. 'Umar an-Namarī has related to us, relating from Shu'ba, from Abū Isḥāq, from al-Barā', who said that the Apostle of Allah—upon whom be Allah's blessing and peace—had hair which hung to the lobe of his ear, and I saw him in a red *ḥulla* than which I have never seen anything more beautiful. Musaddad has related to us, relating from Abū Mu'āwiya, from Hilāl b. 'Āmir, from his father, who said: "I saw the Apostle of Allah—upon whom be Allah's blessing and peace—at Minā, preaching from a she-mule and wearing a red cloak, while 'Alī—with whom may Allah be pleased—was in front of him interpreting for him."

On wearing black

Muḥammad b. Kathīr has related to us, relating from Hammām, from Qatāda, from Muṭarrif, from 'Ā'isha—with whom may Allah be pleased—who said: "I made for the Apostle of Allah—upon whom be Allah's blessing and peace—a black cloak which he put on, but when he sweat in it he found that there was a smell from the wool so he threw it away." I think that he added [in reporting this Tradition] that pleasant smells pleased him (i.e. the Prophet).

On fringes

'Ubaidallah b. Muḥammad al-Qurashī has related to us, relating from Ḥammād b. Salama, reporting from Yūnus b. 'Ubaid, from 'Ubaida Abū Khidāsh, from Abū Tamīma al-Hujaimī, from Jābir, who said: "I came to the Prophet—upon whom be Allah's blessing and peace—and he was cloaked in a *shamla* [1] whose fringes fell to his feet."

[1] A *shamla* is a long cloak that covers the whole body.

On turbans

Abū'l-Walīd aṭ-Ṭayālisī and Muslim b. Ibrāhīm and Mūsā b. Ismāʿīl have related to us, saying: Ḥammād related to us, from Abū'z-Zubair, from Jābir, that the Apostle of Allah—upon whom be Allah's blessing and peace—on the year when Mecca was conquered, entered wearing a black turban. Al-Ḥasan b. ʿAlī has related to us, relating from Abū Usāma, from Musāwir al-Warrāq, from Jaʿfar b. ʿAmr b. Ḥuraith, from his father, who said: "I saw the Prophet—upon whom be Allah's blessing and peace—in the pulpit, wearing a black turban whose ends hung down between his shoulders." Qutaiba b. Saʿīd ath-Thaqafī has related to us, relating from Muḥammad b. Rabīʿa, relating from Abū'l-Ḥasan al-ʿAsqalānī, from Abū Jaʿfar b. Muḥammad b. ʿAlī b. Rukāna, from his father, that Rukāna wrestled [one day] with the Prophet—upon whom be Allah's blessing and peace—and the Prophet threw him. Said Rukāna: "I heard the Prophet—upon whom be Allah's blessing and peace—say: 'Turbans wound around hats are what distinguish us from the polytheists.'" Muḥammad b. Ismāʿīl, client of the Banū Hāshim, has related to us, relating from ʿUthmān al-Ghaṭafānī, relating from Sulaimān b. Kharabūdh, relating from an old man of the people of Madina, who said: "I heard ʿAbd ar-Raḥmān b. ʿAuf say: 'The Apostle of Allah—upon whom be Allah's blessing and peace—put on me a turban whose tails hung before me and behind me.'"

On wearing the ṣammā' [1]

ʿUthmān b. Abī Shaiba has related to us, relating from Jarīr, from al-Aʿmash, from Abū Ṣāliḥ, from Abū Huraira, who said: "The Apostle of Allah—upon whom be Allah's blessing and peace—forbade the use of two [styles of] garment, that in which if a man were to squat he would expose his pudenda to the heavens, and that where the garment is worn so that one of his sides is bare while he throws the garment over his shoulder." Mūsā b. Ismāʿīl has related to us, relating from Ḥammād, from Abū'z-Zubair, from Jābir, who said: "The Apostle of Allah—upon whom be Allah's blessing and peace—forbade the [wearing of the] ṣammā' and squatting on the heels in a single garment."

[1] A *ṣammā'* is a garment which covers the whole body and has no opening at the side through which an arm may be raised.

On unfastening the buttons

An-Nufailī and Aḥmad b. Yūnus have related to us, saying: Zuhair related to us, relating from ʿUrwa b. ʿAbdallah, who said: Ibn Nufail b. Qushair Abū Mahal al-Juʿfī related to us, relating from Muʿāwiya b. Qurra, relating from his father, who said: "I came to the Apostle of Allah —upon whom be Allah's blessing and peace—at the head of a party of men from Muzaina and swore allegiance to him, and behold his *qamīṣ* was hanging [open]. I made my act of allegiance to him and then thrust my hand in at the collar of his *qamīṣ* and touched the seal."[1] Said ʿUrwa: "Never did I see Muʿāwiya or his son but their buttons were unfastened, neither in winter nor in summer did they ever fasten their buttons."

On wrapping oneself in one's cloak

Muḥammad b. Dāwūd b. Sufyān related to us, relating from ʿAbd ar-Razzāq, reporting from Maʿmar, who said that az-Zuhrī reported ʿUrwa as saying that ʿĀ'isha —with whom may Allah be pleased—said: "While we were sitting in our house about midday someone said to Abū Bakr[2] —with whom may Allah be pleased—: 'Here is the Apostle of Allah —upon whom be Allah's blessing and peace—wrapped in his cloak, coming at such an hour as he never used to come to us.' Then along came the Apostle of Allah—upon whom be Allah's blessing and peace—, asked permission, which was granted him, and entered."

On Traditions about letting the izār[3] hang down

Musaddad has related to us, relating from Yaḥyā, relating from Abū Ghifār, relating from Abū Tamīma al-Hujaimī, from Abū Juraiy Jābir b. Sālim, who said: "I saw a man whose advice the people took and refused to say anything save on his advice, so I said: 'Who is this?' They answered: 'The Apostle of Allah—upon whom be Allah's blessing and peace.' I said: 'Upon you be peace, O Apostle of Allah.' This I said twice, but he said: 'Do not say, 'Upon you be peace,' for that is the greeting for the dead, but say: 'Peace be upon you''. I said: 'You are

[1] I.e. the mole or birthmark on the Prophet's body which was considered to be the seal of prophethood.
[2] He was ʿĀ'isha's father. See p. 121.
[3] *izār* is often translated "waist cloth." It is the garment which covers the body from the waist downwards. See p. 499.

the Apostle of Allah?' He answered: 'I am the Apostle of Allah, Who, if you invoke Him when distress has befallen you will remove it from you. Who if you invoke Him when a year of drought has befallen you will give you verdure. Who if you are in a desert waterless land and your riding beast has gone astray will, if you invoke Him, bring her back to you.' I said: 'Impose the conditions on me.' He answered: 'Never abuse anyone grossly.' So never after that did I ever use gross abuse to anyone, freedman or slave, camel or sheep. He said: 'Do not think slightingly of any service rendered you. If you are talking with your brother and you turn a pleasant countenance to him that is a service. Keep your *izār* up to half way down your leg, or if you disdain that then to the ankle. Beware of letting the *izār* hang down, for that is a symbol of pride, and Allah does not love pride. Should a man use bad language to you and upbraid you for something he knows about you, do not upbraid him for something you know about him, for he is already suffering from the mischief of that.'" An-Nufailī has related to us, relating from Zuhair, relating from Mūsā b. ʿUqba, from Sālim b. ʿAbdallah, from his father, who said that the Apostle of Allah—upon whom be Allah's blessing and peace—said: "On the Day of Resurrection Allah will not look upon that person who trails his robe out of pride." Abū Bakr said: "But one side of my *izār* usually falls down, without there being any remissness in that I had not been careful of that. He [i.e. Muḥammad] replied: 'You are not one of those who do it from pride.'" Mūsā b. Ismāʿīl has related to us, relating from Abān, relating from Yaḥyā, from Abū Jaʿfar, from ʿAṭā' b. Yasār, from Abū Huraira, who said: "While a man was praying with his *izār* hanging down, the Apostle of Allah—upon whom be Allah's blessing and peace—said to him: 'Go and perform your ablutions.' He went and performed his ablutions and came back, but [the Prophet again] said: 'Go and perform your ablutions.' A man said to him: 'O Apostle of Allah, what is the matter with you, ordering the man to go and perform his ablutions?' When he was silent [the Prophet] said: 'He was praying with his *izār* trailing. Allah does not accept the prayer of man who trails [his garment].'" Ḥafṣ b. ʿUmar has related to us, relating from Shuʿba, from ʿAlī b. Mudrik, from Abū Zurʿa b. ʿAmr b. Jarīr, from Kharasha b. al-Ḥurr, from Abū Dharr, from the Prophet—upon whom be Allah's blessing and peace—that he said: "There are three with whom Allah will not speak, at whom He will not look, on the Day of Resurrection, whom He will not justify, but for whom there will be a painful punishment." I said: "Who are they, O Apostle of Allah?" "They have fallen short. They are in loss", he replied, and said this three times. "Who are they who have fallen short and are in loss?", I asked. He replied: "He who trails [his garment], he who reminds others of a gift, and he who markets [worthless] goods with an oath false or wicked." Musaddad has related to us, relating from Yaḥyā, from Sufyān, from al-Aʿmash, from Sulaimān b. Mus'hir, from Kharasha b. al-Ḥurr, from Abū Dharr, from the Prophet—upon whom be Allah's blessing and peace—this same Tradition, but the former adds: "A *mannān* [1] is one who never gives a thing without reminding folk of it."

Hārūn b. ʿAbdallah has related to us, relating from Abū ʿĀmir, i.e. ʿAbd al-Malik b. ʿAmr, relating from Hishām b. Saʿd, from Qais b. Bishr ath-Thaʿlabī, who said: "My father, who was one of those who sat with Abū'd-Dardā', informed me that there was a man in Damascus of the Companions of the Prophet—upon whom be Allah's blessing and peace—named Ibn al-Ḥanẓalīya. He was a man who kept much to himself and but seldom sat in company with folk. His life consisted mostly of prayers, and when prayers were over he would set himself to *tasbīḥ* and *takbīr* [2] till he returned to his family. He passed by us while we were with Abū'd-Dardā', who said to him: '[Give us] a word by which we shall be benefitted and you will not be harmed.' He said: 'The Apostle of Allah—upon whom be Allah's blessing and peace—sent out a *sarīya*,[3] so I went out [thereon]. Now a man from among them came and sat down in the gathering where the Apostle of Allah—upon whom be Allah's blessing and peace—was sitting, and said to a man beside him: 'Had you seen us when we and the enemy met, when So-and-So charged and gave a blow, saying—: Take that from me. I am the Ghifārī youth—what would you have thought of his words?' He answered: 'The only opinion I have is that he thereby annulled his reward.' Another man heard that and said: 'But I see no harm in that.' Thereupon they began disputing till the Apostle of Allah—upon whom be Allah's blessing and peace—heard it, whereat he said: 'Glory be to Allah, there is no harm in his being given his reward and being praised.'" I saw that Abū'd-Dardā' was pleased with that. He raised his head and said to him: 'You really heard that from the Apostle of Allah—upon whom be Allah's blessing and peace?' 'Yes,' said he. [Abū'd-Dardā'] ceased not to make him repeat it till I said: 'Let him kneel upon his knees.' [4] He passed by us another

[1] This is the word used in the previous Tradition.

[2] *tasbīḥ* consists in repeating the phrase *subḥān Allāh* (glory be to Allah), and *takbīr* in repeating the phrase *Allāhu akbar* (Allah is very great). See pp. 153, 502.

[3] A raiding party sent out to seek a caravan to raid and bring back the booty to the Muslims in Madīna.

[4] I.e. let him alone so that he may go on with his prayers.

day and Abū'd-Dardā' again said to him: '[Give us] a word by which we shall be benefitted and you will not be harmed.' So he said: 'The Apostle of Allah—upon whom be Allah's blessing and peace—said to us: 'He who squanders money over horses is like a man who stretches out his hand with a charitable alms which he does not bestow.'" He passed by us yet another day, and Abū'd-Dardā' said to him: '[Give us] a word which will benefit us but will not harm you.' So he said: 'The Apostle of Allah—upon whom be Allah's blessing and peace—said: 'What an excellent man Khuraim al-Asadī would be if he did not wear his luxuriant hair so long and trail his *izār*.' This word reached Khuraim, whereat he took a reaping-knife with which he cut off his luxuriant hair till it reached only to his ears, and pulled up his *izār* till it reached but half way down his legs.' Then another day he passed by us, and again Abū'd-Dardā' said to him: '[Give us] a word by which we shall be benefitted and you will not be harmed.' He said: 'I heard the Apostle of Allah—upon whom be Allah's blessing and peace—say: 'When you present yourselves before your brethren have your saddles in good shape and also your clothing, so that you appear as though you were beauty-spots among the people, for Allah does not like what is unseemly or foul.'" Saith Abū Dāwūd: "Thus did Abū Nu'aim give it from Hishām, but he said: 'That you may be like a beauty spot among the people.'"

On pride

Mūsā b. Ismā'īl has related to us, relating from Ḥammād, and Hannād, i.e. Ibn as-Sarī, has related to us from Abū'l-Aḥwaṣ al-Ma'nī, from 'Aṭā' b. as-Sā'ib,— [then] Mūsā said: from Salmān al-Agharr, and Hannād said from al-Agharr Abū Muslim, from Abū Huraira, who, according to Hannād said that the Apostle of Allah—upon whom be Allah's blessing and peace—said: "Allah—mighty and majestic is He—has said: 'Grandeur *(kibriyā')* is My upper garment *(ridā')* and greatness *('aẓma)* is My lower garment *(izār)*, and whosoever contends with Me for even one of them, him will I cast into the Fire.'"[1] Aḥmad b. Yūnus has related to us, relating from Abū Bakr, i.e. Ibn 'Ayyāsh, from al-A'mash, from Ibrāhim, from 'Alqama, from 'Abdallah, who said that the Apostle of Allah—upon whom be Allah's blessing and peace—said: "No man who has in his heart a mustard grain's weight of pride will ever enter Paradise,

[1] There is a play on words here, for both *kibriyā'* and *'aẓama* also have the meaning of "pride", so that the proud man is the one who will be cast into the Fire for assuming to himself what belongs only to Allah.

and no man who has in his heart a mustard grain's weight of faith will ever enter Hell." Saith Abū Dāwūd: "Al-Qasmalī relates from al-A'mash the same Tradition." Abū Mūsā Muḥammad b. al-Muthannā has related to us, relating from 'Abd al-Wahhāb, relating from Hishām, from Muḥammad, from Abū Huraira, that a man came to see the Prophet—upon whom be Allah's blessing and peace. Now he was a handsome man, and he said: "O Apostle of Allah, I am a man who delights in what is beautiful, and I have been given thereof what you see, so that I do not like anyone to surpass me even in the latchet of my sandal—or maybe he said 'thong of my sandal'—Is that pride?" "No", [answered the Prophet], "pride is when there is slighting of rights and a despising of folk."

THE FORTY TRADITIONS OF AN-NAWAWĪ[1]

Praise be to Allah, Lord of the worlds, eternal Guardian of the heavens and the earths, Ruler over all creatures, who sent to responsible beings the Messengers—upon whom be His blessing and peace—that they might bring them guidance and make clear to them the religious laws, [accompanying this] with decisive proofs and clear arguments. Him do I praise for all His favours, and from Him do I beg increase of His kindness and His generosity. Also I bear witness that our Master Muḥammad is His servant and His Apostle, His Beloved and His friend, the most excellent of created beings, who was honoured by [being given] the great Qur'ān, [a Book which is] the miracle that will endure throughout the passing years, and by [being given] the right practices *(sunan)* which enlighten those who seek to be directed in the right way, who is distinguished for the all-embracing [wisdom of his] discourse, and for [his] forbearance in religion. May Allah's blessing and peace be upon him, and upon the rest of the Prophets and Messengers, upon the families of them all, and upon all other righteous persons.

It has come to us on the authority of ʿAlī b. Abī Ṭālib, and ʿAbdallah b. Masʿūd, and Muʿādh b. Jabal, and Abū'd-Dardā', and Ibn ʿUmar, and Ibn ʿAbbās, and Anas b. Mālik, and Abū Huraira, and Abū Saʿīd al-Khudrī, [all Companions of the Prophet], with all of whom may Allah be pleased, [coming] by many channels and varied lines of transmission, that the Apostle of Allah—upon whom be Allah's blessing and peace—said: "Whosoever preserves for my community forty Traditions concerning matters of this religion, Allah will raise up on the Last Day in the company of the Jurists and the Theologians."[2]

[1] *Matn al-Arbaʿīn an-Nawawīya fi'l-Aḥādīth aṣ-ṣaḥīḥa an-nabawīya*, Cairo, 1350 A. H. Yaḥyā b. Sharaf ad-Dīn an-Nawawī, d. 676 A. H. = 1278 A. D., was a famous writer on Jurisprudence. This collection of 42 Traditions, commonly known as "the Forty" *(al-Arbaʿīn)*, is widely known and used throughout the Islamic world. It has been translated into Persian, Turkish, Urdu and Malay, and been made the subject of innumerable Commentaries. The "Forty" are commonly memorized by school children from Morocco in the West to the Philippines in the East.

[2] During the events of the "Day" after the general resurrection people will be assem-

According to another line of transmission [this Traditions reads]: "Allah will raise him up a Jurist and a Theologian." As transmitted by Abū'd-Dardā' [it reads]: "I will be an intercessor and a witness for him on the Day of Resurrection." As transmitted by Ibn Mas'ūd [it reads]: "It will be said to him: 'Enter Paradise by any Gate you please.'"[1] As transmitted by Ibn 'Umar [it reads]: "He will be recorded in the company of the Theologians and raised up in the company of the Martyrs." The professional transmitters [of Traditions] are agreed that the above is a weak Tradition [2] even though the lines [by which it has been handed down] are numerous.

The Theologians—with whom may Allah be pleased—have composed innumerable works on this matter [of the Forty Traditions]. To my knowledge the first among them to write thereon was 'Abdallah b. al-Mubārak. Then came Muḥammad b. Aslam aṭ-Ṭūsī, the Divine devoted to his Lord. Then there was al-Ḥasan b. Sufyān an-Nasāwī, and Abū Bakr al-Ājurrī, and Abū Bakr Muḥammad b. Ibrāhīm al-Iṣfahānī, and ad-Dāraquṭnī etc. etc. etc., and others too numerous to mention both among the older writers and among the moderns. And now I have sought Allah's help in assembling forty Traditions in imitation of these predecessors, the outstanding Traditionists and scholars of Islam. The Theologians have agreed that it is permissible to make use of a weak Tradition when it concerns a matter of meritorious works, yet in spite of this I have not relied on the [above recorded] Tradition, but rather on the saying of him—upon whom be Allah's blessing and peace—(i.e. the Prophet Muḥammad), in the genuine Traditions: "Let him among you who [was present and] saw, inform him who was absent", and on his saying: "May Allah brighten life for any man who hears what I say, pays heed to it, and passes it on just as he heard it."

Among the Theologians are some who have assembled forty [Traditions] concerning the principles of religion *(uṣūl ad-dīn)*, while others

bled in companies, some of honour some of dishonour. The Jurists who have occupied themselves with Islamic Law, and the Theologians who have occupied themselves with theology will have distinguished places of honour.

[1] Many Traditions tell how when the Judgment is over and the Blessed are sent on to their eternal abode in Paradise they find that there are many gates, each gate reserved for the entrance of some special group who are to be honoured in that way. The Tradition here means that such a man may make his own choice of Gate. The Martyrs mentioned immediately after are a specially honoured group. On these various gates see pp. 89-91.

[2] The specialists in the "Science of Tradition" scrutinized the lines of transmission by which any given tradition came down from the Companions of the Prophet, and classified them as "excellent", "good", "fair", "weak", "poor", etc.

[have made their collection] with reference to the derivative matters of religion *(furū')*. Some [have made collections of forty Traditons] about [the matter of] Holy War, some about ascetic practices, some about rules of conduct, others about practical sermonizing. All these are pious purposes, so may Allah be pleased with such as have purposed them. My thought, however, was to assemble forty [Traditions] more important than any of these, viz. forty Traditions which would include all the above-mentioned [subjects], and each Tradition of which would set forth one of the great points of religious belief. [I shall choose such Traditions as those which] the Theologians have referred to as "the pivot of Islam", or "the half of Islam", or "the third thereof", or some such title. Then I shall insist that each of the forty be a "genuine" [Tradition], for the most part such as will be found in the [books called] "Genuine" *(Ṣaḥīḥ)* of al-Bukhārī and of Muslim.[1] I shall record them without the *isnāds* [2] in order to make it easier to memorize them and to make them more generally profitable—if Allah wills—and after them I shall add explanations of any obscure expressions in them.

Everyone who is eager to attain the world to come ought to know these Traditions because of the important matters they contain and the indications they give of all things in which obedience [to Allah is necessary]. This will be apparent to anyone who reflects on the matter. On Allah is my reliance, and He is my trust and my stay. His is the praise and the grace, and with Him is success and protection.

The first Tradition

From the Commander of the Faithful, Abū Ḥafṣ 'Umar b. al-Khaṭṭāb (the second Caliph)—with whom may Allah be pleased—who said: "I heard the Apostle of Allah—on whom be Allah's blessing and peace—say: 'Works [will be rewarded] only in accordance with the intentions, so each man will receive only according to what he intended. Thus he whose migration [from Mecca to Madina] was for the sake of Allah and His Apostle [will be rewarded for] a migration for the sake of Allah and His Apostle, but he whose migration was for the sake of some worldly thing

[1] The collections of al-Bukhārī (d. 257 A. H. = 870 A. D.) and Muslim (d. 262 A. H. = 875 A. D.) are both entitled *Ṣaḥīḥ*, and are often referred to as *aṣ-Ṣaḥīḥān*, "the two Genuines." No Tradition that is found in these two collections would be disputed by any orthodox Muslim. Muslim is a man's name as well as meaning any follower of the religion of Islam.

[2] Each Tradition in these collections consists of two parts, the *matn* or text, and the *isnād* or chain of authorities by whom it was handed down from the time of the companions of the Prophet to the collectors of the canonical collections.

he might gain, or for a wife he might marry, his migration [will be rewarded] according to that for the sake of which he migrated.'" This is related by both al-Bukhārī and Muslim in their [books called] *Ṣaḥīḥ*, which are the soundest collections of Tradition ever made.

Second Tradition

Also from 'Umar—with whom may Allah be pleased—who said: "While we were one day sitting with the Apostle of Allah—on whom be Allah's blessing and peace—there appeared before us a man with a very white garment and very black hair. No traces of journeying were visible on him, and none of us knew him. He sat down close by the Prophet—upon whom be Allah's blessing and peace—rested his knees against his, put his palms on his thighs, and said: 'O Muḥammad! inform me about Islam.' Said the Apostle of Allah—upon whom be Allah's blessing and peace—: 'Islam is that you should testify that there is no deity save Allah and that Muḥammad is His Apostle, that you should say the prayers, pay the legal alms, fast during Ramaḍān, and go on pilgrimage to the House (i.e. the Ka'ba at Mecca) if you can find a way to do so.' Said he: 'You have spoken truly.' We were astonished at his thus questioning him and telling that he was right, [but he went on to] say: 'Inform me about faith.' [Muḥammad] answered: 'It is that you should believe in Allah and His angels and His Books and His Messengers (Apostles) and in the Last Day, and that you should believe in the decreeing of both good and evil.' He said: 'You have spoken truly.' Then he said: 'Inform me about best behaviour.' [Muḥammad] answered: 'It is that you should serve Allah as though you could see Him, for though you cannot see Him yet He sees you.' He said: 'Inform me about the Hour.' [Muḥammad] said: 'About that the one questioned knows no more than the questioner.' So he said: 'Well, inform me about the signs thereof (i.e. of its coming).' Said [Muḥammad]: '[They are] that the slave-girl will give birth to her mistress, that you will see the barefoot ones, the naked, the destitute, the herdsmen of the sheep building arrogantly high houses.' Thereupon [the man] went off. I waited a while, and then the [Prophet] said: 'O 'Umar, do you know who that was?' I replied: 'Allah and His Apostle know better.' He said: 'That was Gabriel. He came to teach you your religion.'" Muslim relates this.

Third Tradition

From Abū 'Abd ar-Raḥmān 'Abdallah the son of 'Umar b. al-Khaṭṭāb—with whom may Allah be pleased—who said: "I heard the Apostle of

Allah—upon whom be Allah's blessing and peace—say: 'Islam has been built upon five things—on testifying that there is no god save Allah, and that Muḥammad is His Apostle; on saying prayers; on giving legal alms; on pilgrimage to the House; and on fasting during Ramaḍān.'" Both al-Bukhārī and Muslim relate this.

Fourth Tradition

From Abū 'Abd ar-Raḥmān 'Abdallah b. Mas'ūd—with whom may Allah be pleased—who said: "The Apostle of Allah—upon whom be Allah's blessing and peace—who is trustworthy and one who is considered to speak veraciously, reported to us [in these words]: 'Verily the creation of any one of you takes place when he is assembled in his mother's womb; for forty days [he is] as a drop, then he becomes a clot, in the same way, and then in the same way a mass. Then an angel is sent to him, who breathes the spirit into him. Four words of command are given [to this angel], viz. that he write down his fortune *(rizq)*, his life-span, his works, and whether [at Judgment] he will be among the wretched or the happy. By Allah, than whom there is no other deity, one of you may work the works of the people of Paradise till there is naught but an arm's length between him and it, when that which has been written will outstrip him so that he works the works of the people of the Fire and enters therein. Or one of you may work the works of the people of the Fire till there is naught but an arm's length between him and it, when that which has been written will overtake him so that he works the works of the people of Paradise and enters therein.'" Both al-Bukhārī and Muslim relate this.

Fifth Tradition

From the Mother of the Believers, Umm 'Abdallah 'Ā'isha (the Prophet's girl-wife)—with whom may Allah be pleased—who said: "Said the Apostle of Allah—upon whom be Allah's blessing and peace—'Whosoever introduces into this affair of ours (i.e. Islam) something that does not belong to it is a reprobate.'" Both al-Bukhārī and Muslim relate it. According to one line of transmission in Muslim [it reads]: "Whosoever works a work which has for it no command of ours is a reprobate." [1]

[1] This Tradition in either of the forms above is a warning against "innovation" *(bid'a)*, the fear of which has ever been present to the Muslim theologians. See pp. 154, 255.

Sixth Tradition

From Abū ʿAbdallah an-Nuʿmān son of Bashīr—with both of whom may Allah be pleased—who said: "I heard the Apostle of Allah—upon whom be Allah's blessing and peace—say: 'Verily what is lawful is obvious, and what is unlawful is obvious, but between the two are matters which are ambiguous and about which many people know not what to do. He who is on his guard with respect to the ambiguous things keeps his religion and his honour clean, but he who falls in the ambiguous things falls into the unlawful, just like the shepherd who pastures [his flock] round about the forbidden area is on the way to pasturing them in it. Is it not a fact that every ruler has a forbidden area [of his own], and is not Allah's forbidden area His sacred place? Is it not a fact that in the body there is a mass through whose healthiness the whole body is healthy, and through whose being diseased the whole body is diseased? And is not this the heart?'" Both al-Bukhārī and Muslim relate this.

Seventh Tradition

From Abū Ruqayya Tamīm b. Aus ad-Dārī—with whom may Allah be pleased—[He said]: "The Prophet—upon whom be Allah's blessing and peace—said: 'Religion is good advice.' We said: 'Whose [advice]?' and he answered: 'That of Allah and His Book, and His Apostle, and the Imāms of the Muslims, and the generality of them.'" Muslim relates it.

Eighth Tradition

From Ibn ʿUmar—with whom and with whose father may Allah be pleased—[relating] that the Apostle of Allah—upon whom be Allah's blessing and peace—said: "I have been commanded to wage war on the people till they testify that there is no deity save Allah, and that Muḥammad is the Apostle of Allah, [till they] say the prayers and give the legal alms. If they do that they have preserved their blood and their property from me, save that to which Islam has a right,[1] and their reckoning is with Allah, exalted be He." Both al-Bukhārī and Muslim relate it.

[1] I.e. though they save their lives and continue to hold their property, they must pay to the Muslim rulers the lawful taxes thereon.

Ninth Tradition

From Abū Huraira ʿAbd ar-Raḥmān b. Ṣakhr—with whom may Allah be pleased—who said: "I heard the Apostle of Allah—upon whom be Allah's blessing and peace—say: 'What I have declared forbidden to you, avoid; what I have bidden you do, comply with as far as you are able. What destroyed those [peoples] who were before you was naught but the number of their questionings and their disagreements with their Prophets.'" Both al-Bukhārī and Muslim relate it.

Tenth Tradition

From Abū Huraira—with whom may Allah be pleased—who said: Said the Apostle of Allah—upon whom be Allah's blessing and peace—: "Verily Allah—may He be exalted—is good. He will not accept anything save what is good. Verily Allah has given believers [at the present time] the same command He gave to those whom He sent as Messengers. He—may He be exalted—has said: 'O ye Messengers, eat of the good things [of the earth] and act righteously' (Sūra XXIII, 51/53); and He—may He be exalted—has also said: 'O ye who have believed, eat of the good things which We have provided for your sustenance' (II, 172/167). Then [the Prophet] made mention of the man who lengthens out his journey, who is dishevelled and dusty, but who stretches out his hands to heaven [saying]: "O Lord! O Lord!" Seeing that his food is something forbidden, his drink something forbidden, his clothing something forbidden, his nourishment something forbidden, how shall he be heard? Muslim relates this.

Eleventh Tradition

From Abū Muḥammad al-Ḥasan, son of ʿAlī b. Abī Ṭālib, the grand-son of the Apostle of Allah—upon whom be Allah's blessing and peace—and the child of his daughter—with whom and with his mother may Allah be pleased—who said: "I memorized from the Apostle of Allah—upon whom be Allah's blessing and peace—[the following words]: 'Leave that about which you are in doubt for that about which you are in no doubt.' At-Tirmidhī and an-Nasāʾī [1] relate it, and at-Tirmidhī said: "It is a good and genuine Tradition."

[1] At-Tirmidhī (d. 279 A. H. = 892 A. D.) compiled the *Jāmiʿ*, which is usually reckoned the third of the six canonical Collections of Tradition, and an-Nasāʾī (d. 303 A. H. = 915 A. D.) compiled the *Sunan* which is generally counted the sixth of them.

Twelfth Tradition

From Abū Huraira—with whom may Allah be pleased—who said: Said the Apostle of Allah—upon whom be Allah's blessing and peace—: "One of the excellences of a man's religion is his leaving alone things which are no concern of his." A good Tradition. At-Tirmidhī and others relate it thus.

Thirteenth Tradition

From Abū Ḥamza Anas b. Mālik—with whom may Allah be pleased—who was the servant of the Apostle of Allah—upon whom be Allah's blessing and peace—and who said, [relating] from the Prophet—upon whom be Allah's blessing and peace—that he said: "No one of you [really] believes [in Allah and in His religion] till he wants for his brother what he wants for himself." Al-Bukhārī and Muslim relate this.

Fourteenth Tradition

From Ibn Masʿūd—with whom may Allah be pleased—who said: Said the Apostle of Allah—upon whom be Allah's blessing and peace—"The blood of a man who is a Muslim is not lawful (i.e. it may not be lawfully shed), save if he belongs to one of three [classes]: a married man who is an adulterer; one who owes his soul for another soul (i.e. a murderer); one who abandons his religion, [thus becoming] one who splits the community." Both al-Bukhārī and Muslim relate this.

Fifteenth Tradition

From Abū Huraira—with whom may Allah be pleased—[relating] that the Apostle of Allah—upon whom be Allah's blessing and peace—said: "Let whosoever believes in Allah and in the Last Day either speak good or be silent. Let whosoever believes in Allah and in the Last Day honour his neighbour. Let whosoever believes in Allah and in the Last Day honour his guest." Both al-Bukhārī and Muslim relate it.

Sixteenth Tradition

From Abū Huraira—with whom may Allah be pleased—[who related] that a man said to the Prophet—upon whom be Allah's blessing and peace—: "Admonish me!" He said: "Do not get angry." [The man] repeated the request several times, [but the Prophet only] answered: "Do not get angry". Al-Bukhārī related this.

Seventeenth Tradition

From Abū Ya'lā Shaddād b. Aus—with whom may Allah be pleased—[relating] from the Apostle of Allah—upon whom be Allah's blessing and peace—who said: "Verily Allah has prescribed the best behaviour with regard to everything. So if you kill make it a good killing; if you slaughter make it a good slaughtering; let each one of you put a good edge on his knife and make his victim die quickly." Muslim relates it.

Eighteenth Tradition

From Abū Dharr Jundub b. Junāda al-Ghifārī, and Abū 'Abd ar-Raḥmān Mu'ādh b. Jabal—with both of whom may Allah be pleased—[relating] from the Apostle of Allah—upon whom be Allah's blessing and peace—who said: "Fear Allah wheresoever ye may be; follow up an evil deed by a good one which will wipe [the former] out, and behave good-naturedly to people." At-Tirmidhī relates it, saying: "It is a good Tradition." In some copies he says: "It is a good and genuine Tradition."

Nineteenth Tradition

From Abū'l-'Abbās 'Abdallah b. 'Abbās—with whom and with his father may Allah be pleased—who said: "I was behind the Prophet—upon whom be Allah's blessing and peace—when he said: 'O young man, I will teach you some words [of wisdom]. Keep fast hold on Allah and He will preserve you. Keep fast hold on Allah and you will find Him ever before you. If you have need to ask, ask of Allah. If you must seek help, seek help from Allah. Know that even though the community should make a united effort to benefit you in any matter they would not benefit you in aught save what Allah has prescribed (lit. written) for you, nor were they to make a united effort to harm you in any matter they would not harm you in aught save what Allah has prescribed for you. The pens have been lifted and the pages are dry.'"

At-Tirmidhī relates this and says: "It is a good, genuine Tradition." According to a line of transmission other than that of at-Tirmidhī [it reads]: "Lay fast hold on Allah and you will find Him in front of you. Get acquainted with Allah in days of ease and He will recognize you in days of distress. Know that what missed you could not have hit you, and what hit you could not have missed you. Know that victory comes with patient endurance, relief with anxiety, ease with hardship."

Twentieth Tradition

From Abū Mas'ūd 'Uqba b. 'Amr al-Anṣārī, who was one of those present at Badr—may Allah be pleased with him. He said: Said the Apostle of Allah—upon whom be Allah's blessing and peace—: "Among the things that people comprehended from the words of the first prophecy [was the statement]: 'If it does not cause you to be ashamed, do whatever you wish.'" Al-Bukhārī relates it.

Twenty-first Tradition

From Abū 'Amr, though others call [him] Abū 'Amra, Sufyān b. 'Abdallah ath-Thaqafī—with whom may Allah be pleased—who said: I said: "O Apostle of Allah, tell me somewhat about Islam which I could not ask anyone about save you." He answered: "Say: 'I have believed in Allah,' and then live straightforwardly [in accordance with such a profession]." Muslim relates it.

Twenty-second Tradition

From Abū 'Abdallah Jābir b. 'Abdallah al-Anṣārī—with whom and with his father may Allah be pleased—[who said]: "A man questioned the Apostle of Allah—upon whom be Allah's blessing and peace—saying: 'Is it your opinion that if I pray the prescribed [prayers], fast during Ramaḍān, allow myself what is allowable and treat as disallowed what is forbidden, but do nothing more than that, I shall enter Paradise?' He answered: 'Yes.'" Muslim related this. The meaning of "treat as disallowed" is "avoid," and the meaning of "allow myself what is allowable" is "do it in the belief that it is allowed."

Twenty-third Tradition

From Abū Mālik al-Ḥārith b. 'Āṣim al-Ash'arī—with whom may Allah be pleased—who said: Said the Apostle of Allah—on whom be Allah's blessing and peace—: "Purification is the condition of faith; [the repetition of the phrase] 'Praise be to Allah' will fill the scales [on the Judgement

Day]; [the repetition of] 'Exalted be Allah' and 'Praise be to Allah', will fill all between heaven and earth; prayers will be a light; alms given in charity will be a demonstration; patient endurance will be an illumination; the Qur'ān will be an argument for you or against you. Everyone will come [to the Judgement] with his soul at stake, either sending it to freedom or to perdition." Muslim relates it.

Twenty-fourth Tradition

From Abū Dharr al-Ghifārī—with whom may Allah be pleased—[relating] from the Prophet—upon whom be Allah's blessing and peace—among the things he related from his Lord—magnified and exalted be He—how He said: "O My servants, I have forbidden wrong-doing in Myself, and I have made it a thing forbidden among you, so do not act wrongfully towards one another. O My servants, all of you are astray save him whom I have guided, so ask guidance of Me, I will guide you. O My servants, all of you are hungry save him to whom I have given food, so ask food of Me, I will feed you. O My servants, all of you are naked save him whom I have clothed, so ask clothing of Me, I will clothe you. O My servants, ye sin night and day. It is I who forgive all sins, so ask My forgiveness, I will forgive you. O My servants, ye will never attain to My power of harming so as to harm Me, nor My power of benefiting so as to benefit Me. O My servants, were the first of you and the last of you, those of you who are men and those who are jinn, as good as the most pious heart among you, that would not add aught to My kingdom. O My servants, were the first of you and the last of you, those of you who are men and those who are jinn, as bad as the most sinful heart among you, that would not diminish aught of My kingdom. O My servants, were the first of you and the last of you, those of you who are men and those who are jinn, to rise in a single place and petition Me and I gave to each what he asked, that would not lessen what I have with Me any more than a needle inserted in the ocean [would raise its level]. O My servants, it is your works alone for which I shall hold with you an accounting, and then I shall give the recompense for them, so he who finds good let him praise Allah, and he who finds otherwise let him blame no one but himself." Muslim relates it.

Twenty-fifth Tradition

From Abū Dharr—with whom may Allah be pleased—[who said] that folk from among the Companions of the Apostle of Allah—upon whom be Allah's blessing and peace—said to the Prophet—upon whom be Allah's blessing and peace—: "O Apostle of Allah, the rich people take off all the rewards. They say prayers just as we do, they fast just as we do, but they can give in charity out of the superabundance of their wealth [and so surpass us in storing up merit that will bring rewards]." He said: "Has not Allah appointed for you what you should give in charitable alms? Truly in every *tasbīḥ* there is such an alms, in every *takbīr*, in every *taḥmīd*, in every *tahlīl*,[1] in every bidding do what is right or forbidding the doing of what is wrong; even when one of you maritally approaches his wife there is an alms in that." They said: "O Apostle of Allah, [do you mean to say that] when one of us satisfies his desires [with his wife] there will be for him a reward in that?" He answered: "What is your opinion? Had He put it among the things forbidden it would have been sinful for one, so when He put it among the allowable things there was a reward for it also." Muslim relates this.

Twenty-sixth Tradition

From Abū Huraira—with whom may Allah be pleased—who said: Said the Apostle of Allah—upon whom be Allah's blessing and peace—: "An alms is due each day that the sun rises from every finger-joint of [all] the people. If you straighten out [some trouble] between two individuals, that is an alms. If you help a man with his beast, mounting him thereon, or hoisting up on to it his baggage, that is an alms. A good word is an alms. In every step you take while walking to prayers there is an alms. Whenever you remove something harmful from the path, that is an alms." Al-Bukhārī and Muslim both relate this.

Twenty-seventh Tradition

From an-Nawwās b. Samʿān—with whom may Allah be pleased—[relating] from the Prophet—upon whom be Allah's blessing and peace—who said: "Virtuous innocence is goodness of character, and wickedness is that which is knit to your soul and which you would hate people to get to know about." Muslim related this. According to Wābiṣa b. Maʿbad

[1] These are pious ejaculations used in prayers. *tasbīḥ* is the saying *subḥān Allāh* "glory be to Allah"; *takbīr* is the ejaculation *Allāhu akbar*, "Allah is very great", *taḥmīd* is the phrase *al-ḥamdu li'llāh* "praise be to Allah," and *tahlīl* is our familiar "Hallelujah." See p. 500.

—with whom may Allah be pleased—he said: I came to the Apostle of Allah—upon whom be Allah's blessing and peace—who said: "You have come to ask about virtuous innocence." "Yes", I answered. He said: "Ask your own heart for the answer. Virtuous innocence is that about which the soul and the heart feel tranquil, but wickedness is that which is knit to your soul, and reechoes in your breast, even though folk give their decision in your favour and continue to do so." An excellent Tradition which we have narrated according to the two *Musnads*,[1] that of Aḥmad b. Ḥanbal and that of ad-Dārimī, with excellent *isnāds*.

Twenty-eighth Tradition

From Abū Najīḥ al-ʿIrbāḍ b. Sāriya—with whom may Allah be pleased—who said: The Apostle of Allah—upon whom be Allah's blessing and peace—preached us a sermon whereby our hearts were made afraid and our eyes dropped tears, so we said: "O Apostle of Allah, it is as though this were a farewell sermon, so give us a testamentary exhortation." Said he: "My testamentary exhortation to you is that you have a pious fear of Allah—magnified and exalted be He; that you hearken and obey, even should it be that a slave is appointed as leader over you. He among you who lives long enough will see great disagreement, so take care to observe my *sunna* and the *sunna* of the rightly-guided Caliphs,[2] holding on to them with your molar teeth. Beware of matters newly-introduced, for every innovation *(bidʿa)* is an error." Abū Dāwūd [3] relates it, as does at-Tirmidhī, who says: "An excellent, genuine Tradition."

Twenty-ninth Tradition

From Muʿādh b. Jabal—with whom may Allah be pleased—who said:

[1] A *musnad* is a collection of Traditions where the material is arranged not according to the subject matter of the *matn*, but according to the names in the *isnād*. Aḥmad b. Ḥanbal (d. 241 A. H. = 885 A. D.) was the great Jurist who founded the Hanbalite school Ad-Dārimī (d. 256 A. H. = 869 A. D.) was a native of Samarqand, whose *Musna* was a small collection made for practical juristic purposes.

[2] *sunna* means "customary way of acting", so that in the Qur'ān the way Allah has dealt with former peoples is called "the *sunna* of Allah". To follow Muḥammad's *sunna* is to be a *Sunnī*, as opposed to the people of *Shīʿa* who followed the family of ʿAlī, the Prophet's cousin and son-in-law. The main purpose of the Traditions is to reveal the *sunna* of the Prophet and his Companions. The first four Caliphs were named by later Islam the "rightly-guided" Caliphs, and their period of office in the Caliphate came to be highly idealized.

[3] Abū Dāwūd (d. 275 A. H. = 888 A. D.) compiled the collection known as *Sunan*, which is generally regarded as the fourth of the six canonical collections.

I said: "O Apostle of Allah, tell me of some work [I may do] which will surely bring me into Paradise and keep me far from Hell." He answered: "You have asked about an important matter, yet it is, indeed, an easy matter for him to whom Allah makes it easy. [It is] that you should worship Allah without associating anything with Him, that you should perform the prayers, give the legal alms, fast during Ramaḍān, and go on pilgrimage to the House." Then he said: "Shall I not also point out to you the gates to what is good? [They are] fasting, which is a protection; alms in charity, which quench sin as water quenches fire; and for one to say prayers in the midst of the night." Then he recited: "'Withdrawing their flanks from [their] couches', until he reached [the words] 'they have been doing'" (Sūra, XXXII, 16–17). Then he said: "Shall I not also inform you about the beginning of the matter and its pillar and the peak of its prominence?" I answered: "Surely! O Apostle of Allah." He then said: "The beginning of Islam and its pillar is prayers, and the peak of its prominence is Holy War." Then he said: "And shall I not tell you how to possess all this?" I answered: "Surely! O Apostle of Allah." So he took hold of his tongue and said: "Keep this under control." I answered: "O Prophet of Allah, we indeed are blameworthy for all we speak with it." He said: "May your mother be bereft of you! Will people be prostrated on their faces—or maybe he said on their noses— in the Fire for [any reason] other than the harvest of their tongues?" At-Tirmidhī relates it, saying: "It is an excellent, sound Tradition."

Thirtieth Tradition

From Abū Tha'laba al-Khushanī Jurthūm b. Nāshir—with whom may Allah be pleased—[quoting] from the Apostle of Allah—upon whom be Allah's blessing and peace—that he said: "Truly Allah—may He be exalted—has laid down ordinances, so neglect them not; He has set limits, so do not outpass them; He has marked certain things as forbidden, so do not commit violations with regard to them; and He has said nothing about certain things, as an act of mercy to you, not out of forgetfulness, so do not go enquiring into these." An excellent Tradition which ad-Dāraquṭnī [1] and others have related.

[1] ad-Dāraquṭnī (d. 385 A. H. = 995 A. D.) was a Jurist and Traditionist of Baghdad. He was a critical scholar who proved that some two hundred of the Traditions accepted by both al-Bukhārī and Muslim were quite uncertain.

Thirty-first Tradition

From Abū'l-'Abbās Sahl b. Sa'd as-Sā'idī—with whom may Allah be pleased—who said: A man came to the Prophet—upon whom be Allah's blessing and peace— saying: "O Apostle of Allah, show me a work which if I do it, will make me beloved of Allah and beloved of the people." He answered: "Act abstemiously with regard to this world and Allah will love you; act abstemiously with regard to what people possess and the people will love you." An excellent Tradition which Ibn Māja [1] and others relate, with an excellent *isnād.*

Thirty-second Tradition

From Abū Sa'īd Sa'd b. Mālik b. Sinān al-Khudrī—with whom may Allah be pleased—[who related] that the Apostle of Allah—upon whom be Allah's blessing and peace—said: "Where there is no injury there is no requital." An excellent Tradition which Ibn Māja, ad-Dāraquṭnī and others related as of sound *isnād*, but which Mālik related in his *Muwaṭṭa'*,[2] as of broken *isnād*, from 'Amr b. Yaḥyā, from his father, from the Prophet—upon whom be Allah's blessing and peace—but dropping [the name of] Abū Sa'īd. [This Tradition] has lines of transmission which strengthen one another [so that it may be regarded as of sound *isnād*].

Thirty-third Tradition

From Ibn 'Abbās—with whom and with whose father may Allah be pleased—[relating] from the Apostle of Allah—upon whom be Allah's blessing and peace—that he said: "Where the people to be given what they claim, men would be laying claim to the property of a community and even to their blood. The onus of proof, however, is on the one who makes the claim, and the oath is for him who makes denial." An excellent Tradition, which al-Baihaqī [3] and others have related thus. Part of it is in the two books named *Ṣaḥīḥ* (i.e. in al-Bukhārī and Muslim).

[1] Ibn Māja (d. 274 A. H. = 887 A. D.), a Persian from Qazvin, compiled the *Sunan* which is generally counted as the fifth of the six canonical collections.

[2] Mālik b. Anas (d. 179 A.H. = 795 A.D.) was the Madinan Jurist who founded the Malikite school His *Kitāb al-Muwaṭṭa'* was a small collection of traditions assembled for juristic purposes, and is perhaps the earliest attempt at a *Corpus* of Muslim Law.

[3] The Shāfi'ite Jurist al-Baihaqī (d. 459 A.H. = 1066 A.D.) from Khurāsān attempted in his *Kitāb as-Sunan* to make a complete collection of all Traditions.

Thirty-fourth Tradition

From Abū Sa'īd al-Khudrī—with whom may Allah be pleased—who said: I heard the Apostle of Allah—upon whom be Allah's blessing and peace—say: "When any one of you notices anything that is disapproved [of by Allah], let him change it with his hand, or if that is not possible then with his tongue, or if that is not possible then with his heart, though that is the weakest [kind of] faith." Muslim relates this.

Thirty-fifth Tradition

From Abū Huraira—with whom may Allah be pleased—who said: Said the Apostle of Allah—upon whom be Allah's blessing and peace—: "Do not envy one another; do not vie with one another; do not hate one another; do not be at variance with one another; and do not undercut one another in trading, but be servants of Allah, brethren. A Muslim is a brother to a Muslim. He does not oppress him, nor does he forsake him nor deceive him nor despise him. God-fearing piety is here", and he pointed to his breast. "It is enough evil for a man that he should despise his brother Muslim. The blood, property and honour of every Muslim are inviolable to a [fellow] Muslim." Muslim relates this.

Thirty-sixth Tradition

From Abū Huraira—with whom may Allah be pleased—[relating] from the Prophet—upon whom be Allah's blessing and peace—who said: "Whosoever dispels from a true believer some grief pertaining to this world, Allah will dispel from him some grief pertaining to the Day of Resurrection. Whosoever makes things easy for someone who is in difficulties, Allah will make things easy for him both in this life and the next. Whosoever shields a Muslim, Allah will shield him in this world and the next. Allah is ready to aid any servant so long as the servant is ready to aid his brother. Whosoever walks a path to seek knowledge therein, Allah will make easy for him thereby a path to Paradise. No community ever assembles in one of Allah's houses to recite Allah's Book and carefully study it amongst themselves but tranquility [1] descends

[1] The word used here for "tranquility" is *sakīna*, which is the Hebrew word *shekīnā*, and shows that this Tradition was drawn from the Rabbinic tradition (*Tamid* 32b) of how the Shekīnā descends on those who study the Torah.

to them, and mercy covers them, and the angels surround them, and Allah makes mention of them among those who are with Him. He whose work detains him will not be hastened by his [noble] ancestry." Muslim relates it in these words.

Thirty-seventh Tradition

From Ibn 'Abbās—with whom and with whose father may Allah be pleased—[relating] from the Apostle of Allah—upon whom be Allah's blessing and peace—among the things he related from his Lord—blessed and exalted be He. He said: "Verily Allah has written down the good deeds and the evil deeds." Then he clarified that. "Whosoever purposes to do a good deed but does not perform it, Allah writes it down with Him as a perfect good deed, but if he purposes it and performs it Allah writes it down with Him as ten good deeds, up to seven-hundred fold, or more than that manifold. But if he purposes an evil deed and does not perform it, Allah writes it down with Him as a perfect good deed, and if he purposes it and does perform it Allah writes it down as one evil deed." Al-Bukhārī and Muslim, each in his *Ṣaḥīḥ*, have thus related it word for word.

> So look! my brother, may Allah help us, and take note of how great is the kindness of Allah—may He be exalted. Reflect on this, how that His saying "with Him" points to His great care with regard to it, and His saying "perfect" is for emphasis, not to [point to] the intensity of His care with regard to it. With regard to the evil deed which one purposed, but then abandoned, He says: "Allah writes it down with Him as a perfect good deed", emphasizing this by [the word] "perfect"; whereas if he performs it He writes it down as "one evil deed", where by the word "one" He emphasizes its being made little of, since He does not emphasize it here by the word "perfect". So to Allah be praise and grace. Glory be to Him. Our encomiums to Him we reckon not up. With Allah is success.

Thirty-eighth Tradition

From Abū Huraira—with whom may Allah be pleased—who said: Said the Apostle of Allah—upon whom be Allah's blessing and peace—

"Verily Allah—may He be exalted—has said: 'Whosoever acts with enmity towards a friend of Mine, against him will I indeed declare war. No servant of Mine draws near to Me with anything I like more than that which I have laid on him as an incumbent duty, and a [true] servant of Mine will continue drawing near to Me with supererogatory acts of worship so that I may love him. Then when I am loving him I am his hearing with which he hears, his seeing with which he sees, his hand with which he takes [things], his foot with which he walks. If he asks of Me I shall surely give him, and if he takes refuge with Me I will surely give him refuge.'" Al-Bukhārī relates it.

Thirty-ninth Tradition

From Ibn 'Abbās—with whom and with whose father may Allah be pleased—[who related] that the Apostle of Allah—upon whom be Allah's blessing and peace—said: "Verily Allah has for my sake overlooked the mistakes and forgetfulness of my community, and what met with His disapproval on their part." An excellent Tradition which Ibn Māja and al-Baihaqī and others have related.

Fortieth Tradition

From Ibn 'Umar—with whom and with whose father may Allah be pleased—who said: "The Apostle of Allah—upon whom be Allah's blessing and peace—took me by the shoulder and said: 'Be in this world as though you were a stranger or a traveller.'" Now Ibn 'Umar used to say: "When evening comes on you do not expect morning, and when morning comes do not expect evening. Take from your health [a preparation] for your sickness, and from your life for your death." Al-Bukhārī relates this.

Forty-first Tradition

From Abū Muḥammad 'Abdallah b. 'Amr b. al-'Āṣ—with whom and with whose father may Allah be pleased—who said: Said the Apostle of Allah—upon whom be Allah's blessing and peace—"No one of you is a true believer till his desire follows the line of that with which I have come." It is an excellent Tradition, and a genuine one, which we have related in the *Kitāb al-Ḥujja*,[1] with a genuine *isnād*.

1 An earlier work by the author of this collection of "Forty" Traditions.

Forty-second Tradition

From Anas—with whom may Allah be pleased—who said: I heard the Apostle of Allah—upon whom be Allah's blessing and peace—say: "Allah—may He be exalted—has said: 'O son of Adam, so long as you call upon Me, and hope in Me, I will forgive you for all that comes from you, caring not. O son of Adam, should your sins reach the horizon of the sky, even then if you asked My forgiveness I should forgive you. O son of Adam, were you to come to Me with sins [so many they would] well nigh fill the earth, and then meet Me without associating anything with Me, I should come to you with a like size amount of forgiveness.'" At-Tirmidhī relates it, saying: "It is an excellent, genuine Tradition."

TRADITIONS ON BEGINNINGS

(A) THE CREATION STORY FROM AL-KISĀ'Ī[1]

The story of the Tablet and the Pen

Said Ibn ʿAbbās—with whom may Allah be pleased—: The first thing that Allah created was the Preserved Tablet[2] on which is preserved [a record] of all that has been and all that will be till the Day of Resurrection. No one knows what is on it save Allah, Most High. It is of white pearl *(durra)*, and Allah created for it from [another] jewel *(jawhara)* a Pen whose length is a five hundred year's journey, whose point is split, and from which light flows as ink flows from the pens of this world. Then a call came to the Pen,[3] "Write!", whereat the Pen from terror at the summoning trembled and shook so that there was a quavering in its *tasbīḥ*[4] like the rumbling of thunder, then it entered on the Tablet all

[1] Almost every religion has its own account of the beginnings of things, its story of the creation and its picture of how the universe is formed, and it is generally true that much of the religious literature of a people is unintelligible without some understanding of this story and this picture. This is particularly true in the case of Islam, whose literature is full of casual references to matters concerned with the Muslim account of the beginnings of the world and of man. It will be noticed at the first glance how closely in basic structure it follows the Biblical creation story, but for understanding Islam its divergences therefrom are even more important than its agreements. This story can be found, with a wealth of variant detail, in many well-known books, but the account by al-Kisā'ī in his *Qiṣaṣ al-Anbiyā'*, is translated here because it gives the story in a simpler, more straightforward manner than in some of the older and more famous sources.—Al-Kisā'ī was a writer of the Vth century A.H. (XIth century A.D.), and the text of his work has been edited by I. Eisenberg, *Vita (sic) Prophetarum, auctore Muḥammed ben ʿAbdallah al-Kisā'ī* (Lugduni-Batavorum, 1922–23), where the creation story is on pp. 6–34.

[2] Sūra LXXXV, 22 refers to this *lawḥ maḥfūẓ*, which is the Qur'ānic equivalent of the celestial Record Book often mentioned in Jewish and Christian legend.

[3] This is said to be the pen referred to in Sūra XCVI, 4 and LXVIII, 1. Al-Kisā'ī frequently uses this indirect expression "a call came" to avoid the anthropomorphism involved in saying "Allah said to . . ." but in every such case we are to understand that it is Allah who speaks.

[4] *tasbīḥ* means to ejaculate the phrase *subḥān Allāh*, "glory be to Allah". It is orthodox

that Allah bade it enter of all that is to be till the Day of Resurrection. So the Tablet was filled up and the Pen ran dry and he who is to be fortunate was made fortunate and he who is to be unfortunate was made unfortunate.[1]

The story of the creation of the water

Said Ibn ʿAbbās—with whom may Allah be pleased—: Then after that Allah created a white pearl *(durra)* the size of the heavens and the earths with seventy thousand tongues, with every tongue of which it uttered *tasbīḥ* to Allah in seventy thousand languages. Kaʿb said that it also had eyes [so large] that were the mountain chains [2] to be cast into them they would seem like flies on the mighty ocean. Then Allah called to it and it so trembled in terror at that call that it became running water one part of which billowed up against the other. He (i.e. Kaʿb) said that everything comes in time to a halt in its *tasbīḥ* save water which never halts, its restlessness and its movement being its *tasbīḥ*, Allah having for that reason given it a superiority over all other created things, making it their origin, as He has said (XXI, 30/31): "And from water We have produced every living thing." Then a call came to the water, "Be still!" So it became still, waiting expectantly for Allah's command. It was then pure water with no turbidity.

The story of the creation of the throne and the footstool

Then Allah created the Throne *(ʿarsh)* out of a green jewel whose size and whose light no one can describe, and it was put on the billowing waves of the water. Wahb said that none of the former Scriptures failed to mention the Throne *(ʿarsh)* and the footstool *(kursī)* for Allah created them from two mighty jewels. Kaʿb said that the Throne has seventy thousand tongues with which it glorifies Allah in a variety of languages. It was [set] upon the water, as He says (XI, 7/9): "Now His Throne was upon the water." Ibn ʿAbbās said that every architect builds the foundation first and later sees to the roof, but Allah created

---

belief that all created things from highest to lowest have their peculiar way of constantly ascribing *tasbīḥ* to the Creator of all.

[1] I.e. all the fortune man enjoys during his earthly life and all the misfortune with which he meets were written for him on the Tablet at the beginning of all things.

[2] Lit. "the motionless mountains", the word *rawāsī* being a reminiscence of such Qur'ānic passages as XIII, 3; XV, 19 which speak of Allah setting the firm mountains on the earth to hold it steady.

the roof first, since He created the Throne before He created the heavens and the earth.[1] He said that then Allah created the Wind *(ar-rīḥ)*, giving it wings the size and number of which no one save Allah knows, and He commanded it to bear up the water on which the Throne was, and it did so. So the Throne was upon the water and the water was upon the wind. Then, said he, Allah created the Throne-bearers who at present are four, but when the Day of Resurrection comes Allah will aid them with four others, as the Most High has said (LXIX, 17): "And above them eight on that day will bear the Throne of thy Lord." They are of such a size as to be beyond description, and each of them has four forms, one in the form of a human, which makes intercession for the sustenance of men, another in the form of a bull, which makes intercession for the sustenance of domestic animals, another in the form of a lion, which makes intercession for the sustenance of the wild beasts, and one in the form of an eagle, which makes intercession for the sustenance of the winged creatures.[2] Ibn ʿAbbās—with whom may Allah be pleased—said that the footstool *(kursī)* [3] is of a jewel other than that jewel from which Allah created the Throne. Wahb said that associated with the Throne are angels, some kneeling on their knees, some standing on their feet, bearing the Throne on their necks, but sometimes they get weary and then the Throne is borne up solely by the might of Allah. [He taught that] the *kursī* is from the light of the Throne, but others say that the *kursī* is Allah's knowledge and that the *ʿarsh* is His knowledge with regard to His creation, but this is false, in the light of what Abū Dharr al-Ghifārī [4] has related of how he asked the Apostle of Allah—on whom be Allah's blessing and peace—which was the most excellent verse in the Qur'ān, and he answered: "*Āyat al-kursī*" (the Throne Verse, i.e. II, 255/256). Then he said: "The seven heavens would be in the *kursī* like a bracelet in the desert wastes, and the *ʿarsh* is as much superior to the *kursī* as the *kursī* is to that bracelet."

Kaʿb al-Aḥbār—with whom may Allah be pleased—said that then Allah created a serpent of huge size to encircle the Throne, its head being of white pearl *(durra)*, its body of gold, its eyes of jacinths, and the size

1 The reference is to a well-known tradition about the Throne being the roof of the seven heavens.

2 C.f. Ezekiel, chapters I and X.

3 In the Qur'ān *ʿarsh* and *kursī* seem to mean the same thing, for both words mean "throne", but in the later literature a distinction is made. Isaiah LXI, 1 speaks of heaven being God's throne and the earth His footstool. Cf. Matt. V, 34, 35.

4 He was one of the early Muslims, a Companion of the Prophet who is quoted as the source for a good many Traditions. See *Ency. Islam*, I, 83.

of that serpent no one knows save Allah. It has four thousand wings made of different kinds of jewels, and at every feather of its wings stands an angel with a jewelled javelin in his hand offering *tasbīḥ* and *taqdīs*[1] to Allah, but when this serpent offers *tasbīḥ* its *tasbīḥ* drowns out that of the angels. Whenever it opens up its mouth the heavens and the earth are lit up by lightning, and did not this serpent utter its *tasbīḥ* very gently all creatures would be thunder-struck by the mightiness of its voice. It is said that it gave a salaam to our Prophet Muḥammad—upon whom be Allah's blessing and peace—on the night of his Ascension *(miʿrāj)*,[2] giving him the good news that he and his community should enjoy every good thing. He said (i.e. Kaʿb) that the *ʿarsh* is the throne of might and greatness whereas the *kursī* is the throne of majesty and splendour, for Allah actually has no need of them since He existed before they were created and He is in no place neither is He on any place.

The story of the creation of the earth with its mountains and seas

Said Kaʿb al-Aḥbār—with whom may Allah be pleased—: When Allah desired to create the earths He ordered the wind to blow the waters so that one part was dashing against another, then when it was all tossed about and foaming, its waves rearing and its spray mounting up on high, Allah bade some of the foam *(zabad)* to harden so that it became dry land *(yābis)* from which He created the earth on the surface of the water in two days, as the Most High has said (XLI, 9/8): "Say, and are ye disbelieving in Him who created the earth in two days?" Then He gave command to the waves and they stood still, so they are the mountains which He set as tent-pegs *(awtād)*[3] for the earth. This is as the Most High has said (XXI, 31/32): "And We set on the earth firm mountains *(rawāsī)* lest it should move with them", for were it not for the mountains the earth would not stand firm with its inhabitants. He said that the roots of these mountains are joined on to the roots of Mount Qāf, which is the mountain that surrounds the earth.[4]

Then Allah created seven seas. The first of them is called Baiṭash, and it is the one which surrounds the earth beyond Mt. Qāf. Beyond it is a sea named al-Aṣam, beyond it a sea named Qainas, beyond it a sea

[1] *taqdīs* is the ejaculating of the cry *quddūs*, i.e. "holy', holy', holy'".
[2] See p. 621.
[3] A reference to Sūra LXXVIII, 7.
[4] The various forms of the Qāf legend are discussed by Streck in *Ency. Islam*, III, 614–616.

named as-Sākin, beyond it a sea named al-Mughallib, beyond it a sea named al-Mu'annis, and beyond that a sea named al-Bākī which is the last of the seven seas. Each sea thus surrounds the sea which precedes it and the others are like canals around it. In these seas are creatures whose number none knows save Allah Most High. Allah created their various types of food on the fourth day, as the Most High has said (XLI, 10/9): "And measured out their food therein in four days to satisfy all cravings."

There are also seven earths. The first is named ar-Ramaka and beneath it is the destroying wind, the wind with which Allah destroyed 'Ād,[1] held in check there by seventy thousand angels. It is inhabited by a community [of people] called al-Muwashshim, who are subject to punishment and reward. The second is called Khalada. In it are the various types of torment reserved for the Damned, and it is inhabited by a community [of people] called aṭ-Ṭamīsh, whose food is their own flesh and whose drink is their own blood. The third is called 'Araqa, in which are scorpions that resemble mules [in size], with tails like javelins each having three hundred and sixty jars of poison so virulent that if one single jar were placed on the surface of the earth the whole world would be annihilated by it. Its inhabitants are a community [of people] called al-Qais, whose food is dust and whose drink is *thuddā'*.[2] The fourth is called al-Ḥarbā, in which are the serpents [prepared for the torment] of the Damned. [In size] they resemble mountains and each serpent has fangs like tall palm trees such that any earthly mountain stung by one of them would be flattened out. Its inhabitants are a community [of people] called al-Jilla, who have neither eyes nor feet nor hands, but have wings like the wings of the *qaṭāt* and die only of old age. The fifth is called Malthām in which are the rocks of brimstone to be hung on the necks of unbelievers, so that when kindled the fuel will be on their chests and the flame in their faces. This is as the Most High has said (II, 24/22): "whose fuel is men and rocks", and again (XIV, 50/51): "fire shall cover their faces". Its inhabitants are a community [of people] called al-Ḥajla who are not very numerous because they eat one another. The sixth is called Sijjīn[3] in which are the Registers of the Damned together with [the record of] their filthy works, as the Most High has said (LXXXIII, 7): "Nay but the register of the evil-doers is in Sijjīn." In it is a community [of people] called al-Qaṭāṭ who are in the form of birds and who worship Allah as He really

[1] Sūra LI, 41. The 'Ād were a semi-mythical people of ancient Arabia.
[2] I.e. the juice of a desert plant notorious for its bitterness.
[3] See Sūra LXXXIII, 7.

ought to be worshipped. The seventh is called ʿAjiba. It is the dwelling-place of Iblīs and in it is a community [of people] called al-Khaṣūm who are black and short of stature but have claws like those of wild beasts. These are they who will be given power over Gog and Magog to destroy them.[1]

Now the earth was rolling about with its peoples like a ship [on the waves] so Allah sent down to it an angel so huge and so mighty that none could be greater, bidding him go beneath them (i.e. the seven earths) and bear them on his shoulders, putting out one of his hands to the east and the other to the west to take hold of the ends of the earth to east and west. There was, however, no place on which to rest his feet, so Allah created for him out of green corundum a rock *(ṣakhra)* cubical in form and in the midst of which were seven thousand holes each containing a sea such as no one but Allah could describe. He gave command to the rock and it entered under the feet of the angel as a resting place for his feet. But then there was no support for the rock, so Allah created a mighty bull with forty thousand heads and as many eyes, ears, noses, mouths, teeth, and legs, and bade him bear the rock, so he bore it on his back and on his horns. Now the name of that bull is ar-Rayyān. But there was no resting place for the bull's feet, so Allah created for him a mighty fish *(ḥūt)* so large that because of his size no one can see him [as a whole], with numerous eyes and [a nose so large that] it is said that if all the seas were put in one of his nostrils they would be like a mustard seed in the desert wastes. Allah bade him be a support beneath the bull, and he did this. The name of that fish is Bahamūth.[2] For his support Allah set the water, and beneath the water the air and beneath the air the darkness which belongs to all the earths. The knowledge of creatures cannot reach to what is below the darkness.

Then Allah created intelligence *(ʿaql)*. He said to it: "Advance!", whereupon it advanced. He said to it: "Retreat!", whereupon it retreated. So He said: "By My might and My majesty, nothing I have created is dearer to Me than thee. By thee I shall take, and by thee I shall give. By thee I shall reward and by thee I shall punish." Said the Prophet—upon whom be Allah's blessing and peace—when he was asked how intelligence could be such a fine thing when [there were so many] sins committed: "Allah will forgive [a man's] sins, but the excellence of intelligence will remain and he will enter Paradise." Said he—upon whom be Allah's

1 One of the signs of the approaching end of the world is the appearance of the hosts of Gog and Magog who will devastate far and wide but at the prayer of Jesus will be destroyed. See p. 352.

2 This is the Behemoth of the Book of Job.

blessing and peace—: "The intelligent man is the trustworthy man, the one who keeps silent, from whose evil the people are safe. Allah on the Day of Judgment will not punish the intelligent man as He will punish the fool. The fool is he who has a lying tongue and meddles in what does not concern him, even though he may be a person who can read and write." Said he—upon whom be Allah's blessing and peace—: "There is no more beautiful adornment for a man than intelligence, nor is there anything worse then ignorance." Said Abū Huraira—with whom may Allah be pleased—: "He who grieves much today will rejoice tomorrow, whereas he who rejoices much today will grieve tomorrow. He who considers that one man is superior to another save in the matter of good health is a fool, but the intelligent man on the Day will attain degrees[1] not to be obtained by those who fast or by those who stay up at night for prayers, for those whose endeavour is most deserving are those who have exercised their intelligence best." It is said that Ka'b al-Aḥbār in making his last testament to his son said: "O my son, there is nothing that is better than an intelligence adorned by knowledge, knowledge adorned by continence, continence adorned by firm conviction, firm conviction adorned by gentleness, gentleness adorned by politeness, politeness adorned by humility, humility adorned by godly fear, godly fear adorned by divine guidance. So, my son, be a man with these qualities and you will surpass the mightiest men."

The story of the creation of the heavens and the angels

Said Ibn 'Abbās—with whom may Allah be pleased—: Then Allah bade the spray which had mounted up from the [billowing] waters to rise high in the air where He created from it the heavens in two days and what is between them in four days. Then the heavens out of fear of the majesty of Allah split asunder from the earth and there came to be seven heavens and seven earths. This is as the Most High has said (XXI, 30/31): "Do not those who disbelieve see that the heavens and the earth were a single mass but We split them asunder?" The Most High has also said (XLI, 12/11): "so He made them seven heavens in two days", i.e. with their rising sun and moon and stars.

The first heaven is of green emerald *(zumurruda)*. Its name is Birqi' and it is inhabited by angels in the form of cattle over whom Allah has

[1] These *darajāt*, "grades, degrees, ranks" are decided by each man's accounting at the Judgment, and indicate the higher or lower position he will occupy in Paradise as decided by his merits. There are many traditions about the high rank in the next life that may be assured by diligent observance of various practices of piety.

appointed an angel called Ismā'īl who is their guard. The second is of ruby *(yāqūta ḥamrā')*. Its name is Faidūm and it is inhabited by angels in the form of ospreys *('iqbān)*, the angel in charge of them being called Mīkhā'īl who is their guard. The third is of topaz *(yāqūta ṣafrā')*. Its name is 'Awn and it is inhabited by angels in the form of eagles *(nusūr)*, the angel in charge of them being called Ṣa'adyā'īl, who is their guard. The fourth is of silver. Its name is Arqalūn and it is inhabited by angels in the form of horses, the angel in charge of them being called Ṣalṣā'īl, who is their guard. The fifth is of red gold. Its name is Ratqā and it is inhabited by angels in the form of Ḥūrīs.[1] The angel in charge of them is called Kalkā'īl who is their guard. The sixth is of white pearl *(durra)*. Its name is Rafqā and it is inhabited by angels in the form of the Wildān,[2] the angel in charge of them being called Shamkhā'īl who is their guard. The seventh is of glistening light. Its name is Gharībā and it is inhabited by angels in the form of humans, the angel in charge of them being called Rizqā'īl, who is their guard. Ka'b al-Aḥbār—with whom may Allah be pleased—said that these angels never cease from *tasbīḥ* and *taqdīs* whether standing, sitting, bowing or prostrating, as the Most High has said (XXI, 20): "They utter *tasbīḥ* night and day unceasingly."

'Abdallah b. Salām said that these are the Karūbīyūn, the Rāḥānīyūn, the Ṣāffūn, the Ḥāffūn, the Rāki'ūn and the Sājidūn.[3] There are some among them who have a position between mountains of light where in an exalted station they utter *taḥmīd*[4] and *taqdīs* to Him. Wahb said that above the seven heavens are Veils and in those Veils are angels so numerous that one knows not another, all of them uttering *tasbīḥ* to Allah in different languages [and with a sound] like peals of thunder. Ibn 'Abbās—with whom may Allah be pleased—said that above the Veils are yet other angels whose feet pierce down through the seven heavens and the seven earths and a five hundred years' journey beyond that so that their feet are away down below the lowest part of the seventh earth like white banners.

Ka'b in giving a description of Gabriel said that he had the position

1 These Ḥūrīs *(ḥūr 'īn)* are mentioned several times in the Qur'ān (e.g. LVI, 22; LII, 20; XLIV, 54) as the beauteous celestial spouses promised the Blessed in Paradise.

2 Just as the Ḥūrīs are the celestial maidens the Wildān are the celestial youths, cf. Sūras LVI, 17; LXXVI, 19.

3 These are different classes of angels. The Karūbīyūn are the Cherubs, the Rāḥānīyūn are apparently the same as the Rūḥānīyūn, i.e. the Spiritual Ones, often referred to as a class of angels, the Ṣāffūn are "those ranged in order" (XXXVII, 1), the Ḥāffūn are "those who circle round" (XXXIX, 75), the Rāki'ūn are "those who bow down" and the Sājidūn "those who prostrate themselves".

4 *taḥmīd* is the uttering of the ejaculation *al-ḥamdu li'llāh*, "praise be to Allah".

of superiority among the angels, and is the Faithful Spirit[1] who has four wings each provided with a hundred wings, and besides these he has two green wings which he does not spread save when he is destroying cities. All his wings are of different kinds of jewels. Moreover he has a bifurcated beard, gleaming front teeth, is white bodied but black haired, his body being like white snow. His feet are immersed in the light and his figure fills up all between the East and the West. ʿĀʾisha—with whom may Allah be pleased—said: "O Kaʿb, I heard the Apostle of Allah say: 'O Lord of Gabriel, Michael, Isrāfīl, forgive me.' Now Gabriel and Michael I have heard mentioned in the Qurʾān, but tell me about Isrāfīl." He answered: "I will tell you about him, and about others, O mother of the Faithful. Isrāfīl is a very mighty angel. He has four wings, with one of which he blocks up the East and with another the West, with the third he blocks up what is between heaven and earth and with the third he cloaks himself from the grandeur of Allah. His two legs are down below the lowest parts of the seventh earth and his head reaches up to the support of the feet of the Throne. Between his eyes is a Tablet [made from] a jewel, and whenever Allah wants to issue a new command to His servants He orders the Pen to write [that command] on the Tablet, which then descends to [its place] between the eyes of Isrāfīl, who then passes the Tablet on to Gabriel, who is [the angel] nearest to Isrāfīl, and he carries out Allah's command." That is what the Most High has said (VIII, 42/43): "That Allah may accomplish a matter [He has decided] is to be done."

Kaʿb said that behind the Frequented Fane[2] there are angels whose number none knows but Allah, over whom Allah has appointed an angel having seventy thousand tongues with which he utters *tasbīḥ* to Allah, and above him are other angels, above whom are still greater angels between whom and them hang veils that these may not burn up those lower than themselves. Above these again are mighty angels from whose mouths as they utter *tasbīḥ* drop live coals from which Allah creates other angels who fly around in the air uttering *tasbīḥ*, and between whom and the angels are veils lest they burn up those lower than themselves with those coals. Above all these there is an angel in human form who, if Allah permitted him, would find it easy to swallow up all the heavens and earths. He is the Spirit *(ar-Rūḥ)* about whom Allah says

[1] The Faithful Spirit *(ar-rūḥ al-amīn)* is mentioned in Sūra XXVI, 193 as the one who brought down revelation to Muḥammad.

[2] This is the celestial Kaʿba directly above the earthly Kaʿba at Mecca and the central shine for the worship of the angels. Its name comes from Sūra LII, 4.

(LXXVIII, 38): "On a day when the Spirit and the angels will stand, in due order arranged, they will not speak, save him to whom the Merciful may give permission." Even above him there are angels greater in might than any others and more fervent in *tasbīḥ*. Ibn ʿAbbās—with whom may Allah be pleased—said that Allah has angels constantly travelling about in the air in numbers which none knows save Allah, who gather where humans assemble to remember [Allah] and to offer supplication, taking under their safe keeping the petitions of the Muslims.

It is related that the Prophet—upon whom be Allah's blessing and peace—one day said to Gabriel: "O Gabriel, I should like to see you in your mighty form in which Allah created you", but Gabriel answered: "O beloved of Allah, I have a terrifying form such as no one could look on without fainting away." Said he—upon whom be Allah's blessing and peace—: "Surely! but I should like to see you in your mighty form." Gabriel answered: "O beloved of Allah, where would you want to see me?" Said he: "Outside Mecca in *(al-Abṭaḥ)* the torrent bed." He replied: "But, O beloved of Allah, al-Abṭaḥ would not be wide enough for me." He said: "Then by Mt. ʿArafāt."[1] So the Prophet made his way to ʿArafāt where, lo! with a rustling and a great rumbling he appeared in a form which blotted out the horizon. When the Prophet saw him he fell down in a faint, so Gabriel changed himself back to his first form, came to the Prophet, and embraced him and kissed him, saying to him: "Be not afraid, O beloved of Allah, for I am thy brother Gabriel." Said the Prophet: "You spoke the truth, O my brother, O Gabriel, for never did I imagine that any creature of Allah's had a form like that." Gabriel replied: "Then, O beloved of Allah, what would it have been like if you had seen Isrāfīl? For then my form would have seemed to you a small and feeble thing."

Kaʿb al-Aḥbār said that in the seventh heaven is the Swollen Sea[2] in which are angels holding in their hands javelins the length of any one of which is a year's journey. Over this Sea Allah has appointed an angel named Mīkā'īl[3] whom no one knows how to describe save Allah. Were he to open his mouth the heavens would be in it like a mustard seed on the ocean, and were he to look down on the inhabitants of the heavens and the earths they would be burned up by his light. He is the viceroy *(qā'im)* over the Swollen Sea and its angels. Kaʿb went on to

[1] A place six hours to the east of Mecca where the Muslims assemble for special ceremonies at the annual Pilgrimage. See pp. 192, 499-500.

[2] *al-baḥr al-masjūr* is mentioned in Sūra LII, 6.

[3] This is the Arabic form of Michael.

say that as for the Angel of Death his name is 'Azrā'īl and his dwelling is the lowest heaven. For him Allah has created assistants to the number of all those who are to taste of death. His legs are at the boundary of the lowest part of the seventh earth and his head is in the seventh heaven high up by the last Veil, while his face is always facing the Preserved Tablet. He has three hundred and sixty eyes, every eye being made up of three eyes and he has three hundred and sixty tongues, each tongue being composed of three tongues. He also has three hundred and sixty hands each composed of three hands, and three hundred and sixty legs each composed of three legs. His wings are four, one to the east, one to the west, one at the limits of the Veils and one at the boundary of the lowest part of the seventh earth. He keeps gazing at the Preserved Tablet where every created thing is pictured before his eyes and he does not take the spirit of any created thing till its fortune has had fulfilment and its allotted span has been completed. The spirits of true believers he takes with his right hand and puts in 'Illīyūn,[1] but the spirits of unbelievers he takes with his left hand and puts them in Sijjīn [to wait] until the "sudden coming comes."[2]

The story of the creation of sun and moon

Wahb said that then Allah created the sun and the moon. The sun He created from the light of the Throne, but the moon He created from the light of His veil. Ka'b used to say that the sun and the moon will be brought forth on the Judgment Day as though they were two bulls and will both be cast into Hell fire. When word of this reached Ibn 'Abbās he was angry and said: "Ka'b is lying. Allah Most High eulogized the sun and moon by His saying (XIV, 33/37): 'And He has subjected to you the sun and the moon in their continuous course', so how could He cast them into Hell fire?" Wahb b. Munabbih—with whom may Allah be pleased—said that Allah—exalted be He—has appointed over the sun and the moon angels who send them along [their courses] in proper measure and hold them back in proper measure, which is what the Most High has said (XXII, 61/60): "He causes the night to enter into the day and causes the day to enter into the night", so that as the one of them decreases the other increases. The people of the Torah (i.e. the Jews) say that Allah began the work of creation on Sunday and finished on Saturday, when He took His seat upon the Throne, so they take that as

1 See Sūra LXXXIII, 18 and for Sijjīn v. 7 of the same Sūra.
I.e. the Last Day. See Sūra LVI, 1; LXIX ,15.

their holy day *('īd)*. The Christians say that the beginning fell on a Monday and the ending on a Sunday, when He took His seat on the Throne, so they take that as their holy day. Ibn 'Abbās said that the beginning was on a Saturday and the ending on a Friday, so the taking His seat was also on a Friday and for that reason we keep it as a holy day. Said the Prophet—upon whom be Allah's blessing and peace—: "Friday is the mistress among the days. It is more excellent in Allah's sight than the 'Īd al-Fiṭr or the Aḍḥā [1] day. On it occurred five special things, viz. on it Adam was created, on it his spirit was breathed into him, on it he was wedded, on it he died, and on it will come the Hour. No human ever asks his Lord for anything on Friday but Allah gives him what he asks." Another version of this Tradition reads: "[What he asks], so long as it is not something forbidden", and on it the Hour will come."

The story of the creation of Paradise and Hell

Ibn 'Abbās—with whom may Allah be pleased—said that then Allah created Paradise, which consists of eight gardens. The first is the House of Majesty *(Dār al-Jalāl)* made of white pearl *(lu'lu')*. The second is the House of Peace *(Dār as-Salām)* made of ruby. The third is the Garden of Resort *(Jannat al-Ma'wā)* made of green chrysolite *(zabarjad)*. The fourth is the Garden of Eternity *(Jannat al-Khuld)* made of yellow coral *(marjān)*. The fifth is the Garden of Delight *(Jannat an-Na'īm)* made of white silver. The sixth is the Garden Firdaws [2] made of red gold. The seventh is the Garden of Rest *(Jannat al-Qarār)* made of refined musk. The eighth is the Garden of Eden *(Jannat 'Adn)* made of reddish pearls *(durr ashqar)*.

Paradise has two double-leaf gates between whose leaves is the distance between heaven and earth. It is built of alternate bricks of gold and silver, its paving-stones are of musk, its dust of ambergris, its grass of saffron, its palaces of pearl *(lu'lu')*, its upper chambers of jacinth, and its doors of jewels. Ibn 'Abbās—with whom may Allah be pleased—said that the most excellent of the rivers of Paradise were six, viz. the river of Mercy, which runs through all the gardens, whose pebbles are pearls *(lu'lu')* and whose water is whiter than milk and sweeter than honey; then the stream

[1] These are the two great festival days of the Muslim year. The 'Īd al-Fiṭr is the feast day after the conclusion of the Ramaḍān month of fasting, and the day of the Aḍḥā, i.e. the day of sacrifices, often called Qurbān Bairam, is the day when the pilgrims outside Mecca offer their sacrifical victims. See p. 497.

[2] *firdaws* is the Arabic form of the Greek word *paradeisos* from which comes also our word Paradise.

al-Kawthar on whose banks are trees of pearl *(durr)* and jacinth, and which belongs especially to our Prophet Muḥammad—upon whom be Allah's blessing and peace—as the Most High has said (CVIII, 1): "We, indeed, We have given thee abundance *(al-Kawthar)*." Then comes the river of Kāfūr, then the river at-Tasnīm, then the river as-Salsabīl, then the river ar-Raḥīq al-makhtūm.[1] Besides these there are rivers whose number none knows save Allah Most High, for they are more numerous than the stars of the sky, a fact which holds also of its castles. The eight Gardens have gates of gold, jewel-encrusted and inscribed. On the first gate is written: "There is no deity save Allah and Muḥammad is the Apostle of Allah." On the second gate is written: "The Gate of those who pray the five prayers, observing perfectly the ablutions and prostrations." On the third gate is written: "The Gate of those who justify themselves by the purity of their souls." On the fourth Gate is written: "The Gate of those who encourage the doing of what is approved and discourage the doing of what is disapproved." On the fifth gate is written: "The Gate of him who holds himself back from lusts." On the sixth gate is written: "The Gate of those who perform the greater and the lesser Pilgrimage." On the seventh gate is written: "The Gate of those who go out on Holy War." On the eighth gate is written: "The Gate of those who desire", i.e. those who avert their eyes [from unseemly things] and perform good works such as showing due affection to parents and being mindful of one's kin. By these gates will enter those whose works have been of the kind written on them.

He said that in Paradise also are the Ḥūrīs *(ḥūr 'īn)*, white with wide black eyes, whose beauty and loveliness no one is able to describe save He who created them. Among these Ḥūrīs are some such as no eye has ever seen nor ear heard of nor the heart of man ever imagined. In it also are things to ravish the soul, to delight the eye, and enjoyments which will never be cut off and whose number has no end, all prepared by Allah for His good and devoted servants.

A description of Jahannam [2]

Wahb b. Munabbih—with whom may Allah be pleased—said that Jahannam has seven stages separated from one another by a five hundred years' journey. In each stage are seventy thousand kinds of torment,

[1] These are all derived from words mentioned in the Qur'ān. *kāfūr* is "camphor" and is mentioned in LXXVI, 5. *tasnīm* occurs in LXXXIII, 27, and *salsabīl* in LXXVI, 18, while *ar-raḥīq al-makhtūm* meaning "choice wine sealed up" is found in LXXXIII, 25.

[2] *jahannam* is the Qur'ānic name for Hell. It is derived from the Ethiopic and corresponds to the Biblical word Gehenna.

fetters, bonds, manacles, chains, as well as *samūm*,[1] *ḥamīm*, and *zaqqūm*.[2] The first [stage is called] Jahannam. The second is Laẓā,[3] and is for idol-worshippers. The third is al-Ḥuṭama,[4] which is for [the hosts of] Gog and Magog and such unbelievers as resemble them. The fourth is as-Saʿīr [5] which is for Satan [and his followers], as the Most High has said (LXVII, 5): "And We have prepared for them the torment of as-Saʿīr." The fifth is Saqar [6] which is for those who do not pray and those who do not give the legal alms, as the Most High has said (LXXIV, 42/43 ff.): "They will ask them (i.e. the wicked): 'What led you into Saqar?' They will say: 'We were not of those who prayed, nor were we feeding the unfortunate, but we were engaging in dispute with those who so engaged, and we were treating as false the Day of Judgment, until the certainty came upon us.'" The sixth is al-Jaḥīm [7] which is for the Jews, the Christians and the Zoroastrians. The seventh is al-Hāwiya,[8] which is for the hypocrites, as the Most High has said (IV, 145/144): "Verily the hypocrites will be in the lowest reaches of the Fire." All this is taken from the words of the Most High (XV, 44): "It has seven gates and to each gate is one section of them assigned."

Ibn ʿAbbās—with whom may Allah be pleased—said that Paradise is to the right of the Throne and Hell [9] to the left, and it (i.e. Hell) has seven heads. Kaʿb al-Aḥbār said that it has seven reaches *(aṭbāq)*, seven portals, and seven heads, in each head of which are thirty-three mouths, each mouth having tongues whose number none knows save Allah Most High with which it offers to Allah various kinds of *tasbīḥ*. It contains trees of fire whose thorns are like longspears which blaze hotly with fires, and fruits of fire on each of which is a serpent which catches the unbeliever by his eyelids and lips so that his flesh falls down at his feet. In it are *zabānīs* [10] in whose hands are maces of iron whose heads are set

[1] *samūm* is "burning wind" and *ḥamīm* "scalding water", both in LVI, 42/41.

[2] Just as in Paradise there is a celestial tree whose fruits are the food of the Blessed, so in Hell there is an infernal tree whose fruits are the food of the Damned. This is Zaqqūm, which is mentioned in Sūras XXXVII, 62/60; XLIV, 43; LVI, 52.

[3] *laẓā* means "a blazing fire", and is mentioned in Sūra LXX, 15.

[4] *ḥuṭama* means "a vehement fire", and is mentioned in Sūra CIV, 4 and 5.

[5] *saʿīr* means "a kindled fire", and is mentioned frequently in the Qur'ān. See Sūra LXVII, 5, 10, 11; XLII, 7/5; XXXV, 6.

[6] *saqar* means "a scorching fire". See Sūra LIV, 48; LXXIV, 26, 27.

[7] *jaḥīm* means "an ardent fire". See CII, 6; LXXXIII, 16; LXXXII, 14.

[8] *hāwiya* means "pit, abyss", and is mentioned in Sūra CI, 9/6 ff.

[9] The words he uses here are Garden and Fire, words which are very commonly found as synonymns of Paradise and Hell.

[10] The Zabānīya are mentioned in Sūra XCVI, 18 and are regarded as the assistants of Mālik, the Grand Chamberlain of Hell. See pp. 23-24.

with three hundred and sixty spikes of fire, any spike of which would be more than jinn and men together could carry. Over them are angels, as the Most High has said (LXXIV, 30): "over it are eighteen" who never disobey the command of their Lord but who do whatever He bids them (LXVI, 6).

The story of the creation of the Jinn and the Jānn, their early history and the service of Iblīs

Wahb said that when Allah had created the fire known as as-Samūm, which is a fire having neither heat nor smoke, He created from it the Jānn, as the Most High has said (XV, 27): "But the Jānn We created earlier from the fire of the samūm." He said that Allah created him a mighty creature, naming him Mārij. From him he created his wife whom He named Mārija. He approached her and she bore to the Jānn a son whom he called Jinn, from whom all the various tribes of the Jinn have branched off, to whom Iblīs the accursed belongs. He said that to Jānn were born males and to Jinn females,[1] so they married the males with the females and thus they came to be seventy thousand tribes and anon increased till they were as numerous as the sands. Now Iblīs married a woman from among the children of the Jānn called Rawḥā daughter of Shalshā'īl the son of the Jānn. She bore him at a single birth Balāqīs and Quṭruba, then at a single birth Faqṭas and Faqṭasa. Thereafter the children of Iblīs increased till they became innumerable. They used to walk "on their faces" like grubs and ants and gnats and locusts and birds, and they used to have their dwelling in caves and desert places, in meadows and hillocks, in pathways and dunghills, in privies and wells, in streams and sepulchral vaults, in underground crypts and in every foul and dark place so that the lands came to be filled with them. Presently they took on themselves the forms of animals such as mules, donkeys, camels, cattle, sheep, dogs and wild beasts. Now when the earth became filled with the progeny of Iblīs Allah set the Jānn to dwell in the air below the sky and the Jinn's children in the lowest heaven, bidding them worship and be obedient, as the Most High has said (LI, 56): "And I have not created jinn and men save that they might serve Me."

Then Allah spoke to the angels, saying: "I have created two dwelling places, one of them from My mercy and one of them from My wrath,

[1] Obviously the author takes Jānn to be a single individual and Jinn a similar individual, whereas both are generally regarded as collective names. Mārij is derived from LV, 15/14 which, however, reads: "And He created the Jānn from a smokeless flame *(mārij)* from a fire." Sūra XVIII, 50/48 says that Iblīs was of the Jinn.

so have a look at them both." Thereupon the angels took a look at Jahannam, gazing at its pillars, it stages and its various kinds of torment, and they asked Allah to inform them for whom this was. So Allah gave the Fire power of speech and it said: "I have been created as a dwelling place and as a torment for betrayers and deniers of the uniqueness of Allah—exalted be He." Then they looked at the Garden and what Allah has prepared there for its inhabitants, and they said; "O our God, for whom hast Thou created this dwelling?" Allah bade the Garden speak in reply, whereupon it spoke, using the words of the Most High (XXIII, 1): "Happy now are the believers." They replied: "You have been created for us, for we are believers", but the Garden [went on with the succeeding verses of that Sūra] saying: "Those who in their prayers are humble, and those who from vain talk turn away, and those who are doers of charitable acts, and those who guard their pudenda, save with their wives or the slave-girls whom their right hands possess, where they are blameless, but those who go beyond that are transgressors, and those who tend to their trusts and their covenants, and those who are watchful over their prayers, these it is who will be the inheritors, who will inherit Firdaws, therein to be continually." At this they (i.e. the angels) were assured that it was created for other than themselves. Then Allah Most High said to them: "I have created this dwelling for those who obey me among those whom I shall have created by My command and by My hand, into whom I shall have breathed of My spirit, to whom I shall have made My angels do obeisance, and whom I shall make superior to all My creatures."

Now the heaven used to boast itself over the earth, saying to it: "My Lord has raised me above you, so I am the highest created thing and I am the dwelling place of the angels. Moreover in me are the Throne and the Footstool and the Pen and the sun and moon and stars, in me are the store-houses of Mercy and it is from me that revelation descends to you." Said the earth: "O my God, Thou didst spread me out as an earth and didst intrust me with the production of trees and plants and springs. Thou didst set on my back the mountains, and didst create on me various kinds of fruits, so why does the heaven boast itself over me because of Thy creating in it the angels who utter *tasbīḥ* to Thee? I am in a state of loneliness because there are no creatures on me who make mention of Thee." Then a call came to the earth: "Be quiet! I am going to create on thee a figure whose beauty has no like, whom I shall endow with intelligence and tongue and teach of My own knowledge, and to whom I shall send down some of My angels. Then with these will I fill thy belly and thy back, thy east and thy west. So, O earth, boast thyself of that over My heaven." Then the earth was quieted, and at that time it was white and pure as though it were white silver.

Now the children of the jinn looked down at the earth and all the beasts of prey thereon, and they asked Allah to send them down to it. He gave them permission to go on condition that they would serve Him and not disobey Him. They gave Him a covenant agreement to that effect and came down, all seventy thousand tribes of them. They worshipped Allah as He has a right to be worshipped for quite a long time, but then they commenced acts of disobedience and the shedding of blood, so that the earth cried for help against them, saying: "My emptiness to me seems preferable to having on my back those who disobey Thee." Then Allah said to the earth: "Be silent! for I am going to send to them a messenger." Kaʿb said that the first messenger (or Apostle) whom Allah sent to the children of the Jānn was ʿĀmir b. ʿUmair b. al-Jānn, but him they killed. Then He sent to them Ṣāʿiq b. Nāʿiq b. Mārid, but him also they killed. So it went on till He had sent eight hundred Prophets over eight hundred years, a Prophet a year, but they killed them. Seeing that they treated the messengers as liars Allah suggested to the children of the Jinn who were in the sky that they descend to earth and fight with the children of the Jānn who were there. So they descended, bringing with them the accursed Iblīs, and fought with the children of the Jānn till they drove them into certain lowlands of the earth. They themselves then worshipped Allah as he ought to be worshipped, and the worship offered by Iblīs was more fervent than theirs so that because of the fervency of his worship Allah raised him to the lowest heaven where he worshipped Allah for a thousand years and became known als al-ʿĀbid (i.e. the worshipper). Then Allah raised him to the second heaven, and so it went on in that way till Allah Most High had raised him to the seventh heaven. It is said that it was on a Saturday that he entered the lowest heaven, a Sunday when he entered the second, a Monday when he entered the third, and so on until it was a Friday when he entered the seventh heaven, having worshipped Allah for a day in each heaven though each of those days was a thousand years in length. Thus Iblīs—accursed be he—occupied an important position among the angels, so much so that whenever Gabriel or Michael or other angels passed by him they would say to one another: "Allah has certainly given this servant [of His] a fervency in worshipful obedience such as has not been given to any of the angels." Now quite a long time after this Allah bade Gabriel go down to earth and take a handful thereof from its east and its west, from its plain country and its mountains, that He might create therefrom a new creature whom He would make superior to all His other creatures. Iblīs—accursed be he—knew about this, so he too went down, stood in the midst of the earth and said to it: "O earth, I have come to you as a sincere adviser." Said the earth: "And what may be your advice, O chief of the abstemious ones?" He said: "Allah is desirous of creating from you a creature whom He will make superior to all His [other] creatures, but I fear that that creature will disobey Allah and He will punish him by the Fire. Now Gabriel has been sent to you to take a handful, so when he comes to you adjure him not to take anything from you." So when Gabriel—upon whom be peace—came down, the earth called to him, saying: "O Gabriel, by the right of Him who sent you to me, take no handful of anything from me, for I fear that Allah may create from me a creature who will disobey Him and be punished by the Fire." Gabriel trembled at that adjuration so he returned without taking anything from it and informed Allah Most High about the matter, although He already knew about it. So He sent Michael to bring a handful, but the case with him was the same as it had been with Gabriel. So Allah sent ʿAzrāʾīl, the Angel of Death. When he made to take a handful the earth adjured him as it had adjured Gabriel—upon whom be peace—but the Angel of Death said to it: "By the might of my Lord and His majesty, I shall not disobey any command He has given me." Then he took a handful of it from all its uplands, mossy earth, sweet earth, salty earth, bitter earth, good earth and bad earth, and earth of all colours, and all the children of Adam owe their creation to that handful. When the Angel of Death returned with that handful he stood in his place for forty years without speaking. Then a call came to him from Allah Most High: "O ʿAzrāʾīl what have you accomplished?" though He well knew. So he told Him of all that had passed between him and the earth. Then Allah said: "By My might and My majesty I will assuredly create from what you have brought a creature whose spirit [and those of his descendants] I will give you the authority to take since you do not show much mercy." Then Allah appointed one half of that handful for Paradise and one half for Hell. Said Allah: "I am Allah. I decide [what is to happen] and no one may condemn Me."[1]

The story of the creation of Adam

Wahb b. Munabbih—with whom may Allah be pleased—said that Allah Most High created Adam's head [out of material] from the first earth,

[1] Or possibly it means: "No one may decide otherwise than I decide", or even: "I prescribe what is to be, but no one prescribes to Me."

his neck from the second, his chest from the third, his arms from the fourth, his belly and back from the fifth, his thighs and rump from the sixth, his legs and feet from the seventh, and He named him Adam because He had created him from the skin *(adīm)* of the earth. Ibn ʿAbbās said that Allah Most High created him from the various districts *(aqālīm)* of the earth, his head from the dust of the Kaʿba, his breast from the dust of ad-Dahnāʾ,[1] his belly and his back from the dust of India *(al-Hind)*, his arms from the dust of the east and his legs from the dust of the west. Wahb b. Munabbih said that Allah Most High created in him nine orifices, seven in his head, namely, his two eyes, his two ears, his two nostrils and his mouth, and two in his body before and behind. In the nose Allah created the sense of smell, in his mouth the sense of taste, in his hands the sense of touch, in his eyes the sense of sight, in his ears the sense of hearing, in his feet the sense of walking. Moreover He created in his mouth a tongue by which he might speak and also four incisor teeth, four *rabāʿīs* (i.e. the teeth near the incisors), four canine teeth and sixteen molars. Then He set in his neck eight vertebrae and in his back fourteen, in his right flank eight ribs and in the left seven. One of these ribs He made crooked because of His foreknowledge that out of it He would create Eve. Then He created the heart, setting it in the left side of the chest, created the stomach over against the heart, and set the lungs as a fan for the heart. Also He created the liver, setting it on the right side, and in it He placed the gall-sack. The spleen He created in the left side dependent on the liver, and created two kidneys one above the liver and the other above the spleen, putting the midriff between below the cartilage of the chest into which He made the ribs enter. Also He created bones, so that in the shoulders there are bones, in the chest bones, in the fore-arm two bones, in the palm five bones, and in each finger three bones save the thumb which has but two bones, both hands being the same in this. In the hips He set two bones and in the thighs two bones, in the knee two bones, in the lower leg two bones, in the ankle two bones, in the foot ten bones, and in each toe three bones save the big toe which has but two, both legs being the same in this. Then He placed in him the veins which take their rise from the aorta which is the home of the blood and causes the blood to flow throughout the body. There are various kinds of veins. Four supply the brain, four the eyes, four the ears, four the nostrils and four the lips. There are two veins in the temples and two

[1] The Dahnāʾ is the great sandy desert of South Arabia. Kaʿba, of course, stands for the Ḥijāz.

in the tongue, two supply the teeth and two the molars, two veins supply the blood from the brain to the kidneys and two veins take the cold blood up from the kidneys to the brain, seven serve the neck and seven the chest, while ten supply the stomach and the remaining veins supply the rest of the body. They are widely dispersed [in the body] and no one knows their number save Allah.

The tongue is the interpreter and the two eyes are the lamps. The two ears are hearing devices and the nostrils breathing holes. The two hands serve as wings and the two feet as means of travel. The liver is the seat of compassion and the spleen the seat of laughter, the two kidneys are the seat of crafty stratagems and deceit, while the lungs are a fan and the bowels a store-house. The heart is the mainstay of the body so that if it is disordered the whole body is disordered while if it is sound the whole body is sound.

Wahb b. Munabbih said that when Allah had created Adam in this form He bade the angels take him off and set him down at the gate of Paradise at a place where the angels would be passing by. He was at that time a body without any spirit therein. This is as the Most High has said (LXXVI, 1): "Did not a long time pass over man when he was not something of which mention is made?" i.e. he was not something properly formed. Ka'b said that the angels were astonished at his strange shape and form for they had never seen anything like him. Iblīs also used to gaze long at him, saying: "Allah has not created this one save for some momentous affair." He (i.e. Ka'b) said that perhaps he entered into his hollow interior, saying: "He is a weak creature. He has been created of clay and is hollow and a hollow creature needs must take food." It is reported that one day he said to the angels: "Do you not know that Allah has given this creature superiority over you?" They answered: "We are obedient to the command of our Lord and will not disobey Him." Whereat he said: "If he is given superiority over me I shall make him disobey Him, and if I am given superiority over him I shall destroy him."

The story of the introduction of the spirit into Adam's body

Ka'b al-Aḥbār—with whom may Allah be pleased—said that the spirit *(rūḥ)* of Adam was not like the spirits of the angels nor those of other creatures, but was a spirit to which Allah gave superiority over all His creatures, which is as the Most High has said (XV, 29): "So when I have fashioned him and have breathed into him of My spirit, then fall down before him in obeisance." [This spirit] is that of which the Most High said

(XVII, 85/87): "They will question thee about the spirit, Say! the spirit is part of the affair of my Lord." Allah gave command that it be plunged in all the lights, and then He commanded it to enter into the body of Adam but gradually not hastily. The spirit saw a narrow entrance, a narrow orifice, so it said: "O Lord how shall I enter?" Then a call came: "Enter unwillingly and come out unwillingly",[1] so the spirit entered from the top of the head [and came down] to the eyes, whereat Adam opened them and began to look at his body of clay but he was not able to speak, and he looked up at the awnings of the Throne where was written: "There is no deity save Allah, and Muḥammad is truly the Apostle of Allah." Then the spirit got to his ears and he began to hear the *tasbīḥ* of the angels in the air. Then the spirit began to go around in his head and his brain, while the angels were looking at him waiting for the moment when they would be ordered to do obeisance, for they would do obeisance to him, though Iblīs had determined to do otherwise, as indeed Allah had informed the angels before the creating of Adam, which is what the Most High says: "When thy Lord said to the angels: I am going to set on the earth a vice-gerent", and: "Lo! I am creating a man from clay, so when I have fashioned him and have breathed into him of My spirit, then do ye fall down before him doing obeisance."[2] Anon the spirit reached the cartilage of the nose so he sneezed and that sneeze opened up the closed passages, whereupon Adam said: "Praise be to Allah who passeth not away", this being the first word that Adam—upon whom be peace—spoke. Then the Majestic One called to him: "May thy Lord have mercy on thee, O Adam. For this did I create thee and it shall be for thee and thy posterity to say what thou hast said."

Ibn 'Abbās—with whom may Allah be pleased—said that there is nothing distresses Iblīs more than to hear folk say: "Allah bless you", when they hear anyone sneeze. Then the spirit moved on into the body of Adam until it reached his legs. Now Adam had become flesh and blood and bone and veins and sinews and intestines save that his feet were still of clay, so when he struggled to stand up he was not able. That is what the Most High has said (XXI, 37/38): "Man is created of haste." When the spirit got to the legs and feet Adam stood upright, and it is said that this was on a Friday towards sunset when the spirit had completed five hundred years [moving gradually] into the body of Adam. It is related

[1] The meaning is that the unwillingness of the spirit to leave the body when summoned by the Angel of Death is parallel to its unwillingness to enter the body at creation.

[2] This is a combination of two Qur'ānic passages. The first is II, 30/28 and the second is XXXVIII, 71, 72.

that Jaʿfar b. Muḥammad aṣ-Ṣādiq [1] said that the spirit was in the head of Adam for a hundred years, in his chest for a hundred years, in his back for a hundred years, in his thighs for a hundred years, and in his legs and feet for a hundred years.

The story of the angels doing obeisance to Adam

Wahb said that when Adam stood upright the angels looked at him and [it seemed to them] as though he were of white silver. Then Allah Most High bade them do obeisance. The first who stepped forward to do obeisance to him was Gabriel—upon whom be peace. Then came Michael, then Isrāfīl and ʿAzrāʾīl and all the angels. Ibn ʿAbbās—with whom may Allah be pleased—said that this obeisance to Adam took place on a Friday just as the sun began to decline from the meridian and the angels remained in an attitude of obeisance till the *ʿaṣr* (i.e. the time of afternoon prayers), so Allah made that day a holy day for Adam and his children till the end of time, a day in which Allah will assuredly give him an answer to his petitions, namely on the twenty-four hours from Thursday night through Friday,[2] and a day on every hour of which Allah will release seventy thousand persons from Hell fire. Iblīs, however, out of pride and envy refused to do obeisance to Adam—on whom be peace. Allah said to him (XXXVIII, 75 ff.): "O Iblīs, what hindered you from doing obeisance to him whom I have created with My own hands? Are you too proud? Or are you one of the high ones?" Iblīs answered: "I am better than he is. Thou didst create me of fire but hast created him of clay, and fire can eat up clay. Moreover I worshipped Thee in the summits of heaven along with the Cherubs and the Rūḥānīs and the Ḥāffūn and the Ṣāffūn and those who draw near." Allah said: "I knew beforehand that from My angels I should have obedience but from you disobedience, so all the long years of your worship will avail you naught because of My foreknowledge about you. I have made you despair [3] of all good for ever and ever and have made you accursed, afflicted, banished, a stoned, accursed Satan." At that his nature was changed into the nature of

[1] He is the sixth Shīʿa Imām, who died at Madina in 148 A.H. = 765 A.D. He is considered the most deeply versed of the Imāms in the theological sciences. See *Ency. Islam*, I, 993.

[2] I.e. the Muslim day ends at sunset, the hours after sunset belonging to the next day. The text here has "Friday evening" which is our Thursday evening but to them the evening hours which belong to the Friday.

[3] There is a play on words here. His name is *Iblīs* and the verb used is *ablasa*, suggesting that his name is derived therefrom.

Satan. The angels gazed on his evil appearance and smelt so disagreeable an odour from him that they leapt at him with their spears, saying: "Accursed! accursed! stoned! stoned!" The first of them to stab at him was Gabriel and after him Michael, then Isrāfīl and the Angel of Death and the angels in all the quarters. He meanwhile was fleeing before them till they cast him into the Swollen Sea. Then the angels of the Swollen Sea hastened towards him with their spears, which are spears of fire, and ceased not stabbing at him with their spears till they drove him into the Euphrates where he was hidden from the eyes of the angels. Now all the angels were troubled and the heavens atremble at the audacity of Iblīs—accursed be he.

The story of how names were given to Adam by inspiration

Allah taught Adam all the names [of things] so that he knew all languages, even the language of fish and frogs and all that is on land and sea. Ibn ʿAbbās—with whom may Allah be pleased—said that Adam spoke seven hundred languages, the most excellent of which is Arabic. Then Allah bade the angels carry Adam on their shoulders that he might be high above them, while they were saying: "Quddūs! Quddūs! we will not depart from obedience to Thee." So they took him through the paths of the heavens while other angels stood in ranks round about him, and each time he passed a rank of them he would say: "Peace be to you"; to which they would reply: "And to you be peace and the mercy of Allah and His blessing, O choice one of Allah, His preferred one and the masterpiece of His creation." Ibn ʿAbbās said that in the highest reaches a pavilion of ruby and emerald was set up for him and whenever Adam passed by a seat of the angelic chiefs or place of the Prophets he would mention its name and the name of its occupant. Then the angels returned him to his Lord—majestic is He.

The story of how Adam stood up to preach

Then Allah bade Gabriel—upon whom be peace—summon the angel ranks to assemble before Adam that he might address them. So Gabriel—upon whom be peace—called them and there assembled before him all the inhabitants of the heavens, making around him twenty thousand rows each row adorned in a different manner, while Adam was given a voice which would reach them all. Then there was set up for Adam—on whom be peace—the pulpit of consideration *(minbar al-karāma)* with its seven steps, and he was clothed that day in a garment of silk brocade *(sundus)* as light as air with two girdles encrusted with jewels and selvaged with musk and ambergris, while on his head was a golden crown, jewel-encrusted and having four corner points each set with a magnificent pearl whose brightness would put out the light of sun and moon. On his fingers were rings of honour while around his waist was the belt of approval *(riḍwān)* the light from which reached to all the upper chambers in Paradise. In this splendid array Adam took his stand on the pulpit. Allah had already taught him all the names [of things] and had given him a rod of light so that the angels stood in awe of him, saying: "O our God, hast Thou created any creature superior to this?" Allah Most High answered: "O My angels, he whom I created with My own hands is not as those whom I created by saying to them 'Be! and they were.'"

So Adam stood upright on his pulpit and greeted the angels, saying: "Peace be to you O ye angels of my Lord, and the mercy of Allah and His blessing." The angels replied: "And to you be peace, O choice one of Allah and masterpiece of His creation." Then a call came to him from before Allah Most High: "O Adam, for this did I create you, and this greeting of peace shall be the greeting for you and your descendants till the end of time." Wahb b. Munabbih said that this peace greeting has never spread among a people without their becoming assured of escaping punishment. It is related that Ibn ʿAbbās—with whom may Allah be pleased—said that the Apostle of Allah—upon whom be Allah's blessing and peace—once said: "Shall I point out to you something which if you do it will assure you of entrance to Paradise?" They replied: "Assuredly, O Apostle of Allah." He said: "Feed the hungry, spread peace abroad and pray for me at night when other folk are sleeping, and you will enter the Garden in peace." Ibn ʿAbbās—with whom may Allah be pleased—said that Iblīs weeps when he hears a Muslim giving the peace greeting to his brother Muslim, and says: "Ah, woe is me! they will not separate ere Allah has forgiven them both."

Then Adam began his sermon. He commenced by saying: "Praise be to Allah", so that has become a customary expression among his children. Then he made mention of what he knew about the heavens and the earths and all that Allah had created in them, first, however, eulogizing Him for having given him the power of speech and for having revealed these matters to him. At this Allah said to the angels (II, 31/29): "Inform Me of the names of these if ye are those who speak the truth", i.e. the names of the created things which Adam had mentioned. The angels confessed their inability, saying: "Glory be to Thee, we have no knowledge save what Thou dost teach us. It is Thou who art the Knowing, the Wise" (*ibid*, 32/30). Then Allah said: "O Adam, tell them their names", so Adam began to tell them the names of all the things Allah had created by land and sea, even [such small things as] the pearl and the gnat. The angels were greatly astonished by this so Allah said: "Did I not say to you that I know the unseen things of the heavens and the earth, and I well know both what ye show openly and what ye have been concealing?" (*ibid.* 33/31), i.e. what Iblīs was thinking about being disobedient. Then Adam came down from his pulpit, having had his handsomeness and his beauty increased by Allah. A bunch of grapes from Paradise was brought to him and he ate thereof, this being the first celestial food he had eaten. When he had finished he said: "Praise be to Allah", whereat Allah said: "For this did I create thee O Adam, and it shall be customary for thee and for thy children to the end of time."

Then slumber overcame him and he slept, for there is no rest for the body save in sleep, but the angels were terrified, saying: "Sleep is the brother of death. This one will die." When Iblīs heard that Adam had taken food he rejoiced, saying: "I shall be able to seduce him." Wahb b. Muhabbih said that sleep is a sign of death but waking up is a sign of resurrection. The Children of Israel once asked Moses—on whom be peace—: "Does our Lord sleep?", so Allah spoke by revelation to Moses, saying: "Were I to go to sleep the heavens would fall down upon the earth and the whole world would be annihilated." Ibn ʿAbbās said that the Jews once asked our Prophet Muḥammad—upon whom be Allah's blessing and peace—about that matter, whereupon Allah Most High sent down (II, 255/256): "Allah, there is no deity save Him, the Living, the Self-subsistent. Slumber takes Him not, nor sleep." They said: "O Muḥammad, do the inhabitants of Paradise sleep?" and he—upon whom be Allah's blessing and peace—answered: "They sleep not, for sleep is the brother of death and they do not die. Likewise the inhabitants of the Fire neither sleep nor die, nor do they grow old and feeble but they keep on being punished."

The story of the creation of Eve

While Adam slept Allah Most High created Eve from one of the ribs of his left side, namely that crooked rib. She is called Eve *(Ḥawwā')* because she was created from a live person *(ḥayy)*. This is as Allah has said (IV, 1): "O ye people, show piety towards your Lord, who created you from a single person, and from that person created his spouse." Eve was of the same height as Adam and equally splendid and beautiful. She had seven hundred locks of hair intertwined with jacinths and sprinkled with musk, was auburn haired,[1] of even stature, with wide black eyes, thin skinned, white complexioned, with henna-dyed palms, and hanging locks so long you could hear their rustling. She had ears pierced for ear-rings, was so plump her thighs chafed as she walked, and was of the same form as Adam save that her skin was more tender, her colouring lighter, her voice sweeter, her eyes wider and darker, her nose more hooked, her teeth whiter. When Allah Most High had created her He sat her by Adam's head. Now Adam had seen her in his dream that day and love for her had taken possession of his heart, so [when he woke up and saw her] Adam said: "O Lord, who is this?" The Most High answered: "This is My handmaid Eve." Said he: "O Lord, for whom hast Thou created her?" He answered: "For him who will take her in faithfulness and be joined with her in thankfulness." Said he: "O Lord, I will take her under those conditions, so marry me to her." So He married him to her before He let him enter the Garden.

It is related that ʿAlī b. Abī Ṭālib—with whom may Allah be pleased—said that Adam saw her in a dream in which she spoke with him, saying: "I am Allah's handmaid and you are Allah's servant, so ask my hand in marriage from your Lord." ʿAlī—with whom may Allah be pleased—said: "Make your marriages a good thing, for women in themselves have neither benefit nor harm, they are but a trust from Allah to you, so do not be contentious with them." Kaʿb al-Aḥbār—with whom may Allah be pleased—said that Adam saw her in a dream and when he woke up he said: "O Lord, who is this Thou hast delighted me by bringing near?" The Most High replied: "This is My handmaid and thou art My servant, O Adam. Nothing I have created is dearer to Me than you two if you obey Me and serve Me. Now I have created for you two a dwelling which I have named My Garden. Whosever enters it is truly My friend, and he who does not enter it My enemy." At this Adam was seized with fear and said: "O Lord, do you have an enemy, when you are Lord of the heavens and the earths?" The Most High replied: "Had I wished that all creatures be My friends I could have had it so, but I do what I will and withhold what I wish." Said Adam: "O Lord, this maidservant of Thine, Eve, for whom hast Thou created her?" Allah Most High replied: "O Adam, I have created her for thee, that thou mayest dwell along with her and not be alone in My Garden." Said Adam: "O Lord, marry her to

1 *shahlā'* which means a colour of dark blue mixed with red.

me." The Most High replied: "O Adam, I will marry her to thee on condition that thou dost teach her the principles of My religion and be thankful to Me for her." Adam was content with this, so a chair made of a jewel was set for Adam, on which he sat while the angels gathered together, and Allah signified to Gabriel that he should be the affiancer. So the Lord of the worlds was the *walī*, Gabriel the *khāṭib*,[1] the angels the witnesses, Adam was the bridegroom and Eve the bride, and thus Eve was married to Adam under covenant of obedience and piety and good works, while the angels showered down upon them celestial confetti *(nuthār)*.

ʿAbdallah b. ʿAbbās—with whom may Allah be pleased—said: "Make public your wedding ceremonies, for that is a custom from your father Adam. Nothing is more pleasing to Allah than marriage, and nothing so moves Him to anger as divorce. Whenever a true believer bathes after accomplishing the marital act Iblīs weeps, saying: 'This person has removed his sin, has satisfied his desire, and has continued in the custom of his father Adam.'" Then the Most High said to Adam: "Now remember My favours to you, for I have made you the masterpiece of My creation, have fashioned you a man according to My will, have breathed into you of My own spirit, made My angels do obeisance to you and carry you on their shoulders, have made you the preacher to them, have loosened your tongue to all languages, had you up on the pulpit of approval where you were preacher to the Ṣāffūn, the Ḥāffūn, the Cherubs, the Rūḥānīs and those who draw near. All this I have done for you as glory and honour, so beware of this Iblīs whom I have made to despair, and whom I have made accursed since he refused with disdain to do obeisance to you. Now as a special honour I have joined you with My handmaid Eve, and there is no greater blessing, O Adam, than a pious wife. Moreover, two thousand years before I created you I had built for the pair of you a dwelling place which you may enter under covenant and pledge[2] to Me."

The story of Adam's taking a covenant

Allah had presented this *amāna* to the heavens and the earths before He presented it to the angels, as the Most High has said (XXXIII, 72): "We indeed presented the *amāna* to the heavens and the earth and the moun-

[1] This represents a regular Muslim wedding ceremony. The *walī* or guardian is the one who gives the woman to the man; the *khāṭib* or affiancer is the one who acts for the man, and the transaction must take place in the presence of witnesses.

[2] The two words are *ʿahd* and *amāna* both of which mean a covenant agreement. *ʿahd* is connected with the verb "to enter into a compact", and *amāna* with the verb "to trust to, to confide in".

tains." It was that they would be rewarded for the doing of good and punished for the doing of evil. They, however, refused to accept it, so this *amāna* was presented to Adam, Allah saying: "If you are obedient I shall reward you with good things and let you live for ever in the Garden, but if you abandon the covenant *('ahd)* with Me I shall drive you out of My dwelling and punish you with My Fire." Said Adam: "O Lord, I accept Thy covenant *('ahd)* and pledge *(amāna)* and testament *(waṣīya)*." The angels were amazed at Adam's acceptance of the *amāna*, as the Most High has said (XXXIII, 72): "We indeed presented the *amāna* to the heavens and the earth and the mountains but they refused to bear it and were afraid of it, but man undertook to bear it, and [proved] unjust, foolish."

Ibn 'Abbās—with whom may Allah be pleased—said that between the taking of the *amāna* and the eating from the tree there was only the space of time between midday prayers and afternoon prayers. Then Allah showed Adam and Eve a picture of Iblīs so that they looked at his form and were told (XX, 117/115): "Truly this one is an enemy to thee and to thy wife, so let him not drive you both from the Garden, that thou shouldst become wretched." Then Allah called: "O Adam, it is of My covenant and My pledge to you both that you may enter this Garden and eat to your fill therefrom wherever you wish, only draw not near to this tree lest you become transgressors" (cf. II, 35/33). Adam accepted this covenant completely, so Allah signified to Gabriel that he go to Riḍwān, the Grand Chamberlain of Paradise, and have him bring out Adam's steed which He had created five hundred years before creating him. Ka'b al-Aḥbār said that Allah had created Adam's steed from camphor and musk and saffron and in all the Garden there was no steed save Burāq [1] better than this steed of Adam—on whom be peace. Wahb b. Munabbih—with whom may Allah be pleased—said that the superiority of Burāq to the other animals of Paradise is like the superiority of our Prophet Muḥammad to the other prophets. As for Adam's steed it was created from the musk of the Garden mixed with the water of al-Ḥayawān,[2] its mane was of coral *(marjān)*, its forelock of jacinth and its hooves of chrysolite *(zabarjad)*.

Gabriel went to Riḍwān who thereupon opened the gate of the gardens

[1] Burāq was the steed on which Muḥammad was taken on his heavenly journey on the night of the Mi'rāj. See p. 621. In some texts this steed of Adam is called al-Maimūn (the auspicious) and this word is used here also in speaking of the animal a few lines further on.

[2] This is one of the streams (or some say fountains) of Paradise.

and called: "O auspicious steed, come!" So it came with *tasbīḥ* and *taqdīs* and *tahlīl* until it stood before Gabriel, saddled with a saddle of emerald and chrysolite, and bridled with a bridle of jacinth. It had wings made of different kinds of jewels. Gabriel—upon whom be peace—brought it along till it stood before Adam, who was amazed at its beauty. Then he mounted on its back while Gabriel took it by the bridle, and he said: "Praise be to Allah who has placed at our service such things as these." The steed from below him answered: "You have spoken well, O Adam, no one ought to ride me save him who is a thankful servant." Then a call came to Adam: "You have given thanks for what was given by your saying: 'Praise be to Allah.'"

A she-camel *(nāqa)* was then brought for Eve. Allah had said to it "Be!" and it was, and Eve mounted it. So Adam on his steed started moving towards the Garden, Eve coming behind him on her *nāqa*, with angels to right and to left, before and behind, while the Cherubs and the Rūḥānīs set themselves in rank with their spears and their banners, till they reached the gate of Paradise. The angels were commanded to have Adam stop at the gate of Paradise, where Allah Most High called: "O Adam, you have had a look at the inhabitants of heaven, but have you seen any who resemble you in beauty of form?" He answered: "O Lord, I have not seen among them anyone who resembles me, nor anyone to whom Thou hast given what Thou hast given me. So glory be to Thee, how great is Thy dignity." Allah Most High said: "O Adam, you are dearer to Me than they are if you obey Me and are content with My covenant and do not become an unbelieving tyrant." In all that Adam accepted the *amāna* and did not ask his Lord for protection or help, so Allah called the angels to witness regarding him. Thus Adam and Eve were there crowned and coronetted and honoured.

(B) THE FALL OF ADAM [1]

Khālid b. Khidāsh has informed us, relating from Khālid b. ʿAbdallah, from Bayān, from ash-Shaʿbī, from Jaʿda b. Hubaira, who said: "The

[1] Translated from Ibn Saʿd, *Kitāb aṭ-Ṭabaqāt al-kabīr*, Vol. I (Leiden, 1905), pp. 11–16.—Abū ʿAbdallah Muḥammad ibn Saʿd (d. 230 A.H. = 845 A.D.) was the Secretary of that al-Wāqidī who assembled the Traditions about the Prophet's *Maghāzī* or warlike expeditions. His *Ṭabaqāt* is a kind of enormous Biographical Dictionary, in which he assembles what the Traditionists had to hand down about the predecessors of the Prophet, about the Prophet and his family, and about the early Muslim worthies. Since Adam was not only the first man but the first Prophet the work starts off with him.

tree by which Adam was seduced was the vine, and it has been set as a seduction for all his progeny."

Khālid b. Khidāsh has informed us, relating from ʿAbdallah b. Wahb, from Saʿīd b. Abī Ayyūb, from Jaʿfar b. Rabīʾa and Ziyād the client of Muṣʿab, who said: The Apostle of Allah—upon whom be Allah's blessing and peace—was asked about whether Adam was a prophet or an angel, and he replied: "Nay, he was a prophet who was addressed."

Khālid b. Khidāsh has informed us, relating from ʿAbdallah b. Wahb, from Ibn Lahīʿa, from al-Ḥārith b. Yazīd, from ʿUlaiy b. Rabāḥ, from ʿUqba b. ʿĀmir, that the Apostle of Allah said: "As regards Adam and Eve men are like a deficient grain measure which they will never succeed in filling. On the Day [of Judgment] Allah will not question you about your noble descent or your pedigree, but the noblest of you in Allah's sight will be the one among you who is the most pious."

Hāshim b. Muḥammad has informed us, relating from Ubaiy, from Abū Ṣāliḥ, from Ibn ʿAbbās, who said: "Adam departed from Paradise between the time of noon prayers and the time of afternoon prayers, and was sent down to the earth. He had been dwelling in Paradise for half a day of the days of the Other World, i.e. five hundred years of those days whose measure is twelve hours, for a day there is a thousand years as people count them in this world.[1] Adam was cast down on a mountain in India called Naudh, and Eve fell at Judda.[2] Adam brought down with him some of the scented air of Paradise which clung to the trees and valleys and filled all that place with perfume. It is thus that the perfumes [known to us] are derived from that scented air of Adam—upon whom be Allah's blessing and peace. It is said that there was sent down along with him some of the myrtle *(ās)* of Paradise, also the Black Stone, which was whiter than snow, and Moses' rod, which was of celestial myrtle wood, ten cubits long, i.e. the height of Moses—upon whom be Allah's blessing and peace—as well as some myrrh and some frankincense. Afterwards there was sent down to him the anvil, the blacksmith's hammer and pinchers. Then, from where he had fallen on the mountain, Adam looked and saw an iron shoot growing on the mountain-side, and he said: 'This is from this' (i.e. the anvil etc. were of the same material as this shoot of metal he saw sticking out). So he began to break down with the hammer trees that had grown old and had dried up, and

[1] See Sūra XXXII, 5/4 and II Pet. III, 8.

[2] Naudh is commonly thought to be Adam's Peak in Ceylon, and Judda is the modern sea-port of Jidda on the Red Sea coast, where until recent days Eve's grave used to be a site for visitation by the pious.

upon them he heated that shoot till it melted. The first thing he hammered out of it was a long knife with which he might work. Then he fashioned an earthern oven *(tannūr)*, the very one that Noah later inherited [1] and the one that boiled over in India [2] bringing the punishment."

When [presently] Adam went on pilgrimage [to Mecca], he placed the Black Stone on Abū Qubais [3] where it gave light to the inhabitants of Mecca on dark nights just as the moon gives light [on clear nights]. About four years before Islam the Quraish brought it down from Abū Qubais, but meanwhile it had become black because of menstruous women and polluted persons mounting up to it and rubbing it with their hands. Adam made the pilgrimage on foot from India to Mecca forty times.

When Adam fell [from Paradise he was so tall] his head rubbed the [vault of the] sky so that he became bald, and from that his progeny have inherited [a tendency to] baldness. All the land beasts fled in terror of his tall stature and from that day became wild beasts. If Adam stood up while he was on that mountain he could hear the voices of the angels and perceive the sweet breezes of Paradise, so he was reduced in stature to sixty cubits, which was his stature till he died. Adam's beauty was possessed by none of his descendants save Joseph.

Adam spoke forth and said: "O Lord, I was near neighbour to Thee in Thy dwelling-place. I had no other Lord than Thee nor any companions save Thee. There I used to feed in luxury and dwell wheresoever I pleased, but Thou didst cast me down to this holy mountain. Even there I used to hear the voices of the angels and see how they went around Thy Throne, and could perceive the breezes and scent of the Garden, but Thou didst cast me down to the earth, and hast reduced me to sixty cubits, cutting me off from that hearing and seeing and making me lose the scented breezes of Paradise." Then Allah—blessed and exalted is He—answered him: "It was because of your rebellious disobedience, O Adam, that I did this to you." Then when Allah noticed the nakedness of Adam and Eve He bade him slaughter a ram of the sheep from among the eight couples that Allah had sent down [to Him] from heaven. So Adam took a ram

[1] Sūra XI, 40/42; XXIII, 27.

[2] One set of Traditions says that the boiling over was the beginning of the Flood which destroyed all that was not in Noah's ark, and that this boiling over commenced in India.

[3] Abū Qubais is the mountain to the east of Mecca. See Burton's *Pilgrimage*, II, 160, 173. The Black Stone, set in an angle of the Ka'ba at Mecca, is one of the main objects of veneration during the pilgrimage rites at the Holy City. The above, however, is only one of the many legends about its origin. See. p. 501.

and slaughtered it, then he took its wool which Eve spun. Then he and Eve wove. Adam wove for himself a gown *(jubba)* and he made for Eve a shift and a head-cloth *(khimār)*, which clothes they then put on. They had come together at Jamʿ, for which reason it is called Jamʿ and had recognized one another at ʿArafa, which is the reason it is called ʿArafa.[1] They wept for two hundred years over what had passed from them, not eating or drinking for forty days. Then they ate and drank, being at that time on Naudh, the mountain on which Adam had fallen.[2]

He did not approach Eve for a hundred years. Then he approached her and she conceived and was pregnant and brought forth at her first delivery Cain and his twin-sister Labūd. Then she again became pregnant and bore Abel and his twin-sister Aqlīmā. When they matured Allah commanded Adam to marry the first pair to the second and the second to the first so as to keep the cohabitation between pairs of a different birth. Now Cain's sister was fair-favoured but Abel's sister was ill-favoured. Adam told Eve what he had been commanded to do and Eve passed the word on to her two sons. Abel was well-pleased but Cain was displeased and said: "Nay, by Allah! Allah has not commanded any such thing. This command emanates from you, O Adam." Said Adam: "Then do you two bring an offering, and for whichever of you has the more right to her Allah will send down a fire from heaven to devour his offering." To this they both agreed. Abel, who was a herdsman, ran and got the best youngling of his flock and with it butter and milk. Cain, who was a cultivator, took a measure of his poorest produce, and both of them, along with Adam, ascended the mountain, i.e. Mount Naudh. There they set forth their offerings, and Adam set himself to make supplication to his Lord. Cain was [meanwhile] saying to himself: "I care not whether He accepts mine or not, Abel will never marry my sister." Then fire came down from heaven and devoured Abel's offering but avoided Cain's offering because he was not pure of heart. Thereupon Abel went off and Cain came upon him while he was with his flocks, saying: "I am assuredly going to kill you." "And why will you kill me?", [Abel] asked. "Because", said he: "Allah accepted [the offering] from you but did not accept from me, returning my offering to me, and because you are marrying my fair-favoured sister while I have to marry your ill-favoured sister, and because

[1] Jamʿ and ʿArafa are places in the environs of Mecca, ʿArafa being the hill visited as one of the essential rites of the annual pilgrimage. These are folketymologies. The verb *jamaʿa* means "to unite together", and the verb *ʿarafa* "to know, to recognize", so these place names are given this fanciful explanation. See pp. 499-500.

[2] Legend says that having met with Eve again on his pilgrimage to Mecca Adam took her back with him to India.

after today people will be saying that you are better than I am." Abel said to him (V, 28/31): "Even shouldst thou stretch forth thy hand to kill me, yet I am not stretching forth my hand towards thee to slay thee. I fear Allah, Lord of mankind (29/32). I desire that thou shouldst be liable for the sin of [slaying] me as well as for thine own sin, so that thou becomest of the people of the Fire, for that is the recompense of those who do wrong." When he says: "for the sin of me" he means "when you have killed me you will add the guilt of my murder to the sin that was upon you before you killed me". So he killed him "and became one of those who repent" (V, 31/34). [Cain] left him [lying there], not concealing the body, so "Allah sent a raven to dig in the ground that it might show him how he might hide the shame of his brother" (V, 31/34). He had killed him in the evening and he went out in the morning to see what he could do, and there was a living raven digging [a hole as a grave] for a dead raven. He said: "Ah! woe is me, am I incapable of being like this raven and hiding the shame of my brother" (V, 31/43) as it has concealed the corpse of its brother? Thus he called "Ah!" for himself "and became one of those who repent" (V, 31/34). Thereupon Cain took his sister by the hand and went down from the mountain, i.e. from Naudh, to the foot of the mountain.

Adam said to Cain: "Go! never cease to be in fear, and never put trust in anyone you see." Now it so was that never did any of [his] sons pass by him without shooting at him. It happened that one of Cain's sons who was blind was with a son of his when the son said to the blind man: "Here is your father, Cain", whereat the blind man shot at his father Cain and killed him. The son of the blind man said: "Alas, O my father, you have killed your father", at which the blind man raised his hand and smote his son so that the son died. Said the blind man: "Woe is me! I have killed my father by my shooting, and I have killed my son by my smiting."[1]

Then Eve conceived again and bore Seth and his twin-sister ʿAzūrā. He was called Hibatallah, a name derived from that of Abel.[2] When [Eve] bore him Gabriel said to her: "This is Allah's gift to thee in place of Abel."[3] In Arabic [the name is] Shith, in Syriac Shāth and in Hebrew Shīth.[4] It was to him that Adam—upon whom be Allah's blessing—gave

[1] Cf. Gen. IV, 23.

[2] The Arabic form of the name Abel is *Hābīl*, and what is meant is that this is composed of two parts *Hāb* = a gift, an *īl* = God, so *Hibatallah*, which means "gift of Allah" would be the same name.

[3] Cf. Gen. IV, 25.

[4] Actually in Hebrew it is *Shēth* and in Syriac *Shīth*.

his last testament. On the day when Seth was born Adam was one hundred and thirty years old. Then Adam covered her again and she conceived a brisk foetus. As she moved about with it it would say: "She has risen. She has sat down." Satan came to Eve in a form other than his own, saying: "O Eve, what is this that is in thy womb?" "I know not", she answered. He said: "Maybe it is an animal like one of these." She answered: "I know not." Then he went from her, till presently when she grew heavy he came to her and said: "How do you find yourself, O Eve?" She answered: "I fear that maybe it is what you made me afraid of. I am unable to stand up straight when I arise." He said: "What would you think about this? If I make supplication to Allah, and He makes him a human like Adam and you, will you name him after me?" "Surely", she replied, so he went from her. Then she said to Adam: "Someone came and informed me that what is in my womb is an animal like one of these. I find that it is very heavy and fear that it may be as he says." Adam and Eve had no other anxiety save this until she gave birth to him. This is [what is meant by] the words of Allah—blessed and exalted is He—(VII, 189): "They both called upon Allah, [saying]: 'If Thou wilt give us a proper[1] [child], we shall indeed be among the thankful.'" This was their prayer before she bore him. When she gave birth to a perfectly shaped boy [Satan] came to her and said: "Are you not going to name him as you promised me?" "What is your name?", she asked. Now his name was ʿAzāzīl and had he given this name she would have recognized him, so he said: "My name is al-Ḥārith." So she named [the child] ʿAbd al-Ḥārith, whereupon he died. Saith Allah (VII, 190): "Then when He gave them a proper [child] they two gave Him partners in what He had given them. Exalted far is Allah from that with which they associate Him."

Then Allah spoke by revelation to Adam [saying]: "I have a sanctuary *(ḥaram)* directly beneath My Throne, so go and build Me thereon a House and go around it the way you have seen the angels going around My Throne. It is there that I will hearken to your prayers and to those of your descendants who are obedient to Me." Said Adam: "Ah Lord, how shall I do that, for I have not the strength for it, neither have I the directions for it?" So Allah appointed for him an angel who went with him to Mecca. Now it so was [as they journeyed on their way] that whenever Adam passed by a watered meadow or a place that pleased him, he would say to the angel: "Let us stop here [awhile]", and the

[1] The word *ṣāliḥ* here is ambiguous. It is generally taken in a moral sense and translated "good", "upright", but it could mean, as it is taken in this Tradition, "proper" in the physical sense.

angel would say: "It is your place." [This went on] till they arrived at Mecca, and every place at which they stopped [on the way] became a centre of civilized life, while every place they by-passed remained a desert, a wilderness. Then he built the House of [materials] from five mountains, from Sinai, Olives, Lebanon, and al-Jūdī,[1] and its foundations from Ḥirā'.[2] When he had finished building it the angel led him out to 'Arafāt and showed him all the rites of pilgrimage *(manāsik)* such as the people perform them today. Then he brought him back to Mecca where he circumambulated the House seven times, and he then returned to India, where he died on Naudh.

Seth said to Gabriel: "Pray over Adam," but he replied: "Do you step forward and pray over your father and pronounce thirty *takbīrs*,[3] five of them as in [ordinary] prayers and twenty-five special as an honour to Adam." Adam did not die till he saw his sons and his sons' sons numbering forty thousand in Naudh. Adam saw among them much fornication, wine-drinking and evil doing, so in his testament he directed that the children of Seth should not intermarry with the children of Cain. The sons of Seth laid Adam in a cave and set over it a guard that none of the sons of Cain might draw near to him, so those who came and sought pardon for him were the sons of Seth. The length of Adam's life was nine hundred and thirty six years.

Now a hundred handsome youths of the sons of Seth said: "How would it be if we had a look at what the sons of our uncle are doing?" meaning the sons of Cain. So the hundred went down to the evil women of the sons of Cain and the women detained those men. Such time as Allah willed elapsed and then another hundred said: "How would it be if we went to have a look at what our brothers are doing?" So they went down the mountain to them and the women detained them also. Then all the children of Seth went down and rebellion and disobedience came to exist, for they intermarried and intermingled and the children of Cain multiplied till they filled the earth. They were those who perished by drowning in the days of Noah.

Seth the son of Adam begot Anūsh and many others. It was to [Anūsh] that Seth gave his testament. Anūsh begot Qaināri, to whom he gave his testament, and many others. Qaināri begot Mahlālīl, to whom he gave

1 The mountain on which, according to Sūra XI, 44/46, Noah's ark came to rest.
2 The mountain near Mecca where Muḥammad received his first revelation and the call to his mission. See p. 284 ff.
3 *takbīr* is the pronunciation of the phrase *Allāhu akbar*, "Allah is very great". See p. 153.

his testament, and many others. Mahlālīl begot Yāridh, who is al-Yāridh, to whom he gave his testament, and many others. It was in his day that idols came to be made and some departed from Islam. Yāridh begot Khanūkh,[1] who is the Prophet Idrīs—upon whom be peace—and many others.

Ḥajjāj b. Muḥammad has informed us, relating from Ibn Juraij, from Mujāhid, in explanation of His words (IV, 1): "and from him he created his spouse," that Eve was created from the *quṣairā* of Adam—upon whom be Allah's blessing and peace—the *quṣairā* being the shortest rib. It was [done] while he was asleep, and when he awoke he exclaimed: "Aththa", which is the Nabataean for "woman".[2] Muḥammad b. ʿAbdallah al-Asadī has informed us, relating from Sufyān b. Saʿīd ath-Thawrī, from his father, from a client of Ibn ʿAbbās, from Ibn ʿAbbās, who said: "She was called Eve because she was the mother of every tribe."[3] Hishām b. Muḥammad b. as-Sā'ib al-Kalbī has informed us, on the authority of his father, from Abū Ṣāliḥ, from Ibn ʿAbbās, that Adam was cast down to India and Eve to Judda, so he journeyed to find her till he came to Jamʿ, where Eve drew near *(izdalafa)* to him, for which reason that place has the name of Muzdalifa,[4] and since they came together at Jamʿ that place is called Jamʿ.

[1] This is an attempt to reproduce the word *Ḥanōk*, the Hebrew name of Enoch.
[2] The Aramaic word for "woman" is *atthā*, and the Nabataean language was a dialect of Aramaic.
[3] *ḥayy* means a "tribe", but it is also the word for "living", "life", and Eve in Arabic is *Ḥawwā'*, which is here taken to be from that same root.
[4] Muzdalifa is another of the important places where ceremonies are performed during the annual rites of Pilgrimage. See p. 504.

TRADITIONS ABOUT THE END

(A) ON DEATH AND THE HEREAFTER [1]

On the terror and distress of death

Saith the Faqīh [2] Abū'l-Laith as-Samarqandī—on whom may Allah have mercy—: Muḥammad b. Faḍl has related to us, relating from Muḥammad b. Ja'far, relating from Ibrāhīm b. Yūsuf, relating from al-Khalīl b. Aḥmad, relating from al-Ḥusain al-Marwazī, relating from Ibn Abī 'Adī, from Ḥumaid, from Anas b. Mālik, who told how the Apostle of Allah —on whom be Allah's blessing and peace—said: "Whosoever has a loving desire to meet with Allah is one whom Allah has a loving desire to meet." By meeting with Allah he means arriving in the after life, and by having a loving desire he means that when the true believer is in such a state at [the moment of] the death-pangs that he cannot be responsible for [his] faith, he will be given the good news that Allah is well-pleased with him and [will grant him] His Paradise, whereupon to die will be more desirable to him than to live. By Allah's meeting him he means that He will pour out upon him His grace and give bountifully of His gifts. The reason why we have explained [the word] "love" as we have is because, as usually understood, it refers to an inclination of the soul such as it is not at all fitting to [ascribe to] Allah—exalted be He. [The Prophet's statement continued] "but he who is disinclined to meet with Allah is one whom Allah is disinclined to meet". That is, when an unbeliever thinks of the punishment that has been prepared for him, he weeps for his doom and is disinclined to die, so Allah is disinclined to meet with him. The meaning of "disinclined" when used of Allah's relations with a man is that He puts him far from His mercy, and wills his punishment, but it has

[1] From the *Tanbīh al-Ghāfilīn* (The Arousement of the Heedless), by Abū'l-Laith as-Samarqandī (d. 373 A.H. = 983 A.D.). Taqaddum Press edition (pp. 7–25 of the second edition, Cairo, 1324 A.H. = 1906 A.D.).

[2] A *faqīh* is properly one learned in *fiqh* (jurisprudence), and so in the first instance a jurist, but it is commonly used as a title for a religious leader.

nothing to do with painful emotions, the attribution of which to Allah —exalted be He—would not be fitting. An-Nawawī says that the meaning of the Tradition is not that their loving desire to meet with Allah is the cause of Allah's loving desire to meet with them, nor that their disinclination is the cause of His disinclination, but is intended to describe clearly those folk who desire to meet with Allah when Allah desires to meet with them. This is all he says, and its purport obviously is that "loving desire" is an attribute of Allah, and a human's loving desire for his Lord issues from it and is a reflection thereof, like the reflection of water on a wall. Support is given to this [interpretation] by the Tradition in which he—upon whom be peace—says: "When Allah loves a man He keeps him busy with Himself." That His loving them precedes their loving Him is indicated in the Qur'ān. May Allah cause us to taste of this loving desire to meet with Him, and be generous to us therein. [When the Prophet made the statement given above] they said: "But, O Apostle of Allah, we are all disinclined to die." He answered: "That is not disinclination. Whenever a believer comes to die a messenger of good tidings *(bashīr)* [1] will appear, bringing to him from Allah—exalted be He—news of the good to which he is going, so there will be nothing for which he has greater loving desire than for the meeting with Allah—exalted be He—and Allah will have a loving desire to meet with him. But when an iniquitous man—or some related that he said, an unbeliever—comes to die, a messenger of ill-tidings *(nadhīr)* will appear, bringing him news of the evil that awaits him, so he will be disinclined to meet with Allah, and Allah disinclined to meet with him."

Muḥammad b. Faḍl has related to us from Muḥammad b. Jaʿfar, relating from Ibrāhīm b. Yūsuf, relating from Wakīʿ, from ar-Rabīʿ b. Saʿīd, from Muḥammad b. Sābiṭ, from Saʿīd b. Ḍābiṭ, from Jābir b. ʿAbdallah, who told how the Prophet—on whom be Allah's blessing and peace—said: "Relate [religious traditions] from the Children of Israel. There is no crime in that, for they are a people among whom marvellous things have happened." Then he himself began to relate, and said: "Once there was a group of the Children of Israel [who, as they were walking along] came presently to a grave-yard. They said: 'Let us set ourselves to prayer, and then make supplication to our Lord, and maybe He will allow one of the dead to come forth to inform us about dying.'

[1] The two words *bashīr* and *nadhīr*, used in this Tradition, are said to have become technical terms in pre-Islamic Mecca, the *bashīr* being the announcer of good news of a caravan's safe arrival, and the *nadhīr* being the announcer of the bad news that a caravan had been lost.

So they set themselves to prayer and made supplication to their Lord, and while they were engaged in so doing a dark mulatto raised his head out of one of the graves, saying: 'Ho! you there! what do you want? By Allah, though I died ninety years ago the bitterness of dying[1] has not left me till this moment. Make supplication to Allah for me that He let me be again as I was [among the living].'" Now there were between his eyes the scars of *sujūd*.[2] Muḥammad b. Faḍl has related to us, relating from Muḥammad b. Ja'far, relating from Ibrāhīm b. Yūsuf, relating from an-Naḍr b. al-Ḥārith, from al-Ḥasan, who told how the Prophet —upon whom be Allah's blessing and peace—said: "For a true believer the distress and anxiety of dying are equivalent to that from three hundred sword strokes."

Saith the Faqīh—on whom may Allah have mercy—: One who is assured of death, and knows that it will inevitably come upon him, should prepare for it by the performance of good works and the avoidance of evil works, since he knows not when it may come upon him. The Prophet —upon whom be Allah's blessing and peace—spoke clearly about the distress and bitterness of dying as a word of wholesome advice from him to his community, so that they might prepare themselves for it, and bear with patient endurance *(ṣabr)* the distresses of this world, for endurance of the distressess of this world is easier than [to endure] the distress of dying, and the distress of dying belongs to the torments of the Hereafter, and the torments of the after life are more severe than the torments of this life.

'Abdallah b. Musawwar, the Hāshimite, relates how a man came to the Prophet—upon whom be Allah's blessing and peace—saying: "I have come to you that you may teach me some of the wonders of learning." The Prophet asked: "What have you done with regard to the head of learning?" "And what may the head of learning be?", asked he. The Prophet answered: "Do you know the Lord, mighty and majestic?" "Yes", he replied. "Then", said the Prophet, "what have you done about giving Him His due?" "What Allah has willed", he answered. "And do you know death?" asked the Prophet. "Yes", answered he. "Then what have you done in preparation for it?" asked the Prophet. "What Allah has willed", answered he. So the Prophet said: "Go and put in practice

[1] *marārat al-mawt* is one of the many expressions used for the death-pangs or the agony of death.

[2] In the act of *sujūd* (prostration) the forehead always touches the ground, and it is a pious conceit that those who pray much work up a callous on their foreheads at the place where it touches the ground in *sujūd*. The point here is that the scars showed he was a very pious man, yet his piety had not saved him from the bitter pangs of death.

what that involves, then come and I will teach you of the wonders of learning." When, after some years, he came back, the Prophet—upon whom be Allah's blessing and peace—said: "Put your hand upon your heart. Now, what you would not desire for yourself do not desire for your brother Muslim, and what you would desire for yourself desire also for your brother Muslim. This is one of the wonders of learning." Thus has the Prophet—upon whom be Allah's blessing and peace—made it quite plain that making preparation for death belongs to the head of learning, so it is best to busy oneself therewith.

ʿAbdallah b. Musawwar the Hāshimite related that the Apostle of Allah—upon whom be Allah's blessing and peace—recited this verse (VI, 125): "Whomsoever Allah desires to guide, his breast He enlarges to Islam, but whomsoever He desires to lead astray, his breast He makes narrow, contracted." Then he said: "When the light of Islam enters the heart it becomes at ease and is enlarged." Someone asked: "And is there any [outward] sign of that?", to which he answered: "Yes! a withdrawing from the abode of the illusory, a coming back to the abode of the eternal, and a making preparation for death before it comes upon one."

Jaʿfar b. Burqān has related from Maimūm b. Mihrān that the Prophet—upon whom be Allah's blessing and peace—said to a man, as he was exhorting him: "Lay hands on the opportunity for five things before five; on your youth before you become decrepit; on your health before you become sick; on your leisure before you become busily occupied; on your wealth before you become poor; and on your life before you die." In these five [precepts] the Prophet—upon whom be Allah's blessing and peace—has gathered up much wisdom, for a man is capable of works during the period of his youth of which he is incapable in the years of his old age. If a youth becomes accustomed to doing deeds of disobedience he cannot refrain from them in his elder years, so a youth in the period of his youthfulness ought to become accustomed to the doing of good deeds, and then that will be easy for him when he has become old. He said: "on your health before you become sick", for a healthy person carries through effectively matters which concern his property or his person, therefore a healthy person ought to seize the opportunity his healthiness gives him to be diligent in using his property and his body for righteous works, for should he fall sick his body will become weak for [doing deeds of] obedience and he will be able to utilize but a third of his property. "On your leisure before you are busily occupied." He means that by night one is at leisure but by day is busily occupied, therefore one ought to say prayers at night during the period of his leisure, and fast by day while he is busy, more especially during the days of winter, for it is related that the Prophet—upon whom be Allah's blessing and peace—said: "Winter is rich in booty for the believer; long are its nights for his rising for prayers, and short are its days for his fasting." According to another line of transmission what he said was: "Long is the [winter] night, so shorten it not by your sleeping; bright is the day, so dim it not by your sins." He said: "on your wealth before you become poor", meaning that if you are well-pleased with the provision Allah has allotted you, lay hold of that and do not covet what is in the hands of [other] people. He said: "on your life before you die", because so long as a man is alive he is capable of works, but when he is dead there is an end to his works. Therefore a true believer ought not to squander his days, which pass so quickly, but should seize the opportunity of such days as remain to him. A Persian sage has said: "When you are a child you play with the children. When you are a youth you are made careless by worldly pastimes. When you are old you have become weak. So when will you do works for Allah—exalted be He?" He means that you will not be able to serve Allah after you are dead. Only during your life are you able to be diligent in making preparation for the approach of the Angel of Death, being mindful of him all the time for he is not unmindful of you.

'Alī—with whom may Allah be pleased—related that the Prophet—upon whom be Allah's blessing and peace—saw the Angel of Death at the head of a man of the Anṣār, so the Prophet—upon whom be Allah's blessing and peace—said to him: "Be gentle with my friend, for he is a true believer." He answered: "Be of good cheer, O Muḥammad, for I am gentle with every true believer. By Allah, O Muḥammad, if any of the family starts screaming when I am taking a man's spirit, I say: 'What is this screaming? By Allah, we are doing him no injustice. We have not come before his time. We have not accelerated his fate, so what sin are we committing in taking him? If you are well-pleased with what Allah has done you will receive your reward, but if you are displeased or sore afflicted [by it], you are committing sin and being rebellious. You have no cause for discontent with us, and we are going to return for you, so let him who will beware beware, for there are no dwellers whether in hair tents or in villages, whether on land or on sea, but we examine their faces five times daily and at night, so that I know them both small and great, know them individually. By Allah, O Muḥammad, did I desire to take the spirit of a gnat I could not do it till Allah gave me commandment to take it.'"

Abū Sa'īd al-Khudrī related that the Prophet—upon whom be Allah's blessing and peace—once saw some people laughing, to whom he said: "Were you to remember more frequently the Disperser of Delights [1] that would divert you from what I see." Then he said: "Keep frequently in mind the Disperser of Delights", i.e. the Angel of Death, and added: "The grave is naught but one of the meadows of Paradise, or [if not that] it is one of the pits of Hell." 'Umar—with whom may Allah be pleased—once said to Ka'b [al-Aḥbār]: "O Ka'b, relate to us something about dying." He said: "Dying is like a thorny tree being pushed into a man's insides, so that every thorn takes hold of a vein therein, and then dragged out by a man mighty of strength, so that what is rent is rent and what remains remains." It is told of Sufyān ath-Thawrī that when anyone made mention in his presence of dying he would be good for nothing for days, so that if he were asked about anything he would say: "I don't know. I don't know."

A certain sage has said that there are three things an intelligent person should never forget, viz. the ephemeralness of this world whose years come to an end, death, and misfortunes from which one can never be safe. Ḥātim al-Aṣamm—on whom may Allah have mercy—said: "There are four things whose value none comprehend save four: youthfulness, whose value none but the aged comprehend; wellbeing, whose value none comprehend but the afflicted; health, whose value only the sick comprehend; and life, whose value none comprehend but the dead." Saith the Faqīh—on whom may Allah have mercy—: This agrees with the Tradition we have recorded above about laying hold of five before five.

It is related of 'Abdallah b. 'Amr b. al-'Āṣ, that he said: "My father was always saying how it amazed him to note that though death kept coming to men in the possession of their intelligence and having the use of their tongue, no one ever gave a description of what it was like. When death came to him he was in the possession of his intelligence and had the use of his tongue, so I said to him: 'O father mine, you used to say how amazed you were that though death came to men in possession of their intelligence and having the use of their tongue, yet no one ever described it.' He answered: 'O my son, dying is too awful to be described, yet I shall describe somewhat of it to you. By Allah, it is as though Mt. Raḍwā [2] were on my shoulders, as though my spirit were being drawn through a needle's eye, as though a box-thorn bush were in my belly, as though the sky had fallen on the earth with me between them.' Then he added: 'O my son, my life has fallen into three periods. At the first

[1] *hāzim al-ladhdhāt*, one of the many names given the Angel of Death.
[2] A mountain in the environs of Mecca.

I was one of those who urged folk to kill Muḥammad—upon whom be Allah's blessing and peace. What a woe it would have been had I died at that period. Then Allah guided me to Islam and Muḥammad—upon whom be Allah's blessing and peace—became the most beloved of mankind to me, and he appointed me over the troops. Would that I had died at that period and had the supplication and the prayers of the Apostle of Allah over me. Then after his day we got occupied with worldly affairs, and I know not how my situation will be with Allah—exalted be He.' So, [said 'Abdallah], I did not go away from him till he died—may Allah have mercy on him."

Shaqīq b. Ibrāhīm said: "Folk concur with me in words on four things but disagree with me on them in deed. The first is that they say: 'I am the slave of Allah—exalted be He', but they act as though they were free agents. The second is that they say: 'Allah is the one responsible for our sustenance', yet their hearts are not tranquil save when they are in possession of the things of this world. The third is that they say: 'The after life is better than this life', yet they gather wealth for a worldly life. The fourth is that they say: 'It is certain that we shall die', yet they perform the works of people who [imagine that they] do not have to die." It is related of Abū'd-Dardā', though some give it as from Abū Dharr and others from Salmān al-Fārisī, with all of whom may Allah be pleased, though the common opinion is that it is from Abū Dharr, that he said: "Three things so amaze me that I have to laugh, and three things so grieve me that I have to weep. The three that move me to laughter are, first the man who is putting his hope in this world while death is looking for him"—i.e. he keeps on hoping and does not think about death. "The second is that man who carelessly overlooks but is himself not carelessly overlooked"—i.e. he is careless about death whereas the resurrection is immediately ahead of him. "The third is the man who laughs heartily though he does not know whether Allah is displeased with him or well-pleased with him. As for the three that make me weep; they are firstly, separation from the beloved ones"—he means the dying of Muḥammad and his Companions—with all of whom may Allah be pleased; "secondly, the sudden comer", he means the coming of death; "and thirdly, the standing[1] before Allah, not knowing whether my Lord will order me to Paradise or to the Fire."

[1] The word used is a technical term in eschatological texts for the event after the general resurrection when all creatures will be assembled at the place of Judgment, where they stand in fear and trembling and sweat awaiting the appearance of the Divine Judge and the beginning of Judgment.

It is related that the Apostle of Allah—upon whom be Allah's blessing and peace—said: "Did the animals, i.e. domesticated beasts, know what you know about dying you would never eat fat meat."[1] It is recorded that Abū Ḥāmid al-Laffāf said: "One who reminds himself frequently of death gains three precious things, viz. an urge to speedy repentance, a contentment with his daily provision, and a liveliness in worship, whereas one who is forgetful of death will be punished for three things, for postponing repentance, for not being content with a sufficiency, and for laziness in [matters of] worship."

It is recorded that Jesus—on whom be peace—used to raise the dead, by Allah's permission. Some of the unbelievers said to him: "You have been raising to life those who had but recently died and who maybe were not quite dead. Raise to life for us someone who died in ancient times." He said to them: "Choose whomsoever you will." They replied: "Raise for us Shem, Noah's son." So he went to [Shem's] grave, prayed a prayer of two *rak'as*, and made supplication to Allah—exalted be He—whereupon Allah raised to life Shem the son of Noah, and lo! his head and beard had gone white. They said: "What is this? Folk used not to go grey in your time." He said: "I heard the summons, and I thought it was the resurrection, so out of fear my head and my beard went white." Someone asked: "How long have you been dead?" and he answered: "Four thousand years, yet the anguish of dying[2] has not left me."

Someone has said that no true believer ever dies without life and the possibility of returning to this world being presented to him, but so great is the distress of dying that all are averse from it save the martyrs,[3] for they find no distress in dying and greatly desire to return so that they may fight and be killed a second time. It is told of Ibrāhīm b. Adham—on whom may Allah have mercy—that someone said to him: "Would that you would sit so that we might hear somewhat from you." He replied: "I am busily occupied with four things, but when I am finished with them I will assuredly sit with you." He was asked: "And what are they?" He replied: "The first is that I am thinking about the day of the covenant *(mīthāq)*[4] when Allah took a covenant from the children of Adam,

[1] I.e. they would be so terrified that they would always be thin and lean.

[2] *sakarāt al-mawt* is another of the many expressions for the agony of death.

[3] Here specifically those who have fallen in Holy War are meant.

[4] The reference is to a well-known Tradition which related that when Allah had created Adam He stroked his loins (or his back) and drew out therefrom the life-principles of all his descendants yet to be, and took covenant from them that He alone was to be worshipped. This is sometimes called "the first life", and is said to be referred to in such Qur'ān passages as VII, 172/171 ff.; XL, 11; XLI, 21/20. It was on this

[for it was then that] Allah—exalted be He, illustrious be His majesty, and hallowed be His names—said: 'These are for Paradise, and I care not, while these are for Hell, and I care not,' for I do not know in which of the groups I shall be. The second is that I am thinking about the child when Allah has ordained his creation in his mother's womb, breathing the life-principle *(rūḥ)* into him, and the angel who is appointed in charge [1] says: 'O Lord, is he to be one of the unfortunate or one of the fortunate?' for I do not know what the answer was in my case at that time. The third is when the Angel of Death will come [for me], for when he is ready to take my spirit *(rūḥ)*, he will say: 'O Lord, is it to be among the Muslims or among the unbelievers?', and I do not know what the answer will be in my case. The fourth is that I am thinking about that saying of Allah—praised and exalted be He—(XXXVI, 59): 'Separate yourselves out this day, O ye sinners', [2] for I do not know in which of the two groups I shall be."

Saith the Faqīh: Blessed is he to whom Allah gives provision of understanding, rouses from the slumber of heedlessness, and leads to ponder over the matter of his end. Let us, therefore, ask Allah to appoint us a good ending, to grant us an ending that is accompanied by a message of good tidings, for there is a message of good tidings from Allah—exalted be He—for the true believer when death comes to him, and it is the words of the Most High (XLI, 30): "Verily, those who have said: 'Our Lord is Allah', and then have kept the straight course, on them will the angels descend [saying]: 'Fear not! Grieve not! But rejoice in good tidings of the Garden which ye have been promised.'" By keeping the straight course he means believing in Allah and in His Apostle, and standing firm in the faith, though others say that it means performing the required duties and avoiding things forbidden. Yaḥyā b. Muʿādh ar-Rāzī—on whom may Allah have mercy—said that to keep the straight course meant to have one's deeds match one's words, while others say that it means maintaining true orthodoxy.[3] The descending of the angels means that they come

---

occasion that Allah decreed who from among Adam's descendants were to gain Paradise and who were to fill Hell. See p. 382.

[1] This is the Angel of the Wombs. Tradition says that when any child is conceived this angel asks the Lord three questions, viz. whether it is to be a male or a female, what the length of its life span is to be, and whether its fate is to be among the fortunate or the unfortunate, i.e. whether it is for Paradise or for the Fire. According to the Lord's answer he writes these things, which cannot be altered.

[2] This verse refers to the event at Judgment commonly known as the Great Separation, familiar to us under the symbolism of the sheep and the goats.

[3] Lit. keeping straight in the *sunna* and the *jamāʿa*, on which see p. 376.

down at his death with the message of good tidings. What he is not to fear or grieve about is the prospect of what is before him in this world, and what he is to rejoice about is the Garden which Allah has promised by the tongue of the Prophet—upon whom be Allah's blessing and peace.

Some say that the message of good tidings at death has five aspects. The first is for believers in general, who receive the message: "Fear not that the punishment will be everlasting", i.e. you will not remain in torment for ever, because the Prophet and the righteous [persons] will intercede for you; "grieve not lest you miss the reward, but rejoice in good tidings of the Garden", i.e. that you will assuredly go to Paradise. The second is for the sincere devotees *(al-mukhliṣūn)*, who receive the message: "Fear not that your works will be rejected, for your works are accepted; grieve not about missing the reward, for you will have a double reward; and grieve not about things you may have done subsequent to your repentance." The third is for the penitents, who receive the message: "Fear not about your sins, for they have been forgiven you, and grieve not that you may miss the reward because of anything you may have done subsequent to your repentance." The fourth is for the ascetics *(zuhhād)*, [who receive the message]: "Fear not the assembling and the accounting [at Judgment], and grieve not about there being any diminution in your doubled reward, but rejoice in the good tidings that you go to Paradise without any accounting and without [having to go to Gehenna for] any torment." The fifth is for the theologians *('ulamā')* who teach the people, if they teach them well and live in accordance with their own teaching. They will receive the message: "Fear not the terrors of the Day of Judgment; grieve not, for He will recompense you for what you have wrought, and rejoice in good tidings of the Garden, which is for you and for those who imitate your example." Blessed is he whose ending is accompanied by a message of good tidings, for there will be such a message of good tidings only for such as have been true believers and whose works have been good. To such the angels will descend [at death], and they will say to the angels: "Who are ye? Never have we seen faces more beautiful, nor [smelled] an odour more pleasant than yours." They will say: "We are your friends *(awliyā')*,[1] i.e. your guardians, who used to write down your deeds during your earthly life, but now we are to be your *awliyā'* in the after life."

[1] Plu. of *walī*, which means a friend, a beloved, a tutor, a patron, a guardian, and in some contexts a saint. It may be noted that the Guardian Angels are being identified here with the Recording Angels, though generally they are kept distinct. See pp. 276–277, 314–315.

Seeing that all this is so an intelligent person ought to awaken from the sleep of heedlessness, and the sign of such an awakening from the sleep of heedlessness is seen in four things. The first is that a man becomes uncovetous, uneager about the things of this world. The second is that he becomes covetous of the things of the next world, in eager haste for them. The third is that he becomes knowledgeable and diligent in things pertaining to religion. The fourth is that in his relations with people he shows sincerity and tactfulness. It has been said that the most excellent of men is he who is found in possession of five good qualities, the first being that he abounds in worship of his Lord, the second is that it be evident that he is serviceable to people, the third is that folk have no fear of being harmed by him, the fourth is that he does not put his hope on what is in men's hands, and the fifth is that he makes preparation for death. Be it known to you, O my brother, that we are created for death, so there is no running away from it. Allah—exalted be He—has said (XXXIX, 30/31): "Thou indeed art mortal and they are mortal", and again He has said (XXXIII, 16): "Say: 'Flight will not benefit you at all if ye are fleeing from death or from being killed'", so it is incumbent on each Muslim to make preparation for death before it comes. Allah—exalted be He—has said (II, 94/88 ff.): "Then wish for death if ye are those who speak truth. But they will never wish for it because of what their hands have sent forward." Allah—exalted be He—here makes it clear that the one who speaks truth desires death, but the false speaker flees from death because of the evil of his works. The truth-speaking believer has made preparation for death, so he wishes for it, yearning for his Lord, as is related of Abū'd-Dardā', how he said: "I love poverty, out of humility towards my Lord; I love sickness, as a redemption for [my] sins; and I love death, out of yearning for my Lord."

It is related of 'Abdallah b. Mas'ūd—with whom may Allah be pleased—that he said: "There is no soul, innocent or wicked, to which death is not a good thing. If it is innocent, Allah—exalted be He—has said (III, 198/197): 'What is with Allah is a good thing for the innocent', and if it is wicked, Allah—exalted be He—has said (III, 178/172): 'We respite them only that they may increase in guilt, and for them is humiliating punishment.'" Anas b. Mālik has related that the Prophet—upon whom be Allah's blessing and peace—said: "Death is the believer's rest." Ibn Mas'ūd has related that the Prophet—upon whom be Allah's blessing and peace—was asked: "Who is the most excellent of believers?" He answered: "That one of them who has the best character." Someone else asked: "And who is the most sagacious of believers?", to which he answered: "That one of them who remembers death most often and makes the best preparation for it." The Prophet—on whom be Allah's blessing and peace—has said: "The sagacious man is he who brings himself under judgment and labours for what is after death. The profligate is he who follows his own desires and puts vain hope in Allah", i.e. that He will forgive him.

On the torment and distress of the tomb

Al-Khalīl b. Aḥmad has related to us, relating from Ibn Muʿādh, relating from Ḥusain al-Marwazī, relating from Abū Muʿāwiya aḍ-Ḍarīr, from al-Aʿmash, from al-Minhāl b. ʿAmr, from al-Barāʾ b. ʿĀzib, who said: We went out with the Apostle of Allah—upon whom be Allah's blessing and peace—[to join] the funeral procession of a man from the Anṣār. When we came to the grave it was not yet dug [completely], so the Prophet—upon whom be Allah's blessing and peace—sat down, and we also sat round about him, and it was as though the birds were over our heads.[1] In his hand was a rod with which he kept digging in the ground. Presently he raised his head and said: "Seek refuge with Allah from the torment of the tomb." This he said twice or thrice, and then went on: "When a man who is a true believer is drawing near to the next world and is about to be cut off from this world, there descend to him angels whose faces are white as the sun, bringing with them a shroud from Paradise and celestial aromatics, and take their seat just within his vision. Then the Angel of Death arrives, takes a seat at his head and says: 'O thou tranquil soul, come forth to Allah's favour and forgiveness.'" "Then", said the Prophet—upon whom be Allah's blessing and peace—"it comes forth, flowing as easily as a drop from a water-skin, whereupon [those angels] take it, not leaving it in his hand more than the twinkling of an eye ere they take it, [wrap it] in the aforementioned shroud and aromatics so that the odour from it is more redolent than the finest musk to be found on the face of the earth, and mount up with it. There is not a single angel group whom they pass [as they mount upwards] but asks: 'What sweet-smelling spirit is this?', and they reply: 'This is the spirit of So-and-So', using the finest names for him. Anon they come with it to the gate of the lowest heaven and ask that it be opened for it. It is opened to them and the chief personages in each heaven receive it and accompany it to that which lies beyond it, till finally they arrive with it at the seventh heaven. There Allah—exalted be He—says: 'Write its

[1] An idiomatic phrase, meaning to wait in a state of anxiety.

record in ʿIlliyūn [1] and return it to the earth from which I created men, into which I make them return, and out of which I shall bring them a second time' (Sūra, XX, 55/57). The spirit is then returned to its body, whereupon two angels [2] come to it and ask it: 'Who is thy Lord?' It replies: 'Allah is my Lord.' They ask: 'And what is your religion?' 'Islam is my religion', it replies. Then they say: 'And what say you about this man who was sent [on a mission] among you?' and it answers: 'He is the Apostle of Allah, upon him be Allah's blessing and peace.' They ask: 'What works have you?', and it answers: 'I have read Allah's Book, believed it, and in it put my trust.' Then a herald will call: 'He has believed My servant [i.e. Muḥammad]. Spread for him a bed *(firāsh)* from the Garden, clothe him in a celestial garment, open for him a door giving on the Garden through which may come to him its breezes and its aroma, and expand his grave for him as far as eye can reach.' Then there approaches him a sweet-smelling man of handsome countenance, who says to him: 'Good tidings of that which will please you. This is your day that you were promised.' He will ask: 'And who are you?', to which the answer will come: 'I am your pious works.' Then [the deceased] will say: 'O Lord, bring on the Hour that I may be again with my family and my servants.'" The Prophet—upon whom be Allah's blessing and peace—continued: "But when an unbeliever is drawing near to the next world and being cut off from this world, there descend to him from heaven angels whose faces are black, bringing with them hair-cloth, and take their seats just within his vision. Then the Angel of Death arrives, takes a seat at his head and says: 'O thou pernicious soul, come forth to Allah's discontent and wrath.' Thereupon his soul is scattered through all his members and [the angel] drags it forth like the dragging of an iron spit through moist wool, tearing the veins and the sinews. Thus he takes it, but it is not in his hand more than the twinkling of an eye ere [those angels] take it, put it in the hair-cloth where the odour from it is like the stench of a decomposing carcass. They mount up with it and there is not a single angel group whom they pass but asks: 'What impure spirit is this?' They reply: 'This is the spirit of So-and-So', using the least worthy name for him. Anon they come with it to the gate of the lowest heaven, and ask that it be opened for it, but it is not opened for it." At this point the Apostle of Allah—upon whom be Allah's blessing

[1] Sūra LXXXIII, 18–21. It is said to be a place in the uppermost heaven where the record of the righteous is kept.

[2] These are Munkar and Nakīr, the blue-eyed questioners of the dead. See pp. 214, 417, 436–437.

and peace—recited this verse (VII, 40/38): "The gates of heaven will not be opened for them, nor will they enter the Garden till a camel passes through a needle's eye." [He continued]: "Then Allah will say: 'Write his record in Sijjīn,[1] then let his spirit be thrown out.'" At this point [the Prophet] recited (XXII, 31/32): "He who associates anything with Allah will be as though he fell from the sky and the birds snatched him away and the winds blew him to some remote place." What he meant is that he is rejected. "So his spirit is returned to his body, whereupon two angels come and sit by him. They ask him: 'Who is your Lord?', and he replies: 'Alas! I know not.' They ask him: 'And what is your religion?', to which again he replies: 'Alas! I know not.' They ask: 'Well, what do you say about this man who was sent [on a mission] among you?', but again he replies: 'Alas! I know not.' Thereupon a herald cries from heaven: 'He has given My servant [Muḥammad] the lie. Spread for him a bed from the Fire, clothe him in fire, open for him a door giving on the Fire, through which its heat and smoke may enter to him, and contract his grave so that his ribs pile on one another.' Then there approaches him a man, ugly of countenance, ill dressed and foul smelling, who says to him: 'Receive tidings of that which will grieve you. This is your day that you were promised.' He will ask: 'And who are you?', to which [the man] will reply: 'I am your evil deeds', whereat he will say: 'O Lord, let not the Hour arrive. O Lord, let not the Hour arrive.'"

The Faqīh Abū Ja'far has related, relating from Abū'l-Qāsim Aḥmad b. Ḥamza, relating from Muḥammad b. Salama, relating from Abū Ayyūb, relating from al-Qāsim b. al-Faḍl, from al-Ḥarrānī, from Qatāda, from Qusāma b. Zuhair, from Abū Huraira—with whom may Allah be pleased—that the Apostle of Allah—upon whom be Allah's mercy and peace—said: "When a true believer draws near his end angels come to him with a silk cloth in which are musk and bundles of sweet basil. His spirit comes forth as easily as as a hair from a batch of dough, and hears the words: 'O tranquil soul, return to your Lord, well-pleasing and well-pleased. [Go on] to the mercy and favour of Allah—exalted be He.' When his spirit has been drawn forth and placed in the musk and sweet basil the silk cloth is folded and sent with it to 'Illiyūn. As for the unbeliever, when he draws near his end, angels come to him with a cloth of hair in which are coals of fire. His spirit is painfully dragged out, and hears the words: 'O thou pernicious soul, come forth displeased and displeasing. [Go on] to Allah's contempt and punishment.' When his

[1] Sūra LXXXIII, 7–9.

spirit has been drawn forth and placed in those coals, which hiss like boiling kettles, the cloth is folded over and sent with it to Sijjīn."

The Faqīh Abū Ja'far has related, on his line of transmission from 'Abdallah b. 'Umar—with whom may Allah be pleased—that when a true believer is placed in his grave the grave is expanded for him seventy cubits, is strewn with sweet basil and hung with silk. If he should be one who has memorized somewhat of the Qur'ān the light of that will suffice him, but should he have nothing [of the Qur'ān memorized] a light equivalent to that of the sun will be put in his grave, and he himself will be like a bride sleeping who will not be wakened save by her best beloved, and who will rise from her sleep as though she has not slept her fill. As for the unbeliever, his tomb will be contracted till it squashes him, and serpents will be sent against him the size of Bactrian camels' necks, which will devour his flesh till none is left on his bones. Also angels of chastisement will be sent to him [who are] deaf and dumb and blind, [and who have] with them hooked staves of iron with which they beat him, but they cannot hear his voice so as to be touched with mercy, nor can they see him so as to pity him. Moreover the fire of Hell will be presented to him morn and eve.

Saith the Faqīh—on whom may Allah have mercy—: He who would escape from the torment of the tomb must hold fast to four things and avoid four things. The four things to which he must hold fast are the careful observance of prayers, almsgiving, reading (or recitation) of the Qur'ān, and much ascription of praise *(tasbīḥ)*, for these things will light up his grave and cause it to expand. The four things that he must avoid are speaking falsely, perfidy, slandering and [defilement from] urine. It is related that the Apostle of Allah—upon whom be Allah's blessing and peace—said: "Keep yourselves free from [defilement by] urine, for most of the torment of the tomb is due to that." It is also related that the Apostle of Allah—upon whom be Allah's blessing and peace—said: "Four things on your part make Allah discontent, viz. trifling during prayers, slips in recitation [of the Qur'ān], sex indulgence while fasting, and laughing while in a grave-yard." It is related of Muḥammad b. as-Sammāk that he gazed upon a cemetery and said: "Let not the silence of these graves deceive you, for many are those being afflicted therein; and let not the sameness of these graves deceive you, for no contrast could be more striking than that to be found in them." So an intelligent person ought to meditate much upon the grave before he enters it.

Sufyān ath-Tahwrī—on whom may Allah have mercy—has said: "He who meditates much on the grave will find it a meadow from the meadows of Paradise, but he who is heedless about the grave will find it a pit from the pits of Hell." It is related that ʿAlī—whose face may Allah honour—said in one of his sermons: "O servants of Allah, death is death and there is no escape from it. If you go forward towards it it will take you, and if you flee from it it will overtake you. Death is knotted to your forelocks. Let him who so wishes rush forth, let him who so wishes make haste, but behind you is a greedy one who is seeking you, namely, the grave. Is it not true that the grave is either a meadow of the meadows of Paradise or a pit of the pits of Hell? Is it not true that each day it speaks out three times, saying: 'I am the house of darkness; I am the house of loneliness; I am the house of the worms?' Is it not true that beyond that day is a Day yet more distressful, a Day on which a child will grow grey-headed, on which an old man will become as drunken, on which the nursing mother will forget her nursling and every pregnant woman drop her burden, on which you will see men staggering drunkenly though they are not drunk, but the punishment of Allah is severe?[1] Is it not true that beyond that Day there is a Fire whose heat is terrific, whose deeps are unplumbable, whose water is purulent matter *(ṣadīd)*,[2] and in which Allah's mercy is not?" As he said this the Muslims wept bitterly, but he went on: "Yet beyond this Day there also is Paradise stretching wide as the heavens and the earth, prepared for the God-fearing."[3] May Allah protect both us and you from the painful torment and grant us and you to dwell in the pleasant abode.[4]

It is related that Asīd b. ʿAbd ar-Raḥmān said: "I have been told that when a true believer dies and is being borne [to the grave] he says: 'Hurry along with me'; when he is being put into the tomb chamber the earth addresses him, saying: 'I used to love you when you were on my back, but now you are even dearer to me.' When an unbeliever dies, however, and is being borne [to the grave], he says: 'Take me back', and when he is being put in the tomb chamber the earth addresses him, saying: 'I used to hate you when you were on my back, but now you are even more hateful to me.'" It is related that ʿUthmān b. ʿAffān—with whom may Allah be pleased—once stood by a grave and wept. Someone said to him: "You oft make mention of heaven and hell but do not weep, yet you are weeping at this?" He replied: "The Apostle of Allah—upon whom

1 See Sūra XXII, 2 and LXXIII, 17.
2 Sūra XIV, 16/19.
3 See Sūra III, 133/127.
4 *dār an-naʿīm*, here used as a general name for Paradise, though in some texts it is said to be the name of one of the seven stages of Paradise.

be Allah's blessing and peace—used to say: 'The grave is the first station among the stations of the after-life, if one escapes [the terrors of] that one those that come after it are easier, but if one does not escape it those that come after it are more severe.'"

It is related that 'Abd al-Ḥamīd b. Maḥmūd al-Ma'walī said: I was sitting with Ibn 'Abbās—with whom may Allah be pleased—when some folk came to him saying: "We left home to go on pilgrimage, having with us a friend of ours, but when we reached the quarter of Dhāt aṣ-Ṣifāḥ he died. So we laid him out and then went to dig a grave with a burial chamber for him, but immediately a black snake [appeared and] occupied the burial chamber. We left it and dug in another place, but again a black snake occupied the burial chamber. So we left that and dug a third grave, but once more a black snake occupied the burial chamber, so we had to abandon it and have come to you [to ask what we should do]." Said Ibn 'Abbās—with whom may Allah be pleased—: "That is some deed of his, [something] he was wont to do. Go and inter him in one of them, for, by Allah, were you to dig the whole earth you would find that [snake] in it. Then [go and] inform his folk about it." They went and interred him in one of them, and when they got back home they went to his family to take to them his effects which they had brought along with them, and they asked his wife what deed it could have been he was doing. She answered: "He was a grain-merchant dealing in wheat, and every day he used to take out sufficient for his own daily provision, and cut up sugar-cane to the like amount, or radish pods, i.e. the stems of these articles of food, and put it in [to replace what he had taken]."

Saith the Faqīh—on whom may Allah have mercy—: This story proves that perfidy is one of the causes of the torment of the tomb, and so it is a warning to everyone who hears it to make a lively effort to refrain from perfidious actions. It is said that the earth gives five calls every day. At its first call it says: "O child of Adam, you are walking on my back, but your journey is to my belly." At its second call it says: "O child of Adam, you are eating all sorts of things on my back, but the worms will eat you in my belly." At the third it says: "O child of Adam, you are laughing on my back, but you will weep anon in my belly." At the fourth it says: "O child of Adam, you are rejoicing on my back, but ere long you will be grieving in my belly." At the fifth it says: "O child of Adam, you are sinning on my back, but anon you will be tormented in my belly." 'Amr b. Dīnār has related that there was a man of the people of Madīna who had a sister living in the environs of the city who grew sick, and whom he used to visit. Presently she died, so she was laid out and borne to her grave. When they had buried her and he had returned home he remembered that he had forgotten a wallet which he had had with him. So he got hold of a friend and the two of them went back to the grave where he dug and found his wallet. Then he said to the [other] man: "Turn your face while I have a look at how my sister is doing." Removing a little of what was over the burial chamber [1] [he looked in] and lo! the grave was blazing with fire, so he returned [what he had removed], levelled off the grave and went home. Going to his mother he said: "Tell me about the kind of deeds my sister used to do." She said: "Why do you ask about your sister now that she is dead?" He said: "Tell me, nevertheless." So she replied: "Your sister used to be dilatory at prayers, and say prayers when she was not properly in a state of ritual purity. Also when folk were sleeping she used to go and put her ear to the neighbours' doors and come away with tales about them." That is, she used to listen to conversations that she might go about giving malevolent reports, which is one of the causes of torment in the tomb. So let everyone who desires to be safe from the torment of the tomb be on his guard to avoid slandering and other sins, that he may escape its torment and have an easy interrogation from Munkar and Nakīr.

Allah—exalted be He—has said (XIV, 27/32): "Allah will stablish those who believe by a declaration that stands firm both in this worldly life and in the after life." Al-Barā' b. 'Āzib—with whom may Allah be pleased—has related that the Prophet—upon whom be Allah's blessing and peace—said: "When a Muslim is interrogated in the grave let him testify that there is no deity save Allah and that Muḥammad is His servant and His Apostle, for that is what Allah means by (XIV, 27/32): 'Allah will stablish those who believe by a declaration that stands firm both in this worldly life and in the after life.'" This stablishing *(tathbīt)* will be effective for the sincere, obedient believer in three situations. The first is when he is brought face to face with the Angel of Death. The second is when he is being interrogated by Munkar and Nakīr. The third is when he is being questioned at the reckoning on the Day. The stablishing when he is brought face to face with the Angel of Death will consist of three things; firstly in his being preserved from unbelief and helped to stand firm in *tawḥīd*,[2] so that his spirit is drawn out while he is in

[1] In a normal Muslim burial care is taken to leave room for some freedom of movement in the *laḥd*, or burial chamber, so this is generally a deeper trench or maybe a niche in the grave, and is covered with slabs before the earth is filled into the grave. It is in this *laḥd* that the corpse must sit up for the questioning by Munkar and Nakīr. See p. 209 and 436–437.

[2] Lit. "making one", that is in maintaining the Divine uniqueness and unity.

Islam; secondly, the angels will give him a message of good tidings of mercy; thirdly, he will be allowed to see his place in Paradise. The stablishing in the grave also consists of three things; firstly, that Allah —exalted be He—will suggest to him the true answers, so that he may reply to the two [questioning angels] in a way well-pleasing to the Lord; secondly, that He will cause all fear, terror and consternation to slip away from him; and thirdly, that as he sees his place in Paradise the grave will become for him one of its meadows. Finally, the stablishing at the reckoning also consists of three things; firstly, that Allah will suggest to him a plea with regard to everything about which he is questioned; secondly, that the reckoning will be made easy for him; and thirdly, that his slips and offenses will be overlooked. Some say that this stablishing takes place on four occasions, the first of which is at death, the second is in the grave so that he answers fearlessly, the third is at the reckoning, and the fourth is at the Bridge, so that he may pass over as rapidly as lightning.

Should anyone raise a question about this interrogation in the grave, and ask how it can be, the answer is that the theologians *('ulamā')* have discussed this matter and there is great variation in what has been handed down about it. Some say that it is the spirit that is questioned apart from the body, and that only then does the spirit reenter the body as far as the chest. Others say that at that time the spirit is between the body and the shroud. For all this proof texts can be brought, but among the learned the correct attitude is for a man to acknowledge that there is to be a questioning in the tomb but not to bother himself about the manner of it, saying rather that Allah knows best about how it takes place. We shall know for sure about it only when it has happened to us. When anyone denies the interrogation by Munkar and Nakīr he denies it for one of two reasons. He may say that the intellect cannot accept its possibility since it is contrary to nature, or he may say that it is something that is possible, but is not certain. If he says that intellectually it is not possible, then his statement is tantamount to denying prophecy and considering miracles as worthless, for the messengers were all of Adam's race and their nature like the nature of other men, but they saw angels and had revelation come to them. The sea was divided for Moses—on whom be peace—and his rod became a serpent, both things which are contrary to nature, so one who denies this puts himself outside of Islam, wheresoever it may be that he entered it. If he says that it is possible but is not certain, we have related Traditions about this matter which are sufficient to convince anyone who has heard them. Moreover in Allah's

Book there is proof of it, for Allah—exalted be He—has said (XX, 124/123 ff.): "And whosoever turns from My reminder will have a narrowness of life, and We will round him up blind on the Day of Resurrection", where quite a number of exegetes say that the narrowness of life referred to here is the interrogation in the tomb. Allah—exalted be He—has said (XIV, 27/32): "Allah will stablish those who believe by a declaration that stands firm in this worldly life and in the after life."

Saith the Faqīh—on whom may Allah have mercy—, the Faqīh has related to me on his line of transmission from Sa'īd b. al-Musayyib, from 'Umar—with whom may Allah be pleased—that the Apostle of Allah—upon whom be Allah's blessing and peace—said: "When a believer has entered his grave there come to him the two *fattāns* [1] of the tomb, who make him sit up in his grave and interrogate him while he is still listening to the patter of the sandals of the mourners who have just turned their backs to go away. They ask him: 'Who is thy Lord? What is thy religion? Who is thy Prophet?' He will answer: 'Allah is my Lord. Islam is my religion. Muḥammad is my Prophet', at which they will say: 'Allah stablishes thee, then there is consolation.' This is what Allah —exalted be He—has said (XIV, 27/32): 'Allah will stablish those who believe by a declaration that stands firm both in this worldly life and in the after life', i.e. Allah will cause them to stand firm on a statement of the truth, whereas Allah will lead wrong-doers astray, namely, the unbelievers, whom He will not help to a statement of the truth. When an unbeliever or a hypocrite has entered his grave they ask him: 'Who is thy Lord? What is thy religion? Who is thy Prophet?', and he replies: 'I do not know.' Thereupon they say: 'You do not know!', and they smite him with a *mirzaba* [2] [such a blow] as can be heard by all creatures save jinn and men."

Abū Ḥātim has related from Ibn 'Umar—with whom may Allah be pleased—that the Apostle of Allah—upon whom be Allah's blessing and peace—said: "O 'Umar, how will things be with you when there come to you the two *fattāns* of the tomb, Munkar and Nakīr, two angels black [of face] and blue [of eyes], whose tusks rend the earth, whose hair is so long that they tread on it, whose voices are like the rumbling thunder, and their glances like the rapid lightning?" 'Umar—with whom may Allah be pleased—replied: "O Apostle of Allah, shall I have my intelligence and be such as I am today?" "Yes", answered [the Prophet].

[1] *fattān* is from a root meaning "to put to the test", "to try", and in many of the Traditions Munkar and Nakīr are called the two *fattāns* of the tomb. See p. 437.
[2] A *mirzaba* is an iron bar somewhat like a crow-bar.

"Then", said ʿUmar, "I shall satisfy them for you, by permission of Allah—exalted be He", and the Prophet—upon whom be Allah's blessing and peace—said: "ʿUmar will indeed do all right."

Abū'l-Qāsim b. ʿAbd ar-Raḥmān [b. Muḥammad] ash-Shābādhī has related to me on his line of transmission from Abū Huraira—with whom may Allah be pleased—that the Prophet—upon whom be Allah's blessing and peace—said: "No dying man ever passes away without bellowing so that every animal near him can hear it, though men cannot, for could they hear it they would faint away. Then when he is being borne off to his grave, if he is a pious man, he says: 'Hasten along with me, for did you know what good there is ahead of me you would want to precede me.' If he is otherwise he says: 'Hasten not with me, for did you know what the evil to which you are forwarding me is you would not hurry me.' Then when the [pious man] is laid in his grave there come to him two angels black [of face], blue [of eyes], who approach him from the head, but his prayers say: 'You cannot come at him from here, for how many a night has he sat up in vigil out of fear of this resting-place.' Then they approach him from the direction of his legs, but filial piety comes forth and says: 'You will not come at him from our direction for on us he used to walk, rising up out of fear of this resting-place.' Then they will approach from his right side, but his charitable acts will say: 'You will not come [at him] from my direction for with me he used to distribute alms in charity out of fear of this resting-place.' Then they will approach from his left side, but his fasting will say: 'You will not come [at him] from my direction for he used to hunger and thirst out of fear of this resting-place.' So he will be wakened as a sleeper is awakened, and will be asked: 'Do you see this man who has been saying what he says about your state?' He will ask: 'Who is he?', and the answer will be: 'Muḥammad—upon whom be Allah's blessing and peace.' Then he will say: 'I testify that he is the Apostle of Allah—on whom be Allah's blessing and peace.' So they will say to him: 'You have lived as a true believer, and have died as a true believer.' Then his grave will be enlarged and strewn with every token of Allah's generosity to the extent that Allah wills." So let us ask Allah's assistance and protection, [praying] that He give us refuge from straying, misleading desires and from heedlessness, and give us refuge from the torment of the tomb, for the Prophet himself—upon whom be Allah's blessing and peace—used to seek refuge with Allah therefrom.

It is recorded that ʿĀ'isha—with whom may Allah be pleased—said: "I was entirely ignorant about the torment of the tomb till a Jewish woman came to me and begged something of me. I gave it to her, whereat she said: 'May Allah give thee refuge from the torment of the tomb.' I imagined that what she said was some Jewish nonsense till the Prophet —upon whom be Allah's blessing and peace—came in and I mentioned the matter to him, whereat he informed me that the torment of the tomb is a reality." It is thus incumbent on every Muslim to seek refuge with Allah—exalted be He—from the torment of the tomb, and make preparation for the grave by pious works before he enters it. That is an easy enough matter for him so long as he is in this world, but when he has entered the grave, though he earnestly desires permission to perform just one good deed, no such permission will be given him, but he will continue in regret and contrition. So an intelligent person ought to think about the state of affairs of the dead. The dead may earnestly desire permission to say a prayer of two *rak'as*, or permission to say even once: "There is no deity but Allah: Muḥammad is the Apostle of Allah", or permission to make one single ascription of praise, but no such permission will be given them, and they will be lost in amazement at the living who fritter away their days in idleness and heedlessness. So, O my brother, do not waste your days which are your chief riches. While you continue able to use your chief riches you can use them to profit, for the goods of the after life are unsaleable in this day of yours. Be diligent, therefore, in gathering goods of the after life at a time of dull market, for a day is coming when such goods will become very precious. Seek therefore to increase them in a day of dull market [looking forward] to a day when they will be precious, for you will not be able to go to seek them on that day. Let us ask Allah—exalted be He—to help us in making preparation for a day of poverty and need, and that He put us not among those who regret, seeking to return but getting no response [to their prayer]. May He ease for us the pangs of death and the distress of the tomb, for us and for all the Muslims, male and female. He is the most merciful of those who show mercy. He is our sufficiency, and how splendid a trustee. There is no power and no might save in Allah, the High, the Mighty One.

On the dread events and terrors of the resurrection

Saith the Faqīh—on whom may Allah have mercy—: Al-Khalīl b. Aḥmad has informed us, on information from Yaḥyā b. Muḥammad b. Ṣā'id, relating from Muḥammad b. al-Manṣūr aṭ-Ṭūsī, relating from Yaḥyā b. Isḥāq aṣ-Ṣāliḥ, relating from 'Abdallah b. Lahī'a, from Khālid b. Abī 'Imrān, from al-Qāsim b. Muḥammad, that 'Ā'isha—with whom may Allah be pleased—said: "I said: 'O Apostle of Allah, will the friend remember his friend on the Day?' 'Yes', said he, 'save at three points, at the Balance, till he knows whether he is weighing light or weighing heavy, at the fluttering down of the *ṣuḥuf*,[1] till he knows whether he will be given his in his right hand or in his left, and when an *'unuq*[2] emerges from the fire, envelops them and says: 'I am put in charge of three, in charge of him who has invoked any other deity along with Allah, in charge of every obstinate tyrant, in charge of everyone who refused to believe in the Day of Reckoning.' Around such it will enfold itself and cast them into the deeps of Gehenna. Gehenna has [over it] a bridge *(jisr)*, finer than a hair and sharper than a sword, fitted with hooks and grappling irons. Over this the people have to pass. Some will cross like rapid lightning, some like swift blowing wind, some escape safe and sound, some lacerated and torn, and some are thrown prostrate on their faces in the Fire.'"

Muḥammad b. al-Faḍl has related to us, relating from Muḥammad b. Ja'far who said, Ibrāhīm b. Yūsuf has informed us, giving information from Abū Mu'āwiya, from al-A'mash, from Abū Ṣāliḥ, from Abū Huraira—with whom may Allah be pleased—that the Prophet—upon whom be Allah's blessing and peace—said: "There will be forty years between the two blasts [on the Trump], during which time Allah will send down water from heaven, like human semen, whereby bodies will grow as vegetables grow." A trustworthy reporter has informed me on his line of transmission from Abū Huraira, indeed by many different lines of transmission from Abū Huraira—with whom may Allah be pleased—that the Apostle of Allah—upon whom be Allah's blessing and peace—said: "When Allah—exalted be He—had finished creating the heavens and the earth He created the Trumpet *(aṣ-ṣūr)*. He gave it to Isrāfīl who [since then has been standing with it] set at his mouth gazing with unwavering glance towards the Throne waiting expectantly to be ordered [to sound it]." I said: "O Apostle of Allah, what is the Ṣūr?" "It is a horn of light", he replied. I said: "O Apostle of Allah, what is the manner of it?" He said: "It is of enormous circumference. By Him who sent me as a Prophet with the truth, its circumference is as big as the span of heaven and earth. Three blasts will be blown on it." Some lines of transmission say "two blasts", a blast for destruction and a blast for resurrection. The Tradition according to Ka'b says two blasts, but that

[1] Lit. "sheets", which contain the record each has to present at Judgment.

[2] *'unuq* is literally "neck", or a "column" such as the trunk of a tree. In eschatological Traditions it refers to a column of fire that will emerge from Hell and turn into an infernal monster.

according to Abū Huraira —with whom may Allah be pleased—says there are three, a blast for consternation, a blast for smiting, and a blast for resurrection.

Allah—exalted be He—will give command to Isrāfīl to blow the first blast. He will blow it, whereat all in heaven and earth will be terrified. This is the word of Allah—exalted be He—(XXVII, 87/89): "And a day when the trumpet will be blown and whosoever is in heaven or on earth will be terrified, save those whom Allah wills." Then the earth will be shaken, every nursing mother will forget her nursling, every pregnant female will cast her burden, and you will see men drunkenly reeling though they are not drunk, but the punishment of Allah is severe (XXII, 2). Youths will become grey-headed (LXXIII, 17), and the satans will depart hastily in flight. This is that of which Allah—exalted be He—has spoken (XXII, 1, 2): "O ye people, show piety towards your Lord. Verily the quaking of the Hour will be a terrible thing. When ye see it every nursing mother will forget her nursling, every pregnant female will cast her burden, and you will see men drunkenly reeling though they are not drunken, but the punishment of Allah is severe." They will remain in this condition [of consternation] such time as Allah wills. Then Allah —exalted be He—will give command to Isrāfīl, and he will blow the blast of smiting, whereat all the inhabitants of heaven will be smitten as well as the inhabitants of earth. That is, the inhabitants of heaven and earth will all die, save those whom Allah wills. This is what Allah—exalted be He—has said (XXXIX, 68): "There will be a blast on the trumpet and everyone in the heavens and everyone on earth will be smitten, save those whom Allah wills." The exception here refers to the spirits of the martyrs. Others say it refers to Gabriel, Michael, Isrāfīl and the Angel of Death —on all of whom be Allah's blessings. Then Allah—mighty and majestic is He—will say to the Angel of Death: "Who now remains of My creatures?", though He knows very well. He will answer: "O Lord, Thou art living, for Thou diest not. Also Gabriel, Michael, Isrāfīl and the Throne Bearers remain, and I remain." Then Allah—exalted be He— will command the Angel of Death to take their spirits. Thus it is given in the account from al-Kalbī and in the account from Muqātil, but in the account from Muḥammad b. Kaʿb, from a certain man, from Abū Huraira—with whom may Allah be pleased—it runs: that Allah—praised and exalted be He—will say: "Let Gabriel, Michael and Isrāfīl die, and let the Throne Bearers die." [When they have passed away] Allah—mighty and majestic is He—will say: "O Angel of Death, who of my creatures remains?" He will reply: "Thou art the Living One who diest not, and there remains [beside but] thy feeble servant the Angel of Death." Then He will say: "O Angel of Death, did you not hear My statement that every soul shall taste of death? (III, 185/182). Thou art one of My creatures whom I created for that which thou seest. Now die." So he will die.

In another Tradition it is related that [Allah] will command him to take his own spirit, so he will proceed to a place between heaven and hell and himself draw out his own spirit, giving such a shriek that were any creatures alive they would die at the sound thereof. He will say: "Had I known that the drawing out of the spirit caused such distress and bitterness as this, I would have been compassion itself while drawing out the spirits of true believers." Then he will die, and there will be no single creature left. Then Allah—mighty and majestic is He—will say to the lower world: "Where are the kings and the sons of kings? Where are the tyrants and the sons of tyrants? Where are those who devoured My good things and yet worshipped other than Me?" Again Allah—exalted be He—will say: "Whose is the kingdom today?" No one will answer Him, so He—praised and exalted be He—will answer Himself, and say: "It belongs to Allah, the One, the Overcomer." Then Allah—exalted be He—will command the heaven to send down rain, and it will send down rain like human semen for forty days till everything is covered to a depth of twelve cubits. By that water Allah will make all creatures grow [again] in the manner vegetables do, till their bodies are perfected and have become again as they formerly were. Then Allah—exalted be He—will say: "Let Isrāfīl come to life, along with the Throne Bearers." So they will come to life at Allah's command—exalted be He—and Allah will give command to Isrāfīl, who will take the trumpet and put it to his mouth. Then Allah—exalted be He—will say: "Let Gabriel and Michael come to life", whereat they will come to life at Allah's bidding. Then Allah—exalted be He—will call for the spirits, who will be brought, and He will put them into the trumpet. Thereupon Allah—exalted be He—will give command to Isrāfīl, who will blow the Blast of Resurrection, whereat the spirits will fly out like bees, filling all the space between heaven and earth. The spirits will penetrate into the earth to their [appropriate] bodies, which they will enter through the nostrils, and straightway the earth will be rent from over them." At this point the Prophet—upon whom be Allah's blessing and peace—said: "I shall be the first over whom the earth will be rent." Another tradition says that when Allah—exalted be He—raises Gabriel, Michael and Isrāfīl to life they will descend straightway to the tomb of the Prophet—upon whom be Allah's blessing and peace—taking with them Burāq [1] and garments from Paradise. Then the earth will be rent above him and the Prophet —upon whom be Allah's blessing and peace—will look at Gabriel and say: "O Gabriel, what day is this?" He will answer: "This is the Day of Resurrection. This is the Day of al-Ḥāqqa.[2] This is the Day of al-Qāriʿa."[3] He will ask: "O Gabriel, what has Allah done with my community?", to which Gabriel will answer: "Rejoice! You are the first over whom the earth has been rent." Then Allah—exalted be He—will command Isrāfīl to blow on the trumpet, "and lo! they will be standing up, looking around" (XXXIX, 68).

We return now to the Tradition from Abū Huraira—with whom may Allah be pleased—who said: They will come quickly forth therefrom (i.e. from the earth that has been rent) to their Lord as newly-begotten.[4] He means that they will come forth from their graves barefooted and naked [as newly born babes are]. Then they will stand at a single place of standing for the space of seventy years, during which Allah will not look at them nor judge among them. They will weep till tears are exhausted and then will weep blood. Moreover they will sweat till they are so immersed that they could swim in it. When the sweat rises to their chins they will be summoned to the assembling. This is what Allah—mighty and majestic is He—speaks of (LIV, 8): "hastening with necks outstretched to Him who summons," i.e. they will be watching, making their way, hastening. When all creatures have assembled, jinn and men and others, then while they are still standing they will hear a mighty voice from heaven which will terrify them. Then the heavens will be rent and the angels of the lowest heaven will descend, to the number of all who are on earth, and will take up their stations. The people will say: "Is our Lord with you?", meaning by that, is the order for the reckoning with you? They will answer: "No! but He will come", meaning that His order for the reckoning will come. Then the inhabitants of the second heaven will descend to stand in a rank behind the inhabitants of the lowest heaven. Then the angels who inhabit the third heaven will descend, and so on till the angels of all the seven heavens have descended, each double the number of the previous group, and they will stand encircling the inhabitants of earth.

[1] This is the steed on which he made his Night Journey from Mecca to Jerusalem. See pp. 336, 621.
[2] "That which is due", Sūra LXIX, 1–3.
[3] "The striking", Sūra CI, 1 ff.
[4] Sūra XXXVI, 51. The word is *yansilūn*, which Bell translates "trickling down".

Saith the Faqīh: Muḥammad b. al-Faḍl has related to us, reporting from Muḥammad b. Ja'far, reporting from Ibrāhīm b. Yūsuf, reporting from Muḥammad b. al-Faḍl, from al-Ajlaḥ, from aḍ-Ḍaḥḥāk, who said: "Allah—exalted be He—will give command to the lowest heaven, which will be rent so that all the angels in it will descend and encircle the earth and all that is therein. [The same will happen in the case of] the second and all that are in it, then the third and all that are in it, then the fourth and all that are in it, then the fifth and all that are in it, then the sixth and all that are in it, then the seventh and all that are in it, so that there will be seven ranks of angels, one within the other, and the dwellers on earth will not be able to turn in any direction without finding seven ranks of angels there. This is what Allah—exalted be He—has said (LV, 33): "O company of jinn and men, if you are able to pass through any of the regions of heaven and earth, then pass through; but ye will not pass through save by authorization." He has also said (XXV, 25/27): "And a Day when the heaven is broken up with the clouds, and the angels come descending down."

Abū Huraira—with whom may Allah be pleased—has related that the Prophet—upon whom be Allah's blessing and peace—will say: "O company of jinn and men, I gave you sincere advice. It is naught but your works that [you find there] in your sheets, so let him who finds good render praise to Allah—exalted be He—and let him who finds otherwise blame none but himself." Then Allah will give command to Gehenna, whereat an *'unuq* will come forth, tall, long-necked, dark and with the gift of speech. Allah will say (XXXVI, 60–64): "O children of Adam, did I not make a covenant with you that ye should not serve Satan? He, indeed, is a manifest enemy to you—[and did I not say] worship ye Me? This is a straight path? But now, indeed, he has led astray a great host of you. Did ye then have no sense? This is Gehenna with which ye were threatened. Roast in it today because of the way ye were disbelieving." Thereupon the peoples will fall on their knees, which is as Allah—exalted be He—has said (XLV, 28/27): "And you will see each community kneeling, each community summoned to its Book."[1] Then Allah—exalted be He—will give judgment among the wild beasts and domesticated animals till He has avenged the hornless sheep on that which possesses horns, after which He will say [to the animal groups]: "Be dust,"[2] [on hearing which

[1] The "Book" in this verse is generally taken to mean its Scripture which was sent to it along with its Prophet, for every community, according to Qur'ānic teaching, had a Prophet.

[2] The animals will thus have no place in Paradise or Hell. They are given proper

each] unbeliever will say: "Would that I were dust." Then [Allah] will give judgment among men.

Nāfi' has related from Ibn 'Umar—with whom may Allah be pleased—that the Prophet—upon whom be Allah's blessing and peace—said: "People will be assembled on the Day naked and barefooted as their mothers bore them." 'Ā'isha—with whom may Allah be pleased—asked: "The men and the women?" "Yes", replied [the Prophet], whereat 'Ā'isha said: "How shocking it will be for them to be looking at one another", but he slapped her on the shoulder and said: "O grand-daughter of Abū Quḥāfa, folk will be too occupied [with more serious matters] on that day to look [at one another], for their gaze will be fixed on the heavens. Forty years will they stand neither eating nor drinking, standing in sweat up to their ankles, in the case of some of them up to their shanks, some up to their waists, and some will spend the period of the standing with it up to their mouths so that it bridles them. Then the angels on both sides of the Throne will arise, and Allah—exalted be He—will give command to a herald who will call: 'Where is So-and-So the son of So-and-So?' At this the people will look up, i.e. they will raise their heads at that voice, and the one who is called will come forth from the place of standing. When he is standing before the Lord of the worlds [Allah] will say: 'Where are those he has wronged?' Then they will be called man by man, and those whom he has wronged will be given compensation out of his store of good deeds. On that day there will be no question of dinars or dirhams [1] but only a taking from the store of good deeds and an adding to the store of evil deeds. They will not cease giving compensation out of his [store of] good deeds till he has no good deeds left, and then [if further compensation still is necessary] they will take from their evil deeds and add them to his. If his store of good deeds has been thus exhausted He will say to him: 'Go off to your mother Hāwiya' (CI, 9/6) i.e. Gehenna, 'for no one is wronged today, Allah being swift at reckoning' (XL, 17), i.e. He is quick at settling the recompense. On that day there will be no angel who draws near [the Throne], no Prophet who has been sent on a mission, no martyr, but will think, when he sees how strict the accounting is, that none will escape save such as may be preserved by Allah—exalted be He."

---

judgment with its evening out of all injustices, so that even the hornless ewe is avenged for any injury done her by the horned beasts, but when this has been seen to the animals are annihilated.

[1] We should say "dollars and cents". The *dīnār* and the *dirham* were coins in use in the Islamic world, both being words derived from the Greek.

Muʿādh b. Jabal—with whom may Allah be pleased—has related that the Prophet—upon whom be Allah's blessing and peace—said: "The two feet of no human will slip till he has been questioned about four things, about the days of his life, in what he spent them; about his body, with what he wore it out; about his learning, how he acted in accordance with it; and about his wealth, where he gained it and on what he spent it." It is related of ʿIkrima that he said: "The father will cling to his child on that Day, saying: 'O my son, it was I who begot you in the world, and was a father to you'; whereat [the son] will speak him fair. He will say to him: 'O my son, I am in need of but an atom's weight of your good deeds that may be I can escape from what you see.' But his child will say to him: 'I am terrified for myself by the like of what terrifies you, and indeed, I am not able to give you anything.' Then he will cling to his wife, saying to her: 'I was your husband in the world', whereat she will speak him fair. He will say to her: 'I beg of you give me but one good deed as a gift, that maybe I can escape from what you see.' But she will reply: 'I cannot do that. I am terrified for myself by the like of what terrifies you.' Then Allah—mighty and majestic is He—will say (XXXV, 18/19): 'And should a heavily burdened one call [someone else to help with] its load, naught of it will be borne [for him] even though [the one called on] be a near relative'; i.e. no one burdened with sins will get anyone to carry for him aught of his sins." Ibn Masʿūd—with whom may Allah be pleased—has related that the Prophet—upon whom be Allah's blessing and peace—said: "The unbeliever will be bridled by his sweat (i.e. he will be immersed in it up to his mouth) till he cries: 'O Lord have mercy on me, even though it be [by sending me] to the Fire.'"

Saith the Faqīh Abū Jaʿfar—on whom may Allah have mercy—: Muḥammad b. al-Faḍl has related to us, relating from Mu'ammal, relating from Ḥammād, from ʿAlī b. Zaid, from Abū Naḍra on his line of transmission from Ibn ʿAbbās—with whom may Allah be pleased—that the Apostle of Allah—upon whom be Allah's blessing and peace—said: "There has never been a Prophet but had [the promise of] one prayer that would assuredly be answered, and hastened [to have it fulfilled] in this world. I, however, held mine back to use it to intercede for my community on the Day. Am I not the *Sayyid*[1] of the children of Adam? Yet I boast not about that. Am I not the first over whom the earth will be rent? Yet I boast not about that. Shall I not on the Day bear in my hand the Standard of Praise,[2] under which Adam [will come to

[1] Master or Lord.

[2] A number of Traditions tell how when the Judgment is over, and creatures are to be

stand] as well as other men? Yet I do not boast about that." Then he said: "The grief and distress of the Day will keep growing more severe for men, so they will go to Adam—on whom be peace—saying to him: 'O father of mankind, make intercession for us to your Lord, that He may judge us.' But he will reply: 'I am not the one for that. I got driven out of Paradise because of my sin, so I can be occupied this day with none but myself. Go to Noah, for he was the first of the Messengers.' So they will go to Noah, saying: 'Make intercession for us to your Lord, that He may judge us.' But he will say: 'I am not the one for that. I prayed a prayer which brought about the drowning of the inhabitants of the earth, so I can be occupied this day with none but myself. Go to Abraham whom Allah took as a friend.' So they will go to Abraham, saying: 'Make intercession for us to your Lord, that He may judge us.' But he will say: 'I am not the one for that. I told three lies while professing Islam.'" Said the Apostle of Allah—upon whom be Allah's blessing and peace—: "They were three statements by uttering which he defended Allah's religion. The first of them was that to which Allah—exalted be He—refers (XXXVII, 88/86 ff.): 'He gave a look at the stars, and said, in truth I am sick.' The second was [when he said] (XXI, 63/64): 'Nay but this big one among them did it.' The third was his saying that his wife was his sister."[1] [The Tradition goes on]: "So I can be occupied today with none but myself. Go to Moses with whom Allah spoke as man to man.' So they will go to Moses, saying: 'Make intercession for us to your Lord, that He may judge us.' But he will answer: 'I am not the one for that. I wrongfully killed a man,[2] so I can be occupied today with none but myself. Go to Jesus, who is Allah's Spirit and His Word.'[3] So they will go to him and will say to him: 'Make intercession for us to your Lord, that He may judge us', But he will answer: 'I am not the one for that. I and my mother have been taken for two gods beside Allah, so I can be occupied today with none but myself. How does it seem to you? If anyone of you were to put some merchandise in a sack and then seal the sack, could he get at

---

sent to their eternal destiny, there will be various groups of them each with its standard bearer, who bears its standard or banner. The most important of all these banners will be the Standard of Praise. See pp. 331, 334.

[1] He pretended sickness in order to avoid participating in worship of the stars; when he smashed the idols he pretended that the big idol had done the smashing. The third lie is not mentioned in the Qur'ān but refers to the story in Gen. XX. In all these, however, he was supposed to be so speaking in order to defend True Islam.

[2] The reference is to the killing of the Egyptian who was beating the Israelite (Exod. II), a story which is mentioned in the Qur'ān in Sūra XXVIII, 15/14.

[3] Jesus is called the *rūḥ*, or Spirit of Allah, and His *kalima*, or Word in IV, 171/169.

what was in the sack without breaking the seal?' They will answer: 'No, indeed', and he will say: 'Verily, Muḥammad—upon whom be Allah's blessing and peace—is the one with whom the Prophetic succession was sealed. He has come to this day in which Allah has forgiven him his former and his latter sins.[1] Go to him.'" "Then", said the Apostle of Allah—upon whom be Allah's blessing and peace—"the people will come to me, and I shall reply: 'Assuredly! I am the one for it. I am the one for it', for Allah gives permission to whom He will and [to him with whom] He is well-pleased, and He delays as long as He wishes to delay. Then when Allah is ready to judge His creatures a herald will call: 'Where is Muḥammad—upon whom be Allah's blessing and peace—and his community?' Thus we, the last, will be the first." He means that they were the latest people in the world [to form a religious community], but they will be the first [to go up] for reckoning on the Day. "Then I and my community will arise, the [other] peoples will open a way for us, and we will move along all in white, glistening white as a consequence of our ritual purifications, so that the other peoples will say of us: 'This community seems almost to be made up of Prophets.' Then I shall advance to the Gate of Paradise and ask that it be opened. [The gate-keeper] will ask: 'Who is this?', and I will reply: 'I am Muḥammad, the Apostle of Allah.' At that he will open for me, I shall enter and fall down in obeisance before my Lord, and praise Him with such praises as none has ever used in praising Him before me, nor will any ever praise Him with such after me. Then the words will come: 'Raise your head. Speak and you will be heard. Ask and it will be given you. Intercede and your intercession will avail.' So I shall raise my head and intercede for everyone in my community in whose heart is a grain or an atom of faith." He means anyone who has unwavering belief *(yaqīn)*, and makes profession that there is no deity save Allah, and that Muḥammad is the Apostle of Allah.

It is related that ʿUmar b. al-Khaṭṭāb—with whom may Allah be pleased—once entered the mosque where Kaʿb al-Aḥbār was relating [religious tales] to the people. He said: "O Kaʿb, arouse our fears." So [Kaʿb] responded: "By Allah, there are with Allah angels who have been standing since the day He created them without ever bending their spines, and there are others doing obeisance without ever raising their heads, [and thus they will continue] till the blast is blown on the trumpet, ever saying in unison: 'Glory be to Thee, Allahumma, and all praise. We

[1] A reference to Sūra XLVIII, 2. Muḥammad is called "seal of the Prophets", in XXXIII, 40.

have not worshipped Thee as we ought to have worshipped nor as Thou hast a right to be worshipped.' By Him in whose hand is my soul, Gehenna will be brought near on the Day panting and braying *(zafīr wa shahīq)*,[1] until when it approaches and is quite near it will commence such a braying that there will be no Prophet or martyr who will not straightway fall down on his knees, and every Prophet, every just person *(ṣiddīq)*, every martyr will cry out: 'O Lord, I beg only for myself.' Abraham even will forget Ishmael and Isaac and will say: 'O Lord, it is I, Thy friend Abraham.' So, O son of al-Khaṭṭāb, were you to be on that Day in possession of the good works of seventy prophets you would still think that you would not escape." At this the people wept till they were choking. When ʿUmar—with whom may Allah be pleased—saw this, he said: "O Kaʿb, make us rejoice." Said Kaʿb: "Be of good cheer, for Allah has three hundred and thirteen ordinances *(sharīʿa)* and if a man appears on the Day with but one of them along with the word of sincere belief,[2] Allah will assuredly cause him to enter Paradise. By Allah, did ye know the reality of Allah's mercy—exalted be He—ye would not procrastinate about works."

O my brother, make preparation for such a Day as this by pious works and by avoiding acts of disobedience, for ere long you will come face to face with the Day of Resurrection when you will regret the days of your life that have passed away. Be it known to you that when you die your resurrection has virtually taken place. It is as al-Mughīra b. Shuʿba said: "Ye keep saying 'the Resurrection', 'the Resurrection', but the resurrection of each one of you is at his death."[3] It is recorded that ʿAlqama b. Qais attended a man's funeral and standing at his grave said: "Is it not a fact that this man has already had his resurrection?" His sole reason for saying this is [that he recognized] that when a man dies he has already come face to face with the matter of the Day of Judgment, because [in the grave] he will see Paradise and Hell and the angels, but will not be able to perform any works whatsoever, so he is in the same position as one who is present at the Day of Judgment. Death has put a seal on his works and he will rise on the Day in the same condition as he was when

[1] *zafīr* is said to be the sound produced by an ass when it commences to bray, and *shahīq* is the sound it makes when bringing the braying to an end. See p. 231.

[2] *kalimatu'l-ikhlāṣ*, i.e. the credal statement that there is no deity save Allah, and Muḥammad is the Apostle of Allah. The 313 ordinances are perhaps to be regarded as a reminiscence of the Jewish notion that the Torah contains 613 commandments.

[3] The reference is to the doctrine of a Double Judgment. There is a judgment passed on each individual immediately he dies, which is a forecast of the final judgment at the general resurrection.

he died, [neither better nor worse]. So blessed is he whose sealing up is with what is good.

Abū Bakr al-Wāsiṭī has said: "There are three victories, that of life, that of death and that of the Day. The victory of life is that one should live in obedience to Allah—exalted be He. The victory of death is that one's spirit should be drawn forth while he is repeating the *shahāda*, 'there is no deity save Allah', but the real victory, the victory of the Day, is the good-tidings when one is taken from one's grave and given the good-tidings of Paradise." It is recorded that Yaḥyā b. Mu'ādh ar-Rāzī—on whom may Allah have mercy—heard one recite at his assembly this verse (XIX, 85/88 ff.): "A Day when We shall gather the godfearing to the Merciful One like an embassy", that is, like a band of riders, "and drive sinners to Gehenna like a herd", that is, like a thirsty band on foot. Then he said: "O people, go gently, go gently! Tomorrow you will be at the Standing place, assembling, assembling! From the ends [of the earth] will ye be brought in, troop by troop. Ye will have to stand before Allah one by one. Ye will be questioned about your deeds, letter by letter. The saints will be led to the Merciful One, band by band. The disobedient will be driven to Allah's punishment, herd by herd, and will enter Gehenna, party by party. And all this when the earth has been pounded flat, bit by bit, and thy Lord has come with the angels, rank on rank (LXXXIX, 21/22 ff.), and Hell will be brought in on that Day, alas! alas!"

O my brethren, alas for you because of a Day whose duration is fifty thousand years (LXX, 4). It is the Day of Quaking (LXXIX, 6), the Day of Portending (LIII, 57/58), the Day of Resurrection, the Day of Sorrow and Regret. That is a dreadful day when men will arise to [meet] the Lord of the worlds. It is the Day of going into the particulars of the account, the Day of Reckoning, the Day of Weighing, the Day of Interrogation. It is the Day of the Quake (XXII, 1), the Day of the Shout (L, 42/41), the day of that which is due (LXIX, 1–3), the Day of the Striking (CI, 1), the Day of the Arousing (XXXV, 10). It is a day when a man will see what his hands have sent forward (LXXVIII, 40/41), the Day of the Overreaching (LXIV, 9), a day when folk will come forward separately to be shewn their works (XCIX, 6), a day when faces will be whitened and faces will be blackened (III, 106/102), a day when a patron will avail naught for a client (XLIV, 41), a day when their craftiness will profit them nothing (LII, 46), a day when no parent can make satisfaction for his offspring nor offspring make any satisfaction at all for his parent (XXXI, 33/32). It is a day whose evil is ready to fly abroad (LXXVI, 7), (i.e. is ready to spread abroad and scatter). It is a day when excuses will avail not the wrong-doers, but theirs will be the curse and the evil dwelling (XL, 52/55). It is a day when every soul will come to dispute in its own defence (cf. IV, 109), a day when every nursing mother will forget what she has nursed, when every pregnant female will cast her burden, when you will see men reeling drunkenly though they are not drunk, but the punishment of Allah is severe (XXII, 2).

Muqātil b. Sulaimān has said that on the Day creatures will stand for a hundred years in sweat up to their mouths, then for a hundred years in darkness, gravely perplexed, then for a hundred years they will rage before their Lord, quarrelling with one another. It is said that the duration of the Day is fifty thousand years, but for the true believer who is sincere it will pass like the passing of a single hour. So take heed, O man of intelligence, to bear with patience the distresses of this world, in obedience to Allah, that He may ease for you the distresses of the Last Day. Allah it is who aids to that which is right.

A description of the fire and its inhabitants

Saith the Faqīh Abū'l-Laith—on whom may Allah have mercy—: The Faqīh Abū Ja'far has related to us, relating from Muḥammad b. 'Aqīl al-Kindī, relating from al-'Abbās ad-Dūrī, relating from Yaḥyā b. Abī Bakr, who said: Sharīk has informed us on the authority of 'Āṣim, from aṣ-Ṣāliḥ, from Abū Huraira—with whom may Allah be pleased—that the Apostle of Allah—upon whom be Allah's blessing and peace— said: "The Fire was stoked for a thousand years till it became red. Then it was stoked for a thousand years till it became white. Then it was stoked for a thousand more years till it became black, so that it is black as the darkest night." It is related of Yazīd b. Marthad that his eyes were never free from tears for he was continually weeping. He was asked the reason for this, and he replied: "Were Allah to threaten me that if I committed sins He would shut me up in a bath-house for ever it would be right for me to weep continually, so how much the more when He has threatened to shut me up in a fire that has been stoked for three thousand years."

Saith the Faqīh—on whom may Allah have mercy—: Muḥammad b. Ja'far has related to us, saying: Ibrāhīm b. Yūsuf has related to us, saying: Abū Mu'āwiya has informed us on the authority of al-A'mash, from Mujāhid—with whom may Allah be pleased—who said: "In Gehenna are pits in which are snakes the size of Bactrian camels' necks, and scorpions the size of black mules. The Damned [1] are driven towards

[1] Lit. "the people of the Fire", i.e. those condemned to be in the Fire for ever.

these serpents who seize them by their lips and skin them from the hair [of their heads] to the nails [of their toes and fingers], and the only way they can escape from them is by rushing into the Fire." ʿAbdallah b. Jubair has related that the Prophet—upon whom be Allah's blessing and peace—said: "Truly in the Fire are snakes the size of camels' necks which sting [so viciously] that one stung by them will feel the burn thereof for forty years, and in it are scorpions the size of mules which also sting so that one stung by them will feel the burn for forty years." Al-Aʿmash has related from Zaid b. Wahb, from Ibn Masʿūd—with whom may Allah be pleased—that he said: "This [earthly] fire of yours is only one seventieth part of that Fire, which, were it to smite the sea twice would render it quite useless to you." Mujāhid said: "This [earthly] fire of yours takes refuge [with Allah] from the Fire of Gehenna." Said the Prophet—upon whom be Allah's blessing and peace—: "The weakest punishment a man has in the Fire is that of his feet, which are put into two sandals of fire, which cause his brains to boil like a copper cauldron, make his ears and molar teeth glow like live coals, and his entrails [melt and] flow out at his feet. He will think that he is the most cruelly tormented of the Damned, but really his is the weakest punishment."

[The Faqīh] saith: Muḥammad b. al-Faḍl has related to us, saying, Muḥammad b. Jaʿfar informed us, on the information of Ibrāhīm b. Yūsuf, on the information of Abū Ḥafṣ, from Saʿīd, from Qatāda, from Abū Ayyūb al-Azdī, from ʿAbdallah b. ʿAmr b. al-ʿĀṣ—with whom may Allah be pleased—that the Damned will supplicate Mālik,[1] but he will not answer them for forty years, and then he will reply to them: "Ye are to remain" (XLIII, 77), i.e. they are to continue there for ever. Then they will supplicate their Lord, saying: "Take us out of it, and if we return [to our evil ways] then indeed we are wrong-doers" (XXIII, 107/109), but He will give them no answer for twice as long as the duration of the world, and then will reply to them: "Be ye driven into it, and speak not to Me" (XXIII, 108/110). Said he: "By Allah, after that the people will not say a single word. Thereafter there is naught but a panting and braying *(zafīr wa shahīq)* in the Fire, their voices resembling the voices of asses which begin with a panting and finish on a braying." Qatāda said: "O people, is there any escape for you from this? Could you support this with fortitude? O people, obedience to Allah is easier for you, so be obedient to Him."

It is said that the Damned will fret impatiently for a thousand years,

[1] The angel set as Grand Chamberlain over the affairs of Hell. See p. 633.

but it will do them no good, so they will say: "In the world we used to get solace if we endured things patiently", so they will endure with patience for a thousand years, but it will not lighten the torment for them. Then they will say: "It is all the same whether we fret with impatience or patiently endure; there is no escape for us. Then for a thousand years they will beg from Allah—exalted be He—refreshing showers, because of their thirst and the severity of the torment, hoping to get relief from some of the heat and the thirst. When they have been making humble entreaty for a thousand years, Allah, exalted be He—will say to Gabriel: "What is it they are asking for?", and Gabriel will answer: "O Lord, Thou knowest best about them. They are asking for refreshing showers." Then there will appear to them a red cloud and they will think that they are going to have rain, but it will shower upon them scorpions the size of mules which will sting them so sorely that the pain thereof will not go from a man for a thousand years. Again they will pray to Allah—exalted be He—for a thousand years, [asking] Him to grant them the gift of refreshing showers. Then a black cloud will appear to them and they will say: "This is a rain cloud", but it will shower against them snakes the size of camels' necks, the pain from whose bite will not go from a man for a thousand years. This is the meaning of that saying of the Most High (XVI, 88/90): "We have added to them punishment on punishment because of their evil doing"; i.e. because of their unbelief and disobedience to Allah—exalted be He. So let him who wishes to escape Allah's punishment and attain His reward take heed to endure patiently the distresses of this world, in obedience to Allah—exalted be He—and avoiding acts of disobedience and worldly desires, for Paradise is set around with things men dislike and Hell is set around with things men desire.

Muḥammad b. al-Faḍl has related on his line of transmission from Muḥammad b. Ja'far, relating from Ibrāhīm b. Yūsuf, relating from Ismā'īl b. Ja'far, from Muḥammad b. 'Amr, from Abū Salama, from Abū Huraira, that the Prophet—upon whom be Allah's blessing and peace—said: "Allah—mighty and majestic is He—summoned Gabriel and sent him to Paradise, saying: 'Have a look at it and see what I have prepared therein for its people.' He came back and said: 'By Thy might, no one will hear about it but will enter it.' Then He surrounded it with disagreeable things and said: 'Go back to it and take another look.' [Gabriel] returned and said: 'By Thy might, now I am afraid that no one at all will enter it.' Then He sent him to the Fire, saying: 'Take a look at it, and what I have prepared therein for its people.' [Gabriel] returned to Him and said: 'By Thy might, no one who has heard about it will ever enter it.' Then [Allah] surrounded it with things men lust after, and said: 'Return to it and have another look at it.' When he came back he said: 'By Thy might and Thy majesty, I am afraid there is no one but will enter it.'" [It is related that] the Prophet—upon whom be Allah's blessing and peace—said: "Mention whatever you like about the Fire, and it will be much worse than anything you mention about it."

[Saith the Faqīh], my father has related to us, relating from al-'Abbās b. al-Faḍl al-Marwazī, relating from Mūsā b. Naṣr, from Muḥammad b. Ziyād, from Maimūn b. Mihrān, who said: "When Allah revealed this verse (XV, 43): 'Gehenna, indeed, is the place appointed for them all', Salmān put his hand on his head and ran out. He kept on running for three days, being unable to bear it, till they brought him back." Yazīd ar-Raqāshī has related from Anas b. Mālik that Gabriel came to the Prophet—upon whom be Allah's blessing and peace—at an unwonted hour and with a changed countenance. Said the Prophet—upon whom be Allah's blessing and peace—: "How is it that I see your countenance changed?" He answered: "O Muḥammad, I have come to you in that hour when Allah has given command that the bellows blow up the Fire. No man who knows that Gehenna is a reality, that the fire [therein] is a reality, that the torment of the tomb is a real thing and that Allah's punishment is even greater [than that], ought to be in tranquillity [1] till he is secure therefrom." Said the Prophet—upon whom be Allah's blessing and peace—: "O Gabriel, describe Gehenna to me." He replied: "Very well. When Allah—exalted be He—created Gehenna He had it stoked for a thousand years till it grew red. Then He had it stoked for another thousand years till it grew white. Then He had it stoked for another thousand years till it went black. So it is black as the darkest night, but its flames and its burning coals may never be put out. By Him who sent thee with the truth, were a space the size of a needle's eye to come open the heat therefrom would burn up the inhabitants of the earth to the last one. By Him who sent thee with the truth, were one of the garments of the people of Hell to be hung between heaven and earth the stench and the heat therefrom would kill off all the inhabitants of earth to the last man, so great would they find its heat. By Him who sent thee as a Prophet with the truth, were one cubit of that chain which Allah—exalted be He—has mentioned in His Book (LXIX, 32) laid upon a mountain it would melt all the way down through to the seventh earth. By Him who sent thee as a Prophet with the truth, were it to be punishing a man in

[1] Lit. "cool of eye". The parallel idiom, to be "hot of eye" refers to a state of restless anxiety.

the West a man in the East would be burned up by the violent [heat] of that punishing. Its heat is terrific, its bottom afar, its ornaments are of iron, its drink is *ḥamīm* and *ṣadīd*,[1] its garments are cut out of fire. It has seven gates [2] for each of which is separated out a sector of men and women." Said [the Prophet]—upon whom be Allah's blessing and peace—: "Are they like our gates?" [Gabriel] answered: "No! they open one below the other, gate after gate, between them a seventy years' journey, and each gate is seventy times hotter than that which preceded it. Allah's enemies are driven to it and as they reach its gate the Zabāniyya [3] meet them with fetters and chains. The chain is inserted into a man's mouth and brought out at his rectum. His left hand is fettered to his neck and his right hand is thrust through his heart and pulled out between his shoulders where it is fastened with chains. Moreover every human will be chained to a satan. He will be dragged on his face while angels beat him with iron cudgels. Whenever in their distress they try to get out of it they will be sent back into it." Said the Prophet—upon whom be Allah's blessing and peace—: "Who are the dwellers in these gates?" (i.e. these seven stages of Hell to which the seven gates give entrance). [Gabriel] answered: "The lowest section has in it the hypocrites, those of the People of the Table who disbelieved,[4] and the people of Pharaoh's household. Its name is Hāwiya.[5] The second section [from the bottom] has in it the polytheists. Its name is Jaḥīm.[6] The third section has in it the Ṣābians. Its name is Saqar.[7] The fourth section has in it Iblīs and his followers, and the Magians. Its name is Laẓā.[8] The fifth section has the Jews in it. It is called al-Ḥuṭama.[9] The sixth section has the Christians in it. Its name is Sa'īr."[10] At this point Gabriel held back out of respect for

[1] *ḥāmīm* is said to mean scalding water (LXXVIII, 25), and *ṣadīd* (XIV, 69) is said to mean purulent matter.

[2] So Sūra XV, 44. Gate, in this Tradition, stands for "stage".

[3] They are the infernal attendants on Mālik. See pp. 23, 24. The fetters and the chains are mentioned in XL, 71/73.

[4] When people asked Jesus to have his Lord send down a table to them, the table was sent, and Allah said (Sūra V, 115) that those who disbelieved after it was sent down would be punished by Him as He had punished no one else in all the worlds. That is why this Tradition puts them in the lowest Hell. Sūra IV, 145/144 puts the hypocrites there, and XL, 46/49 suggests that it is the place for Pharaoh's household.

[5] The name is drawn from CI, 9/6.

[6] LXIX, 30, 31.

[7] LIV, 48; LXXIV, 26 ff. The Ṣābians are mentioned in II, 62/59; V, 69/73; XXII, 17.

[8] LXX, 15. The Magians are the Zoroastrians. They are mentioned in XXII, 17.

[9] The name is derived from Sūra CIV, 4, 5.

[10] Meaning "the blaze". The word occurs in IV, 10/11 and XXXIII, 64, etc. Gabriel is using the present tense but he means, of course, that the Jews and Christians and others will be in these sections after the Judgment.

the Apostle of Allah—upon whom be Allah's blessing and peace—, but he—upon whom be Allah's blessing and peace—said: "Are you not going to inform me about the dwellers in the seventh [or uppermost] section?" So he replied: "In it are those of your community who have committed the mortal sins and have died without having repented." At this the Prophet—upon whom be Allah's blessing and peace—fell down in a swoon, but Gabriel set his (i.e. the Prophet's) head on his own breast until he recovered. When he had recovered he said: "O Gabriel, great is my affliction and violent is my grief. Can it be that any of my community will enter the Fire?" "Yes", said he, "those of your community who are guilty of mortal sins." At that the Apostle of Allah—upon whom be Allah's blessing and peace—wept, and Gabriel also wept. Then the Apostle of Allah—upon whom be Allah's blessing and peace—entered his dwelling and kept aloof from the people, not going out save to the prayer services, where he would say prayers and enter [his dwelling again] without speaking to anyone. [Within the house] he betook himself to prayers and weeping and making humble entreaty to Allah. On the third day Abū Bakr—with whom may Allah be pleased—approached and stood at the door, saying: "Salaam to you, O people of the house of mercy. Is there any way to reach the Apostle of Allah—upon whom be Allah's mercy and peace?" No one answered him, so he went away weeping. Then 'Umar—with whom may Allah be pleased—approached and stood at the door, saying: "Salaam to you, O people of the house of mercy. Is there any way to reach the Apostle of Allah—upon whom be Allah's blessing and peace?" No one answered him, so he went away, and he also wept. Then Salmān the Persian approached and stood at the door, saying: "Salaam to you, O people of the house of mercy. Is there any way to reach my Lord, the Apostle of Allah—upon whom be Allah's blessing and peace?" No one answered him, so he came along weeping, now falling down and now rising again till he came to Fāṭima's house. There he stood at the door and said: "Salaam to thee, O daughter of the Apostle of Allah—upon whom be Allah's blessing and peace." At that time [her husband] 'Alī—with whom may Allah be pleased—was away from home, so he said: "O daughter of the Apostle of Allah, verily the Apostle of Allah—upon whom be Allah's blessing and peace—keeps himself aloof from the people, going not out save for the prayers, neither speaking to anyone nor permitting anyone to enter to him." Fāṭima thereupon put on a striped woollen cloak for walking and made her way till she stood at the door of the Apostle of Allah—upon whom be Allah's blessing and peace—where she salaamed and said: "O Apostle of Allah, it is I, thy daughter Fāṭima." The Apostle of Allah was [at that moment] doing obeisance, weeping, but he raised his head and said: "Why is Fāṭima, the coolness of my eyes, kept away from me? Open the door to her." So the door was opened for her and she entered. When she looked upon the Apostle of Allah—upon whom be Allah's blessing and peace—she wept bitterly at seeing him so pale and so changed [so that it was] as though the flesh of his face had melted through grief and weeping. She said: "O Apostle of Allah, what has come upon you?" He answered: "O Fāṭima, Gabriel came to me, describing to me the stages of Gehenna, and informing me that in the uppermost of them are those of my community who have been guilty of mortal sins. It is that which has made me weep and been the cause of my grief." She said: "O Apostle of Allah, how could they [possibly] enter it?" He replied: "Yea, indeed, angels will drag them to the Fire, but their faces will not be made black, nor their eyes made blue, their mouths will not be sealed up, and they will not be bound with satans, nor will they have the chains and fetters put on them." She asked: "O Apostle of Allah, how will the angels drag them?" He replied: "The men by their beards, the women by their plaits and their forelocks. How many a greyhead of my community will be seized by his beard and dragged to the Fire, crying: 'Alas for the hoary [head]! Alas for the feeble [knees]!' How many a young man will be seized by the beard and driven to the Fire, crying: 'Alas for youthful [strength]! Alas for fair countenance!' How many a woman of my community will be seized by her forelock and dragged to the Fire, crying: 'Alas what ignominy! Alas what dishonour and what shame!' [This will go on] till they are brought before Mālik. When Mālik looks at them he will say to the angels: 'Who are these? No unfortunates have ever been brought before me in so strange a state as these. Their faces have not been made black nor their eyes made blue; their mouths have not been stopped up and they are not bound to satans; nor have fetters or chains been put on their necks.' So the angels will make reply: 'This is the state in which we were bidden bring them before you.' Then Mālik will say: 'O body of unfortunates, who are ye?'"

Another Tradition has it that as the angels drive them along they will keep crying out: "O Muḥammad!", but when they see Mālik, from terror of him they will forget the name of Muḥammad—upon whom be Allah's blessing and peace. So he will say to them: "Who are you?" To which they will reply: "We are those to whom the Qur'ān was sent. We are those who used to fast during Ramaḍān." Then Mālik will say: "The Qur'ān was sent down to the community of Muḥammad—upon whom be Allah's blessing and peace." When they hear the name Muḥammad they will cry aloud, saying: "We are the community of Muḥammad —upon whom be Allah's blessing and peace." So Mālik will say to them: "Did you not have in the Qur'ān warning to abstain from disobedience to Allah—exalted be He?" Then when they are made to stand on the brink of Gehenna and look at the Fire and the Zabāniyya, they will say: "O Mālik, give us permission to weep for ourselves." He will give them permission, and they will weep tears till no more tears remain, when they will weep blood. Mālik will say: "How beautiful is this weeping! Would that it had taken place in the world! Had this weeping been done in the world out of fear of Allah, the Fire would not have had possession of you today." Then Mālik will say to the Zabāniyya: "Cast them down into the Fire." When they are cast into the Fire they will with one accord cry out: "There is no deity save Allah", whereat the Fire will recoil from them. So Mālik will say: "O Fire, seize them", but it will reply: "How can I seize them when they are saying that there is no deity save Allah?" Again Mālik will say to the Fire: "Seize them", but again it will reply: "How can I seize them while they are saying that there is no deity save Allah?" Then Mālik will say: "Yes, but the Lord of the Throne has given command for that", and then the Fire will take hold upon them. There are some of them it will take hold of up to their feet, others up to their knees, others up to their waists, others up to their throats, but when the Fire wants [to seize] their faces Mālik will say: "Burn not their faces for often in the world they were prostrated in obeisance to the Merciful, and burn not their hearts for often did they thirst in the month of Ramaḍān."

They will remain in [Gehenna] for such a period as Allah pleases, saying [continually]: "O most merciful of those who show mercy! O all-Merciful! O Benevolent One!" When Allah has carried out His judgment [on them] He will say: "O Gabriel, how are the disobedient of the community of Muḥammad—upon whom be Allah's blessing and peace—doing?" To which he will reply: "Allahumma, Thou knowest best about them." Then He will say: "Go and have a look at the state they are in." So Gabriel—upon whom be peace—will go to Mālik, who is on a *minbar* of fire in the midst of Gehenna. When Mālik sees Gabriel —upon whom be peace—he will rise out of respect for him, and will say: "O Gabriel, what brings you to enter this place?" He will answer: "What have you done with the troop of disobedient ones from Muḥammad's community?" Mālik will say: "How dreadful is their condition! How straitened is their place! Their bodies have been burned and their flesh devoured, all save their faces and their hearts in which faith is shining."

Then Gabriel will say: "Lift for me the cover from over them that I may look at them." So Mālik will give command to the warders *(khazana)* who will lift the cover from over them. When they see Gabriel in all the beauty of his form they will recognize that he is not one of the angels of chastisement, so they will say: "Who is this servant, more beautiful than anyone we have ever seen?" Mālik will answer: "This is Gabriel, who has an honourable position with his Lord, and who used to bring revelations to Muḥammad—upon whom be Allah's blessing and peace." When they hear the name of Muḥammad—upon whom be Allah's blessing and peace—mentioned, with one accord they will cry aloud and say: "O Gabriel, give Muḥammad—upon whom be Allah's blessing and peace—greeting from us, inform him that our acts of disobedience have separated us from him, and tell him in what a dreadful condition we are." So Gabriel will go off and take his stand before Allah—exalted be He. Allah—exalted be He—will ask: "And how did you see Muḥammad's community?'" He will answer: "O Lord, how dreadful is their state! how straitened is their place!" [Allah] will say: "Did they ask you for anything?" He will reply: "Yes, O Lord, they asked me to give greeting for them to their Prophet and inform him of their dreadful condition." Then Allah—exalted be He—will say: "Well, go and inform him." So Gabriel will go off to the Prophet—upon whom be Allah's blessing and peace—whom [he will find] in a tent made of a white pearl with four thousand doors each with two golden *miṣrā'*.[1] He will say: "O Muḥammad, I have come to you from the troop of disobedient ones of your community who are being punished in the Fire, who give you greeting and say: 'How dreadful is our condition! how straitened is our place!'" Then Muḥammad—upon whom be Allah's blessing and peace—will go to a place beneath the Throne and fall down doing obeisance. There he will eulogize Allah—exalted be He—with such eulogies as no one has ever eulogized Him before, and Allah—exalted be He—will say: "Raise your head. Ask and it will be given you. Intercede and your intercession will be effective." Then he will say: "O Lord, the unfortunate ones of my community. Thy judgment on them has been fulfilled. Thou hast taken vengeance on them. Accept now my intercession for them." So Allah—exalted be He—will say: "I have accepted your intercession for them, so go to the Fire and draw out therefrom whosoever will say: 'There is no deity save Allah.'" Thereupon the Prophet—upon whom be Allah's blessing and peace—will make his way [there]. When Mālik sees

[1] That is it is a folding door with two valves hinged on either side, which is entered by forcing the valves *(miṣrā')* apart where they come together in the middle.

the Prophet—upon whom be Allah's blessing and peace—he will rise up out of reverence for him. He will say: "O Mālik, what is the condition of the unfortunates of my community?", to which [Mālik] will answer: "How dreadful is their condition! how straitened is their place!" Then Muḥammad—upon whom be Allah's blessing and peace—will say: "Open the gate and raise the cover." When the inhabitants of Hell [1] see Muḥammad—upon whom be Allah's blessing and peace—with one accord they will cry aloud, saying: "O Muḥammad, the Fire has burned our skins, it has burned our livers." Then he will draw them all out, but alas! they will have become coals, eaten indeed by the Fire. So he will lead them to a river hard by the gate of Paradise called the "River of Life", in which they will wash and from which they will emerge youths, beardless but with kohled eyes, their faces like the moon, but on their foreheads will be written: "The Gehenna folk: emancipated by the Merciful from the Fire." Then they will enter the Garden. When the [other] inhabitants of Hell see that the Muslims have been withdrawn therefrom they will say: "Would that we had been Muslims, for then we too might have been withdrawn from the Fire." This is what the Most High has said (XV, 2): "Maybe those who have disbelieved will wish: 'Would that we had been Muslims.'"

It is related that the Apostle of Allah—upon whom be Allah's blessing and peace—said: "Death will be brought in as though he were a black and white ram, and the question will be asked: 'O inhabitants of Paradise, do you recognize death?' They will look at him and recognize him, whereupon the question will be asked: 'O inhabitants of Hell, do you recognize death?' They too will look at him and recognize him, whereupon he will be slaughtered between Paradise and Hell. Then a voice will come: 'O inhabitants of Paradise, [it is] eternal, death is no more. O inhabitants of Hell, [it is] eternal, death is no more.'" That is the saying of the Most High (XIX, 39/40): "Warn them of the day of sighing, when the affair will be decided." Abū Huraira—with whom may Allah be pleased—said: "Let not a profligate fellow feel content with any pleasure [he is having], for behind him is a greedy seeker", that is Gehenna, [of which Allah has said (XVII, 97/99)]: "Whenever it dies down We increase for them the blaze", but Allah—praised and exalted be He—knows best.

A description of the Garden and its inhabitants

Saith [the Faqīh]: Muḥammad b. al-Faḍl has related to us, relating from

[1] The phrase *ahl an-nār*, "people of the fire", is quite general but apparently it means here only the Muslims who are in the topmost stage of Gehenna.

Muḥammad b. Jaʿfar, relating from Ibrāhīm b. Yūsuf, relating from Muḥammad b. Yaḥyā b. al-Faḍl, from Ḥamza b. az-Ziyād the Kūfan, from Ziyād aṭ-Ṭā'ī, from Abū Huraira—with whom may Allah be pleased—who said: "We asked: 'O Apostle of Allah, of what was Paradise created?', and he answered: 'From water.' We said: 'Tell us about the construction of Paradise.' He answered: 'A brick of gold, then a brick of silver, the mortar for it being of the finest musk. Its dust is of saffron, its pebbles are of pearl and jacinth. Whosoever enters it will lead a joyous life which knows no despair, and will live there eternally for he will never die. His clothes will not wear out, nor will his youthfulness fade away.' Then the Prophet—upon whom be Allah's blessing and peace—said: 'There are three whose supplication will not be rejected, viz. a just Imām, a faster when he comes to break his fast, and the supplication of one who has been wronged, for [the supplication of] this latter rises above the clouds, so that the Lord—majestic is He—sees it and says: 'By My might and My majesty, I shall certainly give thee aid, even though after some time.'"

Muḥammad b. al-Faḍl has related to us, relating from Muḥammad b. Jaʿfar, relating from Ibrāhīm b. Yūsuf, relating from Ismāʿīl b. Jaʿfar, from Muḥammad b. ʿAmr from Abū Salama, from Abū Huraira—with whom may Allah be pleased—that the Prophet—upon whom be Allah's blessing and peace—said: "In Paradise there is a tree in whose shade a rider could ride for a hundred years without getting out of it. Recite if you will: 'and shade extended' (LVI, 30/29). In Paradise there is what eye has not seen, what ear has not heard, what has not even occurred to the heart of man. Recite if you will: 'no soul knows the consolation which is secretly laid up for them' (XXXII, 17). Verily a place the size of a whip-lash in Paradise is better than this world and all that is in it. Recite if you will: 'he who escapes the Fire and is brought into the Garden, he indeed, enjoys felicity' (III, 185/182)." It is related of Ibn ʿAbbās—with whom may Allah be pleased—that he used to say: "In Paradise are dark-eyed maidens [of the kind] called *luʿba*,[1] who have been created from four things, from musk, ambergris, camphor and saffron, stirred into a dough with water of life. The Mighty One said to these: 'Be!', and they were. All the Ḥūrīs love them dearly. Were one of them to spit into the ocean its waters would become sweet. On the throat of each of them is written: 'He who would desire to have the like of me, let him do works of obedience to my Lord.'" Mujāhid said that the ground of Paradise is of

[1] The word means a "plaything", "toy", "puppet".

silver, its dust of musk, the trunks of its trees are of silver, their branches of pearl and emerald, their leaves and fruits hang low so that he who would eat standing can reach them, and likewise he who would eat sitting or even lying can reach them. Then he recited (LXXVI, 14): "Its fruit clusters hang low", i.e. its fruits are near so that both he who is standing and he who is sitting can reach them. Abū Huraira—with whom may Allah be pleased—said: "By Him who sent down the Book to Muḥammad—upon whom be Allah's blessing and peace—the dwellers in Paradise increase in beauty and handsomeness as in this world they increase in decrepitude."

Ibrāhīm b. Aḥmad has related to us, relating from al-Ḥasan b. Naṣr, relating from Asad b. Mūsā, relating from Ḥammād b. Salama, from Thābit al-Bunānī, from 'Abd ar-Raḥmān b. Abī Lailā, from Ṣuhaib, that the Apostle of Allah—upon whom be Allah's blessing and peace—said: "When the Blessed have entered Paradise, and the Damned have entered the Fire, a herald will call: 'O ye inhabitants of the Garden, ye have a promise with Allah which He wishes to fulfil to you.' They will say: 'What can it be? Has He not made heavy our balances, made white our faces, brought us into Paradise, and saved us from Hell?' Then the Veil will be withdrawn and they will look upon Him, and by Him in whose hand is my soul, no gift He gives them is more precious to them than this look at Him." Anas b. Mālik—with whom may Allah be pleased—said that Gabriel came to the Prophet—upon whom be Allah's blessing and peace—with a white mirror on which was a black spot. Said the Prophet—upon whom be Allah's blessing and peace—: "O Gabriel, what is this white mirror?" "It is Friday", he replied, "And the black spot is the Hour, which will arrive on a Friday. Thereby you and your community are honoured above those who preceded you, for on it people will have to follow you." He means the Jews and the Christians. "In it there is an hour when no believer will ask Allah—exalted be He—for any good without Allah answering him, not seek refuge from any evil without Allah giving him refuge therefrom. Among us it is called the Day of Increase." The Apostle of Allah—upon whom be Allah's blessing and peace—asked: "What is the Day of Increase?" He replied: "Verily, thy Lord will choose a valley in al-Firdaus [1] in which are hillocks of musk. When Friday comes it will be set around with minbars of light for the Prophets, with minbars of gold set with rubies

[1] Firdaus is one of the stages of Paradise, some say the highest stage. The word itself is the Arabic form of our word "Paradise". See p. 63.

and emeralds for the just,[1] the martyrs and the righteous. Then the dwellers in the Upper Chambers *(ghuraf)* will descend and sit behind them on the hillocks, all being gathered unto their Lord, praising and eulogizing Him. Then Allah—exalted be He—will say to them: "Ask of Me." They will answer: "We ask that Thou shouldst be well-pleased [with us]." He will say: "I am well-pleased with you. It is My being well-pleased with you that has given you the freedom of My dwelling-place and has brought you to My consideration." Then He will reveal Himself to them so that they may see Him. Thus there is no day more precious to them than Friday, the day when He increases [the token of] His regard for them.

In another Tradition it is related that Allah—exalted be He—will say to His angels: "Feed My saints", whereupon various kinds of food will be brought, in every bite of which they will find a different pleasure from that which they found in any other. When they have had their fill of eating, Allah—exalted be He—will say: "Give My servants drink", whereupon drinks will be brought, in every sip of which they will find a different pleasure from that which they found in any other. When they have finished, Allah—exalted be He—will say to them: "I am your Lord. I have made My promise to you come true. Now ask of Me and I will give it you." They will reply: "O our Lord, we ask that Thou shouldst be well-pleased [with us]." This they will say two or three times, whereupon He will say: "I am well-pleased with you, but today I have an increase. I shall favour you with a token of regard greater than all that." Then the Veil will be removed and they will look upon Him for such a period as Allah wills. Then they will fall on their faces in a prostration [of obeisance], remaining prostrated for such a time as Allah pleases, whereat He will say to them: "Raise your heads. This is no place for worshipping." At that they will quite forget all the other enjoyment they have been having, for to see [their Lord] will be to them the most precious of all their joys. Then they will depart, and [as they move away] a breeze will blow from beneath the Throne across a hill of white musk scattering that musk on their heads and on the manes of their horses. When they get back to their households their spouses will notice that their beauty and splendour are greater than when they left them, so their spouses will say: "You have returned more handsome than you were [when you went]."

Saith the Faqīh—on whom may Allah have mercy—: When he speaks

[1] In many Traditions the just *(ṣiddīqūn)* and the righteous *(ṣāliḥūn)* are treated as specially honoured groups in the After Life, in much the same way as the martyrs are.

about the Veil being lifted he means the veil which is over them,[1] i.e. the screen which prevents them from seeing Him. As for his statement that they will look upon Him, some say [it means] that that they will look on a token of His regard such as they had not previously seen. Most of the learned, however, say that it is to be taken according to its surface meaning, and that they will actually see Him, though we know not how, save that it will not be in any anthropomorphic manner, just as here on earth they know Him but not in an anthropomorphic manner.

ʿIkrima has said that the Blessed, both men and women, will be as youths aged three and thirty, their stature will be sixty cubits, which was the stature of their father Adam—on whom be peace. They will be youthful, hairless,[2] with kohled eyes, each provided with seventy garments every one of which will change its colour seventy times each hour. Each will [be able to] see his face in her face, i.e. in the face of his spouse, in her chest and in her leg, and she will [be able to] see her face in his face and chest and leg. They will not [have any need to] spit or blow their noses, still less to commit any of the more indecorous acts. In the Traditions it is recorded that were a female among the inhabitants of Paradise to thrust her hand through the sky vault it would light up all that is between heaven and earth.

The sage Abū'l-Faḍl al-Ḥaddādī has related to us, relating from Muḥammad b. Yaḥyā al-Marwazī, relating from Muḥammad b. Nāfiʿ an-Naisābūrī, relating from Muṣʿab al-Karrām, relating from Dāwūd aṭ-Ṭā'ī, from al-Aʿmash, from Thumāma b. ʿUqba, from Zaid b. Arqam, who said: "There came a man of the People of the Book to the Prophet—upon whom be Allah's blessing and peace—and said: "O Abū'l-Qāsim,[3] do you pretend that the inhabitants of the Garden eat and drink?" "Surely", he replied, "by Him in whose hand is my soul, every one of them will be given the capacity of a hundred men in eating and drinking and coition." Said [the man]: "But one who eats and drinks has a need, whereas Paradise is too fine a place for there to be in it anything so malodorous." [Muḥammad] replied: "A man's need there will be satisfied by perspiring, which will be as odoriferous as musk."

[1] In the older Islamic texts it is quite clear that the thought was of a Veil (or a series of veils, for some said there were 70,000 of them), which veiled Allah from the sight of the angels. The Faqih is here suggesting a more sophisticated theory according to which the veil is over them not over Allah.

[2] The reference is to superfluous hair which Muslims are accustomed to remove from the body, but which they will not have to trouble about in Paradise for it will not appear on their bodies.

[3] See p. 93.

Muḥammad b. al-Faḍl has related to us on his line of transmission from Abū Muʿāwiya, from al-Aʿmash, from Abū'l-Ashras, from Muʿattib b. Sumaiy, regarding the words of Allah, exalted be He (XIII, 29/28): "Happiness *(ṭūbā)* for them and a fine place of resort." Ṭūbā,[1] he said, is a tree in Paradise, [so huge] that there is no dwelling therein but is shaded by one or other of its branches. It has fruits of various kinds, and on it alight birds the size of Bactrian camels. Should anyone [of the Blessed] desire [to eat of] one of these birds he merely summons it and it will fall on his tray [cooked in such a fashion] that he may eat from one side of it boiled [2] meat and from the other roasted, then [when he has finished] it will become a bird again and depart. Al-Aʿmash has related from Abū Ṣāliḥ, from Abū Huraira—with whom may Allah be pleased—that the Prophet—upon whom be Allah's blessing and peace—said: "The first batch of my community to enter Paradise will be like the moon on the night of its fullness. Then those who follow next will be like the brightest stars in heaven, then after that in [various] degrees *(manāzil)*. They will not urinate, nor defecate, nor spit, nor blow their noses. Their hair combs will be of gold, their censers [3] of aloes-wood, and what they give off in perspiration will be musk. They will all be the same size, sixty cubits tall like their father Adam—on whom be peace."

Ibn ʿAbbās—with whom may Allah be pleased—has related that the Apostle of Allah—upon whom be Allah's blessing and peace—said: "The inhabitants of Paradise will be youthful, hairless, beardless, having no hair save on their heads and their eyebrows and eyelashes. They will be fringeless, that is, having no pubic hair and no hair under the arms. They will be of the stature of their father Adam, sixty cubits, the age of Jesus son of Mary, which was thirty-three, white of colour and wearing green garments. One of them has only to place a table before himself when a bird will approach and say: 'O Saint of Allah, have I not drunk from the fountain Salsabīl [4] and fed in the meadows of Paradise beneath

[1] *ṭūbā* is a word borrowed from the Syriac. Muḥammad used this word which he had doubtless heard used by the People of the Book with whom he was in contact, but later Muslims, not understanding the word, invented this explanation that it is the name of the huge celestial tree which appears in the eschatological picture of the earlier religions. See p. 395.

[2] Lit. "shredded", i.e. boiled so well that it comes away easily in shreds. The word used for "tray" is *khuwān*, which is a Persian word for a tray with little feet such as is commonly used for serving food.

[3] A *mijmara* is a little vessel for fumigation, and the meaning here is that its coals will be fed with aloes-wood.

[4] A spring in Paradise mentioned in Sūra LXXVI, 18. Some say that it is one of the two springs mentioned in LV, 50.

the Throne, eating of its fruits? so the taste [of the flesh] on one side [of me] is that of boiled meat and that on the other side is of roasted meat.' He will eat of it what he pleases. Every such saint will have seventy garments each of a different colour. On their fingers they will have ten seal-rings. On the first [seal] will be inscribed: 'Peace be upon thee for the patient endurance thou hast shown' (XIII, 24). On the second will be: 'Enter then in peace and in all security' (XV, 46). On the third will be: 'That is the Garden which ye have been given as an inheritance for what ye have been doing' (XLIII, 72). On the fourth will be: 'Removed from you are [all] griefs and anxiety.' On the fifth will be: 'We have clothed you with ornaments and vestments.' On the sixth will be: 'As spouses We have given you the Ḥūrīs' (cf. LII, 20). On the seventh will be: 'Therein for you is whatever the souls desire, whatever delights the eyes, and therein shall ye be for ever' (cf. XLIII, 71). On the eighth will be: 'Ye have matched the prophets and the just persons.' On the ninth will be: 'Ye have become youths who will never grow old.' On the tenth will be: 'Ye are dwelling as neighbours to One who harms not [His] neighbours.'"

Saith the Faqīh—on whom may Allah have mercy—: He who desires to attain these blessings must set himself sedulously to five things: (1) to restrain his soul from all acts of disobedience. Allah—exalted be He—has said (LXXIX, 40, 41): "and restrained the soul from desire; verily the Garden will be his dwelling-place"; (2) to be content with but little of this world, for in the Traditions it is said: "Abandonment of this world is the price of Paradise"; (3) to be eager to do acts of obedience, holding fast to every act of obedience, for maybe that act will be the ground for his forgiveness and his making sure of Paradise. Allah has said (XLIII, 72): "That is the Garden which ye have been given as an inheritance for what ye have been doing." Also in another verse He says (LVI, 24/23): "A recompense for what they have been doing." The only reason for their attaining what they have attained was their acts of obedience;[1] (4) to love pious folk and good people, mix with them and sit in their company, for any one of such when he has been pardoned may make intercession for his friends and his brethren. Thus it is related that the Prophet—upon whom be Allah's blessing and peace—said: "Make many brethren, for every such brother will have an intercession [he may use] on the Day"; (5) to make frequent supplication, asking Allah—exalted

[1] As acts of disobedience have evil recompense so acts of obedience will have a good recompense.

be He—to grant him the good gift of Paradise and make his ending a good one.

One of the sages has said: "To rely on this world in spite of the recompense to be faced is foolish. To give up being diligent in works when one knows what their recompense is is [to show oneself] an incompetent. In the Garden there is a rest that will not be found save by those who know no rest in this world, and in it there are riches that will not be found save by those who have abandoned the excesses of this world, limiting themselves to its simple things." It is related that a certain ascetic used to eat naught but greens and salt without any bread. Someone said to him: "So you have limited yourself to this?" ["Yes"], he replied, "the fact is that I have exchanged this world for Paradise, but you have exchanged this world for a dung-heap." What he meant was: "You feed on the good things [of the world], so you are for the dung-heap, but I eat [only enough to enable me] to perform the [required] acts of obedience that maybe I may come to the Garden."

It is told of Ibrāhīm b. Adham—on whom may Allah have mercy—that he wanted to enter the public baths, but the bath-keeper stopped him, saying: "You cannot enter without paying a fee." Ibrāhīm wept and said: "Allahumma, they will not give me permission to enter the dwelling of satans [1] without payment, so how am I ever going to enter without payment the dwelling-place of prophets and just persons?" Recorded in one of the revelations sent down by Allah—exalted be He—to one of His Prophets—on whom be peace—[are the words]: "O child of Adam, thou dost purchase the Fire at a high price, but wilt not purchase the Garden at a cheap price." The interpretation of this is that an evil doer who wants to offer hospitality for some evil purpose will pay out a hundred or two hundred [dinars] for it and think nothing of it, though he is really purchasing the Fire at that high price, but should he have to offer hospitality for Allah's sake at [the cost of] a dirham or two, and some of the destitute are summoned there, he would think that a grievous thing, though it is the price of Paradise.

It is related that Abū Ḥāzim said: "Were entrance to Paradise to be [gained] only by giving up all that one loves of this world that would be easy, and were escape from Hell to be [secured] only by putting up with all that is disagreeable to one that would be easy, so how then when Paradise may be gained by giving up only a thousandth part of what one loves, and when Hell may be escaped by putting up with only a thousandth

[1] It is commonly believed that the public baths are one of the favourite resorts of the satans (*shayāṭīn*).

part of that which one finds disagreeable?" Yaḥyā b. Muʿādh ar-Rāzī said: "To give up this world is hard, but to give up Paradise is still harder, yet giving up this world is the dowry [1] for Paradise." From Anas b. Mālik—with whom may Allah be pleased—[comes the Tradition] that the Prophet—upon whom be Allah's blessing and peace—said: "Whosoever asks Allah—exalted be He—for Paradise three times, saying: 'The Garden, Allahumma!' will assuredly enter Paradise, and whosoever seeks protection from Hell three times, saying: 'The Fire, Allahumma!' He will protect from Hell." So let us ask Allah—exalted be He—to protect us from the Fire and cause us to enter the Garden. Were there no delight in Paradise beyond that of meeting one's brethren and foregathering with them that would be excellent enjoyment, so how will it be when [we find] in it all the varieties of blessedness that there are there?

Anas b. Mālik relates that the Prophet—upon whom be Allah's blessing and peace—said: "In Paradise there are market-places in which nothing is bought or sold. Folk will gather there group by group and reminisce on how things used to be in this world, how there used to be services of worship for the worship of the Lord, how this world had its poor and its rich, how folk used to die, and how after decomposition they reached Paradise." A trustworthy person has told us on his line of transmission from Asbāṭ, from as-Suddī, from Abū Murra, that Ibn Masʿūd—with whom may Allah be pleased—said: "All people will be sent to the Bridge after they have been standing around the Fire, and will cross the Bridge according to their works. There are some who will cross like lightning, some who will cross like the wind, some will cross [as swiftly] as a bird, others as [fast as] a fine horse, others like a fine camel, but some will cross like a man running, and last of all a man walking on the big toes of his feet, whom presently the Bridge shakes off. The Bridge is slippery, unstable, sharper than a sword-edge, fitted with prickles like the thorns of a tragacanth bush, and on both its sides [stand] angels armed with fiery prongs wherewith they snatch at the people. Some there are who cross safely, but some get across all lacerated, and there are others who fall all torn into the Fire. Meanwhile the angels are saying: 'O Lord, save! save!'. Finally there will cross over that man who is the last to find entrance to Paradise. When he has got across the Bridge he sees from afar a gate of Paradise, but he does not see any place for him in the Garden when he looks in, so he will say: 'O Lord, let me stay here.' [Allah] will reply to him: 'But if I let you stay

[1] *mahr*, the common word for the "bride price", which is an essential item in the arrangements for a Muslim marriage.

here maybe you will be asking Me for some other place.' 'Nay, by Thy might!', he will say, so He will let him stay there. Then from afar he will notice the stages *(manāzil)* of Paradise, and what he has been given will seem contemptible in comparison with what he sees, so he will say: 'O Lord, set me down there.' [Allah] will reply: 'But if I set you down there you will be asking Me for some other place.' 'Nay, by Thy might', he will say, so He will set him down there. Then he will see afar off the fourth heaven, and when he sees the fourth heaven, even from afar, everything he has been given will seem contemptible to him, but he will hold his peace and ask for nothing. [Allah] will say: 'Are you not asking for anything?', and he will reply: 'I did ask, till I was ashamed.' Then Allah will say: 'What you have is ten times as much as all the world.' Yet that man is the one who has the humblest place in Paradise." ʿAbdallah b. Masʿūd said that the Prophet never told that story without laughing so that he showed his molar teeth. In the Traditions it is related that such human women as get to Paradise are, by reason of their works in this world, superior to the Ḥūrīs. Allah—exalted be He—has said (LVI, 35/34 ff.): "We have produced them and made them virgins, beloved wives, of equal age, for those of the right hand."

(B) ON THE REPENTANCE OF IBLĪS (SATAN)[1]

Said the Imām Aḥmad [b. Ḥanbal]: ʿAffān has related to us, on the authority of Ḥammād b. Salama, from ʿAlī b. Zaid, from Anas [b. Mālik], that the Apostle of Allah—upon whom be Allah's blessing and peace—said: "The first to be clothed with a garment from Hell-fire [after Judgment] will be Iblīs. He will put it on his sides and trail it after him, while his progeny follow him. He will cry out, lamenting his distress, and they lamenting their distress,[2] till they arrive at Hell. There he will again lament his distress and they their distress, but one will say to them: 'Call not today for one destruction but for many destructions'" (XXV, 14/15).

From Ḥudhaifa [we have record] that the Apostle of Allah—upon whom be Allah's blessing and peace—said: "By Him in Whose hand is my soul, even he who religiously has been impious and has lived foolishly will certainly enter Paradise. By Him in Whose hand is my soul, Allah on the Day of Resurrection will assuredly forgive with such an all-embracing

[1] From Taqī ad-Dīn al-Maqdisī's *Kitāb al-Istiʿādha min ash-Shaiṭān* (Cairo, 1311 A.H.), pp. 143, 144.

[2] *thubūr* means both "distress" and "destruction", as in Sūra XXV, 14/15.

forgiveness that even Iblīs may hope to be included in it." Aṭ-Ṭabarānī relates this as transmitted from Saʿd b. Ghailān, but it is not a well-known Tradition.[1] We have already noticed the fact that Iblīs says prayers, and that he once said: "What I hope from my Lord is that when He has cleared Himself of His oath He may pardon me."[2]

From ʿAbdallah b. ʿAmr b. al-ʿĀṣ [we have record] that the Apostle of Allah—upon whom be Allah's blessing and peace—said: "When the sun rises from its setting-place[3] Iblīs will fall down doing obeisance, calling out and loudly crying: 'O my God, command me to do obeisance to whomsoever Thou wilt.'[4] Then his assistants will gather themselves together to him and say: 'O our Master, what humble entreaty is this?' He will answer: 'I asked my Lord only that I might be respited till the time appointed (XV, 36–38), and this is the time appointed.' Then the Beast of the Earth will come forth from aṣ-Ṣafā,[5] from a cleft in aṣ-Ṣafā. It is said that the first place on which it will set its foot will be Antioch, where it will come upon Iblīs and slap him." At-Ṭabarānī relates this, but with a weak chain of authorities *(isnād)*.

Said Sufyān b. ʿUyaina: When the verse (VII, 156/155): "My mercy is wide enough for everything" came down, Iblīs stretched out his neck and said: "I am included in everything", so the verse went on: "so I decree it for those who show piety, who pay the legal alms *(zakāt)*, and for those who believe in Our signs." At this the Jews and the Christians stretched out their necks and said: "We believe in the signs, and we pay legal alms." So Allah—exalted be He—drew it away from Iblīs and from the Jews and Christians, and appointed it exclusively for this [Muslim] community by [going on in the next verse]: "for those who follow the *ummī* Prophet".[6] This is a proof that Iblīs acknowledged Allah, as the Imām Aḥmad[7]

[1] *majhūl* means a Tradition from someone not famous as a collector of Traditions, or some source about whom the later authorities knew little or nothing.

[2] Allah had vowed that He would fill Hell with him and those who followed him (VI, 18/17), so he expresses the hope that when Allah has done this, and so has fulfilled that oath, He may pardon him.

[3] This rising of the sun from the West, and the appearance of the Beast, shortly to be mentioned, are among the signs of the approaching end of all things.

[4] It was his disdainful refusal to do obeisance to the newly created Adam when Allah so commanded him and all the angels (XV, 31 ff.) that brought about his fall and expulsion from Paradise, so now that the end is imminent he expresses his willingness to do obeisance to anything.

[5] Aṣ-Ṣafā is a hill within the city boundaries of Mecca, and is concerned with one of the ceremonies of the annual pilgrimage. See Burton's *Pilgrimage*, II, 244 ff.

[6] On the *ummī* Prophet see p. 314, n. 2.

[7] I.e. Aḥmad b. Ḥanbal, the founder of the Ḥanbalite school. The Isḥāq presently to be mentioned is probably Abū Yaʿqūb Isḥāq al-Kawsaj.

expressly says, quoting as evidence for it the words of the Most High (XV, 39): "He (i.e. Iblīs) said: 'O my Lord, inasmuch as Thou hast turned me away.'" Isḥāq, however, says: "He did not acknowledge Allah, and anyone who says that he acknowledged Allah is in unbelief." Now either the statement of Aḥmad had not reached him, or Isḥāq's statement had not reached Aḥmad. The truth of the matter is that on the one hand he acknowledged Allah, recognizing the existence and power of the Creator, but on the other he accused Him of deficiency, which was due to his ignorance of what Allah may do or may refrain from doing. Partly he acknowledged Allah, as the Imām Aḥmad says, yet without giving absolute acknowledgment of Allah, as Isḥāq says. Al-Ḥakam b. Isḥāq has said: "It has come to us that Allah—exalted be He—sends down with the rain more angels than all the number of the children of Iblīs and the children of Adam. They watch where every rain-drop falls and what grows there." Ibn Jarīr[1] relates this [when commenting on] the words (XV, 21): "And We do not send it down save by fixed measure." [It is reported] from Anas that the Prophet—upon whom be Allah's blessing and peace—said that Gabriel had informed him that one of the angels is put in charge of every drop of rain that falls from heaven to put it in its proper place.

[1] He means the Commentator aṭ-Ṭabarī in whose *Tafsīr* it will be found in vol. XIV, p. 14 of the edition published at Cairo (1330 A.H. = 1911 A.D.).

CANON LAW

INTRODUCTION

Besides Qur'ān and Tradition there were two further sources on which the theologians of Islam could draw in their endeavours to work out a complete "rule of life" for the guidance of the Muslim community, viz. *Ijmā'*, or the consensus of the community, and *Qiyās*, or logical deduction. A theologian who engaged in the task of drawing rules of conduct from these sources was called a *mujtahid*, and among the Shī'a there are still *mujtahid*s, for the Shī'a regard the "door of *ijtihād*" as still open. Among the Sunnī Muslims, however, there grew to be a feeling that the "door of *ijtihād*" had become closed, and that for all practical purposes a Muslim would find a sufficiently explicit rule of life if he attached himself to the system expounded by the School of one of the great Sunnī theologians.

Many famous scholars had laboured at working out a comprehensive system that would cover the whole life of a Muslim, but only four have succeeded in gaining any wide acceptance. These are the Ḥanafite system, which goes back to the work of Abū Ḥanīfa (d. 767 A.D.), the Mālikite, which derives from Mālik b. Anas (d. 795), the Shāfi'ite, coming from the teaching of ash-Shāfi'ī (d. 819), and the Ḥanbalite, which was taught by Aḥmad b. Ḥanbal (d. 855). Each of these systems is called a *madhhab*, and though not precisely a "sect" or a "denomination" in our Christian sense, a *madhhab* represents something of the same group-distinction as we recognize between Methodists and Presbyterians.

Each *madhhab* has its *qāḍīs* who give decisions in matters of practical judgment for the guidance of Muslims in their religious and civil life, and *muftīs* who give decisions on matters of theoretical judgment where questions come up for decision. Since these decisions, although legal decisions, are also concerned with religious matters, they fall under what we should call Canon Law.

A *FATWĀ* OF AL-GHAZZĀLĪ AGAINST THE ESOTERIC SECTS

Theoretically there is no separation of Church and State in Islam, and in actual practice there has been none until quite modern times when Western influences have in some areas brought about a certain separation of the two. One result of the Church-State unity in Islam has been the curious fact that every great Muslim theologian is necessarily also a Jurist, and every great Jurist is necessarily a theologian. The fame of al-Ghazzālī (d. 505 A.H. = 1111 A.D.) is as a theologian and a philosopher, but he was also a jurist who wrote technical works on Muslim Jurisprudence. A Muftī is both a religious and a civil official who writes decisions on questions of the theoretical application of the religious law *(sharī'a)* to problems which arise for the individual or the community. Such a written decision is a *fatwā*. During the Seljuk period (1055–1180 A.D.) the esoteric *(bāṭinī)* sects among the Shī'a Muslims seem to have been indulging in unusual extravagances, and were a considerable concern to the Sunnī rulers at Baghdad. It was in response to a request from the youthful Caliph al-Mustaẓhir (1094–1118 A.D.), or his advisors, that al-Ghazzālī wrote his treatise *Kitāb Faḍā'iḥ al-Bāṭiniyya*, (On the Disgraceful Doctrines of the Esoteric Sects), the eighth chapter of which contains his *fatwā*, his decision as a jurist on the question of what standing the members of such sects had in the Muslim community and how they should be treated.

The text here translated is No. 24 in the extracts from the *Faḍā'iḥ* published by Ignaz Goldziher in his study *Streitschrift des Ġazālī gegen die Bāṭinijja-Sekte* (Leiden, 1916). Goldziher in his discussion of it remarks that al-Ghazzālī is a good deal milder and more lenient to the Bāṭinīs than are the judgments on them to be found in other works of Muslim theology and jurisprudence.

CHAPTER EIGHT

A clear legal decision as to their standing; whether they (i.e. the Bāṭinīs) are to be declared unbelievers and sinners whose blood may be shed. What this Chapter is concerned with is juristic decisions [concerning them], the purport of which we may summarily set forth under four heads.

*

I

As to their being declared unbelievers,[1] *i.e. those who are to be considered to have gone astray and to be in error*

Whenever we are questioned about them, whether it be about some individual from among them or a group, and are asked: "Do you give judgment that they are unbelievers?", we are not hasty to declare them unbelievers till we have made inquiry into their beliefs and [examined] their declarations, [till we] have been able to confer on the matter under judgment and are able to expose their beliefs in an equitable statement that we can base on their own testimony. Then when we have ascertained the truth of the matter we give such decision as is necessary.

Their declarations fall into two categories, one of which makes it necessary to declare that they are in error, are astray, and are guilty of innovation *(bidʿa)*, and the other of which makes it necessary to declare that they are unbelievers and [the community must] be cleansed of them.[2]

With regard to the first category which makes it necessary to declare that they are in error, are astray, and are guilty of innovation, it is where we encounter those unlearned folk who believe that the leadership (Imāmate) belongs by right to the *Ahl al-Bait*,[3] and that he who should rightly have it in our day is their Pretender.[4] Their claim is that in the first century the one who should rightfully have had it was ʿAlī – with whom may Allah be pleased – but he was wrongfully deprived of it. Along with that they claim that the *Imām* is [divinely] preserved from any error or slip, for needs must he be impeccable. Nevertheless they do not believe that it is lawful to shed our blood (i.e. the blood of the Sunnī Muslims), nor do they believe that we are in unbelief. What they believe about us [Sunnīs] is that we are iniquitous folk whose minds have erroneously slipped from comprehension of the truth, or that we have turned aside from following [their Imām] out of obstinacy and [a spirit of] troublesomeness. It is not permissible to shed the blood of a person [in this first category], nor to give judgment that he is in unbelief because he

[1] I.e. they fall under the category of *kāfir*, with all the legal and religious consequences of belonging to that category.

[2] He means that some of their statements involve only heresy, which though wrong does not make them unbelievers and cut them off from the Muslim community, whereas other statements involve such unbelief as cuts them off from the community of believers. On *bidʿa* see p. 146.

[3] "People of the House", i.e. the family of the Prophet.

[4] I.e. the current ʿĀlid pretender.

says such things. The judgment concerning him is rather that he is astray and is guilty of innovation, so he should be chidden for his going astray and for his innovation in regard to those opinions about the Imām. That he should be judged to be in unbelief, and the shedding of his blood considered permissible, because of these declarations is not [admissible]. Judgment should be confined to the declaration that he is astray, for he does not express belief in any of the [erroneous] teachings of their sect, such as we have related, concerning certain theological beliefs and matters of resurrection and judgment.[1] With regard to all such matters they express no beliefs other than those we express ourselves, differing from us only to the extent we have related above.

Should someone ask: "But do you not declare them to be in unbelief because of what they say about the leadership (Imāmate) in the first years [of Islam], how that it belonged by right to ʿAlī, not to Abū Bakr and those who succeeded him, but he was wrongfully deprived of it, for in this they go contrary to the consensus *(ijmāʿ)* of the Muslims?"—our answer is: We do not deny the dangerous nature of this opposition to the consensus, and for that reason we go beyond charging them with being in undisguised error, limited to matters consequential to certain questions, (and charge them) with leading others astray, causing heresy and introducing innovation, but we do not go so far as to declare them in unbelief. This is because it is not clear to us that one who goes against the consensus is [necessarily] an unbeliever. Indeed there is difference of opinion among the Muslims as to whether the proof [of a doctrine] can rest on consensus alone. An-Naẓẓām and his group [2] rejected consensus entirely, holding that no proof could ever be based on it, so we would never declare that a person who was in doubt about this matter was in unbelief. Thus we confine ourselves to declaring that they are in error and are astray.

Should someone ask: "But do you not declare them to be in unbelief because of what they say about the impeccability of the Imāms, since being [divinely] preserved from all error and slip with regard to both lesser and greater sins is one of the peculiarities of the prophetic office, so that they are ascribing something peculiar to the prophetic office to someone other than the Prophet—upon whom be Allah's blessing and peace?"—we answer: This does not necessarily involve unbelief. To in-

[1] In earlier chapters of this Treatise he had described their erroneous teachings about humans being divinized, and denying the Qur'ānic teachings about the resurrection and the Final Judgment. Not all *Bāṭinīs* went so far as this.

[2] See Tritton, *Muslim Theology*, pp. 89–95; Macdonald, *Muslim Theology*, pp. 140 ff.

volve that they would have to be guilty of attributing the prophetic office to some other person who came after him (i.e. Muḥammad), contrary to the established doctrine that he is the Seal of the Prophets, or attributing to someone other than [Muḥammad] the function of making abrogations of his religious law. Impeccability is not one of the peculiar characteristics of the prophetic office, nor is the ascription of it [to someone] like the ascription [to that person] of the prophetic office. There are groups among our friends who teach that impeccability with regard to the lesser sins is not with certainty to be ascribed to a Prophet. They quote as evidence [for their teaching] the words of the Most High (XX, 121/119): "But Adam rebelled against his Lord and went astray", and many a story about the Prophets. He who expresses his belief in a sinful man, [declaring] that he is obedient [to Allah] and [divinely] preserved from evil, is doing no more than one who expresses belief about an obedient man, [declaring] that he is a sinner who persists obstinately in doing mischief. If then a man who expresses belief that a just man is a sinner is no deeper in error than one who expresses belief that a peccable creature is impeccable, how can the latter be judged to be in unbelief? The judgment that may be rendered is that he is a fool, and is expressing belief in a matter for which there could scarcely be visible evidence, and a matter for which no indication is given by any perception or compulsion of the intellect.

Should someone ask: "But were one to express the belief that Abū Bakr and 'Umar—with whom may Allah be pleased—and a group of the Companions, were evil men, even though he did not express his belief that they were unbelievers, would you judge such an one to be in unbelief?"—our answer is: We should not judge such an one to be in unbelief, we should give judgment only that he was a perverse person, astray, and in opposition to the consensus of the community. How could we judge him to be in unbelief when we know that Allah, Most High, did not lay down even for him who falsely charges a virtuous person with adultery more than eighty stripes? Moreover we know that this judgment includes all men, bringing them all under a single judgment, so that were one falsely to charge Abū Bakr or 'Umar with adultery [his punishment] would not be increased beyond the limit Allah, Most High, has textually laid down in His Book,[1] nor did they themselves (i.e. the Companions) make any claim to be distinguished in any special way beyond what was laid down for folk in general.

[1] Sūra XXIV, 4.

Should someone ask: "Then were anyone to say plainly that Abū Bakr and 'Umar—with both of whom may Allah be pleased—were in unbelief, ought he to be set down in the place of one who calls any other of the Muslim leaders, or Qāḍīs, or Imāms who came after them, an unbeliever?" —we answer that thus do we teach. To charge them with unbelief is no different from charging unbelief to any other of the leaders or Qāḍīs of the community, nor, indeed, to any individual Muslims who profess Islam, save in two matters. Firstly, it would be going against and contradicting consensus, though, indeed, one who charges them with unbelief because of some perplexity might not even be contradicting reliable consensus. The second is that there are many Traditions handed down concerning them, according to which they are promised Paradise, are eulogized, have judgments expressed as to the soundness of their religion and the steadfastness of their convictions, and declaring that they have precedence over the rest of humanity, so that if these Traditions have reached [the ears] of the one who makes the charge [of unbelief against them], and in spite of it he expresses his belief that they are in unbelief, then he himself is an unbeliever, not because of his charging them with unbelief, but because he is giving the lie to the Apostle of Allah—upon whom be Allah's blessing and peace—and, by general consent, anyone who treats any word of his sayings as a lie is an unbeliever. Wherever it is possible to overlook [these two matters, viz.] treating these Traditions as false and going against the consensus, then to declare them (i.e. Abū Bakr and 'Umar) to be in unbelief is on the same level as declaring any others of the Qāḍīs, Imāms, or leaders of the Muslims to be in unbelief.

Should someone ask: "Well, what is your teaching with regard to one who declares a fellow Muslim to be in unbelief, is he an unbeliever *(kāfir)* or not?"—our answer is: If he was aware that this [fellow Muslim] believed in the Divine unity, had confident trust in the Apostle—upon whom be Allah's blessing and peace—and held the other proper doctrines, then whensoever he declares him to be in unbelief with regard to these doctrines, he is an unbeliever, since he is expressing the opinion that the true religion is unbelief and is untrue. On the other hand, if he thinks that this [fellow Muslim] believes that the Apostle was false, or that he (i.e. the fellow Muslim) denies the Maker, or is a dualist, or some such thing which necessarily involves being in unbelief, and so, relying on this opinion of his, declares him to be in unbelief, then he is in error in his opinion with regard to this person, but he is right in declaring that anyone who believes what he thinks this person believes is in unbelief. To think a fellow Muslim is in unbelief is not to be oneself in unbelief, any more than to think an unbeliever is a Muslim is to be in unbelief. Such thoughts as these may be either erroneous or correct, which is evidence of ignorance with regard to the true state of some particular person, but it is not a condition of a man's religion that he know the Islam of every Muslim or the unbelief of every unbeliever. Indeed there is no individual person who could be imagined, ignorance about whom would harm his religious standing. Nay more, if a person believes in Allah and His Apostle, diligently performes his acts of worship, and yet has never heard the names of Abū Bakr and ʿUmar, but dies before hearing them, he would nevertheless die a Muslim, for belief in [what is told about] them is not among the essentials *(arkān)* of religion, such that any mistake with regard to what must be attributed to them would necessarily strip him of his religion.

But here one must seize the bridle of theological argumentation *(kalām)*, for to dive into this diving-pool would lead to intricacies and stir up ancient bigotries where maybe not all minds would be prepared to accept the truth as it comes out in accordance with the demonstration, so firmly rooted in them are customary beliefs in which they were brought up, and which have been confirmed by the persistence of habits which have become instinctive and whose removal is well-nigh impossible. In a word, a discussion of what things would necessarily involve unbelief and ejection [from the community], and what would not necessarily involve this, would require at least a volume, even though one treat it but summarily. So let us confine ourselves in this treatise to our more important object.

The second category is that of declarations which necessarily involve their being declared to be in unbelief. These are their beliefs that we have mentioned above,[1] to which may be added their belief that we [the Sunnīs] are in unbelief, so that it is lawful to plunder our property and shed our blood. This necessarily involves their being declared to be in unbelief. This is unavoidable since they know that we believe that the world has a Maker, Who is One, powerful, knowing, willing, speaking, hearing and seeing, Who has no similitude;[2] that His Apostle is Muḥammad b. ʿAbdallah—upon whom be Allah's blessing and peace—who spoke the truth in all that he told about the resurrection and judgment, and about Paradise and Hell. These are the doctrines which are pivotal

[1] He refers to his previous exposition of their erroneous beliefs about humans being divinized, and their explaining away many eschatological statements, in the Qur'ān and the Traditions, concerning resurrection and judgment.

[2] He quotes Sūra XLII, 11/9, "naught is there like Him".

for sound religion. Should anyone give it as his opinion that they are in unbelief then it is he who is an unbeliever, a matter about which there is no doubt. So if in addition to this there is added [belief in] any of their opinions which we have mentioned, such as maintaining that there are two deities, denying the last Judgment, or disavowing Paradise and Hell and the resurrection, any one of these would necessarily involve a man being declared to be in unbelief, whether he came from them or from some other sect.

Should someone ask: "Well, what about a man who believes in the Divine unity and denies all association *(shirk)*,[1] yet feels himself free to interpret allegorically particular matters concerning Judgment and Paradise and Hell, not denying them, but actually agreeing that obedience, fulfilling the law, keeping oneself from forbidden things and from lust, are a cause for one's attaining [future] bliss, and that giving way to lust, and disobeying the law in what it commands and forbids, would lead the one guilty of them to [future] distress, yet expressing the opinion that 'bliss'[2] refers to the spiritual pleasures whose enjoyment far exceeds any physical enjoyment derived from taking food or sexual intercourse, things in which the animals share but which angels are far above. Such bliss [this man asserts] can be obtained only by contact with angelic intellectual faculties, and can be enjoyed only by attaining that perfection, whereas bodily pleasures are contemptible and ignoble things in comparison therewith. Also, in his opinion, the distress [with which the wicked are threatened] means a man's being deprived of that great and exalted perfection in spite of his longing for it and passionate desire to have it, the pain of which makes the pain of physical fire a thing of no account. What is found in the Qur'ān [about these matters he thinks], is by way of similitude, set forth for the common folk whose understanding is too limited to conceive of such [spiritual] delights. Had the Prophet in his efforts to attract and to frighten [3] gone beyond things to which they were accustomed and for which they longed or of which they were terrified, he would not have aroused in them any impulse to seek [the one] or flee [the other]. So he made mention of such enjoyments as were most in

[1] *shirk* is the sin of associating any other with Allah in such a way as to prejudice His absolute uniqueness.

[2] The words he uses, *sa'āda* for "bliss", and *shaqāwa* for "distress", are technical words in common use in eschatological tractates which describe the future life of reward for the Blessed and punishment for the Damned.

[3] The technical terms are *targhīb*, i.e. inciting them to follow the right way by describing future enjoyment, and *tarhīb*, e.i. terrifying them from following the wrong way by describing future punishments.

honour among them, namely those which appeal to the senses, e.g. the [celestial] spouses *(ḥūr)* and the palaces, which the sense of sight would enjoy, and the feastings and wivings which would slake the appetites, though really Allah has [in store] for His pious servants better things, [finer] than language could describe or minds could think. Allah, indeed, has said so, according as His Prophet—upon whom be Allah's blessing and peace—has related: 'I have prepared for My pious servants what eye has not seen, what ear has not heard, and what has not even entered man's heart to think', whereas all these [above mentioned] things that can be perceived by the senses have entered into man's heart, or at least may enter into the heart. One who takes this position argues that what leads to the employment, [to describe] the pleasures and pains, of similitudes drawn from things familiar to the common folk is like what leads to the employment of expressions of an anthropomorphic nature when describing the attributes of the Most High. Were they (i.e. the common folk) told the absolute truth and an attempt made to describe to them the majesty of Allah, which is beyond our ability to describe or name, by saying to them: 'The Maker of the world exists, but is neither an essence nor an accident nor a body, is neither connected with the world nor unconnected with it, is neither within it nor outside it, that the directions of space are limited to six and all other directions are empty of Him, that He is not occupying any of them, so that He does not occupy the interior of the world, nor is He absent from the exterior of the world', why men would lose no time in denying that such a Being existed, for their intellects would be incapable of accepting as true the existence of One whom the imagination and the senses reject. So [such people] are told things which lead to the formation of images, that there may be firmly implanted in their souls the unshakeable belief that He actually exists, whereat they quickly assent to the commands out of desire to exalt Him, and avoid acts of disobedience from fear of Him. Now what is your judgment on one who takes this path?" —our answer is: To teach that there are two deities [1] is obvious unbelief, so there is no hesitation about [giving a pronouncement on] that. As for the rest, the investigator may perhaps hesitate, and say that if they recognize the actuality of the bliss and the distress, and [agree] that obedience is the way to the one and disobedience the way to the other, then disagreement about how these are to be particularized is like disagreement over the various measures of reward and punishment, and just as that does not necessarily involve one's being declared to be in unbelief,

[1] Such as there would be if a human were divinized, as the Bāṭinīs taught was at times the case.

so is it with regard to disagreement about the particularization. Our own preference and the opinion on this matter to which we give our voice is that there should be no hesitation in declaring anyone who expresses belief in any of the above ideas to be in unbelief. This is because it is clearly giving the lie to the Master of the religious law and to all the words of the Qur'ān from beginning to end, for the description of Paradise and Hell does not occur there merely once or twice, and is not given by way of allusion *(kināya)*, rhetorical augmentation *(tawassuʿ)* or literary figure *(tajawwuz)*, but in clear terms about which there is nothing doubtful or subject to suspicion. The Master of the religious law meant them to be understood in their literal sense, which means that this [allegorizing] is not a [legitimate] interpretation, but is [tantamount to] declaring [the revelation] to be false. That clearly is unbelief which ought to be unhesitatingly declared such. Likewise, we know for sure that in the days of the Companions if anyone had plainly stated his rejection of [belief in] Paradise and Hell, in the Ḥūrīs and the [celestial] palaces, they would have lost no time in putting him to death, considering that such views as his gave the lie to Allah and His Apostle.

Should someone say: "Yes, may be they used to do [such things as] that, and made every effort to close the door against such statements, since the common weal demands that [the common folk] be not addressed save in such a way as suits their understanding, will make an impression on their souls, and will arouse their impulses. If these notions thus literally expressed were removed, while their intelligences fell short of grasping [the notion of] intellectual delights, they might deny [the Qur'ānic] basis and disown the [idea of] rewards and punishments, so that for them there would fall away all distinction between obedience and disobedience, between unbelief and faith"—our answer is: What is fully recognized is the consensus of the Companions in declaring such a person to be in unbelief and putting him to death for having publicly stated such things, yet we do not go beyond [giving judgment] that one who plainly states such things must be declared to be in unbelief and must necessarily be put to death, for about that there is general agreement. There remains your statement that the reason why they declared such [a person] to be in unbelief was regard for the common weal, and this is mere surmise and opinion which contributes nothing to the case. Nay more, we know for sure that they used to consider such [statements] as giving the lie to Allah and to His Apostle and a rejection of what was set forth in the religious law, even though it was not something which the intelligence had to reject.

Should someone ask: "But did you yourself not travel this road [when you were dealing] with the images which are presented in connection with [exposition of] the attributes of Allah—exalted be He—, e.g. in connection with the verse of sitting,[1] the Tradition about the coming down,[2] the word 'foot' where it says that the Almighty put His foot in the Fire,[3] the expression 'image' *(ṣūra)*, where he—upon whom be peace—said that Allah created Adam in His own image,[4] and in other such Traditions, perhaps more than a thousand of them, yet you know that the pious early believers were not in the habit of allegorizing these literal expressions, but used to take them in their literal sense. You did not declare anyone who denied the literal acceptation [of these passages], and allegorized them, to be in unbelief, but you professed your belief in the allegorical interpretation and plainly stated this"—our answer is: How can one avoid this [suggesting of] equivalences when the Qur'ān states quite plainly that "He has no similitude" (XLII, 11/9), and the Traditions which indicate the same thing are more than can be numbered? We are aware that in the days of the Companions had anyone stated plainly that Allah—exalted be He—is not confined by space, is not limited by time, is not in contact with matter nor separated therefrom by any distance measurable or immeasurable, that He is not subject to transfer, whether going or coming, appearing or disappearing, that it is impossible that He should be among things that settle down or are transferred [from place to place] or that are firmly fixed [in a place], and so on with the other expressions which [are used to] deny anthropomorphic attributes, they would have considered such statements the very essence of [true effort at maintaining] the Divine unity and transcendence.[5] Yet were a person [who asserted these things] to deny the [literal acceptance of the] Ḥūrīs and the palaces, the [celestial] rivers and trees, the Zabāniyya, and the Fire [of Hell], that would have been counted among the various classes of falsity and denial, but there is no equivalence between the two cases.

We have already drawn attention to the difference [between them] in

[1] In several passages of the Qur'ān (e.g. II, 29/27; VII, 54/52; X, 3; XIII, 2, etc.), it says that after having completed the work of creation Allah "took His seat" *(istawā)* on His Throne. Muḥammad was doubtless only reproducing a detail he had learned from the Creation stories told by adherents of the older religions, but the problem of the "sitting" *(istiwā')* has greatly exercised Muslim theologians. See p. 358.

[2] The reference is to Allah's "coming down" to take His seat for the Final Judgment.

[3] See p. 391 in the translation from *Baḥr al-Kalām.*

[4] Here again the Prophet is reproducing a detail heard from accounts of the creation told by the People of the Book. Cf. Gen. I, 26; V, 1; IX, 6 : I Cor. XI, 7.

[5] The technical terms here are *tawḥīd,* "declaring [Allah] to be one", and *tanzīh,* "declaring [Allah] to be aloof from all other things".

the chapter where we refute [the teachings of] their sect, [where we point out] two aspects thereof. One of them is that the expressions regarding the Judgment, Paradise and Hell are stated so plainly that there is no allegorizing them or avoiding them otherwise than by removing them or treating them as false, whereas the expressions regarding such matters as the sitting, the image, and so forth, are commonly used metaphorical, rhetorical figures *(tawassuʿāt)*, which may be interpreted allegorically. The other is that there are intellectually satisfying arguments which hinder belief in anthropomorphism and in [notions of] descent, movement, spatial fixation [with reference to Allah], and indicate their impossibility with a clarity that leaves no room for doubt. On the contrary there is no intellectually satisfying proof that what is promised with regard to Paradise and Hell in the after life cannot possibly happen. Nay, indeed, the eternal Power knew all about these [promises] and had them in His control. They are things which in themselves are quite possible, and the eternal Power will not fail to bring about that which in itself is possible. How then can you confuse this with the expressions used of the attributes of Allah—exalted be He?

To treat this question fully would demand the divulging of some of the secrets of religion did we set ourselves to fathom its profundities and desire to uncover its hidden depths. Since that, however, has presented itself unexpectedly in the course of the discussion, without being purposely raised, let us confine ourselves to the measure we have reached in this section, and concern ourselves with the more important matters that are our object in this treatise. We have made clear in the present section who among them are to be declared to be in unbelief and who not, who [among them] are to be declared astray and who are not.

II

The regulations with regard to those of them who are judged to be in unbelief

A concise statement [of the position] is that they are to be treated in the same manner as apostates [1] with regard to blood, property, marriage,

[1] A *murtadd*, "apostate", is one who has been a Muslim but then has renounced Islam. The blood of an apostate may be shed without hesitation, his property is forfeit, his marriages void, animals slaughtered by him are not ritually acceptable as food for Muslims, legal obligations to him need not be fulfilled, and none of his cult performances are of any avail. See Zwemer, *The Law of Apostasy in Islam* (New York, 1916).

slaughtering, execution of judgments and the performing of cult practices. With regard to their spirits *(arwāḥ)* they are not to be treated in the same way as one who was an unbeliever by origin, since the Imām [1] gives a choice, when it is the case of one who was an unbeliever by origin, between four expedients, viz. [extending to him] grace, [allowing him the chance of] ransom, enslaving [him], or putting [him] to death, but he gives no option in the case of an apostate. Such persons may not in any circumstances [merely] be reduced to slavery, or allowed to offer the poll-tax payment, or be shown grace or allowed to ransom themselves with all that involves. The only [treatment for such] is that they be put to death and the face of the earth cleansed of them. This is the judgment on those Bāṭinīs who have been adjudged to be in unbelief. Neither the permissibility nor the necessity of putting them to death is limited by being [confined to when we are] in a state of war with them, but we may take them unawares and shed their blood, so that [all the more] when they are involved in fighting is it permissible to kill them. But if they belong to the first group against whom there is no judgment that they are in unbelief, the position is that in being engaged in fighting they are associating themselves with agressors, and an agressor may be killed since he is coming out to fight, even though he be a Muslim, save that should he turn his back to make his escape, such as flee are not to be followed nor are their wounded to be killed off. As for those about whom we have given judgment that they are in unbelief there is to be no hesitation about killing them whether they make a show of fighting or merely appear in order to justify themselves.

Should someone ask: "Would you put their women and children to death?"—our answer is: As for the children, No! for a child is not to be blamed, and their judgment will come. As for the women, we ourselves would [favour] the putting them to death whenever they plainly state beliefs which are [in the category of] unbelief, in accordance with the decision we have already rendered. For the female apostate is, in our opinion, deserving of death, in accordance with the inclusive [2] statement of him—upon whom be Allah's blessing and peace—[in which he says]: "Whosoever changes his religion, put him to death." It is allowable, however, for the leader of the community to follow in this matter the result of

[1] He means the Imām ash-Shāfiʻī, to whose school he himself belonged, and who dealt with the question of apostates in his *Kitāb al-Umm*, I, 227–234.

[2] The statement is inclusive or general *('umūmī)* since it does not specify male apostates. The reference is to a well-known canonical Tradition quoted in the law books under the section on apostasy. See Aḥmad b. Ḥanbal, *Musnad*, I, 217.

his own deliberations, and if he thinks that he should follow the way of Abū Ḥanīfa [1] with regard to them and refrain from putting the women to death, the question is one that belongs to the realm of individual deliberation and decision. When the children reach the age of discretion Islam is to be presented to them, and if they accept it they are to be accepted as Muslims and the swords which were at their necks are to be returned to their sheaths. If, however, they persist in their unbelief, assuming as their own the faith of their fathers, we extend the swords of the true religion to their necks, treating them as we do apostates.

As regards property, the regulation concerning it is the same as that with regard to the property of apostates. Whatever is taken in conquest, save the corpses of horses and riders, falls wholly [under the category of] "apostate spoils", which the leader is to distribute rightfully to those to whom such spoils are due, in accordance with the principles of division given in the words of the Most High (LIX, 7): "What Allah has given as spoil to His Apostle from the [goods of the people] of the towns belongs to Allah and His Apostle, etc."[2] Such corpses of horses and riders [3] as are taken may well be treated as booty is treated and distributed to the rightful recipients thereof, in accordance with the principles laid down in the words of the Most High (VIII, 41/42): "and know that when ye have taken anything as booty, a fifth of it belongs to Allah, etc.".[4] This is one of the regulations of the jurists for the treatment of apostates, and it is the best decision that has been given with regard to the case of such persons, though there has been much confused discussion about it and about questions connected with [their] property. When they die their property cannot be inherited, nor can one of them inherit from another. They cannot inherit from a true believer, nor can a true believer inherit their property, even though there should be a kinship between them, for

[1] The founder of the Ḥanafite school was milder in his treatment of apostates than ash-Shāfi'ī to whose school al-Ghazzālī belonged.

[2] The whole verse reads: "What Allah has given as booty to his Apostle from the [goods of the] people of the towns is for Allah and for the Apostle, and for the kinsman and the orphans, and the unfortunate and the wayfarer, that it be not passed around among the rich among you. What the Apostle gives you, take, and what he makes forbidden to you, leave alone. Show piety to Allah. Allah, indeed is severe in punishment."

[3] What is meant is the trappings and accoutrements of horses and riders, not the flesh of the corpses.

[4] The whole passage reads: "And know that when ye have taken anything as booty, a fifth of it belongs to Allah and to His Apostle, to the kinsman and the orphans, the unfortunate and the wayfarer; if you have believed in Allah and in what We sent down to Our servant on the day of al-Furqān (i.e. the battle of Badr), the day when the two parties met, for Allah is powerful over everything".

the inheritance relationship between unbelievers and Muslims is severed. Cohabitation with their women, however, is forbidden, for just as marriage with a female apostate is illegal, so is marriage with a Bāṭinī woman who professes belief in the infamous teachings which, according to our judgment, are a reason for one being declared to be in unbelief, and which we have particularized above. Even should she be a woman who had professed [the true religion] and then been absorbed into their sect the marriage is immediately made void if [this becomes known] before she has been touched, but after she has been touched [the declaring void] must wait till the completion of the *'idda*.[1] Should she return to the true religion, separating from the false believers before the *'idda* period has elapsed according to the computation of its duration, the marriage will continue to be valid, but if she persists and continues [in false belief] till she has completed the period and the *'idda* has been fulfilled the annulment of the marriage may be reckoned from the time of her apostasy.

Whenever a Bāṭinī who has been judged to be in unbelief contracts a marriage with a woman belonging to the true faith, or with one from the people of his own faith, the marriage is an invalid one and is not binding. Nay more, his disposal of his property by sale, and all other such legal contracts [into which he may enter are considered as] rescinded, for the opinion we are supporting in this *fatwā* [favours] the judgment that the possessions of an apostate have ceased to be [his] by reason of his apostasy.

Closely connected with the unlawfulness of such marriage contracts [as the above], is the unlawfulness of slaughtering [2] [by a Bāṭinī]. No act of slaughtering by any one of them is legally valid any more than a slaughtering by a Magian or a Manichee [3] is valid. Slaughtering [for food] and marriage contracts are very similar [in their juristic aspects] and both are unlawful when associated with any group of unbelievers save Jews and Christians, in whose case there is a relaxing of the strictness because they are People of a Book which Allah sent down to a faithful Prophet whose trustworthiness is apparent and whose Book is well known.

[1] The *'idda* is the period a married woman must wait after separation from one husband before she can be married to another in order to make sure that she is not with child by the first husband.

[2] The word used here *dhabīḥa* actually means the animal slaughtered, but the reference is to the ritual slaughtering of animals for food, for a Muslim may not eat of flesh food unless the animal has been slaughtered in the approved way.

[3] *zindīq* is a word that has been used for various heretical groups, especially those which taught a Dualism, but since the Zoroastrians (Magians) are specifically mentioned in this passage, *zindīq* here would seem to mean Manichee. See p. 386.

As for the execution of [legal] judgments in connection with them, (i.e. with Bāṭinīs), it is invalid and [such judgments are] not to be carried out. Also their testimony is to be refused, for these are all matters whose validity is conditional on the person concerned being a Muslim, for which reason no one among them who has been judged to be in unbelief can properly have part in such matters. Furthermore their cult performances are useless. Neither their fastings nor their prayer services have any value, nor do their pilgrimages or almsgivings count for anything, so that whenever one of them repents and cleanses himself of his [erroneous] beliefs, and we are satisfied that his repentance is genuine, then he must make up all the cult performances that have slipped by and were performed while he was in a state of unbelief, just as is incumbent in the case of an apostate [who returns to the faith]. This is as much as we wished to draw attention to in connection with their legal position.

Should someone ask: "But why have you associated them so closely with apostates, seeing that an apostate is one who had taken upon himself the true religion and embraced all that it involved, but then departed from it, discarding it and denying it, whereas these people had never at any time accepted the truth, but grew up in this belief? Why then did you not rather associate them with those who were unbelievers by origin?" —our answer is: What we have made mention of is quite plain in the case of those who have adopted their religious opinions, or have changed over to them, professing belief in them after having professed belief in their opposites, or after separating themselves therefrom. As for those who were brought up in their belief, receiving it by what they heard from their fathers, they are children of apostates, for their fathers or their fathers' fathers needs must have adopted this [false] religion after separating themselves from [the true religion], for [the Bāṭinī doctrine] is not a belief associated with a Prophet and a revealed Book, like the belief of the Jews and the Christians, but belongs to those specious innovations associated with the heterodox and heretical movements of these modern, all too lax, epochs. Now the judgment against the heretic is just the same as the judgment against the apostate, differing from it in no respect.

There remains then only the case of the children of apostates. With regard to them, some say that they are [to be considered as] following [their parents] in apostasy, [their case being the same] as the children of unbelievers in a community conquered by the sword, and the children of the Dhimmīs.[1] In this case when they come of age it is required that

[1] When a place is conquered by the Muslim armies its inhabitants are offered Islam, and if they accept it they are taken into the Muslim community. Should they refuse

they accept Islam, otherwise they are put to death, for it is not acceptable that such should be allowed to pay the poll-tax or be taken as slaves. Others, however, say that they are like those who were unbelievers by origin, since they were born in unbelief, but if when they come of age they choose to continue in the unbelief of their fathers it is permissible to let them live on under the poll-tax or reduced to slavery. Others say that they are to be judged as belonging to Islam, for the blameworthiness of the apostate arises from [the fact that he did have] attachments to Islam. So if [the child] grows up quietly the judgment that he is in Islam holds until [he reaches the age when] Islam is offered to him, then if he pronounces [the credal formula] that settles the matter, but if he then reveals the unbelief of his parents he is at once to be returned to that condition. This latter is the opinion we ourselves prefer with regard to the children of the Bāṭinīs, for any one of the attachments to Islam is sufficient [as ground on which] to give a judgment as to the Islamic standing of the children. Such attachment to Islam remains with every apostate, and therefore he is blameworthy in his state of apostasy, according to the laws of Islam. Moreover he—upon whom be Allah's blessing and peace—has said: "Every child is born in the *fiṭra*,[1] it is his parents who make him a Jew or a Christian or a Magian." So these are to be judged to be in Islam, then when they come of age the face of the truth will be unveiled to them and they will turn away from the disgraceful teachings of the Bāṭinī sect. That will be disclosed to him who pays attention, as fully as he is able to grasp and as quickly as could be expected. But if he refuses to have any other than the religion of his fathers then he may be judged to be in apostasy as from that moment and treated as apostates are treated.

III

On the acceptance and rejection of their repentance

We have associated these people (i.e. the Bāṭinīs) with the apostates in all other matters of judgment, and [as you know], the repentance of an

---

to accept Islam, those among them who belong to the People of the Book may take the status of *dhimmīs* (or *ahl adh-dhimma)*, i.e. people of a protected community, who pay the poll-tax *(jizya)*, but the others suffer the consequences of unbelief, i.e. the men are put to death and the women and children are at the disposal of the conquerors. The point here is that in a conquered territory the children of Dhimmīs are assumed to be Dhimmīs and the children of unbelievers assumed to be unbelievers.

[1] *fiṭra* means that which is natural. Since Islam is claimed to be a reinstitution of the original natural religion of mankind, this Tradition means to say that every child if left to himself would grow up naturally a Muslim. Aḥmad b. Ḥanbal, *Musnad*, II, 233.

apostate is to be accepted. This is a matter about which there is no doubt. Indeed it is best not to hurry the matter of putting them to death until after having sought to have them repent, and presenting Islam to them, even urging it insistently on them. But in cases of repentance on the part of Bāṭinīs, or any heretic *(zindīq)* suspect of unbelief, who thinks that *taqīya* [1] is religiously correct, and believes that to act the hypocrite, and profess quite other than one really believes when in terror of death, is right, there is a difference of opinion among the theologians as to what should be done.

Some think that [their repentance] should be accepted, since he—upon whom be Allah's blessing and peace—has said: "I have been commanded to fight the peoples till they say: 'There is no deity save Allah.' So if they say this they have, as far as I am concerned, preserved their blood and their property, save what is due thereon." Also the religious law considers that "religion is built only on that which is apparent," so we give no judgment save on that which appears, Allah being the One to take cognizance of secret matters. What guides [us in this matter] is that when an unwilling person makes profession of Islam under the threat of the sword, fearing for his life, we know from the context of his situation that what he is thinking is quite other than what he is openly professing, but we accept his profession of Islam, paying no regard to what is known from the context as to his secret feelings. Another guide [for us] is what has been related about Usāma [one of the Companions of the Prophet], how he put an infidel to death, drawing the sword against him after he had uttered the credal statement *(kalima)* of Islam. [2] The Apostle of Allah—upon whom be Allah's blessing and peace—took this amiss, whereat Usāma said: "But he said that only out of fear of the sword." [Muḥammad]—upon whom be Allah's blessing and peace—replied: "And did you know what was in his heart?" By this statement he has drawn attention to the fact that [we human] creatures are not acquainted with hidden things, so that what is shown openly is the only point to which legal responsibility can be attached. A still further guide is the fact that this kind is one kind of unbeliever, and as the way to repentance and to return to the true religion is to be closed against no kind of unbeliever, that rule will hold here.

Others are of the opinion that the repentance of such a person should not be accepted. They claim that were this door to be opened it would be

[1] The doctrine of *taqīya* is one which teaches that it is correct to conceal one's real religious beliefs at such times as they might bring one's life into danger.

[2] I.e. he had uttered the formula: "There is no deity save Allah, and Muḥammad is the Apostle of Allah", which is still today the normal confession of Islam.

quite impossible to prevent their heresy and subdue their evil, for one of their secret principles is to practise *taqiya* in religion and to seek to conceal their unbelief when in danger [of their lives]. So if we should treat them in this way [by accepting their professions of repentance], they will not refrain from uttering the profession of faith *(kalima)* of the true religion and making a show of repentance when they are conquered. Thus they will make a custom of that, [making profession] outwardly, but inwardly making mock of the true believers. As for the Tradition [quoted above, those who take this position argue that] it had reference only to such kinds of unbelievers as followed a religion which did not permit them to profess openly that from which they differed. Anyone who openly accepts Islam thereby abandons Judaism or Christianity. This is their belief, and so you can see them being cut to pieces little by little with swords yet persisting in their unbelief, refraining from coming into agreement with the Muslims by [uttering] the profession of faith *(kalima)*. But he whose religion allows him to utter the credal statement of Islam without thereby abandoning his own religion, but on the contrary seeing in such an act the essence of his own religion, how can we believe in his repentance with regard to what is the essence of his religion? When making such a public statement is fulfilling a condition of his own religion how can that be abandoning his religion?

This is the argumentation [as we find it] set forth by both sides, and we have dealt in detail with the matter in [our] tractate [entitled] *Shifā' al-ʿAlīl fī Uṣūl al-Fiqh,* so for the moment we shall confine ourselves to making mention of the position we took up on this disputed point about which there has been so much discussion. We teach that there are various cases of penitents [coming] from this particular error. The first case is where one of them hastens to make a show of repentance when there has been no fighting or pressure or compulsion, but [he comes] because he wants to and chooses [to repent], coming of his own free will and wanting to join [our religion], without there being any danger to his life. The repentance of such a one ought to be accepted, for if we look at the exterior of his profession of faith *(kalima)* we believe that it corresponds to essential Islam, and could we look at what is hidden within it would in all probability be in compliance and agreement. For we do not know at the moment of anything that would be inciting him to practise *taqīya,* for according to their own teaching it is only permissible to make a profession of some belief contrary to their own by way of *taqīya* when it has been proved that there is real danger, whereas to do it when there is a choice [of not having to resort to it] would be the foulest of greater sins. This [decision of ours] is supported by a command of universal application, namely, [the command] that the door to orthodox belief must never be closed against them. How many a common man has been deceived by evil imagination and seduced by someone's words, and then has been roused, either by himself or by someone else, [to see] the truth, and has made up his mind to return thereto and take it up again after having abandoned it. So the way to the orthodox path may never be closed against those who have gone astray or have become rebellious.

The second case is where one of them accepts Islam under threat of the sword, but belongs to the common and unlearned folk among them, and is not one of their propagandists *(duʿāt)* or teachers of delusion *(ḍullāl)*. The repentance of such a one is also to be accepted, for in the case of one who has not been prepared [by them] for propaganda work the harmfulness of his unbelief is confined to himself, so whenever one of them makes a profession of [the true] religion it may be that he is speaking truly both in what appears and in what is hidden. Such an unlearned common man imagines that taking on religions and beliefs is like [the taking on of] engagements and compacts, which are entered into of choice, which one makes at a particular time for some benefit or other and then at another time dissolves. [In the case of such a person] the inner feelings correspond with the outer expression whether it is a matter of undertaking an obligation or a matter of declining it. Thus you see many male and female slaves, who have been taken as prisoners in the lands of the unbelievers and brought into Muslim territory, who make profession of [their masters'] religion, giving thanks to Allah for the right guidance that has been decreed for them and for cleansing them from the filthiness of unbelief and error. Were they to be asked the reason why they changed religion and accepted the true in place of the false, they would not know any reason for it save the desire of being agreeable to their masters, thus complying with the demands of their situation. But then that [outer profession] makes its imprint on their inner beliefs as we can see and bear witness. If then it is well known that a common man is quick to make such changes [in religion] and we treat him as honest in [making] his change over to the true religion, just as we treat him as being honest in forsaking it when he makes profession of belief in something contrary to the true religion, then we have the alternatives, either to avert our eyes from the unbeliever who is pretending to hide [his unbelief] and do not put him to death, feigning ignorance about him, or to hasten to put to death one who is outwardly a Muslim [since he has made the profession], and may be one inwardly if he has [really] determined upon what he is professing.

There is no great harm in averting the eyes from the unbelief of an unbeliever, where [such a one] has no propagandist mission to fulfil and there is in him no wickedness that would spread abroad. How many a time we have shown ourselves favourable to unbelievers and have overlooked [their unbelief] when accepting their money—and that [friendly relationship with unbelievers] is not a forbidden thing. But to run the risk of putting to death one who is [at least outwardly] a professed Muslim, and who may be one inwardly, that is a dangerous thing.

The third case is where we get hold of one of their propagandists, who is known to believe in the false teachings of their sect, yet who adopted it without really believing in it, [doing it] in order to be able to win the hearts of people and turn their regards to him out of desire for leadership and lust for worldly vanities. This is one whose wickedness is to be feared, and his case hinges on the opinion of the leader [of the community], who must observe attentively the attendant circumstances of his situation, and seek to discover his inward thoughts from what he lets appear outwardly. He must seek to make clear whether what he declares is an acknowledgment of the truth and a confession of it after he has tested it and discovered [what it really is], or whether [his declaration] is hypocrisy and [a case of] *taqīya,* for in the attendant circumstances of his condition there will be that which will indicate this. The best thing, without a doubt, is that the leader should be neither under absolute obligation to put him to death, nor forbidden to put him to death, but should be given freedom to use his own discretion. If his opinion inclines to the belief that the man is following the path of *taqīya* in what he is doing let him put him to death, but if his opinion inclines to the belief that the man has come to see the truth and has realized the evil of the falsely specious teachings which he was propagating before he repented, then let him overlook him for the present, and if there remain some doubts about him, let him put over him someone who will watch how he acts and search out his inmost thought, and then let him decide the man's case in accordance with what becomes clear to him about him. This way of handling such a case is nearest to the observance of justice and the furthest from bigotry and unfair treatment.

IV

A device for getting out of oaths sworn to them, and compacts made with them, when they have secured such by [our] response

Should someone ask: "What do you teach regarding compacts and covenants with them, and oaths that have been sworn to them by response to request? Are these binding? Is it permissible to violate them, or obligatory to violate them, or is this something forbidden? Also should the one who swore [such an oath to them] violate it, is he for that reason in [a state of] disobedience such as requires atonement, or does it not require it? [You are aware] how many persons there are who have made compacts [with Bāṭinīs], and given an oath in confirmation, so that they have been deceived into involving themselves in their dubious affairs, and then when the error of [these people] has been revealed to them and they would wish that they be shown up and their shameful ways made plain, they are prevented [from doing anything] by the solemn oath they had given as assurance, so there is pressing need for teaching [them] some device whereby they may get release from such oaths"—our answer is: The getting rid of such oaths is possible, and there are different ways [that may be used] according to the different circumstances and wording [of the oaths].

The first is where the one who has sworn the oath has become aware of the dangerous nature of the oath [he has given] and the possibility [occured to him] of including in it some ambiguousness [of statement] and grounds for circumvention, so that he thereupon mentioned to himself words [of possible exception], namely, saying: "If Allah wills." Then, [if he has used such words in giving the oath] he will not have to fulfil his oath, there is nothing to hinder him from violating it, and should he violate it the violation involves him in no legal obligation at all. This judgment holds for any oath that was followed by such a formula of exception, as for example, when you say: "I will assuredly do so and so, if Allah wills" and such as saying: "If I do so and so, then my wife is divorced, if Allah wills", and so in similar cases.

The second is when he undertakes in his oath to do something though his intention is to do the opposite of that which he was asked, thus concealing his intention of doing the opposite of what he has said. This concealment may be in such a form as that which is implied in the utterance. Now this is a matter between him and Allah—great and majestic is He—so he may go contrary to the surface meaning of his statement and follow what its hidden meaning and intention involve. Should someone object that in an oath what is relied upon is the intention of the one who was binding [another] by the oath, for were reliance to be on the intention of the one who takes the oath, and he be allowed to insert exceptions, then the oath would be declared invalid in any assembly of judges, since no one who takes an oath before them can insert some hidden intention or secret exception, for that would lead to the voiding of all rights—our answer is: Actually the reliance will always be on the intention of the one who takes the oath and any exception he may make, for he is the one who swears the oath and the one who makes him swear is offering him the oath, nevertheless he is under sentence to follow the intention of the one who seeks to bind him so that right may be guarded and preserved. Necessity demands that he be under this sentence. This is always so when one is rightly taking an oath in accordance with the religious law and all is being performed in harmony therewith. But where one is being unjustly compelled, or has been cruelly and tyrannously deceived, then it is not so, and the matter of the one who took the oath thereanent may be considered from the point of view of the taker of the oath [rather than from that of the offerer], for the very reason why equitable consideration must be given to the point of view of him who requires an oath is the seriousness of the matter [for which such an oath is required], and any matter which empowers the unjust to demand fulfilment of an oath against the weak members of the Muslim community by any sort of deceit or dissembling must be referred back to the rule [of equity].

The third case is when he looks at the language in which the oath was expressed and finds that [the one who required of him the oath] said: "Upon thee is the compact of Allah and His covenant, also those which were taken from the Prophets and the just, so if you reveal the secret you do not belong to Islam or to the Muslims", or "[if you do you will be] one who does not believe in Allah, Lord of the worlds", or "[if you do] all your property will become alms." No oath whatsoever expressed in these terms will hold good. If one says: "Should you do such and such then I belong not to Islam, nor to Allah and His Apostle", this would not be an [acceptable] oath, for he—upon whom be Allah's blessing and peace—has said: "He who swears an oath, let him swear by Allah or keep silent." Now an oath by Allah is that one should say: "Wallāhi" or "Tallāhi" (i.e. by Allah), or some such expression. We have investigated exhaustively the [question of] explicit oaths in [our treatise entitled] *Fann al-Fiqh,* and the expressions mentioned above [as offered by him who required the oath] are not among those [considered as belonging to explicit oaths]. Neither is [it acceptable for] a man to say: "On me is Allah's covenant and compact, and that which Allah took from the Prophets,"[1] for should Allah not take his covenant and his compact

[1] Sūra III, 81/75 speaks of the covenant *(mīthāq)* which Allah had with the messengers He sent to mankind. See pp. 204–205, 382.

there would not be any other statement in the oath to make it binding. As a matter of fact, Allah—exalted be He—would not accept their covenant if it involved concealing the secrets of unbelievers and of folk who are astray in error. Nor indeed is such a compact as this like the compact of Allah, so it does not make anything obligatory. It is the same should a man say: "If I do so and so then my property is an alms", for that would not put him under any obligation unless he phrased it: "I put myself under obligation to Allah to distribute my property in alms." This is the oath of anger and importunity, and one may be released from it, according to the preferred opinion, by [the usual manner of] redemption of an oath.[1]

The fourth is for him to look into the matter about which he has taken the oath, and if there should be in the transcript of the compact any expression such as we have mentioned, e.g. their [habit of] saying: "Now you will conceal the secret of Allah's *walī*,[2] assist him and never disobey him", then let him reveal the secret whenever he wishes, and he will not be an oath-breaker. What he swore to conceal was the secret of the *Walī* of Allah—exalted be He—and that he has concealed, for what he revealed was the secret of the enemy of Allah. It is the same when they say: "You will aid his near relations and his followers", for that again has reference to the [true] *Walī* of Allah, and not to the one whom the offerer of the oath has in mind, for he is Allah's enemy and not His friend. Should it be that he indicates some particular person or mentions him by the name by which he is generally known, saying: "You will conceal my secret", or "You will conceal the secret of So-and-So, the *Walī* of Allah", or "You will conceal the secret of this person who is the *Walī* of Allah", then, if we have regard to the one described and indicated [in these phrases] it may be declared that he does not become an oath-breaker by disclosing the secret. It is as though one should say: "I will purchase from you this ewe", while he is pointing to a stud-mare, which would not be a proper [legally acceptable statement of the transaction proposed]. The preferred opinion in our eyes is that oath-breaking takes place only when that which is indicated is something with which one is well-acquainted and is so particularized [in the statement of the oath] that there can be no prevarication about it, [and that means] something much better than the

[1] There is a section in the books on Muslim Jurisprudence which deals with the question of what atonement may be made to redeem a mistaken oath.

[2] *walī* means "one who has been set in charge of", and among the Bāṭinīs the *imām* was commonly called the *walī* as the successor of 'Alī, who was the prime *walī* of Allah. *walī* also means "close friend", and in this passage both meanings are in mind. See pp. 206, 314.

false description above mentioned. This is not the same as if one were to say: "By Allah, I will assuredly drink the water of these wastes" when there is no water in them. Such an oath could not be fulfilled by reason of the absence of that with which the oath was concerned. Similarly were one to omit the relationship to the wastes and mention only "this water", pointing with the hand, it could not be fulfilled because of the absence of that with which it is here concerned. Were one to confine oneself to saying that one would not disclose the secret of this person, or the secret of Zaid,[1] it would be [an oath to be] kept, even though one refrained from saying that he was the *Walī* of Allah. Whenever an oath of this kind has been taken the disclosure of the secret is permissible, nay more, the disclosure of the secret is obligatory, but he must needs offer redemption, i.e. the [normal] atonement for a [broken] oath. It will be sufficient if he feeds ten unfortunates, giving each of them a *mudd*[2] of food, or if he is unable to do that then that he fast for three days. This is the least thing he can do about it. There is no need to go more carefully into the matter of seeking devices for release beyond the measure [we have given here], for it is a matter easily forgiven. One is not guilty of disobedience by violating such an oath, for he—upon whom be Allah's blessing and peace—has said: "He who binds himself by taking an oath and then sees something other that is better than it, let him go for what is better, but let him give redemption for his oath." One who swears that he will fornicate, or that he will omit prayers, is under obligation to violate his oath, but he must make redemption. This case [we have under consideration] belongs to that same category.

The fifth case is when the one who swears the oath omits intention and exception, and the one who demands the oath omits any expression such as "compact" or "covenant" or "*Walī* of Allah", so that it is an explicit oath "by Allah" and involves divorce and manumission, both of the slaves he already has and his wives, and whatever [of either] he may possess from then on to the end of his life, and should he break the oath he must perform a hundred pilgrimages, fast a hundred years, pray a thousand *rak'as*, give a thousand dinars in alms, and so on. His way [to release] from an oath "by Allah" is the feeding of ten unfortunates, or, if that is not possible, fasting as we have previously

[1] This does not mean any particular Zaid. The Arab grammarians were accustomed to use the names Zaid and 'Amr in their illustrative examples just as two names, as we might use John and George, and from the grammarians the usage became general. Here it means only the secret of any particular person.

[2] For the *mudd* see note 3 on p. 492.

mentioned. This will also give him freedom from the matter of alms and pilgrimages and fastings and prayers when he breaks the oath, for such an oath is an oath of anger and importunity which does not necessarily have to be fulfilled. As for what is concerned with divorcing such wives and manumitting such male and female slaves as he may come to possess, that [type of oath] is invalid [in any case] and not to be concluded, so let him break it and marry whom he pleases when he pleases. There can be no divorce before marriage nor manumission before possession, but if he has in his possession a slave whom he fears he will have to free, then the way for him to take is to sell him to his wife, or to his son or his friend, and after he has disclosed the secret (of the Bāṭinī) get him back into his possession again by purchase or by asking him as a gift or any other way he likes. There is surely no one who does not have a friend in whose friendship and faithfulness he can trust, who would buy [such a slave] from him and then return him to him whenever he wished.[1] In the matter of his wife, if he has sworn to divorce her [should he break his oath to the Bāṭinī], let him put her away for a dirham which she or a stranger possesses,[2] and then, after discovering the secret, renew the marriage with her and be in security from concern with divorce after that.

Should some one ask: "But suppose he had already uttered two divorce pronouncements [against her] so that there remained to him but one more[3] pronouncement, then such a putting away [as you describe] would make her forbidden to him till she had gone through a marriage with another husband, then what could he do?"—our answer is: The way for him to take is to say [to her]: "Whensoever it may be that you suffer my repudiation, you have been repudiated thrice before it," then when he breaks the oath no repudiation will be involved. This is [what is known as] the circular oath, by which one frees oneself of the guilt of oath breaking, and which will prevent any divorce from taking place.

Should someone say: "But the scholars differ on this point, so maybe a pious man would not approve of embarking on suspicion of divorce!" —our reply is: If the questioner is a stickler for having a legal decision then there is [available for him] the decision of the *muftī* which he must follow. A written statement on divorce is peculiar in this that the *muftī*

[1] The point here is that some of the authorities regarded the manumission of a slave as the proper redemption or expiation of a broken oath.

[2] I.e. make use of a ruse by which it would appear that she has been divorced.

[3] A Muslim husband does not have to institute legal proceedings to get rid of his wife, it is sufficient for him to pronounce thrice the words of repudiation, and she is automatically divorced. Thereafter he can take her back again only after she has consummated marriage with another male and been divorced by him.

is the one responsible for the divorce not the one seeking the decision. If the *muftī* is a *mujtahid*[1] he can reach a decision by exercising his own judgment, and if the exercise of his judgment leads to that [decision to divorce] then the divorce is inevitable. Then the man will have to choose between exchanging her for another or refraining from disclosing their secret. Nevertheless he must abandon their belief, for to refrain from disclosing what they have said does not mean agreeing with them in religion. Only agreeing to believe what they believe would mean that. If he speaks out on behalf of his own belief and summons them to it, if he gives up their error outwardly and inwardly, he is actually under no obligation to proclaim what he has heard from them, since no one is in duty bound to make public the story of the unbelief of every unbeliever.

These are the devices for freeing oneself of an oath [sworn to a Bāṭinī]. Some of those who discuss this question go so far as to say that no oath given to them is to be fulfilled under any circumstances, but such statements are due to deficient examination of juristic regulations. The only [judgment] which accords with a proper regard for jurisprudence and the regulations of the religious law is that which we have recorded—and that is that.

[1] A *mujtahid* is one who goes back to the original sources and comes to his own independent conclusion on the solution of a problem in jurisprudence, as against those who rely on decisions given by earlier authorities. See p. 253.

THE SĪRA

INTRODUCTION

The Corpus of Traditions recording the sayings and doings of the Prophet was compiled in the first instance, as we have seen, in the interests of jurisprudence, and only somewhat later in the interests of doctrine. There was, however, at a comparatively early date, some interest in the life story *(sīra)* of the Prophet. In part this was connected with the striving for prestige in Islam, this being to some extent dependent on how early one had accepted Islam, and how valiantly one had fought for the new religion. From this arose the *maghāzī* books, recounting the warlike expeditions of the Prophet, and recording the prowess of those who had fought therein under his command. In part, however, it was due to the interest of new Muslims who had not known Muḥammad in the flesh and were eager to learn of the various events in his career as a Prophet of Allah. We have references to early *maghāzī* books by Abān b. ʿUthmān (c. 100 A.H.), Shuraḥbīl b. Saʿd (d. 123), Wahb b. Munabbih (d. 110), and even have that by al-Wāqidī (d. 207).[1] We also hear of early biographies by ʿUrwa b. az-Zubair (c. 94 A.H.), Mūsā b. ʿUqba (d. 141), and az-Zuhrī (d. 125). The earliest of which we possess any considerable part, however, is that by Ibn Isḥāq (d. 151), which survives in long extracts in aṭ-Ṭabarī's *Annales*, and in a recension by Ibn Hishām (d. 218).[2] By this time the process of idealization of the Prophet had got well into its stride. As time went on pious imagination greatly developed this idealization till in the later popular *Lives* of Muḥammad there has gathered around his figure as great a mass of legend and wonder tales as had earlier gathered around the figure of the Buddha in the *Jātakas*, or around the figure of Jesus in the apocryphal Gospels.[3]

[1] Edited by A. von Kremer in the *Biblioteca Indica* (Calcutta, 1856). Wellhausen summarized the material in the London MS in his *Muhammed in Medina* (Berlin, 1882).

[2] Edited by F. Wüstenfeld, 2 vols. (Göttingen, 1858–60), translated into German by G. Weil (Stuttgart, 1864), and now into English by A. Guillaume (London, 1955).

[3] It is still of some interest to read some of this material in S. W. Koelle's *Mohammed and Mohammedanism* (London, 1889).

THE COMMENCEMENT OF THE PROPHET'S REVELATIONS [1]

On how the Prophet began his prophethood with true visions

Said Ibn Isḥāq: Az-Zuhrī has related from 'Urwa b. az-Zubair how 'Ā'isha told him that the first steps in prophethood of the Apostle of Allah—upon whom be Allah's blessing and peace—when Allah wished to honour him and by him shew mercy to His servants, were in the way of true visions. Never would the Apostle of Allah—upon whom be Allah's blessing and peace—see a vision in his sleep but it came like the breaking of the dawn. She said: "And Allah gave him a love of solitude, so that he liked nothing better than to be alone by himself."

On how stones and trees gave greeting to the Prophet

Said Ibn Isḥāq: It has been related to me by 'Abd al-Malik b. 'Abdallah b. Abī Sufyān b. al-'Alā' b. Jāriya ath-Thaqafī, who remembered [hearing] it from some of the learned, that when Allah wished to honour the Apostle of Allah—upon whom be Allah's blessing and peace—and start him off on his prophetic mission, it so was that when he went out to relieve himself he would go some distance till the houses were far from him and he had arrived at the deep valleys of Mecca, at the low part of its wadies, that the Apostle of Allah—upon whom be Allah's blessing and peace—would not pass by a rock or a tree but it would say: "Greeting to you O Apostle of Allah." Said he: The Apostle of Allah—upon whom be Allah's blessing and peace—would look around him, to right and to left and behind, and would see nothing but trees and stones. So the Apostle of Allah—upon whom be Allah's blessing and peace—would remain there looking and listening for such time as Allah willed he should remain. Then Gabriel brought him what came to him from Allah's favour, and it was at Ḥirā' in the month of Ramaḍān.

[1] Ibn Hishām, *Sīrat an-Nabī*, ed. Wüstenfeld, pp. 151–155; ed. Muḥyi'd-Dīn 'Abd al-Ḥamīd, I, pp. 252–259.

The beginning of Gabriel's coming down

Said Ibn Isḥāq: Wahb b. Kaisān, client of the az-Zubair family, related to me, saying: I heard 'Abdallah b. az-Zubair saying to 'Ubaid b. 'Umair b. Qatāda al-Laithī: Relate to us, O 'Ubaid, about the beginnings of the Apostle of Allah's prophethood, when Gabriel came to him. Then 'Ubaid said, and I was there present while he was relating it to 'Abdallah b. az-Zubair and the people with him: "The Apostle of Allah—upon whom be Allah's blessing and peace—used to repair to Ḥirā' for a month every year. This was in accordance with the custom of the Quraish in the Jāhiliyya to practise *taḥannuth.*" Now *taḥannuth* means *tabarrur* (the practising of piety). Said Ibn Isḥāq: Abū Ṭālib said:

"By Mt. Thaur, and Him who set Mt Thabīr in its place,
And by one who ascends, to go up into Ḥirā' and come down."

Saith Ibn Hishām: The Arabs say *taḥannuth* and *taḥannuf*, meaning Ḥanifism by both, making interchange of *th* and *f*, as they do in *jadath* and *jadaf,* both of which mean "grave". Said Ru'ba b. al-'Ajjāj: "Were my stones with the graves", using *ajdāf* for "graves" where he meant *ajdāth.* This line is from an *urjūza* of his, and the verses quoted above are from an ode of Abū Ṭālib which I shall mention, if Allah so wills, in its place. Saith Ibn Hishām: Abū 'Ubaida has related to me that the Arabs say *fumma* instead of *thumma* for "then," giving a *f* in place of *th.*

Said Ibn Isḥāq: Wahb b. Kaisān has related to me [saying]: 'Ubaid said to me that the Apostle of Allah—upon whom be Allah's blessing and peace—used to repair [to Ḥirā'] on that month every year and feed all such poor as came to him. When the Apostle of Allah—upon whom be Allah's blessing and peace—had ended that month of retreat the first thing he would do on his return from his retreat was to visit the Ka'ba before he entered his own house. He would circumambulate it seven times, or as often as Allah willed, and then would go on to his house. [This continued] till it was the month in which Allah desired to honour him and in the year in which He sent him [as a Prophet]. The month was Ramaḍān, and the Apostle of Allah—upon whom be Allah's blessing and peace—went out to Ḥirā' as he had been wont to go for his retreat, and with him was his family. When it was the night on which Allah would honour him with Apostleship and provide a mercy for His servants thereby, Gabriel came to him by Allah's command. Said the Apostle of Allah—upon whom be Allah's blessing and peace—: "He came to me while I was sleeping, [bringing] with [him] a cloth *(namaṭ)* of silk-brocade *(dībāj)* on which was writing. He said: 'Read!', but I answered: 'I do not read.' Then he smothered me with it till I thought I should die; then freeing me, he said: 'Read!' I answered: 'But I do not read.' Again he smothered me with it till I thought I should die; then, freeing me, he said: 'Read!' But I said: 'I do not read.' So he smothered me with it till I thought I should die, and then, freeing me, said: 'Recite!'[1] So I said: 'What then shall I recite?', saying that only to save myself from having him do again to me the like of what he had been doing. He said: 'Recite, in the name of thy Lord who has created; created man from clots of blood. Recite, seeing that thy Lord is the most generous, Who has taught by the pen, taught man what he did not know' (Sūra XCVI, 1–5). So I recited it, and then he stopped and departed from me. I awoke from my sleep and it was as though a writing were written on my heart. Then I went off till I was in the midst of the mountain, where I heard a voice from heaven, saying: 'O Muḥammad, thou art the Apostle of Allah, and I am Gabriel.' I raised my head towards the heaven to look, and behold, there was Gabriel in the form of a man, with winged feet, on the horizon of heaven, saying: 'O Muḥammad, thou art the Apostle of Allah, and I am Gabriel.' I stood looking at him, neither advancing nor retreating. Then I began to turn my face from him around the horizon of the heaven, but I could not look in any direction without seeing him just the same. So I continued standing, not going forward nor moving backward, till Khadīja sent her messengers to seek for me. They went as far as the heights of Mecca and returned to her [without any news], while I was standing in that place. Then he departed from me and I departed from him, returning to my family. I came to Khadīja and sat in her lap seeking refuge with her. She said: 'O Abū'l-Qāsim, where have you been? By Allah I sent my messengers to seek you, and they went even as far as the heights of Mecca and returned to me [without news]'. Then I related to her what I had seen, and she said: 'Rejoice, O son of my uncle, and be constant. By Him in whose hand is the soul of Khadīja, I hope that you will be the Prophet of this people.'" Then she rose up, put on her garments, and went to Waraqa b. Naufal b. Asad b. 'Abd al-'Uzzā b. Quṣayy, who was a cousin of hers. This Waraqa had become a Christian and had read the Scriptures, and he had hearkened to the people of the Torah and the Injīl. To him she

[1] It is the same imperative *iqra'* which means either "read" or "recite". The orthodox tradition is that Muḥammad could neither read nor write, and so there is the double use of the word here, the angel bidding him read, and since he could not read telling him the words that he might recite them.

told what the Apostle of Allah—upon whom be Allah's blessing and peace—had told her of what he had seen and heard. Said Waraqa: "Holy *(quddūs)*! Holy! By Him in whose hand is the soul of Waraqa, if you are telling me the truth, Khadīja, there has come to him the great *Nāmūs* [1] which used to come to Moses, so assuredly he is the Prophet of this people. Tell him, therefore, that he must be constant." Thereupon Khadīja returned to the Apostle of Allah—upon whom be Allah's blessing and peace—and told him what Waraqa had said. When the Apostle of Allah—upon whom be Allah's blessing and peace—had completed his retreat and gone off, he did as he had been accustomed to do, visit the Ka'ba and circumambulate it. Waraqa b. Naufal met him as he was circumambulating the Ka'ba and said to him: "O son of my brother, tell me about what you saw and heard." So the Apostle of Allah—upon whom be Allah's blessing and peace—told him, and Waraqa said to him: "By Him in whose hand is my soul, you are assuredly the Prophet of this people, and there has come to you the great *Nāmūs* which came to Moses. You will be called a liar, ill-treated, driven out and fought against. If I live to see that day I will lend Allah such aid that He will recognize it." Then he bent his head to him and kissed the top of his head. At that the Apostle of Allah—upon whom be Allah's blessing and peace—returned to his dwelling.

An account of how Khadīja tested the proof of the Prophet's revelations

Said Ibn Isḥāq: Ismā'īl b. Abī Ḥakīm, the client of the az-Zubair family related to me that he had it on the authority of Khadīja that she said to the Apostle of Allah—upon whom be Allah's blessing and peace—: "Arc you able, O son of my uncle, to inform me when this friend who comes to you is coming?". "Yes, surely", said he. Then she said: "If he comes, inform me of it." So when Gabriel came to him as was his wont, the Apostle of Allah—upon whom be Allah's blessing and peace—said to Khadīja: "O Khadīja, this is Gabriel, who has come to me." Said she: "Rise, O son of my uncle, and sit on my left thigh." So the Apostle of Allah—upon whom be Allah's blessing and peace—rose and sat there. She said: "Do you see him?". "Yes", said he. Then she said: "Change over and sit on my right thigh." So the Apostle of Allah—upon whom be Allah's blessing and peace—did so, and changed over to sit on her right

[1] This is the Syriac word *nāmūsā*, "Law", which itself is but the Greek word νόμος.

thigh. She asked: "Do you see him?". "Yes", said he. Then she said: "Change over and sit in my lap", so he changed position and sat in her lap. She asked: "Do you see him?". "Yes", said he. Then she uncovered herself and removed her veil *(khimār)*, while the Apostle of Allah—upon whom be Allah's blessing and peace—was sitting in her lap, and she then asked: "Do you see him?". "No", said he. Then she said: "O son of my uncle, be constant, rejoice, for by Allah, he is an angel and is no satan." Said Ibn Isḥāq: "I told ʿAbdallah b. Ḥasan this *ḥadīth,* and he said: "I heard my mother Fāṭima, daughter of Ḥusain, relate this *ḥadīth* from Khadīja, save that I heard her say that she placed the Apostle of Allah—upon whom be Allah's blessing and peace—inside her shift, whereupon Gabriel went off and she said to the Apostle of Allah: 'Verily this is an angel, he is no satan.'"

The beginning of the revelation of the Qur'ān

Said Ibn Isḥāq: The beginning of the coming down [of revelations] to the Apostle of Allah—upon whom be Allah's blessing and peace—was in the month of Ramaḍān. Says Allah (II, 185/181): "The month of Ramaḍān in which was sent down the Qur'ān as a guidance for men, and as evidential signs of the Guidance, and the Furqān." Allah also said (XCVII, 1ff.): "We, indeed, sent it down on the Night of al-Qadr", and so on to the end of that Sūra. He has said (XLIV, 1ff.): "ḤM. By the Book which makes clear. Lo! We have sent it during a blessed night. Lo! We were warning. Therein each wise affair is disposed of. An affair from Us. Lo! We have been sending [envoys]." Also He has said (VIII, 41/42): "If ye have believed in Allah and in what We sent down to Our servant on the day of the Furqān, the day the two groups met", i.e. the meeting of the Apostle of Allah—upon whom be Allah's blessing and peace—and the polytheists on the day of Badr.

Said Ibn Isḥāq: Abū Jaʿfar Muḥammad b. ʿAlī b. al-Ḥusain related to me that the Apostle of Allah—upon whom be Allah's blessing and peace—met with the polytheists at Badr on Friday morning the seventeenth of Ramaḍān.

Said Ibn Isḥāq: It was then that revelation [in the true sense] began to come to the Apostle of Allah—upon whom be Allah's blessing and peace—and he was believing in Allah, putting full trust in what came to him from Him, receiving it with glad welcome, and for its sake he bore what he was given to bear of the favour of men or their disfavour. For the prophetic office has its burdens and its troubles which none can bear or handle save those among the Apostles who have force and resolution, with the aid and succor of Allah, for what they meet with from the people and [come up against] the way in which what they bring from Allah is rejected. So the Apostle of Allah—upon whom be Allah's blessing and peace—went on at the command of Allah in spite of the opposition and the harsh treatment he was to meet with from his people.

THE GREAT GHAZWA OF BADR [1]

(The Prophet is now head of a community in Madīna, to which he fled from Mecca in the year 622 A.D. It is now his second year in Madīna and his Muslim followers are in dire economic straits. To relieve this he has organized raids on the commerce of the Meccans, attempting to capture their caravans as they went up to or returned from the markets in the north. Where he himself commanded the raid it was called a *ghazwa*, where he appointed another to lead it was called a *sarīya*. He had attempted to capture a very large and rich caravan on its way north, but the caravan leaders had outwitted him. The story now picks up at the point when he gets news that the caravan is on its way back.)

That great caravan against which he—upon whom be peace—had gone out against while it was journeying to Syria, but which he did not overtake, and for whose return he ceased not to be on the watch, did not long delay. So when he heard that it was returning he called the attention of his companions to it, saying: "This is the caravan of Quraish. Go out against it, and maybe Allah will give it you for booty." Some of them responded, but others held back, thinking that the Apostle—on whom be peace—would not desire war. He showed no special anxiety about this, but said: "Whoever has his mount ready let him ride with us", and he did not delay for those whose mounts were not present. So he departed when three nights of Ramaḍān had elapsed, after having appointed over Madina ʿAbdallah b. Umm Maktūm. There were with him three hundred and thirteen men, some two hundred and forty from the Anṣār and the rest from among the Emigrants. They had with them two mares and seventy camels which they rode in turns. The standard bearer was Muṣʿab b. ʿUmair al-ʿAbdarī.

Now when Abū Sufyān [2] heard of this coming out of the Apostle of Allah—upon whom be Allah's blessing and peace—he hired a rider to go

[1] A *ghazwa* is a military expedition led by the Prophet in person. This account is translated from the popular book *Nūr al-Yaqīn fī Sīrat Sayyid al-Mursalīn*, by Muḥammad al-Khuḍarī, third edition (Cairo, 1326 A.H. = 1908 A.D.), pp. 113–132.

[2] The Meccan chieftain who was in charge of the caravan coming back to Mecca from the north.

to the Quraish and give them the news. When they heard of it they were much disturbed, being afraid for their merchandise, so they went out quickly, and there did not remain behind a single one of their notables save Abū Lahab b. ʿAbd al-Muṭṭalib, and he sent al-ʿĀṣ b. Hishām b. al-Mughīra in his stead. Umayya b. Khalaf also wanted to remain behind because of a tale that Saʿd b. Muʿādh had told him when [Saʿd] was a visitor a little after the Hijra, for he told [him] as al-Bukhārī relates: "I heard from the Apostle of Allah these words: 'Verily they will kill you.'" He asked: "At Mecca?", but he answered: "I do not know." For this reason [Umayya] was afraid and swore he would not go out, but Abū Jahl cried shame on him and ceased not [doing so] till he went out, determining to return after a little. But Allah's will is above every will, so his destiny drove him to his death in spite of himself. Likewise a party of the notables decided to procrastinate, and this was held a shame to them, whereupon the men of Quraish decided unanimously on going out. So out they went on rough beasts and tame ones, and before them went the singing women singing satires *(hijā')* on the Muslims.

"Thus did Satan make their deeds seem fine to them, saying: 'You will not meet with a conqueror today from that people, seeing that I am with you'" (VIII, 45/50). But Allah made that act of Satan a proverbial one from which the intelligent folk who come after them may take warning, as He says in Sūrat al-Ḥashr (LIX, 16): "Like Satan when he said to man: 'Do not believe', and when he did not believe, he said: 'I am innocent in regard to you. I fear Allah, Lord of the worlds.'" Thus was his work in this battle. "So when the two parties came face to face [Satan] took to his heels, saying: 'I am innocent in regard to you: I see, indeed, what ye do not see. Verily, I fear Allah, for Allah is a dreadful punisher'" (VIII, 48/50).

Now the number of the polytheists who went out [from Mecca] was nine hundred and fifty men, accompanied by a hundred horses and seven hundred camels.

As for the Apostle of Allah—upon whom be Allah's blessing and peace—he did not know anything of what the polytheists were doing, nor was his incursion directed towards anything other than the caravan. So he camped by the houses of the water-carriers outside Madina, reviewed the army, and sent back all who were unfit for war. Then he sent two men to spy out news of the caravan. When he reached Rawḥā' news came to him of the marching of the Quraish to protect their caravan; also his two spies brought him news that the caravan would reach Badr on the morrow or the day after the morrow. So he—upon whom be peace—

gathered together the leading men of his army and said to them: "O my people! Verily Allah has promised me one of the two parties, so you will get either the caravan or the trumpet [of battle]."

It was then made clear to him—upon whom be peace—that some of them desired [it to be] the unarmed party, viz. the caravan, in order that they might provide for themselves out of the riches it contained, though they had said: "Have you not promised us fighting? Then let us get ready." In confirmation of this came His word—exalted be He—in Sūrat al-Anfāl (VIII, 7): "And when Allah promised you that one of the two parties should be yours, but you were desiring that the undefended one might be yours."

Then Miqdād b. al-Aswad—with whom may Allah be pleased—rose up and said: "O Apostle of Allah: lead on to whatever Allah has commanded you, for by Allah, we will not say to you what the Children of Israel said to Moses (V, 24/27): 'Go up, thou and thy Lord, and fight, verily we will rest here'; on the contrary [we say]: 'Go up, thou and thy Lord, and fight, and we will be fighting with you.' By Allah! were you to make us go to Burk al-Ghamād we would fight along with you all the same till you should reach it." So [the Apostle] invoked Allah's blessing on him. Then he—upon whom be peace—said: "Advise me, O people", meaning by that the Anṣār, because there was the possibility of the pledge of ʿAqaba [1] being understood to mean that it was not incumbent on them to aid him save so long as he was among them [in the city], for, as a matter of fact, it does read: "O Apostle of Allah, we are free of obligation to you until you reach our home, but when you have reached there you are in our protection, and we will protect you from whatever we protect our own children and our women-folk."

At that, Saʿd b. Muʿādh, chief of the Aus,[2] said: "It is as though you need us, O Apostle of Allah." "Assuredly", he replied. So Saʿd said: "Indeed we have believed in you and trusted you and have given you our promises. So lead on to whatever Allah has laid upon you, and by Him who has sent you with the truth, were you to confront us with this river and ford it, we would ford it with you, and there would be no murmur from us should you fall in with our enemy tomorrow. Verily we are

1 The Pledge of ʿAqaba was the undertaking given by the groups from Madīna who were responsible for inviting Muḥammad to leave Mecca and take up his abode as the community leader in their city.

2 The Aus and the Khazraj were the two main Arab tribal elements in the population of Madīna. The members of the community who were under covenant to help Muḥammad, no matter what their tribal affiliation might be, were the Anṣār, and the Emigrants were the group who had followed him from Mecca to Madīna.

patience itself in face of battle, and are the essence of steadfastness at the encounter. Maybe Allah will reveal to you in us that which will rejoice you (lit. cool your eyes). So march on under the blessing of Allah." At that his face—upon him be peace—lit up, and he was pleased with those words, saying, as al-Bukhārī relates: 'Rejoice! By Allah, it is as though I see the fates [1] of the people." From this saying the people knew that war must come to pass, and as a matter of fact it did come to pass.

Now Abū Sufyān, when he learned of the coming forth of the Muslims against him, left the beaten track and journeyed following along the sea shore and so escaped. Then he sent to the Quraish to inform them of this and advising them to return home. But Abū Jahl said: "We will not return till we have reached Badr. We will rest there three days, we will slaughter the animals and eat food and drink wine, so the Arabs will hear about us and will not cease to fear us for ever." Then said al-Akhnas b. Sharīq the Thaqafite to the Banū Zuhra, with whom he was an ally: "Return home, ye people, for verily Allah has saved your property." So they returned, and thus it was that no Zuhrī and no 'Adawī witnessed Badr. The army, however, journeyed on till they reached the valley of Badr, where they descended at the bank farthest from the city, in loose soft soil.

As for the army of the Muslims, when it drew near to Badr, he—upon whom be peace—sent 'Alī b. Abī Ṭālib and az-Zubair b. al-'Awwām to find out the news. By chance they encountered some of the Quraish water-carriers, among whom was a youth of the Banū al-Ḥajjāj and a youth of the Banū al-'Āṣ, both of them Sahmites,[2] so they brought them along to where the Apostle—upon whom be peace—was standing praying. There they questioned them about themselves, and they said: "We are water-carriers for Quraish. They sent us out to draw water for them." But ['Alī and az-Zubair] beat them, because they thought that the two youths belonged [to the caravan] of Abū Sufyān. Thereupon the two youths said: "We belong to Abū Sufyān", so they left them alone. When the Apostle—upon whom be peace—had finished his prayers he said: "When they told you the truth you beat them, but when they lied to you you left them alone. They were telling the truth, by Allah, for they belong to the Quraish." Then he said to them: "Give me news about the Qur-

[1] Lit. "wrestling places", a reference to the battle field where their fates would be worked out.

[2] I.e. both the tribes to which these youths belonged were members of the greater tribe of Sahm b. 'Amr, who in ancient days had possessed the springs (or wells) of Ghamr in Mecca.

aish." They said: "They are there behind this sand dune." He asked them: "How many are they?" They answered: "We do not know." So he said: "How many do they sacrifice every day?" They answered: "Some days nine, some days ten." He said: "Then the host is between nine hundred and a thousand." Then he asked them about what notables of Quraish were in the army and they mentioned to him a great number of them, whereupon he—upon whom be peace—said to his friends: "This [means that] Mecca has literally thrown to you its choicest sons."

Then they journeyed until they descended at the brink of the valley nearest to Madīna, but far from water, in marshy land. The Muslims soon began to be thirsty, some of them being ceremonially impure and some of them even defiled, so Satan tempted them by his whispering, and had not Allah's grace and mercy been with them their steadfastness would have been overthrown, for he said to them: "What do the polytheists anticipate with regard to you save that thirst will choke you and your strength go from you, so that they may deal with you as they please?" Therefore Allah sent down to them rain till the valley overflowed. They drank and they made little reservoirs on the bank of the valley, where they washed and performed their ablutions and filled the water-skins. Also [by reason of this rain] the ground grew compact so that their feet were firm on it. On the other hand this rain was a misfortune for the polytheists for the earth [where they were] grew muddy so that they were hardly able to advance. There is confirmation of this in His words—exalted be He—(VIII, 11): "When He made rain from heaven descend upon you, with which He might purify you and remove the filth of Satan from you, and that thereby He might gird up your hearts and make firm your feet."

Then Allah caused His Apostle to see the enemy in his dream—as He made them see him—at the time of battle few in number, in order that the Muslims might not be faint-hearted, and that Allah might bring to pass a matter that had been determined. He said—exalted be He—in Sūrat al-Anfāl (VIII, 43/45): "When Allah shewed you them in your dream as few; and had He shewed you them as many you would have been faint-hearted and would have disputed about the affair; but Allah preserved [you]—verily Allah knows the secrets of the breasts. And when He made them appear few to your eyes at [your] meeting, and made you [appear] small in their eyes, that Allah might bring to pass a matter that had been determined. To Allah all things return."

Then the army of the Muslims marched till they reached the water nearest Badr, when al-Ḥubāb b. al-Mundhir, one of the Anṣār, said to him, and he was [a man] renowned for the soundness of his judgment:

"O Apostle of Allah, is this the place that Allah has appointed for you [as a place] from which we may neither go forward nor retreat, or is [your selection of this place but] a matter of opinion or military tactics and stratagem?" [The Apostle] answered: "Indeed, it is but a matter of opinion and tactics and stratagem." So [al-Ḥubāb] said: "O Apostle of Allah, this is no place for you. Go up with the people till you come to the water nearest the host [of the enemy], for I know the abundance and extent of its waters. Let us descend there and break up what other wells than it there are. Then we will build upon it a reservoir which we will fill with water to drink while they do not [have anything to] drink." Said the Apostle—upon whom be peace—: "Verily you have given excellent counsel." So he went up until he reached the water nearest the host [of the enemy], where he gave orders about the wells which were behind him, so that they were broken up that the polytheists' hope of drinking after the Muslims might be cut off. Also they built a reservoir at the place where they descended.

Then Sa'd b. Mu'ādh, chief of the Aus, said to him: "O Prophet of Allah, shall we not build for you a booth in which you may stay, and arrange beside you your mounts? Then we will fall on the enemy, and if Allah—exalted be He—gives us strength and we conquer our enemies, that will be what we desired, but should the opposite happen you could mount your steed and follow with those who are behind us, for [behind us are] several tribes who left you, O Apostle of Allah, who are quite as strong in love to you and in obedience to you as we are, who were eager for and desirous of doing battle, and had they thought that you would meet with war they would not have left you, only they thought that it was [merely a matter of] the caravan. [Should the battle go against us] Allah will use them to protect you, and they will advise you well and fight along with you." Said he—upon whom be peace—: "What better thing could Allah have ordained than that?" So they built a booth for him on top of a hillock overlooking the field of battle. When they had assembled, he—upon whom be peace—straightened their lines, putting them shoulder to shoulder, so that they became like a solid wall. Then he looked over towards the Quraish, and said: "Allahumma, this Quraish has come out in its arrogance and boastfulness to oppose Thee and to make Thy Apostle a liar. Allahumma, [grant me] that victory which Thou didst promise."

At that very moment disagreement broke out among the leaders of the army of the polytheists. [The reason for this was that] 'Utba b. Rabī'a desired to restrain the people from war and be himself responsible for the blood of his ally 'Amr b. al-Ḥaḍramī, who had been killed during the *sarīya* under ʿAbdallah b. Jaḥsh, and himself bear whatever loss there might be from the caravan, so he made an announcement to the people to this effect. But when news of it reached Abū Jahl he called him a coward, and said: "By Allah, we will not return till Allah has decided between us and Muḥammad."

Now before the battle started in earnest there sprang out from the ranks of the polytheists al-Aswad b. ʿAbd al-Asad al-Makhzūmī, and said: "I call Allah to witness that I will drink of their cistern, or break it up, or die in the attempt." So there went out against him Ḥamza b. ʿAbd al-Muṭṭalib and struck him a blow that cut off his foot with half his leg, so he fell on his back and dragged himself to the cistern that he might reach it and fulfil his vow. Ḥamza followed him and killed him. Then he—upon whom be peace—stood up and encouraged the people in steadfastness and patience. Part of what he said was: "Verily patience in time of calamity is one of the things wherewith Allah drives away care and gives assuagement from grief."

The fighting began by individual combats. There came forth from the ranks of the polytheists three men: ʿUtba b. Rabīʿa with his brother Shaiba and his son al-Walīd, and they called for opponents. There went out against them three of the Anṣār, but they said: "There is nothing between us and you, we desire only adversaries from our cousins." Thereupon he—upon whom be peace—sent out ʿUbaida b. al-Ḥārith b. ʿAbd al-Muṭṭalib against the first, Ḥamza b. ʿAbd al-Muṭṭalib against the second, and ʿAlī b. Abī Ṭālib against the third. As for Ḥamza and ʿAlī they killed their opponents, but ʿUbaida and ʿUtba exchanged blows and each wounded his opponent, so the two companions of ʿUbaida set upon ʿUtba and killed him. They carried off ʿUbaida from between the lines, wounded, the marrow running from his leg, and laid him down near the resting-place of him—upon whom be peace and Allah's blessing. Then the Apostle of Allah stretched out his noble leg and put his (i.e. ʿUbaida's) cheek upon it, promising him [the honour of] martyrdom, and saying: "I greatly desire, by Allah, that Abū Ṭālib were alive that he might know that we are more worthy than he was himself of his words:

> 'And we shall protect him till we die at his side,
> E'en though we forget both our sons and our wives.'"

After the individual combats had come to an end, he—upon whom be peace—stood up between the ranks to straighten them, using a rod that was in his hand. Now he passed by Sawād b. Ghazīya, an ally of the

Banū an-Najjār, who was standing out from the line, so he struck him on the stomach with his rod, saying: "Stand up straight, O Sawād." He said: "You have hurt me, O Apostle of Allah, and yet you came for truth and justice. Give me then my recompense on your person." So the Apostle—upon whom be peace—uncovered his own stomach and said: "Take your recompense, O Sawād." Then Sawād stepped forward and kissed his stomach, whereat he—upon whom be peace—said: "Why did you do that?" He answered: "O Apostle of Allah, you see what has been happening. I desired, therefore, that my last experience should be that of my skin touching your skin." So [the Apostle] called a blessing on him.

Then he—upon whom be peace—began to admonish the army, saying: "Do not attack until I bid you. If the people surround you then shoot at them with arrows but do not draw swords till they strike at you." Then he urged on them patience and steadfastness, and returned to his booth along with his companion Abū Bakr, and his sentinel Sa'd b. Mu'ādh was standing at the door of the tent with his sword girt on. The prayer of the Apostle—upon whom be peace—at that time was, as is recorded in the *Ṣaḥīḥ* of al-Bukhārī: "Allahumma, I remind Thee of Thy oath and Thy promise. Allahumma, shouldest Thou desire [to forget it] Thou wilt not be worshipped". Thereupon Abū Bakr said: "That is enough for you. Verily Allah will accomplish for you what He promised you." So he—upon whom be peace—went out from his booth, saying [as he went]: "All of them will be put to flight, and they will turn their backs" (LIV, 45). Then he—upon whom be peace—in order to encourage the army, said: "By Him in whose hand is Muḥammad's soul, there is no man who shall fight today and die while patiently enduring, whether retreating or advancing, turning not back, but Allah will take him to Paradise, and whosoever kills a victim, his is the booty." Thereupon 'Umair b. al-Ḥumām spoke up, and in his hand was a bunch of ripe dates that he was eating: "Luck! Luck! There is nothing between me and entrance to Paradise save the being killed by one of these." Then he cast away the dates from his hand, took his sword and fought till he was killed.

The battle grew fierce and the fray waxed hot, but Allah helped the Muslims by His angels as an encouragement to them, and that their hearts thereby might be eased. Not an hour passed ere [the hosts of the polytheists] were all put to flight and turned their backs, so the Muslims followed them, killing [some] and taking [others] prisoner. Of the polytheists about seventy were killed. Among those of the Quraish were 'Utba and Shaiba, the two sons of Rabī'a, and Walīd b. 'Utba, who were killed in the individual combats before the battle. Also [among them] were

Abū'l-Bakhtarī b. Hishām and al-Jarrāḥ the father of Abū 'Ubaida, whom his own son killed after having avoided him, but he would not take warning. Also among the killed were Umayya b. Khalaf and his son 'Alī. A band of the Anṣār along with Bilāl b. Rabāḥ and 'Ammār b. Yāsir determined on killing them, the two latter being incited to that by what Umayya had done to them in Mecca. Also among the slain was Ḥanẓala b. Abī Sufyān, and also Abū Jahl b. Hishām whom two young men of the Anṣār beat grievously because they had heard of his bitter opposition to the Apostle of Allah, but he was killed by 'Abdallah b. Mas'ūd. Among the slain was Naufal b. Khuwailid, whom 'Alī b. Abī Ṭālib killed, also 'Ubaida and al-'Āṣī the two sons of Abī Uḥaiḥa Sa'īd b. al-'Āṣ b. Umayya, and very many others also. As for the prisoners they were likewise seventy, of whom he—upon whom be peace—killed on his return 'Uqba b. Abī Mu'aiṭ and an-Naḍr b. al-Ḥārith, who had been among those at Mecca who had mocked most at him. This battle took place on the 17th of Ramaḍān, which was the day the Qur'ān commenced coming down a whole year before.

Then he—upon whom be peace—gave orders that the dead should be removed from the place where they fell—[a matter] about which the Apostle had had news before the battle took place—to the brook Badr. [This he did] because it was a custom of his—upon whom be peace—on his raids that whenever he passed by a human corpse he would order it to be buried, without asking whether [the man] were a believer or an unbeliever. When they came to 'Utba the father of Abū Ḥudhaifa, one of the earliest converts to Islam, his (i.e. Abū Ḥudhaifa's) face changed. The Apostle—upon whom be peace—noticed this, and said: "Maybe a certain grieving for your father has entered you." "Nay, by Allah", he answered, "But I knew my father for a man of intelligence, patience and goodness, and I greatly desired that Allah would lead him to Islam, so when I saw how he died that grieved me." Then the Apostle—upon whom be peace—called down a blessing on him.

Then he—upon whom be peace—called for his mount and rode it till he reached the edge of the place where the [corpses of the] polytheists had been thrown, and he began to call upon them by their names and the names of their fathers: "O So-and-So the son of So-and-So, would you not have done better to have been obedient to Allah and to His Apostle? We indeed have received what our Lord promised us. Have you received truly what your Lord promised?" 'Umar said [to Him]: "O Apostle of Allah, what you are addressing are bodies without souls." He replied: "By Him in whose hand is Muḥammad's soul, you do not hear what I am saying better than they do." 'Ā'isha—with whom may Allah be pleased—asserts that what he said was: "They know now that what I said to them is the truth", and then she recited (XXVII, 80/82): "Verily you will not make the dead to hear" (XXXV, 22/21), "And you are not one who makes those in the tombs hearken." She said: "They will know that when they take possession of their places in the Fire" (Tradition from al-Bukhārī).

Then he—upon whom be peace—sent bearers of the good news. 'Abdallah b. Ruwāḥa was sent to the people of 'Āliya,[1] and Zaid b. Ḥāritha was sent to the people of Sāfila, riding on the Prophet of Allah's she-camel. Now the Hypocrites[2] and the Jewish unbelievers had been spreading dreadful tales about the Apostle and the Muslims, [as is] the custom of enemies in publishing bad news, desiring thereby [to create] dissension among the Muslims, but those bearers of good news came with [tidings] that pleased the people of Madina. It was just at the moment they were returning from the funeral of Ruqaiya, the daughter of the Apostle of Allah and wife of 'Uthmān.

Anon the Apostle of Allah himself returned, but straightway there broke out dissension among some of the Muslims over the division of the spoils. The young men said: "We bore the burden of the fighting so it (i.e. the booty) is certainly ours." But the old men said: "We helped you, so we share with you." Since such disagreement is one of those things that lead to weakness and the growth of enmity and bitter hatred in hearts, tending to break up unity, Allah sent down against this discord the first part of Sūrat al-Anfāl (VIII, 1): "They will ask you about the spoils. Say: The spoils belong to Allah and the Apostle. So fear Allah and settle this among yourselves, obeying Allah and His Apostle, if ye are true believers." Thus did the light of the Qur'ān shine on their hearts, and they came to agreement after they had almost had a schism, and they left the [matter of the] division of the spoils to the Apostle of Allah, to distribute as he willed according as the Qur'ān commanded. So he—upon whom be peace—divided it justly, foot-soldier with foot-soldier and horseman with horseman, and he gave a place in the division to some who were not present [at the battle] because of matters that had been assigned to them, viz. Abū Lubāba al-Anṣārī, because he had been left

[1] These places are villages on the outskirts of Madīna, whence word would be sent into the city.

[2] The word is used here in a technical sense for those people in Madīna who only outwardly accepted the position of authority of Muḥammad in their city, but in their hearts were annoyed that he had been invited there from Mecca, and who in secret opposed him and his followers at every turn.

behind over the people of Madina, and al-Ḥārith b. Ḥāṭib, because the Apostle had left him behind over the Banū ʿAmr b. ʿAuf to enquire into the truth of a matter, [news of which] had reached him, and al-Ḥārith b. aṣ-Ṣimma and Khawwāt b. Jubair, because they two had broken [their legs] at ar-Rawḥāʾ and so could not walk, and Ṭalḥa b. ʿUbaidallah and Saʿīd b. Zaid, because they two had been sent to seek news and did not get back till after the battle, and ʿUthmān b. ʿAffān, because the Apostle of Allah had left him behind with his daughter Ruqaiya to nurse her, and ʿĀṣim b. ʿAdī, because he had been left behind over the people of Qubāʾ and ʿĀliya. Likewise he gave a share to those who were killed at Badr. They were fourteen, among them ʿUbaida b. al-Ḥārith b. al-Muṭṭalib b. Hāshim, who had been wounded in the first combats and who—may Allah be pleased with him—died at the return of the Muslims from Badr and was buried at aṣ-Ṣafrāʾ.

Now when he drew near to Madina—upon him be peace—the maidens met him with tambourines, singing:

"The full moon has risen upon us
From the folds of Wadāʿ.
It is incumbent on us to give thanks
For as long as a petitioner may call upon Allah.
O thou who hast been sent to us,
Thou hast come with a command that is to be obeyed."

THE STORY OF THE REBUILDING OF THE KAʿBA [1]

How the Apostle of Allah decided for the Quraish about the placing of the Stone

When the Apostle of Allah—upon whom be peace—was thirty-five years of age it so happened that the Quraish came to an agreement to rebuild the Kaʿba. They were anxious to do this so that they might roof it over, but they were afraid [to make a start at the task] of pulling it down. It was [at that time] only a loose stone structure somewhat above a man's height, and they desired to raise it and roof it over. The reason for this was that some men had been stealing the treasure of the Kaʿba which used to be [deposited] in a well in the midst thereof. He with whom the treasure was found was one Duwaik, a client of the Banū Mulaiḥ b. ʿAmr b. Khuzāʿa. Saith Ibn Hishām: The Quraish cut off his hand, though their opinion was that those who had stolen it had deposited it with Duwaik.

Now the sea had cast up at Jidda a ship belonging to a Byzantine merchant which was quite smashed up so they took its timber and prepared it for the roofing. At Mecca there was a man, a Coptic carpenter, and part of the material to repair it was at their disposal, but there was a snake which used to come out of the well in the Kaʿba, in which they had been wont to deposit the gifts brought each day thereto, to bask in the sun on the walls of the Kaʿba. It was one of the things they were afraid of because no one could draw nigh it without its raising its head, hissing and opening its mouth, so that they were afraid of it. One day while it was sunning itself on the wall of the Kaʿba as was its wont, Allah sent a bird which snatched it up and took it off. Then Quraish said: "We hope that that means that Allah is pleased with what we have proposed. We have here a serviceable craftsman, and we have timber, and now Allah has attended to the snake for us."

When they had come to an agreement about the matter of pulling it down and rebuilding it, there arose Abū Wahb b. ʿAmr b. ʿĀ'idh b. ʿAbd b. ʿImrān b. Makhzūm, (saith Ibn Hishām: ʿĀ'idh was the son of ʿImrān b. Makhzūm), and took from the Kaʿba a stone, but it leapt from

[1] From Ibn Hishām's *Sīrat an-Nabī*, ed. Wüstenfeld (Göttingen, 1858), I, pp. 122–126; ed. Muḥyi'd-Dīn ʿAbd al-Ḥamīd (Cairo, 1937), I, pp. 209–216.

his hand and returned to its place, so he said: "O people of Quraish, do not put into the building of it anything you have gained save what is good. Let no whore's hire be put into it, no product of usury, nothing that has been gained by oppressing any of the people." Some attribute these words to al-Walīd b. al-Mughīra b. ʿAbdallah b. ʿAmr b. Makhzūm. Said Ibn Isḥāq: ʿAbdallah b. Abī Najīḥ al-Makkī related to me that he was told on the authority of ʿAbdallah b. Ṣafwān b. Umayya b. Khalaf b. Wahb b. Ḥudhāfa b. Jumaḥ b. ʿAmr b. Huṣaiṣ b. Kaʿb b. Lu'aiy that he saw a son of Jaʿda b. Hubaira b. Abī Wahb b. ʿAmr circumambulating the House and asked about him. He was told: "This is a son of Jaʿda b. Hubaira." Thereupon ʿAbdallah b. Ṣafwan said: "The grandfather of this fellow—meaning Abū Wahb—was the one who took a stone from the Kaʿba when the Quraish had agreed to demolish it, but it leapt from his hand and returned to its place, whereupon he said: 'O people of Quraish, put not into the building of it anything of your gain save what is good. Put in no whore's hire, no product of usury, nothing gained by oppressing any of the people.'" Said Ibn Isḥāq: Abū Wahb was a maternal uncle of the father of the Apostle of Allah—upon whom be Allah's blessing and peace—and was a noble. It is of him the Arab poet says:

"Had I couched my camel at [the dwelling of] Abū Wahb
Her saddle would have gone at noon satisfied with his generosity.
A foremost man, of the chiefs of Lu'aiy b. Ghālib,
When their genealogies are brought forth, he is among the top ones,
Refusing to tolerate any injustice, quick is he to be generous.
Both his grandfathers were among the choicest branches,
Huge is the ash-mound beneath [his] cooking pot, he fills his porringers
With bread loaves, which he piles up like hair-plaits."

Then the Quraish divided up the Kaʿba into lots. The side in which is the door fell to the Banū ʿAbd Manāf and Zuhra. What was between the Black corner and the Yemenite corner fell to the Banū Makhzūm and the tribes of Quraish who had joined themselves to them. The rear of the Kaʿba fell to the Banū Jumaḥ and Sahm the sons of ʿAmr b. Huṣaiṣ b. Kaʿb b. Lu'aiy, the northern wall fell to the Banū ʿAbd ad-Dār and the Banū Asad b. al-ʿUzzā b. Quṣaiy and the Banū ʿAdī b. Kaʿb b. Lu'aiy, it being the Ḥaṭīm wall. Then [when all was ready] the people were afraid to demolish it and kept away from it. Al-Walīd b. al-Mughīra said: "I will give you a start in pulling it down", so he seized a pick-axe, stood over against it, and said: "Allahumma! You [O Kaʿba] are not a thing to be feared" *(turaʿ)*. Saith Ibn Hishām: Others give it *tariʿ*, i.e. you will not be firm, "Allahumma! we desire naught but what is good." Then he pulled down the part near the two corners. At that the people left it for that night, saying: "Let us see. If anything happens to him we will not pull down any more of it but will restore it as it was, but if nothing happens to him, then Allah is pleased with what we are doing and we will pull it down." Al-Walīd arose unharmed after his night's rest and came early to his work of pulling down, so the people pulled down with him, until when they had finished their demolition they came to the foundations, the foundations of Abraham, and reached green stones like camels' humps each one sticking to the other.

Said Ibn Isḥāq: One of the relaters of traditions has told me that a man of Quraish, one of those who was engaged on the demolition, stuck a crowbar between two of these stones in order to lift out one of them, but when the stone was moved all Mecca threatened to fall, so they left that foundation alone. Said Ibn Isḥāq: I have been told that the Quraish found in the corner[-stone] a document in Syriac, and they knew not what it was till a man of the Jews read it to them. It was as follows:

> "I am Allah, Lord of Bakka.[1] I created it on the day when I created the heavens and the earth and formed the sun and moon. And I set around it seven angels, Ḥanīfs. It will not perish till its two Akhshab hills pass away. A blessing to its inhabitants is it in water and in milk."

Saith Ibn Hishām: Its two Akhshabs mean its two hills. Said Ibn Isḥāq: And I have been told that in the Maqām they found a writing in which [was written]:

> "Mecca is the sacred House of Allah. Its prosperity comes from three paths. The first to profane it will not be one of its own people."

Said Ibn Isḥāq: Laith b. Abī Sulaim says that forty years before the coming of the Prophet they found a stone in the Kaʿba on which was written, if what he says is true, "Whosoever sows good will reap happi-

[1] Wüstenfeld's text reads *Mecca*. In Sūra III, 96/90 Mecca is called Bakka, which is said to be the ancient name of the city. Ḥanīf is another Qur'ānic word, for Abraham is in several passages said to be a Ḥanīf, one who rejected all polytheism. Muslim tradition is that Abraham and Ishmael built the Kaʿba.

ness, and whosoever sows evil will reap repentance. Would you do evil deeds and reap the reward of good deeds? Nay! as grapes are not gathered from thorns."

Said Ibn Isḥāq: Then the Quraish tribes assembled for the rebuilding, each tribe assembling by itself. Then they went on with the reconstruction until the building work reached the place of the Corner.[1] About this (i.e. about the setting of the Black Stone in its place there) they disputed, each tribe wanting to be the one to lift it into its place rather than have some other do it, so they drew apart from one another to confer and prepared to fight it out. The Banū ʿAbd ad-Dār brought a bowl filled with blood and they and the Banū ʿAdī b. Kaʿb b. Luʾaiy made a compact unto death, plunging their hands into that bowl, for which reason they were called "the blood-covenanted". In this fashion the Quraish remained for four or five nights, but then they assembled in the shrine, took counsel together and sought some equitable solution. Some of those who hand down tradition say that Abū Umayya b. al-Mughīra b. ʿAbdallah b. ʿUmar b. Makhzūm, who was that year the oldest man among all Quraish, said: "O people of Quraish, agree among yourselves in this matter about which ye are divided, [let us agree] that the first man who enters the door of this shrine will decide the matter for you." To this they agreed, and the first man to enter was the Apostle of Allah—upon whom be Allah's blessing and peace. When they saw him they said: "This is al-Amīn (the faithful); we are content. This is Muḥammad." When he reached them they told him about the matter, and he said: "Bring me a cloak." So one was brought. Then he took the stone and with his own hands put it therein. Then he said: "Let each tribe take one side of the cloak, then raise all together." They did this until when they had brought it to its place he put it in with his hand and it was built over. The Quraish used to call the Apostle of Allah—upon whom be Allah's blessing and peace—al-Amīn, before the coming of the revelations. When they had finished with the building operations and had built it as they desired, az-Zubair b. ʿAbd al-Muṭṭalib said, with reference to the matter of the snake on whose account the Quraish had been afraid to [start to] rebuild the Kaʿba:

"Amazed was I to see the eagle swoop down
Towards the snake, and it trembled before her.
It had been hissing [at her],

[1] I.e. the corner of the building in which the Black Stone, the old Arabian cult-object of the Kaʿba, is set. See pp. 191, 501-502.

And occasionally made little darts.
When we came to lay a foundation it attacked,
Scaring us from building operations, and it was feared indeed.
And when we were afraid of being harmed, there came
An eagle, whose dart [at it] was successful.
She drew it to her, then made free
For us the building, nothing now hindering.
So we hastened to do the building.
With us were the base stones and the binding soil.
Next morning we raised the foundations thereof,
And to make ourselves all equal no one wore his gown.
By this [building] did the [divine] King glorify the Banū Lu'aiy,
For there is no escaping the fact that it originated with them.
There also the Banū 'Adī hastened indeed,
And Murra, though Kilāb preceded them.
By this did the [Divine] King prepare for us glory,
For with Allah is reward to be sought."

The Ka'ba in the time of the Apostle of Allah—with whom be Allah's blessing and peace—was eighteen cubits in size and was robed with Qabāṭī cloth. Later it was robed in streaked cloth [of the kind] called Burūd. The first to robe it in silk brocade was al-Ḥajjāj b. Yūsuf.

THE PROPHET'S FAREWELL SERMON [1]

"O ye people, hearken to what I have to say, for I do not know whether I shall ever meet you again in this place after this year. O ye people, consider your lives *(dam)* and your property as inviolable to one another till ye meet your Lord, as sacred among you at this day and this month, for you are assuredly going to meet your Lord and He will question you about your deeds. I have delivered [2] [the message committed to me]. Let each one who has had a deposit entrusted to him be careful to render it back to the one who has entrusted him with it. All interest *(ribā)* is to be remitted, though in retaining your capital you do no injustice nor do you suffer any injustice.[3] Allah has decreed that there be no usury *(ribā)*,[4] so all the interest [owing to] ʿAbbas b. ʿAbd al-Muṭṭalib [5] is to be remitted. Moreover, all the blood-wit *(dam)* [6] incurred during pre-

1 In the year 10 A.H. (630–631 A.D.), when the pilgrimage month came around, Muḥammad made his final pilgrimage to the shrines in the Holy City, and at Munā on the 11th of the month he addressed the assembled pilgrims. Since the Prophet died only a few months after this, later piety has made the address into a farewell sermon in which the Prophet, as it were, gave his last testament to his community. As such it has been highly regarded by later generations of Muslims, and the text of the "sermon" is extant in various forms. That translated here is from Ibn Hishām's *Sīra* (pp. 968, 969 in Wüstenfeld's edition = Ṭabarī, *Annales*, ed. de Goeje, I, 1753–1755). Other texts will be found in Wellhausen's *Wāqidī (Muhammed in Medina*, pp. 430–432), Ibn Saʿd, *Ṭabaqāt*, II, i, 133, 134 (ed. Mittwoch); Ibn ʿAbd Rabbihi, *al-ʿIqd al-farīd*, II, 157, 158; *as-Sīra al-Ḥalabiyya* (Cairo, 1321), III, 298, 299. See also Caetani, *Annali dell'Islam*, II, 77, and Sir Wm Muir's *Life of Muhammad* (ed. T. H. Weir, Edinburgh, 1912), pp. 472–474.—Ibn Hishām quotes from his main source, Ibn Isḥāq, how the Prophet performed the pilgrimage that year, and explained to his community how the pilgrimage rites *(manāsik)* were to be performed under this new religion of Islam. Then he addressed them, and after having offered praises and laudations to Allah, he began the sermon.

2 For this duty of the messengers to deliver their message, see Sūra XXIX, 18/17; III, 20/19; LXIV, 12.

3 This is quoting Sūra II, 279.

4 See Sūra II, 275/276 ff.

5 This was Abū'l-Faḍl al-ʿAbbās, an uncle of Muḥammad, who was a rich merchant and money-lender in Mecca. See *Ency. Islam*, I, 9, 10.

6 Though he says only "blood" the reference is to the blood-feud, and he means that any blood-feuds contracted in the pre-Islamic period are automatically cancelled when

Islamic days is to be remitted. The first blood-wit I remit is that of Ibn Rabīʿa [1] the son of al-Ḥārith b. ʿAbd al-Muṭṭalib. He was suckled among the Banī Laith and then the Hudhail killed him, and he is the one with whom I make a beginning in this matter of blood-wit from the pre-Islamic period."

"Now, O ye people, Satan has already despaired of his ever being worshipped in this land of yours, but if he is obeyed in matters other than that he will be well-pleased with deeds of yours of which you think lightly, so guard against him by your religion. O ye people, the practice of intercalation [2] is but an increase in unbelief whereby those who disbelieve go astray. One year they make it profane and one year they make it sacred. They make profane what Allah has made sacred and make sacred what Allah has made profane. Yet time has been going on its cyclic round at the same speed it was given on the day when Allah created the heavens and the earth. The number of months with Allah is twelve months.[3] Four of these are sacred, three following one another [4] and Rajab of Muḍar, which is between the two Jumādās and Shaʿbān."

"O ye people, ye have rights ye may claim of your women and they have rights they may claim of you. The right you may claim of them is that they permit no one to tread your carpets who would be unwelcome to you, and that they commit no open immorality. If they do, Allah gives you permission to withdraw yourselves from their beds and to beat them, though not excessively,[5] but if they desist therefrom they have a right to their sustenance and to their clothing as is suitable. Treat women kindly for they are with you as helpmeets who can do nothing for themselves, [remembering] that you have possession of them only as a trust from Allah, and have the freedom of their pudenda only because of certain words [6] of Allah."

---

men become Muslims, so that nothing is owing under Islam for blood shed in pre-Islamic days.

[1] He was a youthful kinsman of Muḥammad.

[2] Lit. "postponement". He is quoting Sūra IX, 37, which refers to the custom in pre-Islamic days of bringing the lunar year into harmony with the solar calendar by intercalating the necessary days, and to do this postponing at the beginning of the sacred month. See Axel Moberg's *An-Nasī' in der islamischen Tradition* (Leipzig, 1931).

[3] Sūra IX, 36.

[4] These are Dhū'l-Qaʿda, Dhū'l-Ḥijja and Muḥarram, the eleventh, twelfth and first months of the Islamic calendar. Rajab is the seventh month and falls between the two Jumādās, which are the fifth and sixth, and Shaʿbān, which is the eighth. It is called Rajab of Muḍar because this great tribal group is said to have held it in special honour in ancient Arabia.

[5] Sūra IV, 34/38.

[6] The reference is to II, 222, 223.

"Consider well what I am saying, O ye people, for I have delivered my message and have left among you that which, if you lay hold upon it, will keep you from ever going astray, viz. a clear command, a book of Allah, and the custom *(sunna)* of His Prophet. O ye people, hearken to what I say and consider it well. You have been taught that every Muslim is a brother to every other Muslim, so that the Muslims are brethren, and it is not lawful for a man to take from his brother anything save what he may give him out of the kindness of his soul, so do not do wrong to yourselves."

"Allahumma! have I delivered my message?"

It has been related to me that the people responded: "Yes." Then the Apostle—upon whom be Allah's blessing and peace—said: "Allahumma! bear witness."

THE MIRACLES OF THE PROPHET[1]

ʿAffān b. Muslim has informed us, relating from Ḥammād b. Salama, relating from ʿAlī b. Zaid, from Abū Zaid, that the Apostle of Allah—upon whom be Allah's blessing and peace—was at al-Ḥajūn and was in grief and distress. He said: "Allahumma, show me this day a miracle, after which I will not care who among my people treats me as false." Now there was a tree ahead on the road leading on to Madina, so he summoned it, and, separating itself from the earth, it came till it was before him and salaamed to him. Then when he commanded it it returned [to its place]. He said: "After this I care not who among my people treats me as false."

Al-Faḍl b. Dukain has informed us, relating from Ṭalha b. ʿAmr, from ʿAṭā', who said: It has reached me that the Prophet—upon whom be Allah's blessing and peace—was on a journey, when he suddenly felt the desire to relieve his bowels, or to satisfy his need, but he could find nothing to conceal him from the people. Then he noticed two trees in the distance, so he said to Ibn Masʿūd: "Go and stand between them and say to them: 'The Apostle of Allah has sent me to you to have you join yourselves together so that he may satisfy his need behind you.'" Ibn Masʿūd went and said this to them, whereat the one of them joined itself to the other and he was able to satisfy his need behind them.

Wakīʿ has related to us, relating from al-Aʿmash, from al-Minhāl b. ʿAmr, from Yaʿlā b. Murra, who said: I was with the Prophet—upon whom be Allah's blessing and peace—on a journey, and when we dismounted at a stopping-place he said to me: "Go to those two small date-palms and say to them: 'The Apostle of Allah—upon whom be Allah's blessing and peace—commands you to join together.'" So I went to them and said that to them, whereat the one of them sprang across to the other so that they were joined together. Thereupon the Prophet—upon whom be Allah's blessing and peace—went over, took cover [behind them], and satisfied his need, after which each of them sprang back to its place.

[1] Translated from Ibn Saʿd's *Kitāb aṭ-Ṭabaqāt al-kabīr* (Leiden, 1905), I. i, pp. 112–126.

Ismāʿīl b. Abān al-Warrāq has informed us, relating from ʿAnbasa b. ʿAbd ar-Raḥmān al-Qurashī, from Muḥammad b. Zādhān, from Umm Saʿd, from ʿĀʾisha, who said: I said [one day]: "O Apostle of Allah, you go to the privy yet nothing of what you void is ever seen." He answered: "Do you not know, O ʿĀʾisha, that the earth swallows up what comes from Prophets so that nothing [of what they void] is ever seen?"

Muslim b. Ibrāhīm has informed us, relating from al-Ḥārith b. ʿUbaid, relating from Abū ʿImrān, from Anas b. Mālik, who said that the Apostle of Allah—upon whom be Allah's blessing and peace—said: "While I was sitting, one day, Gabriel entered and struck me between the shoulders. I arose [and went] to a tree in which was something like two bird's nests, in one of which he seated himself while I sat in the other. [The tree] thereupon began rising, mounting upwards till it shut off the East and the West, and had I so wished I could have touched the [vault of] heaven. On my side I was all upset till I looked at Gabriel. There he was [as steady] as a tightly-clinging saddle-cloth, which made me recognize how well he knew Allah. He opened for me a gate in the heavens so that I saw the great light. Then the veil whose border is of pearls and jacinths descended before me [1] and Allah revealed to me what He willed to reveal."

Muslim b. Ibrāhīm has informed us, relating from al-Ḥārith b. ʿUbaid al-Iyādī, relating from Saʿīd b. Iyās Abū Masʿūd al-Jurairī, from ʿAbdallah b. Shaqīq, from ʿĀʾisha, who said: The Prophet—upon whom be Allah's blessing and peace—was carefully guarded until this verse (V, 67/71) was revealed: "And Allah will defend thee from the people." At that, she said, the Apostle of Allah—upon whom be Allah's blessing and peace—put his head out from the tent and said to them, [i.e. to those on guard]: "O folk, depart, for Allah has undertaken to guard me from the people."

Al-Faḍl b. Dukain has informed us, relating from Ṭalḥa b. ʿAmr, from ʿAṭāʾ, from the Prophet—upon whom be Allah's blessing and peace—who said: "We are a band of Prophets; our eyes sleep, but our hearts sleep not." Hawdha b. Khalīfa b. ʿAbdallah b. Abī Bakra has informed us, relating from ʿAuf, from al-Ḥasan, that the Prophet—upon whom be Allah's blessing and peace—said: "My eyes sleep, but my heart sleeps not." [2]

[1] The reference is to the famous Veil which always hangs between Allah and His creatures. Even to the archangels He speaks only from behind the Veil lest they should perish at the sight of His glory. Cf. I Tim. VI, 16.

[2] The heart was considered to be the seat of the intelligence, so this does not mean that their affections never slumbered, but that though the bodies of the Prophets might lie in sleep their minds were always awake.

Al-Ḥajjāj b. Muḥammad al-Aʿwar has informed us on the authority of Laith b. Saʿd, from Khālid b. Yazīd, from Saʿīd b. Abī Hilāl, from Jābir b. ʿAbdallah, who said: The Apostle of Allah—upon whom be Allah's blessing and peace—came out to us and said: "In a dream I saw as though Gabriel were at my head and Michael at my feet, each of them saying to the other: 'Coin a parable for him.' So one of them said: 'Hearken, for thine ear hath heard, and understand, for thy heart hath grasped. The parable for thee and for thy community is that of a king who took a piece of ground, built thereon a dwelling in which he set a table, and then sent a messenger to summon the people to his supper. Some of them responded to the messenger, but some took no notice. Now the king is Allah, the piece of ground is Islam, the dwelling is Paradise, and thou, O Muḥammad, art the messenger. Whoever responds to you, O Muḥammad, will enter Islam, and whoever enters Islam will enter Paradise, and whoever enters Paradise will feast on what is therein.'"

Saʿīd b. Muḥammad ath-Thaqafī has informed us, on the authority of Muḥammad b. ʿAmr, from Abū Salama, who said: The Apostle of Allah—upon whom be Allah's blessing and peace—used not to eat what was given in alms but would eat what was given as a gift. Now a Jewish woman gave him as a gift a roasted sheep, of which he and his companions started to eat, but it cried out: "I am poisoned." Thereupon he said to his companions: "Withdraw your hands, for it has informed [us] that it is poisoned." [Immediately] they withdrew their hands, but Bishr b. Barā' died. The Apostle of Allah—upon whom be Allah's blessing and peace—sent for her, asking [her]: "What led you to do this that you have done?" "I wanted to know [for sure]," she answered. "If you were a Prophet it would do you no harm, but if you were [setting yourself up as] a king I would have relieved the people of you." He gave orders and she was put to death.

Saʿīd b. Sulaimān has informed us, relating from Khālid b. ʿAbdallah, from Ḥusain, from Sālim b. Abī'l-Jaʿd, who said: The Apostle of Allah—upon whom be Allah's blessing and peace—sent out two men on a certain affair of his, but they said: "O Apostle of Allah, we have not with us sufficient provision [for such a journey]." He answered: "Ask for a water skin to be brought to me." A water-skin was brought to him and he bade us fill it. Then he tied it and said: "Go along till you reach such and such a place, for there Allah will provide for you." So they went off [and journeyed] till they came to that place to which the Apostle of Allah—upon whom be Allah's blessing and peace—had bidden them go, and when they untied their water-skins [they found] therein milk and fresh goat's cheese *(zubd ghanam)*, so they ate and drank their fill.

Hāshim b. al-Qāsim Abū'n-Naḍr al-Kinānī has informed us, relating from ʿAbd al-Ḥamīd b. Bahrām, who said: Shahr, i.e. Ibn Ḥawshab, has related to me, relating from Abū Saʿīd al-Ḥaḍramī, who said: [One day] while a man from Aslam was with a little flock of his, beating down leaves for them in the wilderness of Dhū'l-Ḥulaifa, a wolf came raiding on him and snatched away a sheep from his flock. The man shouted at it and cast stones at it until he recovered from it his sheep. Then the wolf approached till it squatted sitting on its tail opposite the man and said: "Do you not fear Allah! snatching away from me a sheep that Allah had given me as my provision for the day." Said the man: "By Allah, till this day I have never heard of such a thing." Said the wolf: "What is it that astonishes you?" "The thing that astonishes me", he answered, "is a wolf addressing me." Said the wolf: "But you have overlooked something more astonishing than that. Here is Allah's Apostle—upon whom be Allah's blessing and peace—in the palm-groves among these stony tracts telling the people about things that have been and about things that are going to be, yet here you are following your flock." When the man heard these words from the wolf he drove along his flock, urging them gently along, till he brought them into Qubā', one of the villages of the Anṣār, where he asked about the Apostle of Allah—upon whom be Allah's blessing and peace. He came upon him in the house of Abū Ayyūb and told him the story about the wolf. Said the Apostle of Allah—upon whom be Allah's blessing and peace—: "You are telling the truth. Be present this evening, and when you see the people assembled, tell them about that." This he did, and when [the Prophet had] prayed the [evening] prayers and the people were assembled, the Aslamī told them the story about the wolf. Said the Apostle of Allah—upon whom be Allah's blessing and peace—: "True! True! True! Such wonders as that precede the Hour." This he said three times. [Then he continued]: "By Him in whose hand is Muḥammad's soul, it will come about that a man from you will be away from his family, journeying by night or by day, and his whip or his staff or his sandal will inform him of what has happened to his family since he left them."

Hāshim b. al-Qāsim has informed us, relating from ʿAbd al-Ḥamīd b. Bahrām, who said: Shahr related to me, relating from ʿAbdallah b. ʿAbbās, who said: While the Apostle of Allah—upon whom be Allah's blessing and peace—was sitting in the courtyard of his house at Mecca, ʿUthmān b. Maẓʿūn passed by and smiled at the Apostle of Allah—upon whom be Allah's blessing and peace. Said the Apostle of Allah—upon whom be Allah's blessing and peace—: "Will you not sit?" "Assuredly", said he. So the Apostle of Allah—upon whom be Allah's blessing and peace—sat over against him, and while he was conversing with him, the Apostle of Allah—upon whom be Allah's blessing and peace—fixed his gaze on the sky, looking for a while at the sky. Then he began to lower his eyes till his gaze was fixed on the ground to his right. The Apostle of Allah—upon whom be Allah's blessing and peace—was meanwhile quite withdrawn from his guest 'Uthmān [and occupied] with that spot where his gaze was fixed. Then he began to nod his head like one who is following what is being said to him, while Ibn Maẓ'ūn was watching. When this was ended and he had assented to what was said to him the gaze of the Apostle of Allah—upon whom be Allah's blessing and peace—went once more to the sky as it had the first time, and his gaze followed him till he disappeared from sight in the sky. Then he reoccupied himself with [the matter] of his visit with 'Uthmān as at the first. 'Uthmān said: "O Muḥammad, while I was sitting here with you I did not expect to see you do what you did this morning." Said he: "And what did you see me doing?" He answered: "I saw you fix your gaze on the sky. Then you shifted it to your right and were so occupied with it that you neglected me, and you began to nod your head as though you were assenting to something that was said to you." Said he: "Did you perceive that?" "Assuredly", answered 'Uthmān. So the Apostle of Allah—upon whom be Allah's blessing and peace—said: "There came a messenger from Allah just now while you were sitting [with me]." "A messenger from Allah?", he asked, and [the Prophet] said: "Yes." "And what did he say to you?", he asked. "He said", answered [the Prophet], "Allah commands justice and kindliness and the giving to kinsfolk, and He forbids sensuality, reprobate conduct and greediness. He warns you, in order that maybe you will take heed" (XVI, 90/92). Said 'Uthmān: "That was when the faith was fixed firm in my heart and I came to love Muḥammad."

Hāshim b. al-Qāsim has related to us, relating from 'Abd al-Ḥamīd b. Bahrām, relating from Shahr, who said: Ibn 'Abbās said that one day a party of Jews was present with the Apostle of Allah—upon whom be Allah's blessing and peace—and they said: "O Abū'l-Qāsim, tell us about some hidden matters of which we will ask thee and which no one but a Prophet would know." "Ask me about whatever you wish", he answered, "but give me Allah's bond *(dhimma)*, and that which Jacob took from his sons,[1] that if I tell you anything and you recognize [that it is

[1] The reference is to Sūra II, 133/127.

true] you will follow me in Islam?" They answered: "Thus shall it be"; so he said: "Ask whatever you wish." They said: "Inform us about four hidden matters of which we shall ask you. Inform us what food it was that Israel declared forbidden to himself before the coming down of the Torah.[1] Inform us how a woman's semen differs from a man's and how male and female are derived therefrom. Inform us how this *ummī*[2] Prophet [gets revelations] while asleep, and who among the angels is his patron."[3] He replied: "Then take covenant by Allah that if I inform you you will follow me." They gave him whatever covenant and binding promise he wanted, and he said: "I adjure you by Him Who sent down the Torah to Moses, do you know that Israel-Jacob[4] was very ill of a sickness that was long continued, so he took a vow that if Allah would cure him of his sickness he would declare forbidden to himself whatever food and whatever drink he liked best? Now the food he liked best was camel's flesh and the drink he liked best was camel's milk." They said: "Allahumma, that is so." He said: "Allahumma, bear witness against them." Then he said: "I adjure you by Allah, than Whom there is no other deity, He who sent down the Torah to Moses, do you know that a man's semen is thick and white, but a woman's is thin and yellowish, and from whichever of them gets the mastery over [the other] the child is derived? The assimilation is by permission of Allah, but if the man's semen gets the mastery over the woman's then the child is a male, and if the woman's semen gets the mastery over the man's then the child is a female, by Allah's permission." They said: "Allahumma, that is so." He said: "Allahumma, bear witness against them." He said: "I adjure you by Him who sent down the Torah to Moses, do you know that this *ummī* Prophet sleeps with his eyes but his heart sleeps not?" They said: "Allahumma, that is so." He said: "Allahumma, bear witness against them." They said: "Now come along and tell us which of the angels is your *walī*, for it is on that that we will either join ourselves to you or separate from you." He said: "Gabriel, indeed, is my *walī*. Never yet has a Prophet been sent but he was his *walī*." They said: "On that we separate

[1] Sūra III, 93/87 refers to this matter. It is apparently a confused reminiscence of Gen. XXXII, 32.

[2] In Sūra VII, 157/156 ff. Muḥammad refers to himself as the *ummī* Prophet, which Muslim orthodoxy translates "illiterate Prophet" and insists means that he could neither read nor write. It seems, however, to mean no more than that he had no formal instruction in Scripture.

[3] *walī*, "friend", "companion", "guardian", "patron". See pp. 206, 276.

[4] In III, 93/87 and XIX, 58/59 the name Israel is used for the Patriarch elsewhere in the Qur'ān called Jacob. Cf. Gen. XXXII, 28.

ourselves from you. Had any other angel been your *walī* we would have followed you and put our trust in you." "And what", he asked, hinders you from putting your trust in him?". "He", they replied, "is our enemy."[1] Thereat Allah—illustrious be His praises—said (II, 97/91ff.): "Say: whosoever is an enemy to Gabriel, why he it is who has brought it (i.e. the revelations) down upon thy heart by Allah's permission... as though they know not." At that [the Jews] became angrier than ever.

Hāshim b. al-Qāsim has informed us, relating from Sulaimān, i.e. Ibn al-Mughīra, from Isḥāq b. ʿAbdallah b. Abī Ṭalḥa, who said: The Apostle of Allah—upon whom be Allah's blessing and peace—paid a visit to Saʿd and took his siesta at his place. When it was cool enough [to set off] they brought an ass they had, a slow-paced animal of Arab breed, on which they placed a velvet saddle-cloth for the Apostle of Allah—upon whom be Allah's blessing and peace—to ride. Saʿd wanted to have his son mount behind the Apostle of Allah—upon whom be Allah's blessing and peace—to drive the ass, but the Apostle of Allah—upon whom be Allah's blessing and peace—said: "If you are sending him with me let him ride in front of me." "Nay", he answered, "but behind you, O Apostle of Allah." But the Apostle of Allah—upon whom be Allah's blessing and peace—said: "The seat of honour on a beast goes by right to the folk to whom it belongs." Saʿd replied: "Then I shall not send him with you at all. Drive the ass yourself." So he drove it, and it proved a gentle-paced beast, wide-stepping as it travelled along.

Hāshim b. al-Qāsim has informed us, relating from Sulaimān, from Thābit i.e. al-Bunānī, who said: The Munāfiqūn [2] had [one day] gathered together and were talking among themselves, when the Apostle of Allah—upon whom be Allah's blessing and peace—said: "Lo, there are some men among you who have gathered together and have said thus and thus. So rise and seek Allah's forgiveness while I also ask Him to forgive you.' They did not rise, so he said to them: "Why do you not rise and seek Allah's forgiveness, while I also ask Him to forgive you?" This he did three times, and then said: "You will surely rise, or I will name you by your names." [They made no move] so he said: "Rise, So-and-So", whereupon they rose, shamed and convicted.

[1] The archangel Michael was the patron angel of the Jews (Cf. Dan. XII, 1), and the commentators on Sūra II, 97/91 ff. say that the Jews put Michael and Gabriel in opposition to one another.

[2] Lit. "the hypocrites", a name given to the Arab groups in Madīna who were not favourable to the invitation which had led Muḥammad to settle in their city. They had to acquiesce in his leadership but were regarded by the Muslims as only hypocritical supporters of the rule in Madīna. See note 2 on p. 299.

Hāshim b. al-Qāsim has informed us, relating from Sulaimān, from Thābit, from Anas b. Mālik, who said: I was standing by the *minbar*[1] one Friday while the Apostle of Allah—upon whom be Allah's blessing and peace—was preaching, when some of the congregation in the mosque said: "O Apostle of Allah, the rains have failed to come and the cattle are perishing, so make supplication to Allah to give us water." Thereupon the Apostle of Allah—upon whom be Allah's blessing and peace—raised his hands. We could not see a cloud in the sky, but Allah assembled clouds which poured down rain upon us till I saw strong men disquieted as to how they were going to get to their families. It rained incessantly for a whole week till the next Friday, when the Apostle of Allah—upon whom be Allah's blessing and peace—was preaching, and some of the people said to him: "O Apostle of Allah, our houses are coming down, and travellers are being detained, so beseech Allah to remove it from us." Thereupon the Apostle of Allah—upon whom be Allah's blessing and peace—raised his hands and said: "Allahumma, around us, not upon us", whereat what was above our heads cleared till it was as though we were in a tonsure, all around us being rained upon but no rain falling on us.

Hāshim b. al-Qāsim has informed us, relating from Sulaimān, from Thābit, who said: A woman of the Anṣār prepared a morsel of food that she had and then said to her husband: "Go to the Apostle of Allah—upon whom be Allah's blessing and peace—and invite him, but reveal this only to the Apostle of Allah—upon whom be Allah's blessing and peace." So he went and said: "O Apostle of Allah, my wife So-and-So has prepared a morsel of food, and I would like you to come to us." The Apostle of Allah—upon whom be Allah's blessing and peace—said to the people: "Respond now to [the invitation of] the father of So-and-So." Said the man: "Now my legs had not wanted to carry me because of [the meagreness of] what I had left at my house, but here was the Apostle of Allah—upon whom be Allah's blessing and peace—who had come with all the people. I said to my wife: 'We have put ourselves to shame. Here is the Apostle of Allah—upon whom be Allah's blessing and peace—who has come bringing the people with him.' Said she: 'But did I not bid you reveal it only to him?' 'That is what I did,' I replied. She said: 'Well, the Apostle of Allah—upon whom be Allah's blessing and peace—knows best.'" So they came till they filled the house, and filled the quarter. While they were in the house about a handful [of food] was brought in and set down. Then the Apostle of Allah—upon whom be Allah's blessing and

[1] The *minbar* is the equivalent of our pulpit. It is the raised place in the mosque from which the Friday sermon is delivered.

peace—began to spread it out in the vessel, saying whatever it was Allah willed him to say.[1] Then he said: "Draw near and eat, and when one of you has had enough let him make place for his companion." So one man would rise and another sit down till there remained no one in the house but had had enough. Then he said: "Summon to me the people of the quarter." Again one would sit down and one would rise till all had had enough. Then he said: "Summon to me the household." They fared the same, and yet there remained in the vessel as much as there had been [at the first], so the Apostle of Allah—upon whom be Allah's blessing and peace—said: "Eat, and feed your neighbours."

Hāshim b. al-Qāsim has informed us, relating from Sulaimān, from Thābit, who said: I said to Anas: "O father of Ḥamza, tell us something of the wonders you yourself have witnessed, and relate not on any authority other than your own."[2] He said: The Apostle of Allah—upon whom be Allah's blessing and peace—one day prayed the noon prayer and then went and sat on the seat where Gabriel used to come to him. Presently Bilāl came and gave the call to afternoon prayers, so everybody who had a house in Madina went to perform the preliminary ablutions.[3] There remained some men of the Emigrants *(muhājirūn)* [4] who had no house in Madina. A shallow bowl with some water in it was brought to the Apostle of Allah—upon whom be Allah's blessing and peace—into which he put his hand, though the vessel was not wide enough for all his hand. He said: "By these four [fingers] in the vessel." Then he said: "Draw near and perform your ablutions." He kept his hand in the vessel while they performed their ablutions, and there remained not one but finished his ablutions completely. I said: "O Abū Ḥamza, how many do you think they were?". "Between seventy and eighty", he answered.

ʿAffān b. Muslim and Sulaimān b. Ḥarb and Khālid b. Khidāsh have related to us, saying: Ḥammād b. Zaid related to us, from Thābit, from Anas, that the Prophet—on whom be peace—called [one day] for water. Some was brought to him in a wide shallow vessel into which he put his

[1] The reason for this strange unwillingness to give the actual words the Prophet used when performing such a miracle, and disguising them by saying that he said whatever it was Allah willed him to say, is the fear that if the actual words were given they would be used by men as magical formulae.

[2] Anas b. Mālik was a Traditionist and the request here is for Traditions about things he had himself seen and heard, not those he related on the authority of other Traditionists.

[3] The *wuḍū'* which puts one in the state of ritual purification necessary to a prayer service. See p. 466.

[4] Converts to Islam who had left their homes in Mecca to emigrate to Madina, where they could join the Prophet's community.

hand, whereat water began to spurt forth from his fingers like a fountain, so we drank. Said Anas: "I guess that the people [on that occasion] numbered between seventy and eighty." According to Khālid's version the people set about performing their ablutions [with that water].

'Affān b. Muslim has informed us, relating from Ḥammād b. Salama, from Thābit, from Anas b. Mālik, who said: [One day] the time for prayers arrived, so those in the neighbourhood of the mosque set about performing their ablutions. There remained, however, between seventy and eighty whose dwellings were afar, so the Apostle of Allah—upon whom be Allah's blessing and peace—called for a trough in which was some water, though it was not full, put his fingers in it and began to pour out for them, saying: "Perform your ablutions", until all of them had finished their ablutions, yet there still remained in the through about as much as there had been [at the first].

Hishām b. 'Abd al-Malik Abū'l-Walīd aṭ-Ṭayālisī has informed us, quoting from Ḥazm b. Abī Ḥazm, who said: I heard al-Ḥasan say: Anas b. Mālik informed us that the Apostle of Allah—upon whom be Allah's blessing and peace—went out one day on one of his journeys, having some of his companions with him. They went on journeying till the hour of prayers came and the people could find no water wherewith to perform ablutions. They said: "O Apostle of Allah, we cannot find anything with which we may perform ablutions", and the faces of the people shewed how disagreeable a thing this was to them. Presently a man from among them went off and brought a dish in which there was a very little water, but the Apostle of Allah—upon whom be Allah's blessing and peace—took it and performed his ablutions from it. Then he spread his four fingers over the dish and said: "Come along." So the people [came and] performed their ablutions till all the necessary ablutions were completed. He was asked how many there were, and he said: "Seventy, or thereabouts."

Mūsā b. Mas'ūd Abū Ḥudhaifa an-Nahdī has informed us, relating from 'Ikrima b. 'Ammār, from Iyās b. Salama, from his father, who said: We came to al-Ḥudaibiya with the Apostle of Allah—upon whom be Allah's blessing and peace—fourteen hundred of us, and there we found fifty sheep who had nothing to drink. The Apostle of Allah—upon whom be Allah's blessing and peace—sat down at their watering-trough, and either he spat [into it], or he offered supplication, for it became swollen [with water], so that we drank and we watered [the animals].

Khalaf b. al-Walīd al-Azdī has informed us, relating from Khalaf b. Khalīfa, from Abān b. Bishr, from a Shaikh of the people of Baṣra, relating from Nāfiʿ, that he was with the Apostle of Allah—upon whom be Allah's blessing and peace—in a company of about four hundred men whom he had made dismount at a place where there was no water. This troubled the men but they saw the Apostle of Allah—upon whom be Allah's blessing and peace—alighting, so they alighted, when lo! a she-goat with pointed horns came walking along and went to the Apostle of Allah—upon whom be Allah's blessing and peace—who milked her and drew for the company so that their thirst was quenched. Then he said: "O Nāfiʿ, secure her, though I do not think that you will secure her." When the Apostle of Allah said to me: "I do not think that you will secure her", I took a stick which I set firmly in the ground; then I took a rope and tied up the she-goat, making sure of her. Then the Apostle of Allah—upon whom be Allah's blessing and peace—went to sleep, as the people did also, and so I too went to sleep. When I woke up the rope was loose and there was no she-goat, so I went to the Apostle of Allah—upon whom be Allah's blessing and peace—to inform him, saying: "The she-goat has disappeared." The Apostle of Allah—upon whom be Allah's blessing and peace—said to me: "O Nāfiʿ, did I not tell you that you would not secure her? He who brought her is the one who has taken her off."

ʿAttāb b. Ziyād and Aḥmad b. al-Ḥajjāj Abū'l-ʿAbbās, both of whom were from Khurāsān, said, relating from ʿAbdallah b. al-Mubārak, relating from al-Awzāʿī, relating from al-Muṭṭalib b. Ḥanṭab al-Makhzūmī, relating from ʿAbd ar-Raḥmān b. Abī ʿAmra al-Anṣārī, who related that his father had said: We were with the Apostle of Allah—upon whom be Allah's blessing and peace—on a military expedition, when the men's bellies became so lean with hunger that they asked permission of the Apostle of Allah—upon whom be Allah's blessing and peace—to slaughter some of their riding-beasts, saying: "Allah will thereby enable us to satisfy [our hunger]." Now when ʿUmar b. al-Khaṭṭāb saw that the Apostle of Allah—upon whom be Allah's blessing and peace—purposed giving them permission to slaughter some of their riding-beasts, he said: "O Apostle of Allah, how will things be with us if they are slaughtered and we meet the folk [against whom we are out] tomorrow hungry and on foot? Rather, if you think good, summon the men to combine such provisions as they have left, and then do you beseech Allah's blessing thereon, for Allah will through your supplication cause us to satisfy [our hunger], or will give us a blessing by your prayer." So the Apostle of Allah—upon whom be Allah's blessing and peace—sent out a call for what provisions they had left, and the men began to bring in morsels of food, or perhaps something a little more than that. The most that was brought in was a *ṣāʿ* of dates. The Apostle of Allah—upon whom be Allah's blessing and peace—assembled all this, then stood up and made such supplication as Allah willed he should make. Then he summoned the troops [to come] with their provision-bags, and bade them pour in till there remained not a provision-bag among the troops which was not full, yet there was still [food] remaining over. Thereupon the Apostle of Allah—upon whom be Allah's blessing and peace—laughed [so heartily] that his molar teeth showed, and he said: "I bear witness that there is no deity save Allah, and I bear witness that I am the Apostle of Allah. No believer will encounter Allah with these two [statements of faith] but He will shield him from the Fire on the Day of Judgment."

Hāshim b. al-Qāsim has informed us, relating from Sulaimān, i.e. Ibn al-Mughīra, from Thābit al-Bunānī, from ʿAbdallah b. Rabāḥ, from Abū Qatāda, who said: "The Apostle of Allah—upon whom be Allah's blessing and peace—addressed us one evening, saying to us: 'You are going to travel this evening and this night, and if Allah wills you will come to water tomorrow.' So the men set out, not sticking close to one another. For my part I was journeying beside the Prophet —upon whom be Allah's blessing and peace—till well on into the night, when the Prophet —upon whom be Allah's blessing and peace—dozed and slumped forward on his riding beast, so I propped him up, i.e. supported him, without wakening him, so that he sat upright on his beast. We journeyed on, and when night was almost over, the Prophet dozed again and slumped forward on his beast a second time, so again I propped him up, without awakening him, so that he sat upright on his beast. We kept on journeying till when it was about the end of the day-break period he slumped forward more heavily than at either of the two previous times, so that he almost fell off. Again I propped him up, whereat he raised his head and said: 'Who is this?'. 'It is Abū Qatāda', I replied. 'How long have you been journeying with me like this?', he asked. 'I have continued with you like this all night', I replied. 'May Allah guard you the way you have guarded His Prophet', he said, and then he asked: 'Do you think we are concealed from the men? Do you see anyone showing signs he would like to rest?'. 'Here is a rider', I replied, 'and here is a rider.' We gathered together and we were seven riders, so the Prophet—upon whom be peace—turned aside from the road and laid down his head, saying: 'Keep watch for our prayer-time.' He was the first to be awakened by the sun, so we rose up, somewhat afraid, but he said: 'Mount.' So we journeyed till when the sun was well up he dismounted and called for an ablution vessel I had with me in which was some water. We performed our ablutions from it, one after the other, and there still remained some water in it, so the Prophet—upon whom be peace—said to me: 'O Abū Qatāda, take care of this ablution vessel of yours for us, for it will be important.' Then the call to prayers was given, and the Prophet—upon whom be Allah's blessing and peace—prayed two rak'as before [praying] the dawn prayer, after which he prayed the dawn prayer as he was wont to do every day. Then he said: 'Mount', so we mounted, and began to whisper to one another, but the Prophet—upon whom be peace—said: 'What is this you are whispering about apart from me?' We answered: 'O Apostle of Allah [it was about] our neglect of prayers.' 'Do you not have an example in me?' he asked. 'In sleep there is no neglect, but there is neglect when one does not say the prayers till the time for the next prayers has come. If anyone does that let him pray when he comes to [the next prayer-time], and then on the morrow let him pray [the one he has omitted] at its proper time.' Then he asked: 'What do you think the men are doing?' Then [answering himself] he said: 'The men will be up this morning looking for their Prophet. Abū Bakr and 'Umar will say: 'The Apostle of Allah promised you that he would never desert you', so the men will say: 'The Prophet—upon whom be peace—is with you. If they obey Abū Bakr and 'Umar they will be guided aright.' We came up with the men when everything was warming up, or maybe he said, when the day was now bright, and they were saying: 'O Apostle of Allah, we are perishing of thirst.' 'You will not perish', he answered. Then he dismounted and said: 'Bring me my drinking-bowl', meaning his small wooden cup. He called also for the ablution bowl and began to pour [from the drinking-cup into the bowl] and gave them to drink. When the men saw what was in it they prostrated themselves [in reverence], but the Prophet—upon whom be Allah's blessing and peace—said: 'Take your fill. All of you shall drink.' So the Prophet—upon whom be Allah's blessing and peace—set to pouring out and giving them to drink till only he and I were left. He poured and said: 'Drink', 'Nay', I replied, 'I shall not drink, O Apostle of Allah, till you have drunk.' The Prophet—upon whom be Allah's blessing and peace—answered: 'He who pours water for the people has his own turn last.' So I drank, and the Prophet—upon whom be Allah's blessing and peace—drank also. Thus the men went on to [the next] watering-place well-filled with sweet water."

'Abdallah b. Rabāḥ said: "I was in this mosque of yours, this large place of worship, relating this Tradition, when 'Imrān b. Ḥuṣain said to me: 'Look to it, young man. Look to it how you relate, for I was one of the riders that night.' I answered: 'Then, O Abū Nujaid, you know it better.' 'To whom do you belong?', he asked. 'To the Anṣār', I answered. 'Then you know best about your Tradition,' said he, 'go on and relate it to the people.' So I related it to the people, and 'Imrān said: 'I witnessed [the events of] that night, but never have I noted anyone who has preserved [the story as well] as you have preserved it.'"

Fuḍail b. 'Abd al-Wahhāb Abū Muḥammad al-Ghaṭafānī has related to us, relating from Sharīk, from Simāk, from Abū Ẓabyān, from Ibn 'Abbās, who said: "A man came to the Prophet—upon whom be Allah's blessing and peace—saying: 'What makes you a Prophet?'. 'How think you?' he answered. 'If I should ask something of that palm tree and it responds to me, would you believe in me?'. 'Assuredly', said he. So [the Prophet] called to it and it responded to him, whereupon the man became a believer, and accepted Islam."

Hāshim b. al-Qāsim has informed us, relating from Shu'ba, who said: 'Amr b. Murra and Ḥuṣain b. 'Abd ar-Raḥmān have informed me, from Sālim b. Abī 'l-Ja'd from Jābir b. 'Abdallah, who said: "At al-Ḥudaibiya we were overtaken by thirst so we betook ourselves to the Apostle of Allah —upon whom be Allah's blessing and peace—who had before him a small vessel in which was some water. So he milked his fingers into it and said: 'Take, in the name of Allah', whereat water began to flow from his fingers as though they were fountains, so that there was ample for us and we satisfied [our thirst]." Ḥuṣain in his Tradition [about this event] says: "So we drank and also performed our ablutions."

Hāshim b. al-Qāsim has informed us, relating from Sulaimān b. al-Mughīra, from Thābit al-Bunānī, from 'Abd ar-Raḥmān b. Abī Lailā, from al-Miqdād, who said: "I and two friends of mine went out [one time and were] so exhausted that our hearing and our sight were failing, so we presented ourselves to the companions of the Apostle of Allah—upon whom be Allah's blessing and peace—but not one of them would receive us. Finally we went directly to the Apostle of Allah—upon whom be Allah's blessing and peace—and he took us to his place. There were three she-goats there, and the Apostle of Allah—upon whom be Allah's blessing and peace—said: 'Draw enough milk to share among us.' So we drew the milk and each man drank his share, while we put aside for the Apostle of Allah—upon whom be Allah's blessing and peace—his share, saying: 'He will come during the night, and give a salaam that will awake no sleeper nor be heard by anyone who is awake, then he will go to the place of worship and say prayers, then he will come for his drink and drink it up.'" [Said Miqdād]: "Satan came to me that night, saying: 'Muḥammad has gone to the Anṣār who will provide refreshment for him, so he will have his drink with them and have no need for this mouthfull, go on and drink it.' He ceased not enticing me with this till I [got up and] drank it. Then when it got down into my stomach and he knew that there was no way for it to be recovered, he began to make me repent, saying: 'Woe to you! what have you done? You have drunk up Muḥammad's drink. He will come, and when he does not find it he will curse you and you will perish, losing thus both this world and the next.' I was wearing a woollen cloak [so short that] whenever it was raised up over my head my feet showed, and whenever it was down over my feet my head was uncovered. Sleep would not come to me though my companions were asleep. Anon the Apostle of Allah—upon whom be Allah's blessing and peace—came, and gave a salaam as he was wont to do. Then he went to the place of worship and said his prayers, and then came for his drink, uncovered it, and found nothing in it. Thereat he raised his head to the skies, and I said [to myself]: 'Now he is going to curse me and I shall perish.' But he said: 'Allahumma! feed whosoever feeds me, and give drink to whomsoever it may be gives me to drink.' Straightway I caught hold of the cloak, wrapping it closely around me, seized a knife and went out to the she-goats, seeking the fattest of them that I might slaughter it for the Apostle of Allah—upon whom be Allah's blessing and peace. There they were, all of them full-uddered, so I got a vessel belonging to the Prophet's family, which they were not eager to milk into, but I milked into it till the foam reached the top. Then I brought it to the Apostle of Allah—upon whom be Allah's blessing and peace. He said: 'Did not you fellows have your drink last night, O Miqdād?' I said: 'Drink, O Apostle of Allah.' So he drank, and then handed it to me, but I said: 'Drink, O Apostle of Allah.' He drank and then handed it to me, so I took what remained and drank. Then when I was assured that the Apostle of Allah—upon whom be Allah's blessing and peace—had drunk [his fill], and that I had gained [the blessing of] his prayer, I laughed till I fell to the ground. Said the Apostle of Allah—upon whom be Allah's blessing and peace—: 'Confess your sins, O Miqdād.' I said: 'O Apostle of Allah, I was in such and such a state, and I did thus and thus.' Said the Apostle of Allah—upon whom be Allah's blessing and peace—: 'This was none other than a mercy from Allah. Will you not bring me near and waken these two companions of yours that they may partake of it?' I said: 'By Him Who sent you with the truth, since you have partaken of it and I have partaken of it with you, I care not who else partakes of it.'"

Hāshim b. al-Qāsim has informed us, relating from Zuhair Abū Khaithama, relating from Sulaimān al-A'mash, from al-Qāsim, who said that 'Abdallah b. Mas'ūd said: "I am not aware that anyone became a Muslim earlier than I did. The Apostle of Allah—upon whom be Allah's blessing and peace—came to me while I was with the flocks of my family, and asked: 'Is there any milk in your flocks?'. 'No', I answered, ['they are all dry']. He took hold of a ewe, stroked her udder, and she gave down [milk]. So I am not aware that anyone accepted Islam earlier than I did."

'Alī b. Muḥammad b. 'Abdallah b. Abī Saif al-Qurashī has informed us on the authority of Abū Zakarīyā' al-'Ajlānī, from Muḥammad b. Ka'b al-Quraẓī, and from 'Alī b. Mujāhid, from Muḥammad b. Isḥāq, from 'Āṣim b. 'Umar b. Qatāda, from Maḥmūd b. Labīd, from Ibn 'Abbās, from Salmān, who said: "I came to the Apostle of Allah—upon whom be Allah's blessing and peace—while he was attending the funeral of one of his companions. When he saw me approaching he said to me: 'Go around behind me.' Then he removed his cloak and I saw the seal,[1] which I kissed. Then I went around and sat down in front of him. He said: 'Write down [what it is that you want].' So I wrote down: 'Three hundred palm-shoots for planting and forty ounces of gold.' Said the Apostle of Allah—upon whom be Allah's blessing and peace—[to those standing around]: 'Help your brother.' So a man would bring a palm-shoot and then two or three until they had gathered for me three hundred. 'How am I going to plant them?'. I asked. 'Go and dig holes for them with your hand,' he answered. So I dug holes for them. Then I went to him and he came with me and set them in with his own hand till not one of them was left. There remained the [matter of the] gold, and while I was still with him someone brought in as a charitable alms a lump of gold about the size of a pigeon's egg. He said: 'Where is that Persian slave who wrote down [forty ounces of gold]?' I rose up, and he said: 'Take this and help yourself from it.' 'How will this [bit only the size of a pigeon's egg] suffice me?', I asked. Thereupon the Apostle of Allah——upon whom be Allah's blessing and peace—licked it with his tongue, and I weighed out from it forty ounces, yet there was still remaining with me as much as I had given them (i.e. the creditors to whom he owed the forty ounces of gold)."

'Alī b. Muḥammad has informed us, relating from aṣ-Ṣalt b. Dīnār, from 'Abdallah b. Shaqīq, from Abū Ṣakhr al-'Uqailī, who said: "I went to

[1] The reference is to the "seal of Prophecy", a birthmark the Prophet was said to have between his shoulder-blades. See p. 137.

Madina and there met me the Apostle of Allah—upon whom be Allah's blessing and peace—who was walking with Abū Bakr and 'Umar. He passed by a Jew who had a book of the Torah which he was reading to a nephew of his, a sick fellow who was there before him. The Prophet—upon whom be peace—said: 'O Jew, I adjure you by Him who sent down the Torah to Moses and divided the sea for the Children of Israel, do you find in the Torah a description of me, of my qualities, and of my coming?' He shook his head to signify 'No', whereupon his nephew said: 'But I for my part testify by Him Who sent down the Torah to Moses and Who divided the sea for the Children of Israel, that he does find in his book a description of you, of your qualities, your time and your coming. Also I testify that there is no deity save Allah, and that you are the Apostle of Allah.' Said the Prophet—upon whom be Allah's blessing and peace—: 'Separate the Jew from your companion.' The boy then died and the Prophet—upon whom be peace—prayed over him and had him buried."

'Alī b. Muḥammad has informed us, relating from Ya'qūb b. Dāwūd, from a Shaikh of the Banū Jumaḥ, who said: "When the Prophet—upon whom be peace—came to Umm Ma'bad he asked: 'Have you any milk?', 'No', she replied. So he and Abū Bakr retired. In the evening her son came with the lambs and said to his mother: 'What is this group [whose traces] I see retiring?'. 'Some folk', she answered, 'who asked for milk, but I told them that we had no milk.' Straightway her son went after them and made excuses, saying: 'She is only a weak woman. We have that which you need.' So the Apostle of Allah—upon whom be Allah's blessing and peace—said: 'Go then and bring me a female from your flock.' He went and took a she-kid, and his mother said to him: 'Where are you going?'. 'They asked me for a female', he replied. 'But what will they do with her?', she asked (i.e. it was too young an animal to give milk). 'Whatever they wish', he replied. Then the Prophet—upon whom be Allah's blessing and peace—stroked her udder and the flesh around it, whereat it filled with milk, so he milked her till he filled a wooden cup, and left her udder fuller of milk than when he began. He said: 'Take this to your mother and bring me another female from your flock.' So he took the wooden cup to his mother, who said: 'From where did you get this?'. 'It is the milk of such-and-such a she-kid', he answered. 'How so?', she asked, 'no one has ever yet got milk from a toothless female. By Allāt, I believe this must be the Ṣābī [1] who is at Mecca.' Then she

[1] A religious group named the Ṣābians is mentioned in the Qur'ān (II, 62/59; V, 69/73; XXII, 17), where the word seems to refer to some Gnostic sects which still

drank of it. [The youth] then brought him another she-kid which he milked till he filled the wooden cup, leaving her fuller of milk than when he began. He said: 'Drink', so [the youth] drank. Then he said: 'Bring me another.' [The youth] brought one and he milked her and gave Abū Bakr to drink. Then he said: 'Bring me another', so he brought him one and he milked her and drank himself, but he left all of them fuller of milk than when he began."

'Alī b. Muḥammad has informed us, relating from al-Ḥasan b. Dīnār, from al-Ḥasan, who said: "While the Apostle of Allah—upon whom be Allah's blessing and peace—was in his mosque a run-away camel came, put its head in the lap of the Prophet—upon whom be Allah's blessing and peace—and gurgled. Said the Prophet—upon whom be Allah's blessing and peace: 'This camel claims that it belongs to a man who wants to slaughter it as food for his father just now, so it has come asking succor.' A man spoke up [and said]: 'O Apostle of Allah, this is So-and-So's camel, and he was intending to do that.' So he—upon whom be peace—sent for the man and asked him about it. He told [the Prophet] that that was his intention, but the Prophet—upon whom be peace—begged him not to slaughter it, and he agreed."

'Ali b. Muḥammad has informed us, relating from Ḥubāb b. Mūsā as-Sa'īdī, from Ja'far b. Muḥammad, from his father, who said: Said 'Alī —on whom be peace—: "We spent the night one time without any supper. In the morning I got up and went out. Presently I returned to Fāṭima —on whom be peace—and found her grieving. 'What is the matter?'. I asked, and she answered: 'We had no supper yesterday, we have no morning meal today, and there is nothing here for supper.' So I went out and looked around and came across some food and meat that I could buy for one dirham. This I brought to her and she prepared it and cooked it. When she had finished cooking it in the pot she said: 'Would you go to my father and invite him.' So I went to the Apostle of Allah —upon whom be Allah's blessing and peace—who was reclining in the mosque, saying: 'I take refuge with Allah from having hunger as a bed-fellow.' I said to him: 'My father and my mother art thou, O Apostle of Allah. We have a little food at our place, so come along.' Leaning on my arm he entered and there was the pot boiling away. He said [to Fāṭima]: 'Ladle out for 'Ā'isha', so she ladled out into a dish. Then he said: 'Ladle out for Ḥafṣa', so she ladled out into a dish. So it went on till

existed in North Arabia. There are several Traditions which suggest that Muḥammad in the early years of his preaching was at times referred to by his contemporaries as one of these Ṣābians. See p. 234.

she had ladled out for all his nine wives. Then he said: 'Ladle out for your son and your husband.' [When she had done this] he said: 'Ladle out [for yourself] and eat.' So she ladled out and then lifted the pot, and it was still overflowing. Thus we all ate from it as much as Allah willed."

'Alī b. Muḥammad has informed us, relating from Yazīd b. 'Iyāḍ b. Ju'duba al-Laithī, from Nāfi', from Sālim, from 'Alī, who said: "The Apostle of Allah—upon whom be Allah's blessing and peace—when he was still in Mecca, gave orders to [his wife] Khadīja to prepare food for him. Then he said to [his cousin] 'Alī: 'Summon here to me the sons of 'Abd al-Muṭṭalib', so he summoned forty [of them]. Then he said to 'Alī: 'Fetch your food.' Said 'Alī: I brought them some soup but only as much as any man of them could himself have eaten, yet they all partook of it till they could eat no more. Then he said: 'Give them to drink', so I gave them a vessel to drink which was but the measure of the thirst of one of them, yet they all drank of it till they were satisfied. Abū Lahab said: 'Muḥammad has used sorcery on you', whereupon they went off, but he did not call them. Some days passed and then he prepared the like for them, giving me command so that I assembled them and they ate. Then he—upon whom be Allah's blessing and peace—said to them: 'Who will assist me in that on which I am engaged? Who will respond to my call? Such a one shall be my brother and he shall have Paradise.' I answered: 'I will, O Apostle of Allah, though I am in age the youngest of them and the thinnest of leg.' The group, however, was silent. Then they said: 'O Abū Ṭālib, do you not see your son?' He answered: 'Leave him alone. He will never do aught but good to the son of his uncle.'"

'Alī b. Muḥammad has informed us on the authority of Abū Ma'shar, from Zaid b. Aslam and others, that Qatāda b. an-Nu'mān was smitten in the eye, so that it was hanging on his cheek, but the Apostle of Allah—upon whom be Allah's blessing and peace—put it back into its place with his own hand, and thereafter it was the sounder and better of his two eyes.

'Alī b. Muḥammad has informed us on the authority of Abū Ma'shar, from Zaid b. Aslam and Yazīd b. Rūmān and Isḥāq b. 'Abdallah b. Abī Farwa and others, that 'Ukkāsha b. Miḥṣan had his sword snatched away on the day of Badr,[1] so the Apostle of Allah—upon whom be Allah's blessing and peace—gave him a tree stump which in his hand became a sturdy sword of choicest steel firmly wrought.

[1] The day of the great battle with the troops of the Quraish. See p. 290.

ʿAlī b. Muḥammad has informed us on the authority of ʿAlī b. Mujāhid, from ʿAbd al-Aʿlā b. Maimūn b. Mihrān, from his father, who said: ʿAbdallah b. ʿAbbās said that the Apostle of Allah—upon whom be Allah's blessing and peace—used to preach from a wooden block that was in the mosque. When the *minbar* (pulpit) was built and the Apostle of Allah—upon whom be Allah's blessing and peace—mounted it [to preach] the wooden block began to wail, so the Apostle of Allah—upon whom be Allah's blessing and peace—went down to it and embraced it, whereat it was silent.

ʿAlī b. Muḥammad has informed us on the authority of Abū Maʿshar, from Zaid b. Aslam and others, that Surāqa b. Mālik rode out to seek the Prophet—upon whom be Allah's blessing and peace—after he had consulted the divining arrows as to whether he should go out or not go out.[1] He got "Do not go out" three times but he rode off, nevertheless, and overtook them. The Prophet—upon whom be Allah's blessing and peace—prayed [when he saw him approaching] that the feet of his steed might be rooted [to the ground], and they were so rooted. He cried out: "O Muḥammad, pray to Allah to set my steed free and I will depart from you." The Prophet—upon whom be Allah's blessing and peace—said: "Allahumma, if he be speaking the truth free his steed for him", and at that his steed's feet came free.

Muḥammad b. ʿUmar has informed us, relating from al-Ḥakam b. al-Qāsim, from Zakarīyā' b. ʿAmr, from a Shaikh of the Quraish, that when the Quraish wrote a compact against the Banū Hāshim who had refused to hand over to them the Apostle of Allah—upon whom be Allah's blessing and peace—they wrote into the compact that they would neither give nor take in marriage with them, neither buy from nor sell to them, not associate with them in any way nor even speak to them. They continued for three years restricted to their own tribe, save for Abū Lahab, who did not go in with them, though the Banū Muṭṭalib b. ʿAbd Manāf went in with them. When three years had passed Allah informed His Prophet of the state of the document, for a tree-worm had eaten away all the unjust, oppressive sections of it, though the parts which made mention of Allah were untouched. The Apostle of Allah—upon whom be Allah's blessing and peace—mentioned this to Abū Ṭālib, who said: "Is this that you tell me true, O son of my brother?" "Yea, by Allah", said he.

[1] The "going out" was to make an attack on Muḥammad. The usual technique of divining with arrows was to shake up a case in which were three arrows marked "Do it" and "Don't do it" and "Wait awhile", and whichever arrow came out through the hole at the end of the case indicated the answer to the question put to the oracle.

So Abū Ṭālib mentioned this to his brethren, who said to him: "What is your thought about it?" Said Abū Ṭālib: "By Allah, he has never lied to me." They said: "But what do you think [we ought to do]?". "My opinion", he answered, "is that you should put on the finest clothes you can find and then go up to the Quraish and tell them about it before the news reaches them [from other sources]. So they went along until they entered the shrine where they directed themselves towards the reserved place where no one sat but the aged men of the Quraish and their men of high degree. All activity there was suspended that men might hear what they had to say. Said Abū Ṭālib: "We have come about a matter, so respond to it, by Him who is known to you." "You are quite welcome", they replied, "with us [you will find] what will please you. What is it you seek?" He said: "My brother's son has informed me, and never yet has he lied to me, that Allah has empowered the tree-worm over that document of yours that you wrote, so that it has done away with all the injustice, oppression and the severing of blood-bonds that was in it, but has left intact all that makes mention of Allah. If then the son of my brother speaks the truth you are discharged from your evil design, but if he is telling a lie then I will hand him over to you and you can put him to death or let him live as you please." They said: "You have acted equitably in our regard." Then they sent for the document, and when it was brought Abū Ṭālib said: "Read it", but when they opened it up it was as the Apostle of Allah—upon whom be Allah's blessing and peace—had said, all of it devoured save those places where the name of Allah was mentioned. The people were in perplexity, then they lowered their heads, so Abū Ṭālib said: "Is it clear to you now that it was you who began the injustice and the forsaking of relations and the evil?" No one among the people answered back while he upbraided the men of Quraish for what they had done to the Banū Hāshim. They paused a little while, then Abū Ṭālib returned to the tribe and said: "O people of Quraish, for what are we being put in straits and restrained? The matter has been made clear." Then he and his companions entered the curtains of the Ka'ba and went into the Ka'ba where he said: "Allahumma, aid us against those who oppress us, who sever the bonds of blood-relationship and in regard to us make lawful what is unlawful." Then they departed.

'Abdallah b. Ja'far ar-Raqqī has informed us, relating from 'Ubaidallah b. 'Amr, from Ibn 'Aqīl, from Jābir, or some one else, who said: "The first news of the Apostle of Allah—upon whom be Allah's blessing and peace—to come to Madīna was that a woman of Madīna had a familiar spirit *(tābi')* who came to her in the form of a bird and lit on the wall of the house. The woman said: 'Come down and converse with us, and we will converse with thee. Come and give us news and we will give thee news.' It said: 'A Prophet has been sent at Mecca, who has made fornication unlawful for us, and has debarred us from irregular cohabitation.'"

AD-DAMĪRĪ'S DESCRIPTION OF THE PROPHET[1]

Historians record that the first who ever undertook to be a true leader of the [Arab] people was the Prophet—upon whom be Allah's blessing and peace. Allah sent him after a long break [in the succession of messengers] to be a mercy to mankind, and he delivered His message. He strove with true diligence in the cause of Allah, gave proper advice to the people, and served his Lord till death came to him. He is the most favoured of all creatures, the noblest of the messengers, the Prophet of mercy, the leader *(imām)* of convinced believers, who on the Day will bear the Standard of Praise,[2] be the general intercessor, occupy the belauded station,[3] have the pool *(ḥawḍ)*, which many will frequent, and gather under his banner Adam and all who come after him.

He is the best of Prophets, and his community is the best of communities. His companions are, after the Prophets, the choicest of mankind, and his is the noblest of sects. He performed astonishing miracles, possessed great natural abilities, had a sound and powerful intelligence, a most distinguished genealogy and perfect beauty. His generosity was boundless, his bravery unchallengeable, his forbearance excessive, his knowledge profitable, his actions ever honourable, his fear [of Allah] complete, his piety sublime. He was the most eloquent of man, perfect in every respect, and the furthest of all mankind from things base and vicious. Of him the poet has said:

> "None like Muḥammad has the Merciful ever created,
> Nor such, to my thinking, will He ever again create."

[1] Kamāl ad-Dīn ad-Damīrī (750–808 A.H. = 1349–1405 A.D.) was an Egyptian writer who began life as a tailor but became a preacher, and in later life a teacher of the theological sciences. His most famous work is his *Ḥayāt al-Ḥayawān*, a kind of zoological encyclopaedia, in which, however, he included much material of a miscellaneous character. In the section on the *goose* he brings in a brief history of the early Caliphate, in the course of which occurs his famous description of the Prophet. The passage is in Vol. I, pp. 40, 41 of the Cairo edition of 1321 A.H. (= 1903 A.D.).

[2] For this standard see pp. 225-226, 334.

[3] It is mentioned in Sūra XVII, 79/81. For his office as intercessor see pp. 238–239 and for the *ḥawḍ* see p. 349, 534, 615.

'Ā'isha—with whom may Allah be pleased—said: "The Prophet—upon whom be Allah's blessing and peace—when he was at home used to be at the service of his household, i.e. he used to act as servant to them. He used to delouse his own clothes and patch them, mend his own sandals and serve himself. He used to see to the feeding of his own domestic camel,[1] sweep the house, i.e. use the broom on it, tie up the camel,[2] eat with the servant and help her knead her dough, and used to carry his own purchases home from the market." Moreover, he—upon whom be Allah's blessing and peace—used to be continually in grief, ever occupied by anxious thought, never having any rest.

'Alī—with whom may Allah be pleased—said: "I asked the Apostle of Allah—upon whom be Allah's blessing and peace—about his way of life *(sunna)*, and he answered: 'Knowledge is the capital wealth I have; love is my foundation; yearning desire is my ship; remembrance of Allah is my friend; grief is my road-companion, learning is my provision of weapons; patient endurance is my cloak; to be well-pleasing to Allah is my share in the booty; poverty is that of which I boast; asceticism is my profession; sure conviction is my strength; speaking the truth is my intercessor; obedience [to Allah] is my sufficiency; Holy War *(jihād)* is my nature; and that which refreshes my eye is prayer.'"

As for his forbearance, his liberality, his courage, his modesty, his pleasantness in social intercourse, his compassionateness, his clemency, his mercifulness, his piety, his equity, his sedateness, his patience, the dignity of his bearing, his trustworthiness, and his other excellent qualities which can hardly be numbered, they were very many. So the theologians —with whom may Allah be pleased—have composed numerous books about his way of life *(sīra)*, his times, his mission, his warlike expeditions, his personal qualities, his miracles, his good deeds and his characteristics *(shamā'il)*, and should we want to make mention of even a small measure of all this it would take up many volumes, and such is not the purpose of this book of ours.

It is said that his death—Upon him be Allah's blessing and peace—took place after Allah had perfected our religion for us and brought to completion His favour to us, at midday on the 12th of [the month] Rabīʿ al-awwal, in the year 11 A.H. (= 632 A.D.), when he—upon whom be Allah's blessing and peace—was sixty-three years of age. 'Alī b. Abī Ṭālib took charge of washing him [for burial], and he was interred in the chamber of 'Ā'isha, the mother of the believers—with whom may Allah be pleased.

[1] *nādiḥ*, i.e. a beast used for carrying water for the household, generally a camel.
[2] *'aqala* is to bind the forelegs of a squatting camel to prevent it from straying.

MUḤAMMAD AMONG THE PROPHETS [1]

From Ibn ʿAbbās, [who said]: I asked the Prophet: "Where were you when Adam was in Paradise?" He answered: "I was in his loins, and I too fell down to earth in his loins. Also I sailed in the ark in the loins of my father Noah, and was cast into the fire in the loins of my father Abraham,[2] and no two ancestors of mine ever came together for the purpose of begetting but transferred me for the better from pure loins to innocent wombs. Thus there has never been a splitting up of peoples without my continuing on in the better of the two. By the prophetic office Allah made covenant with me, and so in the Torah He has announced me and in the Gospel made known my name.[3] The earth was honoured by [the appearance on it of] my face, as the heavens will be by vision of me. He caused me to ascend to His heaven,[4] and gave me one of His own names, for the Lord of the Throne is *maḥmūd* (praised) and I am Muḥammad.

ʿAṭā' b. Abī Rabāḥ relates from Ibn ʿAbbās how forty men from the Jews of Madina went out of the city saying: "Let us go to see this *kāhin* [5] and rebuke him to his face giving him the lie anent his claim that he is the Apostle of the Lord of mankind." ʿUmar met them, and he was saying: "How excellent is Muḥammad's thought of Allah! How abundant is his thanks to Him for what He has given him!" When the Jews heard these words of ʿUmar they said: "That was not Muḥammad but Moses the son of ʿImrān,[6] with whom Allah spoke." With his hand ʿUmar grabbed

[1] From as-Suyūṭī's *al-La'ālī al-maṣnūʿa* (Cairo, 1317 A.H.), pp. 137–140.

[2] The reference is to the Rabbinic legend which tells how Abraham was cast into the fire by Nimrod, but at God's command the fire became cool and did not burn him. This is told in the Qur'ān in XXIX, 24/23 and XXI, 68, 69.

[3] See p. 398 for another reference to this claim that passages in the Old and New Testaments prophesy the coming of Muḥammad, the passages most commonly adduced are Deut. XVIII, 15 and John XVI, 7.

[4] I.e. on the night of the Miʿrāj. See pp. 393 ff., 621 ff.

[5] The soothsayers of pre-Islamic Arabia were called *kāhins*, this word being the cognate of the Hebrew word *kohen* "a priest". See p. n. 4 p. 36, n. 1 p. 44.

[6] In Exod. VI, 18, 20 ʿAmrām is the father of Moses and Aaron and Miriam, and this name has become ʿImrān in the Qur'ān, where Sūra III, 33/30 speaks of the family of ʿImrān, v. 35/31 calls Moses' mother the wife of ʿImrān.

a Jew by the hair and began to beat him, so the Jews fled. Then they said: "Come along, let us go to Muḥammad and make complaint to him." When they entered his presence the Jews said: "O Muḥammad, we pay the poll-tax, yet we are ill treated." "And who treated you ill?" he asked. "'Umar", they replied, but he said: "'Umar is not the person to treat anyone ill unless he has heard something reprehensible." So he enquired: "O, 'Umar, why did you illtreat these folk?" "If I had had a sword in my hand," he replied, "I should have cut off their heads." "And why?" [the Prophet] enquired. ['Umar] answered: "When I went out from your presence I was saying: 'How excellent is Muḥammad's thought of Allah! How abundant is his thanks to Him for what He has given him!', when these Jews said: 'That is not Muḥammad but Moses the son of 'Imrān.' It was thus that they roused my wrath. Alas for my soul, was Moses better than you?"

Then the Apostle of Allah—upon whom be Allah's blessing and peace—said: "Moses is my brother, but I am better than him, and I was given something more excellent than he was." The Jews said: "This is what we wanted." "What is that?", he asked. They said: "Adam was better than you; Noah was better than you; Moses was better than you; Jesus was better than you; Solomon was better than you." Said he: "That is false. I am better than all these and superior to them." "You are?", asked the Jews. "I am", said he. They said: "Bring a proof of that from the Torah." "I will take 'Abdallah b. Salām",[1] said he, "and let the Torah be between me and them." "Good", they replied. "Now why", he asked, "is Adam better than me?". "Because", they answered, "Allah created him with His own hand and breathed into him of His spirit."[2] "Adam", he replied. "is my father, but I have been given something better than anything he has, namely, that every day a herald calls five times from the East to the West: 'I bear witness that there is no deity save Allah, and I bear witnesss that Muḥammad is the Apostle of Allah.' No one has ever said that Adam was the Apostle of Allah. Moreover on the Day of Resurrection the Banner of Praise [3] will be in my hand and not in that of Adam." "You speak but the truth", they replied, "that is so written in the Torah." "That", said he, "is one."

Said the Jews: "Moses is better than you." "And why?", he enquired.

[1] A Jewish convert to Islam. The point here is that since Muḥammad could not read Hebrew he would have 'Abdallah b. Salām as his witness to check in the Torah any matters to which they might refer.

[2] So Sūra XV, 29.

[3] For this Banner of Praise, see pp. 225-226, 331.

"Because," said they, "Allah spoke with him four thousand four hundred and forty words,[1] but never did He speak a thing to you." "But I", he responded, "was given something superior to that." "And what was that?" they asked. Said he: "Glory be to Him who took His servant by night (XVII, 1), for He bore me up on Gabriel's wing till He brought me to the seventh heaven, and I passed beyond the Sidra tree of the Boundary at the Garden of Resort (LIII, 14, 15), till I caught hold of a leg of the Throne, and from above the Throne came a voice: 'O Muḥammad, I am Allah. Beside Me there is no other deity." Then with my heart I saw my Lord. This is more excellent than that." "You speak but the truth", they replied: "That is so written in the Torah." "That", said He, "makes two."

They said: "Noah is better than you." "And why?", he asked. "Because", they replied, "his ark came to rest on al-Jūdī."[2] "But I", he retorted, "have been given something better than that." "And what was that?", they asked. He said: "Allah—Most High—has said: 'We, indeed, have given thee abundance *(al-kawthar)*' (CVIII, 1), and al-Kawthar is a river in the seventh heaven, springing from beneath the Throne, on whose banks are a thousand thousand palaces, whose grass is saffron, whose pebbles are pearls and jacinths, whose mud is white musk, and it belongs to me and to my community." "You speak but truly", they said, "for thus is it written in the Torah." Said he: "Well, that is three."

They said: "Abraham is better than you." "And why?", he asked. "Because", they replied, "Allah—Most High—took him as a friend."[3] He answered: "Abraham was, indeed, the friend of Allah, but I am His beloved. Do you know why my name is Muḥammad? It is because He derived it from His name. He is *al-ḥamīd* (the praiseworthy), and my name is Muḥammad (the praised), while my community are the *ḥāmidūn* (those who give praise)." "You speak but truly", they replied, "this is greater than that." "That", [said he], "is four."

"But Jesus", they said, "is better than you." "And why?", he asked. "Because", said they, "he mounted up to the acclivity of the temple in Jerusalem,[4] where the satans came to bear him away, but Allah gave command Gabriel who with his right wing smote them in their faces and

[1] This figure is doubtless some reminiscence of Jewish computations of the number of words in the Torah. It was Gabriel who spoke the word of revelation to Muḥammad so the Jews are insisting on the uniqueness of Moses' experience on Sinai, which the Qur'ān admits (VII, 143, 139).

[2] Sūra XI, 44/46. Jūdī stands for Mt. Qardu, i.e. the Gordyene mountains in Mesopotamia in which, according to the Targums, the ark came to rest.

[3] So Sūra IV, 125/124.

[4] This is a confused reminiscence of the Temptation story of Matt. IV, 5 ff.

cast them into the fire." "Nevertheless I", said he, "was given something better than that. I returned from fighting with the polytheists on the day of Badr exceedingly hungry, when there met me a Jewish woman carrying a basket on her head. In this basket there was a roasted kid, and in her sleeve some sugar. She said: 'Praise be to Allah who has kept you safe. I made a vow to Allah that if you returned safely from this warlike expedition I would not fail to sacrifice this kid for you to eat.' Then she set it down and I put forth my hand to it, which caused the kid to speak, standing upright on its four feet, and saying: 'Eat not of me, for I am poisoned.'"[1] "You speak but true", they said. "That is five, but there remains one more, for we claim that Solomon was better than you." "And why?", he asked. "Because", said they, "Allah subjected to him satans, jinn, men and the winds, and taught him the language of birds and insects."[2] "Yet", he replied, "I have been given something superior to that. Allah subjected to me Burāq,[3] who is more precious than all the world. He is one of the riding-beasts of Paradise. His face is as that of a human, his hooves as those of a horse, his tail as that of a cow. He is larger than an ass but smaller than a mule. His saddle is of ruby, his stirrups of white pearl, he is bridled with seventy thousand bridles of gold and has two wings set with pearls and jacinths. Between his eyes is written: 'There is no deity save Allah. Muḥammad is the Apostle of Allah."' You speak truly", they said, "we bear witness that there is no deity save Allah, and that you are His servant and His Apostle."

[1] This story in various forms occurs in a number of the popular biographies of the Prophet. See herein p. 311 and S. W. Koelle, *Muhammed and Muhammedanism*, p. 183, 436.

[2] Sūra XXVII, 16 ff. and XXXIV, 12/11 ff.

[3] Burāq is the steed on whom he made the Night Journey. See pp. 222, 621.

CREEDS AND CONFESSIONS

INTRODUCTION

There is nothing in Islam that quite corresponds to the Creeds and Confessions of Christendom, for in Islam there has never been any such official formulation of the articles of belief and the rules of conduct as were formulated by the Synods and Councils which undertook to define these matters of belief and practice for the various Christian groups. Islam has its credal statements *('aqā'id)*, but they are in all cases the work of individual writers and have no greater authority than that granted by the consensus of believers to their authors. Nowhere in the Qur'ān is there any precise formulation of what one must believe and what one must practice in order to be a good Muslim. There is in the Qur'ān, however, much teaching about God and the world, about angels and men, about sin and righteousness, about prayer and fasting, about belief and practice. Here was the raw material for a formulation, but Muḥammad himself made no formulation beyond such brief statements as that in Sūra IV, 136/135: "Whosoever disbelieves in Allah and His angels and His Books and His messengers and the Last Day has gone far in error". As a matter of fact there could be no final formulation while the Prophet was still alive, for, as his community developed, new revelations were constantly coming, abrogating older ones which proved to be inadequate, making additions and clarifications, and bringing new statements to meet new needs. When he had gone, however, the situation was different. Parties early began to form in the community, each claiming that it represented the true Islam. Even the early political divisions were involved with this question of who was following the true Islam, a fact which raised acutely the question of what was the true Islam. One early group, the Murji'ites, declared that for humans the problem was insoluble, only Allah knew who was a true Muslim and who was not, and that would be revealed at Judgment. Others who thought that there was an answer could but turn to the Qur'ān and the Traditions for the elements of an answer. The evidence of these sources, however, was not always clear, and support could be found in them for various points of view. The Jabarites who denied man's freedom of will and the Qadarites who affirmed it, the anthropomorphists and the transcendentalists, the Jahmites and even such rationalists as the Mu'tazilites could all find there support for their views.

It was when Muslims came into contact with other religious communities in Syria and Mesopotamia, and had to face criticism of their religion by people who had definite formulations of their beliefs, and arguments wherewith to defend them, that they felt the urgency to formulate, as against these other religions, what were the beliefs and practices which constituted the true Islam and marked off Muslims from members of other religious communities, as well as distinguishing true from false Muslims within their own ranks. The commonly quoted *shahāda* or *kalima*, "There is no deity save Allah, and Muḥammad is the Apostle of Allah", is in its way a brief creed, and was the form of witnessing which most readily marked off a Muslim from a non-Muslim, but it does not cover even as much of the ground of belief as the negative statement in Sūra IV, 136/135. The earliest developments of a more adequate statement seem to have been in the negative form of denying that certain positions maintained by other groups are the true Islam. Perhaps as early as 200 A.H. there began to appear in the School of Abū Ḥanīfa (d. 150 A.H.) the beginnings of more definite credal statements. Three such have survived under his name, and are known as *Fiqh akbar I*, *Fiqh akbar II*, and the *Waṣīya* of Abū Ḥanīfa.[1] These laid the groundwork for the later credal statements, confessions, expositions of the articles of belief and catechisms, which we have from Muslim groups of every theological persuasion. The two Schools which finally came to represent standard Muslim orthodoxy are those of al-Ash'arī (d. 935 A.D.) and al-Māturīdī (d. 944 A.D.), and for this reader we have translated afresh the early formulations as well as later creeds and theological statements from both these orthodox Schools.

[1] They have been studied and interpreted by A. J. Wensinck in *The Muslim Creed* (Cambridge, 1932). Short creeds by al-Ash'arī, al-Ghazzālī, an-Nasafī, and a longer statement by al-Faḍālī, are translated in the appendix to D. B. Macdonald's *Muslim Theology* (London, 1903). The credal statement of aṭ-Ṭaḥāwī was translated by E. E. Elder in the *Macdonald Presentation Volume* (Princeton, 1933), and the same author has translated Taftāzānī's Commentary on the Creed of an-Nasafī in *A Commentary on the Creed of Islam* (New York, 1950). The fundamental work of al-Ash'arī, the *Ibāna*, has been translated by W. C. Klein (New Haven, 1940).

FIQH AKBAR I[1]

We do not brand anyone as an infidel because of a sin, nor do we deny that anyone is of the faith.

We bid what is approved and we forbid what is disapproved.

Know that what comes upon you could not have missed you, and what misses you could not have come upon you.

None of the Companions of the Apostle of Allah—upon whom be Allah's blessing and peace—is to be disavowed nor is any one of them to be adhered to as against any other.

The matter of 'Uthmān and 'Alī is to be referred to Allah, for it is He who knows the secret and the hidden things.

Religious learning is superior to scientific learning.

It is a mercy that there should be differences in the community.

Whoever believes in all that he is bidden but says: "I do not know whether Moses and Jesus—upon both of whom be peace—belong among the Messengers or do not belong", is an infidel.

Whoever says: "I do not know whether Allah is in heaven or on earth", is assuredly an infidel.

Whoever says: "I do not admit the torment of the tomb", is of the doomed Jahmite sect.

[1] Translated from the text embedded in Abū Manṣūr's *Sharḥ al-Fiqh al-akbar* (Hyderabad, 1321 A. H. = 1903 A.D.).

THE *WAṢĪYA* OF ABŪ ḤANĪFA [1]

Faith *(īmān)* consists in confessing with the tongue, believing with the mind, and acknowledging with the heart. Confession alone is not faith, for were that faith all the hypocrites would be true believers. Nor is knowledge alone faith for were it faith all the People of the Book (i.e. Jews and Christians) would be true believers. Allah has said with regard to the case of the hypocrites (LXIII, 1): "Allah bears witness that the hypocrites are liars", and with regard to the case of the People of the Book He has said (II, 146/141): "Those to whom We have given the Scripture recognize it as they recognize their own sons."

Faith may neither increase nor decrease, for decrease in it could only be conceived of in terms of unbelief, and increase in it in terms of decrease in unbelief, but how could a single person be at one and the same time both a believer and an unbeliever? The true believer is in truth a true believer and the infidel is in truth an infidel. Faith is not a matter which admits of doubt, nor is unbelief a matter which admits of doubt, for the Most High has said (VIII, 74/75): "These are in truth believers", and "these are in truth unbelievers" (IV, 151/150).

Even the disobedient ones of the community of Muḥammad—upon whom be Allah's blessing and peace—are all of them true believers, and are not [to be classed, because of their disobedience, as] unbelievers.

Works are something other than faith, and faith is other than works. This is proved by the fact that there are numerous occasions when a true believer is granted exemption from works, whereas it is not permissible to say that he is ever exempted from faith. Thus a woman in menstruation or childbirth is granted exemption by Allah—praised and exalted is He—from prayers, but it is not permissible to say that Allah has granted her exemption from faith and bidden her abandon the faith. Also to such the Lawgiver says: "Give up fasting, but make it up later", but it could not be that one

[1] *waṣīya* means "testament", and though this, like *Fiqh Akbar*, is attributed to Abū Ḥanīfa (d. 767 A.D.) it comes from some later writer or writers of his School. It is translated from the text embedded in the *Sharḥ Waṣīyat al-Imām Abī Ḥanīfa* (Hyderabad, 1321 A.H.).

should be told to give up faith and make it up later. Again it is permissible to say: "The poor man is not under compulsion to pay the legal alms", but it not permissible to say that he is not under compulsion to faith.

We confess that the predetermining of good and evil is all from Allah —exalted be He—for should anyone claim that the predetermining of good and evil is from other than He, he would be one who disbelieves in Allah and anulls his own confession of the [Divine] unity.

We confess that works are of three kinds, viz. obligatory, meritorious, sinful. The obligatory are by Allah's command and in accordance with His will, His liking, His good-pleasure, His decreeing, His predetermining, His creation, His judgment, His knowledge, His help and His writing on the Preserved Tablet. The meritorious are not by Allah's command —exalted be He—but are in accordance with His will, His liking, His good-pleasure, His decreeing, His predetermining, His judgment, His knowledge, His help, His creation, and His writing on the Preserved Tablet. The sinful are not by Allah's command but are in accordance with His will, not in accordance with His liking but by His decreeing and His predetermining, by His creation but not by His help, in accordance with His abandoning and His knowledge, but not with His recognition, and in accordance with His writing on the Preserved Tablet.

We confess that Allah—exalted is He—has taken His seat upon the Throne without His having any need [to do this], and without His being settled upon it. He is the preserver of the Throne, and of what is apart from the Throne, without any necessity, for were He under necessity He would not have been able to bring the world into being and order its arrangement, just as creatures [are unable to do such a thing]. Also were He under necessity to sit and settle [there] then where was He before the creation of the Throne? Very far removed is Allah—exalted be He—from any such [necessity].

We confess that the Qur'ān is the speech of Allah—exalted be He—uncreate, that it is His revelation and what He has sent down. It is not He, but neither is it other than He, but in a real sense it is one of His attributes. It is written in examplars, recited by tongues, memorized in breasts, but is not contained in any of these. The ink, the paper, the writing are created things for they are the work of men, but the speech of Allah—exalted be He—is uncreate. The writing, the letters, the words, the verses, are an adaptation of the Qur'ān to human needs, but the speech of Allah—exalted be He—exists in itself, though its meaning comes to be understood through these things. Whoever says that the speech of Allah—exalted be He—is created is a disbeliever in Allah, the Mighty One. Allah—exalted be He—is One who is worshipped, Who continues ever as He was, so that His speech is recited, is written, is memorized, without ever being separated from Him.

We confess that the most excellent person in this community after our Prophet Muḥammad—upon whom be Allah's blessing and peace—is Abū Bakr, the trusty *(aṣ-Ṣiddīq),* then 'Umar, then 'Uthmān, then 'Alī—upon all of whom be Allah's good pleasure. It is as the Most High has said (LVI, 10–12): "Those who have precedence, those who have precedence. They are those who are brought near, [they are] in gardens of delight." Now everyone who has a foremost place is most excellent, and so every godfearing believer loves them and every wretched hypocrite hates them.

We confess that man, along with his works, his confession and his knowledge, is a created thing. Since the doer is a created thing his deeds must even more be created things. We confess that Allah—exalted be He—created the creatures, and that they had no capability [of creating] because they are weak and impotent. Allah is the One who creates them and provides for them, as He has said (XXX, 40/39): "Allah is the One who created you, then made provision for you; then will put you to death, then will quicken you."

Gain is allowable, and to gather wealth is allowable, though acquiring wealth through that which is forbidden is not allowable.

Men belong to three classes: (1) the believer, who is sincere in his belief; (2) the infidel, who is apostate in his infidelity; (3) the hypocrite, who dissembles in his hypocrisy. Now Allah—exalted be He—has laid on the believer work, on the infidel faith, and on the hypocrite sincerity, by His words (IV, 1): "O ye people, show piety towards your Lord", i.e. O ye believers, be obedient, O ye infidels, believe, O ye hypocrites, be sincere.

We confess that ability [to do a thing comes into being] along with the act, not before the act nor after the act, for were it [in existence] before the act man would be able to dispense with Allah at the time of his need, but this would contradict the plain text of Allah's word (XLVII, 38/40): "Allah is the one who is rich, and ye are the poor."[1] Also were it after the act that would be absurd, for there would be the coming to pass of an act without the ability [for its performance], whereas no creature has the

[1] There is here a play on words. The verb "to be able to dispense with" uses the same root as the word for "rich", i.e. man would be sufficiently rich to be able to do without Allah, whereas the Qur'ān denies this, saying that it is Allah who is rich while men are poor.

capability of acting unless the ability has been contemporaneously given him by Allah—exalted be He.

We confess that wiping the two shoes is valid for the one who stays home for a day and a night, and for the one who is travelling for three days and the nights thereof, for thus does the Tradition state [the matter] and anyone who would deny it would be in danger of infidelity, seeing that it is near to a generally recognized report.[1] Shortening [prayers] and breaking [a fast] are allowable on a journey, for there is a text of Scripture where Allah says (IV, 101/102): "When ye are moving about in the land it is no sin on your part that ye shorten the prayers", and about breaking the fast, He has said (II, 184/180): "Should anyone of you be sick, or on a journey, then [fast] a number of other days."

We confess that Allah commanded the Pen to write. The Pen said: "What, O Lord, shall I write?" Allah—exalted be He—said: "Write what is to be till the Day of Resurrection." This is in accordance with His word (LIV, 52-53): "And every thing they do is in the Record Books, where everything whether small or great is written down."

We confess that the punishment of the tomb is something that will take place. There is no doubt about it. We confess that the questioning by Munkar and Nakīr is a reality, because there are Traditions affirming it.

We confess that Paradise and Hell are a reality, that they are already at present created and will never pass away, nor will their inhabitants pass away. This is in accordance with His saying in regard to the believers (III, 133/127): "prepared for those who act piously", and in regard to the infidels (II, 24/22): "prepared for the infidels." He created them (i.e. Paradise and Hell) for reward and for punishment.

We confess that the Balance is a reality, because He has said (XXI, 47/48): "We will set the Balances a just measure on the Day of Resurrection." We confess that the reading of the Book on the Day of Resurrection is a reality, because He has said (XVII, 14/15): "[To each will come the command]: 'Read thy book. Thou Thyself wilt suffice today to assess the reckoning against thee.'"

We confess that Allah will bring these souls to life after death, and raise them up on a day whose measure [of duration] is fifty thousand years,[2] for retribution and rewarding and the paying of what is due, because He

[1] The reference is to a famous matter of controversy as to whether when performing ablutions *(wuḍū')*, one may rub the shoes with the wet hand. A *khabar mutawātir* is a report so well authenticated and so widely recognized that it may be regarded as virtually certain.

[2] See Sūra LXX, 4.

has said (XXII, 7): "For Allah, indeed, will raise up whosoever is in the graves."

We confess that Allah's meeting with the inhabitants of Paradise is a reality, though without this involving Him in any mode, resemblance or place. Also the intercession of our Prophet Muḥammad—upon whom be Allah's blessing and peace—is a reality [available] for everyone who belongs to the inhabitants of Paradise even though guilty of some greater sin.

We confess that 'Ā'isha is the most excellent of the women of the worlds after the great Khadīja [1]—on both of them be Allah's blessing and peace—that she is the Mother of true believers, pure from [any charge of] fornication and innocent of what the Rawāfiḍ say,[2] so that if anyone testifies to a charge of fornication against her he is himself a child of fornication.

We confess that the inhabitants of Paradise [will continue] in Paradise for ever, and the inhabitants of Hell in Hell for ever, for He has said with regard to believers (II, 82/76): "Those are the Companions of the Garden, therein shall they be for ever," and with regard to infidels (II, 81/75): "Those are the Companions of the Fire, therein shall they be for ever."

[1] Khadīja was Muḥammad's first wife whom he married in the days before his mission. 'Ā'isha, the daughter of Abū Bakr, was his girl wife and his favourite among his numerous later wives.

[2] The Rawāfiḍ were the Shī'a supporters of 'Alī and his family, who considered 'Alī's wife Fāṭima, the Prophet's daughter, as the most excellent of women, and were not above spreading tales about 'Ā'isha's reputation to prejudice her position.

THE CREDAL STATEMENT OF AN-NASAFĪ[1]

In the Name of Allah, the Merciful, the Compassionate

The people of the true religion say that real essences of things actually exist and knowledge of them may be verified, contrary to what the Sophists say. For humans the bases of knowledge are three, viz. the unimpaired senses, trustworthy report, and reason. The senses are five, viz. hearing, seeing, smelling, tasting and touching, and by each of these senses comes information about that for which it was appointed. Trustworthy report is of two kinds. One of them is the *mutawātir* report, which is a report established by the tongues of people who could not be imagined to have agreed together on a falsehood. It is the source of necessary knowledge, such as that about former kings in times long past and lands far distant. The second kind is the report of a Messenger aided by miracle, and is the source of inferential knowledge. The knowledge established by it resembles the knowledge established by necessity both in certainty and sureness. As for reason, it is also a basis for knowledge, and what is established by it by immediate perception is necessary [knowledge], as e.g. the knowledge that the whole of a thing is greater than a part of it. What is established by inference is something acquired. Inspiration *(ilhām)* is not, according to the people of the true religion, one of the bases for knowledge of the valid nature of a thing.

The world with all its parts is something originated, because it consists of substances and accidents. The substance is that which subsists in itself, and is either something compounded, that is a body, or uncompounded, like the atom *(jawhar)* which is the particle that may not be further divided. The accident is that which does not subsist in itself but comes to be in bodies and atoms, such as colours, modes of being *(akwān)*,[2] tastes and smells.

[1] Najm ad-Dīn 'Umar an-Nasafī, who died in 537 A.H. (= 1142 A.D.), was a Ḥanafite by rite and a Māturīdite in theology. His credal statement is one of the most popular and has been the subject of numerous Commentaries. It is translated here from the text embedded in the *Sharḥ Sa'd ad-Dīn at-Taftāzānī 'alā'l-'Aqā'id an-Nasafīya* (Cairo, 1321 A.H. = 1903 A.D.).

[2] The commentary says this means such things as combination, separation, movement, rest.

He who brought the world into existence is Allah—exalted be He—the One, the Eternal *(qadīm)*,[1] the Living, the Powerful, the Knowing, the Hearing, the Seeing, the Willing, the Desiring. He is not an accident, nor a body, nor an atom. He is not something formed or limited, or numbered, nor a thing which is portioned out or divided into parts or compounded, nor something that comes to an end. He is not to be described by asking what? or how? He is not confined to any place nor is he affected by time. There is nothing that resembles Him, and there is nothing outside [the range of] His knowledge and His power. Nevertheless He has attributes eternally subsisting in His essence. They are not He nor are they other than Him. They are Knowledge, Power, Life, Might, Hearing, Seeing, Desiring, Willing, Acting, Creating, Sustaining and Speech.

He is one who speaks with a speech which is one of His eternal attributes and is not of the genus of letters and sounds. It is an attribute which precludes silence and defectiveness. Allah—exalted be He—speaks thereby to bid and to forbid and to give information. The Qur'ān is the speech of Allah—exalted be he—uncreate, though it is written in our examplars, preserved in our hearts, recited by our tongues and heard by our ears, yet without inhering therein.

Creating is also an eternal attribute of Allah—exalted be He. It consists in His creating the world and all its parts not in eternity but at the time when it came to exist in accordance with His knowledge and His desire, but it is, in our opinion, not the thing created. Desiring is also an eternal attribute of Allah—exalted be He—subsisting in His essence.

The [beatific] vision of Allah—exalted be He—is a possible thing from the point of view of reason, and is necessarily true from the point of view of Tradition, for there has come down a proof by good report of the fact that believers will have a vision of Allah—exalted be He—in the future abode. So He will be seen, though not in a place, nor in any direction of confrontation, nor by the coming together of light rays, nor with any fixed distance being set between the one who sees and Allah—exalted be He.

Allah—exalted be He—is the creator of all human actions, whether of infidelity or of faith, whether of obedience or disobedience. They are all of them by His desire and His will, by His judgment, His decreeing and His predetermining. Humans may perform actions by choice for which they are rewarded and punished, those of them that are good being by the good-pleasure of Allah—exalted be He—and those of them that are

[1] Lit. "the ancient", i.e. He is eternal in the sense that there never was a time when He was not. See p. 458.

bad not by His good-pleasure. Ability [to perform actions] comes along with the action and is the real power by which the action is performed. This word [ability] refers to the unimpaired functioning of the causes, the instruments, the bodily members [concerned in the performance of actions], and the validity of [the assignment of] legal responsibility is dependent on this ability, for no creature is held responsible for what is not within his capability.

The pain which is experienced by one beaten as a consequence of being struck by some man, or the brokenness of a glass as the consequence of being broken by some man, and such things as that, are all created by Allah—exalted be He—, there being no working on the part of any human in their being created. Likewise the one who is slain dies at his appointed time, for the appointed time is one. A forbidden thing is [in spite of its being forbidden] sustenance [from Allah]. Everyone receives his own sustenance in full, whether it be of that which is permitted or of that which is forbidden, and it is not to be imagined that a man should not eat his own sustenance or that his sustenance should be eaten by someone other than he. Allah— exalted be He—leads astray whom He will and guides whom He will, and it is by no means incumbent on Allah to do that which is best for a creature.

The punishment of the tomb for infidels and for some disobedient believers, the bliss for the obedient in the tomb by that which Allah —exalted be He—knows and desires, the questioning by Munkar and Nakīr, are things established by authoritative proofs. The resurrection is a reality. The Balance is a reality. The Book is a reality. The Interrogation is a reality. The Pool *(ḥawḍ)* is a reality. The Bridge is a reality. Paradise is a reality and Hell is a reality, for both of them are created and presently existing, will endure and not pass away, and their inhabitants will not pass away.

A great sin does not exclude a believing human from the faith nor put him into infidelity. Allah will not forgive anyone who associates another with Him, though He will forgive anything less than that to whom He wills whether of the lesser or the greater sins. It is possible that He may punish a lesser sin or forgive a greater sin, if this does not involve considering lawful [something that is unlawful], for such a considering lawful is infidelity. That the Messengers have the right of intercession is an established truth, and the reports [about this state that it will avail] even in the case of the greater sins. Such believers as commit greater sins will [nevertheless] not remain forever in the Fire.

Faith *(īmān)* consists in putting confident trust in what [the Prophet] has brought from Allah—exalted be He—and confessing it. As for works they increase of themselves but faith neither increases nor decreases. Faith and Islam are one. Whenever a human finds himself exercising confident trust and making confession he may rightly say: "I am a true believer", and he ought not to say: "I am a believer, if Allah wills." One who is happy may become wretched, and one who is wretched may become happy, [in which case] the change will be in the happiness and the wretchedness not in the making happy and the making wretched, for these are attributes of Allah—exalted be He—and there can be no changing in Allah or in His attributes.

In the sending of the Messengers there was wisdom. Allah has sent Messengers of human kind to human kind as bearers of good tidings and as warners, and to make plain to the people what they needed [to know] about matters of this world and of judgment. He aided them by miracles, [i.e. things] which go contrary to what is usual. The first of the Prophets was Adam—on whom be peace—and the last of them was Muḥammad—upon whom be Allah's blessing and peace. An exposition of their number has been handed down in certain Traditions, but it is preferable not to limit oneself to a fixed number in naming them, for Allah—exalted be He—has said (XL, 78): "The stories of some of them We have recounted to thee, but of some We have not", so in mentioning a fixed number one could never be secure against entering among them some who do not belong to them, or omitting from them some who do belong to them. All of them were bringers of information which they transmitted from Allah—exalted be He—speaking the truth and giving sincere advice. The most excellent of the Prophets—upon whom be peace—is Muḥammad—upon whom be blessings and peace.

The angels are servants of Allah—exalted be He—who labour according to His command. They are not to be described as either male or female. Allah has Books which He sent down to His Prophets in which He has made clear what He bids and what He forbids, His promises and His threats.

The Ascension *(miʿrāj)* of the Apostle of Allah—upon whom be Blessings and peace—while awake and in his bodily form, to the heavens and then whatever exalted regions Allah willed, is a reality. The wondrous doings *(karāmāt)* of the Saints are a reality. Such a wondrous doing shows itself in the way of the Saint performing something which violates the usual, as e.g. in his accomplishing a long journey in a short time, in the appearance of food and drink and clothing when he has need of them, in walking on the water or in the air, in the talking of inanimate bodies or animals, in the warding off of a calamity that approaches, in giving the anxious protection against enemies, and other such things. Such a wonder is a miracle on behalf of the Messenger among whose people the one is for whom it appears, for it shows that that individual is a saint, and he could not be a saint unless he were right in his religion, and his religion is a confession of the message of the Messenger.

The most excellent of human kind after our Prophet is Abū Bakr, the trusty *(aṣ-Ṣiddīq),* then 'Umar, the Separator *(al-Fārūq),* then 'Uthmān, lord of the two lights,[1] then 'Alī, the approved. Their Caliphates were in this order. There was a Caliphate for thirty years, then after that kingdom and empire. The Muslims must needs have a Leader *(imām)* who will see to the carrying out of their legal decisions, the maintenance of their laws, the guarding of their frontiers, the equipping of their armed forces, the receiving of what they bestow in charitable alms, the controlling of contenders for power, robbers and highwaymen, the performing of the weekly and the festival prayers, the settling of disputes which arise between individuals, the hearing of evidence in connection with legal rights, the seeing to marriage arrangements for minors of either sex who have no guardians, and the dividing of the spoils. This Imām must needs be a visible person, not someone hidden or expected. He must be of the Quraish, for it is not permissible that he be of any other [tribe], though it is not necessary that he be restricted to the Banū Hāshim or the progeny of 'Alī—with whom may Allah be pleased. It is not laid down as a condition that he be preserved from error, but it is laid down as a condition that he be one of the people of unrestricted complete authority, an administrator, capable of carrying out legal decisions, guarding the boundaries of the territory of Islam, seeing justice done to the oppressed against the oppressor. The Imām may not be set aside because of any evil doing or injustice [on his part].

It is permissible to perform prayers behind any [leader] pious or impious, and to say prayers over [the corpse of] anyone, pious or impious. Mention of the Companions should be confined to what is good [about them]. We testify that the ten to whom the Prophet—upon whom be blessings and peace—gave the joyful tidings are in Paradise. Our opinion favours the wiping of the two shoes whether on a journey or at home. We do not consider date wine as something prohibited. No Saint attains the rank of the Prophets, nor does any creature reach a place where he is beyond [paying heed to] commands and prohibitions. Texts are to be

[1] The two lights are the Prophet's daughters whom 'Uthmān took in marriage.

taken [normally] in their literal sense, so that to turn from that to meanings such as the followers of esoteric doctrine suggest is heterodoxy. To reject the texts is infidelity. To consider disobedience as lawful is infidelity, to make light of it is infidelity, and to make mock of the religious law is infidelity. To despair of Allah—exalted be He—is infidelity, and to consider oneself safe from Allah is infidelity. To put trust in what a soothsayer reports as from the unseen is infidelity. What is non-existent is not a thing. In the prayers of the living for the dead and in giving charitable alms for their sake there is benefit to them.

Allah—exalted be He—answers prayers and supplies needs. The information given by the Prophet—upon whom be blessings and peace—concerning the indications [of the approach] of the Hour, such as the coming forth of ad-Dajjāl, the Beast of the earth, Gog and Magog, the descent from heaven of Jesus—on whom be peace—and the rising of the sun from the West, are a reality. A Mujtahid may make a mistake or he may be right. Messengers of human kind are superior to angelic Messengers but angelic Messengers are superior to the generality of mankind, though the generality of human kind is superior to the generality of angels.

THE CREDAL STATEMENT OF IBN TŪMART

Ibn Tūmart was the Berber Mahdī who in 515 A.H. (= 1121 A.D.) led a revolt in North Africa against the reigning Almoravids, and founded the group, generally known as the Almohades, who carried on his reforms and transmitted his teaching. He had studied Ash'arite theology in Baghdad, where he was particularly impressed by the current teaching of al-Ghazzālī, under the influence of whose ideas he determined to reform the beliefs and practices of his co-religionists in Morocco. He was particularly opposed to what he considered the gross anthropomorphism *(tajsīm)* in the teaching of his contemporaries in North Africa, and their crassly literal interpretation of the Qur'ān. He died in 524 A.H. (= 1130 A.D.), or maybe in 522 A.H.

His doctrine is Ash'arite though he seems to have incorporated certain Shī'ite elements into his teaching. It is said that he dictated a number of tractates of theological and devotional character to his disciples, and some of these tractates attributed to him have survived. This *'aqīda*, or Credal statement, is limited in scope, but has some interest as revealing the "Doctrine of God" associated with his Almohad movement. It is printed as No. 2 in the collection entitled *Majmū'at ar-Rasā'il*, assembled and published in Cairo in 1328 A.H. by Muḥyī'd-Dīn Ṣabrī al-Kurdī, in which it occupies pp. 45–61.

In the Name of Allah, the Merciful, the Compassionate

Praise be to Allah, as is due to Him, and such eulogy as He gave to Himself, and blessing from Him be upon Muḥammad and his family.

(1)

(On the excellence of tawḥīd,[1] *and the necessity for it, so that it is the first thing that must be acquired)*

[It is related] from Ḥumrān, the client of 'Uthmān b. 'Affān, from 'Uthmān b. 'Affān,[2] that the Apostle of Allah—upon whom be Allah's blessing and peace—said: "Whosoever dies in the knowledge that there is no

[1] *tawḥīd* is literally "the making one", and is that section of theology which is concerned with establishing the uniqueness of Allah. Usually it includes also all that we ordinarily would consider under the "Doctrine of God".

[2] He was the third Caliph, a Companion and son-in-law of the Prophet.

deity save Allah will enter Paradise." Also from Ibn 'Umar, from the Prophet—upon whom be Allah's blessing and peace—that he said: "Islam is built upon five things, on maintaining the unity of Allah, on performing prayers, giving alms, fasting [during] Ramaḍān, and the Pilgrimage." Also from Ibn 'Abbās [it is related] that the Apostle of Allah—upon whom be Allah's blessing and peace—sent Mu'ādh to the Yemen, saying: "You are being set over a community of the People of the Book, so let the first thing to which you summon them be to the worship of Allah. If they recognize Allah inform them that Allah has laid as incumbent duties upon them five prayers each day and night. If they conform to that inform them that Allah has laid as an incumbent duty upon them the legal alms *(zakāt)*, to be taken from their property and given to their poor. If they are obedient in that let them possess in security the most precious things they possess." Another line of transmission has [instead of this last phrase, the words]: "And pay heed to the call of the oppressed, for there is no veil between it and Allah."

From this it becomes certain that worship is not genuine apart from faith and sincerity. But faith and sincerity [come not save] by knowledge, knowledge [comes not save] by seeking, seeking [comes not save] by willing, willing [comes not save] by desire and dread, desire and dread [come not save] by promise and threat, promise and threat [come not save] by the religious law, the religious law [comes not save] by trust in the Apostles, trust in the Apostles [comes not save] by the appearance of a miracle, and the appearance of a miracle [comes not save] by the permission of Allah, Most High.

(2)

It is by an intellectual necessity that one comes to know the existence of the Creator—glory be to Him. This necessary truth [1] is something which cannot be subject to doubt and which no intelligent person can reject. This necessary truth may be said to be of three categories, (i) what needs must be; (ii) what may possibly be; (iii) what may not be. What needs must be comprises things which have to exist, e.g. a doer for a deed. What may possibly be comprises things which may or may not actually exist [at any particular moment], e.g. the coming down of rain.

[1] The term is *ḍarūra*. Rational, intellectual knowledge is said to be of two kinds, *ḍarūra*, innate, necessary knowledge, of which we do not know whence or how it comes, and *muktasaba*, or acquired knowledge, which we gain by observation, deduction and instruction.

What may not be comprises things which cannot possibly become actual, e.g. the bringing together of opposites.

These necessary truths are all firmly established in the souls of intelligent beings. It is firmly established in their souls that a deed must have a doer, and that there can be no doubt about the existence of the doer. Of this Allah—blessed and exalted be He—has given a reminder in His Book, where He says (XIV, 10/11): "Is there doubt about Allah, Creator of the heavens and the earth?" The most High thus informs [us] that there is no doubt about the existence of the creator of the heavens and the earth. Now that about which doubt has been removed is obviously something whose existence is known, so by this it becomes an assured thing that the Creator—glory be to Him—is known by innate knowledge (lit. by neccessity of the intellect).

(3)

Also from his own creation man knows of the existence of his Creator, since he knows that he exists [now], though [there was a time when] he was not in existence. It is as the Most High has said (XIX, 9/10): "I created thee before, when thou wast not anything." He also knows that he was created "from base [1] water", as the Most High has said (LXXXVI, 5-6): "Let man then look at that from which he was created. He was created from water that pours forth." Man also knows by innate knowledge that the water from which he was created was of single quality, undifferentiated, uncompounded, unformed, without bone or flesh, without hearing or seeing. Then all these qualities came into existence in him after that they had not been existing. So when he recognizes that they were created he also recognizes that there must have been a Creator who created them, as the Most High has said (XXIII, 12-14): "And indeed We created man of a pith of clay. Then We made him a drop in a safe receptacle. Then We created the drop into a blood-clot, created the blood-clot into a lump, created the lump into bones, and clothed the bones with flesh. Then We produced him another creature. So blessed be Allah, best of Creators."

(4)

From this one deed (viz. the creation of man) the existence of the Creator

[1] Sūra XXXII, 8/7 *mahīn* means "contemptible", "reviled", hence "base".

—glory be to Him—may be known, and the same would be true of a second [deed] and a third, and so on ad infinitum. From the [existence of] the heavens and the earth and all created things the existence of the Creator—glory be to Him—may be known, just as we know from the coming to be of a single movement both the fact that there must have been an agent [who caused the movement], and the impossibility of its having come to be without such an agent. Just as a single deed necessarily demands a doer, so do all deeds, and everything whose existence we know, though previously it had not existed, must be a thing produced. Thus by innate knowledge we know that night and day, men and beasts, cattle and birds, wild animals and beasts of prey, and other species of creatures are things produced, brought into existence after having been non-existent. Now if we know that one single body is a thing produced, we know that all the rest of bodies are things produced, because they are all in the same category with regard to the way in which they occupy space, suffer change, have their possibilities and peculiarities, are contingent and need an agent [who produces them]. Allah, Most High, has given a reminder in His Book that they are created, for He says (II, 164/159): "Assuredly, in the creation of the heavens and the earth, [in] the alternation of night and day, [in] the ships which run in the sea with what may be useful to people, [in] the rain which Allah sends down from the sky, whereby He quickens the earth after its deadness, and spreads abroad in it every [kind of] animal, [in] the changing about of the winds, and in the clouds set to serve between sky and earth, [in all of these] are signs for a people who have intelligence."

(5)

If it is known that they are things brought into existence after having been non-existent, it is also known that a created thing cannot possibly be a creator. Created things are of three categories, (i) rational living beings; (ii) irrational living beings; (iii) inanimate uncomprehending bodies. Now were all the individual rational beings [in the universe] to combine to restore a single finger after it had passed away they would not be able to do it. If rational beings are thus incapable how much more incapable are irrational beings, and if both rational beings and irrational beings are incapable, then inanimate bodies are still further [from being capable]. Thus it is known that Allah is the [sole] Creator of everything. It is as Allah—blessed and exalted is He—has said (XXXIX, 62/63): "Allah is the Creator of everything, and He over everything has charge."

(6)

If it is known that Allah is the Creator of everything, it is known also that He does not resemble anything, since a thing resembles only what is of its own species. The Creator—glory be to Him—cannot possibly be of the species of created things, for had He been of their species He would have been incapable with their incapacity, and had He been incapable with their incapacity it would have been impossible for Him to bring actions to pass. But we have seen that there is innate knowledge that actions do come to pass, and to deny them in spite of their existence is impossible. So hereby it is known that the Creator—glory be to Him—does not resemble that which has been created. It is as Allah—blessed and exalted is He—has said (XIV, 17): "Is then One who creates as one who does not create? Will ye not recollect?"

(7)

If it is known that any resemblance between the Creator and what has been created must be denied, it is also known that the Creator—glory be to Him—exists absolutely. Everything that has a beginning and an end, has defined limits and its proper attributes, must be something that occupies space, suffers change, has possibilities and peculiarities, is contingent and stands in need of a Creator. But the Creator—glory be to Him—has no beginning, for everything that has a beginning has a "before", and what has a "before" has an "after", and what has an "after" has a limit, and everything that has a limit is a thing produced, and everything that is produced needs a creator. The Creator, however—glory be to Him—"He is the First and the Last, the Outward and the Inward, and He knows all things" (LVII, 3). [He is] the First without any beginning, the Last without any end, the Outer without any defined limits, the Inner without any peculiar properties, existing in absoluteness without *tashbīh* and without *takyīf*.[1] Were all intelligent creatures to combine [their intelligences] in order to ascertain how a creature sees or hears or understands they would not be able to do so, even though it is question of but a creature. If they are incapable of ascertaining how this is in the case of a creature, how much more incapable are they in the case of One

[1] *tashbīh* consists in asserting that Allah in any way resembles His creatures. To avoid *tashbīh* we must assert that He is wholly different from anything we can picture in our minds. *takyīf* means assertion that we know *how* He comes to be as He is. To avoid *takyīf* we refuse all speculation as to His *howness*.

Who has no resemblance to any creature and Who cannot be measured by what is intelligible? There is no similitude by which He could be measured. It is as the Most High has said (XLII, 11/9): "There is nothing at all like Him, though He is the One Who hears, the One Who sees." Imagination does not reach Him, nor does intelligence ascertain how He exists. It is as the Chosen one (i.e. Muḥammad)—upon whom be Allah's blessing and peace—said: "I do not understand how to praise Thee. Thou art as Thou hast praised Thyself", [a statement] in which he draws attention to the fact that we cannot say what He resembles or how He exists, while yet recognizing the majesty and greatness of "the Wealthy, the Praiseworthy" (XXII, 64/63). This is the extreme limit of wisdom. May Allah's peace be upon him.

(8)

Intelligence has a limit where it stops and cannot pass beyond. This limit is its incapacity to ascertain how [He exists]. It has no way of passing beyond [this incapacity] and attaining [a knowledge of how He exists], save by *tajsīm* (i.e. giving Him a body like ours and conceiving of Him anthropomorphically), or by *ta'ṭīl* (i.e. depriving Him of His attributes). Those who know Him know Him by His actions, and they refuse any statements of how He, the Majestic One, comes to be, because they know what *tajsīm* and *ta'ṭīl* lead to, viz. that which is impossible. Now whatever leads to the impossible is itself impossible. His deeds bear witness to His existence as Creator, unique in power, so all the ambiguous statements [of the Qur'ān] *(al-mutashābihāt)*,[1] which give rise to suggestions that He might resemble something, or that one might know how He comes to be, such as the verse about His taking His seat (VII, 54/52),[2] and the Tradition about His coming down,[3] and such other ambiguous statements in the Divine law, must be accepted as part of belief just as they are, but [accepted] along with denial of any *tashbīh* or *takyīf*. No one

[1] Sūra III, 7/5 speaks of the Qur'ān containing some verses which are clear and perspicuous, whose meaning is obvious, and others which are obscure and ambiguous, whose meaning is not clear. These latter are the *mutashābihāt*, and one section of the Qur'ānic Masorah consists of lists of these obscure, ambiguous verses.

[2] This is the famous problem of the *istiwā'*, which arises from the fact that in several passages in the Qur'ān (e.g., X, 3; XIII, 2; XX, 5/4), the statement is made that Allah took His seat on the Throne, a statement which caused considerable embarrassment to later exegetes and theologians. See p. 263.

[3] I.e. the descent of Allah on the Last Day to take His place at the Judgment Seat and there judge all mankind according to the record of their deeds.

follows these ambiguous statements in the Divine law [instead of following the clear ones], save him in whose heart is deviation,[1] as Allah, Most High, has said (III, 7/5): "Now as for those in whose hearts is deviation they follow what is ambiguous in it, seeking dissension, seeking its interpretation, whereas none knows its interpretation save Allah. Those well grounded in knowledge say: 'We believe in it [even though we do not understand it]; it is all from our Lord.'" Here the Most High informs [us] that deviators follow what therein is ambiguous, out of desire for dissension, and desire for its interpretation, and He reproves them for that. The Most High also informs [us] that those firmly grounded in knowledge say: "We believe in it; it is all from our Lord", and He praises them for that, bidding the Apostle—upon whom be Allah's blessing and peace—beware of those who follow such parts of it as are ambiguous. It is related from ʿĀ'isha—with whom may Allah be pleased—that she said: "The Apostle of Allah—upon whom be Allah's blessing and peace—was asked about this verse (III, 7/5): 'It is He Who has sent down upon thee the Book, some of whose verses are clear, which are the Mother of the Book, but others are ambiguous. Now as for those in whose hearts is deviation, etc.', and the Apostle of Allah—upon whom be Allah's blessing and peace—said: 'When you see those who follow what therein is ambiguous, [know that] they are those whom Allah has named, and beware of them.'" No one can picture anything in his imagination save in terms of these ten limits, viz. before, after, above, below, to right, to left, in front of, behind, whole and part. But everything that is [pictured] in terms of these is accidental and demands a creator, whereas the Creator—glory be to Him—is the Wealthy, the Praiseworthy (XXII, 64/63).

(9)

If it is known that He exists absolutely, it is also known that He has not with Him any other than Himself in His kingdom, for were there with Him any other than Himself He would necessarily be bound by the limits of accidental things, since the existence of the independent other must be a thing separated out, whereas the Creator—glory be to Him—is neither joined to nor separated from. Could He be described in terms of joining and separation His existence would necessarily be something created, but the existence of the Creator as something created is impossible since

[1] Or "inclination to fall away" from the truth.

it is impossible that essences be reversed.[1] By this, it is known that He is One God, Who has no second with Him in His kingdom, as the Most High has said (XVI, 51/53): "Take not for yourselves two deities. He is only One God: Me, therefore, reverence Me."

(10)

If it is known that He is unique in His oneness, by the might and the majesty He needs must have, known also is the impossibility of anything being lacking in Him, for the Creator must needs be One who lives, One who knows, One who exercises power, One who wills, One who hears, One who sees, One who speaks, without our being able to imagine *how* this comes to be. Could He be described as being deficient in certain respects, then the bringing to pass of certain actions would be impossible for Him, for it is impossible for an ignorant person, one who is incapable, or sleeping, or dead, to be a Creator. The world as a whole bears testimony to the Wealthy, the Praiseworthy, through the fact that in it there is [evidence of] designing and forming, harmony and disharmony, that which is predetermined and that which is freely determined, that which is accurately done and that which is perfectly accomplished, [all testifying to the fact] that He—blessed and exalted is He—is "able to do whatever He wills", One Who "accomplishes that which He intends" (LXXXV, 16; XI, 107/109). He is living, self-subsistent, One whom slumber takes not nor sleep (II, 255/256). He is the One Who knows the hidden and the manifest (IX, 94/95), from Whom nothing whether on earth or in heaven is hidden (III, 5/4). He knows what is in land and sea, and not a leaf falls but He is aware of it (VI, 59). Not the weight of an atom in the heavens or in the earth escapes Him, nor what is less than that or greater (XXXIV, 3; X, 61/62). He has comprehended all things in [His] knowledge (LXV, 12), and has counted all things by number (LXXII, 28). Shall not He who did the creating know? seeing that He is the Kindly, the Well-informed (LXVII, 14).

(11)

If it is known that He necessarily exists in His eternal existence, it is also known that it is impossible that He should change from that state of

[1] That is, if by essence He is Creator that cannot be reversed so that He could be a created thing, just as that which by essence is a created thing cannot by reversal become the Creator.

might and majesty that are necessarily His, because it is impossible that real essences *(ḥaqā'iq)* should be subject to change. Could the necessary suffer change to the possible and the possible to the impossible there would no longer be any matters certainly known. It is therefore necessarily known that He must of necessity continue existing. He has not ceased and He will not cease knowing all things that are produced as they really are in their attributes and their varied species, their times and their numbers, even before they substantially come into being. The One Who knows decreed them in His eternal existence, so they made their appearance by His wisdom, as directed by His decreeing, and they will run their course by His determining, according to a reckoning that may not be thrown into disorder and an arrangement that may not be disarranged.

(12)

Everything that He has predestined and decreed must be and cannot fail to appear. All created things are the result of His predestining and decreeing. The Creator—glory be to Him—caused them to appear just as He decreed them in His eternal existence, without anything being added or subtracted. There can be no substitution for a thing that has been decreed, nor any turning away from that which has been rendered obligatory. He brought them into existence without any intermediary and for no particular cause. He had no partner in the production of them, nor auxiliary in the task of bringing them into existence. He did not produce them from anything that was there with Him in eternity, and He set them in order without any pattern then existing that could be followed. He forged them to be an indication of what He was able to do and what He chose to do, and He set them to work as an indication of His wisdom and His economy (lit. His arranging). "He created the heavens and the earth without being worn out by creating them" (XLVI, 33/32). "His only command when He wishes any thing is to say to it: 'Be', and it is" (XXXVI, 82).

(13)

All the different varieties of creatures who have appeared as existing after they had been non-existent are in the possession of the Creator—glory be to Him. His predestining and decreeing preceded [them], measuring out their allotted portions, marking their tracks, numbering their breaths, setting limits to their terms so that nothing can lag behind its term nor get ahead of it. Nor can anyone die without having received in full his allotted portion, nor can what has been decreed for him be encroached upon. Each will enjoy the riches that have been created for him, and each may expect that which has been decreed as his. He who has been created for bliss will move smoothly into ease of life, and he who has been created for torment will move smoothly into distress.[1] The happy man [was already] happy in his mother's womb, and the miserable man [was already] miserable in his mother's womb. All this is according to His predestining and decree. Nothing escapes His decreeing, and nothing, from an atom upwards, moves in the darkness of the earth [2] apart from His predestining and decree. "With Him everything has its measure. He is the One Who knows the hidden and the manifest, the Great, the Self-exalted One" (XIII, 8/9, 9/10).

(14)

The Creator—glory be to Him—is unique in equity and in welldoing. He guides and He leads astray. He exalts and He humbles. There is no ruler save Him, and no owner beside Him. Injustice and aggression are not laid to the charge of any save such as are under interdiction and judgment for having transgressed the bounds of some owner and disposed of something which they did not themselves own. Such an one is charged with injustice and aggression because there is an interdiction on him with regard to his possessions and a judgment against him for his deeds. But the Creator—glory be to Him—is under no interdiction in His control, nor is there any judgment against Him for His deeds. He is unique in [His] kingdom and oneness, [in His] sovereignty and divinity. He does in His kingdom whatever He wishes, and in His creation he passes sentence as He wills. He punishes whom He wills, and He shows mercy to whom He wills, looking for no reward and fearing no punishment. He owes nothing, and has no sentence against Him. Every act of blessing from Him is a favour, but every punishment from Him is just. "He is not to be questioned about what He does, it is they who will be questioned" (XXI, 23).

(15)

About the names of Allah, most high

He has the most beautiful names (VII, 180/179). "He is the First and the Last, the Outward and the Inward, and He knows all things" (LVII, 3).

[1] The word for bliss is *an-na'īm*, which is a word used in the Qur'ān for Paradise, and the word for torment is *al-jaḥīm*, a word used in the Qur'ān for Hell. See p. 28.
[2] Cf. Sūra VI, 59.

"He is Allah, other than Whom there is no deity, the King, the most Holy One, the Peacemaker, the Faithful, the Guardian, the Sublime, the Mighty, the Proud" (LIX, 23). "He is the High, the Mighty" (II, 255/256), "the Great, the Self-exalted One" (XIII, 9/10), "the Wealthy, the Praiseworthy" (XXII, 64/63), "the Living, the Self-subsistent" (III, 2/1), "He who hears, He who sees" (XVII, 1), "the Knowing, the Well-informed" (LXVI, 3). "He is Allah, the Creator, the Maker, the Fashioner, His are the most beautiful names. To Him gives glory whatsoever is in the heavens and the earth, for He is the Sublime, the Wise" (LIX, 24). The names of the Creator—glory be to Him—are dependent upon His permission. He is not to be named save by the names He has given Himself in His Book, or by the tongue of His Prophet. Matters of analogy, derivation or technical usage do not come in question in regard to His names. A creature may be named "Jurist" or "liberal man" on the ground of his learning or his generosity, but there is no analogy from this to the case of the Creator—glory be to Him. A creature may be named "one who throws" or "one who kills" because of his throwing or his killing, but there is no analogy from that to the case of the Creator—glory be to Him. A creature may be called Zaid or ʿAmr. He is born not having a name, and he adapts himself to his name, but it is not for a creature to give a decision with regard to his Creator or to name Him by a name other than such as He has given Himself in His Book. What He refrains from giving Himself in His Book he will refrain from giving Him, and what He has affirmed for Himself he will affirm for Him, without making any change or [indulging in] *tashbīh* or *takyīf*.[1] We will name Him by His most beautiful names, and by them will we call upon Him. It is as He—blessed and exalted is He—has said (VII, 180/179): "Allah has the most beautiful names, so call upon Him by them, and leave those who deviate with regard to His names; they will be recompensed for what they have been doing."

(16)

What is said in the Divine law about the vision [of Allah] must be confidently believed in. He will be seen without there being any resemblance to creaturely things and without our knowing how.[2] "Sight does not reach to Him" (VI, 103), in the sense that [that would involve that] He has a

[1] Here again *tashbīh* means seeking to establish resemblances between what is true of the Creator and what is true of creatures, and *takyīf* means seeking to know *how* what is affirmed of Him can be.

[2] This is the *tashbīh* and *takyīf* again.

limit or may be encompassed or is subject to contiguousness or separation, for such categories of accidental things cannot be applied to Him. Every specialization involves some diminution or limitation involving an accidental character which must be rejected in the case of His Majesty. He—glory be to Him—is One, with none resembling Him. "He did not beget, and He was not begotten, and no one has ever been His peer" (CXII, 3, 4). "Originator of the heavens and the earth, how should He have a son, seeing that He has had no female companion? He created everything, and He knows everything. That is Allah, your Lord, there is no deity save Him, Creator of everything; so worship Him, for He is in charge over everything. Sight does not reach Him, but He reaches the sight. And He is the Gentle One, the Well-informed" (VI, 101–103).

(17)

On the confirmation of a mission by miracles

By innate necessary knowledge *(ḍarūra)* is known the trustworthiness of an Apostle, through the appearance of signs such as violate the natural order of things and which accompany the proclamation of his message. The proof of this is that the one who claims to have a mission will belong to one of three classes. Either he will come with actions which are customary, such as eating, drinking, wearing clothes, and claim that they are a miracle on his part, but his claim is of no avail because they do not provide any sign of his trustworthiness. Or he will come with actions [involving some unusual skill, but one which] may be attained by [natural] ability or by instruction, such as writing, or building, or sewing, or such like acts, which he claims are a miracle on his part, but his claim is of no avail because nothing which may be attained by [natural] ability or instruction can be considered to be a genuine miracle of an Apostle. Or he may come with actions which violate the usual course of things, such as making the sea divide, or changing a rod into a serpent, or raising the dead, or splitting the moon, and claim that they are a miracle on his part. In such a case his trustworthiness is confirmed, since only the Creator—glory be to Him—could bring them about and cause them to appear as an accompaniment to the proclamation [of the Apostle's message]. The concurrence of the miracle with the proclamation is something that is perceived, and there is no way of refuting things perceived, or of making of no avail things that are [assuredly] known.

Among the miracles of [our] Prophet—upon whom be Allah's blessing and peace—is the Qur'ān. The Faithful Spirit [1] brought it down in clear Arabic speech (XXVI, 193, 195), and Allah made it a sign of his trustworthiness. Said Allah—blessed and exalted is He—(II, 23/21): "And if ye are in doubt about what We have sent down to Our servant, then bring a Sūra like it, and summon your witnesses apart from Allah, if ye are speaking truth." So when they were unable to bring the like of what he brought his trustworthiness was known by necessary knowledge. Allah sent him to mankind as a whole, a bringer of good tidings and a warner (XXXIV, 28/27), a summoner to Allah, by His permission, and a shining lamp (XXXIII, 46/45). He sent him with compassion and mercy, specially endowed him with knowledge and dread, ennobled him with forbearance and wisdom, and guided him to the finest habits. So he delivered the message, made clear the religious law, and brought security. Then there came to him from his Lord firm conviction after religion had been perfected and [Allah's] favour completed. May Allah's blessing and peace be upon him, and on his family, on his Companions, both the Emigrants, and the Helpers, and the Followers,[2] with all of whom may Allah's goodness be till the Day of Judgment.

And praise be to Allah, Lord of the Worlds

1 The "faithful spirit" is Gabriel.

2 The Emigrants were those believers who followed Muḥammad from Mecca to Madīna after he had emigrated to that city in 622 A.D. The Helpers are the Madīnans who joined the new religion and gave the Prophet and his followers asylum in their city. The Followers are the next generation of believers, i.e. the companions of the Companions.

THE *UṢŪL* OF IBN 'UKKĀSHA [1]

Said Muḥammad b. 'Ukkāsha—on whom may Allah have mercy—Mu'āwiya b. Ḥammād al-Kirmānī informed me, quoting from az-Zuhrī, who said: "Whoever bathes himself on Thursday night, prays a two *rak'a* [2] prayer and recites Sūra CXII a thousand times will see the Prophet—upon whom be Allah's blessing and peace—in his dreams." Consequently I kept assiduously at this every Thursday night, praying the prayer of two *rak'as* and reciting Sūra CXII a thousand times, eagerly desiring to see the Prophet—upon whom be Allah's blessing and peace—in my dream, so that I might expose to him [for his criticism] my *Uṣūl.*

Now it happened that one cold night I had bathed and had performed the two *rak'a* prayer, then took to my couch and a dream came to me. So I rose again and bathed and said a two *rak'a* prayer which I finished not long before the dawn. Then I leaned against the wall with my face towards the *qibla,*[3] when lo! the Prophet—on whom be Allah's blessing and peace—came to me. His face was like the moon on the night of its fullness, his neck like a silver ewer in which were golden rods, so to speak. He was wearing two garments of this striped Yemenite cloth, one as an upper garment and one as a lower. He came and sat with his right foot tucked under him and the left foot straight. I wanted to say: "Allah give thee life", but he got in ahead of me and said: "Allah give thee life." I was eager to see his broken front teeth,[4] so he smiled and I saw them.

Then I said: "O Apostle of Allah, the jurists and the theologians disagree with me [about the fundamental principles of our religion] so may I

[1] From al-Malaṭī's *Kitāb at-Tanbīh* (ed. Dedering, Istanbul, 1936), pp. 12, 13.—*uṣūl* is literally "roots" and so means here the fundamental principles of religion. On Muḥammad b. 'Ukkāsha see Ibn Ḥajar, *Lisān al-Mīzān*, V, 286.

[2] For the meaning of *rak'a* see n. 4 on pp. 463.

[3] I.e. the direction of the Holy Shrine at Mecca towards which all Muslims turn in prayer. The "People of the Qibla", soon to be mentioned, means the Muslims, i.e. the people who face in that direction in prayer. See p. 401.

[4] Tradition tells how at the Battle of Uḥud in the year 3 A.H. the Prophet had teeth broken by a stone that struck him in the mouth. See Muir, *Life of Muhammad*, p. 261.

expose to you my *Uṣūl* [for your criticism]?" "Assuredly", said he, so I commenced:

"[The principles of our religion are these], to be ever well-pleased with whatever Allah decrees, to be submissive to His command and patiently endure His judgments, to do what He bids be done and refrain from doing what He has forbidden, to act always as for His eye alone, to believe that both good and evil are by Allah's decree, to avoid all hypocrisy, quarrelling and contention in religion, to rub the two boots,[1] to go on Holy War with the people of the *qibla,* to pray the customary prayers over those of the people of the *qibla* who die, [to confess] that faith is capable of both increase and decrease in word and in deed, that the Qur'ān is the speech of Allah, that one must patiently endure one's Sulṭān [2] such as he is whether just or unjust and not draw the sword against princes even if they act unjustly, that one should never judge any particular believer [3] as certain of Paradise or of Hell, nor ever consider any believer an unbeliever because of some sin, even if he commits the greater sins, that one should reverence the Companions of Muḥammad—upon whom be Allah's blessing and peace." When I came to the "and reverence the Companions of Muḥammad" he wept and even sobbed aloud. [I continued: "And hold] that the most excellent of mankind after the Apostle of Allah—upon whom be Allah's blessing and peace—is Abū Bakr, then ʿUmar, then ʿUthmān, then ʿAlī."

I said to myself: "ʿAlī is his cousin and his son-in-law", but he smiled as though he knew what was in my thought. Three nights in succession I exposed to him these *Uṣūl,* and each time I would stop at "and ʿUthmān and ʿAlī", and he—upon whom be peace—would say "then ʿUthmān, then ʿAlī", repeating this three times, and as I would expose to him these *Uṣūl* tears would flow from his eyes. I myself found such sweetness in my heart and my mouth that I remained eight days taking neither food nor drink, till I became too weak to perform the canonical prayer services, but when I ate that sweetness and delight departed. Allah is my witness and a sufficient witness is Allah.

[1] For this point of dispute see p. 345.
[2] Sulṭān here stands as the symbol of constituted authority in the community.
[3] Lit. "One of the people who confess the uniqueness of Allah". The point is that only Allah knows who, even among Muslims, is for Paradise and who for Hell.

ʻALĪ'S STATEMENT TO ʻABBĀD B. QAIS [1]

ʻAbbād b. Qais came to ʻAlī—whose face may Allah ennoble—and said to him: "O Commander of the Faithful, inform us what the faith *(al-īmān)* is, and what Islam is." He answered: "Yes, O son of Qais. Allah —majestic be His praise—made a beginning of affairs by His knowledge thereof, choosing for Himself what He willed and appropriating what He wanted. Now what He wanted was that He might select Islam, so He appointed it as a religion for His servants. He derived it from His name, for He is as-Salām.[2] So His religion is Islam, which He approved of for Himself and freely gave to him whom He loved best of His creatures. Then He honoured it, made easy its religious ordinances for such as came to it, and strengthened its defences against those who fought against it. Yet how far was any annuller from annulling it! He made it a strength to him who united himself to it, a source of security to him who entered it, a guidance to him who would follow it, a light to him who seeks its illumination, a demonstration to him who takes hold of it, an adornment to him who clothes himself with it, a help to him who professes it, an honour to him who acknowledges it, an argument for him who utters it, a witness to him who engages in disputation about it, a victory to him who argues in favour of it, a knowledge to him who understands it, intelligence to him who transmits it, a judgment for him who executes it, forbearance for him who makes music of it,[3] a sharpening of mind to him who reflects upon it, firm assurance to him who clings to it, intelligence

[1] From *Dastūr Maʻālim al-Ḥikam wa Ma'thūr Makārim ash-Shiyam*, by Ibn Salāma al-Quḍaʻī (Cairo, 1332 A.H.), pp. 114–119. Though put in the mouth of ʻAlī, the cousin and son-in-law of the Prophet, and the First Imām of the Shīʻites, the statement is of much later origin, and is a fair example of the highly rhetorical characterisations of Islam favoured by later Islam. The ʻAbbād mentioned here is probably that ʻAbbād (or ʻUbāda) b. aṣ-Ṣāmit b. Qais al-Anṣārī, who was for a time the Muslim ruler in Ḥomṣ.

[2] In Sūra LIX, 23 one of Allah's names is as-Salām (it is No. 5 in the list of Allah's beautiful names on p. 553), and here by folk-etymology the word *islām* is said to be derived from this name of Allah.

[3] I.e. in his cantillating the Qur'ān.

to him who comes to understand it, a warning to him who is admonished by it, a trusty rope to him who clings to it, a salvation to him who puts his trust in it, a friendship to him who seeks to make peace, a nearness to him who seeks to draw near, and an ease to him who is entrusted with an affair. It is the modesty of him who is filled with godly fear, a mode of entity for him who believes, a security for him who submits himself, and a joy to such as speak the truth."

"Islam is the source of truth, truth is the way of guidance. Its price is good deeds, its benefit is glory, so it is the most far-reaching road and the most brightly shining lamp, a far-shining beacon, a gleaming lantern, a standard lifted high, an easy path, the assembler of ornaments, an ancient number, a stake eagerly desired, a painful vengeance, the goal of those who speak the truth, a clearly evident proof, a mighty affair, and the noblest of riders."

"Now the faith *(al-īmān)* is its well-worn path, piety is its equipment, good deeds are its beacon, chastity provides its lanterns, lovers [of Allah] are its horsemen, death is its standard, this present world is its hippodrome, the resurrection is its *ḥalba*,[1] Paradise is its stake and Hell-Fire is its vengeance. So the refuge of the Blessed (lit. the fortunate ones) is in the faith, and where the Damned (lit. the unfortunate ones) separate themselves out is by disobedience after conclusive evidence has been clearly given them, when the beacon of truth has been made clear to them and the way of guidance. So he who abandons the truth will be in an evil state on the Day of Mutual Deceit.[2] Null will be his argumentation when faced with the enjoyment of the Blessed in Paradise. In faith there is an indication of piety, in piety there is fear of death, in death there is a finishing with this present world, in this world watch is kept for the next world, and in resurrection there is a drawing nigh to Paradise. Paradise is the thing that is regretted by the Damned (lit. inhabitants of Hell), and in mention of the Damned there is a warning to the pious."

"Piety is a goal [to be aimed at]. He who aims at it will not perish, and he who works for it will not repent, because it is through piety that those who succeed reach their success, whereas it was by disobedience that those who perish went astray. Let the pious folk keep this in mind, for at the Resurrection creatures have no way of escape from standing

[1] A *ḥalba* is an assembling of the horses ready to start a horse-race, the *miḍmār*, or hippodrome, is, of course, the area set out for horse racing.

[2] *at-taghābun* is one of the names of the Last Day. It occurs in Sūra LXIV, 9, where Bell renders it "the overreaching".

before the just Judge. There they will quickly go into its arena,[1] racing towards its high winning-post at its farthest end, stretching out their necks towards its caller, having come forth from the depths of their graves and places of entombment to that which is necessarily eternal for all concerned therewith. For the Damned all ways have been cut off and they go forth to a dreadful punishment as their retribution. For them there is no return to this world's dwelling-places, they are deprived of all good things, and of no avail to them will be those whom they chose to obey rather than give obedience to the Great, the Self-exalted.[2] The Blessed, however, enjoy the protection of the faith."

"Faith, O son of Qais, reposes on four pillars, on patient endurance, on assurance, on equity and on earnest striving. Among these patient endurance also reposes on four pillars, on yearning desire, on solicitude, on abstinence and on waiting in expectation. So he who with yearning desires Paradise will be diverted from fleshly lusts, and he who is full of solicitude over Hell-fire will hold back from things forbidden, and he who is abstinent as regards this world will find its misfortunes easy to bear, and he who waits expectantly for death will hasten towards things that are good. So also assurance reposes on four pillars, on the enlightenment of the intelligence, on the warning of telling examples, on the interpretation of wisdom, making clear what the examples mean, [and on the custom of those of former times]. He who makes clear the example understands the custom, and he who understands the custom is as though he were living among those of former times, so that he is guided to that which is right. Equity also reposes on four pillars, on an abundance of knowledge, on a penetrating understanding, on a blossoming of wisdom, and on a luxuriance of judgment. He who understands expounds the propositions of learning, and he who knows opens up a way through the mysterious things of wisdom, and he who opens a way through the mysterious things of wisdom will find that they point him to resources of forbearance so that he will never go astray. So striving earnestly also reposes on four pillars, on bidding that which is approved, on forbidding that which is disapproved, on steadiness in domestic affairs, and on abhorrence of transgressors. He who bids that which is approved strengthens the backs of believers, and he who forbids that which is disapproved spites the hypocrites, and he who is steady in domestic

[1] *miḍmār* is the hippodrome above mentioned, so the horse-racing image is here extended to the scene of final Judgment. The "caller" is the official who calls each race.

[2] These are epithets applied by Allah to Himself in Sūra XIII, 9/10.

affairs fulfils the duties he has to perform, and he who loathes transgressors is angry for Allah's sake—mighty and majestic is He—, and he who is angry for Allah's sake has made majestic His praise."

"That is what the faith is, O son of Qais, and these are its columns and its pillars. Have you understood?" "Yes, O Commander of the Faithful", he replied, "may Allah direct you aright, for, indeed, He has directed you aright."

THEOLOGY

A THEOLOGICAL TRACTATE, THE *BAḤR AL-KALĀM*

Creeds and Confessions give brief statements of the essentials of a religion. More elaborate statements of these matters have, in Islam, taken three forms, (1) Commentaries on the Credal statements;[1] (2) refutations of heresies;[2] (3) systematic theological tractates.[3] Each such tractate will, of course, represent the particular theological position of the author, whether he is a Shī'ite or a Sunnī, an Ash'arite or a Māturīdite, or whatever else. Some of these tractates are very extensive, and many of them have been written by theologians whose names are famous in the history of Islam. To give the non-Muslim reader a true picture of the way in which Muslim theologians have set forth their statements of doctrine it was necessary to translate one tractate as a whole, yet to come within the limits of a *Reader* it could not be one of the longer and more famous tractates. The one selected was the *Baḥr al-Kalām fī 'Ilm at-Tawḥīd*, (Sea of Discussion on the Science of Theology), by Abū 'l-Mu'īn an-Nasafī (d. 508 A.H. = 1114 A.D.), who was a contemporary both of the great theologian al-Ghazzālī (d. 1111 A.D.) and of that Najm ad-Dīn an-Nasafī (d. 1142 A.D.), whose credal statement appears on pp. 347–352. Abū 'l-Mu'īn is a less widely known theologian. He wrote an *'Aqīda* or credal statement, but apparently it has never been published, and is the author of a number of works on theological and polemical subjects. His *Baḥr al-Kalām* has had considerable popularity, and on the title-page of the printed edition he is called "Chief of the People of as-Sunna and al-Jamā'a, sword of the truth and of religion". The translation has been made from the Cairo edition dated A.H. 1329 (= 1911 A.D.), printed at the Press of Faraj-allah Zakī al-Kurdī.

Praise be to Allah, possessor of majesty and nobility, and blessing and peace be upon His Apostle, Muḥammad, the choicest of mankind, and on his family and on his noble Companions.

Saith the Sheikh, the illustrious Imām, a chief of the people of *Sunna*

[1] A good example in English is E. E. Elder's translation of at-Taftāzānī's Commentary on the Credal statement of Najm ad-Dīn an-Nasafī (New York, 1950).

[2] 'Abd al-Qāhir al-Baghdādī's *Moslem Schisms and Sects* has been translated into English, the first part by Kate Chambers Seelye (New York, 1920), and the second part by A. S. Halkin (Tel-Aviv, 1936), but unfortunately the translation of the first part is often unreliable.

[3] A good example in English is Walter C. Klein's translation of al-Ash'arī's *Al-Ibānah 'an Uṣūl ad-Diyāna* (New Haven, 1940).

wa Jamāʿa (approved custom and community),[1] sword of the truth and of religion, Abū 'l-Muʿīn an-Nasafī, on whom may Allah—may He be exalted—have mercy:

Be it known to you that I make my statement of belief as to the fact that Allah—may He be exalted—may be known and my belief in the doctrine of the Divine Unity. I teach that Allah—may He be exalted—is one, unique, primordial, everlasting; that He is eternal, the One Who has no partner, Whom nothing is like and nothing resembles; Who has no shape, against Whom none contents and to Whom none is equal; Who has always been alone, one, unique, single, and Who will always be so for ever. He is the One Who is perfect in His essence, everlasting in His attributes, He Who transcends imperfection. He is the all-knowing One, with Whom there is no forgetfulness, the Omniscient for Whom there are no uncertainties; Who was in existence before space was created, before time and temporality came into being.

It was He Who then created time and the Throne, and on the Throne took His seat, though He had no need of the Throne, nor is the Throne an abiding place for Him, nor His locale; rather it is He Who sustains both Throne and locale, for He is too great for any place to be wide enough for Him, seeing that He is above every place. He knew what was to be before it came to be, and what did not come to be He knew what it would have been had it come to be. His knowledge of things preceded their existence. In His kingdom and in what He wills to be there will never be anything save by His knowledge, His will, His determining and His decree. He exists, as He described Himself in His Book, without image and without assuming shape, just as He has perception of Himself without seeing or act of comprehension.

He—illustrious be His might—said to His Apostle—on whom be blessing and peace—: "Say! He, Allah, is one" (Sūra CXII), where the "He" points to the fact of His [knowable] existence, and is a refutation of those who deny the Divine attributes *(al-muʿaṭṭila)* and the esoteric sects *(al-bāṭinīyya)*; the "One" establishes His unity, refuting the polytheists and the pagans. [So it is with the rest of the words of this Sūra], "the Eternal", which refutes the assimilationists *(al-mushabbiha)*; "He did not beget, and He was not begotten", which refutes the Jews and

[1] This phrase *ahl as-sunna wa 'l-jamāʿa* occurs frequently in this text, and as the author obviously means it to indicate the truly orthodox Muslims as against the various groups of heretics or less orthodox Muslims, we shall translate it consistently as "the truly orthodox". *sunna* means "custom" in the sense of all custom approved as religiously orthodox, and *jamāʿa* means "society of men", in the sense of the society of orthodox believers.

the Christians; "and no one has ever been His peer", which refutes the Zoroastrians who talk of Yazdān and Ahrimān, just as in another place (Sūra, XLII, 11/9). He—may He be exalted—said: "There is nothing [that stands] as His like. He is the One Who hears, the One Who sees."

Now when He had thus revealed Himself and it had become manifest that He must be believed in, there arose questioning as to this belief in Him. Men asked: "What is knowledge [of God]? What is the doctrine of the Divine Unity? What is faith? What is Islam? What is religion?" The answer is, that knowledge [of God] is that you know Him in [His] uniqueness; the doctrine of Divine Unity is that you deny that He has any co-partner, any similar, any contender; that faith is confession with the tongue and firm assurance in the heart of the uniqueness of Allah; Islam is that you worship Allah in this uniqueness; religion is continuing steadfast in these four good positions till death. Allah—may He be exalted—has said (III, 85/79): "Should anyone desire any other than Islam as a religion, it will not be accepted from him, and in the world to come he will be one of the losers."

Be it known that discussion and dispute about religion are allowable, contrary to what the heretics *(al-mubtadi'a)* teach, for they assert that it is not permissible. It is disapproved only when it becomes a matter of vaingloriousness or a mere quest for influence, praise or worldly fame.

Should someone ask: "What is the limitation of knowledge *('ilm)* [in these matters]?" — we answer that the truly orthodox regard the limitation of knowledge as understanding *(ma'rifa)* of what may be known as it is in itself, that is, knowledge such as creatures may have, for Allah's all-inclusive knowledge and information about what a thing is in itself is not to be described as understanding *(ma'rifa)*, for He is always the One Who knows, as we have already made clear. Said He (XVIII, 91/90): "And We had full information about what [forces he had] with him."

The Mu'tazilites teach that knowledge is to be defined as knowledge of the thing in itself. Now this is wrong because the non-existent is not a thing, and does not take the name of "thing", because Allah created things, [and created them] not from a [previously existing] thing, but by saying "Be! and it was" (II, 117/111), whereas we are able to make [things], but not by utterance. So were we to say that it (i.e. knowledge) is understanding of the thing in itself, that would be giving eternity to substances along with Allah, which is the teaching of the unbelieving, impious materialists—whom may Allah curse—for according to them the world is eternal. Allah, however, knows by His knowing, which is one of His eternal attributes, contrary to what the Mu'tazilites [1] teach, viz. that His essence is His knowledge, whereas, as we have already mentioned, Allah is self knowing. According to us He knows His knowledge, seeing that knowing is one of His eternal attributes. He knew what would be before it was, and what is not He knew what it would have been had it come to be. His knowledge of things preceded their existence. He has said (XXVII, 65/66): "No one in the heavens or on earth knows the unseen save Allah." The Rāfiḍites [2] and the Qadarites [3] teach that He does not know things which He has not created and has not brought into existence.

Knowledge (*'ilm*) is superior to intelligence (*'aql*). The intelligence of the Saints is less than that of the Prophets, and the intelligence of the Prophets is less than that of our Prophet, Muḥammad—on whom Be Allah's blessing and peace—, contrary to the teaching of the Mu'tazilites that all men are equal as regards intelligence. It is incumbent upon everyone who is possessed of intelligence and who has reached years of discretion to make use of his intelligence to discover indications that the world has a Maker, just as Abraham—upon whom be Allah's blessings and peace—found such indications, as did also the Companions of the Cave [4]—with whom may Allah be pleased—since "they said: 'Our Lord is Lord of the heavens and the earth; never will we call upon any deity other than Him, for in that case we should have said something outrageous'" (XVIII, 14/13), i.e. a statement far from the truth. Therefore those whom Divine revelation (*waḥy*) has not reached are not [for that reason] excused. This is contrary to the teaching of the Mortifiers (*al-mutaqashshifa*) [5] and the Ash'arites,[6] for our teaching is that Faith (*al-īmān*) is the action of a human under the guidance of the Lord. We do not teach that Faith is either created or uncreated, but we teach that on the human side there is confession with the tongue and confident

[1] These thinkers, whose name means "Seceders", were the followers of Wāṣil b. 'Aṭā', and are commonly referred to as the Rationalists of Islam. See Tritton, *Muslim Theology* (1947), pp. 60 ff.

[2] Rāfiḍites (*rawāfiḍ*) is a general name to cover the various Shī'a sects. See p. 346 and Tritton, *op. cit.*, p. 20.

[3] The Qadarites were the early champions of the doctrine of the free will. *Ibid.*, p. 54.

[4] The reference is to the story in Sūra XVIII where Muḥammad gives his version of the famous Oriental legend of the Seven Sleepers.

[5] This seems to be used as a general term to cover the various ascetic groups in the Muslim community of that day.

[6] The Ash'arites were the followers of Abū 'l-Ḥasan al-Ash'arī, who broke from the Mu'tazilites and founded the system which today is that followed by the great majority of orthodox Muslims. Since the author of the *Baḥr al-Kalām* was a Māturīdite the Ash'arites represent to him the rival school of orthodoxy.

trust in the heart, while on Allah's side there is guidance and help. According to ash-Shāfi'ī [1] the performance of the prime duties of religion *(al-arkān)* is part of Faith. The Mortifiers *(al-mutaqashshifa)* teach that Faith is purely a matter of oral confession without confident trust.

With regard to what has been said above about Faith it may be asked: "Is it from Allah to a human, or from a human to Allah, or some of it from Allah to the human and some of it from the human to Allah?" Should someone teach that it is from Allah to a human, which is the strong point with the Jabarite sect,[2] for they teach that a human is compelled *(majbūr)* either to faith or to unbelief, or should some teach that it is from a human to Allah, which is the strong point with the Qadarite sect, for they teach that humans have capability by what the soul has acquired for itself before the act, so that there is no need for any strength or help from Allah, our answer is that according to our teaching Faith is the act of a human under guidance from the Lord. The instruction is from [the side of] Allah, the understanding and acceptance of the instruction are from [the side of] man. The guidance is from Allah, the being guided and the seeking of guidance are from man. The help is from Allah, the serious endeavour, the constancy and the intention are from man. The generosity and the bestowing are from Allah, the acceptance is from man. That which is from Allah is uncreated, but what is from the human side is created, for Allah in all His attributes is uncreated, whereas humans in all their attributes are created beings, and anyone who does not distinguish clearly the attributes of Allah from human attributes is going astray, is a heretic.

The Voiders *(al-mafrūghiyya)* [3] teach that Faith is from Allah to humans and is uncreated. [They base their teaching on] the statement of Allah (III, 18/16): "Allah bears witness that there is no deity but Himself", so [this statement of Faith] is uncreated, like the Qur'ān. The answer to this is what we have already mentioned. If the objection is raised that if Faith is partly from Allah and partly from a human then there is partnership between the Lord and the slave, which is impossible, the answer is that we teach that the instruction from Allah is the cause of man's salvation, so man is the one caused [to escape] and Allah is the one who causes, and the cause is other than the causer. In the same way

[1] Muḥammad b. Idrīs ash-Shāfi'ī (767–820 A.D.), the founder of the Shāfi'ite rite, the third of the four orthodox rites in Sunni Islam. See p. 265.

[2] The Jabarites were the early supporters of the doctrine of predestination against such supporters of free will as the Qadarites. See D. B. Macdonald, *Muslim Theology*, p. 344.

[3] It is not clear what sect the author is referring to by this name.

sustenance *(rizq)* is the cause of man's continued life, and ablution *(wuḍu')* is the cause of a prayer service being legitimate, yet it is not said to be part of the prayers. Similarly the instruction *(ta'rīf)* from Allah is the cause of man's salvation, and [consists] in the granting of a light in the heart of a believer, so that it is not something shared in partnership. The light of understanding *(ma'rifa)* in the believer's heart is a created thing, for whatever is other than Allah is created, and this goes back to a first principle *(aṣl)*, namely, that the making is not the thing made, and the sustaining is other than the thing sustained (i.e. given sustenance), the creating other than what is created, the instructing other than the matter of instruction *(ma'rifa)* and the bringing into existence other than that which is brought into existence.

The Mu'tazilites and the Mortifiers *(al-mutaqashshifa)* teach that both the instruction *(ta'rīf)* and the understanding *(ma'rifa)* [of the matter of instruction] are created things, while the Voiders *(al-mafrūghiyya)* teach that both of them are uncreated. According to the truly orthodox, however, the *ta'rīf* is from Allah and so is uncreated, while the *ma'rifa* and the *ta'arruf* (i.e. the matter of instruction and the process of being instructed therein), being on the side of man, are created.

Should it be asked: "How Faith is to be described, and what its conditions are?"— we reply that Faith is that you should believe in Allah, in His angels, His Books, His Apostles, in the Last Day, in the resurrection after death, and that the decreeing of both good and evil are from Allah. This is according to the truly orthodox.

The Mu'tazilites teach that evil is wholly from man, for Allah does not decree evil, nor determine it, nor will it, for did He determine evil and then punish men for it, that would be tyranny *(ẓulm)* on His part and injustice *(jawr)*, but Allah is far removed from tyranny or injustice. For this reason they (i.e. the Mu'tazilites) call themselves the people of equity and unity *(al-'adl wa't-tawḥīd)*. We, on the other hand, teach that man is given the option and is capable, that the determining does not compel men to disobedience, just as is the case with knowledge, for determining is an attribute of the Determiner, and the attribute does not compel anyone to action, just as knowledge of tailoring or carpentering does not compel the tailor or carpenter to do [any tailoring or carpentering]. Man has the option and the ability, and in this sense deserves punishment [if he does wrong]. It is as though a master were to say to his slave: "If you enter the house you are free", and he enters the house and is free—a similar case is that of divorce, when divorce takes place—, yet no one says that it was because the oath indicated that he might enter, that, therefore, compelled him to enter. So is it here. Even if the action is by the determination of Allah, no one may say that such determining compelled anyone to act. Another answer is that the determining is one of Allah's secret matters which He has kept hidden from creatures, whereas command and prohibition are Allah's clear proof against His creatures, so that if one ignores His revealed commands when he has the ability [to act], then in that sense he deserves punishment.

The question may be raised: "If we say that Allah determines evil, and man is unable to flee from the determining of Allah, that would mean that the evil is to be attributed to Allah, [would it not?]" — to this we reply that man's action is to be distinguished from Allah's determining. Do you not see that Allah created the instrument for fornication yet the fornication is not to be attributed to Allah? This indicates that though Allah created movement and power in man's soul and man is able [to act] by this capacity of his soul and his will, the movement and the power [when they are activated] are not to be attributed to Allah, even though that was by His determining and by His will. This points to the soundness of our teaching that if Allah did not will unbelief and evil and disobedience and did not determine it, whereas man wills it and does it, then man's will would be predominant over Allah's will, and this [in turn] would mean that a deficiency is to be attributed to Allah, which is unbelief, seeing that all wills are under the will of Allah, and under His desire. Allah has said (LXXVI, 30 = LXXXI, 29): "But ye will not save as Allah wills." It is also pointed to by the fact that were one to say: "My will and desire are other than the will of Allah and His desire", that would be making a claim to Lordship along with Allah, which is unbelief, as 'Alī b. Abī Ṭālib [1]—may Allah honour his face—has said.

So it stands assured that every will comes under the will of Allah. Because Allah knew that Pharaoh and Iblīs [2] would be in unbelief He cursed them. Should we say that He did not desire their unbelief nor did he produce it [that would be saying that] His desire is in contradiction with His knowledge, and this cannot be, for if knowledge is reduced to nothing there remains but foolishness and ignorance, but Allah is far removed from foolishness and ignorance. This [desire], however, is quite distinct from a command, for there is a verse given textually from Allah

[1] The fourth Caliph, and the first Imām of the Shī'a. He was the cousin and son-in-law of the Prophet, having married the Prophet's daughter Fāṭima. His father Abū Ṭālib had been Muḥammad's protector when he was left an orphan.

[2] In the Qur'ān this is the personal name of Satan. It is derived from the Greek word *diabolos*.

[declaring] that He does not command evil. Allah has said (VII, 28/27): "Verily Allah does not command evil deeds (or what is blameworthy)", [1] where the reference is to fornication. Allah has also said (II, 205/201): "and Allah loves not corruption." Here we have a deviation from the rule, because it is possible for Allah to command one with regard to a matter which He does not desire. A case is that of Iblīs—on whom be the curse [of Allah]. He ordered him to do obeisance to Adam,[2] but He did not desire from him any act of obeisance. Also He forbade Adam—on whom be Allah's blessings—to eat from the tree, but He did not desire from him any refraining, nay rather He desired that he eat from the tree. And with Allah is success.

Be it known that Allah created all creatures when He brought them forth from the loins of Adam—on whom be peace—on the day of the Covenant.[3] They were not believers nor were they unbelievers but they were creatures. Then He set before them Faith and Unbelief. Each one who chose Faith and accepted it as belief became a believer, and each one who did not choose Faith became an unbeliever, while each one who responded with words instead of belief became a hypocrite. This was as Allah has said (VII, 172/171): "When thy Lord took from the sons of Adam, from their backs, their progeny, and took their witness against themselves, [saying]: 'Am I not your Lord?', they answered: 'Surely.'" That He said: "Am I not your Lord?", and that they answered: "Surely", would indicate that Allah created them then with bodies as well as souls just as they are now, for question and answer are for bodies along with souls. Then He put them back into the loins of their parents, [and little by little] drew out the children of Adam from him, then the children of his children from his children, and so on till the Resurrection Day, because Allah said: "From their backs."

The Jabarites teach that Allah created the believers as believers and the unbelievers as unbelievers. Therefore Iblīs—upon whom be the curse—

[1] This latter clause is not in VII, 28/27, but is from a similar passage in XXIV, 1.

[2] The Qur'ān in several passages refers to this legend of the angels doing obeisance to the newly created Adam. In Muḥammad's version of the story it was Allah who commanded the angels to do obeisance, but Iblīs refused, and for that reason he was cast out and became the enemy of mankind. Muslim theologians have always been much exercised to explain why Allah should command the angels to do such obeisance to Adam, when obeisance should be tendered to none save Himself.

[3] This event of the Covenant *(mīthāq)*, also known as "the first creation", is the Islamic version of an ancient Oriental notion. It says that after Adam's creation Allah stroked his loins and drew out all his progeny who should be till the end of time, making the division then as to which of them should be believers and which unbelievers, which should inherit Paradise and which go to the Fire. See pp. 204–205, 275.

ceases not to be an unbeliever as he was [from the beginning], and Abū Bakr and 'Umar [1] were believers before there was any Islam. Likewise the Prophets were prophets before any revelation had been given. In that case, curiously enough, the brethren of Joseph must have been prophets at the time of their rebelliousness.[2] The truly orthodox—whom may Allah increase, and among whom we, praise be to Allah, are—teach that they became prophets after that [revelation had been given], and that Iblīs became rebellious by refusing the act of obeisance, and so became an unbeliever by not recognizing that Allah was wise in what He commanded. According to them unbelievers are constrained to unbelief and rebelliousness, and are punished, whereas believers are constrained to obedience and faith. We, however, teach that man is given the option and is capable of either obedience or rebelliousness, being under no constraint, but the aiding or the abandoning *(tawfīq wa khidhlān)* are from Allah, and the decreeing of good and evil are from Allah. This question will be fully discussed in the latter part of this book.

The truth of our position is indicated by Allah's saying (IV, 136/135): "Believe in Allah and in His Apostle." Had they been [already] believers He would not have given them such a command, nor indeed would He have addressed them about the Faith. Had they not had the possibility of choosing there would have been no point to the command. It is also pointed to by the saying of him on whom be Allah's blessing and peace: "I have been bidden make war on the people till they say: 'There is no deity but Allah, and Muḥammad is the Apostle of Allah.' If they say this they will preserve their blood from me and their property, save what is due therefrom,[3] while their accounting is with Allah," for he did not make war on any believer.

The question may be raised: "If capability is granted by Allah to humans at the time of an action, contemporaneous with the action, neither preceding it nor coming after it; if good and evil, faith and unbelief, obedience and rebelliousness, are by the decreeing of Allah, by His

[1] Abū Bakr was the first Caliph in succession to Muḥammad, and 'Umar was the second Caliph.

[2] The point here is that four times in the Qur'ān "the Tribes" are referred to as the recipients of revelation, and thus belong to the prophetic succession. Some have thought that there was a confusion in Muḥammad's mind between the *Twelve* meaning the twelve tribes, and the *Twelve* meaning the Minor Prophets, but it is more likely that he is reproducing the old Rabbinic notion that the Patriarchs were all recipients of revelation.

[3] The reference is to the fact that though they became Muslims they still had to pay out of their property the dues demanded by the religious law for the upkeep of the Muslim social and political order. See p. 147.

determining, His will and His desire, by His aiding, or forsaking, or protecting, then on what ground is man deserving of punishment or reward?" —to this we reply: Be it known that the command to obedience is from Allah, but faith in the obedience is on man's part. The prohibition is from Allah, but the taking of responsibility, the striving and the perseverance are on the human side, so whenever there is found on man's part striving and intention and the taking of responsibility, there comes to him power and capability from Allah contemporaneously with the action, so he deserves reward or punishment for his own deed. In like manner faith is given from Allah, but the accepting is by man; the guidance and instruction are from Allah, but the betaking of Himself, the humble entreaty, the supplication are on man's part. The abandonment in rebelliousness is from Allah, but repentance and seeking pardon are on man's part. The bounteousness is from Allah, but the thanksgiving is by man. If there is found on his part purpose and intention of rebelliousness, abandonment by Allah runs along with his intention and purpose. If on his part there is found constancy and intent to obey, aid from Allah runs along with his intention and constancy, only he is deserving of reward or punishment by reason of the striving, the intention, the taking of responsibility which are human actions and human attributes. Anyone who teaches other than this is astray and is guilty of heresy.

There is another answer, viz. that he is deserving of punishment for disregarding the command and the prohibition, both of which are clear, as we have mentioned.

The question may be asked: "Does a fortunate person ever become unfortunate, and an unfortunate one fortunate, or not?" —our teaching is that he of whom the foreknowledge of Allah is that he be fortunate or unfortunate suffers no alteration [of condition], since His knowledge does not change, but he of whom He knows that part of his life will be unfortunate and part fortunate may have his name written on the Tablet [1] among the fortunate or among the unfortunate, and then that may be changed so that he is written among the unfortunate or the fortunate. Allah obliterates or maintains intact what He pleases, for "with Him is the Mother of the Book" (XIII, 39), whereas were we to say that no unfortunate will become fortunate or no fortunate one become unfortu-

[1] In documents from an early period in Mesopotamia we read of the "tablets of fate" in which things decreed to happen were written. Muḥammad refers to the "Preserved Tablet" in the Qur'ān (LXXXV, 22), which orthodoxy has identified with the "Mother of the Book", and regards as the heavenly Tablet on which all that is to come to pass has been recorded from the beginning.

nate that would be equivalent to nullifying the Scriptures and the Apostles, which is not permissible.

[It may be asked]: Will he whom [the message of] revelation did not reach, though he was an intelligent being, and who therefore did not know about his Lord, be excused or not? According to us he will not be excused, for he should have found some indication [of the existence of his Lord] in the fact that the world has a maker, just as the Companions of the Cave found such an indication, and said (XVIII, 14/13): "Our Lord is the Lord of heaven and earth", or as Abraham—on whom be peace—who found such an indication when he saw the sun rising, and said (VI, 78): "This is my Lord... I am guiltless of this polytheism of yours." The Muʿtazilites teach that it is not incumbent on such a person to seek an indication by his intelligence, though the intelligence is under the necessity of recognizing Allah. The Ashʿarites, and a party of the Ḥanbalites,[1] teach that such a person is excused and is under no necessity to seek for these indications. Their ground for this opinion is the statement of Allah (XVII, 15/16): "It has not been Our wont to punish till We send a messenger."

[The question may be asked]: Is one who does not know the articles *(sharā'iṭ)* of Faith a believer or not? The truly orthodox people teach that he is not a believer so long as he does not know all the articles of Faith, detailing them with his tongue and confidently believing in them in his heart, testifying that there is no deity but Allah, that Muḥammad is His servant and His Apostle, and believing in Allah, in His angels, His Books, His Apostles and in the Last Day, and that the religion of Islam is the best of all religions. [If he does this] then he is a believer, a Muslim.

The Muʿtazilites teach something different from what we have recorded [above], but this is the teaching of Abū Ḥanīfa [2]—on whom may Allah have mercy—for it says in *al-Jāmiʿ al-kabīr* [3]: "If anyone marries a minor, when she come to maturity and she is asked to detail the articles of Faith, if she can detail them then she is his wife, but if she cannot detail them, saying: 'I do not know', let her be divorced from him."

It may be asked: "What indication there is that the world has someone who made it?" —We teach that the existence of a made article is an indica-

[1] The followers of Aḥmad b. Ḥanbal (d. 855 A.D.), the founder of the fourth of the orthodox rites.

[2] Abū Ḥanifa Nuʿmān b. Thābit (d. 767) was the founder of the first of the four orthodox rites.

[3] This work is a famous exposition of the Ḥanafite system written by ash-Shaibānī.

tion of the existence of its maker. The materialists, the Zindīqs [1] and the naturalists—whom may Allah curse—teach that the world has been in existence from all eternity, likewise the drop of semen *(nuṭfa)* [which is the origin of animal life], and the seed which is the origin of vegetation, [have been in existence since eternity], they being [composed] of the four natural elements, viz. the coolness of air, the warmth of fire, the moistness of water, and the dryness of earth. To them this may be said: We have seen things decaying and going to pieces in the winter, as for example trees and grass and herbage, while others do not decay, such as the myrtle, the pine, the juniper and [certain] garden vegetables and seed-produce. Now were it a matter of nature there ought to be no such difference with regard to the ordering of plants and seed-produce. Since, however, there is this difference, it is an indication that it is due to the decreeing of an eternal and powerful Maker. Likewise we see in one and the same place trees whose fruits both in colour and taste are different, though the water, earth, air and heat there are exactly the same. Were nature the sole factor there ought not to be such differences in the fruits and the colours, but there are these differences, and that is an indication that they are due to an eternal, powerful Maker. [The existence of] this efficient cause is brought out in His statement (XIII, 4): "And in the earth are portions neighbouring one another... in which are signs for a people who have intelligence."

Be it known that the names of the [Divine] attributes are of two kinds, attributes of essence and attributes of activity. Attributes of essence are those such as life, power, hearing, seeing, knowledge, speech, will and desire; while attributes of activity are those such as creating, providing, bestowing, favour, being bounteous, doing good, mercifulness and forgiveness. Now our teaching is that Allah with all His attributes is One, with all His attributes and His names is from eternity and to eternity without any distinction of parts, that the attributes of Allah and His names are not He, nor are they other than He, as one is other than ten. Were we to say that these attributes are Allah that would be equivalent to making two gods, whereas Allah is One, He has no partner. Were we to say that these attributes are other than Allah, then these attributes would be contingent, but that is not possible.

Should it be asked: "What indication there is that the attributes of Allah are from eternity and to eternity?" —we reply that had Allah not been powerful in eternity how did He become powerful when He created power?

[1] This word, derived from the Iranian, meant originally the Manichaeans, but then came to mean dualists of all kinds, and finally to mean any heretical group. See p. 267.

How did He become powerful when He created life and hearing and seeing? How did He become knowing when He created knowledge? This would be equivalent to describing Allah as being deficient before the one and ignorant before the other, which is impossible. So also the attributes of activity such as creating, providing, being bounteous, doing good, mercifulness, forgiveness, guidance, are all from eternity and to eternity, being neither He nor other than He, by the same token.

The Ash'arites teach that these [latter] attributes are all contingent. They say that He was not a Creator when He had not yet created, nor a Provider when He had as yet made no provision for creatures. We, on the contrary, teach that it is permissible for Him to be called Creator even when He had not yet created the creation, and to be called Provider even though He had not yet made provision for creatures. Do you not see that one of us who has ability for tailoring is called a tailor even though no tailoring has yet come from him? It is the same here. Since Allah has the ability to create and to provide He may be called Creator and Provider. Do you not see that Allah calls Himself "Master of the Day of Judgment" (I, 4/3), even though He has not yet created the Day of Judgment? Since He is able to create it and bring it into existence He called Himself by that name. It is the same here, save that this answer is here not a strong one. The sound answer is that we teach that these attributes are eternal in His essence for eternity because were they not eternal in His essence for eternity, the essence of the Creator *(al-bārī')* would be the seat of accidentals, which is impossible.

Be it known that existing things are of two classes, eternal and contingent. The contingent is what is other than Allah, and the eternal is Allah—may He be exalted. Linguistically, *eternal (qadīm)* means that which has precedence (i.e. is *al-mutaqaddim)* in existence over other than it. This is so with regard to the attributes of things that have been created, but in reference to the attributes of Allah *eternal* means that which ceases not. Allah is eternal, without beginning, and without ending, who has not ceased (being) and will not cease. In His case it does not mean that He had precedence in existence over other than Himself, as is shown by the fact that did we not teach that Allah is eternal we should have to teach contingency [with regard to Him] and destitution [of attributes], for the opposite of the eternal is the contingent, and a contingent could not be Lord, Creator, Maker, He of Power, so it is necessary for us to deny contingency [with regard to Him], and firmly maintain eternity. This is what the [sacred] text presents in [giving Him] the two names, "the First and the Last" (LVII, 3), meaning that He is continuously without beginning and without end. Yet it is permissible to say that Allah exists, for [to say that He] exists means that He has not ceased and will not cease to be.

It is permissible to say that Allah is One. This is what the text presents where He says (XVI, 22/23): "Your God is one god", and again (CXII, 1): "Say: 'He, Allah, is One', where "one" *(aḥad)* means the existing One who has no parts, whose essence is not subject to division. Allah is not one in the numerical sense, for were He one in the numerical sense He would be subject to division. In that case it would be impossible for Him to be One God, since causation, composition, formation would affect each part of Him, which would be equivalent to saying that an efficient creator comes into being for every part of Him, which is absurd.

It is permissible to say that Allah is a thing. Did we not firmly maintain that He is a thing we should have to maintain destitution *(ta'ṭīl)*, since the opposite of a thing is nothing, so needs must we deny destitution and firmly maintain [that He is] a thing. The Mu'aṭṭila teach that it is not permissible to say that Allah is a thing, for they flee from [any suggestion of the] assimilation [of Allah to created things]. Moreover [they state that] there is a Tradition [which reads]: "Verily Allah has ninety-nine names and whosoever reckons them up will enter Paradise." Now we have reckoned them up, they say, and we have not found among them [the name] "Thing". The answer to this is that we teach that Allah—may He be exalted—gave Himself the name "Thing", for He said (VI, 19): "Say: 'What thing is greatest as a witness?' Say: 'Allah is witness.'" Thus it is demonstrated that it is permissible to confer the name "Thing" on Allah.

According to the truly orthodox people it is permissible for Allah to be spoken of as having a self, because the self is mentioned [in Scripture], and by it is meant the essence, something that exists. Allah has said (XX, 41/43): "And I have made thee for Myself", i.e. for My essential being. Also He has said (III, 28/27): "Allah would have you beware of Himself", i.e. of His essential being. [Again we read] (VI, 116): "Thou knowest what is in my self, but I do not know what is in Thy self." If the Corporealists *(al-mujassima)* [1] say: "If you speak of self then you speak of body", we reply that "body" means a built-up essence liable to qualification by accidents *('araḍ)*, whereas "self" means the essence in itself. Thus from the necessity of giving Him the name "Self" it does not necessarily follow that we are giving Him a body. If they answer: "But we teach that He is a

[1] They were anthropomorphists who taught that the attributes of Allah were like those of men. See Macdonald, *Muslim Theology*, pp. 191, 291.

body unlike [other] bodies, just as you teach that He is a thing unlike [other] things", we reply: If you speak of a body you are speaking of modality *(kaifīya)*, as we have mentioned in the definition of body, and it is not possible to affirm that this is of the essence of the Creator *(al-bāri')*—illustrious be His majesty.

The Assimilationists *(al-mushabbiha)* [1] teach that it is permissible to say that Allah is a light that scintillates. The truly orthodox people, however—whom may Allah succour—teach that He is the creator of light, and the one who causes it to give forth light. Light has colour, so were we to say [what they say] we should be teaching [the doctrine of] assimilation *(tashbīh)*,[2] whereas Allah is far removed from assimilation. Allah has said (XLII, 11/9): "There is nothing [that can be used] as a similitude for Him." They base their teaching on Allah's saying (XXIV, 35): "Allah is the light of the heavens and the earth", where He calls Himself a light. Our reply is that we teach what was taught by Ibn 'Abbās [3]—with whom and with whose father may Allah be pleased—viz. that the meaning is "the One Who lights up the heavens and the earth". Others say that it means, "the One Who guides the inhabitants of the heavens and the earth".

It is permissible in Arabic to speak of Allah having a hand though this is not permissible in Persian. The hand is one of His eternal attributes, without mode of being or assimilation [to the likeness of a human hand], just as are [His] hearing, seeing, knowing, power, desire and speech. Allah is He Who hears without an organ [of hearing], the One Who sees without an eye, knows without an apparatus [of knowing], desires without a heart, speaks without tongue or lips, and in like manner His hand is one of His eternal attributes, without mode [of being] or assimilation or organ. So we confess [to belief in] the hand, and what is intended thereby is what Allah—may He be exalted—intends.

The Mu'tazilites teach that what is meant by [this word] "hand" is naught but power and might, for Allah says (V, 64/69): "Nay, but both His hands are outstretched", where the meaning is His benefactions. We teach that it is not permissible [to say] that what is meant by "hand" is

[1] See A. S. Halkin's translation of al-Baghdādī's *Moslem Schisms and Sects*, pp. 31 ff.

[2] The doctrine of *tashbīh* is that which assimilates Allah to human things, teaching that seeing for Him is like human seeing, or that His taking His seat resembles a human taking his seat. Those who teach *tashbīh* are the *mushabbiha*, who are what we call Anthropomorphists. See p. 363.

[3] The son of Muḥammad's uncle 'Abbās. His own name was 'Abdallah, but he is most commonly known as Ibn 'Abbās. To orthodox Islam he is the greatest of all the early exegetes of the Qur'ān.

only might and power, for Allah said to Iblīs (XXXVIII, 75): "What prevented you from doing obeisance to that which I have created with My two hands", so were what is intended by "hand" only power and might it would mean that there were two powers and two mights, which is impossible, since the might of Allah and the power of Allah are but one, which cannot perish or cease to be, unlike the might of creatures, for our attributes are accidentals, and the accidental does not endure through time and eternity. Allah's might, and His power, however, are not accidentals, do not cease to be, nor do they pass away. It is the same with [the attribute of] speech. Allah is He Who speaks with one speech, and His speech does not suffer interruption.

In the Qur'ān the word "hand" is used in various senses. One of them is *possession,* for Allah has said (LXVII, 1): "Blessed be He in Whose hand is the kingdom", i.e. the kingdom is His possession. One says: "This village is in the hand of So-and-So", i.e. it is in his possession, at his disposal. Another meaning is *favour (minna),* as where Allah says (XLVIII, 10): "Allah's hand is above their hands", i.e. Allah's favour is above their favour, where the meaning is the Divine unity. Or again Allah has said (XXXVI, 71): "We have created cattle for them out of what Our hands have made", i.e. [they are of] Allah's favour and assistance. In the Traditions [we read that the Prophet said]: "Allahumma, do not give any wicked one a hand with regard to me", i.e. [do not give him] favour. Also among its meanings is *rebelliousness,* as where Allah—praised be He—says (XLII, 30/29): "Save for what your hands have gained." [1] Yet another [meaning] is *bodily organ (jāriḥa),* [a word] used of the right and the left hands, though Allah is far removed from having such. To sum up then: Allah's hand has no mode of being, no assimilation to or form of a [human] bodily organ, but is one of His eternal attributes.

The Assimilationists *(al-mushabbiha)* teach that Allah has a form and two hands. They teach that what is meant by the two hands of the Merciful is [that He has] two right hands, for the left hand is inauspicious. Similarly [they hold] that it may be said that He has a leg and fingers. In support of this they quote the saying of the Most High (XXXIX, 67): "The whole earth will be but a handfull for Him on the Day of Resurrection, and the heavens will be folded up by His right hand." The answer [to this] is that the words: "The whole earth will be but a handful for

[1] The text here says: "for what *their* hands have gained", but there is no such passage in the Qur'ān. Most probably what the writer means is this passage in XLII, 30/29, though it is possible that it is a corruption of II, 79/73, "for what their hands have written", where the succeeding words go on to speak of gain.

Him", means that it will be in His possession and in His power, just as one says: "This piece of land is in my grasp", i.e. in my possession. To confirm their notion that Allah has a leg they call in evidence the words (LXVIII, 42): "The Day when the leg will be bared." In the Traditions [we read]: "The hearts of men are between the fingers of the Merciful, Who turns them as He will." Also in the Traditions [we read]: "On the Day of Resurrection Hell will say: 'Is there anything more?', whereupon the Lord will put His foot in it, and it will say: 'Desist! desist!', i.e. I have sufficient. I have sufficient." We teach that what is meant by "leg" is some great and difficult matter. Some say that what is meant by "leg" is Hell's own leg, in accordance with the Tradition which relates that "Hell has thirty thousand heads and in every head thirty thousand mouths", in which case it is quite possible that it has a leg also. As for the Tradition about the hearts of men being between the fingers of the Merciful, what is meant by "fingers" here is influence. Al-Aṣmaʿī [1] mentions this meaning and he is a foremost scholar in matters of language, and whose word is authoritative. [In the above Tradition] it means between two influences from among the influences of the Merciful, viz. helping and abandoning, for he whom Allah helps does the works of obedience, whereas he whom Allah abandons does the works of disobedience. As for the Tradition about the Almighty putting His foot into Hell, the correct reading is [not *qadam* "foot", but] *qidam* "precedence", so that it means those among the unbelievers whom He foreknew [were to enter Hell].

It is not permissible to describe Allah as coming or going, because these two words apply to the attributes of creatures and are indications of contingent beings, so that both are attributes to be denied of Allah. Do you not see how Abraham — on whom be Allah's blessing and peace — saw an indication in that which was moved from place to place (viz. the sun), that it was not a Lord, since [with regard to this incident] Allah says (VI, 76): "But when it set, he (i.e. Abraham) said: 'I love not those that set.'" The meaning of the verse (LXXXIX, 22/23): "And thy Lord comes along, and the angels, rank by rank", is that the commandment of thy Lord will come. Also the verse (LIX, 2): "So Allah came upon them from where they were not expecting", means the killing of Kaʿb b. al-Ashraf.[2] His saying (XVI, 26/28): "Allah came at their building from the

[1] ʿAbd al-Malik b. Quraib al-Aṣmaʿī (d. circa 831 A.D.) was one of the outstanding grammarians of the Baṣrian school. See Huart, *Arabic Literature*, pp. 142, 143.

[2] He was a son of a Jewess, who had joined Muḥammad's party but being disappointde in him went over to the side of his opponents at Madīna. Muḥammad ordered Kaʿb's

foundations", means that He sought to destroy them and root them out, so that of them there remained not one who blew on a fire or dwelt in a house. The reference is to Nimrod, the son of Canaan,[1] whom may Allah curse. The meaning of the verse (II, 210/206): "Can they look for anything other than that Allah will come to them in shadows of clouds along with the angels", is: "after We have given clear indications that He has no likeness and that with Him there is no [such thing as] coming, do they look for His coming in shadows of clouds, and take this as an article of faith that must be believed in?" For this [coming and going] to be one of the attributes of Allah is impossible.

There is a Tradition [which reads]: "Allah descends every midnight of [the month of] Shaʿbān to the lowest heaven and says: 'Is there anyone who is penitent, that he may be forgiven?'" We teach that Allah's descending is His observing and meeting with His servants, meaning that He looks with mercy on His servants. Thus have we received it by transmission from ʿAlī b. Abī Ṭālib—with whom may Allah be pleased. It is like Allah's saying (XV, 9): "We it is, indeed, who have sent down the Reminder", where He did not mean to suggest a real sending down, but meant: "We taught it, and We caused it to be understood." So is it here.

Should some one say: "We to teach that Allah is a composite body that would do us no harm"—we reply [to such a person]: It would do you harm, because the word "body" means a body composed and put together. If you firmly establish [the fact of the] parts then you are teaching that He is not One God, but Allah has said (XVI, 22/23): "Your God is One God." If you disavow this text you are in unbelief, because it would be equivalent to ascribing [the acts of] creating, sustaining, occasioning, forming, to each part of Him, each member of Him, which is as much as to say that He is not One God, and whosoever teaches this is in unbelief.

If you say that some parts of Him are God and some are not God, this would be to bring together Creator and created, provider and provided for, and whoever teaches this is in unbelief. Should someone say that it has been handed down from the Prophet—upon whom be Allah's

---

foster-brother to assassinate him, which he did. This verse is said by the Commentators to refer to the occurrence, and so Allah's coming upon them means the coming of His punishment. See Muir's *Life of Muḥammad*, pp. 245–247.

[1] Nimrod is nowhere mentioned by name in the Qur'ān but is said by the Commentators to be the person referred to in this passage, and in II, 258/260; XXI, 68 ff., as the ruler who was hostile to Abraham as Pharaoh was hostile to Moses. To later Islam he was one of the typical "bad men" of ancient times.

blessing and peace—that he said: "On the night of the Mi'raj [1] I saw my Lord in the loveliest of forms, and He said: 'O Muḥammad, over what should the *mala'* [2] be disputing save over Me?', so I answered: 'I do not know'", our answer is that the words "I saw my Lord" in this Tradition mean: "I saw my Lord Gabriel in the loveliest of forms." Others say that it means: "I saw my Lord while I was in the loveliest of forms." If it is taken to mean that the Lord he saw in the loveliest of forms was Gabriel, that shows the soundness of our teaching.

Allah has said (LIX, 24): "He is Allah, the Creator, the Maker, the Fashioner." If *al-muṣawwir* (he who forms, i.e. the Fashioner), is deliberately read *al-muṣawwar* (i.e. the Fashioned), that is unbelief, and any one who commits that error [unwittingly] has spoiled his prayer. The meaning of the Tradition: "Allah will reveal Himself to those at the Standing [3] in a form they do not recognize, and then reveal Himself in a form which they do recognize", is that [He will be revealed] by a more beautiful attribute. They do not recognize Him [by such an attribute] in the world because in the world they [have been accustomed to] recognize Him by [the fact of His] refraining from punishing [when He might well have punished], and by [His] generosity, so when He shows [Himself in attributes of] authority, and equity, splitting the moon and causing the stars to fall, men will say: "O our Lord, we have not been accustomed to recognize Thee in the world by such attributes." Then He will show refraining from punishing and granting forgiveness, and they will recognize Him by those attributes.

The Karrāmites [4] teach that Allah sat at rest upon the Throne so that it was filled with Him. Their evidence for this is the saying of Allah (XX, 5/4): "The Merciful has taken His seat upon the Throne." Our

[1] The *mi'rāj* is the Ascension of Muḥammad, when one night, on the celestial steed Burāq, and accompanied by Gabriel, he went on a journey through the heavenly spheres and had speech with Allah. See pp. 333 ff.; 621 ff.

[2] *mala'* means "Council of chiefs". Allah has an angelic *mala'* in the heavens, and every ruler had such a *mala'* at his Court on earth. The merchant aristocracy at Mecca also had a *mala'* or Supreme Council. Here the reference seems to be to the heavenly *mala'*.

[3] In the accounts of the events of the Last Day we read that after the Resurrection comes the Assembling, when all are gathered together in their resurrection bodies at the place where Judgment will take place. When they have all been so assembled there will be a period of Standing, while they wait in varying degrees of apprehension and terror for the heavens to be rent and the Judge of all to appear surrounded by His angels who have the record books of men's deeds and who set up the Balances and the Bridge across Gehenna to Paradise.

[4] The followers of Muḥammad b. Karrām (d. 869). See Tritton, *Muslim Theology*, pp. 108 ff.

reply to them is that some of the Commentators say that *istawā* (took seat) means *istawlā,* i.e. "assumed authority", as in Persian one says: *bar ʿarsh pādshāh ast* (the sovereign is on the throne). An indication of this meaning is also given by the words of the poet:

> "A man has taken his seat over ʿIrāq,
> Without sword, and without blood being shed",

where *istawā* (has taken his seat) clearly means *istawlā,* i.e. "assumed authority". From Mālik b. Anas,[1] the Imām of al-Madīna, is recorded the saying: "The taking of the seat is not a matter of which we are ignorant, though how it comes about is a matter we do not understand. Belief in it is incumbent upon us, and questioning about it is heretical innovation." He said to the one who was asking the question: "All I can see is that you are far astray [in error]." He ordered enquiry to be made, and lo! it was Jahm b. Ṣafwān [2] [who asked the question]. Since Allah existed before He created the Throne and it is not permissible to say that He was transferred to the Throne, because [being subject to] transference [from place to place] is an attribute of creatures and one of the signs of things that are contingent, whereas Allah is far removed from that; and since anyone who affirms the sitting [of Allah] at rest upon the Throne must teach either that He is the same size as the Throne, or that the Throne is bigger than He is, or that He is bigger than the Throne. Whichever way you take it the one who says such things is an unbeliever for he has made Him a limited being.

It is related that ʿAlī b. Abī Ṭālib—with whom may Allah be pleased—was asked: "Where was our Lord before the Throne was created?" He—with whom may Allah be pleased—said: "How is it that there is such a question about place, seeing that Allah existed when there was as yet neither space nor time, and He is at the present time just as He was then." So it is related that Jaʿfar aṣ-Ṣādiq [3]—with whom may Allah be pleased—said: "The doctrine of the Divine unity involves three points, viz. that you should recognize that He is not *from* a thing nor *in* a thing, nor *on* a thing, for whosoever describes Him as *from* a thing has described Him as something created, which is unbelief and has no basis; and whoso

[1] Abū ʿAbdallah Mālik b. Anas (d. 795 A.D.), was the founder of the second of the four orthodox rites among Sunni Muslims.

[2] Jahm b. Ṣafwān (d. 746 A.D.), the founder of the heretical group of the Jahmites. He was put to death in 746. See Tritton, *Muslim Theology*, pp. 62 ff.

[3] The sixth of the Shīʿite Imāms, who died in 765 A.D. See D. M. Donaldson, *The Shīʿite Religion,* chapter XII, for an account of his life and work.

describes Him as *in* a thing has described Him as limited, which is unbelief; and whoso describes Him as being *on* a thing has described Him as being in need of being upborne, and that too is unbelief.

What is happening is that the Assimilationists are seizing upon the surface meanings of verses such as (XXVIII, 88): "Everything will perish save His face", and (LV, 27): "but the face of thy Lord, majestic and glorious, will remain", and of obscure Traditions, such as the Prophet's saying that Allah created Adam with His hand, wrote the Torah with His hand, created the Garden of Eden with His hand, planted the tree *ṭūbā*[1] with His hand, and one line of transmission [of this Tradition] adds that He created the camel with His hand. It is related of Muḥammad b. al-Ḥasan[2]—on whom may Allah have mercy—that he used to say: "We believe in Allah, and in what has come from Allah, according as Allah desired, and as the Apostle of Allah—upon whom be Allah's blessing and peace—desired. We do not concern ourselves with how Allah intended it, or with [the reason for] what the Apostle of Allah brought [to us]." This statement is the one preferred by many of the leaders of the community and the theologians of [our] school.

The Jahmites[3]—whom may Allah curse—teach that Allah is in every place, basing their teaching on such verses as (XLIII, 84): "He it is Who is God in the heavens and God on the earth", and (XVI, 128): "Allah is indeed with those who show piety, and with those who are doers of good", and (LVII, 4): "and He is with you wherever ye may be", and (LVIII, 7/8): "No three are ever in private conference but Allah is the fourth of them, nor five but He is their sixth . . . wherever they may be He is with them."[4] The answer [to them] is that the reference in such verses as: "He it is Who is God in the heaven and God on the earth", is to His decreeing and arranging [things in heaven and on earth]. So also His words in (LXVII, 16): "Or are ye safe from Him Who is in the heaven making the earth sink

[1] This is a tree in Paradise of enormous size and miraculous qualities. It is the Islamic equivalent of the commonly found Oriental conception of a "World Tree". The word *ṭūbā* "blessedness," occurs in Sūra XIII, 29/28, and many of the Commentators insist that the reference there is to this tree in Paradise. See p. 244.

[2] He means ash-Shaibānī (d. 805), the fanmous Ḥanafite jurist who is one of our best sources for a knowledge of the teaching of Abū Ḥanīfa.

[3] They are the followers of that Jahm b. Ṣafwān mentioned on p. 394. They are to be cursed because their teacher was critical of both Muḥammad and the Qur'ān, and taught doctrines regarded as heretical.

[4] The text here actually reads: "He is with you wherever ye may be", but is an error of quotation, for the Qur'ānic verse he is quoting has the third person here not the second person. The error doubtless derives from a carrying over of the second personal pronoun from the verse he had previously quoted.

beneath you? so that lo! it is quaking", mean: [are ye safe] from Him the traces of Whose power show in the heavens? Likewise the verse about three not being in secret talk without His being the fourth, refers to His knowledge, and that about His being with you wherever ye may be, also refers to [His] knowledge. If we speak of Him as being in a place, that [teaching] leads to an evil situation, for needs must it be either that all of Him is in each place, or that He is in each place, being split up to this end, or [that He is] in one place as against another. Now that all of Him should be in each place is put out of court by the fact that it would be teaching that there is more than one God and not that there is but one God, yet He is One. That He should be in each place, being Himself partitioned to that intent, is put out of court by the fact that anyone who describes Allah as separated out [into parts] is in unbelief. And that He should be in one place rather than another is put out of court by the fact that it would mean the need of being transferred [from place to place], which is one of the attributes of creatures and a sign of contingent things, whereas Allah is far removed from that.

The Muʿtazilites teach that any vision of the Creator—exalted be He—by the sight is impossible. The orthodox people teach that it is possible. Their (i.e. the Muʿtazilites) proof is Allah's own statement in the story about Moses—on whom be peace—(VII, 143/139): "O my Lord, shew [Thyself to] me that I may look upon Thee. Said He: 'Thou shalt never see Me'", where the particle *lan,* [say the Muʿtazilites], means "not for ever". Similar is the verse (VI, 103): "Vision does not perceive Him, but He perceives vision." It is related that 'Ā'isha—may Allah be pleased with her—said: "I asked the Apostle of Allah—on whom be Allah's blessing and peace—'Did you see your Lord on the night of the Miʿrāj?', and he answered: 'No.' " They, (i.e. the Muʿtazilites) also have an intellectual proof, viz. that if we say that He may be seen, that is equivalent to affirming [that He is in a] place, whereas place cannot be predicated of Allah—may He be exalted.

Our proof [for our view] is that same verse in the story about Moses—upon whom be peace—[where it says]: "O my Lord, shew [Thyself to] me that I may look upon Thee", for had not Moses known that a vision of the Creator was possible he would not have made the request, since Prophets are immune from making impossible requests. There are also such verses as (LXXV, 22, 23): "On that Day [some] faces will be beaming, looking towards their Lord", and (XVIII, 110): "Let whosoever hopes to meet his Lord work a righteous work and associate no one in the worship of his Lord", likewise the verse (XLIII, 71): "Therein for you is whatever the souls desire and will delight the eyes", so did the inhabitants of Paradise desire the vision [of Allah] but could not see Him, that would be equivalent to a contradiction of the word of Allah and [a going back on] His promise. Also it is related of the Prophet—upon whom be Allah's blessing and peace—that he said: "Ye shall see your Lord as ye see the moon on the night of its fullness, and ye shall not be crowded—i.e. not pressed together in a crowd—at the vision of Him." There is also the verse (X, 26/27): "For those who do good there shall be goodness and an increase", where by the "increase" is meant the vision of Allah—may He be exalted.

It is related from Ibn Mas'ūd—with whom and with whose father may Allah be pleased—that he said: "I asked the Apostle of Allah—upon whom be Allah's blessing and peace—: 'Did you see your Lord on the night of the Mi'rāj?', and he answered: 'Yes.'" So the answer to their (i.e. the Mu'tazilites) confused opinions is [as follows]:

In the matter of Allah's saying: "Thou shalt never see me", we do not agree that the particle *lan* means "not for ever", but assert that here it is a particle of time determination. We base this [assertion] on the fact that in II, 95/89 Allah informs [us] that unbelievers will not desire death in this world, by saying: "Never *(lan)* will they wish for it, because of what their hands have sent forward", and then informs us that they will desire death in the next world, by saying (XLIII, 77): "And they will cry: 'O Mālik, would that thy Lord would make an end of us'; but he will say: 'You are to remain.'" From these verses it may be deduced that the particle *lan* [in the passage about Moses] is not used to mean "never at any time." This is clear also [from its use] in the Qur'ānic story about Mary [the mother of Jesus]—upon whom be Allah's blessing and His peace—[where she says] (XIX, 26/27): "Truly, I have vowed to the Merciful a fast, so I shall not *(lan)* speak today to any man", which shows that it does not necessarily mean "not for ever".

In the matter of the verse: "Vision does not perceive Him, but He perceives vision", our teaching is that the text demands the denial of perceiving but does not demand the denial of the vision *(ru'ya)*. As concerns the Tradition from 'Ā'isha—with whom may Allah be pleased—our teaching is that the Prophet—upon whom be Allah's blessing and peace—was informing [her] about His not being seen in this world, so what basis is that for teaching that He will not be seen in the next? With regard to the argument that if we say He may be seen that is equivalent to saying that He is in a place, we reply [by asking the question]: "When is this [the case]?" [The answer is: "Only] if the thing looked at is in a place." So if it (i.e. the thing looked at) is not in a place, then the former [view] is sound, and it is the latter which is to be rejected. Here the One looked at is not in a place, so the necessity of denying place with regard to Him does not involve a denial of the vision *(ru'ya)*. The situation here is much the same as that which we taught with regard to knowledge.

The Qur'ān is Allah's speaking, which is one of His attributes. Now Allah in all His attributes is One, and with all His attributes is eternal, not contingent, [so His speaking is] without letters and without sounds, not broken up into syllables nor into paragraphs. It is not He, nor is it other than He. He caused Gabriel [1] to hear it as sound and letters, for He created sound and letters and caused him to hear it by that sound and by those letters. Gabriel—upon whom be peace—memorized it, stored it [in his mind], and transmitted it to the Prophet—upon whom be Allah's blessing and peace—by bringing down revelation *(waḥy)* and message *(risāla)*, which is not the bringing down of a corporeal object *(shakhṣ)* and a form *(ṣūra)*. He recited it to the Prophet—upon whom be Allah's blessing and peace—the Prophet memorized it, storing it up [in his mind], and then recited it to his Companions, who memorized it and recited it to the Followers, the Followers [handed it on] to the upright, and so on until it has reached us. It is recited by the tongues, memorized by hearts, written in Codices, though it is not contained by the Codices. It may be neither added to nor taken from. Should one burn up the Codices the Qur'ān would not be burned up; just as Allah is mentioned by tongues, recognized by hearts, worshipped in places, yet He is not confined to existence in those places nor in the hearts. It is as He said (VII, 157/156): "Those who follow the Messenger, the *ummī* Prophet, whom they find mentioned in the Torah and the Gospel which they have",[2] for they found [there] only his picture, his description, not his person. Similarly Paradise and Hell are mentioned but they are not actually amongst us. All this [that we have set forth] is according to the school of the truly orthodox.

Moreover we teach that Allah spoke with Gabriel from behind the veil

[1] In Muḥammad's thought Gabriel is the angel of Revelation, so that it is always Gabriel who receives the message from Allah and transmits it to the human messenger who is to transmit it to the community to whom he is sent.

[2] This is Muḥammad's claim that his coming was foretold in the Scriptures of both Jews and Christians. Later Muslims have selected a variety of passages in the Old and New Testaments which they suggest are such prophecies. The two favourite passages are the promise of a coming Prophet in Deut. XVIII, 15, and the promise of the Paraclete in the Gospel of John chapters XV and XVI. See p. 333 n. 3.

(*ḥijāb*). Gabriel heard the speech of Allah from behind the veil, and the Apostle of Allah—upon whom be Allah's blessing and peace—on the night of the Mi'rāj, heard the speech of Allah from behind the veil. He spoke to Adam and to Moses—on both of whom be peace—from behind the veil. Each time that Gabriel came to the Prophet —upon whom be Allah's blessing and peace—that was by command of Allah. Allah taught the Qur'ān to Gabriel—on whom be peace—and then commanded him to take down to Muḥammad such and such a verse or such and such a Sūra. Whenever He bade Gabriel—upon whom be peace—bring down to Muḥammad—on whom be peace—a verse of the Qur'ān, or even a word, that was a reference to His eternal speaking, which is not contingent, for the speech of Allah is not contingent.

The Najjārites,[1] the Mutaqashshifa,[2] the Mu'tazilites and the Jahmites[3] teach that the Qur'ān is a contingent, created thing. They say that the Qur'ān was first spoken on the *lailat al-qadr*,[4] but was not spoken before that. They say that the Qur'ān [contains] commands and prohibitions, and it is not part of wisdom to teach that He commands and prohibits what is not existent, [so the Qur'ān must be a created thing]. The proof of the truly orthodox people that the speech of Allah is not a created thing, is that if we say that it is a created thing needs must we say that He created it either in something other than His own essence or in His own essence. If it was created in other than His own essence the one who uttered it in speech would be that other essence, because the one who utters speech is the one in whom exists the attribute of speaking, and the attribute of speaking, [which we say is an attribute of Allah] would be in that essence, just as "the Black" and "the Red" are names for persons in whom are the attributes blackness or redness. Yet there is no way for His creating it in His own essence, for in that case His essence would be the seat of contingent things, and His essence would thus resemble the essences of creatures and such like. Such an idea, however, is negatived by the saying of Allah (XLII, 11/9): "There is nothing [that can be used] as a similitude for Him, though He is the One Who hears and sees."

1 The followers of Ḥusain b. Muḥammad an-Najjār (fl. 800). On their teachings see A. S. Halkin's translation of al-Baghdādī, pp. 9 ff.

2 See p. 378 n. 5.

3 The followers of Jahm b. Ṣafwān. On their teachings see Halkin, *op. cit.*, pp. 13 ff.

4 "The Night of Power" or "Night of Decree". It is said to be one of the nights at the latter end of the month of Ramaḍān, and Tradition says that it was on this night one Ramaḍān that the material for revelation was brought down from the celestial treasury beneath Allah's Throne to the *bait al-'izza* in the lowest heaven, whence Gabriel transmitted it piecemeal to the Prophet.

With regard to the statement that if the speech of Allah were uncreate He would be commanding and prohibiting what is non-existent, our answer is that we teach that non-existent things may be commanded [and prohibited] in the sense that He said to things before they came into existence: "Come into existence at such and such a time." There is no need to bring in what you [people] say about "like hearing and seeing and knowing", for He is One Who knows eternally all things knowable, the One Who hears all things hearable, the One Who sees all things seeable, even though the things knowable and hearable and seeable were not eternally existing. The meaning of the statement: "He is the One Who hears and sees" in eternity all hearable and seeable things, is that He hears hearable things at the moment of their coming into existence by His eternal faculty of hearing in His eternal essence in eternity. The same holds true with regard to the seeing.

It may be argued that there are other indications that Allah's speech is a created thing. Among such are the verse (XXI, 2): "There comes not to them a fresh warning from their Lord, but they hear it and make mock", since every "fresh" thing is a created one. Also the verse (XLIII, 3/2): "We have made it an Arabic Qur'ān", since everything "made" is a created thing; and the verse (XXIX, 49/48): "But it is evidential in the breasts of those given knowledge", for anything that is in the breasts will be a created thing. Likewise the verse (XV, 9): "It was We who have sent down the Reminder, and We shall keep watch for it", likewise the verse (XXIII, 18): "And We are able to take it away", since anything which needs protecting must be a created thing, and likewise anything that can be removed. Or again the verse (XXXIX, 23/24): "Allah has sent down the best of recitals", where He calls the Qur'ān a *recital.* So it seems firmly established that it is a created thing.

In answer to all this we teach that with regard to XXI, 2 and the "fresh" warning, the meaning is not the coming of a fresh thing but a fresh, youthful person, viz. Gabriel, so the reference is to his bringing the warning. Or we may say that "warning" here really means "warner", so that the reference is to the Prophet—upon whom be Allah's blessing and peace—for he was a fresh prophet. As to XLIII, 3/2 we teach that the verb "made" which is used here really means "create", as in the statement in II, 30/28: "I am going to set a vice-regent on the earth", just as it may mean "describe" in XLIII, 15/14: "Yet they make to Him from among His servants offspring", i.e. they describe them as such. So here "We have made it an Arabic Qur'ān", means: "We have described it and made it clear in the tongue of the Arabs and in their language." The Qur'ān [as such] is not Persian or Arabic, for they are created, contingent things, but it descended in the tongue of the Arabs, just as the rest of the heavenly Books descended in the tongue of each several Prophet and people [to whom the Prophet came]. The Qur'ān as such is eternal, uncreate, and it is not permissible for the eternal to be described by [that which involves] the contingent, though the common people are ignorant of this.

With regard to XXIX, 49/48 and its being in the breasts, we teach that what is meant is that it is memorized in the breasts, not that it is contained there. As for XV, 9 about: "We shall keep watch for it", we teach that what is meant is protecting it from having anything added to it or taken from it, i.e. guarding it from Satan lest he add anything to it or take anything from it. Then as for XXIII, 18 about His being able to take it away, the meaning is to remove all memory of it from the hearts. With regard to XXXIX, 23/24 about its being the best of recitals, we teach that what is meant is that it is better set in order, in which respect it is superior to the speech of creatures.

The people of the *qibla* [1] differ on the question whether the speech of Allah is something that is heard or not. Abū'l-Ḥasan al-Ash'arī [2] taught that it was something that could be heard, an opinion which is accepted by some of the later Sheikhs among our friends (i.e. among the Māturīdites)—on whom may Allah have mercy—, e.g. the Sheikh Abū'l-Qāsim aṣ-Ṣaffārī, the celebrated Imām and ascetic—on whom may Allah have mercy. They use as proof-text the verse (IX, 6): "If anyone from among the polytheists seeks asylum with thee, give him asylum that he may hear the word *(kalām)* of Allah", (i.e. the message of the Qur'ān), which would indicate that His speech *(kalām)* is something that may be heard. The proof on which we rely is the fact that the speech (or speaking) of Allah is an eternal attribute belonging to the essence, and does not come under such considerations as [human] seeing and hearing, the only things that come under hearing are the letters and the sound.

Be it known that the name and the thing named are one, according to the truly orthodox people, so that Allah with all His names is One. The Mu'tazilites and the Mutaqashshifa teach that the name of Allah is other than Allah and is a created thing. We base our teaching on the

[1] The *qibla* is the direction in which worshippers turn in prayer (see p. 68). All Muslims turn towards Mecca for their daily prayers, so that Mecca is their *qibla.* The "people of the Qibla" (more commonly *ahl al-qibla wa'l-jamā'a)* is a term often used to mean the orthodox Muslim community in general.

[2] The founder of the Ash'arite School, which was the rival of the Māturīdite School to which the writer here belongs. See p. 378 n. 6.

verses (XXXIX, 2): "So worship Allah, confining religion solely to Him", and (IX: 31): "Though they are bidden worship only One God." Allah has commanded us to maintain His unity, but if the name of Allah is other than Allah, then the unity we are maintaining is with reference to the name, not to Allah. Yet our object therein is not the [letters] *alif, lām, hā,* but Allah Himself. Said He (XIX, 12/13): "O John, take the Book with strength", at a time when this Book [1] did not have a name. Similarly were one to say the word "free" to his slave, or "divorced" to his wife, the divorcing and the setting free come into effect, but were the name other than the thing named the divorce or the setting free would not come into effect. Similarly if you marry a woman marital rights with the one named are in order, but if the name were other than that which is named, the marital rights would be with the name not with the one named.

The question may be raised: "Did not the Prophet—upon whom Be Allah's blessing and peace—say: 'Verily Allah has ninety-nine names and whosoever recounts them will enter Paradise?' Were the name and the named one there would in that case be ninety-nine gods, which is impossible. In like manner, if the name and the named are one, then were a man to say "fire" his mouth would be burned, and were a man to write the name of Allah on an unclean thing, the essence of Allah would be present on an unclean thing, which is impossible"—we reply that the name points to the individuality of that thing and the meaning of the [above mentioned] Tradition is that the Prophet intended thereby [to recommend] the reciting of the names *(tasmiya)*. The difference between the name and the recital of names is obvious, for the people of each language name Him according to their language, whether it be the folk of Sindh, the Hindus, the Turks, the Arabs or the Persians. In this recital of names there are varieties, and there are various expressions, but Allah is One, just as it is the same person though he may be called [by the various names] Zaid, a learned man, an ascetic, a virtuous fellow, a pious man, a jurist. So is it here, for by whatever name you call Him He is Allah. As for your argument about the fire, our answer is that his mouth is not burned because it is a matter of the naming *(tasmiya)* of the fire, not of the real fire. Similarly with regard to the writing of Allah's name on an unclean substance, our answer is that there it is a matter of writing and naming, so that the essence of Allah is not present on the unclean substance.

[1] The reference in the Qur'ānic verse is to John the Baptist, who, Muḥammad thought, had been given a Scripture Book like the other Prophets.

The truly orthodox people—whom may Allah increase—teach that the [good and evil] fortunes *(arzāq)* of men are portioned out and known, so that nothing can be added thereto by the piety of the pious, nor taken therefrom by the wickedness of the wicked. This [good or ill] fortune which Allah apportions is man's sustenance. The Muʿtazilites teach that it may be increased and decreased. Fortune, according to them, is a matter of possessing *dirhams* and *dīnārs* which are earned by effort. They teach that unlawfully gained fortune *(ḥarām)* is not a matter of Allah's providing, but comes from human action. We teach that ḥarām is a matter of Allah's providing, but that humans deserve punishment for their own deeds. Allah has said (XLIII, 32/31): "It is We Who have divided out among them their sustenance for this world's life." Likewise life's harsh experiences and its trials are by the decreeing and determining of Allah. Allah has said (LVII, 22): "No mischance happens on earth or to yourselves but it is in a Book"; and again (XXXV, 2): "Whatsoever mercy Allah opens up for men no one can hold back, and what He holds back no one can send along"; and again (X, 107): "If Allah touch thee with trouble there is no deliverer from it save Himself, and if He wishes thee good there is no one who can turn back His bounty."

The Muʿtazilites teach that life's harsh experiences and its trials are not by the determining of Allah, but [are due to] man's giving up striving, for Allah neither determines nor desires evil and trials. According to our teaching the medicine is the cause but the healing is from Allah, so that to consider that the healing is from the medicine or from the physician is unbelief. Assuredly the healing must be from Allah, for otherwise one would be assuming a partner with Allah in the healing. Similarly [human] striving is a cause but the fortune is from Allah, so that to consider the fortune as due to the striving is unbelief. Clothes are not the [ultimate] cause of the warding off of heat or cold. He who does the warding off of the heat and the cold is Allah, so that to consider that the warding off of heat and cold is by the clothes is unbelief.

The Jabarites [1] teach that humans have no free will *(istiṭāʿa)*, but are compelled to unbelief and disobedience, just as the wind blows over the grass and bends it to right and to left. The truly orthodox people—whom may Allah aid—teach that man has free will to act himself at the time of the act by Allah's enabling him by His might and aid. Man has power of choice and freedom of will, so that if on his part there is striving, purposing, intending and taking of responsibility for disobedience, then Allah's

[1] See p. 379.

abandoning runs along with his intention and purpose, and so he deserves punishment for his own deed. On the other hand, if he shows all this with regard to obedience, then Allah's help and aid run along with his deed. Were we to teach that Allah compels men to disobedience and then punishes them for it, that would be oppression on His part and injustice. But Allah is far removed from oppression and injustice.

The Muʿtazilites teach that human deeds are all created (or produced) by the human individuals. It is the humans who bring to pass (lit. create) their own deeds whether they be good or ill. According to them the human is a free agent with free will of his own before the deed, and he has no need of being given ability and power by Allah. Now if the human is a free agent with free will of his own before the act, then his deeds are brought to pass by himself. The truly orthodox people—with whom may Allah be pleased, and among whom, praised be Allah, we are—teach that all human deeds are created by Allah. It is Allah who brings to pass (lit. creates) all human deeds, be they good or ill, since the giving ability [to do them] is from Allah, brought into being for the human individuals contemporaneously with the act, not before the deed nor after it. Thus the human individual with all his deeds is [something] created by Allah. This is indicated by the saying of Allah (XXXVII, 96/94): "Allah created both you and what ye make", [a passage] which informs [us] that He created both our persons and our deeds. It is not permissible to take the meaning here to be the things made [by us] from stone or wood, for no one doubts that they are [made of] something created by Allah. Our teaching is that by "and what ye make", he intends "deeds" [of humans], not "things made" [by them]. This is indicated also by His saying (XXVII, 90/92): "Will ye be rewarded save as ye have wrought?", where the clear meaning of the verse demands that [we understand that] both deeds and things made are created by Allah. So if anyone overlooks the true [meaning] it is on him to bring a proof [of the validity of his interpretation].

There is an indication of the soundness of what we teach [in the fact that] were we to say that man brings to pass (lit. creates) his own deeds, that would be equivalent to saying that there are two Creators. Anyone who assents to that is assenting to making association with Allah in His creative activity, and anyone who gives Allah an associate in His creative activity is in unbelief. There is an indication of this in His saying (XXV, 2): "He created everything, and decreed it a decreeing." Likewise there is His saying (XIII, 16/17): "and Allah is the One Who created everything", and a human action is assuredly a thing.

According to the truly orthodox people Faith is confession with the tongue and firm trust in the heart *(qalb)*. Ash-Shāfiʿī—on whom may Allah have mercy—said that Faith is confession with the tongue, firm trust in the heart *(janān)* and the performance of the elementary duties *(arkān)*. The Karrāmites i.e. the followers of Abū ʿAbdallah Muḥammad b. Karrām,[1] teach that Faith is mere confession without firm trust [being necessary]. That standard of guidance, Abū Manṣūr al-Māturīdī[2] —on whom may Allah have mercy—taught that faith is firm trust by itself without any confession [being necessary].

The Karrāmites base their teaching on the surface meaning of that statement of the Prophet—upon whom be Allah's blessing and peace—[in which he says]: "Whoever says: 'There is no god but Allah', will enter Paradise." Ash-Shāfiʿī bases his teaching on the verse (II, 177/172): "Being upright does not consist in turning your faces to the East or the West, etc." Abū Manṣūr [al-Māturīdī]—on whom may Allah have mercy—says that [the word] "faith" means firm trust as such, and there is an indication of this in Allah's saying, in connection with the story of the sons of Jacob—on whom be Allah's blessing—(XII, 17): "Yet thou wouldst not be believing us even were we telling the truth", where the word *ṣādiq* means *muṣaddaq* [as this is used of those in whom firm trust may be placed].

Most of the Sunni Muslims teach that there are five articles of the Faith [which must be held], viz. that one bear testimony [to belief] in Allah and the Apostle, and believe in the Last Day, in the angels, the Book and the Prophets. Our proof that deeds are not [a necessary part of] faith is Allah's statement in (XIV, 31/36): "Say to My servants who have believed that they observe prayer", where He names them believers before the observance of prayer, and thus makes a distinction between faith and prayer. Similar is the saying (V, 6/8): "O ye who have believed, when ye observe prayer wash your faces", where again He calls them believers before [they have] observed prayer. Another indication of this is that if a man should come to have faith before the morning brightened and die before the decline of day he would be among the people of Paradise, but were deeds of observance [a necessary part] of faith he could not be of the people of Paradise for he would not have had [to his credit] such deeds of observance. Such was the case of the Companions of the Cave (in Sūra XVIII), and Pharaoh's magicians (of Sūra VII, 120/117ff.), who, we all agree, are among the people of Paradise, even though they

[1] See p. 393.

[2] Died 944 A.D. He was the founder of the school to which the author of this tractate adhered. See Tritton, *Muslim Theology*, pp. 174 ff.

performed no deeds [of observance]. Thus it is firmly established that deeds [of observance] are not [a necessary part] of faith.

Our prooftext against the Karrāmites is (II, 8/7): "Among the people are some who say: 'We believe in Allah and in the Last Day', but they are not [true] believers", from which it is assuredly established that firm trust is a condition of sound faith. This is also indicated by the words of the Prophet—upon whom be Allah's blessing and peace—[in which he says]: "Whoever says, sincerely and genuinely: 'There is no deity but Allah', will enter Paradise", for in this he makes firm trust a condition. The truly orthodox people teach that if one has faith one will say: "I am a believer, truly and without doubt." The Traditionists [1] *(aṣḥāb al-ḥadīth)* hold that he will rather say: "I am a believer, if Allah wills." Their argument is that if we teach that he should say: "I am a believer, truly so in Allah's sight", that would amount to giving a judgment on the assumption that one has Allah's knowledge with regard to the unseen, for it is Allah [alone] Who knows men's consciences and the final outcome of their affairs, so that no one of whom judgment is given according to Allah's knowledge that he will die an unbeliever will die a Muslim, for Allah's knowledge is not subject to change or alteration. It could be that this man might say: "I am a believer, truly so", whereas in the knowledge of Allah he will die an unbeliever, in which case he would be giving information contrary to the fact as it is in Allah's sight, and this is not permissible.

Our argument is [that it is well known] that the exceptional case gives dispensation from all compacts. This is so in [cases of] divorce, manumission, marriage, commercial transactions, and likewise it gives exemption in the compact of faith. We are all agreed that were a man to say: "If Allah wills, there is no deity but Allah", or: "If Allah wills, I shall testify that Muḥammad is the Apostle of Allah", or: "If Allah wills I I shall believe in Allah and in the angels and the Books and the Last Day", he would be an unbeliever. In like manner, if he says: "If Allah wills, I shall be a believer", he is an unbeliever, for he has a doubt about his faith. This is because every matter that is verified in present or past time leaves no place for exception. Entering the garden [of Paradise], however, is conditional upon dying in faith, which is a matter belonging to future time, so exception there is possible.

The answer to their hesitations is that if [a man] is a believer now he

[1] This was the name given to those groups in Islam who insisted on having a literal basis in Tradition for every matter of religion and who were stoutly opposed to the use of *ra'y*, or opinion based on human reasoning.

will not become an unbeliever so long as no unbelief is found in him. It is the same as [the fact that] he is not called dead now though in the knowledge of Allah he is going to die now. Similarly, in the knowledge of Allah the Hour is coming, but one does not say that it is coming now. Also in the knowledge of Allah this present world is to pass away and the future world is to endure, but one does not say that they are matters verified at the present. There is an indication of the soundness of our teaching in what is related from the Prophet—upon whom be Allah's blessing and peace—how he said to Ḥāritha [1]—with whom may Allah be pleased—: "How are you this morning?" He answered: "I am truly a believer", and he—upon whom be peace—did not raise any objection to this [statement] of his, but said: "Everything has a verification. What is the verification of your faith?" He answered: "I have withdrawn myself from this world, i.e. I have denied it, so that its stones, its lumps of clay and its gold are all the same to me. My day I have made thirsty and my night sleepless. It is as though I see the Throne of my Lord becoming visible, as though I see the inhabitants of Paradise visiting one another therein, and the inhabitants of Hell howling within it." Then he—upon whom be peace—said: "This is a human whose heart Allah has illumined by faith", and to him he said: "Thou hast attained, so persevere."

According to Abū Ḥanīfa and his followers—with whom may Allah be pleased—faith admits of neither increase nor decrease. Ash-Shāfiʿī—on whom may Allah have mercy—taught that it admits both of increase and of decrease. The proof text of the Shāfiʿites is (XLVIII, 4): "That they might have an increase of faith along with their faith." A similar verse is (VIII, 2): "Believers are only those whose hearts thrill [with fear] when they remember Allah, and whose faith increases as His signs are recited to them." So it is related of the Prophet—upon whom be Allah's blessing and peace—that he said: "Were the faith of Abū Bakr (the father of ʿĀ'isha) to be put in the balance along with the faith of my [whole] community, the faith of Abū Bakr would outweigh it all." Similarly it is related from Abū Huraira, and Anas b. Mālik, and Abū Saʿīd al-Khudrī and ʿAbdallah b. ʿAbbās [2]—with all of whom may Allah be pleased—that they reported that the Prophet—upon whom be Allah's blessing and peace—said: "Everyone in whose heart is as much as a barley-seed of

[1] Ḥāritha b. an-Nuʿmān who was neighbour to the Prophet in Madīna, and who provided one after the other the new houses needed for Muḥammad's growing number of wives.

[2] All four were Companions of the Prophet whose names figure prominently in the canonical books of Tradition as the authorities for sayings or actions attributed to the Prophet.

faith will be withdrawn from Hell-fire." A variant says: "as much as an atom of faith." Such a Tradition indicates that faith may increase or decrease.

Our position is that [the word] "faith" means "firm trust", the proof of which we have mentioned above, and so it does not admit of increase or decrease. With regard to the verse XLVIII, 4 about adding increase of faith, we teach that that refers to the Companions [of the Prophet]—on all of whom be Allah's good-pleasure—for the Qur'ān used to come down [in bits] from time to time, and they would believe in it, so that their firm trust in a later passage was something added to that in which they had formerly put firm trust. But in our case this is not so since revelation has ceased. With regard to VIII, 2 we teach that it is a description of believers, and believers differ from one another in degree of obedience but not in the matter of faith. Where it says in that verse: "Whose faith increases", what is meant is assurance not the faith itself. With regard to the Tradition about Abū Bakr—with whom may Allah be pleased—we regard that as an outweighing in reward for he was foremost in [joining the] faith (i.e. he was one of Muḥammad's earliest converts), and the Prophet—upon whom be Allah's blessing and peace—once said: "He who points the way to good is as he who does it." Finally, with regard to the withdrawal from the Fire of everyone in whose heart is an atom of faith, we teach that that Tradition, according to some lines of transmission, reads: "There will be withdrawn from the Fire anyone who has faith in his heart", and it must be taken in accordance with this, as we have before mentioned concerning matters of proof.

The Khārijites [1] teach that anyone who commits a mortal sin is in unbelief. They teach that 'Alī—with whom may Allah be pleased—became an unbeliever by putting to death the oppressors *(bughāt)* and the Khārijites. The Murji'ites [2] teach that disobedience does no harm so long as faith is present and that obedience is without profit if there is unbelief present. The Jabarites [3] teach that men are under compulsion to unbelief and disobedience. The Mu'tazilites teach that by them (i.e. by

[1] The Khārijite group began when after the battle of Ṣiffīn in 36 A.H. = 657 A.D. a goodly number who felt that victory had been thrown away because religious questions had been injected into the conflict withdrew *(kharaja)* from the main body of Muslims and began to regard themselves as the only true Muslims. From that issue it came to be a name to cover a particular type of theological belief in rebellion against the majority opinion. See Tritton, *op. cit.*, pp. 35 ff.

[2] One of the earliest heretical groups to form in the Islamic community. Their name is said to be derived from the verb *arja'a* "to defer", since they held that there was always hope for all men. See Tritton, *op. cit.*, pp. 43 ff.

[3] See p. 379.

unbelief and disobedience) a man departs from the faith but nevertheless does not enter into unbelief.

The Khārijites base their teaching on the verse (VI, 121): "If ye obey them, ye yourselves are polytheists." Similar is the verse (IV, 14/18): "But whoso disobeys Allah and His Messenger, and breaks His bounds, He will make enter the Fire, therein to abide for ever", where the [punishment for] eternity will be only because of his departure from the faith. Likewise there is the saying of him—on whom be Allah's blessing and peace—: "The fornicator, if he was a believer when he fornicated, was not committing fornication, and the thief, if he was a believer when he stole, was not thieving, and the drunkard, if he was a believer when he drank, was not drinking [to intoxication]." There is also another saying of his —on whom be Allah's blessing and peace—: "Prayer is the pillar of religion, so whosoever observes prayer has established [his] religion, and whosoever abandons it has destroyed [his] religion."

We base our teaching on the verse (LXVI, 8): "O ye who believe, repent with a sincere repentance toward Allah", where true repentance can only mean [repenting] from some crime *(ḥauba)*, which is a mortal sin. Similarly we have the saying of him—on whom be Allah's blessing and peace—: "Pray behind both righteous and wicked",[1] for had a man departed from the faith he would not have bidden us pray behind him. With regard to VI, 121 we teach that what is meant by it is obeying [them] in matters of polytheism, for they had been saying: "That which dies of itself is legally permissible [as food] for it has been slaughtered by Allah Himself", whereupon Allah sent down the verse (121): "Eat not of that over which the name of Allah has not been pronounced."[2] As regards IV, 14/18 our teaching is that the one intended there is the unbeliever, for such encroaching on all the bounds would be done by none but an unbeliever. As for the Tradition from the Prophet about the fornicator etc., we teach that this can only be a phrase of customary usage, for one thing which is clear and generally accepted with regard to the times of the Prophet—on whom be Allah's blessing and peace—is the total absence of [such a thing as] fornication then. Finally, with regard to his saying about abandonment of prayer being the destruction of religion,

[1] The point of the Tradition is that at every public service of prayer someone stands out in front as Imām, or prayer-leader, and the others are said to pray behind him. There was some discussion among the orthodox as to whether it was right to pray behind a man who was known to be a sinner or in some way unorthodox, and the present Tradition was produced to answer their scruples.

[2] The point is that the orthodox Muslim may eat of only such flesh as comes from animals killed in ritual fashion.

we teach that what is meant is abandonment of belief in it, so that if one gives up belief in it he has become an unbeliever.

Then [there is the fact that] sins *(dhunūb)* are of various types. There are some which are between men and Allah, (i.e. they are matters about which Allah has by revelation expressed His disapproval). Such are fornication, sodomy, wine-bibbing, lying, slandering, and calumny, where if no news of it has reached men, they may be cancelled by repentance, but if the news has reached men they may not be cancelled by repentance unless the one sinned against pardons the sinner. Similarly if he fornicates with a woman who has a husband and the news reaches him, [his sin] is not cancelled by repentance, unless he (i.e. the husband) pardons him. As concerns a man's giving up praying, almsgiving and fasting, [which are ordinances Allah has commanded men to observe], that is not cancelled by repentance except where satisfaction is rendered [for the observances omitted]. If He wills He will punish him, and that would be but justice on His part, as is indicated by the verse (II, 225): "But He will punish you for what your hearts have earned."

The truly orthodox people—on whom may Allah have mercy—teach that a man is punished for what he has purposed in his heart, for instance, fornication or sodomy, etc., but if he only thought about it and did not purpose [to commit] it, he will not be punished for it. Some teach that he will not be punished in either of the above cases, basing their teaching on a saying of the Prophet—on whom be Allah's blessing and peace—: "Verily Allah will forgive my community for things they have thought over so long as they have not said them or done them." Our teaching is based on the verse (II, 284): "Whether ye disclose what is in your souls or conceal it, Allah will reckon with you for it", i.e. Allah will requite you for it. It is thus firmly established that a man is punished in accordance with his purposing, and the Tradition above-mentioned must be taken as meaning what he thought over but did not purpose. If, however, he purposed [it], then no [forgiveness will be granted].

The Jahmites teach that faith is knowledge in the heart without [any necessary] confession by the tongue. The truly orthodox people teach that knowledge in the heart is not faith so long as there is no confession by the tongue. Our proof text is (V, 85/88): "So Allah has rewarded them for what they said",[1] where the purport of the passage indicates that knowledge in the heart is not faith so long as there is no confession by the

[1] This is obviously the passage meant, though the author has written *aṣābahum* instead of *athābahum*, his *aṣābahum* not being found in this context anywhere in the Qur'ān.

tongue. Of similar purport is the verse (II, 146/141): "Those to whom We have given the Book recognize it as they recognize their own sons, yet a party among them conceals the truth knowingly", and the verse (XXVII, 14): "And wickedly and proudly they denied them (i.e. Allah's signs), though their souls knew them to be true." Thus it is firmly established that mere knowledge is not faith.

The Murji'ites teach that Allah created creatures and set them free, giving them neither command nor prohibition. What has come in the Qur'ān, [according to them], is the form of the command not the command itself, so it is a matter of choice and desirability. Then if [a creature] does good he has a reward, but if he does evil there is no punishment for him. It is, [they say], as Allah has said (II, 60/57): "Eat ye and drink", or again (V, 2/3): "When ye are free [from the pilgrimage prohibition] then hunt."

The reply to them is that we teach that each command accompanied by a threat [of what will happen in the event] of non-compliance therewith, is binding and incumbent, while each command not accompanied by a threat in the event of non-compliance, is a matter of choice and desirability. An instance [will be found] in the case of prayer. Allah has said (XIX, 59/60): "Others came in succession after them who were unmindful of prayer and followed [their] lusts, so anon they will meet destruction." Another instance is alms-giving [concerning which] Allah has said (IX, 35): "A day when their treasures shall be heated in the fire of Gehenna." It is not consonant with the wisdom of the Wise One that He should create creatures left to their own devices and not give them commands and prohibitions. It is as Allah has said (LXXV, 36): "Does man think that he will be left forsaken?", or again as He said (XXIII, 115/117): "Did ye think that We had created you only for a pastime?"

The Murji'ites teach that when the damned enter the Fire they will be in the Fire without torment like a fish in the water, the only difference between the believer and the unbeliever being that the believer in Paradise will have continuous enjoyment of eating and drinking, whereas the damned in the Fire will not have the enjoyment of eating and drinking. This is a false teaching, as indeed is indicated by the words of the Most High (XXXV, 37/34): "And therein (i.e. in Hell) shall they cry aloud [in torment]", and (LXV, 9): "And they tasted the harmfulness of their conduct", and (XLIII, 77): "And they will cry: 'O Mālik![1] would that thy Lord would make an end of us.' He will say: 'Here are ye to remain'",

[1] Mālik is the angel who presides over the torments of the damned in Hell. See p. 231.

and (IV, 56/59): "As often as their skins are well burned We shall give them in exchange other skins [so that the torment can continue]."

The Jabarites teach that man has no free will but is under constraint to unbelief or to faith. They base their teaching on the verse (IV, 129/128): "Ye will never be able to treat your wives alike", where Allah informs them that they will not be able to maintain equable treatment [towards their wives], in spite of the fact that He has laid such equitable treatment on them as a command. Likewise He said (II, 31/29): "Inform Me of the names of these", commanding them [to do this], though He knew that they would not be able. Also He says (LXVIII, 42): "On the Day when the leg will be bared, and they are summoned to do obeisance [but will not be able]", and [note] His words, setting forth what was said by the Prophet—upon whom be Allah's blessing and peace—(II, 286): "O our Lord, do not burden us with what is beyond our capacity", yet were there no such thing as responsibility on the part of those lacking strength there would be no meaning or point to this petition. Similarly we have the statement of the Prophet—upon whom be Allah's blessing and peace—: "Whosoever paints a picture with his hand will be responsible on the Day of Resurrection for breathing a spirit into it, though he is not one who could so breathe [a spirit]."

The answer [to them] with regard to IV, 129/128 is that it concerns equivalence of love in the heart, over which a man has no control, as is related from the Prophet—upon whom be Allah's blessing and peace—how he said: "Allahumma! this is my apportioning with regard to that over which I have control, so do not punish me with regard to that over which Thou hast control but I have no control." A command to act with equity would not be given to one who was incapable [thereof]. As for II, 31/29 our teaching is that what was intended by the words "inform Me of the names" was to point out [their] incapacity, i.e. He commanded them to do this only to show them thereby that they were unable [to do what He asked, and He did this] because they had been thinking that they were more learned than Adam.[1] There is an indication of this in the fact that they were not [considered] deserving of punishment because they left [His request] unanswered. As regards LXVIII, 42 and the day when the leg will be bared, we teach that the meaning is that they are summoned to do obeisance in this present world, and deserve punishment in the next life for leaving it [undone]. As for II, 286 we teach that what is

[1] The reference is to Muḥammad's version of the well-known legend of the envy of the angels at the creation of Adam, and God's reproving them by asking them to name all the animals, a thing which they could not do, whereas Adam did it.

meant is: "Do not make us responsible for what would make continuance of life painful for us." He did not mean by it an original lack of ability. In one of the Commentaries we read: "It means 'do not make us apes and pigs'." Other say [that it means]: "Save us from being metamorphosed; protect us against being swallowed up; spare us from missiles from the sky", and Allah has given this community in general immunity from these three [terrors]. Finally, as concerns the statement of him—on whom be Allah's blessing and peace—about artists having to give a spirit to their creations on the Day [of Judgment], our teaching is that this [threat] is just to keep them reminded of their inability, so that the command [about it] makes punishment something they deserve.

The truly orthodox people—whom may Allah increase—teach that the children of polytheists become servants to the Blessed [in Paradise]. The Mu'tazilites teach that the judgment on them is [the same as] the judgment on their parents, viz. that they remain for ever in the Fire. The theologians of the truly orthodox people differ on this question. Abū Ḥanīfa—with whom may Allah be pleased—said: "I do not know whether they are in Paradise or in Hell." Muḥammad (i.e. ash-Shaibānī) —on whom may Allah have mercy—said: "I know that Allah does not punish anyone when there is no sin [to merit it], and [in my opinion] Abū Ḥanīfa only said: 'I do not know' out of scrupulousness, because of his cautiousness and his modesty in view of the conflicting evidence."

Beings capable of being addressed [by Allah] *(al-mukhāṭabūn)* are of four groups: angels, men, shayāṭīn and jinn.

Angels [are of three classes]. Some of them are in unbelief, and every one of these will be among the Damned and will suffer punishment. Among such is Iblīs, whom may Allah curse. Some are in disobedience but not in unbelief, and every one of these will suffer punishment. This is indicated by the story of Hārūt and Mārūt.[1] Some are in obedience, and every one of these will be among the Blessed, but will receive no reward *(thawāb)*. All the shayāṭīn are among the Damned. All men will be among the Blessed if they are believers. Of the jinn, those in whom is found unbelief will be among the Damned, but whosoever among them repents and believes will gain Paradise, though according to Abū Ḥanīfa —on whom may Allah have mercy—they, like the angels, receive no reward *(thawāb)*. Abū Yūsuf,[2] and Muḥammad (i.e. ash-Shaibānī), and

[1] In Sūra II, 102/96 they are mentioned as two angels in Babylon who teach mankind the magic art. Their story is given in the *Encyclopaedia of Islam* under "Hārūt".
[2] Abū Yūsuf Ya'qūb al-Anṣārī (d. 795) shares with ash-Shaibānī the honour of transmitting the system of Abū Ḥanīfa.

ash-Shāfiʿī—on all of whom may Allah have mercy—teach that they do have a reward.

Abū Ḥanīfa bases his teaching on analogy *(qiyās)*, namely, that even a human does not deserve any reward from Allah for obedience. Yet we have a revelation in the case of the children of Adam, and so analogy may be dispensed with. A slave does not deserve hire when he is working for [his] master. Those who teach that they (i.e. the jinn) do have a reward for obedience are under obligation to produce evidence [in favour of their teaching], though indeed Allah has promised to forgive their sins if they repent, (i.e. the sins of the jinn), as is seen from the verse (XLVI, 31/30): [where the jinn are speaking]: "O our people! Respond to Allah's summoner, and believe in him, that He may forgive you your sins, and rescue you from a painful punishment." Their argument is that if there is punishment for their disobedience, we may know assuredly that there is reward for them if they are obedient. They (i.e. the jinn) do not eat or drink, but they have the sense of smell, and that is their means of obtaining sustenance. They multiply by generation just like humans, and so are affected by all that is connected with [generation].

As regards the generation of the shayāṭīn, some say that they lay eggs from which the young come forth. This is the correct view. In the Traditions it is said that when the shayāṭīn rejoice over the disobedience of the children of Adam they lay eggs out of which come their young. This, however, is a *shādhdha* (i.e. unusual and so suspect) line of transmission. Also in the Traditions we read [an opinion] that a shaiṭān inserts his penis in his anus and it is from there that the young are produced, but that is not a correct view. The correct view is the first [one to be mentioned]. Ibn ʿAbbās—with whom and with whose father may Allah be pleased—said: "Three [groups of humans] are among the brides of the shayāṭīn, viz. the wailing women [who wail at funerals], singing women and drunkards." He meant [by this that the shayāṭīn] embrace them and kiss them. Sexual intercourse does not take place between them and humans, for the shayāṭīn have no hold over humans. The tale that is related about Solomon—on whom be Allah's blessing—how his rule left him for forty days, during which time the shayāṭīn used to have to do with his wives and concubines, so that they gave birth to the Kurdish people who live in the mountains, and that when he recovered his rule he put these women away from him, this tale we say is not true, the correct view being that they did not have intercourse with his wives and concubines.

Wealth is better than poverty. This view is accepted by some of our Sheikhs—on whom may Allah have mercy. The majority of our Sheikhs teach that a poor man who patiently endures is better than a rich man who is thankful. The view is accepted by the jurist Abū'l-Laith—on whom may Allah have mercy. They are all agreed that a poor man who patiently endures is better than a rich man who is a spendthrift or who is niggardly. The proof-text of the first group is (XCIII, 7, 8): "Did He not find thee erring and guide thee? Did He not find thee poor and enrich thee?" i.e. He favoured him (Muḥammad) with riches as He favoured him with guidance. Had poverty been superior there would have been no meaning or point to speaking of doing [him] a favour [by enriching him]. Also [it is a fact that] the Prophets were rich men, e.g. David, Solomon, Joseph, Abraham, Moses and Shu'aib.[1] Also the Companions [of Muḥammad] were rich men. It is related that 'Abd ar-Raḥmān b. 'Auf [2] —with whom may Allah be pleased—divorced his wife in his illness, and his wife agreed to a fourth of her bridal price, which came to 80,000 dirhams. Also it is related of the Prophet—upon whom be Allah's blessing and peace—that he said: "Poverty comes near to being unbelief." Moreover since riches make it possible to bring together [two kinds of worship], worship by means of the soul and worship by means of wealth, then riches is better than poverty. This is the point of that saying related from the Prophet—upon whom be Allah's blessing and peace—: "How blessed is honest wealth in the hand of an honest man."

The proof-text of the second group is (XCVI, 6, 7): "Nay, indeed, man assuredly acts insolently, because he considers himself self-sufficient." Also from the Prophet—upon whom be Allah's blessing and peace—[there is a Tradition according to which] he said: "The keys to the treasures of this world were presented to me, but I could not accept them, saying: 'I will be hungry two days and replete one day.'" Similarly it is related of the Prophet that he said: "Allahumma, cause me to live a poor man, and cause me to die a poor man, and on the Day of Resurrection raise me up among the party of the poor." [They also point to the fact] that some of the Prophets were poor, e.g. Zachariah and John [the Baptist], Jesus and Khiḍr [3] and Elias. Many have related the story of

[1] The Qur'ān tells of this Shu'aib who was sent as a Prophet to the people of Midian. He may be an ancient worthy of old Arabian tradition whom Muḥammad included in the prophetic succession, though some interpreters think that he represents the Biblical figure of Jethro, the father-in-law of Moses.

[2] He was a wealthy Meccan merchant and one of the five converts whom Abū Bakr early brought into Muḥammad's following.

[3] Al-Khiḍr or al-Khaḍir is not mentioned by name in the Qur'ān, but the Commentators say that he is the mysterious figure who appears in the Moses story in Sūra XVIII, 60/59 ff.

how forty prophets died of hunger and vermin in a single day. Our Prophet—upon whom be Allah's blessing and peace—also chose poverty, saying: "Every Prophet has a profession, but I have two professions, earnest striving and poverty; whosoever loves them loves me, and whosoever loathes them loathes me." In the Traditions we read such statements as: "Riches are a cause of gladness in this world, but a cause of tribulation in the next world, whereas poverty is a cause of tribulation in this world, but a cause of gladness in the next." Or again [we read]: "The poor will enter into Paradise half a day before the rich, [a day] which is five hundred of the years of this world." Thus it is firmly established that poverty is the better.

Our reply to their argument, founded on the verse (XCIII, 8): "Did He not find thee poor and enrich thee", is that [it means]: "Enriched thee [O Muḥammad] with contentment", for the riches meant here is riches of the heart not riches of wealth. Or, secondly, [it may mean]: "He enriched thee with knowledge", which is our reply to their statement that the Prophets were rich men. We teach that they were rich in heart, turning not to the world. Even though wealth was in their hands they did not rest at ease because of it, but ate from what they earned themselves. In the Traditions we read: "This world is a cursed thing, and cursed is all that is in it save the learned man or the one who is learning." Another version of this reads: "Save him who remembers Allah." As for the saying of him—on whom be Allah's blessing and peace—: "Poverty comes near to being unbelief," we teach that what is intended here is poverty in regard to learning and patient endurance, not poverty in the matter of wealth.

The Qadarites teach that man had imposed on him ability to acquire *(iktisāb)*, and to seek for wealth. The truly orthodox people teach that if he has the ability [to make gain] then making gain is something permitted, and if he has not the power of gaining nevertheless it is *sunna* for him, while if he is under constraint and has children and little ones [dependent on him] then to make gain is a divine ordinance for him.

The Mutaqashshifa and the Karrāmites teach that gain is a thing forbidden, because it is necessary that we rely only on Allah. Allah has said (V, 23/26): "So put your trust in Allah." To seek for gain is to cast off this putting of trust [in Allah], and that is not permissible, for it is Allah Who provides a man's provision from whence he thinks not. We teach that reliance on Allah is a bounden duty *(farḍ)*, but that to seek for gain does not [necessarily mean that we] cast off reliance [on Him], for to put one's trust is one of the attributes of the heart. It is [having a] confidence in Allah, for [to have] the opinion that one's sustenance is from one's own earning is unbelief and error, while the contrary opinion is religion and the religious law from Allah. This is indicated by what is related from the Prophet—upon whom be Allah's blessing and peace—that he said: "He who seeks this world lawfully, desirous of avoiding mendicancy, labouring for his children, being sympathetic towards his neighbours, will come forward on the Day of Resurrection with a face like the moon on the night of its fullness, whereas he who seeks this world boastfully, avariciously, shall on the Resurrection Day meet with Allah, Who will be wrath with him. "It is indicated also by the fact that the Prophet—upon whom be Allah's blessing and peace—used to store up for his wives sufficient provision for a year. Likewise Allah has said (II, 267/269): "Contribute of the good things ye have gained", and had seeking of gain been forbidden He would not have commanded a contribution [therefrom]. Similarly He commanded the bringing of legal alms *(zakāt)*, and He would not have commanded such alms had the seeking of gain been forbidden. Then there is an indication that the seeking of gain by lawful wealth is not forbidden in the fact that the Prophets—upon whom be Allah's blessing and peace—although they put their trust [in Allah] nevertheless sought for gain. Adam—upon whom be peace—was a farmer; Idrīs [1] was a tailor; Noah was a carpenter;[2] Moses was a hired man to Shuʿaib (= Jethro); Abraham was a cloth-merchant; while Muḥammad—upon whom be Allah's blessing and peace—was a military leader *(ghāzī)*, so that we read in the Traditions: "Allah sent me with the sword in proximity to the coming of the Hour, appointing my portion beneath the shadow of my lance, and appointing humbleness and contemptibleness to such as oppose me."

Then [we teach] that there is no reckoning for the Prophets—on whom be peace—[on the Day of Judgment], no punishment and no questioning of the tomb.[3] Also [we teach] that the ten to whom the Prophet promised Paradise will escape the reckoning.[4] All this, however, refers to the *ḥisāb*

[1] The usual theory is that he represents the Biblical Enoch.

[2] This is an inference from the fact that he constructed the ark out of wood.

[3] It is the orthodox Muslim belief that when the corpse has been laid in the grave and the mourners have departed, two blue-eyed angels named Munkar and Nakīr appear and question the deceased, administering to him comfort or chastisement in accordance with his answers to their questions. At a Muslim funeral one may see someone go up to the corpse just as it is about to be laid in the grave and whisper to it a reminder of the correct answers to be given. See p. 209.

[4] There are various lists extant which purport to be the list of these ten to whom Muḥammad announced that there was no doubt of their reaching Paradise. For one such list see Elder's translation of at-Taftāzānī, *A Commentary on the Creed of Islam* (1950), p. 155.

al-munāqasha (the detailed reckoning), but the *ḥisāb al-farā'iḍ* (the accounting with regard to incumbent duties) will apply to Prophets and Companions [as well as to others]. [With regard to this latter the form of the questioning] is: "You have done thus and so; you have been forgiven thus and so", but with regard to the former it is: "Why did you do thus and so?"

The people of error teach that Allah created all things, and did not leave a single thing even to the present which He did not create [at that time]. All that was created then He [continues to] portion out, so that even the fruits [presently to appear] on a tree are all created [already]. Though they are not apparent and we see them not, yet really they are [already] created. They base their teaching on the verse (II, 29/27): "He it is Who created for you all that is in the earth." The truly orthodox people—on whom may Allah have mercy—teach that He decreed all that is and all that will be till the Day of Resurrection, but He did not create things at the time He decreed them. It was only after that [decreeing] that He began creating them according to times and seasons. He has created [things] in the past, and He will create [things] in the future. This is indicated by His saying (LV, 29): "Every day He is busied about some new work." Also the Prophet—upon whom be Allah's blessing and peace—said: "What He is busied about is causing to live and causing to die, exalting men and humbling them."

It is related of 'Alī—with whom may Allah be pleased—that he was asked about the verse (LV, 29): "Every day He is busied about some new work", and he answered: "What He is busied about is driving out the semen from the loins of the fathers into the wombs of the mothers, then giving it form there, then bringing it forth from the mother's belly into the world, then causing it to die, then raising it up at the Last Day." An indication [of the truth of our position] is the fact that Allah has decreed the Day of Resurrection but it is not yet created, for had it been created we should now be [living] in the Day of Resurrection, but it is not so. Another indication is the fact that Allah created the Pen and said: "Write what is to be till the Day of Resurrection."

The question may be asked as to whether the Pen has life. We teach that it does not have life, but is a solid body which Allah will question as He will question living creatures. If it should be asked what was the wisdom in Allah commanding the Pen to write on the Preserved Tablet all that was to be until the Day of Resurrection, we reply that it was in order that we might know that Allah knows the unseen, and that no one knows the unseen save Allah.

The Muʿtazilites, the Rāfiḍites,[1] and the Jahmites teach that the miraculous doings *(karāmāt)* of the Saints are a deception, but the miracles *(muʿjizāt)* of the Prophets are assured and genuine. In defence of their position they say that were we to teach that the miraculous doings of the Saints are assured [facts], we should be rendering worthless the miracles of the Prophets, since there would then be no difference between Prophets and Saints. They say: "You cannot quote as evidence against us the *karāmāt* of [the Virgin] Mary, e.g. (XIX, 25): "Shake towards thyself the palm-tree trunk, etc.", for that was a *karāma* connected with Jesus—on whom be Allah's blessings—, and the same is true of (III, 37/32): "As often as Zachariah entered the sanctuary to her etc.", for that was a *karāma* connected with Zachariah [2]—on whom be Allah's blessings.

The truly orthodox people—on whom may Allah have mercy—teach that the *karāmāt* of the Saints are possible and do not detract [in any way] from the miracles of the Prophets. In this matter there are three grades [of miraculousness] to be distinguished, viz. the miracles of the Prophets, the miraculous doings of the Saints, and the deceptions of the [Satanic] enemies.

Miracles are called *muʿjizāt* because it is impossible *(yuʿjizu)* for anyone save a Prophet to produce them. Examples are [the transformations of] Moses' rod, [Muḥammad's] splitting the moon, etc. It is this that marks the distinction between a miracle *(muʿjiza)* and a miraculous doing *(karāma)*. Moreover the miracles of the Prophets are witnessed by both Muslims and unbelievers, the obedient, the disobedient and the evil doer, whereas the *karāmāt* of the Saints are witnessed only by another Saint and evil doers see them not. A further distinction is that a miracle may happen whenever the Prophet—upon whom be peace—wishes [to produce one]. He [decides] to produce one, makes supplication to Allah, and the miracle appears for him. A *karāma,* on the other hand, happens only at particular times when Allah wishes it. A third distinction is that in the case of a miracle the Prophet—on whom be peace—recognizes it, knows it [to be a significant sign], and must acknowledge first to himself that his miracle is from Allah, and then [having thus acknowledged this] cause it to appear to others. This is because were he to deny the fact that the miracle is not of his own doing he would be in unbelief. In the case of a

[1] I.e. the Shīʿite groups. See p. 346.

[2] In both the Qur'ānic passages quoted miraculous manifestations are associated with Mary, but the argument is that they appeared not because of Mary, but in the one case because of Jesus and in the other because of Zachariah, both of whom have a place in the Qur'ānic gallery of Prophets.

karāma, however, there is no necessity for the Saint to acknowledge that it is a *karāma,* indeed he may say that it is the *karāma* of some other believer [and not his own at all].

As for the deceptions of the [satanic] enemies, the teaching of the truly orthodox people—whom may Allah increase—is that Allah has given the shayāṭīn ability to put themselves into any form [they please], so that one of them may make himself into a small bird in a man's presence and whisper to the man, [simulating in this and other ways the miraculous signs of Saints and Prophets].

That the *karāmāt* of the Saints are possible is indicated by the story of the Companions of the Cave (Sūra XVIII), for when they came out from the cave their hair had not vanished nor had their clothes become impaired, [in spite of the long years they had been in the cave], but they resembled other folk. It is also indicated by the story of Āṣaf to whom Allah refers in the verse (XXVII, 40): "He who had knowledge of Scripture [said]: 'I will bring it to thee (i.e. to Solomon) in the twinkling of an eye.'"[1] Since it was possible for him to have a *karāma* because of [his association with] Solomon, it is possible for this community (i.e. the Muslims) to have *karāmāt* because of [their association with] the Prophet —upon whom be Allah's blessing and peace.

The Mu'tazilites teach that the shayāṭīn have no hold over humans, nor are they able to whisper to them. Likewise with regard to the jinn they teach that they have no hold over humans. The truly orthodox people teach that they do affect humans both from within and from without. That they do so from within [is clear] from what is related from the Prophet—upon whom be Allah's blessing and peace—how he said: "The shayāṭīn circulate within men [like] the circulation of the blood." Thus it is firmly established that they have a governance from within and whisper to men, inciting them to evil. Their external impression [is made by] causing acts of disobedience to seem well-pleasing to men's hearts. Allah has said (XXVII, 24): "And Satan made well-pleasing to them their works." Should it be asked what wisdom there is in their being able to see us whereas we cannot see them, the answer is that they have been created in such horrible forms that were we to see them we should be unable to take food or drink, so they have been veiled off from us by an act of Allah's mercy. The jinn are created from the wind, and as it is of the nature of wind that it cannot be seen so it is with whatever has been created from it. The angels are created from light, so were we to see them

[1] The Commentators say that he was Āṣaf b. Barakhyā, the vizier of Solomon, who miraculously brought to his Court the throne of the Queen of Sheba.

our spirits would fly out towards them. As for the statement that the soul does acts of disobedience at their instigation, we teach that this is so, and that it is by way of the whispering of the satans. Allah has said (CXIV, 5): "Who whispers into the breasts of men."

To establish the [fact that a Divine] message [has been] sent [to mankind], [we go back to the fact that] since it is well-established that the world has a Maker, powerful, all-Knowing and wise, it was of His wisdom not to leave His servants without commands and prohibitions [by which to guide their lives]. Had he left them thus destitute there would have been no convincing argument *(ḥujja)* against them on the Day of Resurrection, and so He commanded and He forbade. The sole reason why this is done by way of addressing [men] verbally, is because this world is the house of testing, and belief in the unseen is a Divine ordinance, but in this world are the Enemy and the Saint, so had He Himself addressed men in this world there would have been no difference between them. Therefore He addressed men by ambassadors, namely the Apostles. In every age and in each period He has sent to men an Apostle, from the time of Adam to that of our Prophet. For them (i.e. for the ambassadors) He produced miracles, which are contrary to nature and to custom, because it is incumbent on them to give proofs [of their mission].

An indication of the [validity of the] prophetic office of our Prophet Muḥammad—upon whom be Allah's blessing and peace—[is to be found in] the wonderful signs and clear proofs [which he brought]. Among them are the Qur'ān, the splitting of the moon, the yearning of the tree trunk, the stones in his hand uttering praises of Allah, the increase of a little food by the blessing of his prayer. His miraculous gifts in the Qur'ān are of two kinds. One is from the point of view of its language and style, its brevity and its conciseness, comprehending many meanings under few words. The second is from the point of view of the subject matter, for it gave information about the unseen [future]. Thus it actually came about as He had said of it (XLVIII, 27): "Ye will assuredly enter the sacred shrine safely, if Allah wills." Another example is in the verse (LXII, 6): "Then wish for death if ye are truth-speakers." This came about as He had said, because the Jews found [written] in the Torah: "If they wish for death they will die", so they abstained from this.[1] A similar instance is

[1] The reference here is to the claim of the Jews that they were the special friends of God, yet Muḥammad found that they were of all people those most afraid of death, whereas he says that if they were particular friends of God they ought to be glad to die and be with Him. Their reply to him, apparently, was that there was a verse in the Torah which forbade them to wish for death.

[his] summoning the Christians to imprecation, but they refrained from it because they found [written] in the Gospel that if they did that they would be secure. This is referred to in the verse (III, 61/54): "Then say: 'Come let us summon our sons and your sons etc.'"[1]

[It appears] also in the fact that Allah gave information about the history of both former and latter peoples [in the Qur'ān], whereas our Prophet—on whom be Allah's blessing and peace—did not go out [beyond the boundaries] of al-Madīna, nor did he read a single book, nor was he a pupil to any one [who might have taught him these things]. We know that he got his information from the Qur'ān, which derived not from him but only from Allah, so that it is incumbent [on us] to obey in what it commands and refrain from what it forbids.

Then there is an indication that the Qur'ān is a miracle in the verse (XVII, 88/90): "Even though men and jinn were to combine to produce the like of this Qur'ān they would not produce its like." As for the increasing of the little food, the story about it is that Abū Ayyūb, one of the *anṣār*,[2] invited our Prophet—upon whom be Allah's blessings and peace—to be a guest at his house, and slaughtered for him a kid. He had also four measures of flour, and yet [from this scanty provision] all the people of al-Madīna were fed to repletion. The story about the poisoned kid is of course well-known *(ẓāhir)*.[3]

Then [there is the question] whether our Prophet, Muḥammad—on whom be Allah's blessing and peace—is now at the present time an Apostle or not. The Mutaqashshifa and the Karrāmites teach that an accidental does not endure through two periods, and so they teach that our Prophet—upon whom be Allah's blessing and peace—is not now an Apostle [as he was during his lifetime]. Abū'l-Ḥasan al-Ash'arī taught that our Prophet—upon whom be Allah's blessing and peace—is still now at the present time in the Apostolic state, and the state to which a thing belongs

[1] This is a reference to the famous *mubāhala*. It would seem that when the Christians disputed his teaching that Jesus was not superior to Adam, he called on them to bring out their families and he would bring out his family, and both parties would call on Allah to curse the party which was in the wrong about this matter. The Christians, however, would seem to have replied that such a mutual cursing match was forbidden in the Gospels.

[2] *anṣār* means "helpers". When Muḥammad fled from the hostile city of Mecca to make his headquarters at al-Madīna, those Madīnans who pledged themselves to stand by him there were known as the *anṣār*. See p. 365.

[3] A Jewish woman of Khaibar who had lost her husband, brothers and father at the taking of that oasis settlement set a poisoned kid before Muḥammad for his evening meal, and popular tradition says that the kid called out to the Prophet to tell him that it was poisoned. See p. 336 and Sir Wm. Muir's *Life of Mohammed*, p. 379.

replaces the original nature of the thing. Do you not see that the *ʿidda,*[1] which belongs to the matrimonial regulations, replaces the [state of] matrimony. Similarly if a man is engaged at his prayers and is compelled to go to relieve his bowels, and then goes to perform the necessary ritual ablutions, he is still in the state of one at prayer, though he is not actually performing the ritual actions of prayer. Had he continued with the actions of prayer [without going and performing the ablutions] he would have been praying in a state of ritual impurity. In like manner the prophetic office of our Prophet Muḥammad—on whom be Allah's blessings and peace—is [it is true] an accidental, and an accidental does not [normally] endure through two periods, yet he is nevertheless still in the state of those with a message.

An indication that an accidental does not endure through two periods is the fact that if a man prays the mid-day prayer he is no longer said to be at prayer when he has finished it, for were he still at prayer [the acts of] eating, drinking and talking would not be permissible to him. Thus it is firmly established that an accidental has no continuance through two different time periods. We teach that [Muḥammad] is an Apostle at the present time, because were he not an Apostle at the present time the faith of those who become Muslims and believe in him would not be sound. Likewise in the call to prayer we say: "I testify that Muḥammad *is* the Apostle of Allah", and not "I testify that Muḥammad *was* the Apostle of Allah." The same holds true with regard to all the other Prophets —on whom be blessings and peace.

The Muʿtazilites teach that the Miʿrāj [2] did not take place, because in [the Miʿrāj] story are unparallelled Traditions, and a Tradition of this nature is one that must be acted upon[3] but is not necessarily to be believed as an article of faith. The truly orthodox people—on all of whom be Allah's good pleasure—teach that the Miʿrāj to heaven is an authentic fact, for [the Tradition concerning] it is transmitted by most of the Companions of the Prophet—on whom be peace—such as Abū Saʿīd al-Khudrī, Anas b. Mālik, Mālik b. Ṣaʿṣaʿa, Ibn ʿAbbās and Umm Hāni' —with all of whom may Allah be pleased—all of whom taught [the doctrine of the] ascension to heaven.

[1] The *ʿidda* is the period of waiting imposed on a woman. See p. 267.

[2] The ascension of Muḥammad on the celestial steed Burāq, accompanied by Gabriel, through the seven heavens to the presence of the Almighty. See pp. 336 ff.; 621 ff.

[3] The point is that the five prayer periods are popularly supposed to have been fixed during the Ascension, and the pious Muslim has to act in accordance with the regulations for the five daily prayer services, but need not necessarily believe in the story of the Ascension itself.

This [doctrine] is really concerned with two matters, the Isrā' (Night Journey) and the Mi'rāj (Ascension). The *isrā'* was from Mecca to Jerusalem, and the Mu'tazilites do not deny it, since it is based on a Qur'ānic text (XVII,1): "Glory be to Him Who took His servant by night from the sacred shrine [at Mecca] to the further shrine (i.e. the Temple at Jerusalem), whose environs We have blessed, that We might show him [Our signs]". An *isrā'* is a journey by night. Whosoever denies [the reality of] the Isrā' is in unbelief. He (i.e. Allah) used the expression "by night" [in the singular], that it might be known that the Mi'rāj lasted only a single night. The Mi'rāj was from earth to the seventh heaven. Such an event could only be established [as an actual happening] by cogent indications, and the indication that the Mi'rāj is an established fact is what has been related by Umm Hāni'—with whom may Allah be pleased. She said: "The Prophet—upon whom be Allah's blessing and peace—said: 'Shall I not relate to you the most amazing thing I ever saw?' I said: 'Surely! O Apostle of Allah.' Said the Prophet—upon whom be Allah's blessing and peace—'I was sleeping, though my heart was awake, when Gabriel—on whom be peace—came', etc. etc. etc."[1]

There is some difference of opinion as to whether the Prophet—on whom be Allah's blessing and peace—saw his Lord on the night of the Mi'rāj or not. Some say that he saw Him with his heart but did not see Him with his eyes. They base this on the Tradition in which the Prophet—upon whom be Allah's blessing and peace—was asked: "Did you see your Lord on the night of the Mi'rāj?", and he answered: "Glory be to Allah! Glory be to Allah! I saw with my heart, but I did not see with my eyes." There is also the Tradition from 'Ā'isha—with whom may Allah be pleased—who said: "I asked the Apostle of Allah—upon whom be Allah's blessing and peace—about the *ru'yā* (vision), and he answered me like that" (i.e. that the vision was one with the heart not with the eyes). There is also the verse (LIII,11): "His heart did not falsify what he saw", where seeing is attributed to the heart not to the eye.

The Mu'tazilites in denying [the reality of] the Mi'rāj base their teaching on the verse (XVII,60/62): "We did not appoint a vision which We caused thee to see save as a testing for the people." They teach that the Mi'rāj was a part of this vision, for [man's] intelligence cannot accept any such thing [as an ascent to the heavens], and the intelligence is Allah's

[1] This Tradition from Umm Hāni' is so well known and is to be found in so many books that the author here can begin the Tradition, and then say, etc. etc. etc. assured that his readers will know the rest of it as well as we would know the story of Red Riding Hood.

argument *(ḥujja)* against His creatures. Allah has created man with a form that is weighty, and it is of its nature to fall and go downwards [not to ascend]. Going up to the heights is of the nature of birds, so for this reason the Miʿrāj could not have been an actual happening. Our reply is that we teach that any unbeliever may see himself in heaven in a dream, whereas the particular point here in the case of our Prophet—upon whom be Allah's blessing and peace—is that this happened while he was awake. As for the argument that it is natural for man to fall downwards, we agree that this is so, but here it was not that he mounted up himself, but he was taken up, as it says: "Glory be to Him who *took* His servant by night." It does not say that he journeyed on his own account. Do you not see that it is natural for stones and lumps of clay to fall downwards, and yet in spite of this man throws them and makes them mount up into the air. So the Prophet—upon whom be Allah's blessing and peace—since he had Burāq as his mount, Gabriel as his driver, and Allah as his guide, could even more easily ascend to the heavens. In like manner anyone who takes hold of a bow can by it shoot an arrow into the air, and so in the case of the Prophet—upon whom be Allah's blessing and peace—since the Night Journey was his bow, Burāq his mount, Gabriel—on whom be peace—his leader, by Allah's permission it was easier for him to go beyond the heavens.

The Muʿtazilites and the Shīʿites teach that the Throne *(ʿarsh)* is [an expression used for] dominion, and the Footstool *(kursī)*, is [similarly used for] knowledge. Allah has said (II,255/256): "Wide stretches His Throne *(kursī)* over the heavens and the earth", i.e. His knowledge does. The truly orthodox people—on whom may Allah have mercy—teach that it is not permissible to take the Throne to be dominion, for Allah has said (LXIX,17): "And above them eight on that Day will bear the Throne of thy Lord", and dominion could not be thus borne. Similarly it is related of the Prophet—upon whom be Allah's blessing and peace—that he said: "When Allah created the Throne He created the angels, and said to them: 'Bear My Throne!', but they were not able to bear it. Then Allah said: 'Were I to create as many [of you] as there are grains of sand or drops of rain they would not be able to bear it unless they asked help from Me.' They said: 'Allahumma, aid us.' Then they heard a call from Allah, without their knowing how, [saying]: 'Say: There is no strength and no power save with Allah, the High, the Mighty.' So they said that, and they bore the Throne, which then settled on their heads. There are four [of them bearing it] during [the duration] of this world, but there will be eight in the next world, for Allah has said (LXIX,17): 'And above them eight on that Day will bear the Throne.'" The angels who bear the Throne have each four faces. As for what wise purpose was served by the creation of the Throne, there are some who say that it was [created] to be a *qibla* for the prayer services of the angels, so that they raise their hands to the Throne whenever they make supplication. Others say that it is a mirror for the angels into which they look and are able to see everything in the heavens and on earth. [The theologians] differ about the [substance of the] Throne, for there are those who say that it is a couch *(sarīr)* of light, but others say that that is not so, for it is of ruby.

The Mu'tazilites teach that we have over us no [recording] angels or watchers *(ḥafaẓa)*, but Allah knows about all that a man does, and punishes whom He will, or forgives whom He will. There would be need for such watchers only if He were ignorant and did not know about what His servants were doing. But Allah has no need to appoint anyone over them to write down their deeds. We teach that He appointed them over [men] that there might be evidence against each individual on the Day of Resurrection, so that if a man should deny his doings the two angels will testify against him, or if he should forget there will be the [record] book as evidence against him. Should it be asked: "On what do they write?", the answer is that [in a Tradition] aḍ-Ḍaḥḥāk [1] said: "Each day there descend from heaven two angels, each of whom has a sheet *(ṣaḥīfa)*." Mujāhid [2] said: "Your tongue is their pen, your spittle their ink, your body their book." The first statement, however, is more correct, for Allah has said (XVII,14/15): "Read thy book!", which [since this is adressed to the soul at Judgment], indicates that they have [in their hands] something written out. In the final resort, however, the answer is that we believe in what is in the [sacred] text and the Traditions, without busying ourselves with questions of how it can be, even though it be something that both intellect and analogy refuse [to accept as possible]. The truly orthodox people teach that the Watchers are real. Over each one of us are two by day and two by night. Two angels descend [to us] by day and two depart at night. It is not as some teach that each day two angels descend different from those who were there the previous day. An indication of this is in the verse (LXXXII,10,11): "Yet over you, indeed, are guardians; noble ones, those who write", and in the verse (XLIII,80): "Or do they think

[1] Abū'l-Qāsim aḍ-Ḍaḥḥāk b. Muzāḥim (d. 105 A.H. = 723 A.D.), a Follower belonging to the succession of Ibn 'Abbās. He was famous both as a Traditionist and as a transmitter of the text of the Qur'ān.

[2] Abū'l-Ḥajjāj Mujāhid b. Jabr (d. 101 A.H. = 719 A.D.), a Follower belonging to the succession of Ibn 'Abbās. He was more famous in Qur'ānic science than in the field of Tradition.

that We do not hear their secret and their private talk? Nay, indeed, Our messengers beside them are writing down."

The Mu'tazilites teach that when Allah gives the command for the first blast [on the Trump of Doom], heaven and earth, Paradise and Hell, and all spirits will pass away. Then Allah will create them a second time on the Day of Resurrection. They base their teaching on the verse (LVII,3): "He is the first and the last." Since Allah existed in eternity when there was not a single one of His creatures with Him, likewise He must remain at the end, abiding alone, that this name (i.e. the first and the last) may be solely His. The truly orthodox people teach that Paradise and Hell are themselves the House of Eternity, and are for reward and punishment, so they do not pass away. This is indicated by the verse (XXXIX,68): "There will be a blast on the Trump and those who are in the heavens and those who are on earth will expire, save such as Allah wills." [By this exception] He means Paradise and Hell and those who inhabit them, viz. the angels of chastisement and the Ḥūrīs (the heavenly spouses prepared for the Blessed). The truly orthodox people teach that seven things will not pass away—the Throne, the Footstool, the Tablet, the Pen, Paradise and Hell with their inhabitants, and the Spirits.

The Jahmites teach that when the Blessed have entered Paradise and the Damned the Fire, the Blessed will enjoy bliss to the measure of their works, and Allah will cause the Damned to suffer torment to the measure of their works and their unbelief, but then Allah will make an end of Paradise and Hell. They base their teaching on the verse (LVII, 3): "He is the first and the last", which is interpreted as we have already mentioned. There is also a Tradition in which the Prophet—upon whom be Allah's blessing and peace—says: "There will come a day when the wind will bang to and fro the gates of Gehenna, for there will be no one in it." The truly orthodox people teach that Paradise and Hell are the House of Eternity, and are for reward and punishment, so that, as we have already mentioned, they do not pass away. It cannot be that there should be oppression or injustice on the part of Allah, for He has said (IX, 111/112): "Verily Allah has purchased from the believers their souls and their goods on the condition that Paradise be theirs." The Blessed have purchased [Paradise] by their faith, degrees [of beatitude] therein by their works, and the vision [of Allah] by their intentions, whereas unbelievers have purchased the Fire by their intentions and their unbelief. We agree that when a man has purchased a house, and has paid over the price, it is not right for the seller to take it back from him, so that if he should do that he would be guilty of oppression and injustice. Allah, however, is far removed from oppression and injustice. As for the verse (LVII, 3) about Allah being the first and the last, we teach that this is so, but that He endures without anyone causing Him to endure, whereas creatures endure by Allah's causing them to endure, which makes clear the difference between the Creator and the created. With regard to the Tradition [about Hell being empty], we teach that when the disobedient have been drawn out of the Fire and caused to enter Paradise, it remains an empty place in which there is no one.[1] That is the meaning of the Tradition.

The Mu'tazilites teach that being pleased and being angry are not among the attributes of Allah, for with Allah there are no changing states. So in every place [in the Qur'ān] where there is mention of His being pleased or being angry what is meant is Paradise and Hell. The truly orthodox people teach that being pleased and being angry are of the attributes of Allah, being eternal [attributes] though apart from mode or any assimilation [to human emotions], and without any changing from state to state [being involved]. They are [in this] like the rest of His attributes such as willing and hearing and seeing and speech.

An indication that Allah's being pleased is not [just a reference to] Paradise is in the verse (XCVIII, 8/7): "Their recompense is with their Lord, gardens of Eden...Allah will be well-pleased with them, and they with Him." Similarly in verse (IX, 72/73), we read: "goodly dwellings in gardens of Eden, and [Allah's] good pleasure." Likewise with regard to A lah's anger we have the verse (IV, 93/95): "Whosoever kills a believer purposely, his recompense shall be Gehenna... Allah will be angry with him and will curse him." [In all such verses] there is a clear distinction between Allah's good pleasure and Paradise, and between His anger and Hell.

The Commentator Naṣr b. al-Ḥanbalī, the [well-known] Sheikh and Imām, was asked: "Is it a fact that the attributes of Allah are subject to change?" He answered: "The question is a ridiculous one, for Allah in all His attributes is One, in all His attributes is eternal. Were a single one of His attributes to be subject to change those attributes would be contingent, created things, but the attributes of Allah are not created." It is as though they should ask: "Is Allah able to create One like Himself?" The answer to this is that the question is absurd, for Allah is eternal, and if He creates anything that thing is created, so how could it be like Himself? Allah has not created anything in eternity that would be like Himself.

The Jahmites asked the question: "Does Allah know the number of

[1] I.e. Gehenna is only one section of Hell, namely the section in which wicked Muslims are punished, and as all Muslims will some day get to Paradise, there will come a day when this section of Hell will be empty, though others are full.

breaths [to be drawn by] the Blessed and the Damned, or not?" If you answer "No", then you describe Allah as ignorant [of something], and if you answer "Yes", then you are teaching that the Blessed and the Damned will come to an end. The answer to this is that we teach that Allah knows that the breaths of the Blessed and the Damned are not counted, nor do they cease. If it be said [to us:] "By saying that the [succession of the] Blessed and the Damned is not cut off you have made a point of equality between them and Allah", we reply that there can be no point of equality between them and Allah, because Allah was the First, the primordial One without any beginning, the Last, the everlasting One without any ending, whereas the Blessed and the Damned are accidentals, who only continue instead of coming to an end because of Allah's causing them to continue. Allah, on the other hand, continues without being caused to continue by anyone. Thus there is no point of equality between the Creator and the created.

The founder of the Mu'tazilites was a man named Wāṣil b. 'Aṭā'. His follower was 'Amr b. 'Ubaid, a pupil of al-Ḥasan al-Baṣrī [1]—on whom may Allah have mercy—, and then in the days of [the Caliph] Hārūn ar-Rashīd (785–809 A.D.), there appeared Abū Hudhail al-'Allāf,[2] who composed for them a written statement, making clear what their sect taught and assembling their doctrines *('ulūm)*. This book he named *Uṣūl al-Khamsa*, and whenever they saw a man they would say to him: "Have you read the *Uṣūl al-Khamsa*?" If he answered: "Yes", they recognized him as belonging to their sect. The five principles *(uṣūl)* [referred to] were the problems of Equity, Unity, Promise, Threat, and the question of the Intermediate.

(i) Regarding Equity *(al-'adl)* they taught that Allah does not create evil nor does He decree it, for did He create evil and decree it and then punish [men] for it that would be injustice on His part, whereas Allah is the equitable One, to Whom injustice is impossible.

(ii) Regarding the second point they teach that the Qur'ān is a created thing, as are all the rest of His attributes, for if we say that it is uncreate there is an end to His unity.

[1] Abū Sa'id Ḥasan al-Baṣrī (d. 110 A.H. = 728 A.D.) who is one of the most important figures in the history of Islamic thought. He was not only a theologian, but a Ṣūfī master and an important figure in the history of the transmission of the text of the Qur'ān. See Tritton, *Muslim Theology*, pp. 57 ff., and the article on him in the *Encyclopaedia of Islam*. Wāṣil b. 'Aṭā' was one of his pupils, see Tritton, *op. cit.*, pp. 60 ff.

[2] Muḥammad b. al-Hudhail al-'Allāf died in 850 A.D. about a hundred years old. See Tritton, *op. cit.*, pp. 83 ff.

(iii) As regards the third point they teach that if Allah has promised His servants a reward it is not possible for Him to go back on His promise, for Allah "will not fail the appointment" (III, 9/7).

(iv) Also if His promise has been a threat it is not possible that He should not punish them, and leave His threat unfulfilled, since no alteration of the word of Allah is possible.

The truly orthodox people, however, teach that if Allah's promise is a threat it is possible that He punish them not, but forgive and pardon them, and not visit punishment on them. The Muʿtazilites base their teaching on the verse (IV, 93/95): "But should one kill a believer intentionally, his recompense is Gehenna, therein to abide", and the similar verse (IV, 30/34): "We shall roast him in the Fire." The reply to this is that we teach that every mention of a threat by Allah lies under exception, because of the verse (IV, 48/51): "Allah will not forgive the association [of other deities] with Himself, but other than that He will forgive anything to whomsoever He pleases." As to their teaching about His not fulfilling His threat, we teach that this is not a case of non-fulfilment, but is to be considered as a case of generosity and favour on His part. This is quite different from the case where He has promised a reward, for it would be quite impossible for such a promise of His to be broken, since it is something due to man, and were it possible [for the promise to be broken], that would be an act of outrage instead of being counted an act of generosity, a thing which is not to be thought of in connection with Allah. The reply to them on the matter of IV, 93/95 about killing a believer intentionally is that Ibn ʿAbbās said, with reference to the words "his recompense is Gehenna", that [they mean only] should Allah exact recompense. This is indicated by the verse (II, 178/173): "O ye who have believed, prescribed for you is retaliation in the matter of the slain", where He calls him a believer even after he has intentionally slain a man. Our teaching, therefore, is that what is meant [in IV, 93/95] is the case where the killing of the believer was lawful.

(v) Concerning the question of the Intermediate, they teach that he who commits a mortal sin has departed from the faith but nevertheless has not lapsed into unbelief. They base this on the verse (XXXII, 18): "Shall then he who has been a believer be as him who has acted wickedly? They shall not be alike", where a clear distinction is made between the believer and the one doing evil, so that it is clear that the former is not as the latter, nor the latter as the former. The reply is that this verse: "Shall then he who has been a believer etc." was revealed with reference to the case of the hypocrite al-Walīd b.ʿUqba [1]—whom may Allah curse —when he said to ʿAlī—with whom may Allah be pleased—: "If you have a tongue and strength and appearance, well I also have a tongue and strength and appearance." Whereupon ʿAlī—with whom may Allah be pleased—answered: "Be silent! for you are an unbeliever." Thereat Allah sent down this verse concurring with what ʿAlī—with whom may Allah be pleased—had said.

The Muʿtazilites are divided among themselves on [the question of] intercession. Some of them deny absolutely [the possibility of any] intercession. Others maintain that there may be intercession in the case of three groups: (1) those who have avoided the mortal sins but have committed the venial, so that they have need of forgiveness for the venial sins. When they repent there is need for their repentance to be accepted through the intercession of the prophets and the angels, [who intercede] till Allah accepts men's repentance at their intercession; (2) those who have committed mortal sins but have repented thereof. There is need that their repentance be accepted through the intercession of the prophets and the angels, [who intercede] till Allah accepts men's repentance at their intercession; (3) those who have avoided both the mortal and the venial sins but need advance in their grades [2] [of bliss] in accordance with the advance in their works, through the intercession of the prophets and the angels. There is no intercession, however, [that will avail] for other than these three [classes].

The answer [to their arguments] is as follows. With regard to the first group, [we reply that] this is not sound teaching even according to the [doctrine of] their own sect, because, according to them, Allah must forgive entirely the offences of such as have avoided the mortal sins, since He has said (IV, 31/35): "If ye avoid the greater things that ye are forbidden to do, We shall provide atonement for your evil deeds." [For this group] therefore, there is no need for any intercession. With regard to the second group, who have committed mortal sins but have repented and need to have their repentance accepted through the intercession of prophets and angels, we say that again, according to [the teaching of] their own

1 The Commentators say that at the famous Battle of Badr this al-Walīd b. ʿUqba boasted of his great superiority to ʿAlī b. Abī Ṭālib, the son-in-law of the Prophet, and this verse was revealed in answer to his boasting.

2 These grades *(darajāt)* are mentioned in the Qur'ān not infrequently. They affect both the Blessed and the Damned, for there are to be degrees of bliss in Paradise and degrees of torment in Hell in accordance with the outcome of the "Reckoning" at Judgment. Whether the grades can be advanced once Paradise is reached is a disputed point.

sect, this is not sound, for, according to them, if a man repents needs must Allah accept his repentance, so that again there is no need of intercession.

The truly orthodox people teach that intercession is a fact. This is indicated by the saying of the Prophet—upon whom be Allah's blessing and peace—: "My intercession is for those of my community who are guilty of the mortal sins." If the objection should be raised that Allah has said (XL, 18/19): "For wrong-doers there is no ardent friend, nor any intercessor to whom heed will be given", and one guilty of mortal sins is certainly a wrong-doer, as Allah has said (XXXV, 32/29): "Some of them wrong themselves", our reply is that we teach that what is intended by that verse [about there being no intercessor] is the case of unbelievers and associators (i.e. those who associate some other deity with Allah). To such refers also the verse (XXVI, 100, 101): "We have no intercessors nor any warm friend", and that association is wrong-doing appears from the verse (XXXI, 13/12): "Associate naught with Allah. Truly, association [of other deities with Allah] is a mighty wrong."

It may be objected further that there is a Tradition that the Prophet—upon whom be Allah's blessing and peace—said: "My intercession reaches not those of my community guilty of the mortal sins." We reply that we have already quoted the Tradition according to which the Prophet—upon whom be Allah's blessing and peace—says: "My intercession is for those of my community who have committed the mortal sins." If that Tradition is genuine it means [that his intercession will avail] wherever that is lawful. If the objection be raised that we are affirming that intercession [avails] for believers, whereas those who have committed any mortal sin have [thereby] departed from the faith, [supporting our position] by adducing the statement of him—upon whom be Allah's blessing and peace—: "The fornicator is not committing fornication when he fornicates in the state of being a believer", our reply is that he means here: "If that be lawful", since it is related that he—upon whom be Allah's blessing and peace—said to Abū 'd-Dardā'[1]—with whom may Allah be pleased—: "Announce among the folk that whoever will say: 'There is no deity but Allah' will enter Paradise, even though he be a fornicator or a thief."

The Mu'tazilites teach that there will be no Balance, nor accounting,

[1] Abū'd-Dardā' and his wife Umm ad-Dardā' were among the early converts to Islam, and appear constantly in the books of Tradition as sources of information on the sayings and doings of the Prophet.

nor Bridge, nor Pool, nor [final] intercession.[1] A Balance, they say, is something of which a magistrate may have need, or a grocer, but wherever [in the Qur'ān] Allah mentions the balance and the reckoning what is meant is equity *('adl)*. The Balance is [said to be] used to give accurate knowledge of the quantity [each soul has] of good works and of evil works, but [surely] Allah knows all about that. He whose good works are more than his evil works will be ordered to Paradise, and he whose evil works are more than his good works will be sent to the Fire. Such as are among the Blessed (lit. those for Paradise), will not [have to] stand [2] at the Resurrection, nor will they have need of any intercession.

The truly orthodox people teach that all these things are realities; that the Pool and the Balance on [the Day of] Resurrection, and the [stream] Kawthar, [3] and Paradise are [all] realities. [That the Balance is a fact] is indicated by the verse (VII, 8/7): "Whosesoever balances weigh heavy, those are they who will prosper." Said Ibn 'Abbās—with whom may Allah be pleased—: "The Balance has two pans, one in the East and the other in the West." Should someone ask what wisdom there is in [this Whosesoever matter of] the Balance, and why the good and evil deeds should be weighed, since Allah knows all about them, we answer that it is true that Allah knows all about them, but man does not know, so the good and evil deeds are weighed that he may know whether he is for Paradise or for the Fire. If it be asked whether the reading of the [record] books comes first, or the Balance, we reply that there is no Scripture text [available for deciding] this, but the theologians have settled [the question] by way of inference, [and are of the opinion] that the reading of the [record] books comes first. This is indicated by the verse (VII, 8/7): "Whosesoever balances weigh heavy, those are they who will prosper," which indicates that there is no testing [to take place] after the Balance.

The question may be raised as to where the accounting [takes place], and where the Balance will be. We teach that the Balance and the accounting will be at the Bridge. It is there that each individual's good deeds

[1] These are all matters concerned with the events of the Last Day, and as each of them is mentioned in the Qur'ān or Traditions they form part of orthodox belief. On the Day of Judgment the Balance will be set up and when each soul has faced its Record Book there will be a weighing to establish its measure of bliss or of punishment according to the accounting. Then all souls will have to march over the Bridge which has been strung over Hell. The Blessed will move across it to safety, but the Damned will fall from it into Hell. Beyond the Bridge each Prophet has his Pool at which his followers drink to prepare themselves for their entry into Paradise, which opens its gates at the intercession of Muḥammad.

[2] The Standing is another matter of concern at the Last Day. See p. 393.

[3] See p. 633.

and evil deeds will be weighed. He whose balances weigh heavy will proceed [across the Bridge] to Paradise, while he who belongs to the wretched ones will fall from the Bridge like a raindrop into the Fire. There is a Tradition which says that each man stands on the Bridge at seven stations [before he gets across]. At the first station he is questioned about faith; at the second about his major and minor ablutions; at the third about his prayers; at the fourth about his fasting; at the fifth about his pilgrimage; at the sixth about his almsgiving; and at the seventh about filial piety.

The question may be raised that [the Qur'ān] uses the word "balances" in the plural, and how can that be? We teach that each man will have his own individual balance in which his good and his evil deeds will be weighed. Should it be asked how they are weighed, we reply that some say that a man will be weighed against his works. This is in accord with what is related about Ibn Mas'ūd —with whom may Allah be pleased—how [one day] he climbed a tree, and as he was weak in the legs the Companions of the Prophet—upon whom be Allah's blessing and peace—were amused [at the sight]. He—upon whom be peace—however, said: "Are you astonished at the thinness of his legs? On the Balance they will weigh heavier than the heavens and the earth." From this it may be affirmed that a man himself will be weighed against his works. On the other hand it is related that Ibn 'Abbās said: "The good deeds will be written down on a sheet and placed in one pan, while the evil deeds on a sheet will be placed in the other pan." Muḥammed b. 'Alī at-Tirmidhī[1] said: "The works will be weighed apart from the individual. In the case of a Muslim they will be seen [shining] like light, like the sun and moon, but in the case of an unbeliever they will be seen as darkness." Even though works are accidentals Allah is able to give them a form in which it is possible for them to be weighed and seen. The Sheikh, the Imām, the interpreter (i.e. the present author an-Nasafī), says: A man's faith is not weighed, for there would be no opposite to put in the other pan, since the opposite [of faith] is unbelief, and one individual cannot have in him both faith and unbelief.

Some of the Jahmites and the Mu'tazilites teach that Allah has not yet created Paradise and Hell, for it would not become the wisdom of the Wise One to create the House of Blessedness before He has created its inhabitants, or to create the Prison and place of detention before He has

[1] The compiler of *al-Jāmi'*, one of the six canonical collections of Traditions. See p. 80.

created inhabitants for them. Moreover, were they created things they would have to pass away with the passing away of heaven and earth, for they are in heaven and earth, and so, since heaven and earth will pass away, likewise Paradise and Hell [would pass away].

The truly orthodox people teach that Allah has already created both Paradise and Hell, and that they will never pass away, for they are the House of Reward and Punishment, and the House of Reward and Punishment does not pass away, for Allah has excepted them [from destruction] in the verse (XXXIX, 68): "There will be a blast on the Trump, and those who are in the heavens and those who are on the earth will expire, save such as Allah wills", i.e. Paradise and Hell with their inhabitants, such as the angels of chastisement and the Ḥūrīs. [The truth of this position is also] indicated by the fact that since man's reward is already created he is more eager in his service [of Allah], and since his punishment is already created he is more fearful and takes greater care to refrain from disobedience. There is also an indication [of its truth] in the verse (LVII, 21): "A Garden, whose spread is as wide as the heavens and the earth, prepared for those who are pious",[1] and in the verse (II, 24/22): "So fear the Fire, whose fuel is men and stones, prepared for the unbelievers." Were they not both things already created that would be false statement on the part of Allah, and Allah is far removed from such a thing. Another indication is in the fact that Allah has created Paradise above the seven heavens, not in the heavens, so that there is no point in saying that it would have to pass away when the heavens pass away. How could it be said that it is in the heavens when it is a thousand times the size of the heavens? Allah has said (LIII, 14, 15): "At the Sidra-tree of the boundary, beside which is the garden of resort", and the Sidra is above the heavens.[2] Likewise Gehanna and the Fire are below the earth. Allah has said (LXXXIII, 7): "Verily the [record] book of the evil-doers is in Sijjīn", and Sijjīn[3] is beneath the earth, so that the spirits of the unbelievers go there to Sijjīn, while the spirits of the believers and martyrs

[1] This is really a conflate of two Qur'ānic passages, LVII, 21 and III, 132/127.

[2] The Sidra-tree is the Oriental lote tree, and the probabilities are that the tree referred to in Sūra LIII, 14, 15 was a tree growing at some locality near Mecca. The Commentators, however, invariably take it to be a celestial tree of enormous size and marvellous characteristics, so that like the tree Ṭūbā, already mentioned, it is an Islamic variant of the common Oriental conception of the World Tree. See pp. 395, 632.

[3] The word Sijjīn occurs in the Qur'ān only in this Sūra, and there is no certainty as to what it means. Since it may formally be connected with *sijn*, the word for "prison", the usual theory is that it refers to the place where the souls of evil-doers are imprisoned in the lower regions. See p. 628.

go to ʿIllīyūn.[1] Finally there is proof that both Paradise and Hell are already created in what is related of the Prophet—upon whom be Allah's blessing and peace—how he said: "On the night of the Miʿrāj I saw in Paradise such and such, and in Hell such and such", and so on to the end of that Tradition.

The Muʿtazilites, the Jahmites and the Najjārites [2] teach that neither intelligence nor analogy can accept the reality of the torments of the tomb, or the questioning of Munkar and Nakīr.[3] [Their argument is that] if He punishes man it must be either that He torments the flesh without the spirit, or that He causes the spirit to reenter [the body] and then torments it. Now it would be useless to punish the flesh without the spirit for [in that case] it would not feel the pain, yet it is not possible [to think] that He causes the spirit to reenter it and then torments it, for did He cause the spirit to reenter it that would make necessary a second dying, which is not possible, for Allah has said (III, 185/182): "Every soul shall taste of death", and this verse informs men that they will not taste of death more than once. Since these two possibilities are [thus shown to be] hopeless, there remains but the third, namely, that there is no torment in the tomb.

The truly orthodox people teach that the torments of the tomb and the questioning by Munkar and Nakīr are realities, and that the pressure of the grave is a reality,[4] whether a man be a believer or an unbeliever, obedient or reprobate. If he is an unbeliever his torment in the tomb continues till the Resurrection Day, but he gets relief from the torment on Fridays and during the month of Ramaḍān because of the sacred character of these periods. The torment is of the flesh connected with the spirit, and of the spirit connected with the body, so the spirit suffers pain along with the body even though it has gone out from it. Believers fall into two classes. If [the deceased] has been obedient there will be no

[1] This word also is found in Sūra LXXXIII, and since formally it may be connected with the root meaning "high", the generally accepted theory is that as Sijjīn is the prison for evil souls in the lower regions, this is the abode of the souls of the Blessed in the heights.

[2] On the Jahmites and the Najjārites see p. 399.

[3] See p. 417.

[4] The popular tractates on eschatology make much of this question of the *ḍughṭa* or "squeezing" of the deceased in his grave. The common theory is that there is an expanding of the grave for the Blessed so that they lie in ease and quietness awaiting the Trump of Resurrection, while there is a corresponding narrowing ofthe grave, whose pressure and squeezing are a part of the torment to be endured by the evil as they await resurrection. The view expressed in the text is that even the righteous will experience some squeezing to the extent of their lapses from complete righteousness.

torment of the tomb for him, but he will suffer from the pressure and feel the fear and terror therefrom, because Allah has been a gracious benefactor to him but he has not been [truly] thankful for those benefactions. If he has been disobedient he will suffer both the torment and the pressure of the grave, but the torment will be cut off on Fridays. [Others say] that on Thursday nights he will suffer torment for one hour and [suffer] a single squeezing [from the pressure of the grave], after which the torment will be cut off and will not return till the Day of Resurrection.

The spirit, [we teach], will be connected with the body. Even if [the body] becomes dust the spirit will be connected with the dust, so that the spirit and the dust suffer pain together. This is proved by what is related of the Prophet—upon whom be Allah's blessing and peace—, how he said to 'Ā'isha—with whom may Allah be pleased—: "How will you be at the pressure of the grave and the questioning of Munkar and Nakīr?" Then he said [to her]: "O little reddish one, the pressure of the grave and the questioning of Munkar and Nakīr will to the believer be like coryllium to the eye when it is bleary, like the stroking of a mother's hand on the leg of her child." It is also related that the Prophet—upon whom be Allah's blessing and peace—said to 'Umar—with whom may Allah be pleased—: "How will you be when there come to you the two youths of the grave?",[1] and 'Umar answered: "Shall I be like as I am now, my intellect there with me?" "Yes", said the Prophet—upon whom be Allah's blessing and peace—, whereat 'Umar said: "Then I shall not mind it."

There is a proof that the torment of the tomb is something which the intelligence can accept. Do you not see that a sleeper's spirit goes out [from him] and yet remains connected with the body, so that he may suffer pain in a dream, and both the pain and the relief [therefrom] reach him? Also conversations take place in dreams because the spirit is connected with the body. It is related of the Prophet—upon whom be Allah's blessing and peace—that he was asked how the flesh suffers pain in the grave when there is no spirit in it, and he—upon whom be Allah's blessing and peace—answered: "In the same way as your tooth suffers pain when there is no spirit in it." [That is], the Prophet—upon whom be Allah's blessing and peace—informed his [questioner] that the tooth may be

[1] 'Umar was the second Caliph who succeeded Abū Bakr in the year 13 A.H. = 634 A.D. The text here has *fatayān*, "the two youths", but as the reference is obviously to Munkar and Nakīr, who are commonly called *fattānān*, "the two who put to the test", that is probably the word which should be in the text but has been misprinted as *fatayān*. See p. 216.

subject to pain because it is connected with the flesh, even though there be no spirit in it, and so, in like manner after death, because his spirit is connected with his body the body may feel pain.

A proof that the torment of the tomb is a fact is the verse (IX, 101/102): "We shall punish them twice, then they shall be sent back to a mighty[1] punishment", where the word "twice" means the punishment [endured] in this world and the punishment in the grave. It is not permissible to say that what is meant is the punishment in this world and then the punishment on the Day of Resurrection, for the verse goes on to say: "They shall be sent back to a mighty punishment", i.e. the punishment of the Day of Resurrection. It is related that Abū Ḥanīfa[2]—on whom may Allah have mercy—questioned his son Ḥammād about the torment of the tomb, and [Ḥammād] stated that it was a fact. Said [Abū Ḥanīfa]: "What proof have you for your statement?" He answered: "The verse (LII, 47): 'And verily, for those who do wrong, there is a punishment besides that', where the meaning is that there is a punishment besides that of Gehenna", by which he meant the torment of the tomb. It is related that the Prophet—upon whom be Allah's blessing and peace—said that there are three parts to the torment of the tomb, one third of it is due to backbiting, one third to slandering, and one third to [carelessness with regard to] urination.[3] It is firmly established by all these indications that the torment of the tomb is a reality. For the Muslim it is one of the possibilities, for the unbeliever one of the certainties.

Spirits [after death are divided into] four classes:

(i) The spirits of the Prophets come forth from their bodies and take their form, being like musk and camphor. They will be in Paradise, eating and drinking and enjoying themselves, and taking shelter at night in lamps hanging beneath the Throne.

(ii) The spirits of the Martyrs come forth from their bodies and [enter] into the bellies of green birds, eating and drinking and enjoying a pleasant life, as is indicated by the verse (III, 169/163): "Nay, alive with their Lord they happily enjoy ample provision." They too take shelter at night in the lamps suspended under the Throne.

(iii) The spirits of obedient believers are in meadows in Paradise, not

[1] The text here actually says "to a rude punishment", but IX, 101/102 has *'aẓīm*, "mighty". The *ghalīẓ*, "rude", in the text has been wrongly introduced from XXXI, 24/23, which is a parallel passage.

[2] See p. 385.

[3] The point here is that care must be taken that the clothes are not spattered during urination. See Wensinck, *The Muslim Creed*, p. 118, and Elder's translation of at-Taftāzānī, p. 100.

eating or enjoying themselves, but flying around in Paradise. The spirits of disobedient believers are [hovering] in the air between heaven and earth.

(iv) The spirits of unbelievers are in Sijjīn, in the bellies of black birds. Sijjīn is beneath the seventh earth.[1]

The spirits are nevertheless connected with their bodies [which lie in the graves], so that when He punishes their spirits they feel the pain by means of those bodies. Just as the sun is in heaven but its light is on earth, so the spirits of believers are in ʿIllīyūn and its light is connected with [their] bodies. Such a thing as this is possible. Do you not see the sun in heaven while its light is on earth? Likewise the spirit of a sleeper withdraws [from his body], yet in spite of that he feels pain if there was pain in [the dream], and relief therefrom reaches him, so that you can even hear men laugh in [their] dreams. There is an indication [of the truth] of this in the verse (XXXIX, 42/43): "Allah calls in the souls at the time of their dying."

The Muʿtazilites teach that the blood of the people of the Qibla (i.e. Muslims of whatever sect) may be lawfully shed in any one of four cases: (a) when they have committed mortal sins; (b) when they have introduced innovations [into religion]; (c) when they have drawn the sword against the Sultan; (d) when they have set at naught any incumbent duty *(farīḍa)*, i.e. have abandoned its practice, even though a man should consider the abandoning of the practice of such a duty to be lawful, nevertheless, by general consent, his blood may be shed. The truly orthodox people teach that the blood of the people of the Qibla may not be lawfully shed save in one of three cases. Should any one go out acting unjustly against the Sultan, the killing of him is permissible so long as he is making war, but if he abandons it he is to be let alone. This is in accordance with the verse (XLIX, 9): "If two parties of the believers fight one another...etc." Likewise, if anyone is found working corruption in the land, such as a bandit or a highway-robber, as is said in the verse (V, 37/33): "But the recompense of those who make war on Allah and on His Apostle, and spend their efforts in causing corruption in the land", [their recompense is that they be put to death]. So we teach that the shedding of the blood of the people of the Qibla is not lawful save in the cases we have mentioned, or if anyone is found causing corruption in the land by being a

[1] Just as there are seven heavens arching one above the other, so, according to one theory of the cosmos, there are seven earths in layers under one another, and just as there is a supernal region above the seven heavens there is an infernal region below the seven earths.

murderer (lit. a throttler), or anyone who has designs on the wealth or person of another, or is an innovator [in religion], for thereby he invites the people to innovation and so corruption is generated by him.

The truly orthodox people teach that there is no definite stipulation giving the Imāmate to ʿAli b. Abī Ṭālib [1]—with whom may Allah be pleased—nor to his progeny. The Rāfiḍites teach that the Imāmate was given by [a definite] stipulation to ʿAlī—with whom may Allah be pleased—, and that the Prophet—upon whom be Allah's blessing and peace—appointed him [his] executor, so that he was the [sole legitimate and proper] executor of the Apostle of Allah—upon whom be Allah's blessing and peace. The truly orthodox people teach that he was [his] executor in but one special thing, viz. in the matter of settling his finances, and executorship in one particular thing [such as this] does not make him executor for the whole of Islam. He would only have been [his] executor in all things if he had been a general executor, but ʿAlī—with whom may Allah be pleased—was not a general executor.

The Muʿtazilites teach that the making of a testament is an incumbent duty on everyone who comes to die. According to us, if his affairs are in good order and he has settled his finances the making of a testament is not an incumbent duty. He has the choice. If he wishes he may make a testamentary declaration, or if he wishes he may not. If, however, his affairs are not in good order, and he has not settled his finances, then [according to us] a testamentary deposition is an incumbent duty, because of men's rights.

The proof that the Imāmate was not given by definite stipulation to ʿAlī—with whom may Allah be pleased—nor to al-Ḥasan, nor to al-Ḥusain [his sons]—with both of whom may Allah be pleased—is that had there been such a definite text the Companions would have transmitted it to the Followers, the Followers to the pious [of the community], and the pious to us. We do not imagine that the Companions fell short in this [particular matter]. Do you not see that they have transmitted to us the regulations about troops fortifying themselves in hostile country, and other such matters of legal prescription, and the regulations concerning

[1] The two great parties in Islam are the Sunnis and the Shīʿites. The Sunnis have their succession of Caliphs at the head of the community, and by theory the Caliphs are elected, although for the greater part of the time they were members of dynastic groups where each Caliph received the office from that member of his family who preceded him. The Shīʿa groups all claim that the headship in Islam should have been kept in the family of the Prophet, passing from him to ʿAlī, his cousin and son-in-law, whose family has produced the Imāms whom the Shīʿites follow. The name Rāfiḍites, as mentioned on pp. 346, 378, is a general name to cover various Shīʿite sects.

religion which are connected therewith, so that it is most unlikely that they would have fallen short in this [matter of the Imāmate].

Another indication is the fact that when the Prophet—upon whom be Allah's blessing and peace—died, the Companions assembled in the portico of the Banū Sā'id and said: "We heard the Apostle of Allah—upon whom be Allah's blessing and peace—say: 'Whosoever dies seeing not an Imām [ruling] over him, is dying the death of the Times of Ignorance',[1] so it cannot be that a day pass without our seeing an Imām over us, even the Caliph, for he who does not truly see the Imām is in unbelief." The reason why this is so (i.e. why they are in unbelief) is because there are some among the regulations [laid upon all believers] whose being put into operation is bound up with [the presence of the] Imām, e.g. the Friday service [of congregational prayers], the two feasts (viz. those after Ramaḍān and Bairam), and the marriage of orphans. So everyone who disavows the Imām has disavowed the incumbent duties, and anyone who disavows incumbent duties may come to be in unbelief. So one of the Anṣār[2] arose and said: "Let there be an Emir from us, and an Emir from you." Thereupon Abū Bakr—with whom may Allah be pleased— arose and said: "My thought is that 'Alī—with whom may Allah be pleased— is well fitted for that, so my desire is to appoint him." But 'Alī—with whom may Allah be pleased—rose, and drawing his sword, said: "Rise! O Caliph of the Apostle of Allah—upon whom be Allah's blessing and peace. The Prophet—upon whom be Allah's blessing and peace— put you to the fore, so who is there who will put you to the rear? I was with the Apostle of Allah—upon whom be Allah's blessing and peace—yet he did not bid me do anything, but said: 'Bid Abū Bakr lead the people in prayer.' We were well-pleased with what seemed well-pleasing to the Apostle of Allah—upon whom be Allah's blessing and peace—in regard to our religious affairs, so shall we not be well-pleased [with the same person] in regard to our worldly affairs?" He named him Caliph of the Apostle of Allah—with whom be Allah's blessing and peace—because the Prophet—upon whom be Allah's blessing and peace—appointed him (lit. Caliphed him)[3] as his substitute to lead the people in prayers during his last days. So he (i.e. Abū Bakr) led the people in

[1] This phrase which conventionally translates the word *jāhiliyya*, used by Muḥammad for the pre-Islamic period of Arabian history, means that the Arabs of those days were following a way of life in ignorance of the better way of life which was available to men through Allah's revelation of His will to them. See p. 83.

[2] On the *anṣār* or "helpers" see pp. 365, 422. Emir *(amir)* means "prince".

[3] The Arabic title *khalīfa* is from the verb *khalafa*, and *istakhlafa* is "to appoint one as an agent or substitute".

prayer for seven days, according to one line of tradition, or for three, according to another line. At that [the people] swore allegiance to him unanimously, [and Abū Bakr became the first Caliph].

The appointment was duly confirmed, and then they set about burying the Apostle of Allah—upon whom be Allah's blessing and peace. When they had finished with the burying Abū Bakr rose to make a speech. He said: "I have become your Governor! I am not the best among you. Do you accept me?" Then arose 'Alī—with whom may Allah be pleased—and said: "How should we not accept you? seeing that the Prophet—on whom be prayers and peace—put you to the fore, who is he who will put you to the rear?" One day they came upon him (i.e. Abū Bakr) in the market-place selling a chemise of his wife that he might buy food, so they said: "We shall appoint you a salary from the public treasury." They set aside for him two dirhams daily, but he said: "I am but a feeble man, who cannot do two dirham's worth labour, so it would be wrong [for me] to take it." They therefore appointed for him daily a dirham and two dāniqs.[1] This he would take and put in an earthen pot, but secretly he would sell the furnishing of the house [for money] to spend. Then, when the day of his death came, he called for the pot, poured out all that was in it, and said to his daughter 'Ā'isha—with whom may Allah be pleased—: "Return it to 'Umar b. al-Khaṭṭāb—with whom may Allah be pleased—; I make a testamentary declaration to that effect."

He said: "In the name of Allah, the Merciful, the Compassionate. This is what I set forth in my testament, I, Abū Bakr, Caliph of the Apostle of Allah—upon whom be Allah's blessing and peace— on my last day in this world and my first day in the next. I appoint as Caliph over you 'Umar b. al-Khaṭṭāb. If he acts equitably that is what I have thought of him, but if he acts wickedly—none knows the hidden save Allah, [who has said] (XXVI, 227/228): 'Also those who do wrong will know anon with what an upsetting they will be upset.'" All of them were well-pleased with the appointment of 'Umar b. al-Khaṭṭāb—with whom may Allah be pleased—as Caliph, and 'Alī—with whom may Allah be pleased—was exceedingly well-pleased about it.

So his appointment of 'Umar—with whom may Allah be pleased—was confirmed. The only reason why Abū Bakr—with whom may Allah be pleased— chose him was because he had heard the Apostle of Allah—upon whom be Allah's blessing and peace— say: "Follow the example of those who come after me, Abū Bakr and 'Umar"—with both of whom

[1] A dāniq was the sixth part of a dirham. The word is derived from the Persian.

may Allah be pleased. It was ʿUmar who equipped armies and conquered territories. He conquered Khurāsān, and sent Aḥnaf b. Qais to Balkh which he conquered peacefully. It was said to him: "Do not cross to what is beyond the river (i.e. the Oxus)", so he said: "That is the province of ʿUthmān." Then Aḥnaf—with whom may Allah be pleased—went off and died in Merv. The Caliphate of ʿUmar lasted ten years. He was assassinated by Abū Lauza, a Christian slave of Mughīra b. Shuʿba.

Then it became a matter of consultation between ʿUthmān, ʿAlī, Ṭalḥa, az-Zubair and ʿAbd ar-Raḥmān b. ʿAuf. Saʿd—with whom may Allah be pleased—was absent. Ṭalḥa and az-Zubair withdrew, saying: "There is no need for us to be in the matter." Thus there remained but ʿUthmān, ʿAli and ʿAbd ar-Raḥmān. Said ʿAbd ar-Raḥmān: "I give you two my share, so will you permit me to choose one of you two?" They assented and gave him a delay of three days [during which] he was pursuing the people indefatigably in private and in public [to discover their opinions]. This resulted in his opinion being more inclined to ʿUthmān b. ʿAffān, so he said: "I have chosen ʿUthmān b.ʿAffān." Thereupon ʿAlī [officially] swore allegiance to him, as did the other Companions—with all of whom may Allah be pleased. He (i.e. ʿUthmān) was killed by the rabble. The Caliphate of ʿUmar and ʿUthmān—with both of whom may Allah be pleased—lasted twenty-two years, the Caliphate of Abū Bakr—with whom may Allah be pleased—two years, and the Caliphate of ʿAlī—with whom may Allah be pleased—six years. That makes in all thirty years, and there is a Tradition that the Apostle of Allah—with whom be Allah's blessing and peace—said: "After me the Caliphate will last for thirty years, after which it will become a kingdom."[1]

We do not teach that after [the assasination of] ʿAlī the Imāmate was by definite text given to [his sons] al-Ḥasan and al-Ḥusain. The Imāmate is [in our opinion] only assured by general consensus of the Muslims after Abū Bakr—with whom may Allah be pleased—had said: "The Imāmate is from Quraish" (i.e. the tribe to which Muḥammad belonged, and which controlled Mecca in his days). The Rāfiḍites teach that the Imāmate was given by definite stipulation to al-Ḥasan and al-Ḥusain after ʿAlī—with whom may Allah be pleased. The Shīʿites teach that ʿAlī

[1] It is hardly necessary to remark that this is a Tradition invented after the Umayyads had made the Caliphate dynastic, in order to explain that change. The first four Caliphs are commonly referred to as "the rightly-guided Caliphs", and later Islam highly idealized their period of office. The account above of the appointment of these Caliphs is largely fictitious and written under the influence of that idealization of all that happened in their days.

—with whom may Allah be pleased— was the [rightful] successor to the Apostle of Allah—upon whom be Allah's blessing and peace—and that the Emigrants and the Anṣār [1] were in unbelief when they appointed Abū Bakr [to be the first Caliph]. We teach that there is a general consensus that they were good Muslims before the death of the Prophet—upon whom be Allah's blessing and peace—and if anyone says that they were in unbelief after the death of the Prophet—upon whom be Allah's blessing and peace—it is on him to bring proof thereof.

A demonstration that Abū Bakr was the most excellent of the Companions: One proof of it is that [one day] ʿAlī was preaching from the pulpit in Kūfa when his son, Muḥammad b. al-Ḥanafiyya,[2] asked: "Who is the best of the community after the Apostle of Allah—upon whom be Allah's blessing and peace?" He answered: "Abū Bakr." "Then who?" he asked, and [ʿAlī] answered: "ʿUmar." "Then who?" He answered: "ʿUthmān." "Then who?" But he—may Allah be pleased with him—was silent. So [his son Muḥammad] said: "If you wish I will inform you about the fourth. It is you yourself." Then ʿAlī—with whom may Allah be pleased—said: "Your father is a man from among the Muslims." ʿAlī kept silent only because he did not want to praise himself.

Another indication is that the Prophet—upon whom be Allah's blessing and peace—used to seat Abū Bakr—with whom may Allah be pleased—at his right, and ʿUmar—with whom may Allah be pleased—at his left. Now the only possibilities are either that he did this hypocritically or [that he did it] to show preference. Now we cannot imagine that the Prophet—upon whom be Allah's blessing and peace—would do it hypocritically, for he had nothing to fear from either of them. Moreover both of them used to stand opposite him, and there is the fact that towards the end of his life [there were occasions when] he appointed ʿUmar as his deputy. All this points to the fact that he did it on the grounds of merit, for he appointed him as his deputy in the presence of all the Companions, quite otherwise than [was the situation] in the case of the

[1] The Anṣār, as already noted, were the group in Madīna who had invited Muḥammad there from Mecca and had promised him their support in that city. The Emigrants were the followers of Muḥammad who had emigrated from Mecca after he left in order to join his community in the new headquarters at Madīna. See p. 356.

[2] Al-Ḥasan and al-Ḥusain were ʿAlī's sons by Fāṭima, the daughter of the Prophet, but this Muḥammad was his son by a woman of the Ḥanīfa tribe who had been taken prisoner at the battle of Yamāma in 11 A.H. = 633 A.D., and whom ʿAlī had taken into his *ḥarīm*. A party grew up around him later, supporting his claim to the succession after the death of the two sons of Fāṭima.

appointment of Ibn Umm Maktūm as his deputy,[1] for [on that occasion] the Companions were on a warlike expedition with the Apostle of Allah—upon whom be Allah's blessing and peace.

The objection may be raised that it is related of the Prophet—upon whom be Allah's blessing and peace—that he once said to 'Alī—with whom may Allah be pleased—: "Thou art to me the same as Aaron was to Moses—on both of whom be blessings and peace—save that there will be no prophet after me." Now as the deputyship of Aaron [was something which] admitted no possibility of substitution, so the case is here [between Muḥammad and 'Alī]. The reply is that the [Prophet's] honouring him was not in the way you take it to be, for [it is well known that] the Prophet—upon whom be Allah's blessing and peace—[once] appointed 'Alī as his deputy over Madīna while he went out on one of the warlike expeditions, and thereat the evilly disposed said: "Verily the Prophet has turned his face from him and confined him to the house." This grieved 'Alī—with whom may Allah be pleased—, so the Prophet—upon whom be Allah's blessing and peace—said to him: "Thou art to me the same as Aaron was to Moses"—on both of whom be blessings and peace. Another indication [that their interpretation is not sound] is the fact that Aaron died before Moses, and so [their interpretation] would only be sound if he had said: "Thou art to me the same as Joshua son of Nun", for he was the [real] successor to Moses—on both of whom be blessings and peace.

One group of the Rāfiḍites teaches that the revelations [brought by Gabriel] were meant for 'Alī—with whom may Allah be pleased—but Gabriel—on whom be peace—made a mistake in [transmitting] the revelations. Another group of them teaches that ['Alī] was associated with [Muḥammad] in the prophetic office. All of these are unbelievers for they disavow both the text of the Qur'ān and the consensus of the community, for Allah has said (XLVIII, 29): "Muḥammad is Allah's Messenger." Some of them teach that 'Alī was more learned than the Apostle of Allah—upon whom be Allah's blessing and peace—and is in the position [with regard to him] that al-Khiḍr held to Moses—on whom be peace—[in the story in Sūra XVIII]. The answer to this is that saying [of the Prophet] which shows that such knowledge as he (i.e. 'Alī) had was from the

[1] The reference is probably to the expedition against the Banī Naḍīr in the year 4 A.H. Ibn Umm Maktūm was a blind man who could not go with the other Companions on these warlike expeditions, and there are several notices in the accounts of the expeditions which tell how he was left behind as the Prophet's deputy in Madīna while he and the other Companions were absent.

teaching of the Prophet—upon whom be Allah's blessing and peace—, [for he said]: "I am the city of learning and 'Alī is its gate."

Another indication [of the unsoundness of their teaching] is the fact that 'Alī was a saint *(walī)*, but the Apostle of Allah was a Prophet, and a Prophet ranks higher than a Saint. As for al-Khiḍr—on whom be peace—he had direct knowledge [of things divine], for Allah said (XVIII, 65/64): "Whom We had taught knowledge such as We have." He means there knowledge by inspiration *(ilhām)*, so that Moses was superior [to him] since he had [given him] a corpus of religious law and a [Scriptural] book, and he who has a [Scriptural] book and a religious law is superior [to him who has not]. A case in point is that of David and Solomon, where David is the superior.

Another group of them (i.e. the Rāfiḍites) teaches that there is never a time when there is no prophet on earth, and that this prophetic office came by inheritance to 'Alī—with whom may Allah be pleased—and his progeny, so that anyone who does not see that obedience to him [and his progeny] is an incumbent duty is in unbelief. The truly orthodox people teach that there is no prophet after our Prophet—upon whom be Allah's blessing and peace—for this is proved by Allah's words (XXXIII, 40): "and seal of the Prophets". It is related from Abū Yūsuf [1]—on whom may Allah have mercy—that he said: "If a pretender to prophecy comes forward laying claim to the prophetic office, should anyone demand from him proof [of his mission] he would [thereby show himself to] be in unbelief, for he would have disavowed the text [of Scripture]. The same is true of anyone who has doubts about him, for one demands a proof in order to make clear what is true from what is false, but if anyone lays claim to the prophetic office after Muḥammad—upon whom be blessing and peace—his claim cannot be other than false.

The Rāfiḍites teach that the Imām, [i.e. the standard Codex], is the Qur'ān which 'Alī b. Abī Ṭālib—with whom may Allah be pleased—assembled. The truly orthodox people teach that the Imām is the Qur'ān which 'Uthmān b. 'Affān—with whom may Allah be pleased—assembled. When the Prophet—upon whom be Allah's blessing and peace—died, Abū Bakr—with whom may Allah be pleased—assembled the Qur'ān and used to read it, but he did not apply himself to issuing it [in a standard form], because he was busied with warring against the people of Yamāma, and, [moreover], Abū Bakr occupied the Caliphate for only two years. When he died [such a standard Codex] was not issued by 'Umar—with whom may Allah be pleased—because he was busy with the conquest of

[1] See p. 413.

Khurāsān and other places. By the time of 'Uthmān—with whom may Allah be pleased—men had come to differ about the Qur'ān, so 'Uthmān—with whom may Allah be pleased—said: "Ye differ now about the Qur'ān, and those who come after you will differ even worse." Therefore 'Uthmān—with whom may Allah be pleased—sat down and brought out what Abū Bakr—with whom may Allah be pleased—had assembled, and issued it [officially as a standard text] to the Companions—may Allah's good pleasure be upon them all. So it is attributed to 'Uthmān—with whom may Allah be pleased—[only] because it was he who issued it. The Companions—with whom may Allah be pleased—agreed upon that [exemplar as a standard exemplar], so anyone who disavows a [single] verse of the Codex of 'Uthmān—with whom may Allah be pleased—is in unbelief, for the Codex of 'Uthmān—with whom may Allah be pleased—is that on which the Companions agreed—may Allah's good pleasure be on them all.

It must be recognized that all the books [of Scripture] which Allah has sent down [by revelation] to the Prophets and Apostles are the word of Allah uncreate. Of these there were a hundred scrolls *(ṣuḥuf)* and four books. [Of the Scrolls] Allah sent down fifty to Seth the son of Adam—on whom be peace. Thirty were sent down to Idrīs (Enoch)—on whom be peace; ten to Abraham—on whom be peace; and ten to Moses—on whom be peace—before the coming down [to him] of the Torah. It was called the Book of *Tasmiya* (Namings) and was [revealed] before the drowning of Pharaoh, then Allah sent down the Torah after the drowning of Pharaoh. Later Allah sent down the Zabūr to David—upon whom be peace—, and then He sent down the Injīl to Jesus[1]—on whom be peace—who was the last of the Prophets among the Children of Israel. Then Allah—may He be praised and exalted—sent down the Qur'ān to Muḥammad—upon whom be Allah's blessing and peace—, who is the last of the Messengers. Anyone who disavows a [single] verse of any of these Scriptures is in unbelief.

Should anyone say: "I believe in all the Messengers", and then disavow one of the messengers about whom there is no [Scriptural] text, saying: "This one does not belong to them", he would not be in unbelief though he would be in heresy. This holds so long as he does not enter

[1] Injīl is an attempt to reproduce the word "Evangel", and Zabūr would seem to be a corruption of the Hebrew word for a "Psalm". By Injīl Muḥammad meant the New Testament in the hands of the Christians of his day, just as by Torah he meant the whole of the Old Testament in the hands of contemporary Jews. See the articles "The Qur'ān as Scripture" in the *Muslim World* for 1950.

another religion, but if he enters another religion he is an apostate and may be killed. An indication that belief in all the Scriptures is a condition [of true faith] is to be found in the verse (II, 136/130): "Say! we believe in Allah and in what has been sent down to us." Belief in all the Messengers is also such a condition, for Allah has said (II, 177/172): "Being upright is to believe in Allah, and the Last Day, and the angels, and the Books and the Prophets."

Be it known, moreover, that the Prophets—on whom be peace— are one hundred and twenty-four thousand, and the Apostles among them are 313, according to the line of Tradition from Abū Dharr [1]—with whom may Allah be pleased—going back to a statement of the Apostle of Allah —upon whom be Allah's blessing and peace. In some of the Traditions the [number of the] prophets is given as a thousand thousand, or two hundred thousand and more, but the correct thing in this matter is for you to say: "I believe in Allah and in all the Prophets and Apostles, and in all that has come from Allah [by way of revelation] according as Allah willed." By thus doing you will not affirm someone to be a Prophet who was not, nor will you affirm someone not to be a Prophet who was.

One group of the Rāfiḍites teaches that 'Alī—with whom may Allah be pleased—and his Companions will return to this world to take vengeance on their enemies and to fill the earth with equity as it has been filled with injustice.[2] The truly orthodox people teach that no one who has died will return to this world till the Day of Resurrection,[3] for there is no valid indication of any such a return [as a thing to be expected]. The proof of the truth of what we teach is in the verse (XX, 55/57): "From [the earth] did We create you; and into it We shall return you; and from it We shall bring you forth once more", where it does not say "twice". Similar is the verse (XXXVI, 31/30): "Have they not seen how many generations before them We have destroyed? They, indeed, will not return to them." Of similar purport is the saying of him—on whom be peace—: "After death there is naught but Paradise and Hell."

There is a group of the Shī'ites which teaches that wine is not prohibited

[1] Abū Dharr al-Ghifārī, an early convert, on whom see Sir Wm. Muir, *Caliphate*, p. 211.

[2] This is the doctrine that 'Alī is to be the Mahdī who will appear towards the end of time as one of the movements which usher in the final Judgment.

[3] This is carefully phrased so as not to deny the doctrine of the return of Jesus before the Day, for according to the Qur'ān Jesus did not die, but was taken up alive into heaven. Similarly those who teach that both Enoch and Elijah are to reappear and take part in the events which usher in the Day of Judgment rely on the teaching that these persons also escaped death and were translated.

but merely disapproved. Allah has said (V, 93/94): "There is no blame on those who believe and have done righteous works for anything they may have eaten." Likewise they teach that sodomy is lawful, since Allah calls it disreputable but does not actually forbid it in His book. Allah said, [addressing the people of Lot's day] (XXIX, 23/28): "And in your assemblies ye commit what is disreputable." Likewise [this group] considers dancing and singing and poetry as lawful, even saying that this was the teaching of Mālik b. Anas—on whom may Allah have mercy—the Imām of the people of Madīna. The truly orthodox people teach that all such things are forbidden, on the ground of the statement of him—on whom be Allah's blessing and peace—: "All forms of play are forbidden save three: (1) archery; (2) a man's dalliance with his wife; (3) horsemanship." Allah has said (XXIII, 115/117): "Or do ye think that We created you only for amusement?"

As regards wine, we teach that wine is forbidden, for there is a Tradition to that effect, namely the statement of him—on whom be peace—: "Wine has been made a forbidden thing for you, whether little of it or much." So intoxication from any kind of drink is forbidden. Allah has said (VII, 33/31): "Say! my Lord has forbidden only indecencies, both what is open and what is hidden, and the guilty thing, and trespass", where by the "guilty thing" He means wine, as is proved by the verse of the poet:

> "Wine did I drink till my intellect went astray,
> That is how the guilty thing gets away with men's intellects."

The reply to their argument based on the verse (V, 93/94) is that we teach that this verse was revealed concerning a people who were drinking wine after the verse of prohibition had been revealed but before the news of it reached them. They were grieved about the matter so Allah sent down this verse. As regards tambourine-playing we teach that ash-Shāfiʿī—on whom may Allah have mercy—allowed it at weddings for the purpose of announcement but not for amusement.

Some will say that both wine and temporary marriage *(mutʿa)* were considered allowable in the beginnings of Islam, and if we say that that [freedom of action] could be abrogated we are making a retreat from what existed at first, which would make it seem as though Allah ordered a matter and then had another opinion about it. But to initiate [a matter] and then go back [on it] cannot apply to Allah, for initiating and then going back [on a thing] arise from one who is ignorant and does not know the final outcome of affairs.

The reply [to this] is that we teach that we do not agree that in abrogation there is any initiation and then going back, but that on the contrary there is in it both a bringing to fulfilment and completion of the original decision, and a bringing into force of another decision. It thus becomes clear that the first decision was not of eternal validity but was temporal, belonging to that [particular] time, though we [at the time] did not know that. Now, however, it is clear to us that the first decision has come to an end and has been fulfilled. There is an indication of [the truth of] this position in the fact that Allah will raise the dead on the Day of Resurrection, yet one does not say that in this there is an initiation and a going back on anything. Nay rather the decision with regard to the dead has come to its end, and there comes into force another decision. So it is here. It cannot be said that in abrogation there is an initiation and a going back on anything, but rather that in it the decision with regard to what is abrogated comes to an end, and there comes into force the decision concerned in that which abrogates.

Should the question be raised as to what use there is in abrogation, we teach that the usefulness of abrogation lies in its amplifying things, lightening things, and easing things for His servants. An example is [to be found in the case] that at the beginning Allah ordered each of the Muslims to fight with ten of the unbelievers and evil-doers, in the verse (VIII, 65/66): "If there be of you twenty who patiently endure they will overcome two hundred." Then later He lightened the burden, and dropped eight from each ten by saying (VIII, 66/67): "Now has Allah made it lighter for you, and He knows that among you there is weakness." He called it a lightening, and so it is here. The abrogating [decision] is more useful in the present situation because it has to be put into effect in the present situation, and it must be believed in, while the one that has been abrogated does not have to be put into operation in the present situation, but it must be believed in likewise.

The Jews—whom may Allah curse—teach that abrogation of religious law is not possible, but according to the truly orthodox people it is possible. They (i.e. the Jews) offer proof and say that the fact that something is commanded necessarily means that it is helpful, and the fact that something is forbidden necessarily means that it is harmful. If that is so, then the fact that God has given commands and prohibitions in the Torah indicates that it is concerned with something helpful [to humanity]. If then it were possible for Him to forbid something that He has commanded in the Torah, that would mean that He had commanded in the Torah something harmful. But that cannot be, for God is wise, He knows the final outcome of affairs, and it is not possible that His action should be described as foolish.

The reply to this is that we teach that if Allah gives commands about some matter, that necessarily means that it would be helpful at that time, but does not necessarily mean that it would be helpful at all times. An example is [that of] food and drink, which assuredly are helpful in a state of hunger, but are not necessarily helpful in a state of repletion. Another example is [that of the] physician who orders for the sick person different medicines at different times, yet that involves no introduction of a new opinion, but is to ensure real helpfulness at that [particular] time. So it is here. Allah is more compassionate to His servants than is a tender physician, and when He appointed the Torah as a religious law in the time of Moses—on whom be peace—that was something helpful, [and continued such] until the completion of the Mosaic dispensation. Then [after the completion of the Mosaic dispensation] the helpfulness was in the Zabūr until the completion of the Davidic dispensation. Then [after that] the helpfulness was in the Injīl until the completion of the Christian dispensation.[1] Finally the helpfulness was in the Qur'ān in this age of our Prophet Muḥammad—upon whom be Allah's blessing and peace.

One group of the Rāfiḍites teaches that temporary marriage *(mut'a)* is lawful. This [*mut'a* marriage] is the hiring of a woman for intercourse. Allah has said (IV, 24/28): "To those of them ye have enjoyed thereby give their hire," [a verse] which directs payment of hire for the enjoyment [of them] pure and simple quite apart from marriage. The truly orthodox people teach that temporary marriage is forbidden, like as wine [is forbidden]. It was made allowable in a single place under necessity and then abrogated by the verse (XXIV, 2): "The fornicatress and the fornicator, scourge them each a hundred stripes." As for the verse [which they quote], we teach that it was abrogated by the verse (XXIV, 32): "So marry the single females among you."

One group of them teaches that when a man dies and becomes decomposed matter, Allah creates for him another body into which He causes the spirit to enter. Also they teach that the body is to the spirit much as a garment is to the human frame. They base their teaching on the verse (IV, 56/59): "Whenever their skins are thoroughly cooked We will substitute for them new skins." We teach that what is meant is change

[1] This curious idea that the Psalter (Zabūr) and the Gospel (Injīl) comprised a body of legislative enactments such as are in the Torah and in Muḥammad's own Qur'ān, derives ultimately from the mistaken idea Muḥammad had of the nature of Scripture. See the articles "The Qur'ān as Scripture" in the *Muslim World* for 1950.

of form and attributes not change of their essence. There is an indication of [the correctness of] this in the verse (XIV, 48/49): "A day when the earth will be changed to another earth, and the heavens [as well]", by which is meant a changing of its attributes not a changing of its essence.

The Ibāḥites [1] teach that if a man has reached the extreme limit of love [for things divine] the external acts of worship such as almsgiving, prayers, fasting, pilgrimage, etc. fall away so far as he is concerned, so that from then on his worship is by thought, and by his light he mounts up to heaven, enters Paradise, embraces the Ḥūrīs and has intercourse with them. The truly orthodox people teach that anyone who puts belief in this is in unbelief, for even the Prophets do not of themselves mount up to the heavens. It is as Allah said with reference to the case of our Prophet, Muḥammad—upon whom be Allah's blessing and peace—(XVII, 1): "Glory be to Him Who took His servant by night." So also in the case of Jesus—upon whom be peace—(IV, 158/156): "Nay, but Allah raised him to Himself." Also in the case of Adam—upon whom be peace—He said (II, 35/33): "Dwell thou and thy spouse in the Garden", and in the case of Idrīs (=Enoch), He said (XIX, 57/58): "And We raised him up to a high place." So [also] with others than these it is certain that they did not mount up [of themselves].

There are some who teach that Allah created women and wealth to be common property among men, so that if anyone has need of another person's wealth it is proper for him to take it, since Adam and Eve—on both of whom be peace—died and left their wealth equally to us all. The truly orthodox people teach that a Muslim's wealth is not lawful save for his own disposal. Allah has said (IV, 29/33): "And do not consume your wealth among you in vanity, except there be trading by mutual consent on your part." The Traditions available on this matter are many. Among them is the saying of him—upon whom be Allah's blessing and peace—: "It is for the one who makes claim to produce the clear evidence, it is for the one who disavows to take the oath."

Some of them teach that if a man has reached the extreme limit of love [for things divine] it is lawful for him to make use of the wives and handmaidens of other men, for they are as it were the sweet basil [2] [he has been promised that] he shall smell. Such a man, [they teach], is Allah's beloved, and the women and the handmaidens are Allah's, and no lover

[1] These were the "Libertines" of Islamic theology, who, according to their enemies, taught that all things were lawful. They correspond to the Antinomian groups in Christian theology. See Hughes, *Dictionary of Islam, sub voce.*

[2] This is a reference to Sūra LVI, 89/88.

refuses his beloved anything he may desire. The truly orthodox people teach that women are not lawful [for anyone to make use of] save by marriage, nor are handmaidens [lawful in that way] save by ownership, or by marriage should their owner give them in marriage to someone else, for then they would be lawful to that one though they are [still] handmaids of their owner. This [unlawfulness we are speaking of] is indicated by the verse (XXIV, 2): "The fornicatress and the fornicator, scourge each of them a hundred stripes." Now Mā'iz [one of the Companions]—with whom may Allah be pleased— fornicated, so he was stoned", whereas had [the fornication] been lawful the man would not have deserved stoning.

Some of them teach that if a man has reached the extreme limit of love He may commit the mortal sins and Allah will not make him enter the Fire, for no one who enters the Fire, [they teach], will ever come out of it, just as one who enters Paradise [will never be ejected]. This sect of theirs is a vain thing. In answer [to them] we teach that if a man has committed a sin, whether he be a saint or no saint, he is [thereby] subject to the will of Allah. If He wills He may forgive him, or if He wills He may punish him. That will be according to His justice or His generosity [in any particular case]. Allah has said (III, 129/124): "He forgives whom He will, and He punishes whom He will." If He punishes a man to the measure of his sin and then withdraws him from the Fire, out of His mercy or in response to the intercession of the Prophets, that is like [the case of] gold which is put into the fire to remove its dross, so that after his dross [of sin] has been removed he is withdrawn from [the Fire] and not left therein. This is different from the case of the unbeliever, who is like the fuel prepared for keeping the fire alight, and who is there to be burned and for no other reason. The case is different also from that of the Blessed who are for Paradise, since no one enters Paradise save [after having been made] pure from all filth and sinfulness, whether by watching over the soul [so as to avoid sin], or by repentance. See ye not that the Prophet—upon whom be Allah's blessing and peace— has said: "Do you think that Paradise is a common cattle-enclosure? By Allah, ye will never enter in till ye have become like [pure white] hail-stones." The Fire will burn up the uncleanness of sin and remove it from the disobedient believer, in order that he may go out from [the Fire] after this has been removed. This is different from Paradise which does not remove the purity of him who enters that he may go out from it.

Some of them teach that when a man has reached the extreme limit of love, matters of command and prohibition no longer concern him, so he is free to do as he wishes. If a lover of Allah had to choose between unbelief and suicide he would choose to kill himself, for he is a lover of Allah to the extreme limit of love, and everyone who is not a hypocrite is a lover of Allah. The truly orthodox people teach that no human is ever beyond being concerned with matters of command and prohibition. Indeed, he who draws closest to Allah, is the one who is most keenly aware of his legal responsibility in this matter. A case in point is the Prophet [himself]—upon whom be Allah's blessing and peace—who was His lover and His true friend, who stood [worshipping] till his two feet became swollen, yet to whom were issued commands, such, e.g. as His saying (XXXIII, 1): "O thou Prophet, show piety towards Allah, and obey not the unbelievers," and again (LXXIII, 2, 3): "Rise up [worshipping] at night, save a little, half of it," and again [to the Apostles in general] (XXIII, 51/53): "O ye Apostles, eat of the good things, and act righteously." In like manner Adam—on whom be peace—who was His true friend, was nevertheless forbidden to eat from the tree, for He said (II, 35/33): "Draw ye not near to this tree", and when he did eat from it Allah reproved him and drove him from the garden. Similarly when David—on whom be peace—looked at the wife of Uriah Allah reproved him for it.

It is related from 'Ā'isha—with whom may Allah be pleased—that she said: "The Apostle of Allah—upon whom be Allah's blessing and peace—did not have his fill of wheaten bread for three days in succession more than twice in all his life." It is also related that the Prophet—upon whom be Allah's blessing and peace—said: "Seventy Prophets died in one day from hunger and vermin." This [tribulation on earth] is because enjoyment without bearing the anxiety of legal responsibility is promised as [one of the delights] of Paradise, for Allah has said (LXIX, 24): "Eat and drink with full enjoyment by reason of what ye paid in advance in days gone by", where the meaning is: "Ye fasted in days of great heat." Allah ordered His servants to fast, saying (II, 185/181): "So whoever of you sees the month, let him fast in it", and (II, 183/179): "O ye who believe, fasting is prescribed for you." Therefore so long as a man is a believer, possessed of his intelligence, of full age, he is not free from the obligation to fast. So it is with regard to all the other incumbent duties, such as prayer, almsgiving, etc. for Allah has said (II, 43/40): "Now observe prayer, and pay the *zakāt*." There is exemption for one on a journey or sick, for either of whom eating and drinking [during the days of the fast] are allowed by the verse (II, 184/180): "Then a number of other days" (i.e. in place of those missed), and then in the same verse:

"But that ye should fast is better for you." There is an exemption also for the menstruating woman and the woman in childbirth, who is required neither to fast nor to perform the prayers. It is, indeed, allowable for her to fast but not for her to perform the prescribed prayers. Regarding her performing the prescribed prayers there is a prohibition, because of her falling short of fulfilling [the regulations thereof], [1] but there is no prohibition against her fulfilling [the regulations] for fasting.

There are some of them who say that if one has reached the extreme limit of love [for things divine], he has no further concern with command and prohibition. Yet the prophets did not escape such concern, [so some of them take the position], so it is related, that the rank of Saint is higher than the rank of Prophet, but whoever says that a Saint is higher than the Prophet—upon whom be Allah's blessing and peace—is a disbeliever in Allah, the High, the Mighty, [and is one] for whom [is stored up the] "torment of a punishment painful" (XXXIV, 5).

The astrologers teach that affairs of earth are connected with the twelve signs of the zodiac and the seven planets Saturn, Jupiter, Mars, Venus, the Sun, Mercury, and the Moon. They teach that these zodiacal stations and planets govern the affairs of people on earth, so that everyone who knows about that matter (viz. astrology) can recognize what is helpful to himself, is able to incline to what is good for him, and avoid what is bad, and may know when he will die.

The truly orthodox people teach that these zodiacal stations and planets, as well as the sun and the moon, are "bodies under constraint to service" (VII, 54/52), which have no governance over anything, seeing that the One Who governs affairs is Allah. It is as He said (VII, 54/52): "Sun, moon and stars are constrained to service by His command." Someone may say that this science of the stars was considered a true science in the days of Idrīs (Enoch)—on whom be peace—and that anyone who says that it has been abrogated must bring a proof thereof, since there is proof [that it was not abrogated] in what Allah said as He gave information about Abraham (XXXVII, 88/86 ff.): "He gave a look at the stars, and said: 'In truth, I am sick' ", i.e. he found an indication from that look at the stars that he would be sick. The answer is that he knew [already] that he would be sick, since, as the Prophet—upon whom be Allah's blessing and peace—said: "No believer is ever free from times of poverty or sickness or weakness." As regards the days of Idrīs—on whom be peace—we teach that the stars [as a matter of fact] have no

[1] Her condition makes her incapable of having the state of ritual purity demanded for prayers, but no such ritual purity is demanded for fasting.

governance, but that Allah [at that time] gave information in their Book [of Scripture]: "If such and such a star reaches such and such a place, know that such and such will happen", so they recognized in this instruction from Allah. [This science of astrology], however, has been abrogated since the days of Solomon—on whom be peace—[in whose reign on one occasion] the sun returned after night had come on, and the calculation [of the astrologers] was all disordered for them.

He—upon whom be peace and blessings—said [on one occasion]: "Allah has a beautiful custom of giving the lie to astrologers." It is said that an astrologer is as a sooth-sayer, and a sooth-sayer is as a magician, and a magician is as an unbeliever, and an unbeliever will be in the Fire. There is an indication of the vanity of the sciences of astrology and medicine in the verse (XVIII, 51/49): "I did not have them witness the creation of the heavens and the earth, nor the creation of themselves, nor was I taking as helpers those who lead astray." No knowledge is to be attained save by one of two ways, either by ocular evidence, or by being informed by some trustworthy informant. Now the Prophet—upon whom be peace—was given information about it, (i.e. about knowledge), but [ordinary] men in their seeing things are all on the same level, save that some people put their confidence in their own opinions, are forsaken by their intelligence, and so go wildly astray and are in obvious loss. It has been [well] said:"He who would protect himself by his wealth will diminish; he who would protect himself by his character will be humble; he who would protect himself by his intelligence will go astray; but he who protects himself by his Lord will be illustrious."

The astrologers teach that the sun, moon and stars are in the fourth heaven. The truly orthodox people teach, as do the Commentators on the Qur'ān, that they are in the lowest heaven. This is indicated by the verse (XXXVII, 6): "We have adorned the lower heaven with an adornment of stars", and by the verse referring to the story of Dhū'l-Qarnain (Alexander the Great) (XVIII, 86/84): "Until he reached the setting place of the sun, he found it setting in a muddy spring", for [Alexander assuredly] did not reach the fourth heaven.

Now Allah is the One Who guides to the orthodox faith.

AN ISLAMIC CATECHISM, THE *AJWIBA*

Catechisms for the instruction of youth in the principles and practices of their religion are in use in Islamic countries as they are in Christian lands. There are, however, no official Islamic Catechisms formally sanctioned as authoritative by religious bodies and corresponding to such documents as the *Westminster Catechism*, the *Augsburg Confession* or the *Full Catechism* of Philaret. Many Muslim theologians of repute have prepared such catechisms, some of which have had wide use throughout the world of Islam. In more modern days, with the reorganization of the educational system in Muslim countries, what may be regarded as semi-official Catechisms have been issued for use in Schools and given the sanction of local Ministries of Education. A good example is the Turkish *Müslüman çocuğunun kitabı*, compiled by Nurettin Artam and Nurettin Sevin, and printed at Istanbul in 1948 by the Press of the Ministry of Education. Many of these modern Catechisms show an awareness of Western criticism of Islam, but that here translated, the popular *al-Ajwiba al-jalīya*, (the Clear Answers), by Muḥammad b. ʿAbdallah al-Jurdānī, an Egyptian religious leader from Damietta, represents the old standard orthodoxy of the Shāfiʿite rite, little affected by modern ideas. The edition from which the translation has been made is that edited and published by the Cairo bookseller Aḥmad al-Malījī, bearing the imprint: "Fifth edition. Cairo, 1328 A.H." (= 1910 A.D.). 8vo. 72 pp.

CLEAR ANSWERS

to Religious Questions according to the Authorities of the Shāfiʿite Rite

It is an excellent book, of benefit to every student, but especially to the pupils in the higher and elementary Schools, composed by Muḥammad ibn ʿAbdallah al-Jurdānī of Damietta, the Shāfiʿite, whom may Allah—exalted be He—pardon.

In the Name of Allah, the Merciful, the Compassionate

Praise be to Allah for the gracious gift of Faith and Islam, and blessings and peace be upon our Master, Muḥammad, who made clear to us the principles [of religion] and its rules.

He who hopes to attain those things that are desired, Muḥammad ibn ʿAbdallah al-Jurdānī, says:

This book, a work that should be useful to every student, and particularly to the pupils of the higher and elementary Schools, is something that one of my beloved friends has been urging me to write. May Allah grant both him and me a good end. I have named it *Clear Answers to Religious Questions according to the Authorities of the Shāfiʿite Rite*, and I beg Allah—exalted be He—to grant me success in this endeavour by the favour of His Prophet and all his family and Companions. He has power to do whatever He wishes, and to answer He is able.

An exposition of faith

Question: What is Faith *(īmān)?*

Answer: Faith is that you should believe in Allah—exalted be He—and in His angels, His Books, His Apostles and the Last Day, and that you should believe in the predestination of both good and evil.

Q.: What is the meaning of faith in Allah—exalted be He?

A.: It is that you should believe firmly in your heart, be convinced of and confidently affirm that He is the true God who brought into existence all created things, that to Him are to be ascribed the attributes of perfection, that He is free from all defects and inabilities, and that some of His attributes must be known in particular.

Q.: What are those attributes?

A.: They are: existence, primordialness,[1] everlastingness, non-phenomenality,[2] self-subsistence,[3] oneness, power, will, knowledge, life, sensibility,[4] speech, and it is not possible that there be attributed to Him the opposites of these.

Q.: What are those opposites?

A.: They are—non-existence, recentness, ephemeralness, phenomenality,[5] need of anything,[6] plurality, inability, unwillingness, ignorance, death, insensibility,[7] speechlessness. He—may He be exalted—may,

[1] *qadīm*, which means "ancient", i.e. He is eternal in the sense that there never was a time when He was not. The word for "everlastingness" is *baqā'*, which means "abiding", i.e. He is everlasting in the sense that there never will be a time when He will not be. See p. 348.

[2] *mukhālafa li'l-ḥawādith* means "differing from things which are phenomena".

[3] *qiyām bi nafsihī* means "standing up by Himself", i.e. for His subsistence He needs the help of no other.

[4] Lit. "hearing and seeing", i.e. He is able to sense what is going on.

[5] Lit. "likeness to things which are phenomena".

[6] Lit. "need of place and causer".

[7] Lit. "deafness and blindness".

in His own right, do everything that is possible or may leave it undone. Nothing is by any means incumbent on Him [1]—exalted be He. The Most High has said (XXVIII, 68): "Thy Lord creates what He wills, and exercises choice."

Q.: What is the meaning of faith in the angels?

A.: It is that you should firmly believe in and confidently affirm their existence; that they are honoured servants of light nature who never disobey Allah in what He commands them but do what they are bidden; that they are bodies of light, i.e. are created from light, able to take various forms and cover great distances in but a moment of time, and so numerous that Allah Himself—exalted be He—alone knows their number. There are ten of them it is necessary to know by their names.

Q.: Who are the ten?

A.: They are: Gabriel, the one entrusted with revelation; Michael, who is in charge of the rains; Isrāfīl, who has charge of the Trump;[2] 'Izrā'īl, who has charge of the taking of [men's] spirits;[3] Munkar and Nakīr, who are entrusted with the questioning [of the dead] in the grave; Riḍwān, who is the Grand Chamberlain *(khāzin)* of the Garden (i.e. Paradise); Mālik, who is the Grand Chamberlain of the Fire (i.e. Hell); the two recorders of good and evil deeds, whose names are Raqīb and 'Atīd. Among them also are the Throne Bearers who at present are four, but to whom four will be added on the Day.[4]

Q.: What is the meaning of faith in the Books?

A.: It is that you should firmly believe and confidently affirm that they are the speech of Allah—exalted be He—sent down to His Apostles—upon whom be blessings and peace and that all that they contain is truth. Among them are the Torah of our Master Moses, the Injīl of our Master Jesus, the Zabūr of our Master David, and the

[1] Though He has power to do anything yet there is nothing that He *must* do. He can do or leave undone as He chooses.

[2] It is he who will blow the Trump of Doom and the Trump of Resurrection on the Last Day. See p. 220.

[3] *arwāḥ*, the plu. of *rūḥ*, which means "spirit" or "soul", and also is used for the vital principle in living beings.

[4] *yaum al-qiyāma* is "the day of rising up", i.e. our Resurrection Day, but it is commonly used to mean not only the resurrection but the whole series of events of the Last Day, including the preliminaries of Judgment, the Judgment itself and its execution. When it is used in this wider sense it is convenient to translate it simply by "the Day".

Furqān,[1] i.e. the Qur'ān, of our Master Muḥammad. May Allah's blessing and peace be upon him and upon them all.

Q.: What is the meaning of faith in the Apostles?

A.: It is that you should firmly believe and confidently affirm that Allah —exalted be He—sent them to mankind to guide them to the way of the truth, and that four things must be rightly asserted of them, and four things declared impossible on their part.

Q.: What are the four things that must be rightly asserted of them?

A.: They are truthfulness, faithfulness, intelligence and delivery of the message.

Q.: What are the four things that must be declared impossible on their part?

A.: They are untruthfulness, unfaithfulness, stupidity and the concealment of the message. It is permissible to assert of them that they are subject to such human traits as would not lead to any shortcoming in [the fulfilment of] their high office, e.g. [need for] food and drink, any sickness which is not repulsive, walking in the streets, buying and selling, lawful marital intercourse with women, and sleeping with the eye though not with the heart. Allah—exalted be He—supported them by wondrous miracles, such as our Master Moses' changing a staff into a serpent, or water bursting from the fingers of our Prophet —on whom be Allah's blessing and peace. The greatest of his (i.e. Muḥammad's) miracles is the Qur'ān, which men and jinn were incapable of imitating.[2]

Q.: What is the number of the Apostles?

A.: They are many. None knows their number save Allah—exalted be He. Nevertheless it is incumbent to recognize twenty-five of them by their names.

Q.: Who are these twenty-five?

A.: They are Adam, Idrīs, Noah, Hūd, Ṣāliḥ, Lot, Abraham, Ishmael, Isaac, Jacob, Joseph, Shuʿaib, Aaron, Moses, David, Solomon, Job, Dhū'l-Kifl, Jonah, Elijah, Elisha, Zachariah, John, Jesus and Muḥammad. May Allah's blessing and peace be on them all.[3]

[1] *torah* is the Hebrew "Torah", *injīl* is an attempt to represent the Greek *evangelion*, the "Gospel", *zabūr* is apparently meant to represent the Hebrew *mizmōr*, "Psalm", and *furqān*, "that which distinguishes," particularly between good and bad, is a name used for the Qur'ān in II, 185/181; III, 4/2. See p. 447.

[2] This is a reference to such passages as X, 38/39; XI, 13/16; LII, 34, where unbelievers are challenged to produce anything like what Muḥammad is proclaiming.

[3] Most of these names are those of familiar Biblical characters. The unfamiliar names

Q.: What is the Last Day, and what is meant by faith in it?

A.: The Last Day is the Day of Resurrection, and the meaning of faith in it is confident assertion of its reality as a coming event, and of all that it will comprise, such as the resurrection of created beings, their giving an account [of deeds done in the flesh], the weighing of their deeds, their passing over the Bridge, and the entering of some of them justly into the Fire, and some of them by grace into the Garden.[1]

Q.: What is the meaning of faith in predestination?

A.: It is that you should firmly believe and confidently affirm that Allah —exalted be He—decreed both good and evil before the creation, that all that has been and all that will be is by the predetermination of Allah—exalted be He—by His decree and will. In the Traditions [there is a saying] that faith in this drives away both anxiety and grief.

An exposition of Islam

Q.: What is Islam?

A.: It is that you should bear witness that there is no deity save Allah, and that you should bear witness that Muḥammad is the Apostle of Allah; that you should perform the prayers, pay the legal alms, fast [during] Ramaḍān, and go on pilgrimage to the House (i.e. the Meccan shrine) if you are able to make the journey thereto.

Q.: What is the meaning of the two acts of witnessing?

A.: The meaning of the first is that you should know, confidently affirm and acknowledge that there is no true object of worship in existence save Allah—praised and exalted be He. The meaning of the second is that you should know, confidently affirm and acknowledge that Muḥammad is the Apostle of Allah, whom He sent to all mankind. His age at that time was forty years. He is the most excellent of created beings, be they in heaven or be they on earth. He—upon whom be Allah's blessing and peace—was born in Mecca, the en-

---

are: *Idrīs*, who is generally considered to be Enoch; *Hūd* and *Ṣāliḥ*, who are apparently ancient Arabian worthies; *Shu'aib*, who is thought to be Jethro, but who may be but another ancient Arabian worthy; *Dhū'l-Kifl*, "lord of the portion", who is thought by some to be Ezekiel, by others Obadiah, but who again may be but an ancient Arabian worthy. *Zachariah*, it should be noted, is not the Old Testament prophet of that name, but is the father of John the Baptist, who in the list is mentioned immediately after him.

[1] This writer usually writes *janna*, "Garden", when he means Paradise, and *nār*, "Fire", when he means Hell. In translating we shall keep his "Garden" and "Fire" when there seems any particular reason, but shall otherwise use our more common Paradise and Hell.

nobled city, which he left not till he had reached the age of fifty-three years, when Allah—exalted be He—bade him emigrate from it to Madīna, the illuminated. So he emigrated from it to Madīna where he died at the age of sixty-three.

An exposition of his genealogy, his progeny, his wives and his concubines—upon him be Allah's blessing and peace

Q.: What was his genealogy on his father's side?

A.: He was the son of ʿAbdallah, son of ʿAbd al-Muṭṭalib, son of Hāshim, son of ʿAbd Manāf, son of Quṣaiy, son of Ḥakīm, son of Murra, son of Kaʿb, son of Lu'ay, son of Ghālib, son of Fihr, son of Mālik, son of an-Naḍr, son of Kināna, son of Khuzaima, son of Mudrika, son of Ilyās, son of Muḍar, son of Nizār, son of Maʿadd, son of ʿAdnān.

Q.: What was his genealogy on his mother's side?

A.: He was the son of Āmina, daughter of Wahb, son of ʿAbd Manāf, son of Zuhra, son of Ḥakīm, the one mentioned above in the genealogy of his father.

Q.: How many children did he have?

A.: Seven, three males and four females. In order of their birth they were: Al-Qāsim, then Zainab, then Ruqaiya, then Fāṭima, then Umm Kulthūm, then ʿAbdallah, then Ibrāhīm. All of them were by his wife Khadīja, save Ibrāhīm, who was by his concubine, Mary the Copt.

Q.: How many wives did he have?

A.: They were twelve: Khadīja daughter of Khuwailid, Sawda daughter of Zamʿa, ʿĀ'isha daughter of Abū Bakr, Ḥafṣa daughter of ʿUmar, Zainab daughter of Khuzaima, Hind daughter of Abū Umaiya, Zainab daughter of Jaḥsh, Juwairiya daughter of al-Ḥārith, Raiḥāna daughter of Zaid, Ramla daughter of Abū Sufyān, Ṣafīya daughter of Ḥuyaiy, and Maimūna daughter of al-Ḥārith. Some hold that Raīḥāna belongs to the concubines not to the wives.

Q.: How many concubines did he have?

A.: They are three: Mary the Copt, who was presented to him by the Muqawqas, ruler of Egypt; Nafīsa, whom Zainab daughter of Jaḥsh gave to him, and a third; Zulaikha of the Quraiẓa. According to those who hold that Raīḥāna was a concubine they would have been four.

An exposition of prayers

Q.: What are prayers,[1] and what is the meaning of performing them?

A.: Ṣalāt is the technical expression for the words and the acts beginning with the *takbīr* and ending with the *taslīm*,[2] [gone through] in accordance with special regulations. The meaning of performing them is the carrying them through without omitting any of the proper and approved essentials,[3] and avoiding anything that would invalidate [the prayers].

On the number of obligatory prayer services, and an exposition of the times for them, and the customs to be observed both before and after them

Q.: How many prayer services is it necessary to observe each day and night?

A.: Five prayer services are incumbent upon every Muslim who is of age and in the possession of his proper senses. Children should be bidden observe them at the age of seven, and at the age of ten should be beaten for omitting them, that thus they may become accustomed to observe them.

Q.: What is the first prayer service?

A.: It is the morning prayer. The number of its *rak'as* [4] is two, but they are customarily preceded by two *rak'as*. The time for it is [the period] from the breaking of the true dawn [5] till the rising of the sun.

Q.: What is the second prayer service?

A.: It is the midday prayer. The number of its *rak'as* is four, which are

[1] The word is *ṣalāt*, a technical term, derived from Aramaic, and used for formal liturgical prayers as distinguished from *du'ā'* "supplication", which is the word used for extempore prayers. The other technical word here, *iqāma* means "setting up", but perhaps our best translation is "performing".

[2] The *takbīr* is the pronunciation of the words *Allāhu akbar*, "Allah is very great", with which the prayer service begins, and *taslīm* is the pronunciation of the *salām* with which the prayer service ends.

[3] *arkān* are literally "supports", "props", "pillars", and as a technical term the word means those essential parts of any ritual performance which must be observed if the performance is to be valid. See pp. 473-475.

[4] *raka'a* means "to bow down" and a certain complex of recitals and bowings in the prayer service is called a *rak'a*. When one such *rak'a* has been completed it is gone through again and then again to make up the number of *rak'as* obligatory and customary for that prayer service. The number of *rak'as* in any particular prayer service is divided into the *farḍ* which are obligatory, and the *sunna* which are customary.

[5] That is as distinct from what is known as the false dawn. The time given for each of these prayer services states the beginning point and the end point of the period within which that particular prayer service should be performed.

customarily preceded by four and followed by four. The time for it is from the [commencement of the] decline of the sun until the shadow of any elongated object[1] reaches the length of that object.

Q.: What is the third prayer service?

A.: It is afternoon prayer. The number of its *rakʿas* is four, which are customarily preceded by four. The time for it is the period from the end of the noon period till the setting of the sun.

Q.: What is the fourth prayer service?

A.: It is the evening prayer. The number of its *rakʿas* is three, which are customarily preceded by two and followed by two. The time for it is from the setting of the sun till the redness of the evening twilight disappears.

Q.: What is the fifth prayer service?

A.: It is the night prayer. The number of its *rakʿas* is four, which are customarily preceded by two and followed by two, and then by the *witr*,[2] the least number [of *rakʿas*] for which is one *rakʿa* and the most is eleven. The time for it is from the disappearance of the redness of the evening twilight till the breaking of the true dawn.

An exposition of the conditions for the validity of a prayer service

Q.: What are the conditions for the validity of a prayer service?

A.: They are five: that the body of the one who prays be in a state of ritual purity from *ḥadath*; that his body and clothing and the place where he is be in a state of ritual purity from uncleanness;[3] that his pudenda be covered; that he be facing the *qibla*;[4] and that he has entered one of the [prayer] periods explained above.

An exposition of ḥadath, its causes and what is made unlawful by it

Q.: What is *ḥadath*?

1 He means any object whose measurements are not equal. A cube or a sphere, e.g. would be useless for their height, breadth and thickness would all be the same.

2 *witr* means an odd number, but the word is used technically as the name of a prayer service with an odd number of *rakʿas* which it is *sunna* to perform after the night prayers.

3 The impurity of *ḥadath* will be explained in succeeding questions. The other technical term *najāsa* means any uncleanness or filthiness in the commonly understood sense.

4 The *qibla* is the prayer-direction. Wherever a Muslim may be he has to face towards the shrine at Mecca during his services of prayer. See pp. 68 and 474.

A.: It is of two kinds, a lesser, which makes *wuḍu'* or *tayammum* [1] obligatory, and a greater, which makes *ghusl* or *tayammum* obligatory. There are causes for both kinds.

Q.: What are the causes of the lesser?

A.: They are five: (1) anything coming out of the rectum, and anything save semen from the genitals; (2) sleep, save what is possible while sitting upright on the ground; (3) unconsciousness caused by drunkenness, sickness, madness or swoon; (4) touching the human pudenda by the inner palm or the fingers; (5) the coming together of the epidermis of male and female who have reached the age of lustful desire and are not [within the] prohibited [degrees of relationship]. These five things make *wuḍu'* necessary and render five things unlawful [till *wuḍu'* is performed].

Q.: What are those five things?

A.: Prayers, circumambulation,[2] [listening to] the Friday sermon, touching the Holy Book *(muṣḥaf)*,[3] and carrying the same.

Q.: What are the causes of the greater *ḥadath*?

A.: Six things: (1) the emission of semen. This may be recognized either by its [actual] ejaculation, or by the pleasure felt at its emission, or by the presence of its smell, which when it is moist is like the smell of dough or date-palm pollen and when it is dry like the smell of white of egg. (2) Sex intercourse by the insertion of the penis into the vulva or anus, whether of human or animal, and even if no semen descends. (3) Childbirth. (4) Menstruation, namely the blood which comes from the vagina of any female who has reached the age of nine years, the shortest [period of whose flow] is a night and a day and the longest fifteen days, though usually [it lasts] six or seven [days]. (5) After-birth, namely the blood which comes as a consequence of giving birth to a child, the shortest [period of whose flow] is a moment, and the longest sixty days, though usually [it lasts] forty days. (6) Death. These six make *ghusl* necessary, and the first three of them render eight things unlawful till *ghusl* has been performed.

Q.: What are those eight things?

A.: They are the five things already mentioned which are rendered unlawful by the lesser [*ḥadath*, to which are to be added] reading the

[1] *wuḍū'* is ritual ablution by water; *tayammum* is ritual ablution by sand or earth; and *ghusl* is a complete bathing of the whole body. These will be explained later.

[2] I.e. the circumambulation of the sacred shrine at Mecca during the pilgrimage ceremonies. See p. 501.

[3] Lit. "codex", a word used for an individual copy of the Qur'ān.

Qur'ān, tarrying in a mosque, or even frequenting one. Menstruation and afterbirth render twelve things unlawful.

Q.: What are those twelve things?

A.: They are the eight things already mentioned together with fasting, divorce proceedings, marital intercourse, and fondling between the navel and the knees.

An exposition of ritual purification

Q.: What is ritual purification?

A.: It is of five kinds: viz. *wuḍu'*, *ghusl*, *tayammum*, removal of filthiness, and purification after natural evacuations.

An exposition of wuḍu'

Q.: What is *wuḍu'*?

A.: It is the use of pure water on particular bodily members. With regard to it there are elements that are obligatory and others that are customary, and there are things which render it invalid.

Q.: What is pure water?

A.: It is that which has not been defiled, has not been used already for some [other] incumbent duty, whose taste and colour and smell have not been altered by mixture with any other pure thing such as musk, saffron, rosewater or flowers.

Q.: What are the elements in *wuḍu'* which are obligatory?

A.: They are six: (1) the intention *(niyya)*, whose place is in the heart. It is customary for this to be uttered, e.g. by saying: "It is my intention to remove *ḥadath*" or "to perform the incumbent duty of *wuḍu'*"; (2) the washing of the whole face; it is necessary for the intention to accompany the beginning of the washing as a part thereof; (3) the washing of the hands [and arms up] to the elbows; (4) wiping part of the head [with the wet hand]; (5) washing the feet and the ankles; (6) [doing all this in proper] order, so that a beginning is made with the washing of the face contemporaneously with the [expression of] intention, then washing the hands, then wiping the head and then washing the feet. It is also laid down as a condition of its validity that there be no interruption, and that the water flow upon the members.

Q.: What are the customary elements in *wuḍu'*?

A.: They are many. Among them are the cleansing of the teeth with the tooth-stick and washing the palms of the hands at the beginning, and commencing the washing by [pronouncing] the *tasmiya*[1] with the tongue, and expressing intention in the heart of [performing] the customary elements of *wuḍu'* and then uttering it. Among them are the rinsing of the mouth, snuffing water up the nostrils, wiping the whole of the head, washing the ears along with the face-[washing], and wiping them along with the head-[wiping], and likewise after it, with fresh water. [Among them also are] finger-combing the thick hair of the beard and cheeks, though the thin hair needs must be combed with the fingers. Among them is giving precedence to the right over the left in washing the hands and the feet, and rubbing the members and contiguous parts during the washing, and going over whatever has to be washed three times. Also among them is the use of *adhkār*[2] (invocations) over the prominent members.

Q.: What are those invocations?

A.: They are that one should say at the washing of the hands, after the basmala:[3] "Praise be to Allah for Islam and for His grace. Praise be to Allah who has made water a purifying agent and Islam a light. O Lord, with Thee I take refuge from the evil suggestions of the satans,[4] and with Thee, O Lord, I take refuge should they be present. Allahumma, preserve my hands from all disobedience to Thee." So at the time of the rinsing of the mouth one should say: "Allahumma, keep me occupied with remembering Thee and thanking Thee and worshipping Thee in goodly wise." At the snuffing of water into the nostrils [one should say]: "Allahumma, grant that I may smell the perfume of Paradise." At the washing of the face [one should say]: "Allahumma, make my face white on the Day when Thou whitenest and blackenest faces." At the washing of the right arm [one should say]: "Allahumma, grant that I may receive my book in my right hand, and give me an easy accounting."[5] At the washing of the left arm [one should say]: "Allahumma, give me not my book in my left

[1] *tasmiya* or "naming" consists in the pronunciation of a formula invoking the name of Allah.

[2] *dhakara* means "to remember" and so a *dhikr* (plu. *adhkār*) is literally a remembering, but the word is used as a technical term for the calling to mind of the blessings and favours of Allah.

[3] I.e. the phrase: "In the name of Allah, the Merciful, the Compassionate."

[4] There is a reminiscence here of Sūra XXIII, 97/99.

[5] The reference is to Sūra LXXXIV, 7–10: "As for him who is given his book in his right hand, he will be reckoned with by an easy reckoning.... as for him who is given his book behind his back he will invoke destruction." The book in question is each man's record book which he will have to present at Judgment. See p. 219.

hand or behind my back." At the wiping of the head [one should say]: "Allahumma, forbid my hair and skin to the Fire [of Hell]." At the wiping of the ears [one should say]: "Allahumma, make me one of those who hearken to what is said and follow what thereof is best." At the washing of the two feet [one should say]: "Allahumma, make my feet firm on the Bridge [1] on that Day when feet shall slip." It is also good that one should say after completing it (i.e. the *wuḍu'* ablution): "I bear witness that there is no deity save Allah, the One who has no partner, and I bear witness that our Master Muḥammad is His servant and His Apostle. Allahumma, make me one of those who repent, make me one of those who are purified. Glory be to Thee, Allahumma! By Thy praise I bear witness that there is no deity save Thee. Thy forgiveness do I seek. To Thee do I turn in penitence." Then one should recite Sūra XCVII: "We, indeed, sent it down", together with the Throne Verse (II, 255/256), and then pray two *rak'as*, expressing in both of them the intention to observe the *sunna* elements of *wuḍu'*, and the same in the case of *ghusl.*

Q.: What are the things which render *wuḍu'* invalid?

A.: They are the five things which are its cause, as above mentioned. The occurrence of any one of these will make it invalid.[2]

An exposition of ghusl

Q.: What is *ghusl*?

A.: It is bathing the body with pure water along with an expression of intention. Thus one who is polluted [from sex-intercourse] expresses the intention of removing the legal impurity, one who is [impure because] menstruating [expresses the intention] of removing the [legal impurity of] menstruation, the one with after-birth that of removing the [legal impurity of] after-birth. It is quite correct for each one to express the intention of removing all the greater *ḥadath* (i.e. without specifying which particular kind). Conditional for its validity is the running of the water on the body, and the absence of any impediment which would interfere with its reaching it. Among its customary elements are the washing of the palms of the hands beforehand,

[1] The reference is to the Bridge which all have to cross after their deeds have been weighed in the Balance, and from which those who slip fall into Hell. See pp. 433-434.

[2] That is, if *wuḍu'* purification for prayer has been performed and any one of these five things happens before the prayer service is started that *wuḍu'* is invalidated and it has to be performed again for the person to be in a state of ritual purity such as is demanded for prayers.

along with pronunciation of the *tasmiya* by the tongue and an expression of intention in the heart to observe the customary elements of *ghusl*. Then one should rinse the mouth, snuff water into the nostrils, perform a complete *wuḍu'*, and then pour the water on the body, rubbing it and washing it thrice and finger-combing the light hairs. The heavy hair must needs also be finger-combed if otherwise the water would not get well into it.

An exposition of tayammum

Q.: What is *tayammum*?

A.: It is the use of sand *(turāb)*[1] on the face and hands to take the place of [the water of normal] *wuḍu'* or *ghusl* when water is unavailable, or is needed for satisfying the thirst of a venerated animal, or when there is fear of harm arising from its use in cases of sickness or wounds.

Q.: How is it performed?

A.: It is performed by smiting your two palms on the ground or on a pillow or some such mat so that the *turāb* may adhere to them, while you express the intention of doing what is permitted for the requirements of prayer. Then with it you wipe your whole face, occupying your mind the meanwhile with the intention. Then you smite a second time and wipe your arms to the elbows. Conditional for its validity is that it be performed within the proper times for prayer, be preceded by the removal of whatever uncleanness there may be on the body, that this be only by pure sand which itself is dusty, and that there be no impediment which would hinder it from reaching the members. Sunna elements in it are that but little sand be used, that the fingers be separated during the process of smiting, and that the fingers comb one another after the wiping. Any ring [on the fingers] must be removed so that the sand may reach what is beneath it.

Q.: What invalidates it?

A.: It is invalidated by whatever invalidates *wuḍu'*, by the disappearance of that which prevented the use of water, and by the sight of water if *tayammum* was being performed for lack thereof.

Q.: What is accomplished by a single performance of *tayammum*?

A.: By it is accomplished [the fulfilment of the] preliminaries for a single

[1] *turāb* means "dust", but the original regulation in Sūra V, 6/8 ff. seems to have envisaged the use of sand when water was not available.

obligatory cult performance, whether it be of prayer or circumambulation or Friday sermon. If a second such is desired there must be a [separate] *tayammum* for it. As regards the supererogatory (i.e. non-obligatory) cult performances a single performance of *tayammum* suffices for them all, and a *tayammum* performed for an obligatory cult performance may include them also.

Q.: Is there any condemnation for one who practises *tayammum*?

A.: Yes, if he practises *tayammum* because of the cold, or if [he uses the excuse that there is] lack of water and then goes and prays in a place where water will normally be found, though if he prays in a place where water is generally lacking, or where its presence or absence are equally likely, there is no condemnation.

An exposition of [*what is meant by*] *uncleanness and how it may be removed*

Q.: What is *najāsa* (uncleanness)?

A.: It is of three kinds: (1) gross—namely the uncleanness of the dog or the pig or what comes from them; (2) light—namely the urine of a child under two years and whose nourishment has not gone beyond milk; (3) medium—what is other than these, which covers various things.

Q.: What are these various things?

A.: They are many. Among them are manure, urine, blood, pus, vomit, all kinds of fluid intoxicants, milk that is not used for human consumption, *wadā* and *madhā* the former of which is a thick, pearly-white fluid which exudes [from the genitals], usually after urination, but also when one is carrying something very heavy, and the latter a thin, whitish or yellow fluid which exudes [from the genitals], usually when there has been a stirring of lustful desire which has not gone as far as [the orgasm of] pleasure. Among them are any dead things save [the dead bodies of] humans, fish or locusts. Some include among them hair, fur, wool, feathers, since such things have a certain uncleanness. Any part which may be removed from a living animal is [to be treated] like the dead thereof, unclean [if it is unclean], clean [if it is clean], but any part which may be removed from a human, a fish or a locust is clean. Any part which may be separated from other things is unclean save the hair, fur, wool and feathers of what is used as food, for they are clean.

Q.: How may gross [uncleanness] be removed?

A.: Its removal may be effected by washing what has been in contact seven times in pure water, using pure sand *(turāb)* in one [of the seven washings]. Those washings which remove the traces of the thing itself are to be counted as one [washing], and there needs must be six washings after it.

Q.: How may light [uncleanness] be removed?

A.: Its removal may be effected by sprinkling pure water on whatever has been in contact, till it is all covered, even though [the water] does not flow off, provided that the traces of the thing itself had been removed from the place before the sprinkling either by drying it off or by giving a powerful squeeze so that there remain no moisture which can be separated out.

Q.: How may the middling [uncleanness] be removed?

A.: Should it be invisible, namely [an uncleanness] which leaves no certain sign or trace in the way of taste or colour or odour, then its removal may be effected by the running of pure water once over that which has been in contact. Should it, however, be noticeable, namely something that has left a clear sign or trace as described above, then its removal may be effected by the removal of what is noticeable from the place where it has been in contact, even though it be necessary to use some such thing as soap. It is no matter if there remain a colour or an odour which resists removal.

An exposition of istinjā'[1]

Q.: What is the ruling about *istinjā'*?

A.: It is necessary after every voiding of excrement from the anus or the genitals, though not in the case of semen. It is effected by [the use of] water or stones, and the combination of the two is preferable. If one should desire to confine oneself to one of the two then water is preferable. The essential thing in *istinjā'* is to use a sufficient quantity in cleansing the parts that it may reasonably be assumed that the uncleanness has been removed. The sign of this is generally the appearance of hardness after softness. If the *istinjā'* has been by means of stones, because one was confined to that, purification is conditional on five things.

Q.: What are those five things?

A.: They are: (1) that the excrement be not allowed to dry or transferred

[1] Lit. "seeking delivery from". It is the technical term for purification after natural evacuations.

from the place where it came to rest; (2) that there be no foreign matter added thereto; (3) that [the rubbing by the stone] do not proceed beyond the orifice in question; (4) that it be a triple wiping each one of which goes over the place with three clean stones or with three applications of one clean stone; (5) if cleansing is not effected by the three applications then as many more must be applied as will effect it. It is no matter if some trace is left which can only be removed by water or by small pebbles, for that is pardonable.

An exposition of the covering of the pudenda

Q.: What are the pudenda which must be covered during prayer services and likewise during circumambulation [of the Kaʿba]?

A.: In the case of a male or a slave-girl they are whatever is between the navel and the knees. In the case of a free woman it includes all her body save the face and the hands. The covering should be so complete as to prevent any glimpse of its colour. The incumbent thing is that the covering should be from above and from the sides not from below, so that should they be seen from his collar-opening when he is bowing [in the prayer service], for example, that would be harmful, in contradistinction to their being seen from below his gown when he is prostrating, for that would do no harm. It is needful, however, for a woman to cover her legs from below, for were they to be seen from below the bed while she is standing thereon it would be harmful.

Q.: I have come to know about the [covering of the] pudenda during prayers and circumambulation, but what about the pudenda on other occasions?

A.: In the case of a man; as concerns his privacy they are the genitals and the anus, as concerns the view of his women-folk who are forbidden to him and his fellow males they are whatever is between the navel and the knees, as concerns the view of strange women it is his whole body even though he be a decrepit old man. In the case of a woman; as concerns her privacy and the view of men who may [legitimately] enter the *ḥarīm,* and her fellow believing women, they are whatever is between the navel and the knees, as concerns the view of unbelieving women it is all her body save what is normally visible during the daily tasks, viz. the head, the face, the neck, the two arms as far as the upper arm, and the legs as far as the knees, as concerns the view of strange men it is her whole body without anything at all being excepted even though she be an old woman ugly to behold. Everything the viewing of which is forbidden when it is attached [to the person] is equally forbidden when it is unattached, so men are forbidden to look at a woman's hair when it is unattached and vice versa. Everything which is forbidden to the sight is also forbidden to the touch, so a man is forbidden to touch the hand of a woman and vice versa.

An exposition of the qibla and of having it before one

Q.: What is the *qibla* which it is necessary to have before one at the time of prayer services?

A.: It is the illustrious Ka'ba,[1] which it is necessary to have one's breast facing while standing and sitting [during prayers], which one would have before one's face and breast when reclining, before one's face and soles, i.e. the soft lower parts beneath the feet, when lying on one's back. What is taken into account here is a true, accurate facing, with a drawing near to it in thought though far from it in body. [The *qibla*] may be recognized by various things.

Q.: What are these things?

A.: They are many. One of them is to watch for the official *miḥrābs*[2] which are set up to be seen by the one possessing sight, or to be touched by the blind or [by one who is] in the dark. Another is to keep the star called Quṭb[3] behind the left ear if you are in Egypt, behind the right ear if you are in 'Irāq, but the one who is in Yemen keeps it in front of him somewhat to his left, and one who is in Syria puts it behind him somewhat to his left.

An exposition of the essentials of prayer

Q.: What are the essentials *(arkān)*[4] of prayer?

[1] The Ka'ba is the central shrine in the holy city of Mecca. To face the Ka'ba in prayer is commanded in the Qur'ān in II, 142/136 ff.

[2] Every mosque has a *miḥrāb*. Generally it is a niche in the wall, or a mark on the wall, set there to indicate the direction in which one should face in order to be facing the Ka'ba at Mecca.

[3] I.e. the Pole Star.

[4] These are the frequently mentioned "pillars" of prayer. *arkān* is the plu. of *rukn* "pillar", but in legal texts it means those things which must be included in a transaction for that transaction to be legally valid. Here it means those things which must be included in a prayer service for that service to count as a service validly performed. See n. 3 p. 463.

A.: They are thirteen. The first is the standing *(qiyām),* which is incumbent on one who is able. If one is unable [to stand upright] let him pray sitting, if he is unable [to do that] then let him pray reclining, and if he is unable [even to recline] let him pray lying on his back.[1] The second is the intention *(niyya),* namely that one should say: "I express my intention of praying the obligatory morning prayer", or "I express my intention of praying the obligatory noon prayer", and so on. The third is the *takbīra* of making sacred at the first *rakʿa.* It [consists of saying]: "Allah is most great." Needs must the intention be in mind at the time of this *takbīra.*[2] The fourth is the recitation of the Fātiha (i.e. the opening Sūra of the Qur'ān) during the standing position for every *rakʿa.* The fifth is the bowing *(rukūʿ)* at every *rakʿa,* in which one must bend till his palms reach his knees, and pause quietly with his limbs resting in this position at least long enough for [him to say]: "Subḥān Allah" (glory be to Allah). The sixth is the straightening up at every *rakʿa* so that one resumes the standing position and pauses quietly therein. The seventh is the prostration *(sujūd),* twice in every *rakʿa,* in which one places his forehead, his knees, the inner part of his palms and the inner part of his toes to the ground. Needs must the forehead be uncovered and press heavily upon [the ground], while the buttocks are raised higher and he pauses there quietly. The eighth is the sitting *(julūs)* between the two prostrations in every *rakʿa,* and pausing quietly therein. The ninth is the sitting at the final *rakʿa,* viz. the second at morning prayers, the third at evening prayers, and the fourth at the others. The tenth is the testifying *(tashahhud)* during the above-mentioned sitting. It consists in saying *taḥiyyāt* [3] to Allah, then: "Peace be upon thee, O Prophet, and Allah's mercy and blessing. Peace be upon us and upon all pious worshippers of Allah. I bear witness that there is no deity save Allah, and that Muḥammad is the Apostle of Allah." The eleventh is [calling down] blessings on the Prophet—upon whom be Allah's blessing and peace—after finishing the testifying. It [consists in saying]: "Allahumma, grant blessing to Muḥammad." The twelfth is the *taslīm,* [4] which consists in saying

[1] This explains the details in the answer to the question about the *qibla,* where directions are given as to how to face the *qibla* when sitting, reclining or lying down.

[2] It is called the *takbīra* of sanctification or making sacred because by its utterance the one who prays cuts himself off for the time being from profane life and its interests and devotes himself to the world of sacred things till the prayer service is completed.

[3] *taḥiyyāt* are expressions ascribing eternal existence to Allah alone.

[4] Lit. "the giving of peace".

once: "Peace be upon you." The thirteenth is that all the above should be done in proper order as we have mentioned them.

An exposition of the customary elements [1] *in prayer*

Q.: What are the customary elements in saying prayers?

A.: They are of two kinds, known respectively as *ab'āḍ* and *hay'āt.*

Q.: What are the *ab'āḍ*?

A.: They are five things. The first is testifying *(tashahhud)* during the second *rak'a* of every prayer that has three or four *rak'a*s. The second is to pray for blessings on the Prophet after it. The third is to pray for blessings on the Prophet's family after praying for blessings on him in the final act of testifying. The fourth is [to say] the *qunūt* at the rising erect in the second *rak'a* of the morning prayer every day, and at the rising erect during the final *rak'a* of the *witr* during the second half of the month of Ramaḍān. The fifth is to ask blessings and peace on the Prophet, his family and his Companions after the *qunūt.*

Q.: What is the *qunūt*?

A.: It may consist in any formula containing eulogy and supplication, such as: "Allahumma! forgive me, O Forgiving One", but the form preferred is that you should say: "Allahumma! guide me among those whom Thou hast guided; pardon me among those whom Thou hast pardoned; take me as a friend among those whom Thou hast taken as friends; give me blessing in what Thou has bestowed; preserve me from the evil of that which Thou hast decreed, for Thou dost prescribe but no one prescribes to Thee. No one may be humbled whom Thou dost take in charge, nor may any one to whom Thou art hostile be exalted. Blessed art Thou, O our Lord, and exalted. To Thee be praise for what Thou hast prescribed. I seek forgiveness from Thee, and to Thee do I turn in penitence." Then you should say: "May Allah's blessing and peace be upon our Master Muḥammad, and upon his family and his Companions."

An exposition of what is required in a prostration of unmindfulness

Q.: If any one should omit any of the above-mentioned *ab'āḍ* what should he do?

[1] *sunan* which, though not obligatory in the first degree as are the *arkān,* are nevertheless obligatory for a pious Muslim since Tradition says they were the custom *(sunna)* of the Prophet. See p. 154.

A.: There is no obligation in such a case. His prayers are valid whether the omission was witting or unwitting. In either case, however, it is customary for him to perform a prostration of unmindfulness at the end of his prayers before saying the *salām*. This consists of two prostrations with an expression of intention in his heart before prostrating.

Q.: Is this prostration [of unmindfulness] customary on any other occasion?

A.: Yes. It is customary where [the worshipper is afraid that] something may have dropped out, though [in such a case] the doing of it in addition would be unobjectionable. For example, suppose that in a prayer of four *rak'a*s doubt arises [in the worshipper's mind] whether he has performed the *rak'a*s three or four times, since [the validity of the prayer] depends on the correctness of the number, three would be short, so [to make sure] he ought to add a *rak'a*. In such a case a prostration of unmindfulness would be customary. It is customary also in other situations, as for example in the case of the *muṭawwalāt*.[1]

Q.: What are the *hay'āt* of a prayer service?

A.: They are many, but should the one praying omit any of them his prayer service is still valid, and he should make no prostration of unmindfulness on account of them. Among them are the raising of the hands at the *takbīra* of sanctification, and [a similar raising of the hands] at every bowing *(rukū')* and rising erect, also at the standing for the first testifying. Among them is the placing of the palm of the right hand on the back of the left hand below the heart but above the navel during the standing. Another is to sit for a rest each time one rises from a second prostration. Another is to say after the *takbīra* of sanctification: "Great is Allah; very great, and greatly to be praised. Glory be to Allah both in the morning and in the evening." Another is to say the *ta'awwudh*[2] before repeating the Fātiḥa, and the *ta'mīn* after [repeating it], at every *rak'a*. Another is to recite some verses of the Qur'ān after the *ta'mīn* at morning prayers and at the beginning *rak'a*s of all other prayer services. Another is to recite with a loud voice both the Fātiḥa and the portion from the Qur'ān which is recited after it at night and at morning prayers, but to recite them

[1] I.e. prayer services made unusually long. During the month of fasting, e.g. a pious Muslim may undertake prayers of as many as forty *rak'a*s instead of the usual number. In such cases there is always much danger of miscounting, and so the prostration of unmindfulness is customary.

[2] *ta'awwudh* or "taking refuge" is to repeat the phrase: "I take refuge with Allah from Satan the stoned." *ta'mīn* is the pronunciation of the Amen.

softly during the daytime prayers. Another is to pronounce the *takbīr fi 'l-hawā'*[1] at every bowing *(rukūʿ)* and every prostration *(sujūd)*, at the rising from each prostration, and at the first testifying. Another is that at each bowing *(rukūʿ)* one should say three times: "Glory be to my Lord, the Mighty One", and at the rising therefrom: "May Allah give ear to him who praises Him", at the coming erect: "O our Lord, to Thee be praise", at the prostration: "Glory be to my Lord, the Highest One," three times, and at the sitting between the prostrations: "O Lord, forgive me, have mercy on me, restore me, raise me up, give me sustenance, guide me, preserve me and pardon me." Another is to use the completest [possible] form of testifying and praying for blessings on the Prophet—upon whom be Allah's blessing and peace—at the final *rakʿa.*

Q.: What is this completest form?

A.: It is that one should request of Allah *taḥiyyāt, mubārakāt, ṣalawāt, ṭayyibāt,*[2] [saying]: "Peace be upon thee, O Prophet, and Allah's mercy and blessing. Peace be upon us and upon all pious servants of Allah. I bear witness that there is no deity save Allah, and I bear witness that our Master, Muḥammad, is the Apostle of Allah. Allahumma! send blessings on our Master Muḥammad, and on the family of our Master Muḥammad, as Thou didst send blessings on our Master Abraham, and on the family of our Master Abraham; and send blessedness on our Master Muḥammad and on the family of our Master Muḥammad, as Thou didst send blessedness on our Master Abraham and on the family of our Master Abraham in the worlds. Thou art the Praiseworthy, the Glorious One." It is customary that, after [having said] that, one should make in one's own words petition for whatever one may wish, though [to make use of a form of supplication that has been] handed down by tradition is preferable. Such a [traditional] form is: "Allahumma! I take refuge with Thee from the torment of the tomb, from the torment of the Fire, from the trials *(fitna)* of both life and death, and from the *fitna* of the false Messiah."[3] Then one should salaam to his right and to his left, saying at each salaam: "Peace be upon thee and the mercy of Allah."[4]

[1] Lit. "saying *Allāhu akbar* into the air". It means only that the *takbīr* is pronounced aloud at these points mentioned.

[2] I.e. phrases requesting honour, happiness, blessings and good things.

[3] *al-masīḥ ad-dajjāl* is that Antichrist whose appearance and whose success in leading men astray is one of the signs that the Last Day draws near. See p. 352.

[4] These salaams are addressed to the Recording angels who, according to popular belief, sit one at the right shoulder and one at the left. See p. 47.

An exposition of the things which invalidate prayers

Q.: What are the things which invalidate prayers?

A.: They are ten things. (1) The first is the greater or lesser *ḥadath.*[1] (2) The second is the body or clothes of the one who prays or the place [where he is praying] being affected by uncleanness *(najāsa).* (3) The third is the uncovering of his pudenda in any way. (4) The fourth is the utterance of any intelligible sound, or two sounds should they be unintelligible, other than [words of] recollection and supplication.[2] (5) The fifth is the occurrence of [any one of] a number of actions, such, for example, as three steps, or three movements of the foot or the hand or the head. [In this connection] the putting out and drawing back of the hand, if uninterrupted [continuous motions], are counted as one movement, as likewise the raising and lowering of it, even though it is to some other place. The putting out of the foot, however, and the drawing at back are counted as two movements, even though it is an uninterrupted continuous motion, as likewise raising it and putting it down in another place. (6) The sixth is eating or drinking, inserting a pick in the ear, or any such thing as that, which in the case of one fasting would be considered as breaking the fast. (7) The seventh is any turning away from the *qibla.* (8) The eighth is altering the intention. (9) The ninth is the addition of any action to those that are prescribed. (10) The tenth is interrupting [the prayers] even though only by speaking.

An exposition of congregating for prayers

Q.: What is the ruling about congregating for prayer services?

A.: It is a *farḍ kifāya*[3] on adult free men who are performing prayers. The meaning of its being a *farḍ kifāya* is that so long as some do it there is no sin resting on the others [who omit it]. In a big town, however, the disposition [on the part of each believer] to perform it is stipulated, so that the rites of religion may be publicly manifested.

Q.: Are there reasonable excuses which would make its omission lawful?

[1] See pp. 464-466 for the explanation of *ḥadath.*

[2] I.e. the introduction of any speaking of words other than words connected with the prayer service invalidates the prayers.

[3] A *farḍ* is an incumbent duty. Such are said to be of two kinds, (i) *farḍ ʿain*, which is a personal *farḍ* that each must perform personally, and (ii) *farḍ kifāya*, which is a social *farḍ*, a thing which must be performed, though if a certain number perform it there is no obligation on the others.

A.: Yes. The sudden occurrence of rain or sickness or strong winds at night or early morning, or if it is very muddy or very hot or cold, or in the case of one being very hungry or thirsty when food and drink are there ready prepared, or if one has eaten something that causes an unpleasant odour which is hard to remove, or has been busied with preparing a corpse for burial, or with getting rid of *ḥadath,* or where there is a lack of suitable clothes.

Q.: What are the conditions for prayers in congregation?

A.: They are eleven. (1) The first is [an expression of] intention by the one who stands behind the Imām (i.e. the prayer-leader), to imitate or follow or accompany the Imām [in his leadership of the prayers], as though he should say: "[I am] following or imitating the Imām [in this prayer service]." (2) The second is that each should be aware of the actions of his Imām which he must copy, either by seeing [the Imām himself], or seeing the person who is behind [the Imām], or by hearing his voice or the voice transmitted from him. (3) The third is that there should be a possibility of reaching him (i.e. the Imām) by ordinary motion, even though it means turning one's back on the *qibla* if one should be in a mosque, or without turning one's back on the *qibla* if neither are in a mosque.[1] (4) The fourth is that no one should take a position in advance [of the Imām]. (5) The fifth is that no one should be more than three hundred cubits *(dhirāʿ)* behind him, if in any place other than a mosque. (6) The sixth is that no one should get ahead of [the Imām] in the performance of the prescribed actions more than two of such actions. (7) The seventh is that no one should lag behind him for more than that. This is not serious, however, if one has an excuse, such as being slow in recitation, in which case one may be excused for being three of the longer prescribed actions behind him, namely, the bowing *(rukūʿ)* and the two prostrations. (8) The eighth is that the Imām should not be an *aratt,* i.e. one who employs *idghām*[2] where *idghām* is not called for, and so causes a change in consonants, as e.g. if one should say *al-muttaqīm* with doubled *t* [instead of saying *al-mustaqīm*]. (9) The ninth is that he should not be an *althagh,* i.e. one who changes one consonant for another without *idghām,* as, e.g. one who

[1] The point is that there must always be free access between the Imām, who stands a little forward for leading the prayers, and the worshippers. The Imām must never be fenced off in any way from those whom he is leading in worship.

[2] *idghām* is the contraction of two letters into one, as when in English we say *illogical* and *immodest* instead of *inlogical* and *inmodest.* Should we, however, say *iddecent* instead of *indecent,* we should be employing *idghām* where it is not called for.

pronounces *al-ḥamd* with a *h* instead of with a *ḥ*, or one who says *nathta'īn* with *th* instead of [*nasta'īn*] with an *s*. However, if the worshipper is suffering from the same defects there is no harm. (10) The tenth is that there be no cause why the prayers would have to be repeated, as is the case where one performs *tayammum* for lack of water and then prays in a place where water is normally to be found.[1] (11) The eleventh is that there should be no increase in any *rak'a* provided that whoever follows behind the Imām be aware of what the Imām is going to do.

An exposition of the ruling with regard to the masbūq and the muwāfiq

(This short section is concerned with those who come late to congregational prayers and find the Imām has already got so far with the service. It tells them how and where to join in and how much of the service they may count as legally fulfilling their duty to pray. It is not possible, however, to translate it intelligibly into English for those who are not intimately familiar with the various parts of a Muslim prayer service.)

An exposition of Friday prayers

Q.: What is the ruling about Friday prayers?

A.: They are a *farḍ 'ain*[2] on every responsible free male in residence who has no excuse by reason of illness or any of the other excuses mentioned under Prayer in Congregation. A journey which would involve missing them is forbidden after dawn on Friday. It consists of two *rak'as* performed at the time of noon prayers and in substitution therefor. Thus it counts among the five of its day, though if it should be held in a place where there was no need for it then the midday prayers must be performed after it.

Q.: Are there requirements for it beyond the requirements for other prayer services?

A.: Yes. It is conditional on there being an assembly of forty to form a congregation, and that [these forty] be free responsible males of those who habitually dwell in the place, i.e. that they do not [customarily] depart from it either winter or summer save for some special need. [It is conditional also on the prayers] being performed in a

[1] See p. 469-470. The prayer service of such a person would be invalid, and he would have to perform it over again for it to count.

[2] I.e. a personal *farḍ*. See p. 478.

building, and that it be preceded by two *khuṭbas*,[1] each of which has its own essentials [2] and requirements.

Q.: What are their essentials *(arkān)*?

A.: They are five. (1) Praising Allah—exalted be He. (2) Prayer for blessings upon His Prophet Muḥammad—upon whom be Allah's blessing and peace. (3) Exhortation to piety. These three are common to both of them. (4) The fourth is the reciting of a verse [from the Qur'ān] at the beginning of both, though it is *sunna* for it to be [recited again] at the end of the first. (5) Supplication for believers in the second.

Q.: What are the requirements for them?

A.: They are nine, viz. that they both be in Arabic; that they be at noon; that they be listened to by forty persons assembled for them; that the congregation rise for them and sit between them; that they be continuous with the prayer service; that all pudenda be covered; and that there be ritual purity from *ḥadath* and purity from any filthiness of body, clothes or place; that when the preacher mounts the pulpit *(minbar)* those present in the mosque be forbidden from going on with their prayers even though they be obligatory prayers. However, should anyone enter just at that moment, if it is in a mosque he should pray two brief *rak'as* and then take his seat, and should he not have already prayed the earlier prayer service of Friday [3] then let him pronounce the intention of two *rak'as*, thereby observing proper respect. It is customary to bathe on Friday and to adorn oneself with one's best clothes, of which white are the preferred. [Customary also] are the use of such good perfumes as one may have, getting early to prayers, reciting the Sūra of the Cave (XVIII), and calling down numerous blessings upon the Prophet—upon whom be Allah's blessing and peace.

An exposition of prayers for one travelling

Q.: How does one who is travelling perform the prayer services?

A.: It is permissible for him to shorten the midday, afternoon and night prayers by performing two *rak'as* for each, and for him to combine

[1] The *khuṭba* corresponds to the sermon, address, homily of a Sunday service among us.

[2] *arkān*, "pillars", see p. 473.

[3] The earlier prayer would be the dawn prayer whose obligatory *rak'as* are two. The case is that of a man who has come to the mosque for Friday prayer without having as yet performed any prayer for that day.

noon, afternoon and evening prayers with the night prayer at the time for whichever of them he wills, anticipating in the case of the first of them and delaying in the case of the second, but on condition that his journey be a legitimate one for a proper purpose, and that it be two stages or more in length, as, for instance, a journey from Damietta to ar-Rāhibain.[1] Friday [prayer] is like the noon prayer-time in the matter of lumping together the prayers ahead of time if it is put instead of it. To both the shortenings and the combinings, however, there are conditions.

Q.: What are the conditions for the shortening?

A.: They are (1) his expression of intention at the time of the *taḥarrum,* (i.e. his putting himself in a state of remoteness from profane things), (2) the continuance of the journey during the whole of the [time for the] prayer service, (3) that he do not take as prayer-leader anyone who is ignorant about his journey, nor someone who is completing [prayers previously missed]; (4) that he guard against anything which would invalidate his intention to shorten, [and keep so guarding] during the continuance of the prayer.

Q.: What are the conditions for combining in advance?

A.: They are that he have the thought to perform the first completely, and, beginning with that, make the intention to combine with it; that he perform the prayer services continuously allowing for no break between them; and that the journey continue till the contractual time of the last of them.

Q.: What are the conditions for delayed combination?

A.: They are that he express intention to delay at the time of the first [of them], and that the journey continue till the completion of the two prayer services.

An exposition of prayers for the two feasts

Q.: What is the ruling for prayer services for the two Feasts?[2]

A.: They are a verified *sunna.*[3] The [proper] time for them is the period between the rising of the sun and when it commences to decline, but

[1] The author of the Catechism was a native of Damietta on the eastern Mediteranean shore of Egypt, and he mentions a village which is roughly two stages from his home town.

[2] The two feasts in question are the *'īd al-fiṭr*, or the little feast, after the month of fasting *(ramaḍān)*, and the *'īd al-aḍḥā*, or Feast of Sacrifice. See p. 120.

[3] *sunna mu'akkada*, a ratified, confirmed, certain *sunna*.

it is customary for them to be performed after the sun has risen about a spear's length, i.e. seven cubits as judged by the eye. It is desirable that they be performed even if the [proper] time for them has gone by. They consist of two *rakʿas*, with an expression of intention to fulfil the *sunna* of the *ʿīd al-fiṭr* or the *sunna* of the *ʿīd al-aḍḥā*.

Q.: How are they performed?

A.: In the same way as ordinary prayers save that in the first *rakʿa* there are customarily seven *takbīrs* in addition to the *takbīra* of consecration, after the introductory procedures,[1] and before the *taʿawwudh*, and in the second [*rakʿa*] five times after the *takbīra* of arising and before the *taʿawwudh*. It is customary also to intercalate between the two *takbīras* the *bāqiyāt ṣāliḥāt*, i.e. the phrases: "Glory be to Allah"; "praise be to Allah"; "there is no deity save Allah"; and "Allah is most great". It is customary for them to be performed as congregational prayers, and for them to be followed by two *khuṭbas* in form like the two Friday *khuṭbas*. It is customary for the preacher *(khaṭīb)* to pronounce nine *takbīrs* at the opening of the first and seven at the opening of the second, and at the *ʿīd al-fiṭr* to expound to the congregation the regulations about almsgiving at the Feast, and at the *ʿīd al-aḍḥā* the regulations about offering sacrifice. Bathing is customary for both of the Feasts, as well as perfuming the person with the finest of scents, adorning oneself with one's best and most expensive clothes, and enlivening the night preceding each of them with the well-known *takbīr*. It is also customary to introduce this [*takbīr*] after every prayer from the dawn of the day of ʿArafāt until sunset on the last of the days of *tashrīq*.[2]

Q.: What is the form of this *takbīr?*

A.: This much beloved [*takbīr*] is as follows: "Allah is most great! Allah is most great! Allah is most great! There is no deity save Allah. Allah is most great! Allah is most great! To Allah be praise. Allah is most great! Allah is most great! Very great [is He]. Much praise be to Allah. Glory be to Allah, morning and evening. There is no

[1] *al-iftitāḥ*, i.e. "the opening up", a technical word for the commencing section of a prayer service which leads up to the performance of the first *rakʿa*.

[2] The *ʿīd al-aḍḥā* occurs during the month of pilgrimage while the pilgrims are at Mecca, so that those who are at home are in some sense sharing in the peculiarly holy days of those who are performing the pilgrimage. The day of ʿArafāt is the ninth day of the pilgrimage month when the pilgrims assemble on Mount ʿArafāt beyond Mecca, and the days of *tashrīq* are the three days, the eleventh to the thirteenth, when the flesh of the sacrifices at ʿArafāt is drying in the sun. See p. 121.

deity but Allah alone. He fulfilled His promise and aided His servant, strengthened his army [1] and alone put the squadrons to flight. There is no deity save Allah. We will worship none save Him, keeping religion exclusively His even though the unbelievers abhor it."[2] Then one should say: "Allahumma! grant blessings upon our Master Muḥammad, on the Companions of our Master Muḥammad, on the Helpers [3] of our Master Muḥammad, on the wives of our Master Muḥammad, on the descendants of our Master Muḥammad, and peace, even great peace."

An exposition of what needs must be done for a dead person

Q.: What is it that should be done for one who has deceased?

A.: Four things are necessary. The first is that he should be washed, which is done by his whole body being bathed once with pure water. The second is that he should be shrouded after he has been washed. If his estate can afford it there should be three wrappers, each of which covers his whole body, but if that cannot be afforded, then one only. The third is that there should be a prayer service over him. The fourth is that he should be buried in a grave of such a kind as will prevent the smell of his decomposition being noticeable, and will guard him from being dug up and devoured by wild beasts. These four things, however, are obligatory only in the case of a Muslim, other than one who has fallen a martyr on the field of battle, or an untimely birth. In the case of an unbeliever who is a *dhimmī*,[4] or in the case of a martyr who has fallen in battle, only two things are obligatory, viz. the shrouding and the burying. Prayer over them is forbidden, as is also washing in the case of a martyr. As for the untimely birth, if its life has been apparent, then it is treated as though it were an adult, but if life was not apparent, even though its form was apparent, everything save prayer is obligatory. If [it had developed so little that] neither were apparent then nothing is obligatory.

1 The reference is said to be to the battle of Badr. See VIII, 17 and XXXVIII, 11/10.

2 A reminiscence of Sūra XL, 14.

3 *anṣār*, which in this connection probably means the *anṣār* of the Prophet's own day, who had pledged themselves to aid him and his cause when he emigrated in 622 A.D. from his own city of Mecca to their city of Madīna, and who did stand by him there.

4 A *dhimmī* is a member of a protected cult in Muslim lands, who pays a poll-tax and is under certain social and civil disabilities, but who is allowed to profess his own non-Muslim religion. See pp. 268-269.

An exposition of prayers over a dead person

Q.: How are prayers for the dead performed?

A.: You should stand facing the *qibla,* with pudenda covered, ritually pure from all *ḥadath* and uncleanness, having the corpse in front of you. Then you should say: "I express intention of praying four obligatory *takbīra*s over this dead person", or "over such deceased Muslims as are present". Then you should say: "Allah is most great", while keeping in mind this intention. Then you should recite the Fātiḥa, and then say: "Allah is most great", and call down blessings upon the Prophet—upon whom be Allah's blessing and peace— in any form [you please], though it is preferable for it to be [in the form of] the Abrahamic prayer.[1] After this you make supplication for the deceased. Then you should say: "Allah is most great", and salaam to your right and to your left.

Q.: How is supplication made for the deceased person?

A.: It is effected by any form of supplication which has reference to the after life, such as: "Allahumma! have mercy on him", or "Allahumma! forgive him." The most perfect form, however, if it is an adult, is to use the well-known supplication: "Allahumma! this is Thy servant, and the son of Thy two servants, who has departed from the joy and ampleness of this world, from his beloved and his friends therein, into the darkness of the tomb and what will meet him there. He has been wont to testify that there is no deity save Thee alone, that Thou hast no partner, and that Muḥammad is Thy servant and Thy Apostle. Thou knowest better about him than we do. Allahumma! he comes as a guest to Thee, and Thou art the best One to whom to come as guest. He has become a poor man seeking Thy mercy, and Thou hast no need to punish him. We have come to Thee now in earnest supplication as intercessors for him. Allahumma! if he was one who did good increase his good works, and if he was one who did evil then overlook it in his case and meet him with Thy mercy. In Thy good pleasure protect him from the distress *(fitna)* of the tomb[2] and its torment. Enlarge for him his grave, moving back the earth from his sides.[3] Meet him with Thy mercy,

[1] I.e. the prayer in which Allah is besought to bless Muḥammad and his family as He had blessed Abraham and his family. See p. 522.

[2] The *fitna* of the tomb is the questioning of the soul in the grave by the two angels Munkar and Nakīr. See p. 209.

[3] One of the "Torments of the Tomb" described in the popular books of devotion is

which keeps one safe from Thy punishment, till Thou dost resurrect him in safety for Thy Paradise, by Thy mercy, O Thou most merciful of those who show mercy."[1] You should make masculine the pronoun in the case of a male and feminine in the case of a female, save the pronoun for Him to Whom men come as guests, for it is always masculine, since it refers back to an unexpressed attribute, viz. Him who is the most generous of those to Whom men come as guests. If it is the funeral of an infant one should say instead: "Allahumma! make him a predecessor of his parents, an advance payment, a treasure laid up, an exhortation, an object of reflection, an intercessor, and by him make heavy their balances [at the weighing]. Pour out upon their hearts patient endurance, deprive them not of remuneration for him, and distress them not after him."[2] It is also customary that before the *salām* in the case of a funeral prayer, both for an adult and for a child, one should say: "Allahumma! deprive us not of remuneration for him, and distress us not after him, but forgive both us and him."

An exposition of legal alms (zakāt)

Q.: What is *zakāt?*

A.: It is a portion of one's wealth given to the poor and such like, with intent to seek the favour of Allah—exalted be He—in a particular way. It is of two kinds, *zakāt* of property, and *zakāt* of body.

An exposition of zakāt of property

Q.: What is the property on which *zakāt* must be assessed?

A.: It must be assessed on camels, cattle and flocks, provided that they are pasturing, i.e. that they are going out to pasture on common herbage land and are not being used for cultivation or such things, that they reach the assessable number *(niṣāb)*, and that they have been owned for a year. It must be assessed also on gold, silver and

---

the "straitening of the grave" for evil-doers, whereby the sides of the grave so press on their bodies as to crush them. See p. 436.

[1] See Sūra VII, 151/150.

[2] The point is that had the child grown up there would have been a recompense to the parents for him, so the prayer is that they may still find this recompense in other ways now that the child has been taken, and that no other child be later so taken from them by death in childhood.

moveable trade goods, provided that they reach the assessable amount *(niṣāb)* and have been owned for a year. It is assessable also on the fruit of the date-palm, the grape-vine, the grain of the greater fodder plants such as capers, barley, dhurra, rice, lentils, broadbeans, chick-peas, kidney-beans, Indian peas, provided that they appear to be in a healthy condition and reach the assessable amount. In all the above it makes no difference whether they are the property of a mature adult or not.[1]

An exposition of the assessable amount and what is obligatory thereon

Q.: What is the *niṣāb* in the case of camels, and what is the assessment thereon?

A.: For five [camels] the assessment is a year old ewe from the sheep or a two year old she-goat. For ten the [assessment] is two ewes; for fifteen three ewes, for twenty four ewes, for twenty-five a year old pregnant she-camel, for thirty-six a two year old she-camel in milk, for forty-six a *ḥiqqa,* i.e. a three year old she-camel, for sixty-one a *jadhaʿa,* i.e. a four year old she-camel, for seventy-six two milch camels, for ninety-one two *ḥiqqa*s, for a hundred and twenty-one three milch camels, for a hundred and thirty a *ḥiqqa* and two milch camels, and thereafter for every forty a milch camel and for every fifty a *ḥiqqa.*

Q.: What is the *niṣāb* for cattle and what is the assessment thereon?

A.: For thirty of them, whether full-blooded cattle or water-buffaloes *(jawāmīs)*,[2] a *tabīʿ*,[3] i.e. a one year old calf; for forty a *musinna,* i.e. a two year old calf; for sixty two *tabīʿ*s, thereafter for every thirty a *tabīʿ* and for every forty a *musinna.*

Q.: What is the *niṣāb* for flocks and what is the assessment thereon?

A.: For forty of them, whether sheep or goats, a ewe; for a hundred and twenty-one two ewes; for two hundred and one three ewes; for four hundred four ewes; and thereafter for every hundred a ewe.

Q.: What is the *niṣāb* for gold and what is the assessment thereon?

[1] There are several religious obligations from which minors are excused on the ground of their tender years, but in the case of *zakāt,* if the property of a minor reaches the assessable amount and has been his possession for a year, his guardian is under obligation to see that the proper *zakāt* is paid from it.

[2] The original regulation probably had in mind cows, but in Egypt the *jāmūs,* or water-buffalo, is a much more common source of milk supply, and so appears here.

[3] *tabīʿ* means "follower", and so refers to a calf which is still following its mother.

A.: Its *niṣāb* is twenty mithqāls free from alloy and worth twelve Egyptian guineas save an eighth. The assessment on this *niṣāb* is the fourth of a tenth, i.e. half a mithqāl. What is above that is at the same rate.

Q.: What is the *niṣāb* for silver and what is the assessment thereon?

A.: Its *niṣāb* is two hundred dirhams pure, and worth twenty-seven new Egyptian *riyāls* save a third. The assessment on this *niṣāb* is the fourth of a tenth, i.e. five dirhams. What is above that is at the same rate.

Q.: What is the *niṣāb* for trade goods and what is the assessment thereon?

A.: Its *niṣāb* is as the *niṣāb* for gold and silver in the matter of value. The assessment is that you evaluate at the end of the year in which you bought [the goods]. If it was at gold standard you evaluate by that and take the *zakāt* from it, and if it was at silver standard you evaluate by that and take the *zakāt* from it.

Q.: What is the *niṣāb* for fruits and grain and what is the assessment thereon?

A.: The *niṣāb* for them is five camel-loads. The assessment thereon is two tenths for land watered without trouble, otherwise the half thereof. What is above that is at the same rate.

Q.: What is the measure of these five [camel-loads]?

A.: In Egyptian *raṭl*s [1] it is one thousand four hundred and twenty-eight and four sevenths; or in Egyptian measure *(kail)* [2] it is four *irdab*s [3] and a sixth, which is fifty Damietta *kail*s. [Such measures really concern] fruits in their dried state, such as dried dates and raisins, but fruits that are not dried are measured as though they were dry. In the case of the grain it means grain free from rubbish, dirt and the husks that are uneatable.

An exposition of zakāt of the body, which is also called zakāt of breaking the fast (fiṭr)

Q.: What is *zakāt* of the body?

A.: It is a *ṣā'* [4] of the usual provisions of a country, which each person gives for himself. The requirement is that it be his own possession and that it be in excess of his mouth-provisions and the mouth-

[1] The Egyptian *raṭl* is said to be fifteen and three quarter ounces.

[2] The *kail* is a special measure for grain.

[3] An *irdabb* is said to equal five and a half bushels.

[4] A *ṣā'* is a grain measure, said to have meant originally four times the amount that will fill the two hands held together, though now it varies greatly.

provisions of those whom he has to feed on the feast and its final night. Also it must be in excess of what [he needs to sell so as to provide for] his clothing and his dwelling, his domestic servant, furniture, coverings and vessels.

Q.: Is he obliged to give on the part of others than himself?

A.: Yes. It is an obligation on him to give on the part of his wife, his slaves, his poor relations, his domestic servant and the servant of his wife, if they have nothing appointed to them in the way of spendingmoney, clothes or wages.

Q.: What are the conditions for its being obligatory?

A.: Its conditions are that part of Ramaḍān and part of Shawwāl have been reached,[1] though it is valid even if it has been given at the beginning of Ramaḍān. The preferable time for it to be given is after the dawn prayer and before the prayer of the feast [at the close of Ramaḍān].

Q.: What is the amount of the *ṣā'*?

A.: It is four handfulls with the palms held level and joined. Its amount in Egyptian *raṭl*s is four and a half and a quarter and a seventh of an ounce. In Egyptian *kail* measure it is two *qadaḥ*s by the old *kail,* which today is larger than it used to be, as is proved by what the Malikite as-Safaṭī quotes from al-Ujhūrī to the effect that the Egyptian *kail* is a *qadaḥ* and a third and that the Egyptian *rub'* equals three [*qadaḥ*s].[2] Now the Egyptian *rub'* is half a Damietta *kail.* It is manifest that what is meant is sound grain free from clay and other such [impurities].

An exposition of those to whom zakāt gifts may be given

Q.: Who are the recipients of the various forms of *zakāt?*

A.: It may be given to the eight classes mentioned in the Qur'ān (Sūra IX, 60). The first group among them and the one most commonly to be found in this country [consists of] four: The poor *(faqīr)*, the unfortunate *(miskīn)*, the debtor *(ghārim)*, and the traveller *(ibn*

[1] Ramaḍān is the ninth month of the Muslim lunar year and Shawwāl the tenth month. Since it is an alms for the breaking of the fast some part of the fasting month should have been covered before it is given, and the best time is when the next month has already begun. See p. 94.

[2] A *qadaḥ* is a measure of capacity. A *rub'* is literally "a fourth", "a quarter", and is said to measure 3.63 gallons. The authorities he mentions are Yūsuf b. Sa'īd as-Safaṭī, an XVIIIth century writer on Malikite jurisprudence, and his contemporary 'Aṭiya al-Ujhūrī, whose *Ḥāshiya* was finished in the year 1171 A.H. = 1757 A.D.

as-sabīl). An opinion that finds much favour is that *zakāt* of the body may be given to three poor [persons] or unfortunates, though others say that it may be given only to one. It has been handed down from the three Imāms [1] and from later authorities that it is permissible to give the *zakāt* from property also to three of any of those who may have a share. This was the opinion favoured by ar-Rūyānī,[2] whence the *fatwā* [3] declaring this usage in our rite to be free from blame.

Q.: Who is a poor man *(faqīr)?*

A.: He is one who possesses nothing and can earn nothing at all, or he is one who possesses or earns less than half of what would be sufficient for him and for those in his keeping to live in a state that is not immoderate [on the one hand], nor bare subsistence [on the other].

Q.: Who is an unfortunate *(miskīn)*?

A.: He is one who possesses or earns only half of what he needs, or more than half so long as it does not reach the amount that would be sufficient for him. The meaning of "sufficient" in the case of one who is earning is "sufficient for day by day", or in the case of one not earning "sufficient for the rest of his life", which normally lasts sixty-two years.

Q.: Who is a debtor *(ghārim)*?

A.: There are four kinds. The first is he who puts himself into debt in order to prevent dissension between litigants in a crime against body or property. The second is he who has borrowed money for some matter of general advantage such as entertainment of a guest, or the building of a bridge or a mosque. He may be given [from *zakāt*] what he has borrowed for that [purpose], provided that the debt has fallen due and he has not paid it. The third is he who has borrowed for himself in connection with some [pecuniary] embarrassment that was nothing illegal. He may be given [from *zakāt*] the amount of his debt if it has fallen due and he is unable to pay it. The fourth is one who [is in debt because he] has given a guarantee. He may be given [*zakāt* money] if he is in difficulties and the debt is due, whether he was guarantor to a destitute fellow or to a person in easy circum-

[1] The three Imāms are the founders of the three rites, viz. Abū Ḥanīfa, Mālik b. Anas and ash-Shāfiʿī. The author of this Catechism is a Shāfiʿite, which is the rite he means when he speaks of "our rite".

[2] ʿAbd al-Wāḥid ar-Rūyānī, d. 1108 A.D., was a writer on Shāfiʿite jurisprudence.

[3] A *fatwā* is a legal decision rendered by a *muftī* to settle some point of theoretical interest in Muslim jurisprudence. See p. 254.

stances who does not pay what he owes, if his guaranteeing was without this person's permission.

Q.: Who is a traveller?

A.: He is one who is passing along, that is, who is going by the town where the *zakāt* is, or one who is starting on a journey from it. He may be given [from *zakāt*] if he has need, in that he cannot find the wherewithall to provide what he needs for his journey.

Q.: Are there any conditions [laid down] about the one who receives the *zakāt?*

A.: Yes. It is laid down that he must be a Muslim, a free man, not someone dependent on a subvention from a relative or a spouse, and not a member of the Houses of Hāshim [1] or al-Muṭṭalib, for [*zakāt*] is not given to an unbeliever or to a slave or to one dependent on a subvention from a male, nor is it given to a Hāshimite or a Muṭṭalibite even though they are not able to draw their dues from the public Treasury. Some, however, say that it is permissible to give to them if they are unable [to get their dues].

Q.: Is there any need to express intention *(niyya)* when giving *zakāt*?

A.: Yes. It needs to be expressed when giving it, for it is not valid without the expression of intention by the almsgiver as he pays it or sets it aside out of his property. It is sufficient [if the intention is expressed] after [the withdrawal] and before the payment. Expression of intention by one of two partners dispenses the other [from having to express it]. Moreover, expression of intention need only be in the heart, though it is customary to pronounce it aloud. For *zakāt* of property one should say: "This is *zakāt* from my property", and for *zakāt* of body one should say: "This is *zakāt* of my body" or "of my breaking the fast". Should there be some doubt about the intention after it has been paid it is no matter.

An exposition of fasting

Q.: What is fasting *(ṣaum)*?

A.: It is the refraining from breaking the fast for the whole of the day, along with expression of intention.

[1] Members of these Houses would be members of two branches of the Prophet's family, who would normally be provided for out of the public Treasury, and for whom it would be an indignity to accept alms on the same level as the poor.

Q.: What are its regulations?

A.: It is obligatory during Ramaḍān, also for [expiating] a vow, and for atonement, and is approved in other cases.

Q.: How is Ramaḍān recognized?

A.: It is recognized by seeing the new moon [of that month], or by the completion of the thirty days of Sha'bān.[1]

An exposition of the essential conditions for the observance of the Ramaḍān fast

Q.: What are the essential conditions for its observance?

A.: They are three, viz. residence [in a place], having strength for it, and not being in a state of menstruation or going through childbirth. It is permissible for a traveller to break it if he is on a long and lawful journey, and he suffers no disability thereby provided that his journey had begun before the fast, i.e. that he had commenced journeying before dawn [on any day of Ramaḍān], but he must redeem it[2] after completing [the journey]. Also it is permissible for it to be broken by one who is incapable [of carrying it through], if it has caused him some serious indisposition owing to his being sick or old, or a woman being pregnant or nursing. However, an expiation for it is obligatory on the elderly person, or the one who is sick and whose cure is not to be hoped for, and this [expiation] is a *mudd*[3] of food of the usual provisions of the country for every day [of the days he has missed fasting]. If the case is that of a sick person whose cure may be hoped for, [the fast] must be redeemed. The same holds in the case of a pregnant woman or one nursing, if [they break the fast] out of fear for themselves, even though [they may have feared] also for the child. If the fear was only for the child they must make an expiation along with redeeming [the fast]. It is permissible for a woman in menstruation or childbirth to break it for so long as the conditions of being in menstruation or childbirth continue, and such must redeem it after they are ritually purified, but without any expiation.

[1] Sha'bān is the eighth month of the Muslim year and the one which precedes Ramaḍān, so that if the moon happens to be invisible the fact that a full thirty days of Sha'bān have passed is evidence that Ramaḍān has commenced. See pp. 93, 113-114.

[2] To redeem a fast is to perform another fast in its place at some other time.

[3] A *mudd* is a measure, commonly translated as a "bushel." See p. 277.

An exposition of the conditions for the validity of the fast, its essentials, its customary elements, and the things that are considered reprehensible during it

Q.: What are the conditions for the validity of the Fast?

A.: They are four, viz. that one be a Muslim, in possession of his faculties, free from [the impurities] of menstruation or childbirth for the whole day, and unaffected by swooning or drunkenness for any part thereof.

Q.: What are the essentials *(arkān)* of fasting?

A.: They are two, viz. an expression of intention, and abstaining between dawn and sunset from the things that would break it.

Q.: What is the time for the expression of intention?

A.: The time for it embraces the whole night during an incumbent fast, so it is allowable for the expression of intention to be made at any point therein, but it is not allowable during the day, so were one to forget it at night and dawn breaks while he is still forgetful that day cannot be counted for him [as a fast day], so he must refrain during it if it is in Ramaḍān and redeem it after the Feast.[1] In the case of an incumbent fast it is obligatory to particularize the expression of intention, i.e. to mention expressly whether it is [the fast of] Ramaḍān, or [a fast] in expiation of a vow, or as an atonement. As for the supererogatory fasts it is allowable to express the intention for them either by night or by day before it passes away, on condition that there does not precede it anything that would invalidate the fast. In their case it is not obligatory to particularize, and some doubt after sunset about the expression of intention for the previous day is no matter [for concern]. As for doubt during the day, it is harmful if one does not recollect that he has expressed intention, even after some days.

Q.: What are the things that break a fast?

A.: They are four things. The first of them is vomiting. The second is coition in either orifice before or behind. The third is the emission of semen, whether by masturbation or by contact with a female. This breaks it absolutely if [the contact has been such as would] invalidate one's *wuḍū'* ablution,[2] and breaks it even when [the contact was of a kind that] would not have invalidated a *wuḍū'* ablution if [the contact]

[1] I.e. after the 'Id al-Fiṭr which celebrates the ending of Ramaḍān.

[2] See pp. 468-469 for the things which render a *wuḍū'* ablution invalid.

was with lustful desire. The fourth is the appearance of any flux from what is called the hollow of an orifice, such as the mouth, the ear, the nose, the genitals, the anus, the breasts. A breach of the fast by any one of the above is conditional upon its being deliberate, conscious and by choice. For such a breach redemption only is obligatory, save in the case of coition where it is obligatory for the active participant to make an atonement as well as a redemption.

Q.: What is an atonement?

A.: It is the setting free of a healthy [1] believing slave. If that is not possible let him fast for two months in succession. Should he be unable [to do that] let him give in charitable alms sixty *mudd* of the normal provisions of the country to sixty unfortunates or poor persons with expression of the intention to make atonement [for a broken fast].

Q.: What are the customary elements in fasting?

A.: They are three. The first of them is hastening with the breaking [of the fast] when it is evident that evening has come.[2] The preferable thing is to have this precede the evening prayer service even though it be only by some little thing such as ripe dates or dry dates or water or a sweetmeat. The second is to have the *tasaḥḥur* [3] after half the night [has gone], with a view to helping with the fasting, and sufficing with a little food or drink. What is preferable is that it should be with what breaking the fast calls for, and that it be delayed till near the dawn, so that one is finished with it while there are still five degrees of the night remaining. The third is to restrain the tongue from what does not concern one, and to restrain the soul from its lustful desires.

Q.: What are the things disapproved of during a fast?

A.: They are five. The first is chewing, as e.g. the chewing of gum, for whatever crumbles from it and is swallowed with the spittle would cause a breaking of the fast. The second is tasting food even though none of it reaches the stomach, for it might and that would be breaking the fast. The third is frequenting the public baths, for luxury of that kind is out of harmony with fasting. The fourth is the use of the tooth-pick *(siwāk)* from noon till sunset, because it removes the

[1] *salīm*, "sound", "free from defect". I.e. it must not be some sick, decrepit, useless slave one would be glad to get rid of in any case.

[2] The point is that one should avoid any ostentations prolonging of the fast period.

[3] *tasaḥḥara* is "to take the dawn meal". Since the Muslim must fast all day there is generally much eating at night during Ramaḍān, and the regulation here is against a heavy meal before midnight and then sleeping till dawn, but recommending a light meal nearer the dawn as a better preparation for carrying through the day of fasting.

food particles which ought to be left. The fifth is kissing, embracing and fondling, even though it does not bring on an emission, for it might and that is one of the things forbidden during an incumbent fast.

An exposition of the regulations concerning one who delays redeeming a fast, or who dies without redeeming it

Q.: What is the regulation concerning one who has delayed redeeming a fast which he missed in Ramaḍān till the next [Ramaḍān] has come?

A.: If the delay was inexcusable then along with the redemption he must make an expiation of a *mudd* for each day [he did not fast], and this will accumulate as the years do.

Q.: What is the regulation concerning one who dies with a Ramaḍān fast unredeemed?

A.: Should he die after it had been possible for him to have redeemed it, his heir *(walī)* shall undertake the fast for him, or [alternatively] shall set apart every day a *mudd,* if he has not delayed the redemption till another Ramaḍān has come, but should he have [so delayed it], then two *mudd* are obligatory, a *mudd* for the delay and a *mudd* for the omission, i.e. if he has not undertaken a [redemptive] fast for him.

An exposition of the days on which fasting is forbidden and those on which it is customary

Q.: What are the days on which fasting is forbidden?

A.: They are the day of the ʿĪd al-Fiṭr and the day of the ʿĪd al-Aḍḥā,[1] along with the three following days, the day when there is doubt (see p. 492) without any reason, and likewise the second half of [the month of] Shaʿbān,[2] in which fasting is forbidden unless there is some reason other than just that of uniting it to what precedes it.

Q.: What are the days on which fasting is customary?

A.: They are many. Among them are the Monday and Thursday of each week, the white days of each month, i.e. the thirteenth and following days, six days of Shawwāl each year, the days of ʿArafāt and ʿĀsh-

[1] Since these are days of feasting (see p. 482) to fast on them would be inconsistent with the purpose of the days.

[2] Shaʿbān is the month which precedes Ramaḍān, so the prohibition is to prevent voluntary fasts during the weeks immediately preceding the great fast of Ramaḍān, which would savour of ostentation.

ūrā' also, though the fasting of the former covers two years but that of the latter one year.[1]

An exposition of the greater and lesser pilgrimage

Q.: What are the greater and lesser pilgrimage?[2]

A.: They are the visitation of special places for the performance of special rites.

Q.: What are the regulations for them?

A.: The regulations for them are that they are obligatory once in a lifetime if circumstances permit, and each has its essentials *(arkān)* and its obligatory rites.

Q.: What are the conditions under which they are obligatory?

A.: They are five, viz. that one be a Muslim, a free man, of adult standing, in possession of his faculties, and able.

Q.: What is [the meaning of being] able?

A.: It means having sufficient to defray the expenses of the journey [to the Holy City] over and above one's normal obligations, one's dwelling, provision for one's children for the period of going and returning, for the stay in Mecca and the other places for the customary time. It also means that the way must be safe for [the journey to and fro]. In the case of a woman it is laid down that she be accompanied by her husband, or some male who can be with her lawfully, or by two or more trustworthy women. In the case of a blind man [it is conditional] on his ability to procure a guide who will keep with him, lead him and guide him, whether he is mounted or dismounted.

Q.: How are they performed?

A.: They may be performed in [any one of] three ways. The first is [the way of] *ifrād*,[3] i.e. you perform the Ḥajj first and after finishing it you perform the 'Umra the same year. This is the preferred way. The second is [the way of] *tamattu'*,[4] i.e. you perform the 'Umra first, and then after finishing it perform the Ḥajj. It comes next in preference

[1] Shawwāl is the month which follows Ramaḍān. The Day of 'Arafāt is when the pilgrims to the Holy City of Mecca are performing their rites at the Mount of 'Arafāt. 'Āshūrā' falls on the ninth or tenth day of Muḥarram, the first month of the Muslim year; see p. 122.

[2] The *ḥajj* is the greater pilgrimage, and the *'umra*, or visitation, is the lesser pilgrimage.

[3] *ifrād* means performing "one by one".

[4] *tamattu'* means "enjoyment".

to the *ifrād*. The third is [the way of] *qirān*,[1] i.e. you perform both of them together, or [start] with an ʿUmra, and then perform the Ḥajj before beginning its circumambulations, going through the rites of the Ḥajj so that both are completed together. It is incumbent on everyone who does it by way of *tamattuʿ* or *qirān* to offer blood, if he is not among those present in the sacred mosque and does not return to the stations *(mawāqīt)* of the Ḥajj. The ʿUmra of him who performs by way of *tamattuʿ* must take place during the pilgrimage month and he must perform the Ḥajj the same year.

Q.: What is this [offering of] blood?

A.: It is a sheep or goat appropriate for sacrifice, i.e. without defect, a year old if it is a sheep, or two years if it is a goat. What is obligatory is that it be sacrificed and its flesh distributed among the poor and the unfortunate who are on pilgrimage. If [such a sacrificial offering] is beyond the person's means he must fast for ten days, three during the pilgrimage and seven when he returns home to his own land.

An exposition of the essentials (arkān) of the Ḥajj and the ʿUmra and their obligations

Q.: What are the essentials of the Ḥajj?

A.: They are six: (1) sacralization *(iḥrām)* [2] during it; (2) standing at ʿArafāt; (3) circumambulating the Kaʿba; (4) running between Ṣafā and Marwa; (5) shaving the hair from the head; (6) doing these important things in the proper order. [This latter] means that the putting on the *iḥrām* should have precedence over everything else, that the standing should precede the circumambulation and the shaving off of the hair, that the circumambulation should precede the running, if this has not been performed after the circumambulation of arrival.

Q.: What are the essentials *(arkān)* of the ʿUmra?

A.: They are the same as the *arkān* of the Ḥajj, save the standing [at ʿArafāt]. [To observe] proper order is incumbent in all the *arkān*,

[1] *qirān* means "conjunction".

[2] *iḥrām* is "putting oneself in the sacred state", i.e. for the time being removing oneself from ordinary profane life, and devoting oneself to a life of a sacral character. It is symbolized by wearing the peculiar pilgrim dress, which itself is called the *iḥrām*. See p. 104.

namely that one put on the *iḥrām,* then circumambulate, then do the running, then remove the hair.

Q.: What are the obligations of the Ḥajj?

A.: They are five: (1) to maintain the sacralization *(iḥrām)* throughout it from the station *(mīqāt)* [1] onwards; (2) to pass the night at Muzdalifa; (3) to pass the night at Munā; (4) to cast the pebbles; (5) refraining from prohibited things (i.e. things which would invalidate the sacral character caused by the assumption of the *iḥrām*). Some add a sixth, namely the farewell circumambulation, but it is generally agreed that this is a lesser obligation demanded of everyone who wants to leave Mecca whether he be a pilgrim or not. Its omission may be made good by [an offering of] blood similar to the blood [offering] of the *tamattuʿ*.

Q.: What are the obligations of the ʿUmra?

A.: They are two: (1) to maintain the sacralization throughout it from the station onwards; (2) refraining from forbidden things.

Q.: What is the difference between an essential and an obligation?

A.: An essential is an element on which the validity [of the performance] depends and such cannot be made good by an [offering of] blood, whereas an obligation does not have the validity dependent upon it, though he who omits one [of these obligations] is a sinner and must offer blood for his omission.

An exposition of the sacralization

Q.: What is the *iḥrām* which is the first essential element of both the Ḥajj and the ʿUmra?

A.: It consists in an expression of intention to enter into a state of godliness *(nusk),* an expression made in the heart, though it is customary for it to be pronounced aloud, the one intending to make the pilgrimage saying: "I express intention of pilgrimage and to that end have devoted myself [2] to Allah—exalted be He." In like manner the one who is intending to perform the ʿUmra says: "I express intention of visitation, and thereby have devoted myself to Allah

[1] The sacredness of the Holy City extends for a certain distance around it. On each of the roads leading in to Mecca from the various directions there are recognized *stations (mawāqīt)* at which those going on pilgrimage stop, remove their ordinary clothing and assume the pilgrimage dress which they continue to wear till their pilgrimage rites are accomplished. See n. 1 p. 503, and p. 104.

[2] The verb used here is *aḥrama,* which means "to declare a thing sacred", i.e. removed from ordinary profane life and devoted to a period of godliness or sacred life.

—exalted be He." He who is intending to perform by way of *qirān* says: "I express intention of both pilgrimage and visitation, and thereby have devoted myself to Allah—exalted be He." Needs must this expression of intention be at its proper time, viz. from the beginning of [the month of] Shawwāl to the dawn of the day of sacrifice *(yaum an-naḥr)*.[1] Were one to express the intention at some other time it would be a compact [only] for an ʿUmra. Certain things are customary for one who intends to enter on [this state of] sacralization.

Q.: What are these things?

A.: They are that he should perform a *ghusl* with an expression of intention to perform *ghusl* for the purpose of entering [into a state of] sacralization. Then he should clothe himself in a lower wrap *(izār)* [2] and an upper wrap *(ridā')*, both of them white and new. Then he should pray two *rakʿa*s as a *sunna* of the sacralization at some time other than the *karāha*.[3] Then he should express [his] intention, and introduce the *talbiya* [4] immediately after expressing the intention, pronouncing it frequently as long as he is in the state of sacralization, especially at any change of position such as mounting or dismounting, going up or coming down, coming together or separating, welcoming night or welcoming day. The form [of the *talbiya*] is: "Labbaika Allahumma! labbaika! labbaika! Thou hast no partner. Labbaika! Praise and grace are Thine, as is the kingdom. Thou hast no partner." Then when he reaches the sacred area of Mecca, if he is making a Ḥajj or a *qirān* it is customary that he should make a circumambulation of arrival, and if he is making the ʿUmra he should make the circumambulation of the ʿUmra, which is one of its essential elements.

An exposition of the standing at ʿArafāt

Q.: What is the standing *(wuqūf)* at ʿArafāt, which is the second of the essentials of the Ḥajj?

A.: What is desired is the presence of the person in a state of sacralization

[1] That is the tenth day of the twelfth month *(Dhū 'l-Ḥijja)*.

[2] The *izār* is a wrapper that hangs from the waist, and the *ridā'* one that hangs from the shoulders.

[3] That is at a time when such would be disapproved.

[4] The verb *labbā* is said to mean "to answer a call", which in connection with the pilgrimage would mean the summons of Allah to visit the sacred shrine. So the pilgrims as they approach the shrine cry: "Labbaika Allahumma."

on part of its soil, whether sitting, riding or walking, for what is desired is not actual *standing* in the usual sense of the word [but rather being there]. The time for it is from the passing away of the Day of ʿArafāt till daybreak of the Day of Sacrifice.[1] It is sufficient to be present for any part of this time even if only for a moment. It is customary, however, to remain there until sunset in order to have both night and day share in the standing. [The pilgrim] is urged to occupy himself [during the standing] with ejaculations of *tasbīḥ, taḥmīd, tahlīl, takbīr, istighfār* and *talbiya*,[2] along with recitation of the Qur'ān, and calling down blessings and peace upon the Prophet, the Chosen one.

Q.: Should one miss this standing by not reaching ʿArafāt before daybreak, what should he do?

A.: It is obligatory for him to expiate by performing an ʿUmra, a redemption which must be made the following year, and an [offering of] blood similar to the blood-offering of the *tamattuʿ*.

An exposition of the circumambulation

Q.: What is the circumambulation of the Kaʿba which is the third of the essential elements of the Ḥajj, and the second of the essentials of the ʿUmra?

A.: It consists in circling around it. In [the case of] the ʿUmra it comes after assuming a state of sacralization for it, but in the [case of the] Ḥajj it comes after the standing when the first half of the night of sacrifice has passed. It has its conditions and its customary elements.

Q.: What are its conditions?

A.: They are that it be performed seven times within the mosque area in which are the Kaʿba, the Shādharwān [3] and the stone of Ishmael,[4] with the pudenda covered, as is the case for performing prayers, and the purification of the body from *ḥadath*, along with the purification of the body, the clothing and the place of circumambulation

[1] The day they have to be at ʿArafāt is the ninth day of the month Dhū 'l-Ḥijja and the day for the sacrifice is the tenth. For ʿArafāt see pp. 170, 192.

[2] These are all well-known ejaculations used in devotions. *tasbīḥ* is repeating: "Glory be to Allah"; *taḥmīd* is repeating: "Praise be to Allah"; *tahlīl* is repeating: "There is no deity save Allah"; *takbīr* is repeating: "Allah is most great"; *istighfār* is repeating: "I seek forgiveness from Allah", and *talbiya* is to repeat the aforementioned "Labbaika Allahumma", which is said to mean, "Here I am for Thee, Allahumma". See p. 153.

[3] This is the name given to the base of the present Kaʿba. It is a Persian word *shādurwān* meaning the basin for a fountain.

[4] A slab of green stone marking the supposed grave of Ishmael.

from all uncleanness. It should begin at the Black Stone,[1] with the left side of the body opposite it, and walking in the direction of the door of the Kaʿba, keeping it at the left at every step. These conditions are not peculiar to the *ṭawāf*[2] on this occasion, but are general for every *ṭawāf*, even if one is not in a state of godliness *(nusk)*, as, for example, a *ṭawāf* [in fulfilment] of a vow, or a supererogatory [*ṭawāf*] other than that of arrival. There needs must be an expression of intention [in such cases], though for a *ṭawāf* in a state of godliness there is no need for any expression of intention, though one is customary, as a recognition that this is an essential element of a Ḥajj or an ʿUmra. One's purpose to make a *ṭawāf*, however, must needs be expressed, for were one to make a circuit around the Kaʿba without being aware of it, that, [though actually a circumambulation], would not be a valid *ṭawāf*. So there needs must be an expression of intention, whether for an obligatory or for an approved [*ṭawāf*], when one is opposite the Black Stone at the beginning of a circumambulation.

Q.: What are its customary elements?

A.: They are many. Among them is that the walking should be done barefooted, unless there is the excuse of severe heat. Another is that there should be no talking save about things that are good. Another is to get near to the Kaʿba, so long as this is not harmful and does not cause distress by crowding. Another is to touch the Black Stone with the right hand, to kiss it and to place one's forehead on it at the beginning of each circuit. If, because of the crowding, it is not possible to kiss it and place [the forehead on it], then one may confine oneself to touching it, or if that is not possible, then to point one's hand towards it from a distance and kiss the hand after the touching or pointing. Another is to touch the Yemenite corner[3] with one's right hand at each circuit, or if this is not possible to point one's hand towards it from a distance and kiss it after the touching or the pointing. Another is uniting the circuits and dividing them up.

[1] The Black Stone *(al-ḥajar al-aswad)* is a meteorite, apparently reverenced in pre-Islamic days as a sacred stone, and now set in the south-east corner of the Kaʿba and held together by a silver band. See pp. 191, 303.

[2] *ṭawāf* is associated with a verbal root meaning "to walk around a thing", and so is the normal word for "circumambulation". This is a very ancient cult rite found in many religions and was practised at Mecca in pre-Islamic days. Today the "guide" who directs the pilgrims through the complicated rites at the pilgrimage is called a *muṭawwif*, i.e. the one who instructs you how to do the *ṭawāf*.

[3] *ar-rukn al-yamanī* is another sacred stone in the corner facing south.

Another is to walk quickly, to have the left shoulder covered and the right uncovered, and to interpolate remembrances and traditional supplications, so let any one who desires them seek for them in the *manāsik*.[1] It is customary after [the circumambulation] to pray a prayer of two *rak'as* with expression of intention [to fulfill] the customary elements of *ṭawāf*. It is preferable that [this prayer] be performed behind the *maqām*.[2]

An exposition of the running

Q.: What is the running between aṣ-Ṣafā and al-Marwa,[3] which is the fourth of the essentials of the Ḥajj and the third of the essentials of the 'Umra?

A.: It consists in going back and forth between the two, either walking or riding. In the 'Umra it takes place after the circumambulation thereof, and in the Ḥajj after the *ṭawāf* of arrival and before the standing at 'Arafāt. Should one not do it then he may delay it until after the essential circumambulation which is called the *ṭawāf al-ifāḍa*.[4] It has its conditions and its customary elements.

Q.: What are its conditions?

A.: They are: (1) that it be performed seven times. The going from aṣ-Ṣafā to al-Marwa is counted as one, and the return therefrom to aṣ-Ṣafā as another; (2) that it be in the track for running recognized at the present time; (3) that it start from aṣ-Ṣafā on the odd numbers and from al-Marwa on the even; (4) that the whole distance between them be accomplished, either walking or riding, for if a single step be omitted the rite is invalid.

Q.: What are its customary elements?

A.: They are many. Among them is going out to it from the Gate of aṣ-Ṣafā immediately following the circumambulation and such things

[1] It is a mark of piety to ejaculate pious expressions of remembrance of Allah and of supplication to Him while performing the walk around the Ka'ba. One's *muṭawwif* would know what are the correct expressions to use at each point of the circumambulation and it is part of his duty to instruct the pilgrim who needs his help in this matter. The *manāsik* are little booklets explaining the rites of pilgrimage.

[2] The *maqām* is usually called *maqām Jibrā'īl*, or Gabriel's station. It is at the north side of the Ka'ba and supposedly marks the place where the angel Gabriel used to join Muḥammad in prayers.

[3] Ṣafā and Marwa are two hillocks within the city area of Mecca. The running between them is said to commemorate the running to and fro of Hagar trying to find water for the babe Ishmael.

[4] In connection with the pilgrimage the verb *afāḍa* has the technical meaning of "to crowd together from one place to another".

as are connected therewith. Others are the covering of the pudenda, being pure from *ḥadath* and any uncleanness, walking on foot if one is able, doing the times continuously and dividing each time. Another is for a male [but not a female pilgrim] to mount to the height of a man's stature up both aṣ-Ṣafā and al-Marwa, turn towards the *qibla,* and there pronounce the traditional commemoration. This may be done likewise during the walking [between them]. So let anyone who wishes look for it in the *manāsik.*

An exposition of the removal of the hair

Q.: How is the hair removed from the head in this which is the fifth essential of the Ḥajj and the fourth of the 'Umra?

A.: There is no special method. It may be done by any one of the various methods of removing hair, such as shaving, cutting or plucking, but the preferred way is shaving for the male and cutting for the female. The obligation is satisfied by the removal of only three hairs, but it is customary to go over the whole head, shaving it for a male and cutting it for a female to finger-tip length with the exception of the hanging locks *(dhawā'ib),* which are not cut. The time for the removal [of the hair] in the case of one performing the 'Umra is at the time of his completing the running, and it is preferable that it be at Marwa. In the case of one performing the Ḥajj [the time for it] is half way through the night of Sacrifice after the standing, and it is preferable that it be done at Munā early in the forenoon after the casting of the pebbles *(jamrat al-'Aqaba),* and before the *ṭawāf al-ifāḍa.*

An exposition of the stations

Q.: What is the station at which it is obligatory to assume a state of sanctification whether for the Ḥajj or for the 'Umra?

A.: For people coming from Madīna [1] it is Dhū 'l-Ḥulaīfa, called [nowadays] 'Alī's Wells. For those coming from Egypt it is al-Juḥfa, better known as Rābigh. For those coming from Najd of the Ḥijāz, and from Yemenite Najd it is Qarn, a mountain in [the neighbourhood of] aṭ-Ṭā'if. For those coming from Yemenite Tihāma it is Yalamlam, the mountain better known as as-Sa'dīya. For people coming

[1] There are only a few roads leading into Mecca, and pilgrims will normally approach the city by one or other of them. The stations recorded here are all places on these different roads which would be easily recognized by travellers along them as the appropriate places for putting off their daily clothing and assuming the *iḥrām.* They are described in Gaudefroy-Demombynes, *Le pèlerinage à la Mecque* (Paris, 1923), pp. 17–25.

from ʿIrāq and Khurāsān it is Dhāt ʿIrq, a ruined village on one of the roads from aṭ-Ṭā'if.

Q.: Are these five stations especially for the people above mentioned?

A.: No. They are for them and for anyone else who passes that way. When folk reach [these stations] it is obligatory that they put themselves in sacral state there, or when they come over against them to the right or to the left.

Q.: What does a man do who does not come by way of any of these stations that have been mentioned?

A.: If his place of residence is between the sacred precincts and one of these stations it is obligatory for him to put himself in sacral state in his residence, whether for the Ḥajj or for the ʿUmra. If he is in Mecca, and wants to make the Ḥajj, his station is Mecca itself, so he is under obligation to put himself in sacral state at any place therein [where he may be]. Anyone who is in [Mecca], or on the sacred territory, and wants to perform the ʿUmra, his station is the area outside the sacred boundaries of the city, so he must go out there from wherever he is when he wishes to put himself in sacral state. The preferable thing is that he prepare himself for the sacral state at al-Jiʿrāna, a place between aṭ-Ṭā'if and Mecca. The place next most preferable is at-Tanʿīm, known as ʿĀ'isha's mosques, and the next al-Ḥudaibīya, a place on the Jidda road.

Q.: What is the regulation about one who puts himself in a sacral state after passing beyond one of the stations?

A.: His *iḥrām* is legal though he has sinned and must make [an offering of] blood like the blood offering of the *tamattuʿ*. This is if he has passed beyond it while desiring to be in a state of godliness. If he passed beyond it without having had any such desire, but then came to desire it, he is to put himself in a sacral state at the point where the desire came upon him, and there is [in that case] no sin on his part and no need of [an offering of] blood.

An exposition of passing the night at Muzdalifa [1]

Q.: What is this passing the night at Muzdalifa which is one of the obligatory elements of the Ḥajj?

A.: What is intended [by the regulation] is the arrival at any part of it

[1] Muzdalifa is a place roughly halfway between Munā and ʿArafāt, and was an ancient sacred site in the pre-Islamic days. See Gaudefroy-Demombynes, *op. cit.*, pp. 259–263.

after the standing at 'Arafāt, even though only for a moment, during the second half of the night of sacrifice. It is not laid down as a condition that one should stay there, so it suffices to have passed by it at this [specified] time, and it is customary for women and feeble persons to hurry on with the journey from it to Munā, but for others it is customary to remain there so as to be able to perform the morning prayers there. Then they stand at *al-mash'ar al-ḥarām*,[1] which is a small hill at its extremity, busying themselves with commemorations and supplications until the day is bright, and only then go on to Munā. When they enter [Munā] they lose no time in casting the *jamrat al-'Aqaba* and then have their heads shaved or cropped, whereby they secure the first desacralization by which they are released from all the prohibitions of the state of sacralization save those connected with women, viz. contracting a marriage, coition, or the preliminaries thereto. The preferable thing is, for one who is able, to go on to Mecca after this in order to perform a circumambulation and a running [between Ṣafā and Marwa] after it, if he did not perform the running after the *ṭawāf* of arrival. In this way he secures the second desacralization whereby he is released from the rest of the prohibitions. Then after that he may return to Munā in order to pass the night there and cast the pebbles. It is permissible, however, to omit the return to Mecca and to remain in Munā till one has fulfilled all the requirements of passing the night there and casting [the pebbles]. Then when one has finished with that and has entered Mecca he should perform the circumambulation and the running. To delay these beyond the day of sacrifice, however, is disapproved.

Q.: What is the ruling concerning the one who has omitted passing the night [at Muzdalifa]?

A.: His pilgrimage is valid, though he has sinned and must make [an offering of] blood, like the offering of the *tamattu'*.

An exposition of the passing of the night at Munā

Q.: What is this passing of the night at Munā, which is one of the obligatory elements of the Ḥajj?

A.: It consists in being there for the major part of each night of the

[1] Lit. "the sacred bower", another ancient sacred place associated in pre-Islamic days with the god Quzaḥ, the god whose bow was the rainbow. See Gaudefroy-Demombynes, *op. cit.*, p. 261.

nights preceding the three days of *tashrīq*,[1] assuming one has not made the first return [to Mecca], but should one have made that return he drops the third night and likewise the casting of the day following. The major part of each night is interpreted as anything more than half, even if only a moment [or so more than half].

Q.: What is the first return?

A.: It is the journeying from it on the second of the days of *Tashrīq*. Conditional for its validity are that one make the journey after the sun has begun to decline yet before sunset, that it be after the completion of [the rite of] casting, and that one express the intention of returning before departing from Munā. It is thus evident that anyone who wishes to do this will return to Munā after the casting of the *jamrat al-ʿAqaba* and then express his intention, for the *jamra* is not a part of this [rite], but is outside it.

Q.: What is the ruling concerning one who omits this passing the night at Munā?

A.: His pilgrimage is valid though he has sinned. For [his] omission of the three nights he must make [an offering of] blood, like the blood offering of the *tamattuʿ*; for omission of one night [he must distribute] a *mudd*, and for two nights two *mudd*.

An exposition of the jimār and the casting of pebbles at them

Q.: What are the *jimār*[2] at which [pebbles] are to be cast?

A.: They are well known places at Munā, three in number. The first is the *jamra* which is just behind the mosque at al-Khaif. The second is the middle *jamra*, and midway between these there is a pillar that has been built up. The third is the *jamrat al-ʿAqaba*, which is a wall contiguous to the hill.

Q.: What is meant by casting at them?

A.: It is the throwing of stones. This is obligatory at the *jamrat al-ʿAqaba* only on the day of sacrifice, but at all three each day of the three days of *tashrīq* provided one has not made the first return. Should one have done that he is released from the throwing on the third

[1] The days when the flesh of the sacrifices is drying in the sun. See pp. 121, 483.

[2] *jimār* is the plu. of *jamra*, the word already met with in *jamrat al-ʿAqaba*. *jamra* means "a stone", and though the rite is now commonly called "stoning the devil", and associated with a story of how Satan appeared to Adam and later to both Abraham and Ishmael and, by instructions from Gabriel, was driven away by being pelted with small stones, this is really a survival of an ancient rite of lapidation. See Gaudefroy-Demombynes, *op. cit.*, pp. 268-276.

day, as you have already learned from what was said above. The [proper] time for the casting on the day of sacrifice is entered when half the night that precedes it has elapsed, after the standing at ʿArafāt. It is preferable, however, that it be done after the sun has risen a spear's length. The [proper] time for the casting on each of the days of *tashrīq* is entered when the sun has begun to decline. It is preferable however, to do it immediately after the sun has begun to decline, before the noon prayers. The time during which it is permissible to do the casting at all the *jimār* extends to the last of the days of *tashrīq*, so that should one omit the casting on one day it may be made up during what remains of the three days, though it is not valid to make it up after that.

Q.: Are there conditions for the validity of the casting?

A.: Yes. They are: (1) that there be seven [castings] at each *jamra*, even though it be by a single stone which is cast and then picked up [and cast again], though that may not be desirable; (2) that [the casting] be by hand; (3) that it be at the target, which is what is in front of the *jamrat al-ʿAqaba*, and what is around the pillar in the case of the other two, and that it be accurate within three cubits *(adhruʿ)*; (4) that the *jimār* be stoned in proper order during the days of *tashrīq*, beginning with casting at that which is behind the mosque of al-Khaif till its [seven] are completed, then at the middle one in the same manner, and then at the *jamrat al-ʿAqaba*.

Q.: What is the ruling with regard to one who omits this casting?

A.: His pilgrimage is valid, but he has sinned, and must make [an offering of] blood, like the blood-offering of the *tamattuʿ*, if he has omitted it entirely, or has omitted as many as three castings. If, however, he has omitted only one [casting] then [he must distribute] a *mudd*, or if [he has omitted] two, then two *mudd*.

An exposition of things forbidden to one who is in a state of sacralization

Q.: What are the things which the assumption of the *iḥrām* makes forbidden, and which one in a sacral state must leave undone?

A.: They are: (1) the use of perfume for his body or his clothes; (2) anointing the hair of his head or his face with anything that comes under the name of unguent *(duhn)*, such as olive-oil; (3) the removal of anything from his nails or hair from any part of his body; (4) contracting a marriage; (5) marital intercourse or indulging in any of the preliminaries thereto; (6) taking part in hunting free wild animals which are edible, whether killing or [only] injuring; (7) participating in any despoiling of trees or vegetation on the sacred territory, whether by cutting or plucking. In these prohibitions no distinction is made between male and female [for both must observe them]. In addition, however, a male is forbidden in particular to cover any portion of [his] head with anything that could be considered as a recognizable covering, even though it be unsewn. He is also forbidden to cover any [other] member of his body with anything that has been sewn, whether by thread or not. For women there is a special prohibition against covering any part of the face with anything that would touch it, even though it be [something] unsewn. She is also forbidden to cover her arms with long felt gloves though other covering is unobjectionable. An expiation is obligatory for [the violation of] any of these prohibitions, save that [which concerns contracting] a marriage, [for which no expiation is possible].

An exposition of expiation

Q.: What is this expiation?

A.: It varies according to the different things that are forbidden. In the case of [an act of] coition which spoils [the valid performance of] the Ḥajj or the ʿUmra, what is obligatory is [the offering of] a *badana* [1] on the part of the active participant. If that is beyond his means then [let him offer] a cow, or if that is not possible then seven sheep or goats, or if that is not possible let him distribute in charity food to the value of a *badana,* or if that is not possible let him fast a day for every *mudd* [he should have distributed]. Coition which spoils a Ḥajj is that which takes place before the two acts of desacralization, and coition which spoils an ʿUmra is that which takes place before [the ʿUmra] has been completed. One who has [thus] spoiled his Ḥajj must complete it by repeating it the following year, and one who has [thus] spoiled his ʿUmra must complete it by repeating it immediately. In this obligation to complete [a spoiled Ḥajj or ʿUmra] there is no distinction between the active participant in the [act of] coition and the passive, [though the expiation is demanded only of the active participant]. One who has killed [animals] by hunting is under obligation to present as sacrifice the like number [of animals] from the flocks and give [the flesh] in charity, or to reckon up their value and give food to that amount for distribution,

[1] A *badana* is a sacrificial camel offered in Mecca itself.

or fast the number [of days to which] the *mudd* would have amounted. One who has not the like number [of animals from the flock] may choose instead between giving in charity the amount of their value or fasting [in days] the equivalent number of *mudd*. The obligation on one who despoils a tree belonging to the sacred territory is that if it should be a big one [he must offer] a cow, or if it were a small one, about a seventh the size, [he must offer] a sheep. The one who did the despoiling may choose whether he sacrifices the cow or the sheep and gives [its flesh] in charity, or reckons up its value and distributes food to that amount, or fasts for the number [of days] its *mudd* [would have amounted to]. One who perfumes his body or clothes, or anoints the hair of his head or face with an unguent, or cuts three nails or body hairs, or a woman who veils her face or wears gloves, or a man who covers his head or wears on his body anything sewn, or indulges in the preliminaries to coition, or in an [act of] coition after that coition which spoiled [the validity of his performance], or in between the two acts of desacralization, [any one of these] is under obligation [to offer] a sheep which is to be sacrificed and its flesh distributed, or instead to give in charity three *ṣāʿ* to six unfortunates, each of whom must receive half a *ṣāʿ*, or to fast for three days. A person who may have removed only one nail or one hair is under obligation [to offer] one *mudd* of food, and for two hairs or two nails two *mudd*. It should be noted that in the case of a real loss, such as in hunting, expiation therefor is obligatory even though it were done in ignorance or forgetfulness, but in the case of a mere ministering to personal pleasure, such as perfuming or clothing, an expiation is obligatory [only when it was done] with intention and knowledge. In cases where there is a mixture of the two, as in coition, shaving and paring nails, there is a difference of opinion [among the learned theologians], the correct opinion, however, is that coition falls with perfuming, whereas shaving and nail-paring fall with hunting.

An exposition of blameworthy and praiseworthy habits

Q.: I beg of thee to bring this book to a close with the mention of those blameworthy habits which one ought to avoid, and the praiseworthy habits with which one ought to endue oneself.

A.: This, indeed, is a shoreless sea, but there is no harm in mentioning a number of both kinds to the best of one's ability, and maybe I shall thereby attain both reward and forgiveness.

Blameworthy habits

Among them are believing oneself to be perfect, and considering that one has no further need of being instructed or given advice. Another is seeking out peoples' defects, doing them harm, making mock of them, insulting them and besmirching their honour. Another is giving aid in evil, favouring dissensions, open disobedience and persisting therein hoping to be forgiven. Others are covetousness, miserliness, the magnification of anything that one gives [in charity], wastefulness, idleness, pretending poverty when one has sufficient, abasing oneself in the presence of the rich because of their riches. [Others] are pretending great piety but being remiss in worship, immoderate laughter, injustice, proneness to suspicion, frittering away time at meaningless things. [Others are] making accusations of lying or of acting foolishly, name-calling, acting crossly before people, postponing a fixed term, going back on a promise, wrongfully assuming the appearance of the pious. [Others] are love of wicked men and taking them and unbelievers as examples, ignorance, abjuring the truth, quarrelling, unjustly passing judgment, cowardice and rancour. [Others are] profligacy, envy, cheating, love of the world, treachery, hypocrisy, self-admiration, backbiting, slandering, love of leadership, high rank, and fame, thinking oneself superior to one's fellows, evil-thinking, rejoicing in another's evil, gluttony, greediness, too high expectations, being obedient to women, seeking compensation for obedience where there is no need. [Others are] carelessness about remembering Allah—exalted be He—, despairing of His mercy, considering oneself secure from His devices, disregard of relatives, disobedience to parents, undue indulgence in sleep, excessive indulgence in joking, shunning a fellow Muslim, sitting in evil company, and others from which we beg Allah that we may be kept by His grace and favour.

Praiseworthy habits

Among them are keeping silent about what is none of one's business, lowering the eyes from things at which it is not lawful to look, abstaining from unlawful things, being satisfied with what one has, seeking forgiveness oft, reading (or reciting) the Qur'ān and learning what is needful thereto,[1] following the Prophet's customary way of acting, modelling

[1] There are little booklets which give detailed instructions as to the correct method of reading and cantillating the Qur'ān, the approved customs to be observed while one is occupying himself with the Holy Book, and the correct invocations to be used at such times.

one's conduct on that of pious men, being zealous in religious matters, having regard for relatives and being filially obedient to parents, doing good to one's relatives and neighbours, ministering to the necessities of [Allah's] creatures, acting correctly towards both enemy and friend. [Others are] humility, gentleness, compassion, bearing injuries, overlooking the slips of one's brethren, avoiding interference in what occurred among the Companions, leaving the company of the heedless, refraining from slandering anyone's honour, refraining from any calumny against kings but rather praying for their good estate and uprightness. [Others are] having high regard for learned scholars and people of religion, honouring the grey-headed, proper conduct towards Allah—exalted be He—and towards all that He has created, rejecting any word of slander against the honour of a fellow Muslim, honouring the elderly and being merciful towards the young, visiting those in need, providing for guests, spreading peace without rejoicing in the good that arises therefrom, abandoning the world and taking no joy in what it brings. [Others are] treating folk without bias, returning greetings smilingly, being uncovetous of what [you see] in the hands of others, refraining from sitting in the market-places, restraining oneself from interfering in what is due to the dead, being watchful to fulfill all cult duties at their proper time, exerting oneself earnestly in faithful counsel, taking account with oneself for one's actions, being regretful for remissness in commission and omission, banishing ignorance by being instructed and instructing, honouring knowledge and him who seeks it, withdrawing oneself from [indulgence of] one's personal desires. [Others are] compensating for injustices to those who suffered them, peace-making, loving what Allah loves and hating what He hates, fearing Him and showing affection to the kindred of His Apostle—upon whom be Allah's blessing and peace—, maintaining friendly relations with pious people, making humble supplication to Allah—exalted be He—and submitting oneself to Him in all circumstances. [Others are] giving assistance in works of goodness and piety, responding to supplication, aiding the oppressed, relieving those stricken by loss, fasting oft, rising at night [for prayers], being ever mindful of death and preparing oneself for it by performing good deeds and avoiding such as are forbidden, attending funerals and saying prayers thereat, visiting graves and taking warning therefrom, visitation of the sick, stroking the heads of orphans, being well-pleased with Allah's decrees and judgments, exerting oneself to one's utmost in what will be pleasing to Allah, keeping oneself free from what is wicked, loving one's country and exerting oneself for its improvement, being anxious for the benefit of its inhabitants, being serviceable to the poor, sitting with them and helping them financially. [Others are] praying for Muslims that [to them] the hidden may be revealed, rejoicing in the improvement of the community and sorrowing at its corruption, giving first place to what Allah—exalted be He—has advanced and last to what He has given last place, seeking refuge with Him from the fires [of Hell], and seeking His Paradise with yearning. May Allah—exalted be He—make us inhabitants thereof, and grant us the joy therein of looking upon His noble face, by the influence of the high rank of His Prophet—upon whom be the most excellent of blessings and peace.

This is the end of what Allah—exalted be He—has, by His grace and favour, made easy of production by the hand of His poor servant Muḥammad b. ʿAbdallah al-Jurdānī of Damietta, the Shāfiʿite. May Allah, Most High, grant forgiveness to him and to his parents and to all Muslims. Peace be upon the Messengers, and praise be to Allah, Lord of the Worlds. This was brought to completion on Friday, that exalted day, the 28th of the noble [month of] Shaʿbān in the year 1328 of the Hijra of the Master of all creatures—upon whom be Allah's blessing and peace—as well as upon his family and his companions and their followers, until the Last Day. Amen.

[This is the end of the Catechism, but the text continues]

A complement

This is something which the author has added as a supplement to the third edition to complete its usefulness. It concerns a number of things which are disapproved [though they are] of common occurrence among the people, so [much so] that they take no notice of them and take no precautions against their becoming habits, in spite of the fact that in Allah's sight they are most blameworthy, and the punishment for them, did they know, is grievous.

An exposition of things disapproved in mosques

Among them is the very prevalent defectiveness in prayers by omitting the quiet pause at the bowing, the coming erect, the prostration, and the sitting. Another is [the use of] unintelligible pronunciation during the recitation and elsewhere. Another is the delivering of the call to prayer *(adhān)* in sing-song fashion, changing some of its words, pronouncing them unintelligibly, and drawing out [the calling] longer than is right.

Another is [allowing] the presence of women therein in spite of fear of the distraction their presence may cause. Another is the sitting therein of impostors to sell nostrums and to write amulets. Another is the taking of children who play about there. Another is bringing in things without discrimination in spite of the danger of causing uncleanness or defilement. Another is soiling it with food matter even though on the outside. Another is the raising of voices therein with confused recitation. And there are still other things.

An exposition of things disapproved in market-places

Among them are lying about profits, concealing defects, giving short weight or measure,[1] dictating iniquitous conditions, omitting [the legal requirement of] offer and acceptance, being content to give a poor quality article when there has been no advisement that that is permissible. Among them are dealing in musical instruments, in pictures of living creatures, in vessels made of gold or silver, in men's garments of silk, in selling used clothes after shortening them or dyeing them or mending them without the buyer knowing what their condition is. And there are still many other things.

An exposition of things disapproved of in the matter of streets

Among them is the purchasing of a portion thereof and incorporating it in a shop or a house. Another is the building therein of columns, stone benches, or nailed up flattened benches, or planting therein trees. Another is loading pack animals beyond what they can bear. Another is putting thorny things in them or walking in them in such a way as to injure passers by or tear their clothes or make them turn aside from it to a wider street. Another is standing in the way in them in such a manner as to constrict them and cause defilement to passers by more than the measure derived from normal mounting and dismounting. Another is casting out the house sweepings into the upper part of the road, and throwing out water-melon peel and [dirty] water which may cause folk to slip and fall. Similarly [disapproved] is the running of water from the water-pipes through narrow streets. Another is leaving rain-puddles and mud without sweeping them away, and leaving a savage dog at the house door where he may injure passers by. And there are still other things.

[1] Two different words for measure are used here, viz. *kail* which is a measure of capacity, and *dhar'* which is a measure of length.

An exposition of things disapproved at public baths

Among them is the painting of figures of living creatures on their doors and walls. Another is the uncovering of the pudenda therein and looking at them and one rubbing another's thigh and what is beneath his navel without check, in spite of the fact that touching the pudenda of another is just as much forbidden as looking at them. Another is [the practice of] dipping the hand, the waist-wrapper and the dirty drinking-bowl in one's water-basin that holds but little water. Another is wastefulness of water by using more than is necessary or customary without permission. And there are still other things.

An exposition of things disapproved in hospitality

Among them is spending on it unheard of amounts, or doing it for the sake of boasting or vying with others. Another is doing the perfuming [of one's guests] with censers of silver or gold, and feeding them and giving them drink from vessels made of the same. Another is [providing entertainment for one's guests by] musical instruments, or spreading [for them] coverings which have on them pictures of animals. Another is sitting with those who drink wine or wear silk, or put on gold rings, or who laugh immoderately at people, or who spread lies. And there are many other things also.

An exposition of things disapproved of in dwellings

Among them is living evilly with wife and children and servants by everlastingly using the tongue against them, dealing harshly with them and acting illnaturedly. Another is giving permission to a wife and the one in charge of her to go out to the public baths, or to visit graves, or to attend a wedding-feast, knowing or thinking that this outing will not be free from association with reprehensible things, such as the uncovering of the pudenda in the public baths and looking at the pudenda of others, or wailing for the dead *(nauḥ)* and loud weeping at the graves, or listening to musical instruments and directing looks at strangers at wedding-feasts, or walking in the streets and market-places uncovering some part of her body, or such adorning and perfuming of herself as will attract the glances of men towards her and make them incline towards her. Another is leaving the dwellers therein in their ignorance, believing about Allah and His Apostle what is not permissible, not knowing how to observe ceremonial purification and prayer-services or how to preserve themselves from defilement, and so on. Another is noticing them do things that are wrong, such as eating *fasīkh*,[1] speaking against the honour of people, being unnecessarily unclean, and not finding fault with them. Another is allowing children to reach the age of seven years and come to have discrimination without bidding them say the [daily] prayers nor teaching them the Islamic rules of life. Another is seeing young people playing with musical instruments and pictures of living creatures in the forms they have in real life, without forbidding them, and perhaps even having provided these things for them. Another is leaving what falls at meal times from the food so that it gets trodden on by the feet, or sweeping it up and throwing it in some dirty place, likewise throwing the bones after a meal of meat into some dirty place. Another is transmitting what is harmful from one's dwelling to that of his neighbours. And there are many others besides these. In a word, the examples of such disapproved things are numerous, but [to stop to record] what has not been said would delay [us too much], but with Allah is success in [reaching] the most straightforward path, so of Him do we ask a good ending, by the influence of His Prophet—on whom be the most excellent of blessings and peace. Amen. Praise be to Allah, Lord of the Worlds.

[1] *fasīkh* is a popular dish of little salted fish, something like our sardines.

PRACTICAL PIETY

INTRODUCTION

Alongside of its much discussed literature on Systematic Theology and Philosophical Theology Islam has produced a rich body of literature in the area of Practical Theology, i.e. literature concerned with the practical duties of Islam to be observed by a pious practising Muslim, and with the devotional life. A taste of this has already been given in the appendix to an-Nasafī's *Baḥr al-Kalām*, which is concerned with matters of practical religion.

As other religions, Islam has its feasts and festivals and holy days, for which men of learning and piety have written material which may be used to help celebrate these occasions suitably and profitably. Besides the five statutory prayer services each day pious Muslims commonly observe additional prayer services and find many an occasion for the use of supplicatory prayers. Specimens of such, attributed to the Prophet, or to early Muslim worthies, abound in the devotional literature. The person of the Prophet Muḥammad is highly venerated by his followers and there is a very large body of literature celebrating the excellence of the Prophet, and expressing devotionally the believers' reverence for him.[1] Popular Lives of the Prophet, and of his predecessors among the prophets, are also used for devotional reading. Not all Muslims can go to Mecca during the annual pilgrimage season, but even at home they can share in the holiness of that season by pious remembrance of the sanctities of Mecca, and for this manuals are available.

Islam also has its honoured saints who have become the subjects of a not inconsiderable hagiographical literature.[2] Very commonly this type of literature is linked to that of Sufism, which is concerned with the mystical life and philosophy of Islam. This is of sufficient interest to deserve a volume to itself and can be only touched upon in a Reader of such limited dimensions as this.

[1] This has been studied in Tor Andrae's *Die Person Muhammeds in Lehre und Glauben seiner Gemeinde* (Stockholm, 1918).
[2] The two best known collections of this kind are Abū Nu'aim's *Ḥilyat al-Awliyā'*, in Arabic, and Farīd ad-Dīn 'Aṭṭār's *Tadhkirat al-Awliyā'* in Persian.

ON THE DUTIES OF RELIGION [1]

On the legal alms (zakāt) in Islam, and His saying (XCVIII, 5/4): "They were enjoined naught save that they should worship Allah, making religion exclusively His, as Ḥanīfs, and to observe prayer and pay the legal alms, for that is the true religion (dīn)" [2]

Ismā'īl has related to us on the authority of Mālik b. Anas, from his paternal uncle Abū Suhail b. Mālik, from his father, that he heard Ṭalḥa b. 'Ubaidallah say: A man from the folk of Najd came to the Apostle of Allah—upon whom be Allah's blessing and peace—with dishevelled head, the sound of whose voice was audible to us though we could not understand what he was saying till he drew near. Then [we discovered that] he was asking about Islam. The Apostle of Allah—upon whom be Allah's blessing and peace—said that it consisted of five prayer services each day and night. "Shall I be obligated for any more than that?" he asked. "No", answered the Prophet, "unless you undertake some supererogatory prayers yourself." [3] Then the Apostle of Allah—upon whom be Allah's blessing and peace—went on: "There is also the fast of Ramaḍān." Said he: "And shall I be obligated for any other than it?" "No", answered [the Prophet], "unless you undertake something supererogatory." Then the Apostle of Allah—upon whom be Allah's blessing and peace—mentioned to him the legal alms. Said he: "And shall I be obligated for anything beyond that?" "No", replied [the Prophet], "unless you undertake something supererogatory." Thereupon the man turned away, saying: "By Allah! I shall add nothing to it but neither shall I be remiss", whereat the Apostle of Allah—upon whom be Allah's blessing and peace—remarked: "If he is speaking the truth [about that] he will be successful."

[1] From the *Ṣaḥīḥ* of al-Bukhārī (ed. Krehl, Vol. I, pp. 19, 20).

[2] *dīn* is commonly used to mean religion in the sense of the practical cult duties of religion, as contrasted with *īmān*, the beliefs a religious man should hold. The word *ḥanīf* is used several times in the Qur'ān, associated with the true monotheistic faith of Abraham.

[3] *taṭawwa'a* is "to do a thing willingly", and as a technical term refers to those cult acts freely undertaken over and above those that are required of every believer. That is, they are supererogatory works.

PRAYERS

There are two words for prayer in common use among Muslims: *ṣalāt*, which means the formal, liturgical prayer service performed five times a day, after purification of the person and the place, with the face turned towards the sacred shrine at Mecca, and accompanied by bowings and prostrations according to a ritual pattern; and *du'ā'*, or extempore petition and supplication. The word *namāz* is in use in India for the daily liturgical prayer services, but does not denote a further special type of prayer. Within the *ṣalāt* provision is made for *du'ā'* so that individual petitions may be inserted at need, and any ejaculatory prayer that may be uttered by the Believer at any time would be considered *du'ā'*.

Certain stereotyped forms of *du'ā'*, however, are well known throughout the Muslim world. Their contents may seem strange to those brought up to Christian habits of prayer, but they are highly appreciated and very popular among the masses in the Muslim world.

Peculiarly characteristic are the forms of invocation calling down Allah's blessing on the Prophet, his family and his followers, in what we may perhaps call Litanies of Blessing.

The adhān

(The Call to Prayer made by the Muezzin before each of the five daily Prayer services. It is generally called from the minaret of the mosque.)

Allah is very great! Allah is very great! Allah is very great!
Allah is very great!

I bear witness that there is no deity save Allah. I bear witness that there is no deity save Allah. I bear witness that Muḥammad is the Apostle of Allah. I bear witness that Muḥammad is the Apostle of Allah.

Come along to prayer! Come along to prayer!
Come along to salvation! Come along to salvation!
Allah is very great! Allah is very great!
There is no deity save Allah.

(At the dawn prayer, after "Come along to salvation" is added the sentence: "Prayer is better than sleep. Prayer is better than sleep.")

The durūd

(This is a benediction which forms part of the ordinary daily Prayer service.)

O Allah! have mercy upon Muḥammad and on his descendants, as Thou didst have mercy on Abraham and on his descendants. Thou art to be praised, and great art Thou. Oh Allah! bless Muḥammad and his descendants, as Thou didst bless Abraham and his descendants. Thou art to be praised, and great art Thou.

The Du'ā' al-Qunūt

(A prayer, sometimes called *Qunūt al-Witr*, which is recited during the Night Prayer.)

O Allah! from Thee we seek help and the forgiveness of sins. We believe in Thee and in Thee put our trust. We praise Thee, we thank Thee, for we are not of the unthankful. We expel and we withdraw from anyone who does not obey Thee. Thee only do we worship, and to Thee we pray. We seek Thee, we bow down and worship Thee. We hope for Thy mercy and fear Thy punishments. Surely Thy judgments are on the infidels.

A prayer when going out to prayers [1]

Abū Sa'īd al-Khudrī quoted from the Prophet: "If a man on going out to prayers says: 'Allahumma! I beg of Thee by the right of those who make request of Thee; by the right of this journey I am making, for I have not come out for joy or merriment, neither to be seen nor to be heard, but I have come out in fear of Thy wrath and with desire that Thou shouldst be well-pleased, I beg of Thee not to cast me into Hell-fire, but cause me to enter into Paradise, and forgive me my sins, for there is no one who forgives sins save Thee', then seventy thousand angels will go out with him begging forgiveness for him, and Allah will turn a friendly face towards him till he finishes that prayer service."

A bed-time prayer [2]

Before he went to sleep the Apostle of Allah—upon whom be Allah's blessing and peace—used to pray: "Allahumma! It was Thou who didst create my soul, and it is Thou Who wilt call it in at death. It is for Thee

[1] From Ibn Taimīya, *Qā'ida jalīla fī't-Tawassul* (Cairo, 1373 A.H.), p. 111.
From Ibn Qaiyim al-Jawzīya, *Kitāb ar-Rūḥ* (Hyderabad, 1324 A.H.), p. 237.

to put it to death and to quicken it again. Shouldst Thou take it [this night] show mercy to it, and shouldst Thou send it back [to tomorrow's duties], guard Thou it in the same way as Thou hast ever guarded Thy servants the righteous ones."

Pilgrim prayers [1]

"Allahumma! this is the sacred place which Thou didst declare sacred by the tongue of Thy Apostle, so forbid my body to the fire (of Hell), and keep me safe from Thy punishment on the Day when Thou wilt raise Thy servants. Grant me such sustenance as Thou has granted to Thy saints, and keep me standing firm in a well-disciplined life, and in the doing of good, by Thy favour, O Thou most merciful of those who show mercy."

"Allahumma! set a light in my heart, and a light in my sight. Allahumma! expand my breast and ease for me my affair", then let him stand as the Apostle stood among the great rocks which are at the foot of the mountain of mercy.

"Allahumma! let not my standing here be the end of my covenant, but let it be a blessing for me so long as I live. Make me this day one whose petitions are answered, one whose sins are forgiven. Grant me Thy approval and abundant legitimate sustenance such as will be a comfort to me. Bless me in all my affairs, in my family, in my property, in my progeny."

"Praise be to Allah, such praise as befits His favours and is a suitable response to His liberality and His generosity. Of Thee do I ask forgiveness for all my transgressions, both those of which I am aware and those of which I am not aware. Allahumma! to Thee be such praise as will fill the heavens and fill the earth, such as will be agreeable and well-pleasing to Thee. Allahumma! as Thou hast bestowed on me the favour of belonging to those present at the place made sacred by Thy Apostle, where he was the recipient of Thy revelation, let me have the favour of living a well-disciplined life before this noble Prophet. Have him receive me and be well-pleased with me. Make me one for whom his intercession will avail. Grant me the consolation of Thy being well-pleased with me,

[1] Prayers used by Pilgrims during visitation of the holy cities of Mecca and Madīna. Translated from the *Irshād al-Ḥājj* of Muṣṭafā Muḥammad 'Ammāra (Cairo, 1926), pp. 19, 67, 68, 71.

and his being well-pleased, O Thou most merciful of those who show mercy.

Allahumma! there is no one who can debar what Thou dost give nor give what Thou dost debar, nor is there any one who can rescind what Thou hast decreed. Raise high, I beseech Thee, remembrance of me; remit my load [of sin]; set right my affair; enlighten my heart; forgive me my trespasses; bless me in my nature and my habits, in my family, in my property and in my labour. Of Thee I beseech the highest ranks in this life and after death.

Prayers of supplication

(Brief prayers included in the Collections of Tradition as supplications which Muḥammad recommended his followers to use.[1])

Say: "Allahumma! make my inner life better than my outward, but make my outward life a good one. Allahumma! I ask of Thee what is good from that which Thou sendest to men, whether of wealth, or of womenfolk, or of progeny who neither go astray nor lead astray."

Say: "Allahumma! creator of the heavens and the earth, knower of the unseen as well as of the seen, Lord and ruler of everything, I bear witness that there is no deity save Thee. With Thee do I take refuge from the evil of my own self, from the evil of Satan and his snare." Say this when morning comes, when evening comes, and when you go to bed.

Say: "Allahumma! I ask Thee for a tranquil soul which believes in the Meeting with Thee [on the Last Day], is well-pleased with whatever Thou dost decree, and is contented with what Thou dost bestow."

Say: "Allahumma! I am weak, so strengthen me. I am lowly, so exalt me. I am poor so give me good-fortune."

Say: "Allahumma! Thy forgiveness is wider than my transgressions, and Thy mercy is a greater source of hope for me than my own works."

Say when you wake up in the morning: "A Bismillah for myself, for my womenfolk, for my property", and then nothing will go from you.

Whenever morning comes, or evening, say: "A Bismillah for my religion, for my soul, for my son, for my womenfolk, and for my property."

Say: "Allahumma! forgive me; show me mercy; protect me; give me

[1] From as-Suyūṭī's *al-Jāmiʿ aṣ-ṣaghīr min Ḥadīth al-Bashīr an-Nadhīr* (ed. Muḥyi'd-Dīn 'Abd al-Ḥamīd, Cairo, 1352 A.H.). As-Suyūṭī (d. 911 A.H. = 1505 A.D.) was an Egyptian polygraph, whose *al-Jāmiʿ* is one of the more famous epitomes of Muslim Tradition. The prayers are Nos. 6134–6144 (Vol. II, pp. 215, 216).

good-fortune", for these [petitions] will secure for you both this world and the next.

Say: "Allahumma! grievously have I wronged my soul. There is no one save Thee who forgives transgressions, so forgive me with a forgiveness from Thee, and have mercy on me. It is Thou who art the Forgiving, the Merciful."

Say: "Allahumma! guide me and direct me," keeping in mind with regard to guidance the straight course of a path, and with regard to direction the straight flight of an arrow.

A prayer [1]

"Allahumma! of Thee do I ask mercy, a mercy from Thyself whereby my heart may be guided, my affair comprised, my disorder repaired, my unseen future made fitting and my seen present raised higher, my actions purified, my life's direction inspired and my fellowship restored. Preserve me thereby from all evil. Allahumma! give me faith, [give me] such certainty that after it there can be no unbelief, and a mercy whereby I may attain to the honour of Thy regard in this world and the next. Allahumma! I ask of Thee deliverance at the Judgment, the reward of the martyrs, the life of the Blessed, and victory over my enemies. Allahumma! with Thee do I lodge my affair, and if my skill has fallen short or my actions have proved feeble I stand in need of Thy mercy, so I ask of Thee, O Thou decider of affairs, O Thou healer of [men's] breasts, as Thou dost protect [the ship that is] among the waves, protect me from the torment of as-Sa'īr,[2] from calling for destruction,[3] and from the trials [4] of the tomb. Allahumma! whatever it be where my skill has fallen short, my resolution failed, my questing not attained, whether it be some good thing Thou hast promised to one of Thy creatures, or some good thing Thou art giving to one of Thy servants, humbly do I make my request to Thee for it, asking it of Thee for Thy mercy's sake, O Lord of the Worlds."

"Allahumma! Lord of the strong bond [5] and the rightly directed affair,

[1] As-Suyūṭī, *al-Jāmi' aṣ-ṣaghīr*. This prayer is No. 1477 in his collection (Vol. I, pp. 188–190) and is apparently meant to be taken as a prayer which the Prophet taught his followers.

[2] One of the Qur'ānic names for Hell, or for a part thereof. Cf. LXXXIV, 12.

[3] Sūra LXXXIV, 11 speaks of those who on the Day of Judgment will call for destruction. See also XXV, 13/14, 14/15.

[4] A *fitna* is a trial or a testing, and the *fitna* of the tomb is an expression often used for the questioning of the deceased in the tomb by Munkar and Nakīr. See pp. 209, 417.

[5] *ḥabl* is literally a cord or a rope, but is used of Allah's bond in Sūra III, 103/98.

I ask Thee for security on the threatened Day,[1] for Paradise on that Day of eternal things, along with the angels [2] who draw near, along with those who kneel in obeisance, along with those who fulfil [their] covenants. Verily Thou art the Merciful, the Loving, and Thou doest whatever Thou desirest. Allahumma! make us guides who are themselves guided, not those who are astray, nor those who lead astray. [Make us] at peace with Thy saints but inimical to Thine enemies. Let us love with Thy love whosoever loves Thee, but be hostile with Thy hostility to whosoever disobeys Thee. Allahumma! this is the petition, but it is for Thee to answer; this is the endeavour, but reliance is on Thee."

"Allahumma! grant me a light in my heart, a light in my tomb, a light before me and a light behind me, a light on my right hand and on my left, a light above me and a light below me, a light in my hearing and a light in my seeing, a light in my hair and a light in my skin, a light in my flesh, a light in my blood and a light in my bones. Allahumma! magnify for me a light; grant me a light; appoint for me a light. Glory be to Him Who has wrapped Himself in might and is named thereby. Glory be to Him Who has clothed Himself in glory and is honoured thereby. Glory be to Him to Whom alone glory should be ascribed. Glory be to the possessor of bounty and grace. Glory be to the Possessor of glory and honour. Glory be to the Possessor of majesty and nobility."

Prayers of supplication [3]

(1)

"Allahumma! Thou hearest my words and beholdest my position. Thou knowest what I have in secret and what manifest. Nothing of my affair is hidden from Thee. I am the unhappy poor one who is calling for help, calling for assistance, fearful, anxious, acknowledging and confessing his sins. I beg of Thee with the plea of an unfortunate one, beseech Thee with the supplication of a vile sinner, implore Thee with the importunate prayer of a man who is blind, whose neck is bowed to Thee, whose tears overflow to Thee, whose body is abased before Thee, and whose nose is in the dust before Thee. Allahumma! make me not unfortunate in my supplication to Thee, but be kindly to me and compassionate, O Thou best of those who are asked, Thou best of those who give."

[1] *yaum al-wa'id* is one of the many names of the Last Day. It is so called in Sūra L, 20/19.

[2] *shuhūd* literally means eye-witnesses, but here seems to mean the angels who draw near the Throne and witness all the events of the Day of Judgment.

[3] As-Suyūṭī, *al-Jāmi'*, Nos. 1481–1483, 1486–1490 (Vol. I, pp. 190–193).

(2)

"Allahumma! make good that which is between us, unite our hearts and guide us to paths of peace. Grant us escape from the darkness into the light, and cause us to avoid immoralities, both those which appear and those which are hidden. Allahumma! grant us blessing in our hearing, in our seeing, in our hearts, in our wives and in our children. Forgive us, for Thou art the Forgiving One, the Compassionate.[1] Make us thankful for Thy bounty, freely praising Thee for it, gratefully receiving it, and make it perfect for us."

(3)

"Allahumma! to Thee I make complaint of my feeble strength, of my small abilities, my lowly estate. O Most Merciful of those who shew mercy,[2] to whom wilt Thou intrust me? To an enemy who will meet me with frowning face, or to a kinsman whom Thou hast put over my affair? So long as Thou art not discontent with me I am not anxious, save that seeking subsistence from Thee is more favourable for me. I take refuge with the light of Thy noble countenance by which heavens and earth are illumined, the darkness turned to light, and both this world and the next set right, against Thine anger alighting or Thy discontent descending upon me. It is Thine to grant favour so long as Thou art well-pleased. There is no might nor any strength save with Thee."

(4)

"Allahumma! guard me by Islam when I am standing; guard me by Islam when I am sitting; guard me by Islam when I am sleeping, and let no enemy nor any envious person rejoice over me. Allahumma! of Thee do I ask every good whose treasuries [3] are in Thy hand, and with Thee do I take refuge from every evil whose treasuries are in Thy hand."

(5)

"Allahumma! we ask of Thee Thy momentous mercy, Thy constant forgiveness, freedom from all sin, attainment of every virtue, the attainment of Paradise and escape from Hell-fire."

[1] Cf. Sūra II, 37/35.
[2] Allah is so called in Sūra VII, 151/150.
[3] Sūra XV, 21 says: "There is not a thing but with Us are its treasuries", i.e. its storehouses.

(6)

"Allahumma! long let me enjoy my seeing and my hearing till Thou dost make them my heir. Grant me soundness in my religion and in my body, and give me the victory over everyone who oppresses me till Thou dost cause me to see my revenge on him. Allahumma! I have handed myself over to Thee, entrusted my affair to Thee, committed myself to Thy protection, turned my face to Thee alone. There is no refuge and no escape from Thee save [by turning] to Thee. I have believed in Thy Apostle whom Thou didst send, and in Thy Book which Thou hast sent down."

(7)

"Allahumma! with Thee do I take refuge from inability, from sloth, from faintheartedness, from miserliness, from decrepitude, from hardness of heart, from heedlessness, from poverty, from weakness, from destitution. I take refuge with Thee from need, from unbelief, from immorality, from contention,[1] from hypocrisy, from [doing things for the sake of] being heard or seen. With Thee do I take refuge from deafness, from dumbness, from insanity,[2] from elephantiasis, from leprosy and from evil diseases."

(8)

"Allahumma! with Thee do I take refuge from a knowledge that does not profit, from a heart that is not reverent, from a petition that is not heard, from a soul that is never satisfied, from hunger, for it is the worst of bedfellows, from perfidy, for it is the worst of familiars, from sloth, from miserliness, from faintheartedness [3] and from decrepitude. [With Thee do I take refuge from] being recalled to a dependent stage of life, from the trials of ad-Dajjāl, from the torment of the tomb, from the trials of life and death.[4] Allahumma! of Thee do we ask hearts that are truly repentant,[5] humble, walking penitently in Thy way. Allahumma! we ask of Thee Thy constant forgiveness, the disclosing of Thy command, freedom from

[1] *shiqāq*, which, however, could mean "schism".

[2] *junūn* is literally "jinn possession", but may here be used to mean madness in general rather than the special case of madness by spirit-possession.

[3] *jubn* which both here and in the previous prayer has been rendered "faintheartedness", may mean "cowardice".

[4] Again the word is *fitna* as on p. 525. For the *fitna* of ad-Dajjāl, the Antichrist, see p. 477.

[5] Lit. "which cry out 'Alas!'"

all sin, attainment of every virtue, attainment of Paradise and escape from Hell."

(9)

"Allahumma! as I increase in years and my life span is progressively shortening, expand Thy provision for me."

(10)

"Allahumma! I ask Thee for continence and soundness in my worldly life and my religious life, in my family and in my property. Allahumma! curtain off my pudenda, tranquillize my fears, protect me from in front and from behind, from the right hand and from the left, and from above. With Thee do I take refuge against being taken unawares from below."

A LITANY OF BLESSINGS ON THE PROPHET

(From the *Dalā'il al-Khairāt wa Shawāriq al-Anwār fī Dhikr aṣ-Ṣalāt 'alā'n-Nabī al-mukhtār*, by Muḥammad al-Juzūlī, Cairo, 1329 A.H. [=1911 A.D.], pp. 6–8 and 56–72.)

In the name of Allah, the Merciful, the Compassionate

May Allah grant blessings to our master Muḥammad, and to his family and his Companions, and grant peace. O my God, by the high ranking of Thy Prophet, our master Muḥammad—upon whom be Allah's blessing and peace—with Thee, and by his position with Thee, by Thy love for him and his love for Thee, by the secret there is between him and Thee, I ask Thee to grant Thy blessing and peace to him and to his family and to his companions. Increase also, Allahumma, my love for him, and teach me to know what is due to him [from me], and to understand his dignity. Help me to follow him and to maintain his way of life. Bring me into contact with him and grant me to enjoy a vision of him. Assist me by his perfection, and remove from me [all] hindrances and [earthly] attachments, [all] intermediaries and veils.

Adorn my repute with him by a pleasing statement [of it], and give me joy at meeting him. Make me worthy of serving him, and make my prayer for him a light, a bright [light], perfect and perfecting, pure and purifying, dispelling all obscurities and darkness, all doubt and association *(shirk)*,[1] all unbelief, falsehood and sin. Make it a cause for the forgiveness [of sins], and a ladder whereby I may attain the highest position of election and special regard, so that in me there may remain no feeling that there could be a Lord other than Thee. [Grant this] so that I may set myself right with Thee, and be one of Thy special people, holding fast to the way of life of him—on whom be Allah's blessing and peace—, seeking succor from his exalted presence at every time and season.

[1] *shirk*, which is the greatest of all sins in the Islamic catalogue of greater sins, is the sin of associating any other being or thing with Allah in a way which would compromise His uniqueness. See p. 260.

The second ḥizb for Tuesday

Allahumma, I beg of Thee the good of that which Thou knowest, and I take refuge with Thee from the evil of that which Thou knowest, and I beseech Thy forgiveness for all of that which Thou knowest. Thou knowest and we do not know, for Thou art the One Who hast knowledge of the unseen.

Allahumma, be merciful to me in my time with its accompanying distresses, when audacious men trespass on my rights, treating me as a feeble person. Allahumma, set me as of Thyself in a refuge place inaccessible, and in a safe place hard to be reached by any of Thy creatures, where I may be preserved safe till there come to me my allotted term.

Allahumma, grant blessings to our lord Muḥammad, and to the family of our lord Muḥammad, [blessings] to the number of those who pray for him; and grant blessings to our lord Muḥammad, and to the family of our lord Muḥammad, to the number of those who have not prayed for him; and grant blessings to our lord Muḥammad, and to the family of our lord Muḥammad, [to the extent to which] he ought to have been prayed for; and grant blessings to our lord Muḥammad, and to the family of our lord Muḥammad, as he must be prayed for; and grant blessings to our lord Muḥammad, and to the family of our lord Muḥammad, as Thou hast bidden that he be prayed for; and grant blessings to our lord Muḥammad, and to the family of our lord Muḥammad, whose light is from the light of lights, and by the rays from whose heart [all] hearts are ennobled.

Allahumma, grant blessings to our lord Muḥammad, and to the family of our lord Muḥammad, and to the kin of his house, all those just ones. Allahumma, grant blessings to our lord Muḥammad, and to the family of our lord Muḥammad, [seeing that he is] the sea of Thy lights, the mine of Thy secrets, the tongue of Thy plea, the bridegroom of Thy kingdom, the Imām of Thy presence, the seal of Thy prophets. [Grant him such] blessings as shall endure so long as Thou dost endure, and continue as long as Thou dost continue; such blessings as will be well-pleasing to Thee and to him, and by which Thou wilt be well satisfied with us, O Lord of the Worlds.

Allahumma, Lord of the sacred and the profane, Lord of the sacred pilgrimage centre, Lord of the sacred House, Lord of the column and the Maqām,[1] transmit from us greeting to our lord and our master Muḥ-

[1] The references are to places of visitation during the pilgrimage to Mecca.

ammad. Allahumma, grant blessings to our lord and master Muḥammad, lord of the former and the latter peoples. Allahumma, grant blessings to our lord and master Muḥammad at all times and seasons. Allahumma, grant blessings to our lord and master Muḥammad in the highest measure till the Last Day.

Allahumma, grant blessings to our lord and master Muḥammad until [the day when] Thou dost inherit the earth and all that is thereon, for Thou art the best of inheritors. Allahumma, grant blessings to our lord Muḥammad, the *ummī*[1] Prophet and to the family of our lord Muḥammad, as Thou didst grant blessings to our lord Abraham. Thou art the Praiseworthy, the Glorious, so bless our lord Muḥammad, the *ummī* Prophet, as Thou didst bless our lord Abraham. Thou art the Praiseworthy, the Glorious.

Allahumma, grant blessings to our lord Muḥammad, and to the family of our lord Muḥammad, [blessings] as many as Thy knowledge can encompass, Thy pen write, Thy will predetermine. May Thine angels pray for him prayers which will continue as long as Thou dost continue, and endure as long as does Thy grace and Thy doing of good, which are for ever and ever, without beginning and without end, since their continuance suffers no passing away.

Allahumma, grant blessings to our lord Muḥammad, and to the family of our lord Muḥammad, [blessings] as many as Thy knowledge can encompass, Thy book recount, Thine angels witness. Grant Thy approval to his Companions. Be merciful to his community. Thou art praiseworthy and glorious. Allahumma, grant blessings to our lord Muḥammad, and to the family of our lord Muḥammad, and to all the companions of our lord Muḥammad. Allahumma, grant blessings to our lord Muḥammad, and to the family of our lord Muḥammad, as Thou didst grant blessings to our lord Abraham. Bless our lord Muḥammad and the family of our lord Muḥammad as Thou didst bless our lord Abraham and the family of our lord Abraham in the world. Thou art praiseworthy and glorious.

Allahumma, grant blessings to our lord and master Muḥammad, [blessings] to the number that Thy knowledge can encompass. Allahumma, grant blessings to our lord and master Muḥammad, to the number that Thy book can record. Allahumma, grant blessings to our lord and master Muḥammad, to the number that Thy power can carry out. Allahumma, grant blessings to our lord and master Muḥammad, to the number that Thy will can particularize. Allahumma, grant blessings to our

[1] This title *ummī* is given to Muḥammad in the Qur'ān (VII, 157/156, 158). See pp. 314, 618.

lord and master Muḥammad, to the number that Thy command and Thy prohibition can direct. Allahumma, grant blessings to our lord and master Muḥammad, to the number that Thy hearing is wide [enough to embrace]. Allahumma, grant blessings to our lord and master Muḥammad, to the number that Thy sight can encompass. Allahumma, grant blessings to our lord and master Muḥammad, to the number of the remembrances of those who remember him. Allahumma, grant blessings to our lord and master Muḥammad, to the number of times the careless ones have forgotten to remember him.

Allahumma, grant blessings to our lord and master Muḥammad, to the number of the raindrops. Allahumma, grant blessings to our lord and master Muḥammad, to the number of the leaves on the trees. Allahumma, grant blessings to our lord and master Muḥammad, to the number of the beasts in the wilderness. Allahumma, grant blessings to our lord and master Muḥammad, to the number of the creatures in the sea. Allahumma, grant blessings to our lord and master Muḥammad, to the number of the waters in the ocean. Allahumma, grant blessings to our lord and master Muḥammad, to the number of the things over which night sheds its darkness and day sheds its light.

Allahumma, grant blessings to our lord and master Muḥammad in the mornings and in the evenings. Allahumma, grant blessings to our lord and master Muḥammad to the number of the sand grains. Allahumma, grant blessings to our lord and master Muḥammad, to the number there are of women and of men. Allahumma, grant blessings to our lord and master Muḥammad to the extent that will please Thee. Allahumma, grant blessings to our lord and master Muḥammad to the full measure of Thy words [for blessing]. Allahumma, grant blessings to our lord and master Muḥammad to the fullness of Thy heavens and Thy earth. Allahumma, grant blessings to our lord and master Muḥammad [to the number which would amount] to the weight of Thy Throne. Allahumma, grant blessings to our lord and master Muḥammad, to the number of the things which Thou hast created.

Allahumma, grant blessings to our lord and master Muḥammad, [even] the most bountiful of Thy blessings. Allahumma, grant blessings to the Prophet of Mercy. Allahumma, grant blessings to him who intercedes for the people. Allahumma, grant blessings to him who clears up the difficult cases. Allahumma, grant blessings to him who lightens the darkness. Allahumma, grant blessings to him who brings benefit [to his community]. Allahumma, grant blessings to the bringer of mercy. Allahumma, grant blessings to the lord of the Pool to which the people will come to drink.

Allahumma, grant blessings to the lord of the position belauded *(maqām maḥmūd)*. Allahumma, grant blessings to the lord of the entrusted standard. Allahumma, grant blessings to the lord of the place clearly seen.[1]

Allahumma, grant blessings to him to whom are ascribed generosity and liberality. Allahumma, grant blessings to him who in heaven is our master well-praised, and who on earth was our master Muḥammad. Allahumma, grant blessings to him who possessed the beauty spot.[2] Allahumma, grant blessings to him who possessed the sign [of prophethood]. Allahumma, grant blessings to him to whom is ascribed honour. Allahumma, grant blessings to him who is singled out for leadership. Allahumma, grant blessings to him whom the cloud overshadowed. Allahumma, grant blessings to him who could see behind him just as he could see in front of him. Allahumma, grant blessings to the intercessor who will be asked to intercede [for mankind] on the Day of Resurrection.

Allahumma, grant blessings to the lord of supplication. Allahumma, grant blessings to the lord of mediation. Allahumma, grant blessings to him who is the way of access. Allahumma, grant blessings to him who is the lord of virtue. Allahumma, grant blessings to him who has the most exalted rank [among mankind]. Allahumma, grant blessings to him who is the possessor of the staff [of authority]. Allahumma, grant blessings to him who is the possessor of the sandals. Allahumma, grant blessings to him who is the possessor of the convincing proof. Allahumma, grant blessings to him who has the demonstration. Allahumma, grant blessings to him who has the authority [of Allah]. Allahumma, grant blessings to him who has the crown. Allahumma, grant blessings to him who ascended [to heaven on the night of the Mi'rāj]. Allahumma, grant blessings to him who has the sceptre. Allahumma, grant blessings to him who mounts the noble steed. Allahumma, grant blessings to him who rides along on Burāq. Allahumma, grant blessings to him who [on the heavenly journey] pierced through the seven spheres. Allahumma, grant blessings to him who will be the intercessor for all men. Allahumma, grant blessing to

1 The references in these lines are all to matters of eschatology and the preeminent place that Muḥammad is pictured as having in the events of the Last Day. The Pool *(ḥawḍ)* is beyond the Bridge which all have to cross after judgment, and at which they refresh themselves after the dreadful experience of the Bridge, and purify themselves for entrance into Paradise. The *maqām maḥmūd* is the position promised Muḥammad in Sūra XVII, 79/81. After judgment various groups will be led by distinguished persons bearing standards, who will lead them to the clearly seen places prepared for them in Paradise or Hell. See pp. 225–226.

2 The references in this section and those which follow are to the *shamā'il* or "characteristics" of the Prophet. They are set forth in great detail in the many little *shamā'il*-books which are popular devotional reading in Islamic lands.

him in whose hand the food [that he was about to eat] gave glory. Allahumma, grant blessings to him for whom the palm-stock wept and yearned for him as he went from it.

Allahumma, grant blessings to him to whom the fowl of the desert made supplication. Allahumma, grant blessings to him in whose palms the stones sang praises. Allahumma, grant blessings to him to whom the fawn made eloquent supplication. Allahumma, grant blessings to him to whom the bear spake while he was sitting with his exalted Companions. Allahumma, grant blessings to the bringer of good tidings, the warner. Allahumma, grant blessings to him who is the bright-shining lamp. Allahumma, grant blessings to him to whom the camel made complaint. Allahumma, grant blessings to him from whose fingers the clear water gushed forth. Allahumma, grant blessings to the pure one, the purified. Allahumma, grant blessings to the light of lights. Allahumma, grant blessings to him for whom the moon was split.

Allahumma, grant blessings to the one who is sweet and perfumed. Allahumma, grant blessings to the Apostle, who is one of those brought near [the Throne]. Allahumma, grant blessings to [him who is like] the spreading dawn. Allahumma, grant blessings to the [one who is like the] shining star. Allahumma, grant blessings to him [who is like] a bond most firm. Allahumma, grant blessings to him who is the warner for the inhabitants of earth. Allahumma, grant blessings to him who will be the intercessor on the Day of Presentation. Allahumma, grant blessings to him who will give the people refreshing drink from the Pool. Allahumma, grant blessings to him who will bear the Banner of Praise. Allahumma, grant blessings to him who exerted all his energies [in fulfilling his mission]. Allahumma, grant blessings to him who labours with all his strength at what is well-pleasing to Thee. Allahumma, grant blessings to the Prophet who is the seal [of the prophets]. Allahumma, grant blessings to the Apostle who is the seal [of the apostles]. Allahumma, grant blessings to the chosen one, the upright one.

Allahumma, grant blessings to Thy Apostle, Abū 'l-Qāsim.[1] Allahumma, grant blessings to him who had the signs. Allahumma, grant blessings to him who had the proofs. Allahumma, grant blessings to him who had the indications. Allahumma, grant blessings to him who had the wonders. Allahumma, grant blessings to him who had the sign-marks. Allahumma, grant blessings to him who had the demonstrations. Allahumma, grant blessings to him who had the miracles. Allahumma, grant

[1] See p. 93.

blessings to him who had marvels happen to him. Allahumma, grant blessings to him to whom the stones gave greeting. Allahumma, grant blessings to him before whom the trees did obeisance. Allahumma, grant blessings to him at whose brightness the blossoms opened up. Allahumma, grant blessings to him at whose blessedness the fruits became sweet. Allahumma, grant blessings to him the dregs of whose ablution water caused the trees to become green [with foliage]. Allahumma, grant blessings to him from whose light all lights have come forth. Allahumma, grant blessings to him by asking blessings on whom all sins are put away. Allahumma, grant blessings to him by asking blessings on whom the dwellings of the righteous are attained. Allahumma, grant blessings to him by asking blessings on whom the old and the young find mercy. Allahumma, grant blessings to him by asking blessings on whom a pleasant life is assured in this world and the next. Allahumma, grant blessings to him by asking blessings on whom we attain the mercy of the Sublime, the Forgiver. Allahumma, grant blessings to him who is victorious, divinely aided. Allahumma, grant blessings to him who is the selected one, the glorified. Allahumma, grant blessings to our lord and master Muḥammad. Allahumma, grant blessings to him whose footsteps the wild beasts followed closely when he walked in the desert lands. Allahumma, grant blessings to him and to his family, and to his Companions, and perfect peace.

And praise be to Allah, Lord of the Worlds

FRIDAY PRAYERS

While it is not correct to call Friday the Muslim Sabbath, as Sunday is commonly called the Christian Sabbath, since Friday in Islam was in no sense instituted as a day of rest, nevertheless, as the day of special assembly for a special form of worship, with a special service, including a sermon *(khuṭba)*, Friday prayers are in a sense the Muslim equivalent of the holy days of Jews and Christians. There is some uncertainty as to just when the Prophet first instituted Friday prayers, whether just before he left Mecca, or as soon as he settled in Madīna (see Buhl-Schaeder, *Das Leben Muhammeds*, pp. 214, 215), but it was in Madīna that it became a formal religious duty. Its formal regulations bear clear evidence of having been based on the practice of the People of the Book, but the notion, appearing often in the Traditions, that Friday was chosen deliberately as a day preceding the holy days of the Jews and Christians, to be indicative of Islam's precedence, is but a conceit of later piety. The Friday prayer service takes the place of midday prayers, is held in the mosque *(masjid)* as a congregational service, and angels are said to sit at the gate of every mosque to record the attendance and assist at the service (Aḥmad b. Ḥanbal, *Musnad*, II, 239). Both Traditionists and theologians have made much of the practical religious value of the proper observance of Friday.

On observance of Friday [1]

That the assembling thereon is a duty

Sa'īd b. 'Abd ar-Raḥmān al-Makhzūmī has informed us on the authority of Sufyān, from Abū 'z-Zinād, from al-A'raj, from Abū Huraira, as also Ṭā'ūs, from his father, from Abū Huraira, that the Apostle of Allah—upon whom be Allah's blessing and peace—said: "We are the last and yet the first. [We Muslims are] last since they (i.e. the Jews and Christians) were given scripture before us, we being given it later then they were, and [they were given] also this day which Allah—mighty and majestic is He—ordained for them, but they differed about it, i.e. about Friday, so Allah guided us to it so that other communities follow us (i.e. come after us) in this, so that the Jews have Saturday and the Christians Sunday; then Allah brought us along and guided us to Friday. [The order of days as]

[1] From the *Kitāb as-Sunan* of Aḥmad an-Nasā'ī (Cairo, 1312 A.H.), pp. 201–211.

He has appointed them is Friday, Saturday, Sunday, so on the Last Day [when peoples are called in their communities] they will be following after us. Thus in this world we are the last people [to be formed into a religious community] but on the Last Day we shall be the first, those who receive their judgment before [other] creatures."

On the excellence of Friday

Suwaid b. Naṣr has informed us, on the authority of ʿAbdallah, from Yūnus, from az-Zuhrī, who said that ʿAbd ar-Raḥmān al-Aʿraj related how he had heard Abū Huraira say that the Apostle of Allah—upon whom be Allah's blessing and peace—once said: "The sun rises on no better day than Friday, for on it Adam—on whom be peace—was created, on it he was put in the Garden, and on it he was expelled."

On how serious it is to neglect Friday

Yaʿqūb b. Ibrāhīm has informed us, on the authority of Yaḥyā b. Saʿīd, from Muḥammad b. ʿAmr, from ʿUbaida b. Sufyān al-Ḥaḍramī, from Abū 'l-Jaʿd aḍ-Ḍamrī, who was on friendly relations with the Prophet—upon whom be Allah's blessing and peace—that Allah will put a brand on the heart of anyone who passes three Fridays in neglect.[1]

Muḥammad b. Maʿmar has informed us, on the authority of Ḥibbān, from Abān, from Yaḥyā b. Abī Kathīr, from al-Ḥaḍramī b. Lāḥiq, from Zaid, from Abū Sallām, from Ḥakam b. Mīnā', that he heard Ibn ʿAbbās and Ibn ʿUmar relating how the Apostle of Allah—on whom be Allah's blessing and peace—said while in the pulpit: "There will be those who neglect that with which they were entrusted in regard to Friday, on whose hearts Allah will put a seal so that they become of those who neglect."

On proper clothes for Friday

Qutaiba has informed us, on the authority of Mālik, from Nāfiʿ, from ʿAbdallah b. ʿUmar, that ʿUmar b. al-Khaṭṭāb[2] saw a cloak [for sale] and said: "O Apostle of Allah, if I bought this cloak I could wear it on Fridays and for [receiving] delegations when they come to call on you."

[1] The commentary says that this means that if a man neglects the Friday prayer service three Fridays in succession Allah will put a veil on his heart and will withdraw from him His favours.

[2] The second Caliph and father-in-law of the Prophet.

Said the Apostle of Allah—upon whom be Allah's blessing and peace—: "No one would wear that [kind of cloak] but he who has no share in the life to come." Later on some of the same kind [of cloaks] were brought as presents to the Apostle of Allah—upon whom be Allah's blessing and peace—and he conferred one of them on 'Umar. Said 'Umar: "O Apostle of Allah, do you cloak me with it after what you said about 'Uṭārid's cloak [which I wanted to buy]?" The Apostle of Allah—upon whom be Allah's blessing and peace—answered: "I did not cloak you with it for you to wear it yourself", so 'Umar gave it to an uncle of his who was a polytheist in Mecca.

Hārūn b. 'Abdallah has informed me, on the authority of al-Ḥasan b. Sawwār, from al-Laith, who said that they had been informed by Abū Bakr b. al-Munkadir that 'Amr b. Sulaim had related from 'Abd ar-Raḥmān b. Abī Sa'īd, from his father, that the Apostle of Allah—upon whom be Allah's blessing and peace—said: "It is [incumbent] on everyone who has reached puberty to bathe on Friday, to use the tooth-pick and such perfume as he is able."

On the excellence of walking to the Friday assembling

'Amr b. 'Uthmān b. Sa'īd b. Kathīr has informed us, on the authority of al-Walīd, from 'Abd ar-Raḥmān b. Yazīd, from Jābir, that he heard Abū 'l-Ash'ath recounting how he had heard Aus b. Aus, a companion of the Apostle of Allah, say that the Apostle of Allah—upon whom be Allah's blessing and peace—said: "Whoever bathes on Friday and washes his body clean, gets up early and goes out early, walking and not riding as he makes his way towards the Imām, preserving silence and not speaking, will have [written to his credit] for every step the [good] works of a year."

On being early at Friday prayers

Naṣr b. 'Alī b. Naṣr has informed us, on the authority of 'Abd al-A'lā, from Ma'mar, from az-Zuhrī, from al-Agharr Abū 'Abdallah, from Abū Huraira, that the Apostle of Allah—upon whom be Allah's blessing and peace—said: "When Friday comes angels seat themselves on the mosque gates and write down [the names of] those who come to Friday prayers, but when the Imām departs [1] the angels fold the sheets." He added:

[1] The departure of the Imām who has been leading the prayers is the signal that the canonical Friday prayers are over, and anything done after that is in the nature of private devotions.

"The Apostle of Allah also said: 'Of those who go to Friday prayers some are like one who offers a she-camel [as sacrifice], some like one who offers a cow, then like one who offers a sheep, then like one who offers a duck, then like one who offers a hen, then like one who offers an egg.'"[1]

Muḥammad b. Manṣūr has informed us, on the authority of Sufyān, from az-Zuhrī, from Sa'īd, from Abū Huraira, that the Prophet—upon whom be Allah's blessing and peace—announced that when Friday comes there are over each gate of the mosque angels who write down the people [who come] in their order, the first first, and so on, till when the Imām departs they fold the sheets and listen to the devotions, so that of those who go to prayers some are like one who makes an offering of a she-camel, some like one who offers a cow, some like one who offers a ram", and so on till he mentioned the hen and the egg.

Ar-Rabī' b. Sulaimān has informed us, on the authority of Shu'aib b. al-Laith, from al-Laith, from Ibn 'Ajlān, from Sumai, from Abū Ṣāliḥ, from Abū Huraira, that the Apostle of Allah—upon whom be Allah's blessing and peace—said: "Every Friday angels sit at the mosque gates writing down the folk in their order [of arrival], so some are like a man who offers a she-camel, some like a man who offers a cow, some like a man who offers a sheep, some like a man who offers a hen, some like a man who offers a sparrow, and some like a man who offers an egg."

On the time for Friday service

Qutaiba has informed us, on the authority of Mālik, from Sumai, from Abū Ṣāliḥ, from Abū Huraira, that the Apostle of Allah—upon whom be Allah's blessing and peace—said: "He who takes a bath on Friday to wash away defilement[2] and then goes out early [to prayers] is as one who offers a she-camel. If he goes at the second hour he is as one who offers a cow. If he goes at the third hour he is as one who offers a ram. If he goes at the fourth hour he is as one who offers a hen. If he goes at the fifth hour he is as one who offers an egg. When, however, the Imām has departed the angels assemble to listen to the devotions."

'Amr b. Sawwād b. al-Aswad b. 'Amr and al-Ḥārith b. Miskīn have informed us, on the authority of Ibn Wahb, from 'Amr b. al-Ḥārith, from al-Julaḥ the *mawlā* (client) of 'Abd al-'Azīz, that Abū Salama b.

[1] He means that to come early is equivalent to offering some big offering, but to come late is like bringing a small offering, and the later the smaller.

[2] *janāba* means the ritual defilement which must be removed before prayers can be performed with validity.

ʿAbd ar-Raḥmān related from Jābir b. ʿAbdallah that the Apostle of Allah—upon whom be Allah's blessing and peace—said: "Friday has twelve hours during which there is no Muslim who asks Allah for anything but He will give it to him, so keep on asking till the last hour after the afternoon prayer."

Hārūn b. ʿAbdallah has informed me, on the authority of Yaḥyā b. Ādam, from Ḥasan b. ʿAyyāsh, from Jaʿfar b. Muḥammad, from his father, from Jābir b. ʿAbdallah, who said: "We used to perform prayers with the Apostle of Allah—upon whom be Allah's blessing and peace—on Friday and then return and rest our beasts that carried our water." "At what hour?" I asked. He replied: "When the sun began to decline" (i.e. shortly after mid-day).

Shuʿaib b. Yūsuf has informed us, on the authority of ʿAbd ar-Raḥmān, from Yaʿlā b. al-Ḥārith, who said: I heard Iyās b. Salama b. al-Akwaʿ relating from his father, who said: "We used to perform Friday prayers with the Apostle of Allah—upon whom be Allah's blessing and peace—and would return while the walls still had no shadow in which one could take shade."

On the call to prayer for Friday service

Muḥammad b. Salama has informed us, on the authority of Ibn Wahb, from Yūnus, from Ibn Shihāb, who said: As-Sā'ib b. Yazīd has informed me that at first the call to prayers on Friday used to be made when the Imām had taken his seat on the pulpit. This was in the time of the Apostle of Allah—upon whom be Allah's blessing and peace—and of Abū Bakr and ʿUmar, but during the Caliphate of ʿUthmān there came to be so many people [coming to prayers] that ʿUthmān gave orders for there to be a third call to prayer, so that call was given on the Zawrā',[1] and this became the customary thing.

Muḥammad b. Yaḥyā b. ʿAbdallah has informed us, on the authority of Yaʿqūb, who said that his father related from Ṣāliḥ, from Ibn Shihāb, that as-Sā'ib b. Yazīd informed him that ʿUthmān gave orders for the third call to prayer on Friday only when the people in Madīna had increased in numbers, but in the time of the Apostle of Allah—upon whom be Allah's blessing and peace—there was normally only one muezzin and on Friday the call to prayer was given when the Imām had taken his seat.

Muḥammad b. ʿAbd al-Aʿlā has informed us, on the authority of al-

[1] The Zawrā' is said to have been a tall house in the market place at Madīna.

Mu'tamir, from his father, from az-Zuhrī, from as-Sā'ib b. Yazīd, who said: "Bilāl used to give the call to prayer on Fridays when the Apostle of Allah—upon whom be Allah's blessing and peace—took his seat on the pulpit, and when he descended he would stand up for prayers. Thus it was also in the time of Abū Bakr and 'Umar—on both of whom be peace.

On the Friday prayers of one who arrives after the imām has departed

Muḥammad b. 'Abd al-A'lā has informed us, on the authority of Khālid, who said: Shu'ba related to us from 'Amr b. Dīnār, who said: I heard Jābir b. 'Abdallah tell how the Apostle of Allah—upon whom be Allah's blessing and peace—said: "If any one of you should arrive after the Imām has departed let him pray two *rak'as*." Shu'ba said that this referred to Friday prayers.

On the place where the imām is to stand to preach

'Amr b. Sawwād b. al-Aswad has informed us, on the authority of Ibn Wahb, from Ibn Juraij, who was informed by Abū 'z-Zubair that he heard Jābir b. 'Abdallah telling how the Apostle of Allah—upon whom be Allah's blessing and peace—used to lean when he preached on one of the palm trunks used as columns in the mosque, but when the pulpit was constructed and he took his stand on it that palmtrunk was distressed and whined like the plaintive whining of a she-camel so as to be heard by all the people in the mosque, till the Apostle of Allah—upon whom be Allah's blessing and peace—went down to it and embraced it, whereat it became silent.

That the imām should stand up to preach

Aḥmad b. 'Abdallah b. al-Ḥakam has informed us, on the authority of Muḥammad b. Ja'far, from Shu'ba, from Manṣūr, from 'Amr b. Murra, from Abū 'Ubaida, from Ka'b b. 'Ujra who said: [Someone] entered the mosque while 'Abd ar-Raḥmān b. Umm al-Ḥakam was sitting preaching, and said: "Look at this fellow preaching while seated. Allah—mighty and majestic is He—has said (LXII, 11): 'But when they see some merchandise or some sport off they go thereto and leave thee standing.'"[1]

[1] The commentators on this verse recount how one day while the Prophet was preaching in Madīna a returning caravan preceded by music entered the city and all his audience ran out to join in welcoming it leaving the Prophet standing there. The

On the benefit of drawing near the imām

Maḥmūd b. Khālid has informed us, on the authority of ʿUmar b. ʿAbd al-Wāḥid, who said: I heard Yaḥyā b. al-Ḥārith relating from Abū 'l-Ashʿath aṣ-Ṣanʿānī, from Aus b. Aus ath-Thaqafī, that the Apostle of Allah—upon whom be Allah's blessing and peace—said: "Whoever bathes and cleanses his body and comes early to draw near to the Imām, preserving silence and not speaking, will have [written to his credit] for every step the recompense for a whole year of fasting and performing prayers."

On how "stepping over the necks"[1] of people when the imām is in the pulpit on Friday is forbidden

Wahb b. Bayān has informed us, on the authority of Ibn Wahb, who said: I heard Muʿāwiya b. Ṣāliḥ relating from Abū 'z-Zāhirīya, from ʿAbdallah b. Busr, who said: I was sitting by his (i.e. the Prophet's) side one Friday when there came a man who started "stepping over the necks" of people, and the Apostle of Allah—upon whom be Allah's blessing and peace—said to him: "Sit down! you are making a nuisance of yourself."[2]

On the Friday prayer of one who comes in while the imām is preaching

Ibrāhīm b. al-Ḥasan and Yūsuf b. Saʿīd have informed us, the latter quoting from Ḥajjāj, from Ibn Juraij, who said: ʿAmr b. Dīnār informed me that he heard Jābir b. ʿAbdallah say that a man came in one Friday while the Prophet—upon whom be Allah's blessing and peace—was in the pulpit, so [the Prophet] said to him: "Have you performed two *rakʿas* of prayer?" "No", answered he. So [the Prophet] said: "Then perform the *rakʿas*."

On listening quietly to the sermon on Friday

Qutaiba has informed us, on the authority of al-Laith, from ʿAqīl, from az-Zuhrī, from Saʿīd b. al-Musayyib, from Abū Huraira, that the Prophet—upon whom be Allah's blessing and peace—said: "He who on Friday

---

point is that this verse shows that the Prophet used to stand while preaching and that therefore other preachers should stand to deliver their sermons.

[1] This is hyperbole for what we should refer to as "craning the neck to see". It refers to those who in their eagerness to get themselves into a position to see the Imām clearly cause inconvenience to others.

[2] Lit. "you are doing harm", but it is rather the inconveniencing of people that is meant than doing any physical harm.

while the Imām is preaching says as much as 'Be silent!' to his companion has spoken needlessly."

'Abd al-Malik b. Shu'aib b. al-Laith b. Sa'd has informed us, on the authority of his father, from his grandfather, from 'Aqīl, from Ibn Shihāb, from 'Amr b. 'Abd al-'Azīz, from 'Abdallah b. Ibrāhīm b. Qāriẓ, and from Sa'īd b. al-Musayyib, that they both recounted how Abū Huraira said: I heard the Apostle of Allah—upon whom be Allah's blessing and peace—say: "If you as much as say to your companion 'Be quiet!' on Friday while the Imām is preaching, you have spoken unnecessarily."

On the excellence of silence and of refraining from talk on Friday

Isḥāq b. Ibrāhīm has informed us, on the authority of Jarīr, from Manṣūr, from Abū Ma'shar Ziyād b. Kulaib, from Ibrāhīm, from 'Alqama, from al-Qartha' aḍ-Ḍabbī, who was one of the early *qurrā'*,[1] from Salmān[2] who said: The Apostle of Allah—upon whom be Allah's blessing and peace—said to me: "There is no man who purifies himself on Friday as he is commanded and then goes out from his house to make his way to Friday prayers, maintaining silence till the service is finished, but will have that [counted as] atonement for [the sins of] the previous days of the week."

On the Friday sermon (khuṭba)

Muḥammad b. al-Muthannā and Muḥammad b. Bashshār have informed us, on the authority of Muḥammad b. Ja'far, from Shu'ba, who said: I heard Abū Isḥāq relating from Abū 'Ubaida, from 'Abdallah, who said: The Prophet—upon whom be Allah's blessing and peace—taught us the proper *khuṭba* for a marriage,[3] viz. "Praise be to Allah. To Him we turn for help and from Him we seek forgiveness. With Allah we take refuge from the evil in our own selves and from the wickedness of our deeds. He whom Allah guides no one can lead astray, and he whom He leads astray no one can guide. I testify that there is no deity save Allah. I testify that Muḥammad is His servant and His apostle." Then let him read three

[1] Lit. "readers" or "reciters". They were the early authorities on the text of the Qur'ān.

[2] This is Salmān al-Fārisī.

[3] A *khuṭba* is normally part of a marriage ceremony, and what is meant here is that what the Prophet had taught as to the form of a *khuṭba* for a marriage could be taken as a model for the *khuṭba* for Friday prayers.

verses, viz. (III, 102/97): "O ye who believe, fear Allah as He ought to be feared, and die not save as Muslims"; (IV, 1): "O ye people, be in godly fear of your Lord who created you from a single person, from whom He created his wife, and from the twain spread abroad many men and women. Reverence Allah, concerning Whom ye ask questions, and the wombs, for Allah is indeed regardful of you"; (XXXIII, 70): "O ye who believe, fear Allah and speak well-disposed speech." Saith Abū ʿAbd ar-Raḥmān:[1] "Abū ʿUbaida did not hear a thing of all this from his father, nor did ʿAbd ar-Raḥmān b. ʿAbdallah b. Masʿūd, nor did ʿAbd al-Jabbār b. Wāʾil b. Ḥajar."

On the imām making special mention in his sermon of bathing on Friday

Muḥammad b. Bashshār has informed us, on the authority of Muḥammad b. Jaʿfar, from Shuʿba, from al-Ḥakam, from Nāfiʿ, from Ibn ʿUmar, who said that the Apostle of Allah—upon whom be Allah's blessing and peace—was once preaching and said: "When one of you [intends] going out to Friday prayers, let him bathe."

Muḥammad b. Salama has informed us on the authority of Ibn Wahb, from Ibrāhīm b. Nashīṭ, that he asked Ibn Shihāb about bathing on Friday, and he replied that it was *sunna*,[2] for Sālim b. ʿAbdallah related from his father that the Apostle of Allah—upon whom be Allah's blessing and peace—spoke about it from the pulpit.

Qutaiba has informed us, on the authority of al-Laith, from Ibn Shihāb, from ʿAbdallah b. ʿAbdallah, from ʿAbdallah b. ʿUmar, that the Apostle of Allah—upon whom be Allah's blessing and peace—while he was standing in the pulpit, said: "Whoever of you comes to Friday prayer let him bathe [beforehand]." Saith Abū ʿAbd ar-Raḥmān (i.e. an-Nasāʾī): I do not know anyone who follows al-Laith in this *isnād* save Ibn Juraij. The friends of Ibn Shihāb relate from Sālim b. ʿAbdallah from his father rather than from ʿAbdallah b. ʿAbdallah from ʿAbdallah b. ʿUmar.

[1] I.e. an-Nasāʾī himself. This is another example of Ḥadīth criticism. He records the Tradition as it came to him but appends a note denying the authenticity of its transmission from Abū ʿUbaida, who in his judgment is one of three who are said to have received Traditions from their fathers though actually none of them ever heard Tradition from his father.

[2] I.e. not obligatory in the first degree like a thing *farḍ* or *wājib*, but obligatory in the second degree, since it was the custom *(sunna)* of the Prophet.

On the imām, during his Friday sermon, urging [the duty of] charitable almsgiving

Muḥammad b. ʿAbdallah b. Yazīd has informed us, on the authority of Sufyān, from Ibn ʿAjlān, from ʿIyāḍ b. ʿAbdallah, who said: I heard Abū Saʿīd al-Khudrī say that one Friday, while the Prophet—upon whom be Allah's blessing and peace—was preaching, a man came in with worn-out garments. The Apostle of Allah—upon whom be Allah's blessing and peace—said to him: "Have you prayed?" "No", answered he. So [the Prophet] said: "Pray two *rakʿas*." Then he urged on the congregation the [duty of] charitable almsgiving, and they threw in a number of robes, two of which he bestowed on the man. The following Friday he came again while the Apostle of Allah—upon whom be Allah's blessing and peace—was preaching and urging on the congregation the [duty of] charitable almsgiving, and threw in one of his two robes. Said the Apostle of Allah—upon whom be Allah's blessing and peace—:"This man came last Friday with worn-out clothes and when I bade the congregation give charitable alms they cast in many robes out of which I ordered him to be given two, and now today he has come again, and when I bade the congregation give charitable alms he has cast in one of them." Then he called to him, saying: "Take your robes."

On the imām's [1] addressing his subjects while he is in the pulpit

Qutaiba has informed us, on the authority of Ḥammād b. Zaid, from ʿAmr b. Dīnār, from Jābir b. ʿAbdallah, who said: While the Prophet—upon whom be Allah's blessing and peace—was preaching one Friday, a man came in and the Prophet—upon whom be Allah's blessing and peace—said to him: "Have you prayed?" "No", he answered. So [the Prophet] said: "Get up and pray the *rakʿas*."

Muḥammad b. Manṣūr has informed us, on the authority of Sufyān, from Abū Mūsā Isrāʾīl b. Mūsā, who said that he had heard al-Ḥasan say: I heard Abū Bakr telling how he saw the Apostle of Allah—upon whom be Allah's blessing and peace—in the pulpit, having with him [his grandson] al-Ḥasan, and he would be one minute occupying himself with him and another with the congregation, and he said (i.e. to the congregation): "This son of mine is a *sayyid* by whom it may be that Allah will make peace between two great parties of the Muslims."

[1] Here the *imām* must be not just the prayer leader for the day but the head of the community.

On reciting [the Qur'ān] during the khuṭba

Muḥammad b. al-Muthannā has informed us, on the authority of Hārūn b. Ismā'īl, from 'Alī b. al-Mubārak, from Yaḥyā, from Muḥammad b. 'Abd ar-Raḥmān, from the daughter of Ḥāritha b. an-Nu'mān, who said: "I learned by heart Sūra L from the mouth of the Apostle of Allah —upon whom be Allah's blessing and peace—while he was on Friday in the pulpit."

On pointing with the finger during the sermon

Maḥmūd b. Ghailān has informed us, on the authority of Wakī', from Sufyān, from Ḥuṣai, that Bishr b. Marwān raised his hand one Friday when he was in the pulpit, and 'Ammāra b. Ruwaiba ath-Thaqafī abused him [for it], saying: "The Apostle of Allah—upon whom be Allah's blessing and peace—never went beyond this", and he pointed with his forefinger.

On the imām's descending from the pulpit on Friday before he has finished his khuṭba, and on his interrupting it and then resuming it

Muḥammad b. 'Abd al-'Azīz has informed us, on the authority of al-Faḍl b. Mūsā, from al-Ḥusain b. Wāqid, from 'Abdallah b. Yazīd, from his father, who said that the Prophet—upon whom be Allah's blessing and peace—was preaching [one Friday] when [his grandsons] al-Ḥasan and al-Ḥusain wandered in wearing red smocks [so long that they were] making them stumble, so the Prophet—upon whom be Allah's blessing and peace—came down, interrupting his discourse, and carried them out. Then he returned to the pulpit, remarking: "Allah has well said (VIII, 28): 'Your possessions and your children are naught but a trial to you.' I saw these two children stumbling in their smocks and could not refrain from interrupting my address and carrying them out."

On what part of the sermon it is desirable to shorten

Muḥammad b. 'Abd al-'Azīz b. Ghazwān has informed us, on the authority of al-Faḍl b. Mūsā, from al-Ḥusain b. Wāqid, from Yaḥyā b. 'Aqīl, who said: I heard 'Abdallah b. Abī Aufā say that the Apostle of Allah—upon whom be Allah's blessing and peace—used to increase the *dhikr* [1]

[1] *dhikr* "making mention" refers to all the pious ejaculations and phrases, such as "Praise be to Allah", "We take refuge with Allah", etc. in which mention is made of the name of Allah.

and decrease the vain talk, lengthen the prayers and shorten the sermon, and never did he disdain to walk with the widow and the unfortunate and fulfil their need.

On how many khuṭbas there should be

ʿAlī b. Ḥujr has informed us, on the authority of Ismāʿīl, from Sammāk, from Jābir b. Samura, who said: I sat in company with the Prophet—upon whom be Allah's blessing and peace—and never did I see him preach save standing. Then he would sit down, then rise and preach the final *khuṭba.*

On sitting during the interval between the two khuṭbas

Ismāʿīl b. Masʿūd has informed us, on the authority of Bishr b. al-Mufaḍḍal, from ʿUbaidallah, from Nāfiʿ, from ʿAbdallah [b. ʿUmar], that the Apostle of Allah—upon whom be Allah's blessing and peace—used to preach the two *khuṭbas* standing, but would sit between times.

On keeping silence while sitting between the two khuṭbas

Muḥammad b. ʿAbdallah b. Bazīʿ, from Yazīd, i.e. Ibn Zuraiʿ, from Isrāʾīl, from Sammāk, from Jābir b. Samura, who said: I saw the Apostle of Allah—upon whom be Allah's blessing and peace—one Friday preaching. He was standing and then sat down for the interval without saying a word, and then rose to preach the other *khuṭba,* so anyone who relates to you that the Apostle of Allah—upon whom be Allah's blessing and peace—used to preach sitting, is a liar.

On recitation [of the Qurʾān] and dhikr in the second khuṭba

ʿAmr b. ʿAlī has informed us, on the authority of ʿAbd ar-Raḥmān, who said: Sufyān related to us from Sammāk, from Jābir b. Samura that the Prophet—upon whom be Allah's blessing and peace—used to preach standing, then would sit, and then rise and recite some verses [of the Qurʾān] and make mention of Allah—mighty and majestic is He—so his *khuṭba* was moderate [1] and his prayer service moderate.

[1] *qaṣdan,* i.e. taking the middle course, neither too short nor too long.

On standing and talking after coming down from the pulpit

Muḥammad b. ʻAlī b. Maimūn has informed us, on the authority of al-Firyābī, from Jarīr b. Ḥāzim, from Thābit al-Banānī, from Anas, who said that the Apostle of Allah—upon whom be Allah's blessing and peace—used to come down from the pulpit, and should a man turn to him and speak to him the Prophet would stand talking with him till he had said what he had to say, then he would proceed to the place of prayer and say prayers.

On the number [of rakʻas] in Friday prayers

ʻAlī b. Ḥujr has informed us, on the authority of Sharik, from Zubaid, from ʻAbd ar-Raḥmān b. Abī Lailā, who reported that ʻUmar said the Friday Prayer was of two *rakʻas*, the prayer on breaking the fast one of two *rakʻas*, the prayer for the feast of sacrifice one of two *rakʻas*, and the prayer for a traveller one of two *rakʻas*, but [in each case] complete and unshortened and in the tongue of Muḥammad—upon whom be Allah's blessing and peace. Saith Abū ʻAbd ar-Raḥmān: "ʻAbd ar- Raḥmān b. Abī Lailā said that he had not heard this from ʻUmar."

That the Qur'ān reading for Friday prayers ought to be sūras LXII and LXIII

Muḥammad b.ʻAbd al-Aʻlā aṣ-Ṣanʻānī has informed us, on the authority of Khālid b. al-Ḥārith, from Shuʻba, who said he was informed by Mukhawwal, from Muslim al-Baṭīn, from Saʻīd b. Jubair, from Ibn ʻAbbās, that on Fridays the Apostle of Allah—upon whom be Allah's blessing and peace—used to recite Sūras XXXII and LXXVI at dawn prayers and Sūras LXII and LXIII at Friday Prayers.

On reciting sūras LXXXVII and LXXXVIII at Friday prayers

Muḥammad b. ʻAbd al-Aʻlā has informed us, on the authority of Khālid, from Shuʻba, from Maʻbad b. Khālid, from Zaid b.ʻUqba, from Samura, who said that the Apostle of Allah—upon whom be Allah's blessing and peace—used to recite Sūras LXXXVII and LXXXVIII at Friday Prayers.

ON THE VIRTUE OF PIETY[1]

It is related that Abū Dharr—with whom may Allah be pleased—told how the Prophet—upon whom be blessings and peace—said to him: "Be watchful, for you are no better than a red man or a black man save as you exceed such in piety" *(at-taqwā)*.[2] It is related from Jābir—with whom may Allah be pleased—that he said: We sought an exhortation from the Apostle of Allah—upon whom be blessings and peace—during the days of *tashrīq*,[3] and he said: "O ye people, your Lord is One. Is it not a fact that the Arab has no superiority over the non-Arab, nor the non-Arab over the Arab, nor the red over the black, nor the black over the red, seeing that ye are all from a single father, save as one is superior in piety? Verily the noblest of you in Allah's sight is the one who is most pious (XLIX, 13). Has this not reached you?" "Yes, indeed, O Apostle of Allah", they answered. So he said: "Then let him who is present see that it reaches him who is absent."

Said the Apostle of Allah—on whom be blessings and peace—: "When the Day comes Allah—exalted be He—will bid a herald cry: 'Is it not a fact that I have appointed a line of pedigree *(nasab)*[4] and ye have appointed a line of pedigree? I have appointed that the noblest among you is that one among you who is most pious, but ye have appointed it so that ye say: So-and-So the son of So-and-So is nobler than So-and-So the son of So-and-So. Today I am exalting My line of pedigree and humbling your line of pedigree. Where are the pious ones?'" It is related

[1] From al-Birkawī's *aṭ-Ṭarīqa al-muḥammadīya wa's-Sīra al-aḥmadīya* (Cairo, 1357 A.H. = 1935 A.D.), pp. 37, 38.

[2] *taqwā* is often translated "godly fear". It is related to the verb *ittaqā* "to keep or preserve oneself" and so may be rendered "piety". The brown Arabs were accustomed to call a Byzantine a red man *(aḥmar)* and a Sudanese or negro a black man *(aswad)*, so the reference here is to racial pride. See Goldziher, *Muhammedanische Studien*, I, pp. 268, 269.

[3] These are the last three days of the Pilgrimage ceremonies, the 11th, 12th and 13th of Dhū 'l-Ḥijja. See pp. 121, 483, 506.

[4] The word refers to those genealogical trees of which the Arabs were so fond and so proud, whereby they traced back the line of their pedigree to such and such an ancestor and boasted with one another of the nobility of their line.

from Abū Dharr—with whom may Allah be pleased—that he told how the Prophet—on whom be blessings and peace—said: "Wait six days, O Abū Dharr, in expectancy for what will be said to you thereafter." When it was the seventh day he said: "I exhort you to show fear of Allah *(taqwā)* both in your private and your public affairs. If you have done ill [to anyone] then do some good to him, but do not ask anything from anyone. Even should your fortune fall do not grab at security."

From Abū Sa'īd al-Khudrī—with whom may Allah be pleased—there is a Tradition about how a man came to the Prophet—upon whom be blessings and peace—and said: "O Prophet of Allah, give me a word of exhortation." He replied: "See that you have fear of Allah *(taqwā)* for it gathers up in itself all good." From Abū Umāma comes a tradition that the Prophet—on whom be blessings and peace—used to say: "After fear *(taqwā)* of Allah there is no good thing whose benefits a man may enjoy greater than to have a pious wife who when he commands her obeys him, when he looks at her is a joy to him, when he adjures her keeps it inviolate, and when he is absent from her observes faithfully her duty towards both him and his property."

From Ibn 'Abbās—with whom and with whose father may Allah be pleased—there is a Tradition that the Prophet—on whom be blessings and peace—once came in from a military expedition, and summoning Fāṭima said to her: "O Fāṭima, make your own bargain with Allah for I can do nothing for you with Allah." He said the same words to his women-folk and to his kinsmen. Then he said: "The Banū Hāshim [1] are not the foremost people in my community, for the foremost people in my community are those who show piety. The Quraish are not the foremost people in my community, for the foremost people in my community are those who show piety Nor are the Anṣār the foremost people in my community, for the foremost people in my community are those who show piety. You are only men and women and you are like the filling up of a grain measure, so no one has any superiority over another save in piety."

Traditions illustrative of this are numerous, and practical life also shows

[1] The Prophet's own family belonged to the Banū Hāshim. The Quraish was the tribe whose chiefs were dominant in Mecca during the Prophet's youth. The Anṣār were the Madinan groups who had promised to stand by Muḥammad if he left Mecca for Madīna. This Tradition, therefore, reflects the rivalry of the three groups after the Prophet's death, the Legitimists holding that the succession should belong of right to the Prophet's kinsfolk, the members of the old aristocracy claiming that it reverted to the leaders of the Quraish, and the Old Believers that it should be with them since they had called the Prophet to Madīna.

the superior virtue of piety *(taqwā)* over other acts of obedience, because dressing comes after undressing, and adorning comes after cleansing, the former [1] being of little avail without the latter whereas there is avail in the opposite process. It (i.e. *taqwā)* is the foundation of all good qualities, so take a strong hold upon it and bid your people take hold upon it in its finest form, for in it there is happiness in both worlds and bliss in both lives.[2] May Allah—exalted be He—grant both us and you the joy thereof, for He is the Beneficent and the Compassionate, the Bountiful and the Generous.

[1] The words he uses here mean that before putting on elegant clothing it is necessary to take off the ordinary clothing, and before adorning the body one naturally bathes and cleanses it.

[2] He means in this world and the next, and in the life here and that hereafter.

A LITANY OF THE BEAUTIFUL NAMES OF ALLAH[1]

1. Ar-Raḥmān	the Merciful One.
2. Ar-Raḥīm	the Compassionate.
3. Al-Malik	the King.
4. Al-Quddūs	the Holy One.
5. As-Salām	the Peace.
6. Al-Mu'min	the Faithful.
7. Al-Muhaimin	the Overseer.
8. Al-ʿAzīz	the Mighty.
9. Al-Jabbār	the Almighty.
10. Al-Mutakabbir	the justly Proud.
11. Al-Khāliq	the Creator.
12. Al-Bāri'	the Maker.
13. Al-Muṣawwir	the Fashioner.
14. Al-Ghaffār	the Pardoner.
15. Al-Qahhār	the Overcomer.
16. Al-Wahhāb	the Bestower.
17. Ar-Razzāq	the Provider.
18. Al-Fattāḥ	the Opener.
19. Al-ʿAlīm	He who knows.
20. Al-Qābiḍ	the Restrainer.
21. Al-Bāsiṭ	the Extender.
22. Al-Khāfiḍ	the Humbler.
23. Ar-Rāfiʿ	the Exalter.

[1] The use of the rosary *(subḥa)* is widespread in the Islamic world. A complete rosary has ninety-nine beads and a large ending bead called a *yad* (hand), but the commonly used rosary has thirty-three beads and a *yad*, so that it has to be gone over three times to complete the ninety-nine. The *yad* represents the all-inclusive name *Allah* but the others represent the ninety-nine beautiful names of Allah, and one is repeated as an ejaculation as each bead is passed through the fingers. There are many lists of these "beautiful names", e.g. there are three in as-Suyūṭī's *al-Jāmiʿ aṣ-ṣaghīr*, Nos. 2367–2369, and the Traditions tell that Muḥammad declared that anyone who repeats these ninety-nine names is sure of Paradise. The list given here is that dictated by our informant, with the meanings in English that he suggested these names meant to a Muslim at the present day.

24. Al-Mu'izz	the Empowerer.
25. Al-Mudhill	the Abaser.
26. As-Samī'	the Hearer.
27. Al-Baṣīr	He who sees.
28. Al-Ḥākim	the Judge.
29. Al-'Adl	the Just.
30. Al-Laṭīf	the Kindly One.
31. Al-Khabīr	the Well-informed.
32. Al-Ḥalīm	the Forbearing.
33. Al-'Aẓīm	the Great One.
34. Al-Ghafūr	the Forgiving.
35. Ash-Shakūr	the Grateful.
36. Al-'Alī	the High One.
37. Al-Kabīr	He who is great.
38. Al-Ḥafīẓ	the Guardian.
39. Al-Muqīt	the Nourisher.
40. Al-Ḥasīb	the Reckoner.
41. Al-Jalīl	the Majestic.
42. Al-Karīm	the Generous.
43. Ar-Raqīb	the Watcher.
44. Al-Mujīb	He who answers.
45. Al-Wāsi'	the Comprehensive.
46. Al-Ḥakīm	the Wise.
47. Al-Wadūd	the Loving One.
48. Al-Majīd	the Glorious.
49. Al-Bā'ith	the Raiser (of the dead).
50. Ash-Shahīd	the Witness.
51. Al-Ḥaqq	the Truth.
52. Al-Wakīl	the Advocate.
53. Al-Qawī	He who is strong.
54. Al-Matīn	He who is firm.
55. Al-Walī	the Patron.
56. Al-Ḥamīd	the Praiseworthy.
57. Al-Muḥṣī	the Numberer.
58. Al-Mubdi'	the Commencer.
59. Al-Mu'īd	the Restorer.
60. Al-Muḥyī	the Life-giver.
61. Al-Mumīt	the Death-giver.
62. Al-Ḥai	the Living One.
63. Al-Qaiyūm	the Self-subsistent.

64. Al-Wājid	the Discoverer.
65. Al-Mājid	the Sublime.
66. Al-Wāḥid	the One.
67. Aṣ-Ṣamad	the Eternal.
68. Al-Qādir	the Powerful.
69. Al-Muqtadir	He who is able.
70. Al-Muqaddim	the Advancer.
71. Al-Mu'akhkhir	the Retarder.
72. Al-Awwal	the First.
73. Al-Ākhir	the Last.
74. Aẓ-Ẓāhir	the Evident.
75. Al-Bāṭin	the Hidden.
76. Al-Wālī	the Governor.
77. Al-Muta'ālī	the Exalted.
78. Al-Barr	the Beneficent.
79. At-Tawwāb	the Forgiver.
80. Al-Muntaqim	the Avenger.
81. Al-'Afū	He who pardons.
82. Ar-Ra'ūf	the Kindly One.
83. Mālik al-Mulk	Ruler of the kingdom.
84. Dhū 'l-Jalāl wa 'l-Ikrām	Lord of Majesty and Generosity.
85. Al-Muqsiṭ	the Equitable.
86. Al-Jāmi'	the Gatherer.
87. Al-Ghanī	the Rich One.
88. Al-Mughnī	the Enricher.
89. Al-Mu'ṭī	the Giver.
90. Al-Māni'	the Defender.
91. Aḍ-Ḍārr	the Distresser.
92. An-Nāfi'	the Advantager.
93. An-Nūr	the Light.
94. Al-Hādī	the Guide.
95. Al-Badī'	the Incomparable.
96. Al-Bāqī	He who abides.
97. Al-Wārith	the Inheritor.
98. Ar-Rashīd	the Director.
99. Aṣ-Ṣabūr	the Long-suffering.

ON THE EXCELLENCE OF THE BASMALA [1]

Be it known to you that *In the Name of Allah, the Merciful, the Compassionate,* (i.e. the *basmala)* is a word [of such power] that he who knows how to use it rightly will possess no inconsiderable gift, for he who repeats it may attain his highest wish, and he who is assiduous [in repeating it] will be robed with the robe of auspiciousness. This is the word with which Noah made entreaty to his Lord in ancient times, and its blessing *(baraka)* came back upon the hoopoe *(hudhud)*, which was given a crown by the One who hears, the One who knows.[2] He—upon whom be Allah's blessing and peace—said that *In the Name of Allah, the Merciful, the Compassionate,* is the opening sentence of every Holy Book. Abū Nu'aim [3] is reported to have said: Abū Bakr b. Muḥammad at-Tūnisī has related to us, saying: "The theologians of all communities are in agreement that Allah, Most High, commenced every Scripture He sent down [to mankind] with the words *In the Name of Allah, the Merciful, the Compassionate.*"

When Allah, in speaking by revelation to Adam, made use of the *basmala,* Adam questioned Gabriel, [saying]: "O Gabriel, what is this word with which Allah has commenced the revelation?" Said he: "O Adam, this is the word whereby the heavens and the earth came to be, by which the [primaeval] water was set in motion, by which the mountains were established steadfast and the earth made firm, and whereby the hearts of all creatures were strengthened." The reason why the

[1] From 'Abd al-Majīd 'Alī's *at-Tuḥfa al-marḍīya fi'l-Akhbār al-qudsīya* (Cairo, n.d., 1953?), pp. 2–4. The *basmala* is the phrase *bismi'llāhi 'r-raḥmāni 'r-raḥīm* "in the name of Allah", and *tasmiya* is the technical word used for the ejaculation of this phrase as an act of piety. It is, and always has been, freely used on all sorts of occasions by pious Muslims, e.g. as a grace before meat, or a grace after meat, as a phrase of sacralization, etc. In some groups it tended to develop into an equivalent of the Logos, and the tendency to treat it as a single word may still be seen in the *Din Dersleri*, II, p. 3 (Istanbul, 1954), prepared by the Turkish Ministry of Education for use in the elementary Schools. The *basmala* appears at the head of every Sūra in the Qur'ān save Sūra IX.

[2] For the Noah reference see Sūra XI, 41/43, and for the *hudhud* Sūra XXVII, 30.

[3] Abū Nu'aim al-Iṣfahānī (d. 430 A.H. = 1038 A.D.), was the author of the famous work *Ḥilyat al-Awliyā'*, much quoted by writers of devotional tractates.

basmala begins with *b* rather than with any other letter, in spite of the fact that *a* is more excellent, seeing that it is the latter with which Allah's noble name commences, is that it was the first letter pronounced by the progeny of Adam in the world of the spirits on the day [when Allah took covenant with them, saying] (VII, 172/171): "Am I not your Lord? They replied: *Balā* (Yea, indeed)." It has been said in explanation of the fact that it is pointed with a *kasra,*[1] that no one really gets ahead save by being broken and humble, as the poet has said:

He who has humbled his soul has enlivened it and cheered it,
And will pass no night in disquiet, withdrawing from it.
At a time when the winds blow in violent stormy gales
No tree is overthrown save that which is overly tall.

There is a noteworthy thing which the Imām Qāḍī ʿIyāḍ has mentioned in the text of his *Shifā' fī Sharaf al-Muṣṭafā,*[2] namely, that the Apostle of Allah—upon whom be Allah's blessing and peace—once called for a scribe and said: "O scribe, put down the ink-pot and sharpen the pen, then write squarely the *b,* and separate well the points of the *s,* open up the *m,* make clear the Divine Name, and make excellent the *raḥmān* and the *raḥīm,*[3] for there was once a man of the Children of Israel who wrote it, writing it beautifully, and because of it forgiveness was granted him."

It is said that the Scriptures sent down from heaven to earth consist of one hundred and four [Books]. The *ṣuḥuf* (scrolls) of Seth were sixty,[4] the *ṣuḥuf* of Abraham were thirty, the *ṣuḥuf* of Moses before the Torah were ten, then [came down] the Torah, the Gospel, the Psalter and the Furqān. The essential message of all the Scriptures is gathered up in the Qur'ān, the essential message of the Qur'ān is gathered up in its opening chapter *(al-Fātiḥa),* the essential meaning of the *Fātiḥa* is gathered up

[1] In Arabic *In the Name* is written *bism,* where the vowel *i* (the *kasra*) is expressed by a small stroke beneath the letter, i.e. in a humble position as compared with *a* and *u,* which are expressed by signs above their letters, and moreover, *kasra* means "a little bit broken off".

[2] Printed at Constantinople in 1325 A.H.

[3] Pens in those days were reed pens, the "nib" of such a pen being freshly cut for a new task, as we might sharpen a pencil. The directions in the text are for the careful writing in Arabic of the *basmala,* cf. p. 556 n. 1.

[4] There is no mention in the Qur'ān of the *ṣuḥuf* of Seth, though some say they are meant by "the former scrolls" in Sūra XX, 133, but the *ṣuḥuf* of Abraham are referred to in LXXXVII, 19, and the *ṣuḥuf* of Moses in LIII 36/37 as well. The *Torah,* of course, is the Old Testament, and the *Furqān* is one of the names for the Qur'ān (III, 4/2).

in the *basmala*,[1] and the essential meaning of the *basmala* is gathered up in its *b*, whose meaning is: "With Me is all that was, and with Me is all that will be."[2] Some carry it further [and say that] the essential meaning of the *b* is gathered up in its dot, and that this points to the Unity [of Allah], which is absence of any plurality.

The number of letters in the *basmala* as it is written is nineteen, which is the number of the Guardians of Hell Fire, as Allah has said (LXXIV, 30): "Over it are nineteen." Ibn Mas'ūd said: "So let anyone who wants Allah to rescue him from the Zabāniya [3] ejaculate it, so that for every letter of it Allah may appoint a garden", that is, as a preservative from the Fire. It is related that when the Blessed enter Paradise, they will say: "In the name of Allah, the Merciful, the Compassionate. Praise be to Allah who has made His promise come true. He gave us the earth to inherit, and [now] we settle ourselves where we please in Paradise. How fine is the reward of those who do good works" (XXXIX, 74). Also when the Damned enter the Fire, they will say: "Our Lord has not done us any wrong, but we did wrong to ourselves" (cf. III, 117/113; XVI, 33/35). Another noteworthy thing about it is that it consists of four words, and there are four kinds of sinning, viz. sinning by night, sinning by day, sinning in secret and sinning openly, but if one repeats it with sincerity Allah will forgive him all these kinds of sinning. But Allah knows best.

A story to illustrate the auspiciousness of the basmala

It is said that a well-nourished satan once met an emaciated satan. Said the well-nourished one to the emaciated one: "How is it that you have come to be in such a condition?" He answered: "I am with a man who whenever he enters his house says: 'In the Name of Allah', and whenever he eats says: 'In the Name of Allah', and for that reason I am emaciated." Said the well-nourished one: "I am with a man who knows nothing of all that, so I share with him in his eating, in his clothing, in his marital intercourse, and after that I ride on his neck as on a riding-beast." An indication of this [auspiciousness is to be found in] what Abū Dāwūd [4] and at-Ṭirmidhī have related from him—upon whom be Allah's blessing

[1] The *basmalc*, as already mentioned, stands at the head of every Sūra of the Qur'ān except the ninth.
[2] In Arabic the written sign for *b* is a small tooth with a single dot below it, and this *b* besides being a letter of the alphabet is a preposition meaning "with".
[3] They are mentioned in XCVI, 18, and on the ground of this verse were early taken to be the Guardians of the Fire, just as there are angelic Guardians of Paradise. See p. 24.
[4] On him and at-Tirmidhī, see pp. 154, 148.

and peace—[how he said]: "When any one of you eats let him mention the name of Allah, and should he forget to mention the name of Allah at the beginning let him ejaculate it at the close." The *tasmiya* at the drinking of milk, water, honey, broth, medicine, or any of the things that are drunk, is similar to the *tasmiya* at the taking of food. It is a proper *tasmiya* if one says "In the Name of Allah", but should one add "the Merciful, the Compassionate", that is very good.

In [a Tradition] handed down by Muslim,[1] [it says]: "Satan finds to his taste food over which the name of Allah has not been mentioned", and in *al-Ḥiṣn al-Ḥaṣīn*[2] [we read] that someone said: "O Apostle of Allah, we eat but we are not filled." He replied: "Maybe ye eat separately." "Yes", they answered. So he said: "Then come together in company to eat your food, and mention over it the name of Allah, whereat He will give you blessing therein." When a man eats with someone who has some plague or [is afflicted] with elephantiasis, let him ejaculate "In the name of Allah", putting full trust in Allah and relying on Him, [and he will be safe]. It is said that Luqmān[3]—upon whom be peace—saw a piece of something on which was [inscribed] the *basmala*, so he picked it up, and as a consequence Allah honoured him with [the gift of] wisdom.

[1] The compiler of the *Ṣaḥīḥ*. See p. 144.
[2] A well-known book of prayers and devotional exercises by Muḥammad b. al-Jazarī (d. 833 A.H. = 1429 A.D.)
[3] The Arabian Aesop. He is mentioned in the Qur'ān in Sūra XXXI, 12/11 ff.

A PROPHET STORY

One popular form of devotional literature throughout the Muslim world is that known as *Qiṣaṣ al-Anbiyā'*, or Stories of the Prophets. The Qur'ān mentions by name quite a number of the Prophets who preceded Muḥammad in the exercise of the prophetic office, and tells somewhat of their stories, as we see in Sūra XII which tells the Joseph story as Muḥammad had learned it. Just as that Joseph story is made up partly of Biblical reminiscences, partly of details from Midrashic and apocryphal legend, and partly of imaginative elaboration, so these same three elements enter into the much more elaborate stories of the Prophets which found popular favour in later days. There are well-known collections of these stories in Arabic, Persian, Turkish, Urdu and Malay, but the substance of all the collections is much the same.

The story translated here is the Story of Jesus from the best known of all these collections, the *Qiṣaṣ al-Anbiyā'* of Abū Isḥāq Aḥmad ath-Tha'labī, (d. 437 A.H. = 1036 A.D.), popularly known as *al-'Arā'is* or *Kitāb 'Arā'is al-Majālis*, from the edition printed at Cairo in 1921, where it occupies pp. 266–282.

The story has interest not only in showing the figure of Jesus as the Muslims know him and think of him, but like all these Prophet legends of Islam it illustrates admirably both the dominance of the Qur'ān in Muslim thought and the curious way in which material from the Bible and from Jewish, Christian and Iranian legend comes to be woven into the texture of Muslim interpretation of their Scripture. Perhaps even more valuable is the light that such stories as these throw incidentally on what pious Muslims who read this type of devotional literature find religiously satisfying and stimulating.

THE STORY OF JESUS

*Concerning the birth of Jesus—on whom be peace—
and concerning Mary's pregnancy with Jesus—on both of whom be peace—
together with matters connected therewith*

Allah—may He be exalted—has said (XIX, 16): "Make mention in the Book of Mary, when she went apart from her people to an eastern place." Those learned in the affairs of the Prophets say that [this was] three days after Mary had conceived Jesus—on whom be peace—and Mary was at that time a girl of fifteen years, or some say of thirteen years. There was with Mary in the temple [at that time], among the devotees, her cousin on the paternal side, [a man] named Joseph the carpenter. He was a sweet-tempered man, a carpenter [by trade], who distributed alms from the labour of his hands. Now Joseph and Mary had charge of keeping the sanctuary clean, and [it was their custom] when Mary had used up her water and Joseph his, each of them would take his vessel and go to the cave in which the water was, fill up from it and return to the sanctuary.

Now when it was the day on which Gabriel—upon whom be peace—met her, which day was the longest and hottest day of the year, she had used up her water, so she said: "Shall we not go together, O Joseph, and fill up?" He said: "I indeed, have water enough to last me this day until tomorrow." Said she: "But I, by Allah, have no water." Then she took her water pot and went on by herself till she entered the cave, and found hard by it Gabriel—upon whom be peace. Now for her sake Allah had given him the appearance of a perfect man.[1] He said to her: "O Mary, Allah has sent me to thee to give thee a pure child." She said: "I take refuge with the Merciful One against thee, if thou art god-fearing *(taqī)*", i.e. believing, obedient.

'Alī b. Abī Ṭālib—may Allah grant him honour—said that she knew that one who was *taqī* would be merciful and god-fearing, for she thought him a man of Adam's race. 'Ikrima said that Gabriel appeared to her in the form of a beardless youth, with shining face, curly hair and symmetrical form. The learned say that Allah—may He be exalted—sent him in the form of a man only that Mary might not flee from him, and that she might be able to hearken to what he had to say, for had he descended in his own [angelic] form she would have been terrified of him, and would have run away from him and not been able to hearken to what he had to say. Now when Mary took refuge [with the Merciful] against him, he said (XIX, 19–21): "I am only a messenger of thy Lord, [sent to thee] that I may give thee a pure son!" Said she: "How shall I have a child when no man has touched me, and I have never been unchaste?" Said he: "That, saith thy Lord, is easy for Me." When he said that to her she submitted to what Allah had decreed. So he breathed into the neck of her chemise, which she had put off from her. When he departed Mary put on her chemise again and conceived Jesus—upon whom be peace. Then she filled up her water pot and returned to the temple.

As-Suddī and 'Ikrima say that Mary—upon whom be peace—used to remain in the temple as long as she was [ritually] pure, but when her

[1] This and what immediately follows is based on Sūra XIX, 17–19, though in the Qur'ān it is Mary who speaks first, and then Gabriel explains why he is there.

periods came upon her she would go to the house of her maternal aunt [to stay] till she was pure again, when she would return to the temple. Now it was while she was bathing herself after her period that she took [1] an eastern place (XIX, 16) i.e. to the East, because it was in winter and on the shortest day of the year. Al-Ḥasan says that the only reason the Christians take the East as a *qibla* (i.e. prayer direction), is because Mary withdrew to an eastern place, and drew [2] a "veil between herself and them" (XIX, 17), i.e. a curtain. Muqātil says that she put the mountain between herself and her people. It was while she was thus, in this condition, that Gabriel appeared to her and announced Jesus to her, and blew into the opening of her chemise.

Wahb says that at the time she conceived Jesus there was with her one of her kinsmen called Joseph the carpenter, for the two of them used to frequent the temple situated at Mount Zion, a temple which at that time was one of the most celebrated of all their places of worship. At that temple Mary and Joseph the carpenter used to do the menial service. Such menial service thereat was a great honour, and they two used to have the charge of tending it themselves, keeping it in order and cleanliness, nor were there known in their day any more diligent in work or worship than these two.

The first one to notice her pregnancy was the son of her paternal uncle, her companion Joseph the carpenter. When he saw how it was with her he was amazed at it and found it shocking, but he did not know what to do about the matter. As often as he decided to suspect her [of evil] he remembered her piety, her acts of worship and her purity, and [the fact that] she had not been absent from him a single hour. Yet whenever he decided to declare her innocent, he would notice the signs of pregnancy that appeared in her. When this got to weigh too heavily upon him he spoke to her, and the way he began it was this. He said to her: "There is a matter concerning you, [O Mary], that occupies my mind. I have striven to stifle it, but it is too much for me, so I have come to see that to speak about it would be easier for my breast." Said she: "Speak! so long as it is kindly." He said to her: "Tell me, Mary, does a plant grow without a seed [being planted]?" "Yes", said she. He said: "Then, does a tree grow without [being watered by] the rain?" "Yes", said she. He said: "Can there be a child without [the participation of] a male?" Said she: "Do

[1] The text reads *ittakhadhat*, "she took", but it is probably just a scribal error for *intabadhat* "she went aside to", as the Qur'ān reads in this passage.

[2] The text reads *ḍarabat*, but this is probably only a mistake for the *ittakhadhat* which the Qur'ān reads in this place. See previous note.

you not know that Allah—magnified and majestic is He—caused the plant to grow, on the day that He created it, without any seed? so that the seed comes only from the plant which He caused to grow without a seed. And do you not know that Allah—may He be exalted—caused trees to grow without watering, and by decree made the watering to be the life of trees after that He had created each one of them separately? Or do you say that Allah is not able to make the tree grow till He has sought aid from the water, so that had it not been for that [water] He would not have been able to make it grow?" Said Joseph: "I do not say this, but I say that Allah—may He be exalted—is able to do what He pleases. He says to a thing 'Be!' and it is" (II, 117/111). So Mary said to him: "Do you not know that Allah created Adam and his wife without [the participation of] male or female?" "Assuredly", said he. And when she spoke thus to him it entered his mind that maybe what [she was pregnant with] was from Allah, so that it was not proper for him to question her about it. This was confirmed by his noticing how reticent she was concerning it.

So Joseph took on himself the servicing of the sanctuary, relieving her of all the work that she had been wont to do in it, because he saw the thinness of her body, her yellowish colour and spotted face, the swollenness of her abdomen and her failing strength. Now Mount Zion was right at the gate of Jerusalem. I have heard from trusthworthy sources that the tomb of David—on whom be peace—is there, and that there [also] is a church overlooking the spring of Silwān. I asked one of the monks [at that church], and he said: "This is Zion, and this is the temple in which Mary and Joseph used to serve. Also Jesus preached in it, summoning the people to Allah—may He be exalted. Then from here he was removed to the Church of the Resurrection" (i.e. the Church of the Holy Sepulchre), which is a magnificent church at the entrance to Jerusalem. They claim that Jesus—upon whom be peace—when he was killed was buried in it, and after three days rose from it to heaven, so it will last for ever, and it is there that he will descend. But Allah knows best.

Concerning his birth—on him be peace

They say that when Mary grew heavy with child and her confinement drew near, Allah—may He be exalted—spoke to her by revelation, [saying]: "The temple at Jerusalem is one of Allah's Houses, which He has purified and exalted, so that in it His name may be remembered. Therefore, go forth to a place in which you may take refuge." So Mary went to the house of her maternal aunt, the sister of her mother, the mother of John [the Baptist]. When she entered John's mother stood up welcoming her and embracing her. The wife of Zachariah said: "O Mary, do you notice that I am pregnant?" Mary answered: "And you also, do you notice that I am pregnant?" Said the wife of Zachariah: "Verily I feel what is in my womb doing obeisance to what is in thy womb." This is what [was meant by] His saying (III, 39/34): "confirming a word from Allah." While she was staying at the house of her aunt, Allah spoke to her by revelation [saying]: "If you give birth among your people, they will reproach you and stone you, killing both you and your child; so depart from them", i.e. go away. Al-Kalbī said that people said to her cousin Joseph: "Verily Mary has conceived a child by adultery, and the king is about to kill her, for her name has been given to him." So Joseph fled with her, carrying her on a donkey that he had, and there was nothing between her and the saddle of the donkey. Thus did Joseph journey with her until when he was nigh to the land of Egypt, far removed from the land of her people, the birth pangs overtook Mary, causing her to repair quickly to the trunk of a dried-up palm (XIX, 23). Now that was in the winter time.

Al-Kalbī says that while Joseph was on the way he desired to kill her, but Gabriel—upon whom be peace—came to him and said to him: "It is of the Holy Spirit, so do not kill her." The learned differ as to the length of the pregnancy of Mary—on whom be peace—and the time of her delivery of Jesus—on whom be peace. Some of them say that the period of her pregnancy was nine months like that of the rest of women. Others say eight months, and that that was another miracle because no eight months child has lived save Jesus. Others say six months, others three hours, and others say just one single hour. Ibn 'Abbās says that the fact is that she became pregnant and was delivered, and between the pregnancy and the delivery and the departing [to an eastern place] there was only a single hour, [and this we know] because Allah—may He be exalted—has made no mention of any interval between them where He—may He be exalted—says (XIX, 22): "So she became pregnant with him and went apart with him to a remote place", i.e. far from her people. Muqātil says that his mother conceived him in an hour, he was formed in an hour, and was delivered in an hour, while the sun continued its daily course, she being [at that time] a girl of twenty years who had menstruated twice before she became pregnant with Jesus.

They say that when the pangs came upon her she repaired to a palm tree, and it was a dried up palm tree without leaves or stumps of leaves or branches, and the angels surrounded her, encompassing her in ranks, i.e. encircling her. That palm tree was in a place called Bethlehem. When the travail began she cried (XIX, 23): "Would that I had died ere this, and become forgotten, quite forgotten", i.e. a corpse cast out. Then she was called to (XIX, 24, 25): "Do not grieve! thy Lord has set neath thee a rivulet. So shake towards thyself the trunk of the palm tree, it will let fall on thee fresh ripe dates." That is in accordance with what He—may He be exalted—said (XIX, 24): "Then one from beneath her called to her: 'Do not grieve'." Those who read *min taḥtihā* take it to mean Gabriel, who called to her from the foot of the mountain, while those who read *man taḥtahā* take it to mean Jesus [1]—upon whom be peace—who when he came forth from his mother's womb called to her, and by the permission of Allah, spoke to her. They say that when she bore Jesus Allah caused a rivulet of water to flow for her which was cool when she drank [of it], but luke-warm when she used it [for washing]. This is as He —may He be exalted—said (XIX, 24): "Verily thy Lord has set beneath thee a rivulet", i.e. a little stream. Ibn ʿAbbās says that Jesus—though others say it was Gabriel—beat on the earth with his foot, whereat the water appeared and made that palm tree revive after it had been withered, so that it put forth branches, became leafy, bore fruit and matured it. Then she was bidden (XIX, 25): "Shake towards thyself the trunk of the palm tree", i.e. move it to and fro, "it will let fall on thee fresh ripe dates", i.e. tender and moist.

Said ar-Rabīʿ b. Khuthaim: "There is nothing better in my opinion than fresh dates for a woman in confinement, or than honey for a sick man." Also ʿAmr b. Maimūn said: "I know nothing better for a woman, when her labour is hard, than ripe dates", and he recited this verse. ʿĀʾisha—may Allah be pleased with her said: "The Apostle of Allah—upon whom be Allah's blessing and peace—used to chew dates and anoint therewith the mouths of the children of the Companions when they were born." Some of the Rhetoricians in describing the date say: "It is a plaything for the young, and nourishment for the grown ups."

They say that thereupon Joseph the carpenter set off to get firewood and made of it a kind of fence around her, near to her, since the cold was troubling her. Then he kindled the fire for her that she might warm herself thereat, and he broke for her seven coconuts which he had in his

[1] The point is that the unvowelled Arabic words here can be pointed to read with *i* or *a*. In the former case they mean "from beneath her", and in the latter "he who was underneath her", and so have been taken in the one case to refer to Gabriel, and in the other, which is the usual reading, to refer to the babe.

saddle-bag and gave them to her to eat. It is for this reason that the Christians kindle a fire on Christmas night and play with coconuts.

Wahb says that when he—upon whom be peace—was born all the idols in all the earth were turned over on their heads. The devils were terrified, not knowing why this was, so they journeyed in haste till they came to Iblīs—may Allah curse him and be angry with him—where he was sitting on his throne on a green wave, like to the Throne on the day when it was on the waters. They reached him after six hours of the day had elapsed. Now when Iblīs saw them gathering together it terrified him, for he had not seen them all together before that hour since he had dispersed them, for he used only to see them individually. He questioned them, therefore, and they told him that some event had happened in the earth, because of which all the idols had been turned upside down upon their heads. Now there was [in those days] nothing more effective for man's destruction than these [idols], for they (i.e. the devils) used to enter into their hollow [interiors] and speak with them (i.e. the people), arranging their affairs [for them], for they would think that it was [the idols] which spoke with them. When this happened to them, however, they became small in the eyes of the people, who despised them. "So", [said they to Iblīs] "we are afraid that they will not worship [the idols] any more after this. And know that we came not to thee ere we had scoured the earth and encompassed the seas and everything else, yet we did not find increase in anything of that which we desired save ignorance." Then Iblīs said to them: "What can it be save some wondrous affair? So stay in your places." Whereupon Iblīs flew off and tarried away from them the space of three hours in which time he passed by the place in which Jesus was born. When he saw the angels surrounding that place he knew that there was the event that had happened. Now Iblīs—may Allah curse him—desired to come at him from above, but lo! the heads of the angels and their shoulders [stretched] up to the heavens. Then he desired to come at him from beneath the earth, but lo! the feet of the angels were firmly planted. Then he desired to enter between them, but they prevented him from that. There is a confirmation of this in a Tradition from the Prophet—upon whom be Allah's blessing and peace—[where he says:] "Satan pokes with his finger the sides of every child of Adam when he is born, save Jesus son of Mary—upon whom be peace—whom Allah—may He be exalted—veiled off from him. He went to poke [him] but poked the veil."

Wahb says that Iblīs—whom may Allah curse—went to his companions and said to them: "I came not to you till I had traversed all the earth, east and west, land and sea, the surface of the earth and the highest heaven. All this I covered in three hours." Then he told them about the birth of Jesus, and said: "No woman's womb ever encompassed a child before him without my knowing of it, nor gave birth to one except when I was present with her. I do hope that more will be led astray by him than are guided by him, for never was there a Prophet more dangerous to you and to me than this one who is just born."

There came a body of folk that night directing their steps towards him because of a star that had appeared. They had been discussing beforehand that the rising of that star was one of the signs of a birth [mentioned] in the Book of Daniel. So they came forth desiring [to see] him, bringing with them gold and myrrh and frankincense. [On the way] they passed by one of the kings of Syria who asked them whither they were bound, so they told him about it. He said: "And what is the significance of the myrrh and the gold and the frankincense, these things you have brought as gifts for him?" They answered: "They are symbols of him. Gold is the lord of all matter, and likewise this Prophet—on whom be prayers and peace—will be lord of the people of his generation. By myrrh cuts and wounds are cured, and likewise by this Prophet will Allah heal every diseased and sick person. And as the smoke of frankincense enters the very heavens, where no other smoke enters, so likewise Allah will raise this Prophet to heaven, but will raise none other in his generation." Now when they had said that to the king he purposed to himself to kill him, so he said to them: "Go! and when you know his abode inform me of it, for I am eager with a like desire to yours with regard to him." They went on till they came to Mary and presented to her—upon whom be peace—the gifts they had with them. Then they wished to return to that king to inform him of [Jesus'] abode, but an angel met them, who said to them: "Go not back to him nor inform him of his abode, for he desires only to kill him." So they departed by another way.

Mujāhid says that Mary—upon whom be peace—said: "When I was alone with Jesus I used to talk with him and he with me, and when anyone took my attention from him he would say prayers in my womb and I could hear him."

Concerning the return of Mary with her son Jesus to her people in Bethlehem, after her delivery of him

Then, indeed, a party from among her people [made trouble for her], after Allah—may He be exalted—had settled the affair of His handmaiden, and had made easy for her the means of her delivery. Allah said [to her]: "Eat, O Mary, of the ripe dates and drink of the cool water, cool your eyes and compose your spirit, and should you see any man who might question you about your child, or censure you on his account, then say: 'I have vowed to the Merciful a fast'" (cf. XIX, 26, 27) i.e.—a vow of silence. This is how it reads in the text of Ibn Mas'ūd and Anas,[1] and that was because they were wont when they fasted to refrain from food and drink and speech — "So I shall not speak today to any man" (XIX, 26/27). "Then she brought him to her people, carrying him" (XIX, 27/28). Al-Kalbī says that Joseph the carpenter took Mary and Jesus to a cave where he made them remain for forty days until she rose from her confinement. Then he brought her [home], and Mary came carrying him, after the forty days, and Jesus talked with her on the way, saying: "O mother, rejoice, for I am a servant of Allah and His Messiah."

Now when she came to her parents with the child they wept and grieved, for they were pious people. They said: "O Mary, thou hast come with a strange thing" (XIX, 27/28)—i.e. a great abomination. "O sister of Aaron" (XIX, 28/29)— Qatāda said that this Aaron was a pious man of the god-fearing among the Children of Israel, and is not Aaron the brother of Moses. They relate that there followed his bier on the day of his death forty thousand Israelites all of them named Aaron.[2] Wahb says that this Aaron was one of the most debauched of the Israelites and the most renowned for evil ways, so they likened her to him — "thy father 'Imrān was no man of wickedness, nor was thy mother unchaste" (XIX, 28/29) — i.e. a harlot, "so from whence have you this child?" Then Mary made a sign, pointing them to Jesus, that they should speak with him. But they got angry and said: "How shall we speak with one who is in the cradle a babe?" (XIX, 29/30).

Wahb says that Zachariah—upon whom be peace—came to her as she was disputing with the Jews, and said to Jesus: "Speak up in defence of yourself, if you are authorized to do so", whereupon Jesus—upon whom be peace—though he was only forty days old, [spoke up] and said: "Truly,

[1] The *textus receptus* as we have it reads *ṣawman*, but in the Codices of these two early authorities the texts read *ṣamtan*, i.e. "a silence" instead of "a fast".

[2] The point is that in Arabic the word for Mary is *Maryam*, which is the same as the Arabic name of Miriam the sister of Moses and Aaron. Muḥammad confused the two women, as is clear from Sūra III, 33/30 ff.; LXVI, 12, where Mary is called the daughter of 'Imrān, i.e. the 'Amrām who was the father of Moses and Aaron. When this confusion was drawn to the attention of the exegetes of Islam they put forward a number of devices to show that this was not a confusion but that a different Aaron and a different 'Imrān were meant. See p. 333, n. 6.

I am a servant of Allah, He has given me the Book, etc." (XIX, 30/31). He thus confessed to the fact that he was but a servant the first time he spoke, [and in so doing] gave the lie to the Christians and furnished a proof against them.[1] ‘Amr b. Maimūn says that when Mary came to her people with Jesus they took up stones desiring to stone her, [in accordance with the prescribed penalty for adultery], but when Jesus spoke up they left her. It is said that he did not speak again after that until he was of the age of other children. But Allah knows best.

Concerning the departure of Mary and Jesus to Egypt

Allah—may He be exalted—has said (XXIII, 50/52): "We made the son of Mary and his mother a sign, and sent them for refuge to a lofty place, where there was a secure spot and a spring." They say that the birth of Jesus took place after there had been forty-two years of the rule of Augustus, and fifty-one years of the rule of the Ashakānīs, kings of the Ṭawā'if.[2] Dominion at that time was in the hands of the kings of the Ṭawā'if, but the overlordship of Syria and its neighbouring areas was in the hands of Caesar, king of Rome, and the ruler over it on behalf of Caesar was Herod. Now when Herod, king of the Israelites, heard news of the Messiah he determined to kill him. [How the Court got this news] was because they noticed a certain star which had appeared, and they knew [what this portended] by calculations they had in a book of theirs. Consequently Allah sent an angel to Joseph the carpenter, informing him of what Herod was resolved upon and bidding him flee with the child and his mother to Egypt. Allah also spoke by revelation to Mary, [saying]: "Run away to Egypt, for verily if Herod gets his hands on your son he will kill him. Then when Herod is dead return to your land." So Joseph carried Mary and her son upon his donkey until they reached

[1] The Christians of Muḥammad's day apparently insisted that Jesus was the Son of God, and this was one of his great points of controversy with them. So in the Qur'ān he makes Jesus state that he is not a son but a servant of Allah, and this is naturally the "proof text" quoted by later Muslim controversialists in their opposition to Christian teaching.

[2] In the *Shāhnāmeh* the Ashakānīs are the third great dynasty of Persian kings immediately preceding the Sāsānīs. So it would seem to mean the Parthians. In the Arabic Chronicles the *Mulūk aṭ-Ṭawā'if* are generally taken to be the chiefs of the various Arab tribes who after the extinction of the Arsacids ruled with more or less freedom over the territories beyond the Tigris. Here, however, the title would seem to be given to the Parthians. The knowledge the Muslim writers had of this period was very vague and indefinite. See Christensen, *L'Iran sous les Sassanides* (Copenhague, 1944), p. 19.

the land of Egypt, for it was the lofty place which Allah had meant when He said: "We have sent them for refuge to a lofty place, where there was a secure spot and a spring" (XXIII, 50/52).

Abū Isḥāq ath-Thaʿlabī [1] mentions that in interpreting "a secure spot and a spring", ʿAbdallah b. Sallām said that it was Damascus; Abū Huraira said that it was Ramleh; Qatāda and Kaʿb said that it was Jerusalem, though Kaʿb [also recorded the opinion that] it was that piece of land on earth nearest to heaven; Abū Zaid said that it was Egypt; aḍ-Ḍaḥḥāk said that it was a place in Damascus; and Abū 'l-ʿĀliya said that it was Aelia, saying also that *qarār* meant "level ground", and *maʿīn* meant "pure water".[2]

Mary remained in Egypt twelve years spinning flax and gathering the grain after the harvesters. She used to gather the grain with the [babe's] cradle attached to one shoulder, and the vessel in which the grain was to the other shoulder. [This life in Egypt continued] till Jesus reached the age of twelve years.

There is a Tradition from Muḥammad b. ʿAlī al-Bāqir [3]—with whom may Allah be pleased—in which he says that when Jesus was born he was at the age of one day like a child at the age of a month, and when he was nine months old his mother took him by the hand and brought him to the *kuttāb*,[4] where she gave him over to the care of the school-master. The school-master said to him: "Say—In the name of Allah, the Merciful, the Compassionate", so Jesus said it. Then the school-master said: "Say the abc." Jesus—on whom be peace—raised his head and said: "Do you understand what the abc is?" Thereupon he (i.e. the teacher) raised the stick to strike him, but [Jesus] said: "O school-master, do not strike me if you know the [meaning]; if you do not, then ask me and I shall explain it to you." The school-master answered: "Then you explain it to me." So Jesus said: "The *alif* means that there is no deity save Allah; the b means the beauty of Allah; the g means the majesty of Allah; the d means the religion of Allah; of hwz the h is Gehenna, i.e. al-Hāwiya, the w is the wailing of the damned in the Fire, and the z the sighing of the people of Hell; ḥṭy means the removal of sins from those who ask

[1] This is the author of the work from which we are translating. He is referring here to his other great work, a Commentary on the Qur'ān, *al-Kashf wa-'l-Bayān*, which has not yet been printed.

[2] *qarār* is the word we have translated "secure spot", and *maʿīn* the word we have rendered "a spring". Aelia in this connection means the Jerusalem area.

[3] He is the fifth Imām of the Shīʿites.

[4] All over the Muslim world the *kuttāb* is the elementary village school where the children learn to read and write and to recite by heart the Qur'ān.

forgiveness; klmn means the word of Allah uncreate, and that there is no alteration of His word; s'fṣ means measure for measure and part for part; qr*sh*t means that He gathers them when He assembles them, or gathers them together."[1] The school-master said to his mother: "O woman, take your son; he is instructed, and has no need of a teacher."

The exegete al-Ḥusain b. Muḥammad b. al-Ḥusain has related in his *isnād* from Abū Sa'īd al-Khudrī, how the Apostle of Allah—upon whom be Allah's blessing and peace—said: "Jesus' mother sent him to be instructed. The school-master said to him: 'Say the Bismillah', but Jesus said: 'And what is the Bismillah?' Said the school-master: 'I do not know', so Jesus said: 'The b is the splendour of Allah; the s is the illustriousness of Allah; and the m is His kingdom, may He be praised and exalted'". But Allah knows best.

Concerning the appearance and exterior qualities of Jesus

Ka'b al-Aḥbār said that Jesus son of Mary was a man of reddish complexion tending to white. His hair was not lank, nor did he ever anoint his head. Jesus used to walk barefooted and possessed neither house nor ornament, nor merchandise, nor fine clothes, nor possessions save his daily food. When the sun set he would draw up his feet and say prayers until dawn broke. He used to heal the born blind and the lepers, raise the dead to life by permission of Allah, and tell his people what they were eating in their houses and what they were storing up for the morrow (III, 49/43). He used to walk on the water in the sea. His hair was dishevelled, his face thin, [since he was] an ascetic in this world, desirous of the next, and diligent in the service of Allah. He used to wander on the earth until the Jews sought him, desiring to kill him, whereat Allah raised him to heaven. But Allah knows best.

Concerning the miracles of Jesus from his childhood to his becoming a prophet

Wahb said that the first miracle of Jesus which the people saw was when his mother was dwelling in the house of a Dihqān [2] in the land of Egypt,

[1] He goes through the alphabet in its ancient Semitic order, not the modern order of the letters, and from the individual letters or combinations of them draws out these meanings all connected with Islamic doctrine.

[2] *dihqān* is a Persian word, or rather a word derived from the Persian, and means the chief man of a village who exercises magisterial authority therein. See Christensen, *L'Iran sous les Sassanides*, p. 112.

where Joseph the carpenter had set her down when he went with her to Egypt. Beggars used to resort to the house of that Dihqān, and though goods were being stolen from the Dihqān's storehouses he did not suspect the beggars. Mary was distressed over the Dihqān's loss, and when Jesus saw his mother's grief for the losses of her host, he said to her: "O mother, would you like me to tell him where his property is?" She said: "Yes, my son." He said to her: "Then tell him to gather the beggars before me in his house." So Mary mentioned that to the Dihqān and he gathered the beggars before him. When they were all gathered together he picked out two men from among them, one of them blind and the other a cripple, the cripple being borne on the shoulders of the blind. He said to this latter: "Rise up with him", but the blind man said: "I am too weak for that." Then Jesus said to him: "How was it that you were strong enough for it yesterday?" When they heard him say that they beat the blind man till he stood up, and when he rose and stood firmly the cripple was just at the height of the window of the store-house. Jesus said to the Dihqān: "Thus did they scheme with regard to your goods yesterday, for the blind man gave the aid of his strength and the cripple of his eyes." Thereupon the blind man and the cripple said: "He has told the truth, by Allah", and they returned to the Dihqān all his property, which the Dihqān took and put in his store-house. Then he said: "O Mary, take the half of it." She answered: "I am not that sort of a person." Said the Dihqān: "Then give it to your son." She answered: "But he is of more noble estate than I am."

Not long after this that Dihqān arranged a marriage for his son, and made a feast to which he invited all the people of Egypt, whom he feasted for two months. When this was just ended there came to visit him a party of people from Syria about whom the Dihqān had no notice till they arrived. On that day he had nothing in the house to drink, and when Jesus saw his solicitude about it, he entered one of the houses of the Dihqān in which were two rows of earthenware jars. Jesus passed his hand over the mouth of each of them as he was walking and no sooner had he passed his hand over the mouth of a jar than it was filled with drink, until Jesus came to the last of them. At that time he was twelve years old.

Another miracle. As-Suddī says that Jesus—on whom be peace—while he was in the *kuttāb* used to tell the boys what their parents were doing. He would say to a youth: "Run off, for verily your family is eating such and such, and they have set apart for you such and such, and they themselves are eating such and such." So the boy would run off to his family and weep till they gave him that thing. Then they would say to him: "Who told you about that?" and he would say: "Jesus." So they kept their boys away from him, saying: "Do not play with that sorcerer." They gathered [their children] into one house, and when Jesus came seeking them, they said to him: "They are not here." Said he: "Then what is there in this house?" They said: "Oh, pigs." "Even so", said he, and when they opened to them, behold, they were pigs. News of this spread abroad among the Israelites, and the people were in anxiety about it. So when his mother grew afraid for him she put him on a donkey that she had and fled to Egypt.

Another miracle. As-Suddī said that when Jesus and his mother—on both of whom be peace—were wandering in the land, they left the Israelites and dwelt in a [certain] village at a man's house, where he treated them as guests and was good to them. Now the king at that time was an obstinate tyrant. One day the man came home anxious and in grief, and entered his house while Mary was with his wife. Said Mary to her: "What is the matter with your husband whom I see grieving?" She said: "Do not ask me", but [Mary] said: "Tell me, for maybe Allah will relieve his distress at my hand." Said she: "The truth is that we have a king who places on every man among us in turn [the duty of] providing food and wine to drink for him and his armies, and punishes whoever fails to do it. Now today is our day and we have no supplies [on hand]. Said [Mary]: "Tell him not to worry about it, for he did good to us, so I shall bid my son pray for him, and that will be sufficient." Then Mary spoke to Jesus [about the matter]. He said: "If I do that evil will come of it." She answered: "Never mind that, for he has treated us well and with honour." Said Jesus: "Then tell him, when [the king] draws near, to fill up the earthen jars and pots with water, and then tell me." So he did that and called to Jesus, who changed the water in the earthenware pots into meat and gravy, and the water of the jars into wine the like of which the people had never seen.

Now when the king came he ate, and when he had drunk he asked: "From whence is this wine?" He said to him: "From such and such a land." Said the king: "But my wine too is brought from that land, yet it is never like this." So he told him that it was from another land, but when the king saw how muddled and confused he was, he said: "Now tell me the truth." Said he: "I will tell you. I have with me a young man who never asks Allah for anything but He gives it to him. He called on Allah Who made the water into wine." Now the king had a son whom he desired to succeed him, but who had died a few days before. Now he was very dear to the king, so he said: "Verily a man who could call on

Allah and have Him make water into wine could urgently supplicate Him till He raise my son to life." So he called Jesus and talked to him about it. Said Jesus: "Let us not do it, because if he were to come to life [again], evil would assuredly come of it." Said the king: "I care not so long as I see him." Said Jesus: "If I raise him to life will you let me and my mother go wherever we desire?" "Most certainly", said he. So [Jesus] called on Allah—may He be exalted—Who made the young man live again. Now when the people of the realm saw that he was alive again, they fell suddenly on them with the sword saying: "This man devoured us till now he draws near to death he wants to appoint over us his son that he may devour us as did his father." So they began to fight with one another, but Jesus and his mother departed.

Another miracle. Wahb says that while Jesus was playing with the boys a youth sprang upon a small boy, kicked him with his foot and killed him. Then he threw him into the arms of Jesus, who was covered with blood. Then he brought the people on [Jesus], who charged him with it, took him and went with him to the Qāḍī of Egypt. To him they said: "This one has killed the other." Then the Qāḍī questioned him, and Jesus said: "I do not know who killed him, but I am not guilty of it." They desired to fall upon Jesus—on whom be peace—but he said: "Confront me with the boy." They said to him: "And what do you want with him?" Said he: "I want to ask him who killed him." They said: "And how can he speak with you when he is dead?" Nevertheless they took him and brought him to the spot where the boy was killed. There Jesus set himself to prayer, whereat Allah—may He be exalted—raised him to life. Then Jesus asked him: "Who killed you?" He answered: "So and so killed me", mentioning the one who had killed him. Then the Israelites said: "Who is this?" He said: "This is Jesus, son of Mary." They said: "And who is this with him?" He said: "The Qāḍī of the children of Israel." Then the boy died again straightway, and Jesus returned to his mother, a great multitude of the people following him. His mother said to him: "My son, did I not forbid you to act like this?"; but he said to her: "Verily Allah is our protector, and He is the most merciful of those who show mercy" (cf. XII, 64).

Another miracle. 'Aṭā' says that Mary, after she had withdrawn Jesus from the *kuttāb*, set him at various jobs, and finally put him with the dyers, indeed with the chief of them, that he might learn [his trade] from him. There were assembled at his place different [kinds of] garments [to be dyed]. Anon it became necessary for the man to go on a journey, so he said to Jesus: "Now you have learned this profession, and I am about to go off on a journey from which I shall not return for ten days. [Here are] these garments of different colours, and you know the colour that each one of them should be dyed. I want you to be finished with them by the time I come back." Then he departed, and Jesus—on whom be peace—heated up one vat of one colour, and throwing into it all the garments, said: "Be, by permission of Allah, whatever I want you to be." Presently the dyer came back, and behold, the clothes were all in one vat. Said he: "O Jesus, what have you done?" He said: "I have finished with them." Said [the dyer]: "Where are they?" He answered: "In the vat." "What! all of them?" "Yes", said he. "And how is that all of them are in the one vat? You have ruined the garments." Said [Jesus]: "Come and see." So he came, while Jesus drew out a yellow garment, a green garment, a red [and so on] till he had drawn them all out according to the colour he had desired. The dyer was amazed, but he understood that this thing was from Allah—may He be praised and exalted. The dyer said to the people: "Come! see what Jesus—upon whom be peace—has done." Then he and his friends believed in him, and they became the Ḥawārīyūn.[1] But Allah—great and majestic is He—knows best.

On the return of Mary and Jesus—on both of whom be peace—to their own country after the death of Herod

Wahb says that when Herod the king died in the twelfth year after the birth of Jesus—upon whom be peace—Allah, by revelation, gave Mary the news of Herod's death, and bade her return, with her cousin Joseph the carpenter, to Syria. So Jesus and his mother—on both of whom be peace—returned and dwelt in Jebel al-Jalīl in a village called Nāṣira, from whence comes the name Naṣārā.[2] Now Jesus used to master in an hour the learning of a day, and in a day that of a month, and in a month that of a year. When he was thirty years of age Allah spoke to him by revelation, [telling] him that he should come forth to the people and summon them to Allah, speaking to them in parables, curing the sick and the infirm, the blind and the mad, taming the devils, rebuking them and humbling them, so that they used to die for fear of him. He did what

[1] This is the word that Muḥammad uses in the Qur'ān for the disciples of Jesus. It is the Ethiopic word for "disciple" given an Arabic plural, and was doubtless learned by Muḥammad from Abyssinian Christians in humble positions in Mecca in his youthful days.

[2] The Qur'ānic name for the Christians of its day is *naṣārā*, a word about whose derivation there is still some dispute. The author here says that it is derived from the word *Nāṣira*, which is his word for the town of Nazareth in Galilee.

[Allah] commanded him, so the people loved him and inclined towards him as they got accustomed to him, so that his followers increased and his fame grew great. At times [the people] would assemble before him the sick and infirm, as many as fifty thousand in one hour. As many of them as were able to come to him came to him, and those who were not able to come Jesus—upon whom be peace—visited. He used to heal them by prayer alone, on the condition of faith.

His prayer by which he used to heal the sick and raise to life the dead was:

> "Allahumma! Thou art the God of whosoever is in the heavens and whosoever is on earth. There is no God in them save Thee. Thou art the omnipotent One among those in the heavens and those on earth, and there is no omnipotent One in them save Thee. Thou art the king of whosoever is in the heavens and whosoever is on earth, and there is no king in them save Thee. Thou art the ruler of whosoever is in the heavens and whosoever is on earth, and there is no ruler in them save Thee. Thy power on earth is as Thy power in heaven, and Thy authority on earth is as Thy authority in heaven. I pray Thee by Thy honourable names, for Thou hast power over all things."

The story of the ḥawārīyūn—on whom be peace

Said Allah—glorious and exalted be He—(III, 52/45): "Now when Jesus perceived their unbelief he said: 'Who are my helpers towards Allah?' Said the Ḥawāriyūn: 'We are Allah's helpers. We believe in Allah, so bear witness that we have submitted ourselves.'" Allah—may He be exalted—has also said (V, 111): "When I spoke by revelation to the Ḥawārīyūn", i.e. inspired them and directed them that they should "believe in Me and in My messenger, they said: 'We believe; so bear witness that we have submitted ourselves.'" Know that the Ḥawāriyūn were the devout [followers] of Jesus son of Mary, and his saints, those who loved him and aided him and were his helpers. They were twelve men whose names were—Simon, the brass worker, called Peter; and Andrew his brother; and James the son of Zebedee and John his brother; Philip and Bartholomew; Thomas, and Matthew the collector of taxes; James the son of Ḥalfā, and Līyā who was called Thaddaeus; Simon the Canaanite and Judas Iscariot—on them be peace.

The learned differ as to why they were thus called. Ibn 'Abbās said that they were fishermen who were fishing when Jesus passed by and said to them: "What are you doing?" They answered: "We are fishing." He said to them: "Will ye not walk with me that we may fish for men?" They said: "How should that be?" Said he: "We will summon [them] to Allah." They said: "And who are you?" And he answered: "I am Jesus, son of Mary, a servant of Allah and His Apostle." They said: "Will there be any Prophet superior to you?" "Yes", said he, "the Arabian Prophet." So they followed him, and believed in him, and went along with him. As-Suddī said that they were sailors, but Ibn Arṭāt said that they were fullers and were called that name (i.e. Ḥawārīyūn) because they used to whiten clothes, i.e. bleach them.[1]

Ibn Fatḥūya tells us, with an *isnād* from Muṣʻab, that the Ḥawārīyūn were twelve men who followed Jesus, and who were wont when they were hungry to say: "O Spirit of Allah,[2] we are hungry", and he would smite with his hand on the ground, whether it was plain land or hill country, and bring forth for each man two loaves which they would eat. Also when they were thirsty, they would say: "O Spirit of Allah, we thirst", and he would smite on the ground whether plain or hill and bring forth water which they would drink. Then they said: "O Spirit of Allah, who could be in a position superior to ours? Whenever we wish it you feed us; whenever we wish it you give us drink, and we have believed in thee and followed thee." He answered: "Superior to you is he who works with his hands and eats from his earnings." After that they began to make clothes for hire. Ibn ʻAun says that one of the kings [in those days] made a feast to which he invited the people, and Jesus was [sitting] before a platter which never diminished. The king said to him: "Who are you?" He answered: "I am Jesus son of Mary." Said the king: "I will leave my kingdom and follow you", so he went along with those from among them who were following him and they were the Ḥawārīyūn. Others say that this was [not some king, but was] the dyer and his friends, whose story we have already told.

Aḍ-Ḍaḥḥāk says that they were called Ḥawārīyūn because of the purity of their hearts. ʻAbdallah b. al-Mubārak says that they were called Ḥawārīyūn because they were shining bright since on them was the mark of worship with all its light, its whiteness and its radiance. Among the Arabs the root ḥwr signifies intense whiteness, and derived from it are

[1] Being ignorant of the fact that this name is derived from the Ethiopic word for "disciple", the Muslim exegetes have tried to find a derivation of it from Arabic, and that given here is that it is from the root ḥwr, one of whose meanings is "to glisten white", so that *ḥawwara* means "to whiten cloth".

[2] This is dependent on Sūra IV, 171/169 where Jesus is called a Spirit from Allah.

the *aḥwar* and the *ḥūr*.[1] Al-Ḥasan says that [the meaning of] Ḥawārīyūn is Helpers. Qatāda says that they are such folk as are suitable to be successors. An-Naḍr b. Shumail says that Ḥawārīyūn means a man's closest friends and those who assist him in what he wants to do.

There is a saying of the Prophet—upon whom be Allah's blessing and peace—:"Every Prophet has a Ḥawārī and my Ḥawārī is az-Zubair." These were the Ḥawārīyūn of Jesus son of Mary, on whom be peace, and as for the Ḥawārīyūn of this [Muslim] community, we are told by al-Ḥusain b. Muḥammad ad-Dīnawarī in his *isnād* from Sufyān b. Ma'mar, that Qatāda said that all of them were from the Quraish, viz. Abū Bakr, 'Umar, 'Uthmān, 'Alī, Ḥamza, Ja'far, Abū 'Ubaida b. al-Jarrāḥ, 'Uthmān b. Maẓ'ūn, 'Abd ar-Raḥmān b. 'Auf, Sa'd b. Abī Waqqāṣ, Ṭalḥa b. 'Ubaidallah, and az-Ẓubair b. al-'Awwām—may Allah be pleased with them all.

Concerning the virtues of Jesus, and the miracles which his hands performed, from [the start of] his mission, until he was raised up

Among them is [the way in which] Allah aided him by the Holy Spirit *(rūḥ al-qudus)*. The most noble of Speakers has said (II, 87/81): "We aided him by the Holy Spirit." Similarly in the Sūra of the Table (V, 110/109), it says: "And when Allah said: 'O Jesus son of Mary, remember My bounty to thee and to thy mother, when I aided thee by the Holy Spirit.'" There is some difference of opinion as to this [spirit]. Ar-Rabī' b. Anas says that it was the spirit which He breathed into him, so that "spirit" is to be taken as construct to [*al-qudus*], which is an honourable and special name of Allah—glory be to Him—so that [the phrase is equivalent to "Spirit of Allah"] just as one says "the House of Allah" or the "she-camel of Allah". That the *qudus* is Allah—exalted be He—is indicated by His words in (IV, 171/169): "and a spirit from Him", and (LXVI, 12): "and We breathed therein [2] of Our Spirit." Others say that by *al-qudus* is meant purity, i.e. the spirit of purity, and Jesus—on whom be peace—is called "spirit" because loins of male did not contain him, nor did the womb of such as menstruate bring him forth. [Thus] he was none other than a matter from Allah—exalted be He. As-Suddī and Ka'b say that the Holy Spirit is Gabriel, and Gabriel's assistance to

[1] The reference is apparently to the Houris, the fabled maidens of Paradise, whose Qur'ānic name *ḥūr* is the plural of *aḥwar*, which is said to mean "white-eyed", i.e. having the white of the eye intensely white against the black of the pupil. See p. 45.
[2] I.e. into the womb of Mary. The parallel passage in XXI, 91 reads "into her".

Jesus was that he was his familiar and companion, the one who helped him and travelled with him wherever he went, till [finally] he mounted up with him to heaven. Saʿīd b. Jubair and ʿUbaid b. ʿUmair say that *al-qudus* is that greatest name of Allah by which he (i.e. Jesus) used to raise the dead to life and show the people those miracles.

Among [the miracles is the fact of] Allah's teaching him the Injīl and the Taurāt, which he used to recite from memory. This is as Allah—may He be exalted— said (V, 110): "And when I taught thee the Book", i.e. the art of writing, for it is said that there are ten kinds of writing nine of which were [taught] to Jesus, "and the Wisdom, and the Taurāt and the Injīl".

And among them is his creation of a bird from clay, as Allah says, giving the information as from him (III, 49/43): "Verily I have come to you with a sign from your Lord. Out of clay will I make for you as it were the figure of a bird, and I shall breathe into it and it will become a bird, by the permission of Allah." Allah—may He be exalted—also said (V, 110): "When thou didst create from clay as it were the figures of birds by My permission." He was fashioning from clay what was like the figure of a bird, then he would blow into it and it would become a bird by permission of Allah. Actually what he created was a bat, and a bat was chosen because it is the most perfect [kind of] bird in form, and the most effective in strength, since it has breasts and teeth, and gives birth and menstruates and flies. Wahb says that it flew as long as the people were looking at it, but when it got out of their sight it fell dead, in order to mark the distinction between the work of a creature and that of Allah—may He be exalted—and to teach that perfection belongs only to Allah—great and majestic is He.

Among them is the curing of the born blind and the leper, as the Most High has said (V, 110): "Thou didst heal the born blind and the leper by My permission." The leper *(abraṣ)* is the one on whom are leprous scabs, and the born blind *(akmah)* is the one who has been blind from birth and has never seen the light. No such born-blind person existed among the [early] Muslims save Qatāda. The reason why these two [diseases] were selected [for particular mention] was because they were beyond medical help. Medicine was the thing in which men excelled in the days of Jesus, so He caused them to see a miracle of this nature. It is related that Jesus [once] passed by a monastery in which were blind men. He said: "Who are these?" They said: "These are men who were summoned to a court judgment and so destroyed their eyes with their own hands." Said he to them: "What caused you to do that!" They answered: "We were afraid of the issue of the judgment, so we did to ourselves what you see." Said he: "And you [who do such a thing] are the theologians, the sages, the religious teachers, the clergy, [who ought to set people an example]. Rub your eyes with your hands and say: 'Bismillah.'" They did that, and lo! they were standing there seeing [perfectly again].

Among them is his giving life to the dead by permission of Allah. Said the Most High (V, 110): "And thou didst bring forth the dead by My permission." He raised to life several of their dead, among them Lazarus, who was one of his friends. His sister sent to Jesus [saying]: "Lo, your brother Lazarus is dying, so come to him." Now there was between them a three days' journey, and when he and his friends came to him they found that he had already been dead for three days. They said to his sister: "Come along with us to his tomb", so she went with them to his tomb which was in an enclosed rock chamber. Then said Jesus: "Allahumma! Lord of the seven heavens and of the seven earths, verily Thou hast sent me to the Children of Israel to summon them to Thy religion, and Thou hast informed them that I will raise the dead to life by Thy permission, so raise Lazarus." Then Lazarus rose up, came out from his tomb, lived and had children.

And among them was the son of the old dame, whose story is as follows. Jesus while journeying, with the Ḥawārīyūn in his company, passed by a town. He said: "Verily there is a treasure in this town, who will go in and get it for us?" They said to him: "O Spirit of Allah, no stranger ever enters this town but they kill him." Jesus said to them: "Stay ye here till I come back to you." Then he went on till he entered the town. He stopped at a door and said: "Peace be to you, O people of the house. [Here is] a stranger, feed him." An old woman said to him: "Do you not prefer that I leave you alone and go not with you to the Governor, since you say: 'Feed me.'" While Jesus was at the door there arrived the young man, the son of the old dame. Said Jesus to him: "Take me as your guest this night." The young man said to him the same as had the old dame. Said Jesus to him: "But, indeed, if you do this I will see that you marry the king's daughter." The young man said: "Either you are a madman, or you are Jesus son of Mary." He said: "I am Jesus." So he took him in as a guest and he spent the night with him. When morning dawned he said to him: "Go out early, enter the king's presence and say to him: 'I have come to ask the hand of your daughter', and he will order you to be beaten and thrown out." So the young man went and entered the king's presence and said to him: "I have come to ask the hand of your daughter." He immediately ordered him to be beaten, so they beat him and turned him out. The young man then returned to Jesus and told him the news. When it was the next morning he said to him: "Go and ask the hand of his daughter, for verily he will give you less than that [which you got yesterday]." So the young man did as Jesus bade him, and the king had him beaten but less than at the first beating. He returned to Jesus and told him. Then he said to him: "Go to him, for [today] he will say to you: 'I will marry her to you on my condition, and my condition is a palace of gold and silver, and everything in it of gold and silver and emerald. Then say to him: 'I will do that', and if he sends anyone with you, bring him along, for verily you will find it. Only do not say [to him] anything about it." So again [the youth] entered the presence of the king and asked her hand. Said [the king]: "Will you give her a dowry according to my conditions?" "And what are your conditions?" he asked, whereat the king made the conditions just as Jesus had named them. Said he: "Very well, I accept. Send someone to receive it." So he sent men with him, to whom [Jesus] handed over what the king had demanded. The people wondered at this. Then the king handed over to him his daughter, whereat it was the young man's turn to wonder. He said: "O Spirit of Allah, you are able to do a thing like this and yet you are in this [humble] estate?" Jesus said to him: "I give to that which abides preference over that which passes away." Said the young man: "I also will forsake it and will join myself to you." So he withdrew from the world and followed Jesus. Jesus took him by the hand and brought him to his friends, saying: "This is the treasure of which I spoke to you." The son of the old dame continued with him, but presently he died. Jesus passed by his bier while he was lying dead upon it, and Jesus called on Allah, whereat [the youth] sat up on his bier, came down from the necks of the men [who were bearing him to the tomb], put on his clothes, and bearing his bier on his own neck returned to his family, where he lived and had children.

Among them is the daughter of the collector of tithes, i.e. a man who used to take the tithes. He was asked: "Can you revive her, seeing that she died yesterday?" He called upon Allah—mighty and majestic is He—whereat she was raised to life, lived and had children.

Among them was [the raising of] Shem son of Noah. The Ḥawārīyūn said to him as he was telling them about Noah's ark: "Would that you would send to us someone who saw that ship, that he might describe it to us." So he arose and went to a hill *(tall)* which he struck with his hand, and taking a handful of the dust, said: "This is the grave of Shem, Noah's son. If you so desire I shall raise him to life for you." They said: "Surely." So he petitioned Allah by His most wonderful name, and striking the hill with his staff, said: "Come to life, by Allah's permission." Then Shem, Noah's son, came forth from his grave, and lo! one half of his head had gone white. [As he came forth] he said: "And has the resurrection come to pass?" [Jesus] said: "No, but I have evoked you by the most wonderful name of Allah." Now they used not to grow grey at that time [1] [when Shem was still alive on earth]. Shem had lived five hundred years but was [in appearance still] a youth. Then he told them all about the ship [in which he had been with Noah during the flood]. [When he had done that] Jesus said to him: "Die!" Said he: "On condition that Allah ease me [this time] from the pangs of death"; so Jesus made intercession to Allah, and He granted that. An account of this has already been given in the Story of Noah.

Among them is [the raising of] Ezra—on whom be peace. They said to Jesus—on whom be peace—:"Bring him to life, or we will burn thee with fire", and they assembled around him a lot of faggots of grape-vine wood. Now at that time they used to bury their dead in coffins of stone with lids, so they found the grave of Ezra, with his name written on the back thereof. They struggled with it in order to open it but were not able to drag it out from his tomb. They returned to Jesus and told him, so he gave them a vessel of water, saying to them: "Sprinkle his tomb with this water." This they did, whereat the lid opened of itself. Then they brought him to Jesus while he was still [whole] in his shrouds, for the earth does not devour the bodies of Prophets. [Jesus] removed the [grave]-clothes from him and began to sprinkle the water on his body, whereat his flesh and hair began to live again. Then he said: "Come to life, O Ezra, by permission of Allah, Most High", and lo! he sat up, and they all saw that with their eyes. They said: "O, Ezra, what is your testimony about this man?", that is to say, about Jesus. He answered: "I testify that he is the servant of Allah, and His Apostle." Then they said: "O Jesus, intercede with thy Lord for us, that He let him remain with us and be alive [again] among us." But Jesus said: "Return him to his tomb." So they returned him to his tomb where he became dead once more. Then there believed in Jesus son of Mary those who believed, and there resisted those who resisted. Al-Kalbī says that Jesus used to raise the dead to life by [the words]: "O Living One, O Everlasting One."

Among them was his giving information about the unseen. Allah—

[1] The point is that as one from the Patriarchal period he ought to have come out of the grave as dark haired as he entered it, but his head had become partly white because of the "pangs of death".

great and majestic is He—has said (III, 49/53) [giving the words of Jesus]: "And I will reveal to you what ye are eating and what ye are storing up in your houses." Al-Kalbī says that when Jesus healed the born blind and the leper and gave life to the dead, they said: "This is a sorcerer! but tell us what we are going to eat and what we shall store up", so he used to reveal to a man what he was going to have to eat for lunch and for dinner.

Among them was his walking on the water. It is related that he went out on one of his journeys, and with him was one of his friends, a short man who was inseparable from Jesus. When Jesus came to the sea he said: "In the name of Allah, in truth and certainty", and walked on the face of the water. So the short man also said: "In the name of Allah, in truth and certainty", and walked on the face of the water. Thereat he was amazed and said: "Here is Jesus, Spirit of Allah, walking on the water; and here am I walking on the water." Whereupon he began to sink in the water, and called on Jesus for help, so Jesus took him from the water and lifted him out. Then he asked him: "What did you say, little man?" So he told him what had entered his mind, and Jesus said to him: "You had put yourself in a place in which Allah had not put you, so Allah is offended with you because of what you said. Repent, therefore, to Allah because of what you said." So he repented and went back to the rank in which Allah had put him. So fear Allah and do not envy one another.

The Imām Abū Manṣūr al-Ḥamshādhī has related to us with an *isnād* from Muʿādh b. Jabal, that the Apostle of Allah—on whom be Allah's blessing and peace—said: "Did you know Allah with the proper knowledge, you would know a knowledge after which there is no ignorance, but no person has ever attained that." They said: "And did not you, O Apostle of Allah?" He answered: "Not even I." They said: "O Apostle of Allah, it has reached us that Jesus son of Mary walked upon the water." "Yes", said he, "and had he exercised more faith and fear he could have walked on the air." They said: "O Apostle of Allah, we did not think that the Apostles were ever found lacking [in any good quality]." He answered: "Verily, Allah is high above the rank that anyone else may attain to."

A collection of more traditions on the same subject

Wahb said that Jesus—on whom be peace—went out to wander on the earth, and one of the Jews accompanied him. Now that Jew had two loaves and Jesus but one loaf. Jesus said to him: "Let us go shares in our food", and the Jew said: "very well", but when he saw that Jesus had only one loaf he repented of it. Then Jesus commenced to say prayers, so his companion went and ate one loaf. When Jesus had finished his prayer they brought out their food. Said he to his companion: "Where is the other loaf?" Said he: "Why, there was only one loaf." So Jesus ate a loaf, and his companion ate a loaf. Then they went on till presently they came to a tree. Said Jesus to his companion: "Could we not pass the night under this tree till we wake in the morning?" He answered: "Very well." So they passed there the night. In the morning they started on again and [presently] came upon a blind man. [Jesus] said to him: "Do you want me to treat you, so that Allah may restore to you your sight? and will you give thanks to Him?" "Assuredly", said he. So Jesus touched his eyes and prayed to Allah for him, and lo! he was whole. Then said Jesus to the Jew: "By Him who caused you to see the blind man receive his sight, how many loaves did you have?" He answered: "By Allah, there was only one loaf."

Jesus held his peace, and they went on till they met a lame man. To him Jesus said: "Do you want me to treat you, so that Allah may restore you? and will you give thanks to Him?" "Assuredly", said he. So Jesus prayed to Allah, Most High, and lo! the man was sound, walking on his two feet. Then the companion said to Jesus: "Never did I see the like of this." So Jesus said to him: "By Him who caused you to witness the blind man receive sight and the lame man made whole, who is the possessor of the third loaf?" But he swore to him that he had had but one loaf. Jesus held his peace, and they went on till they came to a tumultuous river. Jesus said to him: "I see no bridge nor any boat, so take hold of my girdle from behind and plant your feet in my footsteps." He did so, and they walked over the water. Jesus said to him: "By Him who caused you to witness the affair of the blind man and the lame man, and who now has made the water a highway for you, who is the possessor of the third loaf?" Said he: "Nay, by Allah, there was but one loaf."

Jesus held his peace. Then they went on and came to where some gazelles were feeding. Jesus called a gazelle, killed it, and roasted some of it, which they ate. Then he struck the remains of the gazelle with his staff and said: "Rise, by permission of Allah— great and majestic is He". and behold, the gazelle ran away. "Praise be to Allah", said the man, Jesus said to him: "By Him who caused you to witness this miracle, who was the possessor of the third loaf?" Said he: "But there was only one loaf." Then anon they passed by a cowherd. Jesus called out: "O cowherd, kill for us this calf from among your cattle." Said he: "Send your friend the Jew to take it." So the Jew went and brought it, and he killed it and cooked it while the cowherd was watching him. Said Jesus: "Eat, but do not break the bones." Then, when they had finished, he threw its bones into its skin, and striking it with his staff, he said: "Rise, by permission of Allah." Thereupon the calf arose and bellowed, so Jesus said: "O cowherd, take your calf." He said: "Goodness, who are you?" Said he: "I am Jesus son of Mary." Said he: "Jesus the sorcerer", and he ran away from him. Then said Jesus to his companion: "By Him who gave life to the calf, how many loaves did you have?" He answered: "I had only one loaf."

Jesus held his peace, and they went on till they entered a town, where Jesus went to the lower part of it and the Jew went to the higher. The Jew took Jesus' staff, saying to himself: "Now will I heal the sick and raise the dead." Now the king of that town was afflicted with a chronic disease. The Jew went along calling out: "Who needs a physician?" till he came to the king's gate and was informed of his illness. He said: "Take me in to him and I will cure him, and even if you find that he is dead I will bring him to life." But they said to him: "The king's illness was beyond the skill of the leeches who came before you, and there is no leech who treats him and fails to cure him, but he crucifies him." Said he: "Take me in to him." So they took him in to him, and he beat the king with his staff and killed him. Nevertheless, he kept on beating him with the staff after he was dead, saying: "Rise, by permission of Allah." But he did not rise. Then they took him off to crucify him, but news of that reached Jesus, so he came to him. He, however, was already raised up on the wood, so Jesus said to them: "If I raise your king to life would you be willing to deliver my friend to me?" "Yes", said they. So he prayed to Allah—great and majestic is He—and He raised [the king] to life. Then [Jesus] went and took the Jew down from the wood. Said he: "O Jesus, you are the man who has done me most favour. By Allah I will never separate from you." Jesus said to him: "I adjure you by Allah, Who raised to life the gazelle and the calf after we had eaten from them, and raised this man to life after he had died, and brought you down from the stake after He had crucified you, how many loaves did you have?" He swore by all this and said: "By Allah, I did not have more than one loaf."

Jesus said: "Never mind." Then they went on till they came to a wonderful uninhabited city, in which there was a treasure of three blocks of gold, and where the lions and wild beasts had made their home. Said the man to Jesus: "Is this treasure yours?" Said Jesus: "It is thus. One for me, one for you, and one for him who ate the third loaf." Then said the Jew to Jesus: "I am the possessor of the third loaf, for I ate it while you were saying prayers." Then Jesus said: "All this is yours." Jesus went on and left him looking [at it], for he was not able to carry away even one block of them, for it was far too heavy for him. Jesus said to him: "Leave it, for verily there are people who die because of it." Then was the soul of the Jew distressed, being inclined to the wealth, but disliking to disobey Jesus, and because of his inability to carry away the wealth. So he went along with Jesus. Now while they were going along three men chanced upon that wealth. Two of them said to their companion, the third: "Go to one of these towns and bring us food and drink and beasts of burden on which we may bear away this treasure." Then when their companion had gone one of them said to the other: "What about killing him when he returns, so that we may be but two to divide the treasure?" He answered: "Very well." Also the one who went said to himself: "I shall put poison into the food, so that when they eat thereof and die all the treasure will be mine." So he did that, and when he on his return reached them they killed him. Then they ate the food which he had brought them and they died. Presently, Jesus—on whom be peace—passed by and there they were lying around it slain, so he said: "There is no god but Allah. This is what the world does to its people." Then Jesus raised them to life, by permission of Allah, and they took warning [from what had happened], and passed on without taking any of the wealth. But the soul of the Jew, the companion of Jesus, inclined to that wealth, so he said: "Give me the wealth." Jesus answered: "Take it for yourself. It will be your portion in this world and in the next." When, however, he went to carry it off the earth sank with him, and Jesus—on whom be peace—went on.

Among them is the Descent of the Table. Allah, Most High, has said (V, 112): "When the disciples [Ḥawārīyūn] said: 'O Jesus son of Mary, is not thy Lord able to send down to us a table from the skies?' He said: 'Show piety to Allah, if ye are believers'", and so on to the end of the verse. The theologians differ as to the description of the descent of the table, and as to its use and what was on it. Qatāda relates from Jābir from 'Ammār b. Yāsir, from the Apostle of Allah—on whom be Allah's blessing and peace—that he said: "The table descended and on it were bread and meat." That was because they had asked Jesus for food of which they might eat, yet which would never be consumed. He (i.e. the Prophet) said: "And he said to them: 'Verily I will do this, and it will come to you, provided that you do not steal nor conceal, for if you do that you will be punished.'" He said: "There did not pass a day ere they both stole and concealed." In some of the stories it says that some of them stole from it, so [Jesus] said: "May it not descend any more", so it was taken up and they were metamorphosed into apes and pigs.

Ibn 'Abbās said that Jesus said to the Israelites: "Fast for thirty days, then ask Allah for whatever you want to eat, and He will give it to you." So they fasted for thirty days, and when they had finished they said: "O Jesus, when we work for anyone and have finished the work for him, he always feeds us. Now we have fasted [at your bidding], and are hungry, so pray to Allah that He cause a table to descend to us from heaven." Thereupon Jesus clothed himself with a monk's robe, sat among the ashes and prayed to Allah, Most High, saying (V, 114): "Allahumma, our Lord, send down to us from the skies a table", and so on to the end of the verse. Thereupon the angels came with a table which they carried and on which were seven loaves and seven large fish, and they placed it before them. From it those who came last ate just as [plentifully] as those who came first.

'Aṭā' b. as-Sā'ib and others relate that when the table was placed before the Children of Israel many hands found their way to it, and it included every sort of food save meat. 'Aṭīya al-'Aufī says that a fish descended from heaven, and in it was every kind of food. Qatāda says that the table descended from heaven with fruit [on it] from the fruits of Paradise, and it used to descend even and morn, wherever they were, just as the manna and the quail had to the Children of Israel. Wahb says that Allah sent down loaves of barley and fishes. Someone said to Wahb: "But that would not have been anywhere near sufficient for them." He answered: "True, but Allah doubled the blessing", for one group would eat and go away, while others would come and eat, till all had eaten, and there still remained some.

Ka'b al-Aḥbār says that a table descended from heaven upside-down, with which the angels flew between heaven and earth, and upon which was every kind of food save meat. Muqātil and al-Kalbī say that Allah answered Jesus—on whom be peace—saying: "Lo! I am sending it down to you as you requested, but whosoever eats of that food and does not believe, I will make him an example and a curse and a warning to those who come after them." They said: "We agree", so he summoned Simon, the brass-worker, who was the most worthy of the Ḥawārīyūn, and asked: "Have you any food?" He answered: "I have two small fishes and six loaves." Said [Jesus]: "Give them to me." Then Jesus broke them into little bits, and said: "Sit down in the meadow in rows of ten persons a row." Then Jesus stood up and prayed to Allah, Most High, and Allah answered him, sending down blessing on them, so that they became excellent bread and excellent fish. Then Jesus arose and went and began to distribute to each row what his fingers could carry. Then he said: "Eat, in the name of Allah", whereat the food became so plentiful that it was up to their knees. So they ate what Allah willed [each should eat], and there still remained [food left over] though the people [who had partaken] numbered five thousand and more. Then all the people said: "We bear witness that thou art the servant of Allah and His Apostle."

They asked him another time, and Allah sent down five loaves and two fishes, and he did with them as he had done the first time. Now when they returned to their villages and spread abroad this story they were laughed at by those who had not witnessed it. Such said: "What is this? He has only bewitched your eyes." Thus he whose [salvation] Allah desired He confirmed in his clear-sightedness, and he whose unbelief He desired He returned to his infidelity, and these latter were metamorphosed into apes and pigs, but among them there was no child or woman. Now they remained in this [metamorphosed] state three days, and then died, without having begotten or eaten or drunk – and every metamorphosed person is in like state.

It is related on the authority of 'Aṭā' b. Abī Rabāḥ from Salmān the Persian, that he said: "By Allah, Jesus did not follow worthless fellows, nor did he treat the orphan harshly, nor laugh loudly, nor drive off the flies from his face, nor take anything on his nose twice, nor did he busy himself with trifles. When the Ḥawārīyūn asked him to bring down to them tables of different kinds, he said (V, 114): "Allahumma, send down to us a table from the skies, etc.", "and provide for us upon it food which we may eat, for Thou art the best of providers." Thereupon a red table-cloth descended between two clouds, a cloud above it and a cloud below it, while they were looking at it. It descended, swooping down, till it came to rest before them. Then Jesus wept, and said: "Allahumma, make me one of the thankful ones. Allahumma, make it a blessing, make it not an example and a punishment." They were all looking at it, and they looked at a thing the like of which they had never seen before, nor had they ever experienced a smell nicer than its smell. Jesus said to them: "Let one of you, that one whose works are best, uncover it, make mention of the name of Allah, and eat of it." Simon the brass-worker, the chief of the Ḥawārīyūn, said: "Thou art more worthy to do that than are we." So Jesus stood up and performed his ablutions, prayed a long prayer and wept much. Then he removed the napkin from it and said: "In the name of Allah, the best of Providers" (cf. V, 114), and lo! thereon was a cooked fish, free of scales and spines, floating in gravy, exuding fat, with salt upon its head and vinegar on its tail, with various kinds of vegetables around it except garlic. [Moreover, on it] were five loaves. On one of them was olives, on another honey, on another cheese, on another butter, and on the fifth shreds of dried meat. Said Simon: "O Spirit of Allah, is this of the food of this world or of that of the next?" Jesus—on whom be peace—said to him: "What you see is neither of the food of this world nor of that of the next, but Allah has made it by His almighty power. Eat of what you asked for, and He will assist you and give you of His bounty." They said: "O Spirit of Allah, would that we might see beyond this miracle another miracle." Thereupon Jesus said: "O fish, come to life, by permission of Allah", and the fish began to agitate, its scales and spines returned to it, and they were afraid of it. Jesus said: "What is the matter with you? You ask for a thing, and when it is given to you you dislike it." Then he said: "How afraid I am for you that you will be punished. O fish, return to your former state, by permission of Allah." So the fish again became cooked as it had been. They said: "O Spirit of Allah, be thou the first to eat of it, and then we will eat." Jesus said: "Allah forbid that I should eat of it. Let those who asked for it eat of it." But they were afraid to eat of it, so Jesus summoned the poor and the diseased, the lepers and the mutilated, the afflicted, and said to them: "Eat of what Allah has provided, and may you have joy while the others have tribulation." So they ate of it, and there departed from it thirteen hundred men and women of the poor and the aged, the afflicted and the sick, all of them filled to satiety and belching. Then Jesus looked at the fish, and behold! it was as whole as when it came down from heaven. Then the table mounted up while they were watching it, until it disappeared from their sight. Now there did not eat from it that day any sick man who was not healed, nor infirm man who was not made whole, nor afflicted person who was not relieved, nor poor person who did not become rich and continue rich until he died. Thereupon the Ḥawārīyūn and such as had not eaten repented.

It so was that when it descended there were gathered together the rich and the poor, the small and the great, men and women, crowding towards it, and it continued for forty days, descending in the morning and remaining there being eaten from, till when the shadow turned it would sail upwards, while they were watching it, till it was hidden from them. It used to descend intermittently, coming down one day and not coming down the next, like the she-camel of Thamūd.[1] Then Allah spoke by revelation to Jesus, saying: "Let My table and My provision be for the poor instead of for the rich." The rich were greatly amazed at this, so they doubted and caused the people to doubt it, saying: "Did you really see the table coming down from heaven?" Jesus said to them: "You will perish, so prepare for Allah's punishment." Then Allah spoke by revelation to Jesus, saying: "I have laid stipulations on such as treat it as false. If anyone disbelieves after its descent I shall punish him with such a punishment as none of the people of the world has ever had." Said Jesus—on whom be peace—: "Shouldst Thou punish them, why they are Thy servants, and shouldst Thou grant them forgiveness, it is Thou who art the Sublime, the Wise" (V, 118). Now three hundred and thirty men from among them were metamorphosed while they were sleeping at night on their beds with their wives in their houses, so that they woke up in the morning pigs, going about the roads and the rubbish tips and eating the filth of the courtyards. When the people saw that, they fled in fear to Jesus son of Mary. They wept and he wept for those whose folk had been metamorphosed. Also when the pigs saw Jesus they wept and began to circle around him. Then Jesus began to call them by their names, one by one, and they would weep, making signs with their heads but being unable to speak. They lived three days and then perished.

Among them is what is related about Jesus—upon whom be peace—passing by a man seated at a grave. He kept passing by him and always found him sitting there. He said: "O servant of Allah, how is it that I see you always sitting at this grave?" Said he: "O Spirit of Allah, this woman was such and such to me because of her beauty and her suitability, and I had great trust in her." Said [Jesus]: "Would you like me to pray to Allah to restore her to life for you?" "Yes, indeed", replied he. So Jesus performed his ablutions, prayed a two *rakʿa* prayer, and called upon Allah, Most High, whereupon a blackamoor emerged from the grave as though he were a burnt stump. [Jesus] said to him: "Who are you?" He answered: "O Apostle of Allah, I am a man [who has been] in torment for forty years, and now when I had reached this hour, it was said to me: 'Respond!' so I responded." Then he said: "O Apostle of Allah, the pain of the punishment has been upon me. If Allah would let me return to the world I would give Him a covenant never to disobey Him.

[1] Cf. Sūra LIV, 28. The she-camel produced from a rock was the miracle the Prophet Ṣāliḥ brought as confirmation of his mission to the people of Thamūd. She used to drink from their watering-place on one day and the cattle of the people of Thamūd the next day.

So pray to Allah for me." Then Jesus—on whom be peace—was touched with compassion for him, so he prayed to Allah, Most High, for him. Then he said to him: "Go!" and he went.

Then the one who was [sitting] at the grave said to him: "O Apostle of Allah, I was in error about the grave. Verily this one is her grave." So Jesus—on whom be peace—prayed to Allah, and there came forth from that grave a beautiful young woman. Said Jesus to him: "Do you recognize her?" "Assuredly", said he, "this is my wife." So [Jesus] prayed to Allah, and He gave her back to him. Then the man took her by the hand, [and they walked along] until they came to a tree under which he went to sleep, placing his head in her lap. Now there [presently] passed by her the son of the king, who looked at her, and she looked at him, and each was pleased with the other. He beckoned to her, so she removed her husband's head from her lap and followed the youth. When her husband woke up he looked for her but found her not, so he sought her and was directed towards where she was. Then he clung to her, saying: "This is my wife." But the young man said: "Nay, she is my slave-girl." While they were thus disputing Jesus—on whom be peace—passed by. Said the man: "This is Jesus", and he told him the story. Jesus said to her: "And what do you say?" She said: "I am the slave-girl of this young man, and I do not know the other." Jesus said to her: "Then give us back what we gave you." She said: "I do", and fell dead on the spot. Then said Jesus: "Have you ever seen anything more amazing than this? [Here was] a man whom Allah caused to die while an unbeliever, and then He raised him and he believed. And here you have seen this woman whom Allah caused to die while a believer, then He raised her to life and she became an unbeliever."

Among them is his ascent to heaven. Allah has said (III, 55/48): "O Jesus, I am causing thee to die, and raising thee to Myself and purifying thee from those who disbelieve", and so on to the end of the verse. [He also records] their saying (IV, 157/156): "Truly we killed the Messiah, Jesus, the son of Mary, the messenger of Allah, whereas they did not kill him, and they did not crucify him, but a likeness was made for them", which agrees with His saying (IV, 158/156): "But Allah raised him to Himself, and Allah is sublime, wise."

Al-Kalbī relates from Abū Ṣāliḥ from Ibn ʿAbbās, that Jesus—on whom be peace—met a party of Jews who when they saw him said: "Here comes the sorcerer, the son of the sorceress, the actor, the son of the actress." So thus they abused him and his mother. Now when Jesus saw that he cursed them, saying: "Allahumma, Thou art my God. From Thy spirit did I come forth, and by Thy Word was I created. I did not come to them of my own accord. Allahumma, bring evil on whosoever reviles me and reviles my mother." Allah answered his prayer and metamorphosed those who were reviling him and his mother into pigs. Now when the leader of the Jews and their Prince saw that [sign] he was terrified by it, and was afraid of his prayers. The Jews, therefore, came to the decision to kill Jesus. They came to him that very day and began to question him. He said: "O company of Jews, Allah is angry with you." Then they grew very angry at what he said, and they rushed at him one day to kill him, but Allah—great and majestic is He—sent Gabriel to him, who made him enter a niche in the wall, concealing him in the roof thereof. Then Allah, Most High, took him up from that window-niche. The ruler of the Jews bade one of his companions, a man named Falṭiyānūs, to enter the niche and kill him. When Falṭiyānūs entered he failed to see Jesus, but as he remained a long while away from them they supposed that he was fighting with Jesus in there. Allah, however, cast upon him the likeness of Jesus, so that when he emerged they thought he was Jesus, and they killed him, crucifying him.

Wahb says that Jesus, when Allah informed him that he was to depart from the world, was afraid of death and was distressed, so he summoned the Ḥawārīyūn and made a feast for them, saying: "Come to me to-night, for I have need of you." When they came to him that night he fed them, rising up and serving them. When they had finished eating he began to wash their hands and exhort them and wipe their hands on his garment. At this they were [somewhat] astonished and displeased with him, but he said: "Whosoever rejects anything that I am doing is not of me nor I of him." So they consented to it till he finished. Then he said to them: "Verily, what I have done to you this night in serving you at food and washing your hands with mine, is that you might have an example from me, though you see that I am better than you are. So let not any one of you consider himself greater than another, but sacrifice yourselves for one another as you have seen me sacrifice myself for you. Now the thing that I have to request of you is that you pray to Allah for me, and be instant in prayer that my time may be delayed in coming." But when they betook themselves to prayer, and were desirous of being diligent [therein], Allah sent on them sleep, so that they were unable to pray. He began to awaken them and say: "Glory be to Allah; could ye not endure for one night to help me therein?" They said: "By Allah, we do not know what is the matter with us. We used to stay up late and to sit up much, but this night we were not able to keep awake, for whenever we desired to pray some barrier came between us and it." Then he said: "The shepherd goeth and the sheep are left behind", and he went on saying such things as that, meaning [by them] himself. Presently he said: "One of you will surely disbelieve in me ere the cock crows three times, and one of you will sell me for a few dirhams and will eat the price of me." Then they all went out and dispersed.

Now the Jews were seeking him, so they seized Simon, one of the Ḥawārīyūn, saying: "This is one of his companions", but he denied it, saying: "I am not of his companions", so they left him. Then others seized him, and he denied it likewise. Thereupon he heard the cock's voice, and wept for that grieved him. When it was morning one of the Ḥawārīyūn went to the Jews and said to them: "What will you give me if I guide you to him?" They gave him thirty dirhams, which he took and led them to him. But before that he (i.e. the betrayer) was made to have his semblance for them, so they took him and made him secure by binding him with a rope. Then they started to lead him away, saying: "You used to raise the dead to life, and cure the born blind and the leper, are you not able to free yourself from this rope?" Also they spat on him and put thorns upon him, and they set up a wooden stake on which to crucify him. When they came with him to the stake the earth was darkened, and Allah sent angels who came between them and Jesus. Then He cast the appearance of Jesus upon him who had led them to him, whose name was Judas, so they crucified him in his place, thinking that he was Jesus. Then Allah caused Jesus to die for three hours, after which He raised him to heaven, according to His saying (III, 55/48): "Lo, I am putting thee to death and raising thee to Myself, and purifying thee from those who disbelieve."

When they had crucified him who had taken on the appearance of Jesus, Mary, the mother of Jesus, came with a woman over whom Jesus had prayed so that she was freed from a certain madness, that they might weep over the crucified. Jesus met them and said: "For whom are you weeping?" "For you", they said. "But Allah took me up", said he, "so that nothing has befallen me save good. This [one whom you see crucified] is but another person who has been made to resemble me." Muqātil says that the Jews put Jesus in charge of a man who was to be his jailer and go around with him wherever he went. When Jesus ascended the mount where an angel came and took him up to heaven, Allah threw the similitude of Jesus on the jailer so that the Jews thought that he was Jesus and seized him. He said to them: "I am not Jesus. I am So and So the son of So and So", but they believed him not, and so they put him to death by crucifying him. Qatāda said: "It has been related to us that Jesus, the Apostle of Allah, said to his friends: 'Which of you will take upon himself my likeness so that he may be put to death [instead of me]?' One of the group said: ['Let it be cast] on me, O Prophet of Allah.' So that man was killed, and Allah saved Jesus by raising him to Himself." It is said that the one who took the likeness of Jesus and was crucified in his place was an Israelite named Ashyū' b. Qandīrā. But Allah knows best.

Concerning Jesus' descent from heaven seven days after he had been raised up

Wahb and others among the People of the Book say that when Allah raised Jesus—on whom be peace—to Himself, he remained in heaven seven days. Then Allah said to him: "Lo! your enemies, the Jews, have precluded you from [keeping your] promise to your companions, so descend to them and give them your testament. Go down also to Mary Magdalene for there is no one who has wept for you or grieved for you as she has. Go down, therefore, to her and announce [yourself] to her, that she may be the first one to find you. Then bid her gather the Ḥawārīyūn to you so that you may send them out into the world as preachers summoning [men] to Allah, Most High."

The story of Mary Magdalene was that she was an Israelite from one of the villages of Antioch named Magdalān. She was a pious woman but used to menstruate without ceasing. Many of the nobility of the Israelites had sought her hand in marriage but she had refused them. They thought that she considered herself above them, but that was not the reason, she only wanted to hide from them her infirmity. When she heard about the coming of Jesus—upon whom be peace—and of what diseases and infirmities Allah was curing at his hands, she went to him hoping to be cured. But when she saw Jesus and the dignity with which Allah had clothed him, she felt ashamed. Therefore she went around behind him and put her hand on his back. Jesus said: "Some diseased person has with good intention touched me. May Allah give him what he desires and purify him with my purity." So Allah removed her trouble from her so that she was cleansed and purified.

When Allah bade Jesus descend to her seven days after his ascension, he went down to her, and the mountain blazed with light as he came down. Then she gathered unto him the Ḥawārīyūn, whom he sent out into the world as summoners to Allah. After this Allah took him up, clothed him with feathers, dressed him in light, and removed from him desire for food and drink. So he flew about with the angels around the Throne, being of human and of angelic kind, earthly and heavenly. Then the Ḥawārīyūn dispersed to where he had bidden each of them go. The night in which he descended is the night which the Christians celebrate. They say that he sent Peter to Rome, Andrew and Matthew to the land where the inhabitants eat men, Thomas and Levi to the Orient, Philip and Judas to Qairawān and Africa, John to Ephesus, the place of the Companions of the Cave (cf. Sūra XVIII), the two James to Jerusalem, which is Aelia, the land of the Holy House, Bartholomew to Arabia, i.e. to the Ḥijāz, Simon to the land of the Berbers. Each one of the Ḥawārīyūn who was thus sent out was made able to speak the language of those to whom Jesus sent him.

Ibn Isḥāq says that the Jews sought out the remainder of the Ḥawārīyūn, the companions of Jesus, exposing them to the sun, torturing them and going around with them. Now the king of Rome, who was an idolator, heard about that, for they said to him: "There was a man, among those of the Israelites in subjection to you, against whom they acted evilly and whom they put to death. [This man] used to tell them that he was the Apostle of Allah, and indeed he used to raise the dead to life, and heal their sick, and he created for them from clay the figure of a bird into which he breathed so that by Allah's permission it flew. Moreover he revealed to them the future and performed miracles for them." Said this king of Rome: "And what prevented you from mentioning his affair to me? By Allah, had I known I would have intervened between him and them." Then he sent for the Ḥawārīyūn and took them out of their hands. When they came to him he asked them about the religion of Jesus. They told him about him, so he acknowledged to them [his acceptance of] his religion and received [from them] a likeness of Jesus and the cross on which he had been crucified. This he honoured and guarded because it had been touched by him. Afterwards he made war on the Israelites and killed a great number of them. That was the origin of Christianity in Rome.

The people of the Torah say that Mary bore Jesus when she was thirteen years of age and bore him in Bethlehem in the land of Jerusalem, some sixty-five years after Alexander's conquest of Babylon, and fifty-one years after the king of the Ashakānīs. At the age of thirty Allah [began to] give revelations to him, and He raised him to Himself from the Holy place on the Night of Power in the month of Ramaḍān when he was thirty-three years old. Thus the period of his Prophetic activity was three years. His mother Mary lived six years after his ascension. But Allah knows best.

Concerning the death of Mary, the daughter of 'Imrān, on whom be peace

Wahb says that when Allah, Most High, decided to raise Jesus, He made all the Ḥawārīyūn brothers. Then he commanded two of them, namely, Simon the brass-worker and John, to look after the mother [of Jesus] and never leave her. So they took Mary away with them to Mārūt, king of Rome, summoning him to Allah—great and majestic is He. Now Allah had before this sent to him [the Prophet] Jonah—on whom be peace. When they came to him he ordered Simon and Andrew to be crucified upside-down, whereat Mary and John fled. As they were on the way the searchers found them, and they were afraid, but the earth opened up and they hid therein. Thereupon along came Mārūt, the king of Rome, and his friends, and dug at that place but did not find anything, so they put back the earth, recognizing that this was an affair from Allah. Then the king of Rome asked about Jesus, and they told him about him and he became a Muslim, as we have related. But Allah knows best.

Concerning the descent of Jesus a second time in the Last Days

Allah—may He be exalted—has said (XLIII, 61): "Verily he is a sign of the Hour, so be in no doubt about it." Al-Ḥasan b. al-Faḍl was asked: "Do you find anything about the Descent of Jesus in the Qur'ān?" "Yes", said he, "in the words 'and a grown man' (*kahlan* in III, 46/41; V, 110/109), for he did not reach the *kahl* age in this world [on his first appearance] so that this [expression] 'and a grown man' must refer to the time after his descent from heaven."

Abū Ṣāliḥ Shu'aib b. Muḥammad al-Baihaqī has informed us in his *isnād* from Abū Huraira, how this latter related that the Apostle of Allah —on whom be Allah's blessing and peace— said: "The Prophets are brethren though of different mothers, and their religion is one and the same. I am the nearest of mankind to Jesus son of Mary—on both of whom be peace—because there has been no Prophet between him and me. It will come to pass that the Son of Mary will descend among you as a just ruler. He will descend to my community and be my *khalīfa* over them, so when you see him give him recognition. He will be a man symmetrical in stature, of reddish-white [complexion], lank haired, as though his hair were dripping perfume though it has not been moistened.

He will come down in a greenish-yellow garment, will break crosses and kill swine, will put an end to the poll-tax,[1] will make wealth to abound, will raise the Hallel from ar-Rawḥā' coming for the pilgrimage and the visitation, undertaking them both with zeal.[2] He will make war on behalf of Islam, until in his time he destroys all religions save that of Islam, and there will be thence forward but one single prostration of obeisance, namely that to Allah, Lord of the Worlds. Also in his time Allah will destroy the Antichrist, the lying ad-Dajjāl. There will then be such security on the earth that lions will pasture freely with the camels, tigers with cattle, wolves with sheep, children will play with serpents and no one will do harm to anyone else. [Jesus] will remain on earth for forty years, will get married and have children. Then he will die, and the Muslims will pray over him and bury him in Madīna beside [the grave of] 'Umar. Read, if you will, the words (IV, 159/157): "There are none of the People of the Book but will believe in him before his death, and on the Day of Resurrection he will be a witness against them", i.e. before the death of Jesus. Abū Huraira repeats this three times.

Muḥammad b. al-Qāsim the Persian, has informed us with an *isnād* from Abū Huraira, how he related that the Apostle of Allah said: "When Allah sends down the Messiah Jesus he will live in this community a certain time, and will then die in this city of mine, and will be buried beside the grave of 'Umar. How blessed are Abū Bakr and 'Umar, who will thus be resurrected between two Prophets." My father informed me saying: Al-Ḥusain b. Aḥmad b. Muḥammad b. 'Alī related to me, with an *isnād* from Ibn 'Abbās, that this latter related how the Apostle of Allah—on whom be Allah's blessing and peace—said: "How can Allah destroy a community at whose beginning I am, at whose end is Jesus, and in the middle of which is the Mahdī of the people of my House?"[3]

[1] The significance of this is that under the governance of Islam non-Muslims had to pay the *jizya* or poll-tax. When Jesus descends, as one of the signs of the approaching end of the age, he will himself become a Muslim and will convert all the People of the Book to the religion of Islam. Since this conversion will change all the non-Muslims into Muslims the poll-tax will automatically come to an end.

[2] The Pilgrimage is one of the rites performed by professing Muslims. The *ḥajj* is the greater Pilgrimage, and the *'umra*, or visitation, is the lesser pilgrimage. The Hallel is the welcome cry with which the pilgrim greets the Holy City. See p. 496.

[3] The reference is eschatological. Muḥammad, of course, was the founder of the Muslim community, so he is its beginning. The Descent of Jesus and the end of the Antichrist ad-Dajjāl immediately precede the sounding of the trump which ushers in the Last Day, so the leadership of Jesus in the Muslim community at his Second Coming makes him the end. The coming of the Mahdī is the first of the greater Signs of the approach of the Hour, so his championship of Islam makes him a midway figure between Muḥammad and Jesus.

ON THE MERITS OF MECCA [1]

With regard to the excellent merits [of Mecca], be it known to you that the theologians differ as to whether Mecca—which may Allah, Most High, guard—has the greater merit, or Madīna. In the opinion of Abū Ḥanīfa and ash-Shāfiʿī—on both of whom may Allah have mercy—Mecca has greater merits than Madīna, save that in the latter is the site of the tomb of the Prophet—on whom be Allah's blessing and peace. Mālik, however, says that Madīna has greater merits than Mecca. As regards [the merit of] residing in the vicinity of Mecca the Doctors of religion are also divided. Abū Ḥanīfa and some of the followers of ash-Shāfiʿī, spiritual men who are ever on the watch to guard [the purity of] Allah's religion, go so far as to regard remaining on in Mecca a thing disapproved *(makrūh)*, for did not [the Prophet]—on whom be Allah's blessing and peace—say: "Let him who has finished his pilgrimage make haste to return to his family, a thing which will increase his reward, for too much beholding inevitably brings on weariness and lowers the sense of reverence below what it should be." It was for this reason that he—upon whom be Allah's blessing and peace—said to Abū Huraira: "O Abū Huraira, visit seldom and thou wilt find more love." ʿUmar—with whom may Allah be pleased—said, when he finished the duties of the pilgrimage: "O people of Yemen, [off with you to] your Yemen; O people of Syria [off with you to] your Syria; O people of ʿIrāq [off with you to] your ʿIrāq."

1 From ad-Diyārbakrī's *Tārīkh al-Khamīs*, I, 124–126 (edition of Cairo, 1283 A.H. = 1866 A.D.).

The pilgrimage to Mecca, the Holy City of Islam, is one of the five incumbent duties resting on every professing Muslim, and annually during the month Dhū 'l-Ḥijja, the twelfth month of the Muslim year, crowds of pilgrims from every part of the Muslim world make their way to Mecca to fulfil this duty of pilgrimage, and commonly go on to visit the other sacred city, Madīna, before returning home. There are two forms of pilgrimage, the lesser and the greater. The lesser is the *ʿumra*, or visitation, which can be performed at any time. The greater is the *ḥajj*, or pilgrimage proper, which can be performed only at the specified pilgrimage season. There have been several popular descriptions of the pilgrimage ceremonies written for the interest of non-Muslim readers. This passage from ad-Diyārbekrī may perhaps serve to explain somewhat more clearly the significance the visit to Mecca has for pious Muslims.

It is related of 'Umar—with whom may Allah be pleased—that he was very anxious to prevent the people from increasing [the number of] circumambulations, saying: "I fear lest the people become too familiar with this House *(bait)* so that reverence for it disappear from their breasts." Ibn 'Abbās—with whom may Allah be pleased—said, when he gave preference to residing at Ṭā'if [1] and its environs over [residing in] Mecca: "[This is because] I would rather be guilty of fifty sins — or seventy sins, as it is given in the *Rabī' al-Abrār*[2] — at Rukba than a single sin at Mecca." This Rukba is a well-grassed and watered place between Mecca and Ṭā'if, not far from Ṭā'if. Ibn Mas'ūd—with whom may Allah be pleased—said: "There is no town in which a man will be punished for meditating before acting save Mecca." And he recited this verse (XXII, 25/25, 26): "And the Sacred Shrine which We have appointed for men, alike for the dwellers there and for strangers, so whoever desires infamously to profane it We shall make to taste of painful punishment." ...Moreover, he said that evil deeds done there are doubly bad, just as good deeds done there are doubly good...

Abū Yūsuf and Muḥammad,[3] as well as a group of the followers of ash-Shāfi'ī and many other theologians, are of the opinion that this [remaining on at Mecca] is not a thing disapproved, quoting the words of the Most High (XXII, 26/27): "But make pure My House for those who circumambulate, those who stand", which is an unrestricted command, and the words of him—upon whom be Allah's blessing and peace—:"Mecca and Madīna remove sins as a blacksmith's bellows removes dross from the iron, so I shall be a witness, or an intercessor, on the Day for everyone who patiently endures the hardships, the heat and the distress [involved in dwelling] there." There is also [to be taken into consideration] what is to be found in the Traditions about staying in Mecca being a happiness and leaving it a misfortune.

Some of the theologians, who are watchful about matters of religion, disapprove of any hindrance being placed in the way of one's abiding and dwelling there, because that would be putting a hindrance to obedience and worshipful service of Allah. Moreover it may be argued that to dwell near the Ka'ba enables one to pay it its full due of reverence and

[1] Ṭā'if was a mountain resort some seventy-five miles south-east of Mecca, where even in pre-Islamic days wealthy Meccan merchants had summer residences. See H. Lammens, *La cité arabe de Ṭāif à la veille de l'hégire* (Beyrouth, 1922).

[2] It is a book by the famous twelfth-century exegete and grammarian az-Zamakhsharī (d. 538 A.H. = 1143 A.D.).

[3] Abū Yusūf and Muḥammad ash-Shaibānī were the two main transmitters of the system of Abū Ḥanīfa. See p. p. 413 n. 2, and p. 385 n. 3.

honour, etc., which one would not otherwise be able to do, though if one is unable to pay it such full due as is rightly its, then to depart from it and leave the neighbourhood is better for him in view of what [that inability] would involve of showing deficiency and weariness and neglect of what would honour, exalt and dignify it. This is evident, so if anyone is able to dwell there and remain in such a state as will pay it due honour and reverence, and keep that reverence for it in his eye as undimmed as when he first entered [the city], what a wondrous thing that will be. That, indeed, will be the great bliss [1] and the manifold grace which has no parallel, as the lord of men—upon whom be Allah's blessing and peace—once proclaimed: "To look upon the Ka'ba is an act of worship, and whoever looks upon the House in faith and belief will have his former and latter sins forgiven, and whoever looks upon the House in a spirit of willing obedience, even though he does not circumambulate it nor say the prescribed prayers, will have done what in Allah's eyes is of greater merit than a year's acts of worship during which [year] he has fasted by day and stood up for prayer by night. It is related of Ibn 'Abbās that he said: "I do not know any place in the world save Mecca of which it is written that whoever looks at one of its buildings has done the equivalent of a lifetime of acts of worship or of fasting."

Said he—upon whom be Allah's blessing and peace—: "A prayer performed in this mosque of mine (i.e. the mosque at Madīna) is more meritorious than a thousand prayers in any other mosque save the sacred mosque (i.e. the mosque in Mecca), for a prayer performed in the sacred mosque is more meritorious than 100,000 prayers if one performs it alone, but if one performs it in company with others it is more meritorious than two thousand times two thousand plus 500,000 prayers."... Anas b. Mālik has related that the Apostle of Allah—upon whom be Allah's blessing and peace—said: "A man's performance of prayer in his own house counts as one prayer service. If he prays it in the mosque of his group it counts as twenty-five prayer services. If he prays it in a congregational mosque it counts as five hundred prayer services. If he prays it in the Aqṣā mosque (in Jerusalem) it counts as fifty thousand prayer services, as it does if he prays it in my mosque [at Madīna], but if he prays it in the sacred mosque it counts as a hundred thousand p services." Ibn Māja relates this.

Whoever sits for a single hour facing the Ka'ba with faith and belief in Allah and in His Apostle, and doing honour to the *qibla,* will have the same reward as those who perform the pilgrimage and the visitation (i.e.

[1] This *fawz kabīr* here is a reminiscence of Sūra LXXXV, 11.

the greater and the lesser pilgrimage, the *ḥajj* and the *ʿumra),* as those who go out on Holy War, and as those who stand on guard at the frontiers in the way of Allah. Each day Allah looks three hundred and sixty times at all His creatures, but His first look is at those who dwell in His sacred city of Mecca, His place secure, and to those He sees circumambulating, or standing in worship, or sitting over against the Kaʿba, He grants forgiveness. Thereupon the angels say: "O our God and our Master, there remain only those who are sleeping." And He says: "Join them with the others for they are neighbours of My House." So then the people of Mecca are the people of Allah and the neighbours of His House, and those who have memorized the Qur'ān are the people of Allah, and His favourites.

Said the Apostle of Allah—upon whom be Allah's blessing and peace—: "Whoever performs the visitation (*ʿumra*) in the month of Ramaḍān is as though he had performed the pilgrimage (*ḥajj*) along with me." Ibn ʿAbbās reports that the Apostle of Allah—upon whom be Allah's blessing and peace—said that an *ʿumra* during Ramaḍān was the equivalent of a *ḥajj,* and if a man fasts the month of Ramaḍān in Mecca, fasting completely and staying up at night for prayers as much as he can manage, Allah will write to his credit a hundred thousand Ramaḍāns fasted elsewhere, while for each day and each night thereof he will be allowed a forgiveness and an intercession, and for each day and night [the merit of having] freed a slave and [having provided] a horse's load for the cause of Allah, and also for each day and night thereof a special benefit (*ḥasana*). It is recorded from Ibn ʿAbbās that the Apostle of Allāh—upon whom be Allah's blessing and peace—said: "An *ʿumra* in Ramaḍān fulfils one pilgrimage obligation, or is the equivalent of a pilgrimage with me." This is how Muslim [1] gives it.

ʿAbdallah b. ʿUmar—with whom and with whose father may Allah be pleased—said that he had heard the Apostle of Allah—upon whom be Allah's blessing and peace—say: "If a man circumambulates the House and prays a prayer of two *rakʿas* it is as though he had freed a slave." Ibn Māja relates this, but an-Nasā'ī words it: "If one performs seven circumambulations it is the equivalent of freeing a slave." From Abū Huraira comes the statement that the Prophet—upon whom be Allah's blessing and peace—said: "Whoever circumambulates the House

[1] The point of the Tradition here is that as Ramaḍān is the month of fasting the performance of an *ʿumra* would be particularly arduous, so that though Ramaḍān is not one of the proper months for the *ḥajj* yet an *ʿumra* in that month can be counted as its equivalent.

seven times, uttering no other words than: 'Glory be to Allah!', 'Praise be to Allah!', 'There is no deity save Allah', 'Allah is most great', 'There is no strength nor might save with Allah, the High, the Mighty', will have ten of his evil deeds blotted out and ten good deeds written to his credit, as well as having [his rank in Paradise] raised ten degrees, whereas he who circumambulates but speaks while so doing will wade on his feet through mercy as one wades through water." Ibn Māja relates this.

Ibn ʿAbbās records that the Apostle of Allah—upon whom be Allah's blessing and peace—said: "Whoever circumambulates the House fifty times becomes as free from sin as he was the day his mother bore him." At-Tirmidhī relates this. In an epistle of al-Ḥasan al-Baṣrī [1] there is a statement that the Apostle of Allah—upon whom be Allah's blessing and peace—said: "Whosoever enters the House has entered into Allah's mercy, Allah's protection, Allah's security, and he who departs departs [with assurance of] having received His forgiveness." Ibn ʿAbbās reports that he—upon whom be Allah's blessing and peace—said: "Whosoever enters the House enters into a good deed and departs from an evil deed, having His forgiveness." Al-Baihaqī [2] and others relate this, as they are cited in *al-Baḥr al-ʿamīq*.[3] ʿAbdallah b. ʿUmair records that Ibn ʿUmar used to press close to the two corners *(ruknain)*,[4] so I said: "O father of ʿAbd ar-Raḥmān you are pressing closer to them than I ever saw any of the Companions of the Apostle of Allah press." He answered: "I do it because I heard the Apostle of Allah—upon whom be Allah's blessing and peace—say that to rub against them is an atonement for sin." The way it is given in an-Nasā'ī is "it will ward off sin." Then he (i.e. Ibn ʿUmar) continued: "And I heard him say that if one circumambulates the House for a week it is as though he had freed a slave, and I also heard him say that one does not set down one foot or raise the other [in circumambulating] but Allah removes [from his record] a sin and writes in a good deed." At-Tirmidhī relates this.

Ibn ʿAbbās records that the Prophet—upon whom be Allah's blessing and peace—said: "To circumambulate around the House is like saying prayers, save that in them you speak, so let him who speaks [while

[1] He was one of the most famous theologians and mystics of early Islam (died 110 A.H. = 728 A.D.).

[2] His *Kitāb as-Sunan al-kabīr* is an important compendium of Tradition. He died in 458 A.H. = 1066 A.D.

[3] I.e. aṣ-Ṣāghānī's *al-Baḥr al-ʿamīq fī Manāsik al-Muʿtamir wa'l-Ḥājj ilā'l-Bait al-ʿatīq*, a book concerned with the ceremonies of the Pilgrimage.

[4] He means the Yamanī corner and the Black Stone corner, which the pilgrims press close as they circumambulate the Kaʿba.

circumambulating] say nothing but what is good." At-Tirmidhī relates this. In the book *Rabīʿ al-Abrār* it is recorded that Wahb b. Ward said: I was one night in the sacred precincts praying when I heard from between the Kaʿba and the curtains [1] the words: "To Allah I make my complaint, then to thee O Gabriel, of how those who circumambulate around me cast on me their frivolous conversation, their trifling talk, their merry-making. If they do not make an end of it I shall get so disturbed that every stone in me will fly back to the mountains from which it was hewn." Abū Ghifār said: I performed the circumambulation in the rain along with Anas b. Mālik. When we had finished we went to the *maqām* [2] and prayed a prayer of two *rakʿas*, whereupon Anas said: "Begin works anew, for Allah hath pardoned you. Thus did the Apostle of Allah—upon whom be Allah's blessing and peace—say to us when we circumambulated with him in the rain." Ibn Māja relates this. Abū Huraira has related that the Prophet—upon whom be Allah's blessing and peace—said: "Allah has set seventy angels in charge of the Yamanī corner, and whenever anyone says there: 'Allahumma! I ask pardon of Thee, and well-being in this life and the next! O our Lord, send us blessing in this life and blessing in the next! and protect us from the punishment of the Fire!' they say 'Amen.'"

Said the Apostle of Allah—on whom be Allah's blessing and peace—: "Whoever keeps company with the Black Stone corner [3] keeps close company with the hand of Allah." Ibn Māja relates this. ʿĀ'isha—with whom may Allah be pleased—reports that the Apostle of Allah—upon whom be Allah's blessing and peace—said: "There is no day on which Allah is more likely to free a mortal from Hell-fire than on the day of ʿArafāt. [4] On that day He will draw near, will boast of them to the angels, and will say: 'What do these want?'" Muslim and an-Nasā'ī relate this and an-Nasā'ī adds "a community", i.e. an individual mortal or a community. ʿAbbās b. Mirdās records that the Apostle of Allah—upon whom be Allah's blessing and peace—on the eve of ʿArafāt prayed for forgiveness for his community, and the answer came: "I have forgiven them, all save the oppressor, for I am going to exact vengeance for the oppressed from him." He said: "O Lord, if Thou wilt Thou canst give the oppressed [some special recompense] in

[1] He means the external cloth covering which is annually renewed and with great ceremony hung over the Kaʿba.

[2] I.e. the *maqām Ibrāhīm*, a small sacred place in close proximity to the Kaʿba. See *Encyclopaedia of Islam*, II, 585.

[3] See p. 501.

[4] See pp. 170, 192, 499–500.

Paradise and forgive the oppressor." He received no answer on the eve of 'Arafāt but when morning came at Muzdalifa[1] he repeated his petition and his request was granted, whereat the Apostle of Allah laughed, or maybe the narrator said he smiled. Abū Bakr and 'Umar—with both of whom may Allah be pleased—said: "By my father and my mother, this is no hour in which to be laughing. What has caused you to laugh?" He replied: "When Allah's enemy Iblīs learned that Allah—mighty and majestic is He—had granted my petition and forgiven my community he took dust and threw it on his head, crying 'Woe!' and 'Destruction!' What made me laugh was what I saw of this outburst of his distress." Ibn Māja relates this.

In [the book] *Rabīʿ al-Abrār* it is related on the authority of Muḥammad b. Qais b. Makhrama that whoever dies in one of the two sacred cities will be raised up by Allah on the Day and sent forward in perfect tranquillity. It is related that even an unacceptable pilgrimage[2] is better than [the possession of] this world and all that is in it. It is also said that one whose pilgrimage is unacceptable will nevertheless [because of it] become as free from sins as he was the day his mother gave birth to him, while he whose pilgrimage is accepted by Allah is truly victorious.

[1] A place on the way back from 'Arafāt to Mecca where the pilgrims perform certain rites and spend the night between the 9th and the 10th days of the pilgrimage month. See p. 504.

[2] Quite a number of things, which are all listed in the works of theology and jurisprudence, may occur to render one's pilgrimage invalid, in which case one has the merit of having visited the holy city but cannot count it as having fulfilled the pilgrimage obligation.

FESTIVAL DEVOTIONS

Islam, like other religions, has its feasts as well as its fasts, and the feasts besides being occasions of merry-making are points in the year when it is customary to practise special exercises of devotional character. The five great feasts or festivals of the Muslim year are:[1]

I. The *'Īd al-Fiṭr* at the end of the fasting month of Ramaḍān.
II. The *'Īd al-Aḍḥā* (Feast of Sacrifice) on the 10th day of the month Dhū 'l-Ḥijja, the last month of the year.
III. *Muḥarram*, the New Year's Festival at the beginning of the first month of the year.
IV. *Mawlid an-Nabī*, the Prophet's birthday, on the twelfth of the month Rabī' al-awwal.
V. *Lailat al-Mi'rāj*, the night of the Prophet's Ascension to heavenly places.

Specimens of the special *khuṭba*s preached in the mosques during the celebration of the *'Īd al-Fiṭr* and the *'Īd al-Aḍḥā* can be read in Sell's *Faith of Islam*, 4th ed. (Madras, 1920), pp. 432–438, and the Passion Play commonly performed in celebration of Muḥarram may be read in Sir Lewis Pelly's *Miracle Play of Hasan and Husain* (London, 1879). The specimens offered in this Reader, therefore, are concerned with the celebration of the Prophet's birthday and his Ascension.

THE MANTLE POEM OF AL-BŪṢĪRĪ

The Prophet's birthday falls on the 12th day of the month Rabī' al-Awwal, and quite naturally is kept as a festival day in Muslim countries. It was early marked by special celebrations in the community, and though local custom varies there is a general similarity in the ceremonies for *Mawlid an-Nabī* (Prophet's Birthday). Lane in cap. XXIV of his *Modern Egyptians* gives a good account of how it was celebrated in Egypt in his day. For long one prominent element in the celebration of this festival has been the recitation of panegyrics on the Prophet. Many of these in various languages have been published, some of ancient and some of more recent data. Perhaps the best known of them is the *Burdah*, or Mantle Poem, of the Shaikh Muḥammad al-Būṣīrī (608–694 A.H. = 1211–1294 A.D.). The author was a Berber of the Sanhāja tribe, who lived in Egypt, where he seems to have earned his living as a copyist of manuscripts, though he gained some fame as a poet. The story is that he became partially paralysed and was in great distress, but in a dream one night the Prophet Muḥ-

[1] For a general account see Gustave von Grunebaum's little book, *Muhammadan Festivals* (New York, 1951).

ammad appeared to him and covered him with his striped mantle. When he awoke in the morning he found that his paralysis had disappeared, so in gratitude for his miraculous cure he turned to religion and composed a poem in honour of the Prophet, which he called "Glistening stars in praise of the best of Creatures", but which is commonly known as *al-Burdah*, i.e. the Mantle Poem.

It has become very popular, has been translated into Persian, Turkish, Tatar and the Shilha dialect of Berber, and become the subject of innumerable commentaries. Though popular its literary value is not great, belonging as it does to that decadent style of Arabic verse which delights in exaggerated use of play on words. The various editions differ somewhat in the number of lines, some having a considerable number of interpolations. The present translation is made from a cheap lithograph dated Cairo, 1318 A.H. (= 1900 A.D.), with the commentary of al-Marrākushī on the margin.

A similar poem for popular recital in Turkey on the Prophet's birthday, is Suleyman Chelebi's *Mevlud-i sherif*, translated by F. Lyman McCallum in the Wisdom of the East Series (London, 1943). Even more popular in India and Indonesia has been the *'Iqd al-Jawāhir*, by Ja'far b. Ḥasan al-Barzanjī.

[1]

(On amorousness and complaint about passion)

1. Is it from the remembrance of neighbours at Dhū Salam [1]
   That thou hast mixed with blood the tears that flow from [thine] eyes?
2. Or is it the wind that blows from the direction of Kāẓima?
   Or the flashing of the lightning in the darkness from Iḍam? [2]
3. What ails thine eyes? When thou tellest them to cease they flow.
   And what ails thy heart? When thou tellest it to come to its senses it becomes love-distraught.
4. Does the lover think [his] passion can be hid,
   When it is being declared by his dropping tears and his glowing [heart]?
5. Had it not been for love-passion thou wouldst not have shed tears on the traces of an encampment,
   Nor wouldst thou have lost sleep at remembrance of the *bān*-tree [3] and the mountain tip.

[1] Dhū Salam is said to be the name of a place in Arabia near Madīna.

[2] Both Kāẓima and Iḍam are mountains in the neighbourhood of Madīna.

[3] *bān* is the name given at the present day to the *Salix Aegypta*, or the Egyptian willow, but the Lexicons are uncertain what tree was meant by the ancient poets who so often refer to the *bān*-tree. See line 164.

6. So how canst thou deny [thy] love after evidence has been borne
To it against thee by such faithful witnesses as tears and sickness?
7. Moreover love's passion has written two lines of tears and langour,
Like yellow *bahār* and like red *'anam* on thy cheek.[1]
8. Yea! the phantom of the one I love came at night and kept me wakeful,
For love alternates pleasure with pain.
9. O thou who dost reproach me for a love worthy of an 'Udhrite,[2] excusable
Let me be to thee, for wert thou just thou wouldst not blame.
10. May my [sorry] plight pass over to thee. My secret is not hidden
From such as would traduce, nor will my sickness soon be cured.
11. Good advice hast thou offered me, but I am not hearkening.
A lover, indeed, is deaf to those who reprove.
12. I myself was suspicious of the advice of [my] greying hair as it reproached me,
Though grey hair should be farthest from arousing suspicion as to its advice.

[2]

(On being on guard against the lusts of the self)

13. For indeed my passionate desire for evil takes no warning,
So foolish is it, from the call to caution of grey hairs and waning strength,
14. Nor had it prepared by good deeds proper entertainment
For a guest who has unashamedly drawn near my head.[3]
15. Had I known that I should not duly honour him (i.e. the guest),
I would have concealed from him by *katam*[4] the secret now disclosed.

[1] The *bahār* is also called *'ain al-baqar* or "ox-eye", i.e. *buphthalamum*, a plant with a yellow flower which appears in the spring and is used as a symbol of yellowness. The *'anam* is a kind of carob with a very red flower, so that it is likewise used as a symbol for redness.

[2] The men of the tribe of 'Udhra in the Yemen were famed for the ardour of their love.

[3] This is a poetical way of saying that age has begun to whiten his hair.

[4] *katam* is the name of a plant used in the production of a vegetable dye much used among the Arabs for dyeing greying hair a glossy black.

16. Whom do I have [to help me] restrain from their wrong courses [my] restive passions,
    As the restiveness of horses is restrained by bridles?
17. Think not to break its appetite by unlawful indulgences,
    For food but strengthens the glutton's appetite.
18. The soul is like an infant. If you neglect him he will grow to youthful age still
    Loving to suck the breast, but if you wean him, he will be weaned.
19. So check its desires, and beware lest you let it get the mastery,
    For desire, whenever it gets the mastery, either kills or dishonours.
20. Watch it carefully while it pastures in the [field of] actions,
    And if it finds some pasture to its taste, let it not pasture freely.
21. How often has it found delight in a pleasure which for the man was deadly,
    Since he did not know that there was poison in the dainty.
22. Fear the secret perils both of hunger and of satiety,
    For it may be that hunger is more dangerous than indigestion.
23. Let the tears pour down freely from an eye which has taken its fill
    Of forbidden sights, and cling close to the protectiveness of repentance.
24. Go contrary to both the soul and Satan; disobey them both,
    And if that pair pretend sincere affection in advising thee, be suspicious.
25. Pay no heed to either of them, whether as adversary or as arbiter,
    For well thou knowest the guileful schemes of the adversary and the arbiter.
26. Allah's pardon I ask for preaching apart from practice,
    For thereby I have been providing a genealogy for a childless man.
27. To thee I recommend virtuous action, but do not myself conform thereto.
    Yet what I do not perform myself, how shall I bid thee perform?
28. I have not made any provision before death of supererogatory works,
    Having neither prayed nor fasted beyond the prescribed amount.

[3]

(On praise of the Prophet—on whom be Allah's blessing and peace)

29. I have transgressed the way of life of him who kept vigil at night,
Till his feet in pain complained of the harm [they were suffering].
30. Out of hunger he tightened [the belt] around his stomach, and folded
Beneath the stone[1] a delicate skin on his flanks.
31. High mountains of gold [sought to] entice him
Against himself, but what aloofness he showed them.
32. His need only confirmed his abstinence in regard to them.
Need does not prevail in the case of the virtuous.
33. How could need attract towards this world such an one,
Had it not been for whom the world would not have come out of non-existence?
34. Muḥammad, Lord of the two Worlds, and of the two species having weight,[2]
And of the two [human] groups, Arabs and non-Arabs.
35. Our Prophet, who issued commands and prohibitions, and there is no one
More justified than he to say: "No!" or "Yes!"
36. He is [Allah's] beloved, whose intercession is to be hoped for,
Against each terror among the oncoming terrors.
37. He summoned [the people] to Allah, and those who attach themselves to him,
Are attaching themselves to a rope that will not break.[3]
38. He surpassed the [other] Prophets in physical and moral qualities,
Nor did they approach him in either knowledge or magnanimity.
39. All of them seek to obtain from the Apostle of Allah,
A ladle-full from the ocean or a sip from the continuous rains.
40. They will stand before him at their ranking places,
Like diacritical points of science or vowel signs of wisdom.[4]

[1] The reference is to a story in the *Sīra* of how during the fourth year A.H. there was such a serious shortage of food that the Prophet had to bind a stone on his stomach beneath his girdle to lessen the pangs of hunger.

[2] The two Worlds are this World and the Hereafter. The two species having weight *(ath-thaqalān)* are men and jinn, so called as opposed to the third species, viz. angels, who are light, airy beings.

[3] This is a reminiscence of Sūra II, 256/257.

[4] In a pointed Arabic text the diacritical points distinguish certain consonants and the vowel signs mark the vocalization. What he is saying here is that Muḥammad is the book of science or of wisdom, while the other Prophets are only the diacritical points or the vowel signs therein, useful but not essential.

41. He is the one whose interior and exterior form were made perfect.
    Then the Creator of men chose him as a beloved friend.
42. Far removed [is he] from having any partner in his good qualities,
    For in him the essence of goodness is undivided.
43. Leave aside what the Christians claim for their Prophet,
    And by what you will judge and decide what there is in him to be praised.
44. Ascribe to his person whatever nobility you may desire,
    And ascribe to his dignity whatever grandeur you please.
45. For verily, the excellence of the Apostle of Allah has no bounds,
    So that a speaker might tell of it with his mouth.
46. Were his miracles in accord with his dignity, by their grandeur,
    His name would, when pronounced, resuscitate decayed bones.
47. He did not try us with what would have been beyond our intelligence,
    Being solicitous of us, so we found no difficulty [in accepting him], nor were we suspicious.
48. Understanding of his inner nature surpasses man's comprehension, so there was not found
    Among those near or far anyone but was silent [about it].
49. It is like the sun which appears to the eyes from afar
    To be a little thing, but which dazzles the sight from near at hand.
50. The intelligence of men was in perplexity about his being, so they set forth
    As explanations of him mere phantasies of dreams.
51. So never have I seen, whether near to his real nature,
    Or far therefrom, anything other than obscure babblings.
52. For how, in this world, could his real nature be comprehended
    By people who are asleep and diverted from him by dreamings?
53. Thus the extent of knowledge with regard to him is that he is a man,
    And that of all Allah's creatures he is the best.
54. Every sign which the [other] noble Messengers have produced,
    Was obtained only because of his light which was with them.
55. He is the sun of excellence, they are but its stars,
    Which show their light to folk [only] in the darkness.
56. So that when it rises in the cosmos its guidance embraces
    The worlds, and revives all peoples.
57. How excellent is the person of the Prophet! Good-nature adorns him.
    Cloaked [is he] in beauty, marked by a joyful countenance.

58. Like a flower in delicate freshness; like the full moon in splendour,
Like the sea in bountifulness, and like time in aspiration.
59. Even when he is alone in his majesty, it is as though
He were in the midst of soldiers, with attendants thrown around him.
60. It is as though a pearl hidden in an oyster were
In the two mines of his speech and his smile.[1]
61. No perfume can equal the dust that has gathered on his limbs,
Happy is he who can sniff the odour thereof or can kiss [them].

[4]

(On the birth of him—upon whom be Allah's blessing and peace)

62. The circumstances of his birth gave clear evidence of the excellence of his family origin,
How excellent was his beginning and how excellent his end.
63. [His birth was] on a day when the Persians discovered that they
Had been given warning of coming misfortune and chastisement.
64. For that night the palace of Chosroes was split asunder,
Just as the supporting armies of Chosroes were presently to be, and never mended.
65. And the flames of the [sacred] fire were extinguished, being afflicted
Because of him, and the river, because of grief, forgot its course.
66. While Sāwa was afflicted by the sinking of its lake,
So that he who went to it for water returned in anger and still thirsty.[2]
67. It was as though the fire had taken moisture from the water,
Out of grief, and the water had put on the burning of fire.

[1] I.e. when he speaks or smiles his teeth show like pearls that had been hidden as treasure is in a mine.

[2] The references in these verses are to the portents which appeared in Persia on the night of Muḥammad's birth. Chosroes *(Kisrā)* is used here not as the name of any particular monarch, but as a general name for the Sassanian sovereign, just as we use the word Shah. The cracking of his palace was said to be symbolic of the crack up of the Persian armies in the near future. The sacred fire, attended by the Mobeds, and said not to have gone out for a thousand years, was suddenly and inexplicably extinguished that night, and the Tigris (or some say the Euphrates) was so disturbed that it changed its course. Sāwa is a place between Rai and Hamadhān, and when the waters of its lake suddenly dried up that event spelled disaster to the fine palaces and other buildings around its shores.

68. The jinn also were crying aloud, and lights were seen shining,
While the truth was manifesting itself by signs and by words.[1]
69. [The Meccans, however], were blind and deaf, so the announcement of the good news was not
Heard, and the bright flash of warning was not seen [by them],
70. Even after their soothsayers had informed the people
That their crooked religion would stand no longer,
71. And after they had noticed on the horizon the bright meteors
Falling, just as the idols were tumbling face downwards on the earth,
72. So that there was in the morning, from the path of revelation, a flight
Of the Satans, following precipitately on the traces of one another,
73. As though they were fleeing like the warriors of Abraha,
Or the troops against whom pebbles were thrown by his hands.[2]
74. Cast by him after they had sung praises in the hollow [of his hands],
As he was cast who sang praises in the bowels of that which swallowed him.[3]

[5]

(On the miracles of him—upon whom be Allah's blessing and peace)

75. Trees used to come at his summons, doing obeisance,
Walking towards him on a leg without a foot,
76. As though they were making lines for what would be written
By their branches, writing a beautiful hand as though with a pen.
77. [Another miracle] like it is the cloud which journeyed wherever he journeyed,
Shading him from the heat which at midday blazed like an oven.

[1] The jinn were said to have cried out from Mt. Ḥajūn and from Mt. Abū Qubais announcing the birth of the Prophet, and both the soothsayers of the Arabs, and the religious leaders among the Jews and Christians, recognized the fulfilment of the signs and the prophecies which told of his coming.

[2] Legend says that the Abyssinian troops under Abraha, when they tried to attack Mecca, were driven off by birds sent by Allah. At the battle of Badr, in the year 2 A.H., Muḥammad is said to have cast pebbles at the army of the idolators and put them to flight.

[3] The pebbles in the hollowed hands of the Prophet are likened to Jonah in the belly of the whale, for both, after their praising God, were suddenly shot forth.

78. I swear by the moon that was split [by him], that he possesses
A heart that resembles it [in brightness], and this oath is justified.[1]
79. And I swear by what the cave enclosed of good and noble things,
While the eyes of the unbelievers were blind to him.[2]
80. So the true one and the trusty one were in the cave, and went not out,
While the pagans were saying: "There is no one in the cave."
81. They did not think that doves and spiders, around
The best of creatures, would hover and would spin.
82. Allah's protection made him able to dispense with a double
Coat of mail and with a lofty stronghold.
83. Never have I sought his protection, when fate was doing me injustice,
Without finding with him a protection that was never oppressed.
84. Never have I demanded from his hand some rich thing of the two Worlds,
Without obtaining some precious gift from the best hand that ever gives.
85. Deny not the revelation that came [to him] in his dreams, for he had
A heart which slept not, though his two eyes might sleep.
86. That happened just when he reached the age to assume prophetic office,[3]
When there is no denying that he possessed adult mentality.
87. Blessed be Allah! Revelation is not something acquired [by human means],
Nor because of its mysteries is any Prophet to be a person suspect.
88. How many a diseased person has been cured by the touch of his palm,
And how many a madman loosed [thereby] from his fettering knots.
89. His prayer brought renewed life to a year of drought,
So that in black times it shone like a white spot,

[1] The two references here are to the splitting of the moon, a miracle that he exhibited at the demand of the pagan Meccans, and to the cleansing of his heart during his childhood days, a cleansing which made it bright like the moon.

[2] On the Flight from Mecca to Madīna in 622, Muḥammad and Abū Bakr took refuge in a cave from the pursuit of the Meccans, who failed to perceive them therein, partly because they noticed a dove nesting there and a spider spinning its web. Abū Bakr is the "trusty one" in the next verse.

[3] Tradition says that he was then forty years of age, and that the revelations commenced in the form of true dreams.

90. By a cloud dropping rain so abundantly you would have thought the wide vales,
Had been filled by the sea or by the inundation of ʿArim.[1]

[6]

(On the noble and praiseworthy Qur'ān)

91. Let me go on with my description of the miracles which appeared for him,
Appearing as clear as the fire of hospitality at night on the hills.
92. For the pearl increases in beauty when it is strung,
Though it does not decrease in value when unstrung.
93. Yet in my eulogy I do not hope to reach,
All the noble dispositions and high qualities he possessed.
94. [In his Qur'ān] are verses of truth from the Merciful, newly created,
And yet old as eternity, since they are an attribute of the Eternal.[2]
95. They are not connected with any one time, but inform us
About the life to come as well as about ʿĀd and about Iram.[3]
96. They remain forever with us and so surpass every miracle
Of the [other] Prophets, which came but did not remain.
97. They are clear, leaving no room for ambiguousness,
From which the doubter could take profit, nor do they need any arbiter.
98. Never have they been combatted without the combatant retiring.
Even the most inimical of their enemies have sued for peace.
99. Their eloquence refutes the claims of those who oppose them,
Just as the jealous man drives back the hand of the trespasser from his harem.
100. They have inner meanings as abundant as the waves of the sea,
And superior to its pearls in beauty and in price.

[1] The reference is to the rupture of the great dam at Ma'rib in South Arabia and the consequent inundation of the country. This *sail ʿArim* is mentioned in Sūra XXXIV, 16/15.

[2] Since the Qur'ān is considered to be the Word of God it is said to be eternal, "Speech" *(kalām)* being one of the eternal attributes of Allah, yet in its spoken and written form it is a created thing.

[3] The people of ʿĀd are mentioned several times in the Qur'ān as one of the very ancient peoples who had been destroyed for their wickedness. In Sūra LXXXIX, 7/6 Iram is mentioned as the place where this people once lived.

101. Their marvels may neither be computed nor enumerated,
While they cause no weariness no matter how oft they are repeated.
102. The eye of him who reads them is charmed with them, so I say to him:
"You have hold on the rope of Allah, so hold fast to it."
103. If you read them out of fear of the hot fire of Laẓā,[1]
You will extinguish the heat of Laẓā by introducing their coolness.
104. It is as though they were the Ḥawḍ,[2] at which will be made white the faces
Of the disobedient, when they have come there black as coals.
105. [They are] like the Bridge and the Balances in their equity,[3]
So that apart from them justice cannot be established among men.
106. Be not astonished at the envious person who goes about denying them,
Affecting ignorance when he is the essence of shrewdness and intelligence.
107. The eye that is bleared denies the light of the sun,
And the mouth of a sick person denies that water has any taste.

[7]

(On the night journey and ascension of him—upon whom be Allah's blessing and peace)

108. O thou best of those whose Court is sought by suppliants,
Hastening on foot or on the backs of swift-moving camels,
109. Thou who art the greatest sign for one who considers,
Who art the most munificent blessing to him who knows how to profit.

[1] *laẓā* "flame" is one of the names of Hell (Sūra LXX, 15). In later eschatological treatises, however, it is taken to be the name of the second of the seven stages of Hell.

[2] Wicked Muslims will be punished in Hell for a time, but then they will be let out in batches as they finish their purging. By that time, however, they are burned as black as charcoal, and to fit them to enter Paradise they have to go and be washed at the Prophet's *ḥawḍ* (pool or basin) before the gates of Paradise.

[3] Both the Bridge *(aṣ-ṣirāṭ)* and the Balances *(al-mawāzīn)* belong to the matters of the Last Judgment, and they are symbols of equity, for men's deeds are all weighed at the Balances, and they are screened as they cross the Bridge, the good gaining entrance to Paradise and the wicked slipping from the Bridge into the Fires of Hell. See p. 468.

110. Thou didst travel by night from one sanctuary to another,[1]
As the full moon goes by night through the overspreading darkness.
111. And didst spend the night mounting up till thou didst attain a station,
At a distance of two bow-lengths,[2] a thing never before attained or even sought.
112. There all the Prophets granted thee precedence,
And the Apostles also, the same precedence servants grant to a master.
113. With them thou didst pierce through the seven heavenly spheres,
In a procession wherein thou wert the standard bearer,
114. Until when thou hadst not left any possibility for a competitor
To draw near [thee], nor any place of ascent for one who would mount up,
115. Thou didst make lower in comparison [to thine] every rank, when
Thou wast called, as one exalted, as though one unique, unequalled,
116. That thou mightest enjoy union—what a [mystery] hidden
From eyes! and a secret—what a hidden thing!
117. Thus hast thou taken to thyself every glory without any partner [therein],
And surpassed every rank, without any contestant.
118. How illustrious is the rank of dignity thou hast been accorded!
And how difficult to attain is the favour thou hast obtained!
119. What good news for us, O people of Islam! for we have
From Providence a support which may not be overthrown.
120. When Allah called him, who summoned us to obedience to Him,
The noblest of Apostles, that made us the noblest of communities.

[8]

(On the warlike campaigns of the Prophet—upon whom be Allah's blessing and peace)

121. The announcement of his mission struck terror in the hearts of the enemies,
Just as the barking of dogs scares a flock taken unawares.

[1] Muḥammad's Night Journey *(isrā')* was from the temple at Mecca to the temple at Jerusalem.

[2] He means that the Prophet came as near as two bow-lengths' distance to the Divine Throne. The expression *qāb qawsain* "two bow-lengths", is used in Sūra LIII, 9.

122. He ceased not encountering them on every battle-field,
Until from the spear thrusts they were like meat on the drying-block.
123. They preferred to flee, and thereby almost envied
The limbs which were carried off by the eagles and carrion vultures.
124. Nights would pass without their being aware of how many,
As long as they were not nights of the sacred months.[1]
125. It was as though religion were a guest which had alighted at their courtyard,
With every chieftain lusting for the flesh of the enemy.
126. He (i.e. Muḥammad) would lead along an ocean-like army mounted on swift steeds,
Throwing forward a dashing wave of gallant warriors.
127. Each a volunteer for Allah, believing in Him,
Making assault in an attempt to extirpate and root out the infidels,
128. Until the creed of Islam had among them become
A thing with family blood-ties, after having been but a stranger,
129. Protected for ever among them by the best of fathers,
And the best of husbands, so that it would never be an orphan or a widow.
130. They (i.e. the Muslims) were as mountains. Ask their adversaries about them,
What they saw from them at each encounter.
131. Ask Ḥunain; ask Badr; ask Uḥud,[2]
Seasons of death to them more calamitous than the pestilence.
132. They brought back red the white [swords], after they had been thrust
Into all the black haired locks of the enemies.

[1] By ancient custom the four months of Dhū'l-Qa'da, Dhū'l-Ḥijja, Muḥarram and Rajab were months free from fighting among the Arab tribes. The meaning of the verse is that the warlike expeditions of the Prophet were so continuous that save during the four sacred months his enemies were in such continual terror that they lost count of the nights.

[2] These are three famous battles of early Islam, all referred to in the Qur'ān. Ḥunain was fought in A.H. 8 and is mentioned in IX, 25. Badr was the great battle in A.H. 2. It is mentioned in III, 123/119, and is the subject of the early part of Sūra VIII. Uḥud was fought in A.H. 3 and is the subject of Sūra III, 121/117 ff.

133. They were writing with brown [lances] of al-Khaṭṭ,[1] nor left
Their pens any part of the body [of an enemy] undotted.
134. Bristling with weapons, they had a mark to distinguish them,
[Like as] the rose is distinguished by a mark from the *salam*-bush.[2]
135. The winds of victory bring to you their fragrance,
So that you would think that each armed man was a flower in bud.
136. As though they, on the backs of the horses, were verdure on a hillside,[3]
[Steady] by the strength of their resolution, not by the tightness of their saddle-girths.
137. From terror at their prowess the hearts of the enemy flew away,
So that they could not distinguish between *bahm* (lambs) and *buham* (heroes).
138. When one has help from the Apostle of Allah,
Were he to encounter lions in their dens, they would be silent.
139. Never will you see any saintly one who is not victorious
Through him, nor any enemy [of the faith] who is not broken.
140. He lodged his community in the safe refuge of his creed,
Just as the lion lodges with its cubs in the thicket.
141. How many a dispute have the words of Allah settled
Concerning him, and how many an adversary has the proof overthrown.[4]
142. Let it be a sufficient miracle for you [to see] such knowledge in the illiterate,
In the Times of Ignorance, and such education in an orphan.[5]

[1] He is likening their lances to pens and the bodies of their foes to parchment. *khaṭṭ* means a line of writing, but also al-Khaṭṭ was a place famous for the manufacture of lances. A *ḥarf* means a letter of the Arabic alphabet, many of which were dotted, and *ḥarf* also means a part of the body, so there is double word-play.

[2] The *salam* or *salām* is a bitter, prickly tree of the mimosa family. Legend says that a bright mark of glory glowed on the faces of the Muslim warriors as they charged in battle.

[3] Plants growing on a hill are more firmly rooted than others, but the steadiness of these warriors in their saddles was due not to the tightness of their girths but to their steadiness of purpose.

[4] *burhān* means "evident proof", and the reference is apparently to Sūra IV, 174.

[5] The Times of Ignorance *(jāhilīya)* were the days before Islam in which Muḥammad grew up as an orphan child. In Sūra VII, 157/156 ff. he refers to himself as the *ummī* Prophet, which has commonly been taken to mean "unlettered". See pp. 83, 441, 532.

[9]

(On seeking the favour of the apostle of Allah—upon whom be Allah's blessing and peace)

143. Him have I served by my panegyric, by which I ask pardon for
The faults of a life passed hitherto in poetry and serving [others].[1]

144. Since they have invested me with something whose consequences are to be feared,
As though because of them I were an animal led for sacrifice.

145. Obedient was I to the misdirected passions of youth, and did not
Reach anything [thereby] save sin and repentance.

146. O what soul-loss there was in such trafficking!
It did not purchase religion at the price of the world, nor even bargain.

147. Whoever sells his future life for this transitory [world],
Will discover how he has been defrauded in the selling and the bargaining.

148. Even though I commit a fault, yet unbroken is my covenant
With the Prophet, nor is my tie [with him thereby] cut.

149. I myself have protection from him by being called
Muḥammad, for he is the most faithful of mankind in fulfilling obligations.

150. Should he not at my resurrection take me by the hand,
In his kindness, then say: "O what a slip of the foot!"[2]

151. Far be it from him to disappoint one who hopes for his protection,
Or to let a client return from him unaided.

152. Ever since I began to apply my thoughts to praising him,
I have found him the best of helpers towards my redemption.

153. Riches from him never pass by a hand that is destitute,
Any more than the rain which makes flowers bloom on the hillocks.

[1] The reference is apparently to his two means of livelihood, viz. the composing of profane poetry for the delight of his patrons, and the copying of MSS for his employers. From now on he will use his verse and his pen for religion.

[2] After resurrection all have to attempt to cross the Bridge which is stretched over Hell, and unbelievers and the wicked who are not helped by the Prophet will slip from it into the Fire. See pp. 468, 615.

154. I desired not the flower of this world, such as was plucked
By the hand of Zuhair for his eulogizing of Harim.[1]

[10]

(On communion and presenting petitions for one's needs)

155. O noblest of creatures! I have none with whom to seek refuge
Save thee, when the common fate arrives.[2]
156. Thy dignity, O Apostle of Allah, will not be lessened by me,
When the Generous One appears with the name of Avenger.[3]
157. Indeed, this present world and its counterpart [the Hereafter], are of Thy bounty,
And in Thy science are knowledge of the Tablet and the Pen.[4]
158. O soul, be not in despair because [thy] sins are great,
For under Divine pardon even the greater sins are as little things.
159. Perchance the mercy of my Lord, when He portions it out,
Will come in a measure proportionate to [thy] disobedience.
160. O my Lord, arrange that my hopes be not frustrated
With Thee, and arrange that what I have counted on be not undone.
161. Act kindly with Thy servant in both worlds, for he has
The kind of patience apt to fade when terrors summon.
162. Permit clouds of benediction continually from Thee
To fall upon the Prophet, falling bountifully and gently.
163. [And on his] family and Companions, then on the Followers,[5] for they are
People of piety and purity, forbearance and generosity.
164. So long as the east wind makes the branches of the bān-tree quiver,
And the camel-driver delights the reddish beasts with his song.

[1] Zuhair b. Abī Sulmā was an ancient Arab poet who was munificiently rewarded for singing the praises of the ruler Harim b. Sinān.

[2] He may mean death, or he may mean the Last Day when all are raised together.

[3] The Generous One is one of the titles of Allah, but at Judgment He will appear as the Avenger. "The Avenger" is usually reckoned as the eighty-second among the ninety-nine beautiful names of Allah, and He is called *al-Karīm*, "the Generous" in Sūra LXXXII, 16.

[4] The preserved Tablet (LXXXV, 22) is the heavenly record on which Allah's decrees are all written, and the Pen (LXVIII, 1) is that by which they were written.

[5] The Companions were those who followed Muḥammad during the days of his active ministry. The Followers, or Successors *(at-tābi'ūn)*, were the followers of the Companions.

THE STORY OF THE NIGHT JOURNEY AND THE ASCENSION

by

the Imām Najm ad-Dīn al-Ghaiṭī [1]—on whom may

Allah have mercy

Amen

In the Name of Allah, the Merciful, the Compassionate

While the Prophet—on whom be Allah's blessing and peace—was at al-Ḥijr, near the House (i.e. the Ka'ba at Mecca), reclining between two men (viz. his uncle Ḥamza and his cousin Ja'far b. Abī Ṭālib), lo! Gabriel and Michael came to him, along with another angel (viz. Isrāfīl), and carried him off. They took him to [the well] Zemzem, where they laid him on his back and Gabriel took charge of him from them. According to another line of transmission [of this story, Umm Hāni' said]: "The roof of my house was opened up and through it Gabriel descended." He split [the Prophet's body] from the pit of his throat down to the lower end of his stomach. Then Gabriel said to Michael: "Bring me a basin of Zemzem water that I may purify his heart and set his breast at ease." Then he drew out his heart, which he bathed three times, thus removing everything noxious that was in it, while Michael came and went with the three basins-full of Zemzem water. Then he brought a golden basin filled with wisdom and faith which [Gabriel] emptied into his breast, filling him thus with wisdom, knowledge, assurance and Islam. Then he closed up [his breast] and sealed him between the shoulders with the seal of prophecy.

Then he brought Burāq, saddled and bridled. [Burāq] is a large white riding-beast, standing somewhat higher than an ass but not so high as a mule, who at every step travels as far as its eye can reach. It has constantly moving ears. When it comes to a mountain [which has to be ascended on the journey] it just advances somewhat its hind legs, and when it has to descend it advances its forelegs. It has two wings on its flanks by which it speeds its legs. Burāq was restive [before the Prophet], whereat Gabriel put his hand on its mane, saying: "Are you not ashamed, O Burāq? By Allah, never yet has there mounted you any creature of more honour in Allah's sight than is he." Thereupon it was ashamed, quietened down, and kept still so that he could mount.

The Prophets who had been sent before him had also been wont to

[1] Translated from his *al-Mi'rāj al-kabīr* (Cairo, 1324 A.H. = 1906 A.D.). He was an Egyptian, a pupil of the famous Zakarīyā' al-Anṣārī, and belonged to the Shāfi'ite *madhhab*. He died in 982 A.H. (= 1574 A.D.).

ride it. Saʿīd b. al-Musayyib and others say that it was Abraham's riding-beast on which he used to ride to the Inviolable House (i.e. the Kaʿba at Mecca). Anon Gabriel started off with him, he being at his right hand and Michael at his left. According to Ibn Saʿd Gabriel took hold of his stirrup while Michael held the rein of Burāq. They travelled thus until they reached a piece of land rich in palm trees. [Here] Gabriel said to him: "Descend and say your prayers here." He did so and remounted. Said [Gabriel]: "Do you know where this is that you have said your prayers?" "No", said he, so [Gabriel] said: "You said your prayers at Ṭaiba, to which the emigration will be."[1]

Then Burāq went off with him, going like the wind, putting his hoof where a moment before his glance had been (i.e. every bound covered the distance the eye could reach). Presently Gabriel said to him: "Descend and say your prayers here." He did so and remounted. Said Gabriel: "Do you know where you have just said your prayers?" "No", said he, so [Gabriel] said: "You have said your prayers at Madyan (i.e. Midian), at Moses' tree" (i.e. the burning bush where Moses had his message from God). Burāq went off with him again, going like the wind, but presently Gabriel said: "Descend here and say your prayers." This he did and remounted, whereat [Gabriel] said: "Do you know where you have said your prayers?' "'No", said he, so [Gabriel] said: "You have just said your prayers at Mt. Sinai, where Allah spoke with Moses." Presently he reached a land from which he could see the castles of Syria, and there Gabriel again said: "Descend and say your prayers." He did so and remounted, whereat Burāq went off with him, going like the wind, and [Gabriel] said: "Do you know where that was you said your prayers?" "No" said he. So he said: "You said your prayers at Bethlehem, where Jesus, son of Mary, was born."

Now while he was journeying along thus on Burāq, suddenly he saw an ʿIfrīt from among the jinn aiming at him a brand of fire. Each time he turned he would see him, so Gabriel said to him: "Shall I not teach you words which, when you pronounce them will put out his fire-brand and make him fall on his face?" "Surely!" said the Apostle of Allah—upon whom be Allah's blessing and peace—, so Gabriel said: "Say! I take refuge with the noble face of Allah, and with the perfect words of Allah which none, whether innocent or guilty, may outpass, from the evil of that which descends from heaven and the evil of that which mounts up thereto, from the evil of that which is sown in the earth and the evil

[1] Ṭaiba is a name of Madīna, and the famous "Flight", the emigration *(hijra)* from which Muslim dating is reckoned, was from Mecca to Madīna.

of that which emerges therefrom, from dissensions by night and by day, from misfortunes by night and by day, save that misfortune whose outcome is for good. O Thou Compassionate!" At that [the 'Ifrīt] fell upon his face and his fire-brand went out.

They journeyed on till presently they came to a community who were one day sowing and the next day reaping, for no sooner had they reaped [the grain] than it returned again just as it had been. He said: "O Gabriel, what is this?" Said he: "These are they who exert themselves in the way of Allah—may He be exalted—, to whom good is multiplied seven hundred times. There is not a thing they have expended [in the way of Allah] but He has transformed it so that it has become a sweet odour. Anon he said: "O Gabriel, what is this smell [I perceive]?" "That", said he, "is the odour of the hair-dresser of Pharaoh's daughter, and her children." [One day] as she was doing the hair of Pharaoh's daughter the comb dropped, and she said: "In the name of Allah, may Pharaoh wax old." Pharaoh's daughter said: "Do you have a Lord other than my father?" "Yes", said she. Said [Pharaoh's daughter]: "May I inform my father of that?" "Yes", said she. So she informed her father, who summoned [the woman] and said: "Is it that you have a Lord other than me?" "Yes", said she, "my Lord and your Lord is Allah." Now the woman had two sons and a husband, so he sent for them and enticed the woman and her husband to deny their religion, but they refused. He said: "I shall put the pair of you to death." Said she: "It would be a gift on your part to us if you would put us to death, prepare for us a single tomb, and bury us therein together." Said he: "That shall be yours, along with whatever we may owe you [for your services]." So he ordered a huge bronze cauldron [to be brought] and heated, and then commanded that she be cast therein, she and her children. They cast them in one by one. When they came to the youngest, who was just a nursling, he cried out: "O Mother, hurry me! Do not hold me back! for you are in the right." Thus she was cast in with her children.[1]

It is said that four spoke in the cradle while they were still babes. This [is one of them. The others are], the infant who bore testimony on Joseph's behalf, the friend of Juraij, and Jesus the son of Mary.[2]

Presently they came upon a community who were breaking their own heads, and each time they broke them they returned to their former state

[1] This story is drawn from that of the mother and children in II Macc. VII, 1–41.

[2] The story of the infant and Joseph is mentioned in the Qur'ān, Sūra XII, 26, 27, and that Jesus spoke in the cradle is mentioned in Sūra XIX, 29/30 ff. The infant friend of Juraij belongs to the Oriental legends of St. George. See pp. 55, 568.

[of wholeness], and there was nothing that could give them alleviation from this. Said he: "O Gabriel, who are these?" He answered: "These are those whose heads were dull and sluggish at the appointed times of prayer." Then anon they came to a community who had patches on their bodies before and behind, being driven along like camels or sheep are driven, eating the Ḍarīʿ and Zaqqūm plants [1] and the red-hot stones and rocks of Gehenna. So he said: "Who are these?", and Gabriel answered: "These are those who gave nothing of their wealth to charity, though Allah had not wronged them in anything." Then they came upon a community who had in their hands pots of well-cooked meat and other meat uncooked and foul, yet they were devouring the uncooked foul meat and leaving aside the good well-cooked meat. He asked: "What is this, O Gabriel?" and he replied: "This [community consists of] men belonging to your community (i.e. Muslims), who have good and lawful wives, but they go to some foul woman and spend the night with her till the morning, and women who rise from their lawful good husbands and go forth to spend the night with foul men until the morning."

Then they came to a piece of wood [lying] in the road, which tore every garment or anything else that passed it. Said he: "What is this, O Gabriel?" Said he: "This is a similitude of some folk in your community who sit in the way and block it up." Then he recited (VII, 86/84): "Sit not in every path making promises and turning [men] aside from the way of Allah." Then he saw a man swimming in a river of blood and swallowing down stones. Said he: "What is this, O Gabriel?" and he replied: "This is the similitude of one who takes usury." Then they came upon a man who had amassed a heap of firewood he was quite unable to carry, but who kept adding to it. Said he: "What is this, O Gabriel?" and he said: "This is a man of your community who has with him money on deposit from folk beyond what he can liquidate, and yet he wants still to add thereto." Presently they came upon a community who were cutting off their tongues and lips with iron shears, but as often as they cut them off they returned as they had been, so that there was no respite for them. Said he: "Who are these, O Gabriel?" He answered: "These are preachers of dissension, preachers of your community who say what they do not do." Then they passed by a community who had claws of bronze with which they were lacerating their faces and their breasts. Said he: "Who are these, O Gabriel?" He answered: "These are they who eat the flesh of people (i.e. slander them) and impugn their honour." Then anon they

[1] These plants are mentioned in the Qur'ān as forming part of the food of the Damned in Hell. Cf. LXXXVIII, 6, 7 and LVI, 51–53.

came upon a little stone from which emerged a huge bull. Straightway the bull wanted to return whence he had come out but was not able. He said: "What is this, O Gabriel?" Said he: "This is a man of your community who speaks big words and then repents of them, but is not able to put them back."

Now while he was thus travelling, lo! [a voice] called to him from his right: "O Muḥammad, look at me, I beseech you." He did not answer, but said: "Who is this, O Gabriel?" Said he: "This is an emissary of the Jews. Had you responded to him you would have made Jews of your community." Then as he was travelling along [a voice] called to him from the left: "O Muḥammad, look at me, I beseech you." He did not answer but enquired: "Who is this, O Gabriel?" Said he: "This is an emissary of the Christians. Had you responded to him you would have made Christians of your community." Then as he continued travelling along he came by a woman with arms uncovered and adorned with every adornment Allah has created. She cried out: "O Muḥammad, look at me, I beseech you." He did not turn to her, but asked: "Who is this, O Gabriel?" Said he: "This is the world. Had you responded to her you would have made your community prefer this world to the next." Again as he travelled along he found himself by an old man who called to him, trying to lure him from the way, saying: "Come along, O Muḥammad." But Gabriel said: "Nay! hurry forward, O Muḥammad." So he asked: "Who is this, O Gabriel?" and he answered: "This is Allah's enemy, Iblīs,[1] who wishes to make you deviate [from the path]." Presently he found himself by an old woman at the wayside, who said: "O Muḥammad, look at me, I beseech you." He did not turn to her but said: "Who is this, O Gabriel?" He replied: "There remains not of the life-span of the world save what remains of the life-span of this old woman" (i.e. she represents the duration of this present world).

So they journeyed on until they came to the city of Jerusalem, which they entered by the Yemeni gate. There he descended from Burāq and tethered him to the gate of the Shrine by the ring to which he had been wont to be tethered by the [other] Prophets—on whom be blessing and peace—[when they rode this steed]. Another line of transmission [of this narrative, says] that Gabriel went to the Ṣakhra,[2] which he pierced by placing his finger on it, and then fastened Burāq there. He entered the

[1] A corruption of the word *diabolos*, and a common Qur'ānic name for Satan. See p. 381.

[2] The Ṣakhra is the great rock under the Dome of the Rock in the temple area at Jerusalem, which is thought to be the Navel of the world.

Shrine by a gate through which shine the setting sun and moon, and both he and Gabriel said there a two-rak'a prayer. They had been there but a little while ere many folk gathered, whom the Prophet recognized as the [former] Prophets, some standing in prayer attitude, some bowing, some doing obeisance.[1] Then a muezzin gave the call to prayers, so they arranged themselves for a prayer service, standing in rows and waiting expectantly for some one to lead them [in prayer]. So Gabriel took him—upon whom be Allah's blessing and peace— by the hand and led him forward, and he prayed with them a two-rak'a prayer. According to [a Tradition from] Ka'b it was Gabriel who gave the call to prayer, whereat the angels descended from the heaven, and Allah caused all the Messengers and the Prophets to gather, so that the Prophet—upon whom be Allah's blessing and peace—said prayers with the angels and the Messengers. When he had finished Gabriel said: "O Muḥammad, do you know who they were who said prayers behind you?" "No", said he, so [Gabriel] said: "Every Prophet whom Allah—exalted be He— has sent." Then each Prophet [in turn] eulogized his Lord in a beautiful eulogy, whereat the Prophet—upon whom be Allah's blessing and peace—said: "Each of you has eulogized his Lord, so now I am going to eulogize my Lord." Thereupon he began to say:

> "Praise be to Allah, who sent me as a mercy to the worlds,[2] inclusively, as a bringer of good tidings and a warner;[3] Who sent down to me the Qur'ān in which is an explanation of everything;[4] Who has made my community the best community ever to appear among men,[5] making my community a [mediating] middle community,[6] making them the former and the latter peoples.[7] Who expanded for me my breast, removed from me my burden, and exalted my reputation,[8] making me one who opens and the one who seals."[9]

Thereupon Abraham—upon whom be Allah's blessing and peace—said: "Thus hath He given you [Muslims] the superiority, O Muḥammad."

[1] These are the three main positions for the genuflections which are part of the Muslim ritual of saying prayers. See pp. 473 ff.
[2] Sūra XXI, 107.
[3] XXXIV, 28/27.
[4] XVI, 89/91.
[5] III, 110/106.
[6] II, 143/137.
[7] Cf. LVI, 39/38 ff., 48, 49.
[8] XCIV, 1–4.
[9] Cf. CX, 1 and XXXIII, 40.

At that moment the Prophet—upon whom be Allah's blessing and peace—was seized with the most violent thirst he had ever experienced, so Gabriel—upon whom be peace—brought him a vessel of wine and a vessel of milk. He chose the milk, whereupon Gabriel said to him: "You have chosen according to natural instinct. Had you drunk the wine you would have misled your community, and but few of them would have followed you. Another line of transmission [of this story, says] that there were three vessels, the third having in it water, and Gabriel said: "Had you drunk the water you would have drowned your community." According to yet another line of transmission the third vessel presented to him had in it honey, not water.

Then he saw, at the left of the Ṣakhra, the Ḥūrīs,[1] so he salaamed to them and they returned his salaam. He questioned them and they responded with [such words as] refresh the eye. Then was brought in the ladder on which the spirits of mortal humans mount up [to the heavens]. Nothing so beautiful has ever been seen by [Allah's] creatures. It has one ascent of silver and one of gold. It comes from the [celestial] garden [called] Firdaus, and is set with pearls. To its right are angels and to its left are angels. [On it] he and Gabriel mounted up till at last they came to the gates of the lowest heaven, the one named the Gate of the Guardians. Over it is an angel named Ismā'īl, who is Master of the lowest heaven, dwelling in the air, and never mounting up into that heaven nor coming down on to the earth save on the day of the Prophet's death. Under him are seventy thousand angels, each of whom [in turn] commands a troop of seventy thousand angels.

Gabriel requested that the gate of heaven be opened, so the question was asked: "Who is this?" "Gabriel", said he. "And who is that with you?" "It is Muḥammad", said he. "And has he been sent for?"—another line of transmission uses a different verb for "sent for"—"Yes", said he. So [the questioner] said: "Welcome to him; welcome indeed. Allah give him life as a brother and as a Khalīfa.[2] How excellent a brother! How excellent a Khalīfa! What an excellent arrival!" So he opened [the gate] for the two of them.

Having passed in they saw there Adam—on whom be peace—the father of mankind. He was in the form he had on the day when Allah created

[1] These are the heavenly spouses whom the Qur'ān promises to Believers in Paradise. Cf. XLIV, 54; LII, 20; LV, 72; LVI, 22; XXXVII, 47. See p. 45.

[2] The "brother" is because each of the Prophets was called the "brother" of his community, as in Sūra XXVI, 106, 124, 142, 161; and a Prophet is Allah's Khalifa, or vice-gerent, on earth, as is said e.g. of David in XXXVIII, 26/25.

him in his form.[1] [It was then that] He made pass before him the spirits of the Prophets and of his believing descendants, and he would say: "A good spirit and a good soul, set them in 'Illīyūn." Then He made pass before him the spirits of his unbelieving descendants, and He would say: "A foul spirit and a foul soul, set them in Sijjīn."[2] To his right Adam saw persons and a gate from which came forth a pleasant odour, and to his left he saw persons and a gate from which came forth a foul, stinking odour. So whenever he looked to his right he would laugh and rejoice, but whenever he looked to his left he would grieve and weep. The Prophet —upon whom be Allah's blessing and peace—salaamed to him and he returned the salaam, saying: "Welcome to the good son, to the good Prophet." The Prophet—upon whom be Allah's blessing and peace—said: "Who is this, O Gabriel?" He answered: "This is your father Adam, and these persons are the life-breaths of his progeny. Those of them to the right are to be the people of Paradise, and those of them on the left are to be the people of Hell. So whenever he looks to his right he laughs and rejoices, but whenever he looks to his left he weeps and grieves. This gate which is at his right is the gate of Paradise, and when he looks at those of his progeny who are entering it he laughs and rejoices, but the gate which is at his left is the gate of Gehenna, and when he looks at those of his progeny who are entering it he weeps and grieves."

Then he went on a little and found the takers of usury, the devourers of the property of orphans, fornicators and others, dwelling in a loathsome state, much like what he had previously seen, and even more loathsome. Then he mounted up to the second heaven, where Gabriel asked admission. The question came: "Who is this?" "Gabriel", said he. "And who is with you?" "Muḥammad", said he. "And has he been sent for?" "Yes", said he. So [the questioner] said: "Welcome to him; welcome indeed. Allah grant him life as a brother and as a Khalīfa. How excellent a brother! How excellent a Khalīfa! What an excellent arrival!" Then he opened [the gate].

When they had passed through, behold! there were the two cousins on the maternal side, Jesus son of Mary, and John son of Zachariah. Each of them had garments and hair resembling those of the other, and

[1] The reference is to the legend that before his fall Adam was of great size and astonishing beauty, but was reduced in size and changed in appearance as a consequence of the fall. The "in his form" probably meant originally "in His form" and was a reference to Adam being created in the image of God. The Commentators on al-Ghaiṭī however insist that the "form" is that of Adam.

[2] 'Illīyūn and Sijjīn are used as synonyms for Heaven and Hell. For the words see Sūra LXXXIII, and the note on p. 435.

with them were some of their respective communities. Now Jesus was curly-haired, of medium stature, [in complexion] inclined to a reddish-white, with a head crisp as though he had just come from the baths, i.e. from the Ḥammām. He closely resembles [the well-known figure] ʿUrwa b. Masʿūd ath-Thaqafī. The Prophet—upon whom be Allah's blessing and peace—salaamed to both of them, and they returned the salaam. Then they said: "Welcome to the good brother, to the good Prophet", and they blessed him.

Then he mounted to the third heaven where Gabriel asked admission. The question was asked: "Who is this?" "Gabriel", said he. "And who is with you?" "Muḥammad" said he.' And has he been sent for?" "Yes", said he. So [the questioner] said: "Welcome to him; welcome indeed. Allah grant him life as a brother, as a Khalīfa. How excellent a brother! How excellent a Khalīfa! What an excellent arrival!" So he opened to them [the gate]. When they had passed through, lo! there was Joseph, and with him some of his community. So the Prophet salaamed to him, and he returned the salaam, saying: "Welcome to the good brother, to the good Prophet", and he blessed him. Now he (i.e. Joseph) had been given the one half of beauty (i.e. of all the beauty available for mankind Joseph had half to himself). Another line of transmission [of this story, says] that he was the most beautiful thing Allah had created, outpassing other folk in beauty as the moon on the night of its fullness outpasses the other stars. Said he: "Who is this, O Gabriel?" He answered: "This is your brother Joseph."

Then they mounted up to the fourth heaven, where Gabriel asked admission. The question came: "Who is this?" "Gabriel", said he. "And who is with you?" "Muḥammad", said he. "And has he been sent for?" "Yes", said he. So [the questioner] said: "Welcome to him; welcome indeed. May Allah grant him life as a brother, as a Khalīfa. How excellent a brother! How excellent a Khalīfa! What an excellent arrival!" So he opened to them [the gate]. When they passed in there was Idrīs (i.e. Enoch), whom Allah had raised to an exalted place.[1] [The Prophet] salaamed to him, and he returned the salaam, saying: "Welcome to the good brother, to the good Prophet", and he blessed him.

Then they mounted to the fifth heaven, where Gabriel asked admission. The question came: "Who is this?" "Gabriel", said he. "And who is with you?" "Muḥammad", said he. "And has he been sent for?" "Yes", said he. So [the questioner] said: "Welcome to him; welcome indeed. Allah

[1] See Sūra XIX, 57/58.

grant him life as a brother, as a Khalīfa. How excellent a brother! How excellent a Khalīfa! What an excellent arrival!" Then he opened to them [the gate]. When they passed through there was Aaron, one half of whose beard was white and one half black, and so long was it that it reached almost to his navel. Around him was a community of the Children of Israel to whom he was narrating stories. [The Prophet] salaamed to him, and he returned the salaam, saying: "Welcome to a good brother, and to a good Prophet", and he blessed him. Said he: "Who is this, O Gabriel?" He answered: "This is the man well-beloved in his community, Aaron the son of Amram."

Then they mounted to the sixth heaven, where Gabriel asked admission. Then came the question: "Who is this?" "Gabriel", said he. "And who is with you?" "Muḥammad", said he. "And has he been sent for?" "Yes", said he. So [the questioner] said: "Welcome to him, welcome indeed. Allah grant life to him as a brother, as a Khalīfa. How excellent a brother! How excellent a Khalīfa! What an excellent arrival!" So he opened to them [the gate]. Straightway they began passing by the Prophet and the prophets with whom was a small party, the Prophet and the prophets with whom was a [large] community, and the Prophet and the prophets with whom was only a single person. Then they passed by a great multitude who shut off the horizon. Said he: "Who are all these?" [A voice] said: "Moses and his community; but raise your head." [He did so], and lo! there was a great multitude shutting off the horizon in all four directions, [and the voice] said to him: "These are your community (i.e. the Muslims), and apart from these are seventy thousand [of them] who will enter Paradise without any accounting [being taken]."

When they had passed through there was Moses son of Amram, a brown man, taller than normal as though he were one of the Shanuites,[1] and so hairy that though he wore two shirts the hair would pierce through both of them. The Prophet—upon whom be Allah's blessing and peace—salaamed to him, and he returned the salaam, saying: "Welcome to a good brother, to a good Prophet", and he blessed him. Then he (i.e. Moses) said: "People claim that I am a man more honoured with Allah than this man, but he is more honoured with Allah than I am." Then as the Prophet—upon whom be Allah's blessing and peace—passed beyond him he wept. Someone asked him: "What is it makes you weep?", and he answered: "I weep because a youth who was sent [on a Divine mission] later than I was will have more of his community enter Paradise than will

[1] The Shanū'a were a tribe of South Arabians said to have been remarkable for the number of very tall men among them.

enter from my community. The Children of Israel claim that I am the most honoured of the human race in Allah's sight, but this is a human and he has succeeded me [in that position], though he is in the world and I am in the other world. Even though he may not himself notice it his community is with him here."

There they mounted up to the seventh heaven, where Gabriel requested admission. The question came: "Who is this?" "Gabriel", said he. "And who is with you?" "Muḥammad", said he. "And has he been sent for?" "Yes", said he. So [the questioner] said: "Welcome to him, welcome indeed. Allah grant him life as a brother, as a Khalīfa. How excellent a brother! How excellent a Khalīfa! What an excellent arrival!" Then he opened to them [the gate].

When they had passed through, the Prophet—upon whom be Allah's blessing and peace—found himself right by Abraham, the Friend [of Allah]—upon whom be Allah's blessing and peace—, who was sitting at the Gate of Paradise, on a golden seat whose back was resting against the Frequented Fane.[1] With him were some members of his community. The Prophet—upon whom be Allah's blessing and peace—salaamed to him, and he returned the salaam, saying: "Welcome to the good son, to the good Prophet." Then he said to him: "Bid your community increase their planting in Paradise, for its earth is good and its fields wide." Said he: "And in what does this planting in Paradise consist?" He answered: ["In repeating the pious phrase] 'There is no might and no strength save in Allah, the High, the Mighty.'" According to another line of transmission [of this story, he said]: "Give your community salaam from me, and inform them that the soil of Paradise is good, its waters sweet, and that planting therein consists [in repeating the pious phrases]: 'Glory be to Allah', 'Praise be to Allah', 'There is no god save Allah' and 'Allah is most great.'"

With him there was a community of folk, sitting together, whose faces were white like parchment sheets, and others in whose colour was something [that detracted from its pure whiteness]. Those in whose faces was this something rose and entered a river in which they bathed. When they emerged their colour was somewhat purer, so they entered [another] river in which they again bathed, and when they emerged their colour was somewhat purer. Then they entered a third river in which they bathed, whereat their colour became quite pure like that of their companions. Said he: "O Gabriel, who are these with white faces, and those in whose

[1] This is the celestial Ka'ba, situated directly above the earthly Ka'ba at Mecca, and the Shrine at which the celestial hosts worship. See p. 169.

colour is something? And what are these rivers which they entered and in which they bathed?" He answered: "As for those whose faces are white, they are a community who did not render their faith dubious by wrong-doing, and those in whose faces is something are a community who mingled with their good works others which were evil, but they repented and so Allah has turned to them. As for these rivers, the first of them is Allah's mercy, the second is Allah's grace, and the third Allah has poured for them to drink as a purifying draught." Then [someone spoke and] said: "This is your place and the place of your community", and lo! he was with his community in two groups, one group [clothed] in garments [as white] as though they were parchment sheets, and another group whose garments were dirty. He entered the Frequented Fane, and those who had white garments entered with him, but the others, who had dirty garments, were prevented [from entering], although they were good folk. Then he and those believers who were with him said prayers within the Frequented Fane. This [Fane] is entered every day by seventy thousand angels who will not return to it till the Day of Resurrection. It is directly above the Kaʿba [at Mecca], so that were a stone to break through from there it would fall directly on to it.

The story goes no further with regard to them [after they entered the Fane], but according to another line of transmission this is where he had presented to him the aforementioned three vessels, of which he chose the milk, and Gabriel approved his action, as we have already mentioned. According to one line of transmission [of the story] he (i.e. Gabriel) said: "This is in accordance with your natural instinct and that of your community."

Then he was taken up to the Sidrat al-Muntahā,[1] which is the limit to which anything mounting up from earth may go, for it is restrained by it, and the limit to which anything falling from above (i.e. from the higher celestial spheres) can go, for it is caught by it. It is a tree from whose root proceed rivers of water which goes not stale, rivers of milk whose taste never alters, rivers of wine pleasant to those who drink, and rivers of purified honey,[2] and under whose shade a rider could journey for seventy years without ever getting out of it. Its pods are the size of stone pitchers and its leaves like elephants' ears, one leaf of which would well nigh [be sufficient to] cover this [whole] community. According to one line of transmission [of this story] one leaf of it would give shade to all mankind. On each of its leaves is an angel. It has colours which cannot be described,

1 The Lote-tree of the Boundary. See Sūra LIII, 14, and pp. 395, 435.

2 Sūra XLVII, 15/16 ff.

for whenever there covers it that which Allah bids cover it,[1] they change. According to one line of transmission [of this story] they change to ruby and emerald, and no one is ever able to give a description of it because of its [everchanging] beauty. On it are golden moths, and from its root proceed four rivers, two rivers within and two without. Said he: "What are these rivers, O Gabriel?" He answered: "The two within are two rivers of Paradise, but the two without are the Nile and the Euphrates."

According to another line of transmission he saw Gabriel beside the Sidra, and [saw that] he had six hundred wings, any one of which would shut out the horizon. From his multicoloured wings fell pearls and rubies and [other kinds of jewels] such as are known only to Allah—may He be exalted. Then he came upon the Kawthar,[2] [along whose banks he journeyed] till he entered Paradise, and lo! therein was what eye has not seen, nor ear heard, and what has not entered into the heart of man. On its gate he saw written: "A charitable gift [is rewarded] by ten times [what is given], but a loan by eighteen times [what is lent]." Said he: "O Gabriel, what is the point of a loan being much more highly honoured than a gift in charity?" He answered: "Because the beggar begs [for a charitable gift] when he actually has somewhat of his own, but the man who seeks a loan seeks it only out of [desperate] need."

So he journeyed on and presently came to rivers of milk whose taste never alters, rivers of wine pleasant to those who drink, rivers of purified honey, and there by them were pomegranate trees of pearl whose fruits were the size of buckets. Another line of transmission [of this story, says]: "And there on it were pomegranates the size of the skins of pack-saddled camels, and its birds were like Bactrian camels." [When Muḥammad was telling this story] Abū Bakr said: "O Apostle of Allah, will they be for our enjoyment?" He answered: "I ate of them with full enjoyment, and I hope that you will also eat of them." Also he saw the river Kawthar on whose two banks were cupolas of hollowed pearls, and whose mud was finest grade musk.

Then he was shown Hell, in which are [worked out] the wrath and the anger of Allah, and His vengeance. [So hot is it that] if a stone or a piece of iron were to fall into it they would be consumed. Therein [he saw] a community eating stinking filth, so he said: "Who are these, O Gabriel?" He answered: "These are they who eat the flesh of other people" (i.e. are slanderers). Also he saw Mālik,[3] the Keeper of Hell, who was a grim-

[1] Sūra LIII, 16.
[2] The great celestial river. See Sūra CVIII, 1.
[3] Sūra XLIII, 7. He corresponds to the Biblical Moloch. See pp. 231, 636.

faced man, showing the marks of wrath in his countenance. The Prophet —upon whom be Allah's blessing and peace—proffered him salaam, and then [the gates of] Hell were closed against him, and he mounted up again to the Sidrat al-Muntahā. There there came over him a cloud containing every colour. Gabriel stayed behind, but he—upon whom be Allah's blessing and peace—was taken up to a lofty place where he heard the scratching of the pens [that are writing the decrees of Allah]. There he saw a man [sitting] concealed in the light of the Throne. Said he: "Who is this? Is it an angel?" The answer came: "No." "Is it a Prophet?" The answer came: "No." "Then who is it?" The answer came: "This is a man whose tongue in the world was always moist with the mentioning of Allah, whose heart clave to the mosque, and who never at any time abused his parents."

Then he saw his Lord—glorified and exalted be He—and the Prophet—upon whom be Allah's blessing and peace— fell on his face in obeisance. Thereupon his Lord spoke to him, saying: "O Muḥammad." He answered: "Here am I, O Lord." He said: "Ask!", and [the Prophet] replied: "Thou didst take Abraham as a friend, and didst give to him a great kingdom.[1] Thou didst speak with Moses face to face.[2] To David Thou didst give a great kingdom, causing iron to be soft to him and setting the mountains at his service.[3] To serve Solomon Thou didst set jinn and men and Satans, making the winds do his bidding,[4] and didst give him such a kingdom as none after him had. Thou didst teach Jesus the Gospel and the Torah, didst make him one who could cure the born blind and the lepers and raise the dead to life by Thy permission.[5] Him and his mother didst Thou guard against Satan the stoned, so that Satan had no way to them."[6] Then Allah—glorified and exalted be He—said: "But you have I taken as [My] beloved one."—Says the narrator [of this Tradition]: "In the Torah he is written of as 'Beloved of God'"—"And I have sent you to mankind as a whole, [to be] a bringer of good tidings and a warner.[7] I have expanded for you your breast, removed from you your burden, and exalted for you your reputation,[8] so that no longer shall I be mentioned [by men] but you will be mentioned with me. I have made

[1] Sūra IV, 125/124.
[2] IV, 164/162.
[3] XXXIV, 10.
[4] XXXIV, 12/11 ff.
[5] III, 48/43 ff.
[6] III, 36/31.
[7] XXXIV, 28/27.
[8] XCIV, 1–4.

your community the best community that has appeared among mankind,[1] made it a [mediating] middle community,[2] making them the former and the latter peoples.[3] Moreover I have so arranged it that your people cannot have a sermon without bearing witness that you are My servant and My Apostle. I have appointed among your community some whose hearts will be their Gospels. You have I made the first Prophet to be created, the last to be sent [on his mission], and the first to be discharged [at Judgment]. To you have I given the Seven Mathānī,[4] which I gave to no previous people. Also I gave to you the concluding verses of the Sūra of the Cow,[5] from a Treasury beneath the Throne, which I gave to no previous Prophet. To you have I given al-Kawthar,[6] and I have given you eight portions, viz. Islam, the Hijra, Holy War, almsgiving, fasting [during] Ramaḍān, the [task of] enjoining that which is proper and forbidding that which is improper, and on the day when I created the heavens and the earth I laid as an incumbent duty on you and on your community fifty prayer times, so see that you observe them, both you and your community."

According to another line of transmission [of this matter], the Apostle of Allah—upon whom be Allah's blessing and peace—was given the five prayer services, the concluding verses of the Sūra of the Cow, and forgiveness for anyone belonging to his community who has not [been guilty of] giving Allah a partner of any sort, which is of the sins that destroy.

Then the cloud cleared away and Gabriel took him by the hand, so that he came to himself quickly, and went to Abraham, but [Abraham] did not say to him a thing. So he went to Moses, saying: "How excellent a friend He was to you." [Moses] said: "What have you accomplished, O Muḥammad? What has your Lord laid as an incumbent duty on you and on your community?" Said he: "He has laid on me and on my community fifty prayer services each day and night." Said [Moses]: "Return to your Lord and request from Him some alleviation for you and for your community, because your community will not tolerate that. Before you I have had to inform people [of Allah's command]. I put the Children of Israel to the test, and exercised all my skill with them [to get them to observe something] less onerous than this, but they were too

1 Sūra III, 110/106.
2 II, 143/137.
3 Cf. Sūra LVI, 39/38, 48, 49.
4 XV, 87. The word means "repetitions", but its significance is much disputed.
5 Sūra II, 285–286.
6 CVIII, 1.

weak for it and abandoned it, and your community are folk still weaker in flesh and body, in heart, in seeing and hearing." So the Prophet—upon whom be Allah's blessing and peace—turned to Gabriel, seeking his advice, and Gabriel's advice was: "Yes, if you wish, return." So he returned quickly till he came to the Tree, where the cloud came over him and he fell down doing obeisance. Then he said: "O Lord, make it lighter for my community, for it is the weakest of communities." [Allah] said: "I have removed five." Then the cloud was lifted and he returned to Moses, saying: "He has removed five." But [Moses] said: "Go back to your Lord and ask Him [a further] alleviation for your community, for they will not tolerate that."

So he continued going to and fro between Moses and his Lord, Who would remit for him five, and then another five, until Allah said: "O Muḥammad!" and he answered: "Here am I, at Thy service." Said [Allah]: "They are five prayer services each day and night, but since each prayer service is of the value of ten that makes them fifty prayer services. What I have said does not change, and what I have written is not abrogated. Whoever purposes a good deed but does it not I record it [to his merit] as a good deed, and if he does it I record it as ten [good deeds]. [Likewise] whoever purposes an evil deed but does not do it, nothing at all is recorded against him, and if he does it I record against him a single evil deed." Then [the cloud] lifted and he descended till he came to Moses, whom he informed about it. [Moses] said: "Return to your Lord and request from Him some alleviation for your community, for your community will not tolerate that." Said he: "I have already returned to my Lord till I am ashamed. I am satisfied and I submit." Then a Herald called: "I have signed My [Divine] ordinance. I have lightened [the obligations] for My servants." At this Moses said to him: "Go down [to earth] in the name of Allah." [On his way down] he passed not a group of angels but said to him: "Keep thou to cupping." According to another line of transmission [of this story, they said]: "Bid your community practise cupping."[1]

[As they went down] he said to Gabriel: "How is it that I never come by any of the celestial beings but they welcome me and are laughing with me save one? To him I salaamed, and he returned my salaam, welcomed me and blessed me, but he did not laugh with me." He replied: "That is Mālik, the Keeper of Hell. He has not laughed since he was created. Could he laugh with anyone he would have laughed with you." When he had descended to the lowest heaven he looked at its lowest part, and

[1] He means the practice of blood-letting by the process of cupping.

behold there was a riot of dust and smoke and voices. Said he: "What is this, O Gabriel?" He answered: "These are the Satans. They hover above over the vision of men so that men will not occupy themselves with pondering over [matters of] the kingdom of the heavens and the earth. Were it not for this men might observe the marvels [of celestial matters]."

Then [having reached Jerusalem] he mounted [Burāq, who had been tethered there] to make his way back [to his home in Mecca]. [As he journeyed] he passed by a caravan of camels belonging to [the merchants of] Quraish at such and such a place. Among them was a camel which had on it two sacks, one black and one white. When he came opposite the caravan that animal became scared, turned around and fell, and was injured. Then he passed by [another] caravan which had lost one of its camels, which the Banū So-and-So had picked up. He salaamed to them and someone among them said: "That is the voice of Muḥammad."

Presently he came [home] to his friends at Mecca a little before dawn. When dawn came and he realized that the folk would disbelieve [his story], he sat sorrowful. Anon that enemy of Allah, Abū Jahl, passed by, and [seeing him he] came and sat beside him. Mockingly he asked: "Well, has anything been happening?" "Yes", said [Muḥammad]. "What was it?" he asked. "I was taken a night's journey", said [Muḥammad]. "To where?" asked he. "To Jerusalem", answered Muḥammad. "And you were back here amongst us by morning?" asked he. "Yes", said Muḥammad. Now [Abū Jahl] did not think [it wise] to give him the lie direct, fearing that he might deny [having told] him the story if he summoned his people to him. So he said: "What would you think about my summoning your people? Would you relate to them what you have related to me?" "Surely", said [Muḥammad]. So [Abū Jahl] called out: "O folk of the Banū Ka'b b. Lu'aiy, come hither", whereupon the company hastened to him, coming and sitting before the two of them. Then [Abū Jahl] said: "Relate to your people what you related to me." So the Apostle of Allah—upon whom be Allah's blessing and peace—said: "I was taken at night a night's journey." "To where?", they asked. "To Jerusalem", said he. "And then you were back among us by morning?" they asked. "Yes", said he. Some of them clapped their hands and some of them put their hands to their heads in amazement. There was much clamouring and expression of astonishment at [what he had said], till presently al-Muṭ'im b. 'Adī said: "[O Muḥammad], your affair until this day has been but a trifle, but it is otherwise with what you are saying now. I give my testimony that you are a liar. We beat the livers out of our camels [driving them] to Jerusalem [yet it is] a month going up and a month returning, while you pretend that you did it in a night. By al-Lāt and al-ʿUzzā [1] I do not believe you." Then Abū Bakr said: "O Muṭʿim, evil is what you have said to the son of your brother. You have treated him harshly and given him the lie, but I give my testimony that he is a truth-speaker."

So they said: "O Muḥammad, describe Jerusalem to us. How is it built? What is its appearance? What mountain is near it?", for among the people were those who had travelled to it. So he set about describing it to them, that it was built thus and so, that its appearance was thus, and that such and such a mountain was near it. He continued thus describing it to them till he got confused in the description and became more distressed than he had ever been. Then [a model of] the Shrine was brought, at which he looked till it was set down in front of the house of ʿUqail or ʿIqāl, and they said: "How many doors does the Shrine have?" Now he had never counted them, but he began to look at it and enumerate them door by door, and tell them, while Abū Bakr was saying: "You speak true! You speak true! I testify that you are Allah's Apostle." Finally the people said: "As for the description, he has hit it off, by Allah." Then they said to Abū Bakr: "But do you believe him [when he says] that he went to Jerusalem by night and got back before dawn?" "Yes", said he, "I believe him in what is harder to believe than that. I believe him in the matter of information brought from heaven morning and evening." For this Abū Bakr got the name "Trusty."

Then they said: "O Muḥammad, give us information about our caravan." He replied: "I came upon a caravan of the Banū So-and-So at ar-Rawḥā'. They had lost one of their camels and had gone out to seek for it, so when I arrived at their baggage there was not a single one of them there with it, so I drank a vessel of water that was there. Then I came upon the caravan of the Banū So-and-So at such and such a place, [a caravan] in which was a red she-camel carrying a black sack and a white sack. When I came opposite the caravan that she-camel got scared and fell and was injured. Then I came upon the caravan of the Banū So-and-So at at-Tanʿīm, which was led by an ash-coloured camel on which was a black saddle cloth and two black sacks, and here she is coming to you from the mountain pass." "When will she come in?" they asked. "On Wednesday", said he. When that day came the Quraish went up to look for the caravan, but the day passed and it had not come, so the Prophet—upon whom be Allah's blessing and peace—made sup-

[1] These were two of the great goddesses in the Meccan p antheon. They are mentioned in Sūra LIII, 19.

plication [to Allah], and for his sake an hour was added to the day, the sun being held back [from setting] till the caravan appeared. Then they went out to meet the camels, asking: "Did you lose a camel? ""Yes", they replied. Then they questioned the other caravan, saying: "Did a red she-camel of yours get injured?" "Yes", said they. Then they asked: "Did you have a large water bowl?" A certain man answered: "I, by Allah, set it down, yet no one from among us drank of it, and it was not spilled on the ground." Thereupon they accused him (i.e. Muḥammad) of magic practice, and they said: "Al-Walīd is right."[1] So Allah—glorified and exalted be He—sent down [the verse] (XVII, 60/62): "We did not appoint a vision which We caused thee to see save as a testing for the people."

Finished is the story, to Allah's praise and by His assistance. So may Allah bless our Master Muḥammad, his family and his Companions, and give them sound and abundant peace. Praise be to Allah, Lord of the Worlds.

[1] Al-Walīd, according to the Commentators, was the first one to suggest that Muḥammad was a worker of magic.

SUFISM

Sufism is the mystical theology of Islam. In the modern Islamic world the Ṣūfī life is for the most part embodied in the various Dervish Orders, which provide a way of expression for the religious life quite apart from the official religious cult associated with the mosques or the private religious observances of the individual. There are Dervish "monasteries" where groups of members of an Order live a communal religious life, and there are Dervishes who abandon the common life of men to live as wandering mendicants, but the vast majority of members of any Order live normal daily lives in their homes and at their work, but meet with other members at some centre of their Order at stated times to practise the devotional excercises of the Order, and theoretically to make progress thereby on the Ṣufī way towards the *Unio mystica.*

INSTRUCTIONS TO A POSTULANT

by

the very great Shaikh, Muḥyī 'd-Dīn Ibn al-'Arabī [1]

A tractate on those things a postulant [2] *needs must possess*

In the Name of Allah, the Merciful, the Compassionate

Praise be to Allah, Lord of the Worlds, and well-being to the god-fearing, and may there be no enmity save towards evil-doers. There is no power nor strength save with Allah, the High, the Mighty One. "Allah is our sufficiency and an excellent guardian" (III, 173/167). May the blessings

1 Muḥyī 'd-Dīn Ibn al-'Arabī (1164–1240 A.D.), was born in Murcia in the south of Spain, travelled as a Ṣūfī teacher all over the Islamic world of his day, and was buried in a private sepulchre at Damascus. The tractate translated here is one entitled *Risāla fī Kunhi mā lā budda minhu li'l-Murīd,* which Muḥyī 'd-Dīn al-Kurdī printed as a supplement to his edition of al-Ghazzālī's *ar-Risāla al-laduniya* (Cairo, 1328 A.H.), where it occupies pp. 39–60.

2 Postulant *(murīd)* is the technical word used for a youth being prepared for initiation into one of the Dervish Orders. It corresponds roughly with our word "catechumen". *murīd* means literally "he who desires", i.e. he who is a candidate or novice desiring full initiation into the company of the Ṣūfīs.

and peace of Allah be on our lord Muḥammad, and on his family and his Companions.

You have made enquiry, O Postulant seeking for right direction, about those things you needs must possess, so I reply to you in these pages with regard to that about which you have enquired. Allah has success in His charge.

Be it known to you, O Postulant—may Allah direct both us and you to obedience to Him, and employ both us and you in what is well-pleasing to Him—that [our] relationship to Allah is not to be known save by His acquainting us therewith and putting us in mind of it. Praised be Allah that He has done this. He sent the Messengers and made clear the ways which lead to everlasting happiness, and we believed and trusted. What remains is that we employ ourselves in those works which the faith has imposed and [obey] the laws which it seemed appropriate to believing souls to promulgate.

Now the first thing, O Postulant, you needs must possess is [belief in] the unity *(tawḥīd)* of your Creator, and His aloofness from whatever may not be ascribed to Him. As for His unity [the case is thus]. Were there [beside Him] another deity the proper happening of things would be hindered by [the consequent] differing of desires [between them], and opposition [of the one to the other] in matters of arrangement [about affairs], whether in the bringing them into being or the carrying out of them, and so the orderly disposition of affairs would be quite spoiled. This is as Allah has said (XXI, 22): "Were there gods other than Allah in both of them (i.e. heaven and earth), they would both go to ruin." So pay no heed, O my brother, to anyone who is guilty of association.[1] You have no need to establish proof of the unity, for it is the associator who has declared what he has declared against His being the One. He admits, just as you do, the existence of the Creator, but to what you confess he has added [the notion of] a partner, so it is on him to bring proof for that which he has added, seeing that he acknowledges the essential point of what you maintain. Let this suffice you in the matter of unitarian belief *(tawḥīd)*, for time is precious and [your] intelligence is sound, whereas the one who disagrees [on this matter] has no real substantiation for his [disagreement]. So praised be Allah, the Most High.

With regard to His aloofness,[2] you should pay the more heed to it in

[1] I.e. one who associates any other with Allah so as to impair His uniqueness. To do this is to be guilty of *shirk*, the gravest of all sins. See p. 260.

[2] This "aloofness" means on the one hand the absence of any imperfection in Him, and on the other His being far removed from likeness in any way to created things.

view of the [presence of] the anthropomorphists *(mushabbiha)* and the corporealists *(mujassima)*,[1] who are showing themselves at this time. Therefore, my brother, have recourse to the words of the Most High (XLII, 11/9): "There is nothing that at all resembles Him." Let this be your sufficiency. Every descriptive attribute [applied to Allah] which contradicts this verse is to be rejected in favour of what conforms to this verse, so do not exceed or depart from this position. Likewise in the Sunna come [the words]: "Allah was, and there was nothing with Him", to which the theologians add: "and He is now just as He was", so that He did not acquire from His act in creating the world any attribute which He did not have when the world was not yet existent. So in this matter of aloofness, believe with regard to Him now that the world is in existence, what you would have believed when there was no world, no Throne, nothing save Allah Himself. Exalted is Allah above what evil-doers and apostates say, far exalted (Sūra, XVII, 43/45). Every verse [of the Qur'ān], or Tradition from the Prophet—upon whom be Allah's blessing and peace—may be suspected of [teaching] anthropomorphism, because such is the idiom of the Arabic language, or the manner of speech of him to whom was committed part of that task of delivering a message [from Allah], but what is incumbent on you is to have faith, according to what Allah has taught and has revealed, not according to what you may suspect. Intrust to Allah knowledge of that, for nothing could declare more clearly His aloofness than [His own words]: "There is nothing that at all resembles Him"; for therein He has set Himself as far aloof as He ought to be.

Then, after that, O Postulant, needs must you believe in all the Messengers (Apostles), in what they brought [from Allah in their messages], and in the information they gave about Allah, Most High, whether they are things you know or things you did not know. Then [you must have] love for the Companions—with all of whom may Allah be pleased—confessing their uprightness, and that they are never to be disparaged or evil spoken of, treating no one of them (i.e. the Messengers) as superior to the others, save wherein his Lord has given him superiority in His Book or by the tongue of His Apostle. Moreover, it is incumbent on you, my brother, to honour those who honoured Allah, and [it is well known how] His Messengers honoured Him—may Allah's blessing and peace be

[1] The Muslim Heresiologists have much to say about these teachers of false doctrine. Some of them merely went too far in using human terms in describing Allah, but others taught what we should call incarnation doctrines, holding that Allah at times embodied Himself in creaturely form. See p. 387 ff.

on them. Then you should be submissive to the people of this way *(ṭarīqa)* [1] in all that is related of their words and signs, trusting in all you see of their actions even though it goes beyond your knowledge. They merit this since they have been pleased to accept you as their servant in that knowledge of yours.

Among the things you must possess is [the grace of] thinking good of all men, having a breast free from viciousness, praying for the Muslims, that the hidden may be made clear, serving the *faqīrs* [2] by showing them kindness and bearing their expenses, taking on yourself what might be a harm to them or burdensome to them, and for Allah's sake enduring patiently their tempers.

Among the things you must possess is [the gift of] being silent, save for uttering remembrances of Allah, reciting the Qur'ān, directing the erring into the right way, commanding what is proper and forbidding what is improper, making peace between those who are parting [in enmity], urging [men] to charity, or indeed [using speech] for anything that is good.

Among the things you must possess, O my friend, is [the grace to] seek a suitable brother [postulant] who will stir you up to that in whose path you are engaged. Beware of friendship with the contrary kind.

Among the things you must possess is [the grace to] seek a Shaikh [as a] Director, and [have in your relations with him] that sincerity *(ṣidq)* which is the distinctive mark of a Postulant. If the Postulant acts with sincerity in relation to Allah, Allah will decree for him [a Director] who will take him by the hand, and will change for him every Satan who attacks him into an Angel who will inspire him to good. This is because sincerity is never brought into association with anything without affecting its nature.

Among the things you must possess, O my brother, is [the grace] not to live at the expense of other people, to be a burden to no one, to accept no support from man either for yourself or anyone else, but to practice your own trade and be abstemious in the matter of your living expenses. [Exercise restraint] also in your words and in your glances on all occasions, whether you are moving about or are stationary. Be not extrava-

1 Each Ṣūfi Order is known as a *ṭarīqa* or "way", because it has its own particular spiritual discipline which its members follow. The "words" and "signs" mentioned have reference to the fact that the Postulant as he associates with the older members of his Order may often see and hear things which surpass his understanding, but these things he must submissively accept even though he does not yet understand them.

2 Many of the Dervish Orders have certain members who live the life of wandering mendicants, and such a man is called a *faqīr*, "poor man", because he has forsaken all earthly possessions.

gant in matters of housing or dress or food, for what is lawful [thereof] is but little and leaves no room for lavishness. Be it known to you, my friend, that if a man plant appetites in his soul they will take root there and afterwards are hardly to be rooted out. So the Postulant should know no ampleness or ease of life. All of this is among those things a Postulant needs must possess.

Among the things you must possess, O my friend, is [the grace of doing with but] little food, for [abstinence in] this brings cheerfulness in obedience and drives away laziness. You must be careful to apportion out [your] time by day and by night. As for the hours when the religious law summons you to stand before your Lord they are the five prayer periods for the canonical prayers. But beyond them are the [other] times consecrated by Apostolic custom. So if you are a craftsman labour diligently to make enough in one day to provide for your needs for several days. If you are a business man do not hasten away from your place of prayer after the dawn prayer until the sun has risen, nor after the afternoon prayer till the sun has set. Remember Allah with a collected and humble mind, and you will not miss an opportunity for standing in prayer before Him for some twenty *rak'as*[1] between the midday prayer and the afternoon prayer, and also between the evening prayer and the final night prayer. Be careful to observe four *rak'as* at the beginning of the day and before the noon [prayer] and the afternoon [prayer], and make your *witr*[2] one of thirteen *rak'as*. Do not go to sleep till you are quite overcome [by slumber]. Do not eat save what is needful, nor dress save as is necessary to guard against cold or heat, with the intention of covering the pudenda and removing a peremptory impediment to the worship of Allah. If you are one of those who knows how to write prepare a *wird*[3] for yourself from the Qur'ān in the exemplar *(muṣḥaf)* which you hold in your lap, so that with your left hand you can hold the exemplar and with your right hand follow along the letters, while you gaze at it and raise your voice sufficiently for you to hear yourself. Cantillate the

[1] In the prayer services prescribed for each day there are three parts: (1) the preface; (2) the body of the prayer; (3) the conclusion. The second part consists of stated prayers and genuflections, and when they have been gone through one *rak'a* has been completed. The worshipper then goes back and performs this section over again, and then again, to complete the number of *rak'as* prescribed for that particular prayer service. When the required number of *rak'as* has been completed the worshipper goes on with the third part which concludes the prayer.

[2] A *witr* is a prayer service which has an odd number of *rak'as*, e.g. 3, 5, or 7. See p. 117.

[3] A *wird* is a section or selections from the Qur'ān for private recitation.

Qur'ān, marking the tone of interrogation where a question mark is needed, using an admonitory tone at the verses of admonition, and in every verse taking care to observe the indications for saying: "I take refuge with Allah", or "I ask forgiveness of Allah", and other such details.[1] When you read therein a description of the true believer take a look at how you yourself measure up to that description, and how far you fall short of it, thanking Allah for such measure of it as you possess, and purposing to attain what you lack. Similarly when you read [therein] descriptions of the hypocrites and unbelievers, take a look at whether or not these descriptions fit you yourself.

Among the things you must possess is [the grace of] having an accounting with yourself, a seasonable examination of your inmost thoughts, putting a shamefacedness before Allah as the raiment on your heart, for if you possess a true feeling of shame before Allah you will prevent your heart from harbouring fancies which Allah would find blameworthy, or from being moved with emotions with which Allah, Most High, would not be pleased. We ourselves used formerly to have a Shaikh who was accustomed to record his emotional states during the day in a book that he had, and when night came he would set the pages in front of him and have an accounting with himself for what was written therein. I myself have done even more than my Shaikh did in this matter of restraining my thoughts.

Among the things you must possess is [the grace of] keeping close watch over the passing time, that you may be aware of what time it is, notice what the religious law says you should be doing at that particular time, and do it. If it should be the time for one of the incumbent duties, then perform it; or a time for reciting eulogies, then hasten to do it. If it should be leisure time, busy yourself therein with some form of doing good to which the True One invites you. When you start to perform some religious duty which merits a reward, do not say to yourself that you will live to perform some other duty after it, but treat it as though it were the last duty you will perform in this world ere you meet your Lord. If you do this you will discharge it sincerely, and with that sincere discharge [of duty] comes acceptance.

Among the things you must possess is [the grace of] sitting always in a state of ritual purity, so whenever you have voided perform the lesser ablution, and when you have performed the ablutions, say a prayer of

[1] Part of the instruction of the young in Qur'ān recitation is concerned with the places where it is proper to utter various pious ejaculations. The marking of Selah in the Psalter is perhaps due to a similar custom.

two *rak'as,* save it should be a time in which the saying of prayers is forbidden. Such times are three [1]: at the rising of the sun, at its setting, and when the sun is immediately overhead on any day save Friday. [Friday] is an exception, and prayers are permissible [on that day] even if the sun is immediately overhead.

Among the things you must possess, O my friend, is [the grace of] seeking out the noblest habits, so that wherever it may be that you get news of such a habit you go after it. Likewise [you must possess the grace of searching out] evil habits so that you may avoid them all. Be it known to you that anyone who abandons a noble habit abandons it only because of some blameworthy habit. Be it known to you that habits are of different kinds, just as people are of different kinds, so you must watch which of the noble habits you make use of with Him, for he who acquires the greatest number of kinds is a person who is a means of bringing ease to people and warding off harm—if this accords with the good-pleasure of Allah. So be diligent in this matter, my friend, knowing that they are Allah's creatures, servants under constraint and compulsion in their movements, whose forelocks are in the hand of Him Who causes them to move. The Prophet—on whom be peace—gave us this position, for he said: "I was sent to perfect noble habits for you." So in every place where the religious law says to you: "If you wish you may exact vengeance, or if you wish you may neglect it", or where it says to you: "If you wish you may take compensation"—so you set your soul in the position of an evil deed, since the Most High has said (XLII, 40/38): "The recompense for an evil deed is an evil deed like it"—"or if you wish you may compensate with pardon and the making of peace", then be of those who pardon and make peace, and your reward will be with Allah. Beware of retaliating on anyone who has injured you, for Allah has named this "an evil deed" without qualification, so that if there is evil on the part of the one who wants to retaliate, and an earlier evil on the part of him who wronged him, you have two evils. In every place where the religious law says you should be angry, be angry, for refraining from anger [in such a situation] is not a praiseworthy characteristic, since anger on Allah's behalf is in Allah's sight one of the noble characteristics, and is a most excellent way of acting with regard to Allah—may He be exalted. So blessed be he who acts in such a way and lives in such company, for with Allah you ought to cultivate such habits as He has praised and marked out clearly [as approved by Him].

[1] The reason for these prohibitions is that Muslims may avoid any semblance of being sun-worshippers.

Among the things you must possess is [the grace of] avoiding those who are opposed [to your way of life], and people who are not of your sort, without, however, entertaining any thought of wronging them such as may occur to you, but with the intention of choosing the friendship and company of the True One rather than theirs. Also in your relations with animals let there be tenderness and compassion for them, for they are creatures whom the True One has put under constraint for your service. So do not load them more than they can bear, nor ride them carelessly or with abandon. Similarly with regard to the slaves who are under your hand, [remember that] they are your brethren, whose fore-locks Allah has given you to possess that He may see how you conduct yourself with them. You are His slave—glory be to Him—and you would not like Him to conduct Himself in an evil manner with you. Treat them exactly as He [has treated you], and you will be rewarded for that on the Day when you stand in need of it. If you have a family, treat them with kindness, for all [of us] are children, including yourself. All the command-ments are summed up in this, that whatever you would like the True One to do to you, that do to His creatures, step by step. If you have a son teach him Allah's book (the Qur'ān), for Allah's sake and not for any worldly purpose. Lay upon him the duty of observing the discipline of the religious law and maintaining religious habits. Encourage him in the practice of good works from his childhood so that they may become habitual to him. Plant no desires in his heart, but lead him to hate the ornaments of this present life by teaching him what a mean portion there is in the life to come for those who make friends of it (i.e. of this world's life), and how excellent a portion there is in the life to come for those who abandon it. Yet do this without being niggardly of your own dirhams or possessions.

Among the things you must possess is [the grace of] not frequenting the doors of people in authority, nor keeping company with those who covet wordly things, for such will draw away your heart from Allah. If some affair compels you to seek their company, then transact your business with them in sincerity, and be not afraid of them, for in reality your transaction is with none other than the True One. Whatever you do they will take as a cause for scoffing at you, but do you in all your affairs be intent on directing your thoughts towards Allah, that He may see you through whatever situation you may be in in such a way as will be best for you in your present life.

Among the things you must possess is [the grace of] feeling yourself in the presence of the True One whether you are in activity or at rest.

Impoverish yourself, I urge you, by the giving of alms, both in times of happiness and in times of misfortune, both in distressful days and those of ease, for that is an indication of a heart that trusts in what is with Allah. The miser is a cowardly fellow to whom Satan comes, stretching his expectations, making weary his days, saying to him: "If you spend in alms you will destroy [your situation] and remain with nothing, an example and a warning among your friends and your fellows. Keep your wealth to yourself. Prepare for changing times. Be not deceived by this time of plenty that you see, for you do not know what Allah will bring about in the coming year." Then if it is a season of misfortunes and hard times he (Satan) will say to him: "Keep your wealth to yourself. Give no one any of it, for you do not know when these hard times will end. Think only that this situation may get worse, so keep [your wealth] for yourself, for no one will serve you when you have nothing left, rather people will shun you, you will become a burden on men, and the brightness of your face will disappear." When such Satanic whispering as this keeps on at the heart of a weak man, it leads him to miserliness and niggardliness, intervening between him and the words of the Most High (LIX, 9): "Such as are protected from niggardliness of soul, they are those who will prosper", and His words (XLVII, 39/40): "He who is niggardly is niggardly only against himself." It is the teaching of those of us who are on this Path that if a man has joined himself to the people of Allah and to His Saints, and then acts niggardly, he should be exchanged, [that is], demoted from that position, into which some more generous-spirited person should be put. In regard to this Allah has said in that same verse (XLVII, 38/40): "If ye turn away He will substitute another people for you."

It also intervenes between him and the saying of the Most High (XXXIV, 39/38): "Whatsoever thing ye contribute [as alms], He will replace it", and between him and that saying of the Most High, [where He is recounting] the petition of Moses—on whom be peace— against Pharaoh, in which [Moses] desires that he (i.e. Pharaoh) be destroyed, and petitions Allah to apportion to them niggardliness, saying (X, 88): "O our Lord, wipe out their wealth, and harden their hearts." [As a result] they caused their poor people to waste away till they perished of hunger, whereupon Allah seized them (i.e. the oppressors of the poor). It also intervenes between him and the saying of him—upon whom be Allah's blessing and peace— : "Spend in alms like water, and fear not that the Lord of the Throne will be sparing [in His reward thereof]", and likewise his other saying: "Allah has two angels who at the dawning each day cry out: 'Allahumma, give to everyone who freely spends [in alms] a compensation, and to everyone who withholds a spoiling.'" It also intervenes between him and the attitude of the Prophet—upon whom be Allah's blessing and peace—for he was offered two amounts of treasure, but he chose to refuse them both rather than to take them. Similarly it comes between him and what Abū Bakr—with whom may Allah be pleased—did, when he brought all his wealth in its entirety to the Prophet—upon whom be Allah's blessing and peace—who said: "But what have you left for your family?", and he answered: "Allah, and His Apostle." Also 'Umar—with whom may Allah be pleased—came with half of his wealth, leaving half for his family. So the Prophet—upon whom be Allah's blessing and peace—said to the two of them: "Between you two is what is between your two statements."

To impoverish yourself by almsgiving is a way to secure in exchange the provision of the Provider *(ar-Razzāq)* [1] for this world and the next. Thus everyone who holds back [from generous almsgiving] is showing himself suspicious of Allah, is putting his reliance in his own wealth, and trusting in his dirhams more than he trusts in his Lord. This is a spear-thrust into his faith, so let us ask Allah to heal it. Be careful to observe this liberality in almsgiving in hard times as well as in times of ease, having no fear or terror of poverty, for unhappy is the man who has. Be such an one as the Prophet—upon whom be Allah's blessing and peace—speaks of: "Is not he one who says 'take this' and 'take that' with his money to right and to left?", and Allah will fulfill what He has promised to you, whether you wish it or not, and whether the world wishes it or not, for a bountiful man never perishes. Were it not necessary to be concise we should have gone on giving you further details to strengthen [the argument in what] we have been urging on you.

Take care to repress bursts of anger, for [such repressing] is an indication of a liberal spirit (lit. wideness of heart). If you repress your bursts of anger you are doing something well-pleasing to the Merciful, and ill-pleasing to Satan, while at the same time you are keeping your soul in subjection and in restraint, since it did not finish [what it started]. Also you have brought joy to the one from whom you have restrained your burst of anger in not letting it fall on him, a thing which would have made him bitter and caused him to turn to the True One to obtain justice from Him and a settlement by some ill-treatment or hostility wrought against you. Perhaps the response from him [to your restraint] may be a plea

[1] In Sūra LI, 58 Allah is so called.

that would find acceptance and from which you would gain something that you will find in your balance,[1] and then how great will be the benefit, how intense the joy. If you repress your bursts of anger Allah will not punish you for deeds you do which incur the wrath of Allah, for if you repress your bursts of anger against the one who has done to you something that induces anger and wrath, Allah will requite you for your deed. What more beneficial thing could there be than for you to forgive your brother, put up with his injuring you, and restrain your anger? What Allah desires you to do to others is the very same thing He desires to do Himself to you. So be diligent in this matter for it bequeaths a legacy of love in people's hearts. The Prophet—upon whom be Allah's blessing and peace—has bidden us show love and affection to one another, and this [that we have been speaking of] is one of the greatest inducements to perfect love.

Pay heed to good behaviour, for it is an indication of a true shamefacedness [2] before Allah, Most High, and [a sign] that Allah is highly regarded in the heart of him who behaves well. Gabriel said to the Prophet—upon whom be Allah's blessing and peace—:"What is good behaviour?", and the Apostle of Allah—upon whom be Allah's blessing and peace—answered: "Good behaviour is to serve Allah as though you saw Him", for such good behaviour is an indication that Allah is highly regarded in the heart of him who behaves well. Then he—upon whom be peace—said: "Even though you do not see Him, He sees you." This good behaviour is an indication of shamefacedness before the Beneficent One, who is Allah, Most High. He—upon whom be Allah's blessing and peace—has said that this shamefacedness is something wholly good, for in the case of a believer it is quite impossible that he should have any evil if his heart perseveres unswervingly in this both in this world and the next. If the second indication, viz. having a high regard [for Allah], predominates in the heart of him who is behaving well, it will prevent anyone from having lordship over such a steady heart. So be diligent in acquiring the art of behaving well, and hold fast to this way whose utility we have set forth to you.

Hold fast also to [the practice of] remembering [Allah], and seeking [His] forgiveness, for should it be the consequence of sin it will blot it out and remove it, and should it be the consequence of obedience and good

[1] I.e. the balance in which the good and evil deeds are weighed at the accounting on the Last Day.

[2] *ḥayā'* means "pudency", "bashfulness", a sense of honest shame and a shrinking due to a sense of unworthiness. Sometimes it is used as synonymous with "repentance".

behaviour, it will add light to light and joy to joy. Remembrance [of Allah] keeps the mind collected and the eye pure. If you feel disgusted [with the life of the world], turn to recitation of the Qur'ān, chanting it, and reflecting with careful thought and wonder when you come to verses [expounding His] unity and His aloofness [from creaturely things], making supplication at verses of hope, showing humble submissiveness at verses of fear and threat, and pondering the meaning of the stories told therein, for the Qur'ān never causes any feeling of disgust in him who reads it, because of the infinite variety of hidden meanings to be found in it.

Be at pains to loose from your heart the knot of perseverance [in evil]. You will succeed in this only if you say to yourself as each breath goes from you: "O soul, do you know if there will be another breath coming after this one or not?" for perhaps you may die during this breath, while you are bound up with evil, and Allah has various kinds of punishment for one who dies bound up with evil, such punishments as the firm-standing mountains could not endure,[1] so how could a weakling like yourself? So turn in repentance, [O my soul], to Allah, since you do not know when death will surprise you. Allah has said (IV, 18/22): "The relenting is not for those who do evil deeds till, when death comes nigh, one of them says: 'Now, indeed, I repent.'" The Prophet—upon whom be Allah's blessing and peace—has said: "Allah accepts a man's repentance so long as he is not at the death rattle." How many a person there is whom death has surprised while he was eating, or drinking, or making love with his wife, or sleeping, so that without his being aroused [from what he was doing] his soul was taken, and he died while bound to his sins. So warn your soul by examples such as these, for it is when you multiply such examples that you will loose from yourself the knot of perseverance [in evil ways].

Be careful to have a godly fear of Allah in private and in public, for it will guard you from His punishment, and he who is guarded from Allah's punishment will hasten to do deeds that are well-pleasing to Allah. Allah has said (III, 28/27): "Allah warns you to beware of Himself"; and again (II, 236): "And know that Allah is aware of what is in your minds, so beware of Him." Godly fear *(at-taqwā)* is a word derived from *wiqāya* (keeping watch), and the greatest and most powerful protection is Allah's keeping watch. So guard against what Allah may do by

[1] In eschatological tractates it is not uncommon to find the use of this image of the mountains melting away at the fierceness of the punishments with which Allah will visit wickedness. It is probably based on such Qur'ānic passages as XX, 105; LXXIII, 14; LVI, 5 and 6.

what Allah may do. The Prophet—upon whom be Allah's blessing and peace—said: "I take refuge in Thy approval from Thy wrath, and with Thy pardon from Thy punishment." So guard against Allah by Allah, as he said: "I take refuge with Thee from Thee." Whatever it may be you fear or dread avoid taking the path that leads to it. Acts of disobedience are the paths that lead to wretchedness, just as acts of obedience are the paths that lead to happiness, so guard against the way of wretchedness by the way of happiness, i.e. guard against disobedience by obedience, and guard against the Fire by [making sure of] Paradise, just as you guard against [Allah's] wrath by doing what is approved. Therefore walk in the stations of godly fear. The Most High has said (III, 131/126): "and protect yourselves against the Fire", so walk the way of godly fear as I have sketched it for you, and you will escape, if Allah, Most High, wills.

Beware of negligence. This comes when your soul deceives you [with fair words] about the generosity of your Lord, how He bears with your perseverance in disobeying Him, and when Iblīs (the devil) deceives you by saying to you: "Were it not for your sins and your transgressions how could the Most High show His generosity, His pardon, His mercy, His forgiveness?" This is the most foolish of all his statements, for it is of His generosity, and His mercy, that He directs me to obey Him, and intervenes between me and my transgressing against Him. Satan will also say to you: "Against those who behave well there is no way [for the infliction of punishment],[1] for mercy from Allah has gone ahead of them in the world because of the acts of obedience they have directed towards Him, so when the morrow comes He will show His generosity, His forbearing, His forgiveness and His mercy in regard to your transgressions and your sins." With speeches such as these he will draw you in among the disobedient ones who serve him, so let him not deceive you by talk like this. Keep guard over your soul, and say to him: "As for His forbearance and generosity, and what you have mentioned concerning His pardoning, it is true that had it not been for transgressions and sins the signs of these attributes [of His] would not have been manifest, as you state. The signs are real, and the statements about them true, but do you, O accursed one, want to allure me with regard to His generosity so that I disobey Him, relying on His mercy? How am I to know that I am one of those whom He will pardon, to whom He will show mercy, or forgive? His generosity and His forgiveness, it is true, reach whomsoever of His servants He

[1] Satan is here quoting the Qur'ān, for these words are found in Sūra IX, 91/92.

wills, just as His punishment, His vengeance, His torment will reach a party of His disobedient servants, but I know not to which group I shall belong in doing this deed of disobedience. Perhaps Allah, as He deprived me of repentance for the act of disobedience here, will deprive me of His pardon before my entry into the Fire, and so will punish me. It is true that I shall come out of it if I die a Muslim,[1] yet acts of disobedience increase unbelief, [so that I may not die a believing Muslim]. Did I know for sure that I shall be one of those who will be pardoned and not punished for sin, perhaps I might be led astray by your words. That, however, would be sheer stupidity on my part and an act of foolishness. Nay more, were I to be secure against punishment by Allah that would make it incumbent on me to expend my every effort in being obedient to the Most High out of thankfulness to Him and shamefacedness before Him. He above all is the One before Whom one should feel a sense of shame, so how [would my condition before Him have been] if He had not given me the good news of my being singled out, nor made me secure, but had abandoned me, leaving me in my disobedience uncertain whether I should have His pardon or His punishment? So how should I let myself be deceived by your falsehood and set my soul to obey what is evil?"

Take care also to be continent. That is, avoid everything that would leave an impression on your soul. Said he—upon whom be Allah's blessing and peace—:"Leave what seems suspect to you for that which is not suspect, even though at the time you can find no substitute and have need of it. Make no use of it all, but leave it to Allah, for Allah, the Most High, will give you something better in exchange for it, so be in no haste." If you live in that state of continence which is the foundation-stone of religion and the path to Allah, your works will thrive and your undertakings be successful, your condition in life will prosper, *karāmāt*[2] will hasten towards you, and you will be guarded by divine care in all your affairs. We have no doubt about it. But whenever you turn aside from the path of continence and go straying in every valley [of desire], Allah departs from you and leaves you to yourself, so that Satan gets the mastery of you. So Allah is Allah, my brother, and continence is the continence you are well able [to observe].

[1] The orthodox teaching is that though Muslims who have been evil-doers may go into the Fires of Hell for a time to be punished therein to the measure of their evil, no one who dies a Muslim will remain for ever in damnation, but will, after the torment due for his sins, be released.

[2] *karāmāt* are the special acts of grace of which saints are the recipients. The wondrous experiences and seemingly miraculous events which make up such a large part of the popular *Lives of the Saints* in Islam are their *karāmāt*.

As to abstinence, observe abstinence, and have little desire for the world. Nay rather, annihilate it from your soul utterly. If you cannot escape from seeking it, then cut down what you have to take as provision from it, in the way of things that are lawful, sighing not for [fellowship with] its sons, for it is an accidental thing *('araḍ)*,[1] which will not endure through the two times,[2] so he who sets his desire in it will never attain what he wants. The hopes of that man who desires [the world] are wide-ranging, indeed, but Allah Most High will give him what He has decreed for him thereof, whether he wants or does not want, so he will not cease being anxious about it, full of grief over it, hateful in Allah's sight. He who seeks the world and desires it is like one who drinks water from the sea, the more he drinks the greater becomes his thirst. Let it be sufficient for you, O my brother, that the Prophet—upon whom be Allah's blessing and peace—likened it to a corpse and to a dung-heap. Do any save dogs gather around a corpse? Would you be well-pleased that your soul should belong to that category? No! by Allah, not if you are an intelligent person. So be content with what Allah has allotted you, for He, glory be to Him, will cause that to reach you whether you wish it or not. In His revelation to Moses[3]—on whom be peace—Allah said: "O son of Adam, if you are content with what I have apportioned you I will give rest both to your heart and to your body, and you will be well-spoken of, but if you are not content with what I have apportioned for you, I will give the world dominion over you that you may run about therein as the wild beasts run in the wilderness. Then, by My might and by My majesty, you will attain naught therein but what I have decreed for you, yet will be judged blameworthy."

Suppose, O my brother, that Allah were to give you the world with all its trappings, would you have from it anything more than a house to shelter you, clothes to cover you, and broken pieces [of food] to stay your hunger? Yet this much is obtained even by that one from whom [these trappings] are withheld, and, as against you, he adds [thereto the blessing] of a light accounting and an ease of heart. Beware, O beware, lest you lose your goodly portion with your Lord for an accidental thing that will disappear when you disappear. You might even die at the very first step you take in seeking the world, and then nothing would be accomplished of all your hopes. You know that there are children of this world, and that there are children of the next. He—upon whom be Allah's blessing

[1] I.e. it belongs to accidents not to essences, and so is but a temporal thing.
[2] Viz. this world and the future world.
[3] This is supposed to be a passage from the original Torah given to Moses.

and peace—has said: "Be ye of the children of the next world; be not of the children of this world." Ponder the word of our Lord when you read it, and pay heed to that saying of His (XI, 15/18 ff.): "If any desire the life of this world and its adornment, We shall recompense them therein for their works, and therein they will not be defrauded. These are they for whom there is nothing in the next world save the Fire. Fruitless is what they have wrought therein, and vain what they have been doing." There are also His words (XLII, 20/19): "Whoever wishes to cultivate the next world, to him will We give increase in his cultivating, but whoever wishes to cultivate this world, We shall give him somewhat of it, but in the next world he shall have no portion." With reference to seeking that which is lawful the Most High has said (VIII, 67/68): "Ye desire the chance gain of this world, but Allah desires the next world." Also with reference to one who has desired to cultivate this world and the increase of wealth, He has said (II, 195/191): "Contribute in the way of Allah, and do not with your own hands deliver yourselves over to destruction; but behave well, for verily Allah loves those who behave well."

SOME ACCOUNT OF THE EARLY ṢŪFĪ MASTERS[1]

We shall mention in this section the names of a number of the Masters of this way, beginning with the earliest group and coming on to the later. We shall mention somewhat of their lives and their sayings in which there may be an indication of their origins and their attainments—if Allah wills, may He be exalted.

Ibrāhīm b. Adham

Among them was Abū Isḥāq Ibrāhīm b. Adham the son of Manṣūr of the city of Balkh—may Allah be pleased with him. He was a prince of the Royal House, but he went out one day to hunt and came upon the traces of a fox, or maybe it was a rabbit. While he was following after it a voice from the unseen *(hātif)* called to him: "O Ibrāhīm, was it for this that thou wast created? or is this what thou wast bidden do?" Then another voice spoke from his saddle-bow: "By Allah it was not for this that thou wast created, nor is this what thou wast bidden do." So he dismounted from his riding-beast and chanced upon one of his father's shepherds, whose woollen cloak he took and put on, giving the shepherd his horse and all that was on it. Then he went into

[1] From al-Qushairi's *Risāla fī 'Ilm at-Taṣawwuf*, pp. 8–12 (al-Ḥalabi edition, Cairo, 1330 A.H. = 1911 A.D.).

the wilderness. Anon he came to Mecca, where he frequented Sufyān ath-Thawrī and al-Fuḍail b. ʿIyāḍ.[1] Later he went to Syria where he died. He used to eat from the labour of his hands, [earning his living] as a harvester or a caretaker of gardens or such-like employment.

In the wilderness he saw a man who taught him the greatest name of Allah,[2] which he used thereafter in his prayer. He also saw al-Khiḍr [3]—upon whom be peace—who said to him: "It was none other than my brother David who taught you that greatest name of Allah." It was the Shaikh Abū ʿAbd ar-Raḥmān as-Sulamī who informed us about this—may Allah show him mercy. He said: Muḥammad b. al-Ḥusain b. al-Khashshāb has related to us, on the authority of Abū 'l-Ḥusain, from ʿAlī b. Muḥammad al-Miṣrī, from Abū Saʿīd al-Kharrāz, from Ibrāhīm al-Bashshār, who said: I was a companion of Ibrāhīm b. Adham and I said to him: "Inform me about the beginning of your affair", and the above was what he related.

Ibrāhīm b. Adham was a man of great stature in the matter of godliness. It is related of him that he said: "Be generous with your food and then it is no sin for you not to get up at night [for prayers] or not to fast by day." It is said that his customary prayer was: "Allahumma! change me over from the low estate of being disobedient to Thee to the noble estate of being obedient to Thee." Someone said to Ibrāhīm b. Adham: "Meat has become very expensive." He answered: "Then do you make it cheap", i.e. do not purchase it. It was about this that he recited the verse

"If I find anything expensive, I leave it,
So it becomes the cheapest thing there is, when it is expensive."

Muḥammad b. al-Ḥusain—on whom may Allah have mercy—has informed us, on the authority of Manṣūr b. ʿAbdallah, from Muḥammad b. Ḥāmid, who stated that he heard Aḥmad b. Khaḍrawaih say: Ibrāhīm b. Adham said to a man during the *ṭawāf*:[4] "Know that you will not reach

[1] These were both early Ṣūfī Masters, see Massignon, *Essai*², Index *sub voce* Thawrī and Ibn ʿIyāḍ.

[2] The orthodox insist that this "greatest name" of Allah is one of those given in the Qur'ān, the consensus being that it is *al-ḥai al-qaiyūm*, "the living, the self-subsistent", but the Mystics claim that there is a secret name of Allah which is taught only to the initiates.

[3] A mythical figure, said to be the mysterious figure who appears in the Moses story in Sūra XVIII, 65/64–82/81, who was taken by the Ṣūfīs to be supreme Master of the "way" and whom many of the early Ṣūfīs are said to have met. See Friedländer, *Die Chadirlegende und der Alexanderroman* (Berlin, 1913).

[4] I.e. during the circumambulation of the Kaʿba while on pilgrimage at Mecca.

the grade of the pious *(aṣ-ṣāliḥūn)* till you have passed through six stages. The first is that of locking the gate of the favoured life and opening the gate of the distressful life. The second is that of locking the gate of nobility and opening the gate of lowliness. The third is that of locking the gate of ease and opening the gate of strenuousness. The fourth is locking the gate of sleep and opening the gate of wakefulness. The fifth is that of locking the gate of wealth and opening the gate of poverty. The sixth is that of locking the gate of hope and opening that of getting ready for death."

Ibrāhīm b. Adham was [at one time] caretaker of a vineyard, when a soldier passed by and said: "Give me some of your grapes." He replied: "The owner has given me no order for that", whereupon [the soldier] began to beat him with his whip. He, however, lowered his head, saying: "Beat a head which has been disobedient to Allah", whereat the man refrained and went off. Sahl b. Ibrāhīm said: I used to be a friend of Ibrāhīm b. Adham, and once when I fell ill he spent on me all his money. I, however, had an insatiable appetite so he sold his donkey and spent its price on me. When I recovered I said: "O Ibrāhīm, where is the donkey?" "We have sold it", he answered. So I said: "Then on what am I going to ride?" "On my neck, O my brother", he answered, and he carried me three stages.

Dhū 'n-Nūn

And among them was Abū 'l-Faiḍ Dhū 'n-Nūn the Egyptian. His name was Thawbān b. Ibrāhīm, though others say it was al-Faiḍ b. Ibrāhīm. His father was a Nubian. He died in the year 245 A.H. (859 A.D.). He was a man of surpassing eminence in this matter [of Ṣūfī life], peerless in his time in learning and in godliness, in [the Ṣūfī] state and in [general] culture. He was slandered before al-Mutawakkil,[1] so [the Caliph] demanded that he be brought from Egypt [to Baghdad]. When he entered [the Caliph's] presence he preached to him, whereat al-Mutawakkil wept and sent him back to Egypt. Whenever godly folk were mentioned in the presence of al-Mutawakkil he would weep and say: "If you are mentioning godly men make haste to come to [the name of] Dhū 'n-Nūn." He was a thin, lean man, red-headed, with a beard that did not go white.

[1] The 'Abbāsid Caliph who reigned from 232–247 A.H. (846–861 A.D.) in Baghdad, and under whom there was a return to rather fanatical orthodoxy.

I have heard Aḥmad b. Muḥammad say: I heard Sa'īd b. 'Uthmān say: I heard Dhū 'n-Nūn say: "The main points of *kalām* [1] are four, love of the Majestic One,[2] loathing of the destitute one (i.e. Satan), following that which has been revealed (i.e. the Qur'ān), and being afraid of backsliding." I heard Muḥammad b. al-Ḥusain—on whom may Allah have mercy—say: I have heard Sa'īd b. Aḥmad b. Ja'far say: I heard Muḥammad b. Aḥmad b. Muḥammad b. Sahl say: I heard Sa'īd b. 'Uthmān say: I heard Dhū 'n-Nūn the Egyptian say: "Among the signs of one who loves Allah—sublime and majestic is He—is the following of Allah's beloved (i.e. Muḥammad)—upon whom be Allah's blessing and peace—in his habits, his actions, his commands and his ways." Dhū'n-Nūn was asked about [who were] the inferior men, and he answered: "Those who do not know the path to Allah, and make no enquiry about it."

I heard the Shaikh Abū 'Abd ar-Raḥmān as-Sulamī—on whom may Allah have mercy—say: I heard Abū Bakr Muḥammad b. 'Abdallāh b. Shādhān say: I heard Yūsuf b. al-Ḥusain say: I was present at the *majlis* [3] of Dhū 'n-Nūn one day when there came to him Sālim al-Maghribī, who said to him: "O Abū 'l-Faiḍ, what was the cause of your repentance?"[4] He answered: "A wonder that you could not grasp." Said he: "By the object of thy worship, I beseech thee to tell me." So Dhū 'n-Nūn said: "I was once desirous of going from Cairo to one of the towns, but I fell asleep on the way in a certain desert place. When I opened my eyes, behold, there was a blind lark which had fallen from its nest on to the ground. Then, [as I watched], the earth opened, and from it came forth two bowls one of gold and the other of silver, in one of which was coriander seed and in the other water. So it began to eat from the one and drink from the other. I said: 'That is enough for me. I have repented.' Then I clung close to the gate [of repentance] till Allah accepted me—sublime and majestic is He."

I heard Muḥammad b. al-Ḥusain say: I heard 'Alī b. 'Umar the *ḥāfiẓ* say: I heard Ibn Rashīq say: I heard Abū Dujāna say: I heard Dhū 'n-Nūn

[1] Scholastic theology is what is usually meant by *kalām*, so this is somewhat of a jibe.

[2] Al-Jalīl is one of the names of Allah.

[3] Perhaps we could translate it "reception". It is from the verb "to sit", and refers to the little gatherings of people who would come and sit in the company of some important person.

[4] Anyone familiar with the Methodist Class Meeting, particularly that of our fathers' day, and the fondness there for recounting the occasion of one's conversion from worldliness to the religious life, cannot but be struck with the constant interest these Ṣūfī lives show in the occasions that were the cause of individuals embracing the Ṣūfī way of life.

say: "Wisdom does not dwell in a stomach filled with food." Dhū 'n-Nūn was asked about repentance, and he answered: "The repentance of the generality of folk will be [repentance] for sin, but the repentance of some special folk will be for carelessness."

Ibn ʿIyāḍ

Among them was Abū ʿAlī al-Fuḍail Ibn 'Iyāḍ. He was a Khurāsānī from the neighbourhood of Merv. It is said that he was born at Samarqand and grew up at Abīward. He died at Mecca in [the month of] Muḥarram of the year 187 A.H. (802 A.D.). I have heard Muḥammad b. al-Ḥusain say: Abū Bakr Muḥammad b. Muḥammad b. Jaʿfar informed us, on the authority of al-Ḥasan b. ʿAbdallah al-ʿAskarī, who said: My nephew Abū Dhurʿa has related to us, on the authority of Muḥammad b. Isḥāq b. Rāhawaih who related to us, saying: Abū ʿAmmār has related to us from al-Fuḍail b. Mūsā, who said: Al-Fuḍail was a mischievous fellow who practised highway robbery between Abīward and Sarakhs. The cause of his repentance was that he fell in love with a slave-girl, and while he was one day climbing the wall to get to her he heard someone reciting: "Is it not high time for those who believe to humble their hearts to remembrance of Allah?" (LVII, 16/15). So he said: "O Lord, it is indeed high time." Then he went back and took shelter for the night at a ruined place, but lo! therein was a company of people. Said one of them: "Let us journey", but the group said: "Not till the morning, for that Fuḍail is on the road and will rob us." So al-Fuḍail repented and left them in security. Thereafter he lived close by the Ḥaram [1] till he died. Al-Fuḍail b. ʿIyāḍ said: "If Allah loves a man He increases his griefs, but if He is angry with a man He expands for him his worldly life."

Ibn al-Mubārak said: "When al-Fuḍail died grief disappeared." Al-Fuḍail said: "Were this world in its entirety presented to me and I had no account to settle because of it, yet I would find it as loathsome as any one of you finds a corpse loathsome when he passes by it, [fearing] lest it touch his clothes." Al-Fuḍail said: "I would rather take oath that I am a hypocrite than take oath that I am not a hypocrite." He also said: "To abandon the doing of good works for the sake of people is hypocrisy, but to do works for the sake of people is *shirk* (i.e. associating others with Allah)." Abū ʿAlī ar-Rāzī said: "I was a friend of al-Fuḍail for

[1] He means the sacred precincts in which the Kaʿba stands at Mecca.

thirty years and never did I see him laughing or even smiling save on the day his son 'Alī died. I spoke to him about that and he said: "If Allah likes something then I like that [thing also]." Al-Fuḍail said: "I myself am disobedient to Allah, so I bear the same patiently in the case of my donkey or my servant."

Ma'rūf al-Karkhī

And among them was Abū Maḥfūẓ Ma'rūf al-Karkhī. Ma'rūf b. Fīrūz al-Karkhī was one of the great Masters, whose prayers brought response and at whose tomb cures were wrought. The people of Baghdad say that Ma'rūf's tomb is an approved antidote. He was one of the clients of 'Alī b. Mūsā ar-Riḍā [1]—with whom may Allah be pleased. He died in the year 200 A.H. (815 A.D.) or some say in 201. He was the teacher of as-Sarī as-Saqaṭī to whom he said one day: "If you have need of Allah then adjure him by me." I have heard the teacher Abū 'Alī ad-Daqqāq—on whom may Allah have mercy—say: "The parents of Ma'rūf al-Karkhī were Christians who handed Ma'rūf over to their tutor when he was just a small boy. The tutor used to say to him: 'Say: [He is] the third of three',[2] but he would answer: 'Nay, but He is One.' One day the tutor beat him so excessively that Ma'rūf ran away, whereat his parents said: 'Let him return to us following any religion he pleases and we shall assent to it for him.' Then he became a Muslim at the hands of 'Alī ar-Riḍā, returned to his house and knocked at the door. Some one [from within] asked: 'Who is at the door?' 'Ma'rūf', he answered. They said: 'And in what religion do you come?' 'In the Ḥanīfī [3] religion', he answered. So both his parents also became Muslims."

I have heard Muḥammad b. al-Ḥusain say: I heard Abū Bakr ar-Rāzī say: I heard Abū Bakr al-Ḥarbī say: I heard Sarī as-Saqaṭī say: "In my sleep I saw Ma'rūf al-Karkhī, and it was as though he were beneath the Throne, while Allah—mighty and majestic is He—said to His angels:

[1] I.e. the eighth Imām of the Shī'a Muslims, the son of Mūsā al-Kāẓim.

[2] Sūra V, 73/77 reads: "They most assuredly have disbelieved who say that Allah is the third of three, seeing that there is no deity save One." This is taken to be a reference to Christian teaching, so in the story the tutor is pictured as trying to teach the child what the Qur'ān says is the Christian doctrine.

[3] In the Qur'ān Muḥammad associates the word *ḥanīf* with the religion of Abraham, and as he also associated the new religion he was preaching with the religion of Abraham, which he considered he was restoring in its pure original form, the term "Ḥanīfī religion" came to be used not only for Islam, but as a name for the original religion out of which both Judaism and Christianity had come.

'Who is this?' They answered: 'Thou, O Lord, knowest best.' Whereat He said: 'This Ma'rūf al-Karkhī, drunken with love of Me, and he will not recover save by meeting Me.'" Ma'rūf once said: "One of the companions of Dāwūd aṭ-Ṭā'ī [1] said to me: 'Beware of giving up the work, for it is that which will bring you near to the favour of your Lord.' So I said: 'And what is the work?' He answered: 'Constant obedience to your Lord, and serving and counselling the Muslims.'"

I have heard Muḥammad b. al-Ḥusain say: I heard Muḥammad b. 'Abdallah ar-Rāzī say: I heard 'Alī b. Muḥammad ad-Dallāl say: I heard Muḥammad b. al-Ḥusain say: I heard my father say: "In a dream I saw Ma'rūf al-Karkhī after his death, and I said to him: 'What has Allah done with you?' He answered: 'He has granted me forgiveness.' 'Because of your asceticism and your godliness?', I asked. 'No', he answered, 'because of my acceptance of the warning of Ibn as-Sammāk to stick to poverty and to love the poor.'" The warning of Ibn as-Sammāk is thus told of by Ma'rūf himself: "I was walking along one day in Kūfa, when I came upon a man named Ibn as-Sammāk who was preaching to the people. In the course of his remarks he said: 'He who shuns Allah in all things will be wholly shunned by Allah. He who occupies himself with Allah in his heart, to him will Allah come in His mercy, and will come to him with all the honours of creation. He who is sometimes the one and sometimes the other will have Allah show him His mercy in season.' Now his words struck my heart so I set to occupying myself with Allah, Most High, leaving all with which I had been concerned save the service of my lord 'Alī b. Mūsā ar-Riḍā. I recounted these words [of the preacher] to my lord, who said: 'Let this warning suffice thee, now that thou hast been warned.'" Muḥammad b. al-Ḥusain told me of this story, saying: "I heard 'Abd ar-Raḥmān b. 'Alī, the *ḥāfiẓ*, in Baghdad say: I heard Muḥammad b. 'Umar b. al-Faḍl say: I heard 'Alī b. 'Īsā say: I heard Sarī as-Saqaṭī say that he heard Ma'rūf tell it."

Someone said to Ma'rūf during the illness from which he died: "Make your last will and testament." He answered: "When I die give my shirt away as alms, for I desire to leave this world naked as I entered it naked." Once Ma'rūf passed by a water-carrier who was crying out: "May Allah have mercy on him who drinks." He was fasting [at the time], but he stepped forward and took a drink. They said to him: "But you are fasting, are you not?" "Surely", he replied, "but I put my hope in his prayer."

[1] One of the early Ṣūfī Masters. See Massignon, *Essai*[2], p. 170.

Sarī as-Saqaṭī

Among them was Abū 'l-Ḥasan Sarī b. al-Mughallis as-Saqaṭī, the maternal uncle of Junaid and his teacher. He was a pupil of Maʿrūf al-Karkhī, and was unique in his time in godliness, in matters of the *sunna,* and in the theological sciences. I have heard Muḥammad b. al-Ḥusain say: I heard ʿAbdallah b. ʿAlī aṭ-Ṭūsī say: I heard Abū ʿAmr al-ʿUlwān say: I heard Abū 'l-Abbās b. Masrūq say: It has reached me that Sarī as-Saqaṭī used to be a merchant in the market-place and was one of the friends of Maʿrūf al-Karkhī. Maʿrūf came to him one day bringing an orphan child, and said: "Clothe this orphan." "So", said Sarī, "I clothed him, whereat Maʿrūf was rejoiced and said: 'May Allah make the world an object of aversion to you and give you relief from that in which you are engaged.' Thereupon I arose [and left] the shop, and there was nothing thereafter I had in greater aversion than this world. Thus all I have [of reputation for piety] is derived from the blessing of Maʿrūf."

I have heard the Shaikh Abū ʿAbd ar-Raḥmān as-Sulamī—on whom may Allah have mercy—say: I heard Abū Bakr ar-Rāzī say: I heard Abū ʿUmar al-Anmāṭī say: I heard Junaid say: "Never did I see a more devoted worshipper than Sarī. He reached the age of ninety-eight years without ever being seen lying down save during his last illness." It is related of Sarī that he said: "Sufism is a word that means three things. It is that thing a man's knowledge of which never puts out the light of his godliness, that which never speaks in secret of a knowledge which the plain meaning of Scripture or the *sunna* contradicts, and that wherein favours bestowed never lead a man to remove the veil from things which Allah has made unlawful."

Sarī died in the year 257 A.H. (870 A.D.). I have heard the teacher Abū ʿAlī ad-Daqqāq relating from al-Junaid—on whom may Allah have mercy—that he said: "Sarī asked me one day about love, so I said: 'Some folk say that it is mutual suitability, others say that it is a choosing, while others say this and that.' Then Sarī took hold of the skin of his forearm and tried to stretch it, but it would not stretch, so he said: 'By His might—exalted be He—were you to say that this skin is tight on this arm-bone because of love of it you would be speaking the truth.' Then he fainted away, and his face changed as though it were the rising moon and Sarī were its skin."

It is related that Sarī said: "For thirty years I have been seeking forgiveness for having once said: 'Praise be to Allah.'" Someone asked him: "And how was that?" He replied: "There was a fire in Baghdad one day and a man met me saying: 'Your shop has escaped', so I said: 'Praise be to Allah.' So for thirty years I have been repenting for what I said, for [by saying that] I had been desiring for myself something better than what had happened to [other] Muslims." 'Abdallah b. Yūsuf told me about this, and he said: I heard Abū Bakr ar-Rāzī say: I heard Abū Bakr al-Ḥarbī say: I heard Sarī say that. Also it is related that Sarī said: "I look at my nose in the mirror several times a day fearing lest it may have become black, for I fear Allah's blackening my face because of the things in which I have been engaged."

I have heard Muḥammad b. al-Ḥusain—on whom may Allah have mercy—say: I heard Muḥammad b. al-Ḥasan b. al-Khashshāb say: I heard Ja'far b. Muḥammad b. Nuṣair say: I heard al-Junaid say that he heard Sarī say: "I know a short way of getting to Paradise", so I said to him: "What is it?" He answered: "Ask nothing of anyone, take nothing from anyone, have nothing with you from which you could give to anyone." I heard 'Abdallah b. Yūsuf al-Iṣfahānī say: I heard Abū Naṣr as-Sarrāj aṭ-Ṭūsī say: I heard Ja'far b. Muḥammad b. Nuṣair say: I heard al-Junaid b. Muḥammad say: I heard Sarī say: "I greatly desire to die in some place other than Baghdad." He was asked: "And why is that?", and he replied: "I fear that my grave will not receive me,[1] and so I should be put to shame."

I have heard 'Abdallah b. Yūsuf of Iṣfahān say: I heard Abū 'l-Ḥasan b. 'Abdallah al-Fuwaṭī of Tarsus say: I heard al-Junaid say that he had heard Sarī say: "Allahumma! whatever may be the punishment with which Thou dost punish me, punish me not with the humiliation of the veil (i.e. of being veiled from Thee)." I heard 'Abdallah b. Yūsuf of Iṣfahān say: I heard Abū Bakr ar-Rāzī say: I heard al-Jarīrī say: I heard al-Junaid say: One day I entered to Sarī as-Saqaṭī and he was weeping. I said to him: 'What makes you weep?' He answered: "Yesterday the little girl came to me and said: 'Father, this is a hot night so here is a waterpot I shall hang in this place!' Then my eyes constrained me and I slept, and behold, a maiden, most beautiful of form, came down from heaven. I said: 'For whom are you?' She answered: 'For him who does not drink water cooled in water-pots.' Then she went to the waterpot, cast it to the ground and smashed it." Said Junaid: "I saw the broken pieces. He did not gather them up nor touch them, so the dust collected on them."

[1] This is a reference to tales, quite common in Muslim devotional tractates, of how when men have been uncommonly wicked it has been found impossible to bury them, the ground simply refusing to accept their corpses.

Bishr b. al-Ḥārith

Among them was Abū Naṣr Bishr b. al-Ḥārith the barefoot. He was originally from Merv but came to live in Baghdad and died there. He was sister's son to ʿAlī b. Khashram, and died in the year 227 A.H. (841 A.D.), a man of great reputation. The cause of his repentance was that [once as he was going] along the road he chanced upon a piece of paper on which was written the name of Allah—sublime and Majestic is He—but which had been trodden under foot. He took it up and with a dirham he chanced to have on him he bought some *ghāliya* (a perfume composed of musk and ambergris) with which he perfumed the piece of paper and put it in a chink in a wall. Then he had a vision such as one sees in a dream, and it was as though someone were speaking to him and saying: "O Bishr, you perfumed My name, so I shall assuredly make your name a perfumed thing in both this world and the next."

I have heard the Master Abū ʿAlī ad-Daqqāq—on whom may Allah have mercy—say: Bishr was one day passing along with some folk who said: "This fellow never sleeps at night and breaks his fast only once in three days." Thereat Bishr wept, and when he was asked the reason, he said: "I myself cannot remember ever having spent a whole night sleepless, nor ever having fasted a single day without breaking it at night, but Allah—glorified and exalted is He— puts into mens' minds more than His servant ever does. This is a kindness on His part and an act of grace." Then he went on to tell how he had started on this way of life, as we have already related. I have heard the Shaikh Abū ʿAbd ar-Raḥmān as-Sulamī—on whom may Allah have mercy—say: I heard Muḥammad b. ʿAbdallah ar-Rāzī say: I heard ʿAbd ar-Raḥmān b. Abī Ḥātim say: It has reached me that Bishr b. al-Ḥārith the barefoot said: "I saw the Prophet—upon whom be Allah's blessing and peace—in a dream, and he said to me: 'O Bishr, do you know why Allah raised you up from among your contemporaries?' 'No, O Apostle of Allah', I answered. He said: 'It was because of your following my *sunna,* your doing service to the pious, your giving good advice to your brethren, and your love for my companions and my kinsfolk. It is that which has caused you to reach the stations of the just.'"

I have heard Muḥammad b. al-Ḥusain—on whom may Allah have mercy—say: I heard Muḥammad b. ʿAbdallah ar-Rāzī say: I heard Bilāl al-Khawwāṣ say: "I was once in the wilderness of the Children of Israel when suddenly I was aware of a man walking along with me. I was vastly astonished at this till, presently, it dawned upon me that this was al-

Khiḍr—on whom be peace—so I said to him: 'By the truth of the True One, who are you?' 'I am your brother al-Khiḍr', he replied. So I said: 'I should like to ask you some questions.' 'Ask away', replied he. I said: 'What do you say about ash-Shāfi'ī—on whom may Allah have mercy?' He replied: 'He is one of the *awtād*.'[1] 'And what', I asked, 'do you say of Aḥmad b. Ḥanbal—with whom may Allah be pleased?' 'A trusty man', he answered. 'And what', I asked, 'have you to say about Bishr b. al-Ḥārith the barefoot?' He answered: 'No one like him has been created after him.' Then I asked: 'And what is the cause of my seeing you?' 'Your mother's blessing', he replied."

I have heard the Master Abū 'Alī ad-Daqqāq—on whom may Allah have mercy—say: "Bishr the barefoot once came to the door of al-Mu'āfā b. 'Imrān and knocked. Someone asked: 'Who is it?' 'Bishr the barefoot', he replied, whereat a little girl from within the house said: 'Were I for two dāniqs to buy you a pair of sandals you would lose the name of barefoot'" I heard... Aḥmad b. 'Alī ad-Dimashqī say: Abū 'Abdallah b. al-Jalā' said to me: "I saw Dhū 'n-Nūn and he had the explanation. I saw Sahl[2] and he had the counsel. I saw Bishr b. al-Ḥārith and he had self-restraint." He was asked: "To which of the three did you incline?", and he answered: "To Bishr b. al-Ḥārith, our master." It is said that for many years he had a great longing for broad-beans but never ate any. After his death he was seen in a dream and was asked: "What has Allah done for you?" He answered: "He granted me forgiveness, and He said to me: 'Eat, O you who did not eat. Drink, O you who did not drink.'"

The Shaikh Abū 'Abd ar-Raḥmān has informed us that 'Ubaidallah b. 'Uthmān b. Yaḥyā said: Abū 'Amr b. as-Sammāk has related to us, on the authority of Muḥammad b. al-'Abbās, from Abū Bakr b. bint Mu'āwiya, who said: I heard Abū Bakr b. 'Affān say: I heard Bishr b. al-Ḥārith say: "Forty years long did I long for roast meat but never did I have enough money for it." Someone asked Bishr: "What then did you eat with your bread?" He answered: "I would call to mind good health

[1] *awtād* is the plu. of *watad* "a stake or tent-pole", and is used in the Qur'ān for the mountains which are like tent-pegs pegging out the flat earth (LXXVIII, 7). Likewise it may be used metaphorically of the chief men of any place or community. That may be its meaning here, though among the Ṣūfīs there was a technical use of the word for certain prominent figures who were high in the mystical hierarchy. Ash-Shāfi'ī (d. 204 A.H.) and Aḥmad b. Ḥanbal (d. 240 A.H.) were the founders of two of the four orthodox Sunnī *madhhabs*. See p. 379.

[2] He means Sahl b. 'Abdallah at-Tustarī, another of the early Ṣūfī masters. See Massignon, *Essai*[2], Index, *sub voce* Tostarī.

and use that as a condiment" Bishr... was seen in a dream and was asked: "What has Allah done for you?" He answered: "He has granted me forgiveness and given me the freedom of one half of Paradise, but He said to me: 'O Bishr, had you done obeisance to me kneeling on live coals, you would not have [sufficiently] thanked [Me] for that [praise] of you I have set in the hearts of My servants.'" Bishr said: "No man who demands that the people take notice of him will ever find the true sweetness of the After Life."

GLOSSARY

BOOK LIST

GLOSSARY

adhān—the call to prayers made daily by the muezzin from the mosque.
'adl—equity.
'ahd—a compact, agreement, covenant, or the oath whereby such is made secure.
amāna—covenant agreement, from *amina* "to trust".
amīr al-mu'minīn—Commander of the Faithful, a title of the Caliph.
anṣār—helpers. In particular the people of Madīna who covenanted to aid the Prophet after his *hijra* from Mecca to Madīna.
'aqīda (plu. *'aqā'id*)—a statement of religious beliefs or tenets. A credal statement.
'aql—intelligence, the rational mind in man.
'araḍ—an accidental matter as opposed to an essential matter.
arkān—principles. The plu. of *rukn* q.v.
'arsh—throne; in particular the Throne of the Almighty.
āya—a sign. The word is used for a miracle, and also for a verse in the Qur'ān.
bait—house, and then in a restricted sense a temple or shrine as God's house. *ahl al-bait* "the people of the house" sometimes means the people of Allah's House at Mecca, sometimes the family of the Prophet.
baraka—blessing.
bashīr—a bringer of good tidings.
bāṭinī—a follower of one of the esoteric sects reprobated by orthodox Islam.
bid'a—innovation, and then, in a derived sense, heresy.
daraja (plu. *darajāt*) — a step, degree, rank, grade.
ḍarūra—a necessary truth which may not be doubted.
dhikr—a making mention, particularly of Allah and His praiseworthiness.
dhimmī—*dhimma* is a bond, a *dhimmī* is a member of a protected community, living under bond in a Muslim community.
dīn—(1) religion, more particularly religion as expressed in practice.
(2) judgment, whence *yaum ad-dīn* means "Day of Judgment".
dīnār—a unit of coinage. The word is from the Latin *denarius.*
dirham—a unit of coinage. The word is from the Greek *drachma.*
diya—blood-wit; compensation to the family for a man who has been slain.
du'ā'—supplication, invocation, spontaneous extempore prayer.
durūd—a form of benediction on the Prophet.
faqīr—a poor man; then a member of dervish fraternity under vow of poverty.
farā'iḍ—the plu. of *farḍ* and of *farīḍa.* Duties of religion incumbent on the person or the community.
al-fātiḥa—the Opener; title of the first Sūra in the Qur'ān.
fatwā—a decision of a *muftī* on some matter of the religious law.
fiqh—jurisprudence, so a *faqīh* is properly a jurist whose professional interest is in matters of *fiqh.*
firdaws—Paradise, or the highest section thereof.
fitna—(1) trial, testing; so the *fattāns* are the angels who test the soul after death;
(2) discord, dissension.

fiṭr—"breaking". The 'Īd al-Fiṭr is the feast which ends the fast of Ramaḍān.
fiṭra—a natural disposition.
furqān—that which distinguishes or separates. A name for the Qur'ān.
furū'—"branches", hence derivatives as distinguished from *uṣūl* "roots".
gehenna—see *jahannam* the Arabic name for Hell-fire.
ghazwa—a military expedition. The person taking part in it is a *ghāzī*.
ghusl—bathing, ablution, the greater lustration for purifying the body.
ḥadath—filth, that which causes defilement demanding purification.
ḥadīth—news, a story; then a Tradition embodying the *sunna* of the Prophet.
ḥāfiẓ—one who has memorized the Qur'ān; a professional reciter of the Qur'ān.
ḥajj—pilgrimage; the greater pilgrimage, as contrasted with the lesser, the *'umra*. A man who has completed a pilgrimage is a *ḥājjī*.
ḥanīf—a striver after the true religion.
ḥarām—forbidden; that which must be kept inviolate.
ḥawḍ—a pool or cistern; especially the Prophet's pool in the Hereafter.
hijā'—satire, satirical or vituperative verses.
ḥijāb—a veil; particularly the veils which hide Allah from His creatures.
hijra—emigration; particularly the Prophet's "flight" in 622 from Mecca to Madīna which counts as the starting point of the Muslim era.
ḥujja—a proof, convincing argument.
ḥūrī—one of the *ḥūr 'īn* or celestial maidens of Paradise.
'ibāda—service; then in particular service as an act of worship.
iblīs—*(diabolos)*, a Qur'ānic name for Satan.
'īd—feast or festival day.
'idda—the period a woman who has been married must wait before remarrying.
iḥrām—the act of putting oneself into a sacral state for cult purposes; then the sacred dress assumed by pilgrims when approaching Mecca.
i'jāz—miraculousness. Hence *mu'jiza* is a miracle.
ijmā'—consensus; more particularly the consensus of the Muslim community.
ijtihād—the exercise of independent judgment in deriving rules of conduct from the sources of jurisprudence. See *mujtahid.*
iktisāb—acquisition; the act whereby each individual brings into actuality the deeds foreordained for him to do.
ilhām—inspiration, but of a lesser degree than *waḥy*, for in *ilhām* the subject of inspiration expresses in his own words the ideas given him.
'ilm (plu. *'ulūm*)—knowledge. The plu. is used for "doctrines" and for "sciences".
imām—leader; in particular the leader at prayers. Among the Shī'a groups the succession of Imāms takes the place of the Caliphs among the Sunnis.
īmān—faith, belief; in particular the beliefs of religion as opposed to *dīn* the practices of religion.
isnād—the chain of transmitters through whom a Tradition has been handed down.
isrā'—a night journey; in particular the journey by night from Mecca to Jerusalem associated with the Prophet's ascension.
jahannam—the Qur'ānic word for Genenna or Hell-fire.
jāhilīya—a name, "Times of heathen barbarism", applied to the pre-Islamic period.
jaḥīm—a name for Hell, or for some particular section thereof.
jamā'a—a society of men of a particular persuasion.
jāmi'—a cathedral mosque; a larger mosque suited for Friday prayer services.
janāba—ritual impurity which must be removed before certain cult practices may be performed acceptably.
jihād—striving; particularly Holy War for the extension of Islam.
jinn—spirits, sprites, demons dwelling in the invisible world around mankind.
ka'ba—cube. The central shrine at Mecca.

kāfir—an unbeliever. It is the opposite of *mu'min* a believer.
kāhin (plu. *kahana*)—a sootshayer, diviner, idol priest.
kalām—speech. It is used of the *word* of God, and came to mean scholastic theology which discussed dialectically questions of religion.
kalima—word. Technically it means the short credal statement that Islam consists of believing in Allah and in Muḥammad as His messenger.
karāmāt—the charismata or wonders associated with the lives of the Saints.
kawthar—abundance; then the name for a river in Paradise.
khalīfa—successor; then the Caliph as successor of Muḥammad.
khazana (sing. *khāzin*)—guardians, protectors.
khuṭba—an address, sermon, hortatory speech.
kitāb—something written, a document, a book; in particular Scripture.
koḥl (kūḥl)—a preparation of collyrium for anointing the eyes.
kursī—footstool, low seat. A word used for the Throne of the Almighty.
kuttāb—a village school.
lailat al-qadr—"the Night of Power", one of the final nights of the month Ramaḍān on which, it is believed, the fates for the coming year are fixed.
lawḥ maḥfūẓ—preserved tablet; the celestial original of Scripture.
madhhab—a way of acting, a system of rules to be followed to assure right living.
maghāzī—warlike expeditions, particularly those of the Prophet.
majhūl—a Tradition the authority for which is obscure.
majnūn—possessed by the jinn, crazed.
manāsik—cult rites, particularly those of the pilgrimage.
maqām—a standing-place. The *maqām Ibrāhīm* is a structure near the Ka'ba.
ma'rifa—knowledge, understanding.
masjid—a place for doing *sujūd*, i.e. prostration in worship; a mosque.
matn—the text of a Tradition telling what the Prophet said or did.
miḍmār—a hippodrome.
miḥrāb—a niche in the wall of a mosque to indicate the *qibla* or direction to be faced during a prayer service.
milla—a sect, party, religious group.
minbar—the place in a mosque from which the *khuṭba* is delivered, a pulpit.
mi'rāj—means of ascending, ladder; in particular the Ascension of the Prophet.
mīthāq—covenant; in particular the covenant taken from Adam's progeny while they were still in his loins.
mubāhala—imprecation, an invitation to mutual cursing.
muezzin (mu'adhdhin)—he who gives the *adhān*, calling believers to prayers.
muftī—an official of the religious law who may be called on to deliver a *fatwā* or decision on matters concerned therewith.
muhājir—an emigrant; particularly those who emigrated from Mecca to join Muḥammad after he had settled in Madīna.
muḥtalim—a youth who has attained puberty.
mu'jiza—a miracle, particularly the evidential miracles granted to Prophets.
mujtahid—one who exercises *ijtihād*, i.e. breaking from *taqlīd* or the slavish following of tradition, he works out independently rules of conduct from the original sources of jurisprudence.
mu'min—a believer, one who has the true faith, as opposed to an unbeliever.
murīd—one who desires, i.e. seeks as a postulant initiation into the *ṭarīqa* of one of the Dervish fraternities.
mursal—an envoy, messenger.
murtadd—a renegade, apostate, one who has abandoned the religion of Islam.
muslim—one who has submitted, in particular surrendered himself to the will of Allah by embracing Islam.

mut'a—temporary marriage.
mutakallim—one who studies *kalām*, a scholastic theologian.
mutawātir—a Tradition handed down by many lines of unimpeachable transmitters.
muṭawwif—one who directs the *Ṭawāf*, a guide for the pilgrimage ceremonies.
nabī—a prophet sent by Allah with His message.
nadhīr—a warner sent by Allah to warn mankind.
nāfila—a voluntary good work in excess of what is required by law.
najāsa—uncleanness, that which renders the person ritually impure.
nīya—intention. It is customary at the commencement of any cult act to express intention of performing such and such act.
qadar—the decreeing by Allah of good and evil.
qāḍī—a judge, a minor official who administers the religious law.
qadīm—ancient, primordial, from of old, eternal in the sense that it always has been.
qibla—the point towards which a worshipper faces in prayer.
qiyās—analogical reasoning.
qur'ān—Scripture lesson; then the special name for Muḥammad's Scripture.
rak'a—bowing, prostration. Technically it means a complex of bodily genuflections accompanied by the repetition of liturgical formulae in ritual prayer. Each daily prayer service is made up of a certain number of *rak'as*.
ramaḍān—the ninth month of the Muslim year, the month of the great fast.
rasūl—a messenger, Apostle, one sent with a mission from Allah.
ra'y—opinion.
razzāq—He who provides, one of the names of Allah, as giver of man's *rizq*.
ribā—usury, interest on money.
risāla—message, particularly the message brought by a *rasūl*.
rizq—provision, sustenance, portion, fortune.
rūḥ (plu. *arwāḥ*)—the spirit within man, or Rūḥ the spirit of God.
rukn (plu. *arkān*)—a corner, a corner-stone, a principle.
rukū'—prostration or bowing in a service of prayer.
ru'ya—vision, particularly the Beatific Vision of Allah.
ṣadaqa—charitable alms.
sajda—a prostration of obeisance.
salām—peace, then greeting of peace.
ṣalāt—formal, ritual prayer.
ṣāliḥ—pious, righteous, upright. So the *ṣāliḥūn* are the righteous.
saqar—a name for Hell-fire, or for some special region therein.
sarīya—a warlike expedition.
sha'bān—the eighth month of the Muslim year, immediately preceding Ramaḍān.
sharī'a—the body of regulations which makes up the Islamic religious law.
shayāṭīn—satans, evil spirits, demons.
shirk—the sin of associating any one or anything on an equality with Allah.
ṣiddīq—a trustworthy person.
sidra—the lote-tree; particularly a noted celestial boundary tree.
sijjīn—an infernal prison house for the wicked.
sīra—way of life, particularly the biography of the Prophet.
ṣūfī—one who wears wool; a follower of the mystics' way in Islam.
ṣuḥuf—sheets, scrolls, particularly those of Scripture. Sing. *ṣaḥīfa*.
sujūd—prostration in worship.
sunna—custom, customary way of acting, particularly that of the Prophet.
sūra—a chapter or section of the Qur'ān.
ṣūra—representation, picture, form.
ta'awwudh—the act of taking refuge with Allah, or using a formula thereanent.
taḥiyyāt—expressions wishing one abundance of life.

tahlīl—to raise to Allah the *hallel*. Cf. our familiar Hallelujah.
taḥmīd—to praise Allah by using special formulae of praise.
tajsīm—speaking of Allah in bodily terms, anthropomorphism.
takbīr—to magnify Allah by using formulae of magnification.
takyīf—the error of trying to explain how what is affirmed of Allah can be.
tamjīd—to utter pious phrases in glorification of Allah.
ta'mīn—to pronounce the Amen formula.
tanzīh—to declare Allah aloof and far removed from things earthly.
taqdīs—sanctifying Allah by using formulae of sanctification.
taqīya—concealment, the concealing of one's religious opinions.
taqwā—piety, fear of Allah, godly fear.
ta'rīf—instruction.
ṭarīqa—the way, the spiritual discipline of a Ṣūfī order.
tasbīḥ—to glorify Allah by using phrases of glorification.
taṣdīq—putting full trust in the reliability of someone or something.
tashbīh—the error of asserting that Allah resembles created things in any way.
tashrīq—desiccation of meat in the sun. The name is given to the three days of the pilgrimage when the flesh of the sacrifices is drying in the sun.
tasmiya—the devotional use of the phrase "in the Name of Allah".
taṭawwu'—the performance of works of supererogation.
tathniya—to praise Allah by using expressions of eulogy.
ṭawāf—circumambulation; particularly circumambulation of the Ka'ba at Mecca.
tawḥīd—maintaining the Divine unity.
'ulamā'—men of learning, savants, the theologians and teachers of Islam.
tayammum—ritual purification by fine sand instead of water.
umma—community, social group, people.
'umra—visitation, the lesser pilgrimage to Mecca.
uṣūl—roots, first principles.
waḥy—revelation, where the words as well as the ideas are revealed.
wājib—necessary, incumbent, obligatory.
wakīl—trustee, agent, executor.
walī—he who is contiguous to one, whence it has the meanings: (1) heir; (2) guardian or trustee; (3) friend or companion; (4) saint, who is the friend of and is contiguous to Allah.
waṣīya—testamentary declaration.
wildān—the youthful attendants in Paradise.
wird—(1) a form of liturgical prayer; (2) a selection of Qur'ānic passages for private recitation.
wiṣāl—combining night and day fasting.
witr—an odd number; then prayers with an odd number of *rak'as*.
wuḍū'—the lesser ablution of purification.
zabāniya—the infernal attandants of Hell.
zakāt—legal alms.
zamzam—the sacred well in the environs of the Ka'ba at Mecca.
zindīq—a heretic, a dualist, particularly a Manichee.

BOOK LIST

SUGGESTIONS FOR FURTHER READING

General

T. Arnold and A. Guillaume (ed.), *The Legacy of Islam*, 2nd ed. (Oxford, 1948).
E. E. Calverley, *Islam: an Introduction* (Cairo, 1958).
B. Carra de Vaux, *Les penseurs de l'Islam*, 5 vols. (Paris, 1921–26).
E. Dermenghem, *Muhammad and the Islamic Tradition* (London, 1958).
L. Gardet, *La cité musulmane, vie sociale et politique* (Paris, 1954).
I. Goldziher, *Vorlesungen über den Islam*, 2nd ed. by F. Babinger (Heidelberg, 1925).
M. Gaudefroy-Demombynes, *Muslim Institutions* (London, 1950).
—, *Mahomet (L'homme et son message: naissance du monde musulman)* (Paris, 1957).
G. E. von Grunebaum, *Islam: Essays in the Nature and Growth of a cultural Tradition* (Menasha, 1955).
— (ed.), *Unity and Variety in Muslim Civilization* (Chicago, 1955).
A. Guillaume, *Islam* (London, 1954; Pelican Books).
M. Guidi, "Storia della religione dell'Islam", in Vol. II of Tacchi Venturi's *Storia delle Religioni* (Torino, 1949).
A. Jeffery, *Islam: Muhammad and his Religion* (New York, 1958).
R. Jockel, *Islamische Geisteswelt* (Darmstadt, 1954).
E. Kellerhals, *Der Islam: seine Geschichte, seine Lehre, sein Wesen* (Basel, 1945).
A. von Kremer, *Geschichte der herrschenden Ideen des Islams* (Leipzig, 1868).
R. Levy, *The Social Structure of Islam* (Cambridge, 1957).
A. Mazahéri, *La vie quotidienne des musulmans* (Paris, 1951).
K. Morgan (ed.), *Islam: the Straight Path, interpreted by Muslims* (New York, 1958).
Johs Pedersen, *Islams Kultur* (Copenhagen, 1928).
G. Pfannmüller, *Handbuch der Islamliteratur* (Berlin, 1925).
J. Schacht, *Der Islām; mit Ausschluss des Qor'āns* (Tübingen, 1931).
Ed. Sell, *The Faith of Islam*, 4th ed. (Madras, 1920).
C. Snouck-Hurgronje, *Selected Works* ed. G.-H. Bousquet and J. Schacht (Leiden, 1957).
J. Sauvaget, *Introduction à l'histoire de l'Orient musulman* (Paris, 1946).
A. S. Tritton, *Islam: Beliefs and Practices* (London, 1951).

Pre-Islamic Arabia (the background)

Tor Andrae, *Der Ursprung des Islams und das Christentum* (Uppsala, 1926).
R. Dussaud, *La pénétration des Arabes en Syrie avant l'Islam* (Paris, 1955).
J. Hirschberg, *Jüdische und christliche Lehren im vor- und frühislamischen Arabien* (Krakow, 1939).
Georg Jacob, *Altarabisches Beduinenleben*, 2nd ed. (Berlin, 1897).

A. Jamme, "La Religion sud-arabe pré-Islamique", in Brillant et Aigrain, *Manuel d'Histoire des Religions*, IV, 239–307.

H. Lammens, *L'Arabie occidentale avant l'Hégire* (Beyrouth, 1928).

Th. Nöldeke, "Arabs (ancient)", in Hastings' *Encyclopaedia of Religion and Ethics*, Vol. I, pp. 659–672.

G. Ryckmans, *Les religions arabes préislamiques* (Louvain, 1951).

J. Starcky, "Palmyréniens, nabatéens et arabes du Nord avant l'Islam", in Brillant et Aigrain, Vol. IV, pp. 201–237.

J. Wellhausen, *Reste arabischen Heidenthums*, 2nd ed. (Berlin, 1897).

Muḥammad

Tor Andrae, *Die Person Muhammeds in Lehre und Glauben seiner Gemeinde* (Stockholm, 1918).

—, *Mohammed, the Man and his Faith* (London, 1936 and 1955; New York 1960).

K. Ahrens, *Muhammed als Religionsstifter* (Leipzig, 1935).

R. Bell, *The Origin of Islam in its Christian Environment* (London, 1926).

F. Buhl und H. H. Schaeder, *Das Leben Muhammads* (Heidelberg, 1955).

Régis Blachère, *Le problème de Mahomet: essai de biographie critique du fondateur de l'Islam* (Paris, 1952).

A. Guillaume, *The Life of Muhammad: a translation of Ibn Isḥāq's Sīrat Rasūl Allāh* (London, 1955).

H. Holma, *Mahomet, prophète de l'Islam* (Paris, 1945).

S. W. Koelle, *Mohammed and Mohammedanism critically considered* (London, 1889).

C. A. Nallino, *Vita di Maometto* (Roma, 1946).

D. S. Margoliouth, *Mohammed and the Rise of Islam* (London, 1903).

—, *Muhammad* (in *What did they teach?*) (London-Glasgow, n.d.)

Sir Wm. Muir, *Life of Mohammed;* revised edition by T. H. Weir (Edinburgh, 1923).

A. Sprenger, *Das Leben und die Lehre des Mohammed*, 3 vols. (Berlin, 1861–65).

Qur'ān

(Translations)

J. Rodwell, *The Koran, translated from the Arabic* (London, 1926; Everyman's Library).

R. Bell, *The Qur'ān, translated with a critical rearrangement of the Sūras*, 2 vols. (Edinburgh, 1937–39).

Régis Blachère, *Le Coran: traduction nouvelle*, 2 vols. (Paris, 1949–50).

J. H. Kramers, *De Koran, uit het Arabisch vertaald* (Amsterdam, 1956).

A. Bausani, *Il Corano: introduzione, traduzione e commento* (Firenze, 1955).

(Studies)

R. Bell, *Introduction to the Qur'ān* (Edinburgh, 1952).

H. Birkeland, *The Lord guideth: Studies in primitive Islam* (Oslo, 1956).

Régis Blachère, *Introduction au Coran* (Paris, 1947).

A. Geiger, *Was hat Mohammed aus dem Judentum aufgenommen?* (Leipzig, 1902).

I. Goldziher, *Die Richtungen der islamischen Koranauslegung* (Leiden, 1920).

J. Henninger, *Spuren christlicher Glaubenswahrheiten im Koran* (Schöneck/Brekenried, 1951).

J. Horowitz, *Koranische Untersuchungen* (Berlin, 1926).

A. Jeffery, *The Qur'ān as Scripture* (New York, 1952).
D. Masson, *Le Coran et la révélation judéo-chrétienne: études comparées*, 2 vols. (Paris, 1958).
I. di Matteo, *La divinità di Cristo e la dottrina della Trintià in Maometto* (Roma ,1938).
Th. Nöldeke, *Geschichte des Qorāns*, 2nd ed. by Schwally, Bergsträsser and Pretzl, 3 pts. (Leipzig, 1919-38).
W. Rudolph, *Die Abhängigkeit des Qorans von Judentum und Christentum* (Stuttgart, 1922).
D. Sidersky, *Les origines des légendes musulmanes dans le Coran* (Paris, 1933).
H. U. W. Stanton, *The Teaching of the Qur'ān* (London, 1919).
W. StC. Tisdall, *The Original Sources of the Qur'ān* (London, 1911).
C. C. Torrey, *The Jewish Foundation of Islam* (New York, 1933).

Tradition

Wm. Goldsack, *Selections from Muhammadan Traditions* (Madras, 1923).
I. Goldziher, *Muhammedanische Studien*, 2 vols. (Halle, 1888–90).
A. Guillaume, *The Traditions of Islam* (Oxford, 1924).
J. Robson, *An Introduction to the Science of Traditions* (London, 1953).
A. J. Wensinck, *A Handbook of Early Muhammadan Tradition alphabetically arranged* (Leiden, 1927).

Theology

(Translations of texts)

Miguel Asín Palacios, *El justo medio en la creencia: compendio de Teología dogmática de Algazel* (Madrid, 1929).
L. Bercher, *Al-Qayrawânî: La Risâla: épître sur les éléments du dogme et de la loi de l'Islâm* (Alger, 1945).
E. E. Elder, *A Commentary on the Creed of Islam* (New York, 1950).
A. A. A. Fyzee, *A Shi'ite Creed* (London, 1942).
Max Horten, *Muhammedanische Glaubenslehre* (Bonn, 1916).
W. C. Klein, *Al-Ash'arī's Ibāna* (New York, 1940).
R. J. McCarthy, *The Theology of al-Ash'arī* (Beyrouth, 1953).
J. D. Luciani, *El-Irchad par Imam al-Harameîn* (Paris, 1938).
W. McE. Miller, *Al-Bâbu 'l-Ḥâdî 'ashar by Al-Ḥillî* (London, 1928).
A. Michel et Abdel Raziq, *Cheikh Mohammed Abdou: Rissalat at-Tawhid, exposé de la religion musulmane* (Paris, 1925).
G. F. Pijper, *De Edelgesteenten der Geloofsleer* (Leiden, 1948).

(Studies)

A. Arnaldez, *Grammaire et théologie chez Ibn Hazm de Cordoue* (Paris, 1956)
Miguel Asín, Palacios *Abenházam de Cordoba y su Historia crítica de las ideas religiosas* (Madrid, 1927–32).
D. M. Donaldson, *The Shī'ite Religion* (London, 1933).
L. Gardet et M. Anawati, *Introduction à la théologie musulmane* (Paris, 1948).
Max Horten, *Die philosophischen Systeme der spekulativen Theologen im Islam* (Bonn, 1912).
D. B. Macdonald, *Development of Muslim Theology, Jurisprudence and Constitutional Theory* (London, 1903).
D. S. Margoliouth, *The Early Development of Mohammedanism* (London, 1914).

R. Strothmann, *Die Zwölfer-Schī'a* (Leipzig, 1926).
A. S. Tritton, *Muslim Theology* (London, 1947).
A. J. Wensinck, *The Muslim Creed* (Cambridge, 1932).

Jurisprudence

A. P. Aghnides, *Mohammedan Theories of Finance, with an Introduction to Mohammedan Law* (New York, 1916).
G. Bergsträsser's Grundzüge des islamischen Rechts, ed. J. Schacht (Leipzig, 1935).
E. Bussi, *Principi di Diritto musulmano* (Milano, 1943).
A. Ben-Shemesh, *Taxation in Islam* (London, 1958).
Th. W. Juyboll, *Handleiding tot de Kennis van de Mohammedaansche Wet*, 4th ed. (Leiden, 1930).
M. Khadduri, *War and Peace in the Law of Islam* (Baltimore, 1955).
M. Khadduri and H. J. Liebesny (ed.), *Origin and Development of Islamic Law* (Washington, 1955).
L. Milliot, *Introduction à l'étude du droit musulman* (Paris, 1953).
O. Pesle, *Les fondements du droit musulman* (Casablanca, 1944).
D. Santillana, *Istituzioni di Diritto musulmano malichita*, 2 vols (Roma, 1926–38).
J. Schacht, *The Origins of Muhammadan Jurisprudence* (Oxford, 1950).
E. Tyan, *Histoire de l'organisation judicaire en pays d'Islam*, 2 vols. (Paris, 1938–43); and ed. (Leiden, 1960).
—, *Les institutions du droit public musulman*, 2 vols (Beyrouth, 1954).
S. G. Vesey-Fitzgerald, *Muhammadan Law: an Abridgment* (Oxford, 1931).

Devotional and practical

Tor Andrae, *I Myrtenträdgarden: Studier i sufisk Mystik* (Stockholm, 1950).
P. J. André, *Contribution à l'étude des confréries religieuses musulmanes* (Paris, 1956).
A. J. Arberry, *Sufism, an Account of the Mystics of Islam* (London, 1950).
—, *The Doctrine of the Sufis* (Cambridge, 1935).
Miguel Asín, Palacios, *El Islam cristianizado: estudio del Sufismo* (Madrid, 1931).
—, *La espiritualidad de Algazel y su sentido cristiano*, 4 vols. (Madrid, 1934–41).
J. K. Birge, *The Bektashi Order of Dervishes* (London, 1937).
G.-H. Bousquet, *Les grandes pratiques rituelles de l'Islam* (Paris, 1949).
E. E. Calverley, *Worship in Islam* (Madras, 1925).
T. Canaan, *Mohammedan Saints and Sanctuaries in Palestine* (London, 1927).
D. M. Donaldson, *Studies in Muslim Ethics* (London, 1953).
M. Gaudefroy-Demombynes, *Le pélerinage à la Mekke* (Paris, 1923).
G. E. von Grunebaum, *Muhammadan Festivals* (New York, 1951).
R. Hartmann, *Al-Kuschairis Darstellung des Sufitums* (Berlin, 1914).
Max Horten, *Einführung in die höhere Geisteskultur des Islam* (Bonn, 1914).
E. W. Lane, *Manners and Customs of the Modern Egyptians* (London, 1924; Everyman's Library).
D. B. MacDonald, *The Religious Attitude and Life in Islam* (Chicago, 1912).
L. Massignon, *La Passion d'al-Hallaj, martyr mystique de l'Islam*, 2 vols. (Paris, 1922).
—, *Essai sur l'origine du lexique technique de la mystique musulmane*, nouvelle édition (Paris, 1954).
R. A. Nicholson, *The Mystics of Islam* (London, 1914).
—, *Studies in Islamic Mysticism* (Cambridge, 1921).
J. Pedersen, *Muhammedansk Mystik* (Copenhagen, 1923).
E. T. Tscheuschner, *Mönchsideale des Islam* (Gütersloh, 1933).

Modernism

C. C. Adams, *Islam and Modernism in Egypt* (London, 1933).
H. E. Allen, *The Turkish Transformation* (Chicago, 1935).
G. Antonius, *The Arab Awakening* (London, 1945).
A. J. Arberry and R. Landau, (ed.), *Islam today* (London, 1943).
H. Bammate, *Visages de l'Islam* (Paris, 1959).
R. Charles, *L'âme musulmane* (Paris, 1958).
Kenneth Cragg, *The Call of the Minaret* (New York, 1956).
Louis Gardet, *Connaître l'Islam* (Paris, 1958).
Angelo Ghirelli, *El Renacimiento musulmán* (Barcelona, 1948).
H. A. R. Gibb, *Modern Trends in Islam* (Chicago, 1947).
— (ed.), *Whither Islam?* (London, 1932).
R. Hartmann, *Die Krisis der Islam* (Leipzig, 1928)
Max Horten, *Die religiöse Gedankenwelt der gebildeten Muslime im heutigen Islam* (Halle, 1916).
—, *Die religiöse Gedankenwelt des Volkes im heutigen Islam* (Halle, 1917).
E. Jung, *Le reveil de l'Islam et des Arabes* (Paris, 1933).
M. Laissy, *Du panarabisme à la Ligue arabe* (Paris, 1949).
R. Le Tourneau, *L'Islam contemporain* (Paris, 1950).
A. Nielsen, *Muhammedansk Tankegang i vore dage* (Copenhagen, 1930).
S. G. Wilson, *Modern Movements among Moslems* (New York, 1916).